Thede Kahl, Michael Metzeltin,
Helmut Schaller (Hg.)

Balkanismen heute –
Balkanisms Today –
Балканизмы сегодня

BALKANOLOGIE

Beiträge zur
Sprach- und Kulturwissenschaft

herausgegeben von

Thede Kahl, Michael Metzeltin,
Gabriella Schubert und Christian Voss

Band 3

LIT

Thede Kahl, Michael Metzeltin,
Helmut Schaller (Hg.)

Balkanismen heute –
Balkanisms Today –
Балканизмы сегодня

LIT

Umschlagbild:
Dreidimensionale Getränkewerbung vor der Altstadtkulisse
von Berat (Albanien).
Foto: Thede Kahl, September 2009

Gedruckt auf alterungsbeständigem Werkdruckpapier entsprechend
ANSI Z3948   DIN ISO 9706

Bibliografische Information der Deutschen Nationalbibliothek
Die Deutsche Nationalbibliothek verzeichnet diese Publikation in der
Deutschen Nationalbibliografie; detaillierte bibliografische Daten sind
im Internet über http://dnb.d-nb.de abrufbar.

ISBN 978-3-643-50388-6

©LIT VERLAG GmbH & Co. KG
Wien 2012
Krotenthallergasse 10/8
A-1080 Wien
Tel. +43 (0) 1-409 56 61
Fax +43 (0) 1-409 56 97
e-Mail: wien@lit-verlag.at
http://www.lit-verlag.at

LIT VERLAG Dr. W. Hopf
Berlin 2012
Verlagskontakt:
Fresnostr. 2
D-48159 Münster
Tel. +49 (0) 2 51-620 320
Fax +49 (0) 2 51-23 19 72
e-Mail: lit@lit-verlag.de
http://www.lit-verlag.de

Auslieferung:
Deutschland: LIT Verlag Fresnostr. 2, D-48159 Münster
Tel. +49 (0) 2 51-620 32 22, Fax +49 (0) 2 51-922 60 99, e-Mail: vertrieb@lit-verlag.de
Österreich: Medienlogistik Pichler-ÖBZ, e-Mail: mlo@medien-logistik.at
Schweiz: B + M Buch- und Medienvertrieb, e-Mail: order@buch-medien.ch

Contents / Inhalt / Содержание

III Einzelsprachliche Vergleiche

Vorwort

Spätestens seit Nikolai Trubetzkoy (1923) redet man in der Sprachwissenschaft vom ‚Sprachbund' und im Fall der südosteuropäischen Sprachen vom ‚Balkansprachbund'. Seitdem Kristian Sandfeld in seinem Standardwerk *Linguistique balkanique* (1930) die strukturellen Gemeinsamkeiten der betroffenen Sprachen – die sogenannten Balkanismen – zusammengestellt hat, haben sich mehrere Forscher (z.B. Reichenkron 1962, Schaller 1975, Solta 1980, Asenova 1989, Reiter 1994, Hinrichs 1999, Steinke/Vraciu 1999, Mišeska-Tomić 2006) darauf konzentriert, diese Richtung weiter auszubauen. Neben der Existenz eines Sprachkontakts als Erklärung für die Entstehung der Balkanismen haben bisherige Forscher vor allem auf Länge und Intensität des Kontaktes hingewiesen, um die Entstehung des Sprachbundes erklärbar zu machen. Dabei fokussieren die meisten Darstellungen die Gemeinsamkeiten der Balkansprachen und lassen die Divergenzen weitgehend unberücksichtigt.

Im Gegensatz hierzu hinterfragen die Autoren des vorliegenden Bandes, wie aktuell und angemessen dieser Ansatz heute noch scheint. Diese Frage stellt sich vor allem nach einer langen Phase der politischen Dekonstruktion des Balkanraumes und der Monolingualisierung der einst enger miteinander verflochtenen Sprachen. Durch die Beiträge zieht sich daher die leitende Frage, welche Auswirkungen die Standardisierung der Nationalsprachen Südosteuropas auf die Balkanismen hatte, wobei die oft bewusste Distanzierung von zahlreichen Gemeinsamkeiten, wie z.B. den Turzismen, auffällt.

Die Balkanlinguistik als historisch orientierte philologische Disziplin richtet ihren Blick fast ausschließlich auf die Vergangenheit. Selten wird die Frage gestellt, wie der Zustand des Balkansprachbundes *gegenwärtig* ist und welche Prognosen sich über seine *Zukunft* abgeben lassen. Einige Entwicklungen wie der wachsende Nationalismus, die ethnische Homogenisierung und die damit verbundene Monolingualisierung deuten auf ein Ende des Balkansprachbundes hin. Überlagert wird diese Entwicklung fraglos durch das Entstehen eines neuen Sprachbundes. Die zunehmende europäische Integration hinterlässt auch in den Balkansprachen ihre Spuren und geht in Richtung auf einen Eurosprachbund, der bereits in mehreren Beiträgen thematisiert wird.

Die Autoren des Bandes fragen nicht nach der Bedeutung der Balkanismen als Forschungsgegenstand, sondern als weiterhin existentes sprachliches Phänomen, und versuchen dieses in die Zukunft zu projizieren. Über die Entstehung der Balkanismen herrscht soweit Übereinstimmung, dass die sprachlichen Gemeinsamkeiten auf einen engeren Kontakt zwischen den Balkanvölkern zurückzuführen sind. Die Autoren beschäftigen sich mit den aufgeworfenen Fragen daher aus der Perspektive der Kontakt- und Areallinguistik, wobei die verschiedenen balkanologischen Teildisziplinen wie Albanologie, Rumänistik, Südslawistik und Neogräzistik berücksichtigt werden.

Aus den Beiträgen ergibt sich ein aktuelles Abbild des Balkansprachbundes und der Balkanismen. Die Autoren können somit Handlungsempfehlungen für weitere Aufgaben der Balkanlinguistik geben:

(a) Die traditionellen Balkanismen sind ein Relikt früher Sprachkontaktprozesse; als wirkender Faktor sind sie nicht mehr anzusetzen.

(b) Balkanismen müssen als Phänomene verstanden werden, die einem ständigen Wandel unterworfen sind. Nach dem Wegfall wichtiger Voraussetzungen verliert die ehemalige Konvergenz an Kraft, während durch die europäische Integration neue Formen der Konvergenzen entstehen.

(c) Mit der Bildung der Nationalstaaten haben eine sprachliche Neugliederung der Balkanhalbinsel und eine „Entkontaktierung" ihrer Sprecher eingesetzt. In den neuen Staaten gibt es jeweils eine dominante Herrschaftssprache. Zwar sind sie noch nicht vollkommen monoethnisch und monolingual geworden, aber der Übergang vom Multilingualismus zum Monolingualismus ist überall erkennbar. Die Minderheiten werden von den jeweiligen Herrschaftssprachen dominiert, und ihre Angehörigen sind zwangsläufig mehr oder weniger bilingual.

(d) In der Zukunft könnte ein Eurosprachbund oder auch ein globaler Sprachbund die Nachfolge des Balkansprachbundes in Südosteuropa antreten und daher die Expertise von Sprachbundforschern wie den Balkanlinguisten fordern.

Um sich den verschiedenen aktuellen Fragen der Balkanlinguistik anzunehmen, wurde im September 1993 während des XI. Internationalen Slawistenkongresses in Bratislava die Kommission für Balkanlinguistik des Internationalen Slawisten-Komitees gegründet. Sie führte seitdem eine Reihe von einschlägigen Arbeitstagungen durch (Marburg 1997; St. Petersburg 2001, Sofia 2002, St. Petersburg 2004, Belgrad 2006, Berlin 2008, Veliko Tărnovo 2009, Wien 2010, Iaşi 2011).

Die achte balkanologische Tagung des Internationalen Slawisten-Komitees mit dem Thema „Balkanismen heute – Balkanisms today – Балканизмы сегодня" fand vom 3. bis zum 5. September 2010 in Wien statt und wurde in Zusammenarbeit mit der Österreichischen Akademie der Wissenschaften (Balkan-Kommission) und der Universität Wien (Institut für Romanistik) durchgeführt. Wien mit seiner 1847 gegründeten Akademie der Wissenschaften sowie der Universitäts- und Nationalbibliothek stellte ohne Zweifel den Ausgangspunkt und die traditionell zentrale Forschungsmetropole der Balkanlinguistik dar, äußerlich dokumentiert durch die mehr als hundertjährige Tradition der „Balkanschriften" der Balkan-Kommission. Eng mit Wien verbunden sind für den Balkanologen Namen wie Bartholomäus Kopitar (1780–1844), Franz Miklosich (1813–1891), Vatroslav Jagić (1838–1923), Kon-

stantin Jireček (1854–1918) und Nikolai Trubetzkoy (1890–1938), die in Wien gewirkt haben und für die Entstehung und Entwicklung der Balkanologie entscheidend waren.

Der vorliegende Sammelband stellt in den offiziellen Sprachen des Internationalen Slawisten-Komitees die zahlreichen Facetten der Wiener Tagung zusammen.
Für die Unterstützung der Tagung danken wir dem Magistrat 7 der Stadt Wien
(Referat für Wissenschaft und Forschung), der Balkan-Kommission der Österreichischen Akademie der Wissenchaften und dem Austrian Science Fund (FWF,
Projekt 19406-G03) für ihre großzügige Unterstützung. Für das Zustandekommen
des Bandes bedanken sich die Herausgeber bei allen Beiträgern sowie für die Hilfe
bei der Durchsicht englisch- bzw. russischsprachiger Texte bei Ioana Nechiti und
Anna Kuzmina, für die redaktionelle Mitarbeit bei Frau Petra Himstedt-Vaid sowie
bei Herrn Richard Kisling vom LIT-Verlag für die Publikation in unserer balkanologischen Reihe.

Wien im Februar 2012
Thede Kahl, Michael Metzeltin, Helmut Schaller

Balkanismen in Vergangenheit und Gegenwart –
Theorie und Wirklichkeit

Helmut W. SCHALLER (Marburg a.d. Lahn)

„… Jede Sprachkarte weist eine Unmenge sich kreuzender Isophone, Isoseme, Isomorphen, Isolexen und Isosyntaxen auf, und man [dürfte] auf Grund der zahllosen Isoglossen auch eine unendliche Zahl von Klassifikationen vornehmen […]. Die vielen Kreuzungen der Isoglossen führen uns zu der Erkenntnis, dass sich in jeder Sprache genug Eigenschaften vorfinden, die in anderen, nahen und entfernten Sprachen und Dialekten wieder angetroffen werden können. Wir gelangen somit zu Baudouin de Courtenays Überzeugung vom gemischten Charakter aller Sprachen", schreibt Stefan MLADENOV (1928: 6) in seiner umfangreichen Geschichte der bulgarischen Sprache, die er in dem von Reinhold Trautmann und Max Vasmer herausgegebenen „Grundriss der slavischen Philologie und Kulturgeschichte" in deutscher Sprache veröffentlicht hatte.

Ganz offensichtlich lässt sich, wie mehrfach erörtert (SCHALLER 1975: 123ff.), der Terminus „Balkanismus" nicht auf alle Gemeinsamkeiten der Balkansprachen anwenden. Nach Henrik BIRNBAUM (1965: 43) kommt den lexikalischen Gemeinsamkeiten der Balkansprachen eine „relativ geringe bzw. nur ergänzende Bedeutung als sprachbundbildenden Merkmalen" zu, so dass hierfür vor allem Übereinstimmungen aus dem lautlichen, morphologischen und syntaktischen Bereich in Betracht kommen (BIRNBAUM 1966: 18–19). Bei der Darstellung der Übereinstimmungen der Balkansprachen dürften daher vor allem zwei Kategorien in Betracht kommen:

1. Sprachbundbildende Gemeinsamkeiten von Balkansprachen, die sich auf den lautlichen, morphologischen und syntaktischen Bereich erstrecken, wobei im Einzelnen zu fragen ist, ob diese Merkmale tatsächlich sprachbundbildend sind, sich in der Mehrheit der in Frage stehenden Balkansprachen finden.
2. Gemeinsamkeiten der Balkansprachen, die sich auf den lexikalischen Bereich erstrecken und nicht unbedingt als sprachbundbildend angesehen werden können.

Eine Betrachtung des Begriffes „Balkanismus" als sprachliche Übereinstimmung im Hinblick auf die Möglichkeiten und Grenzen seiner Anwendung auf die Balkansprachen steht in direktem Zusammenhang mit dem Begriff des „Sprachbundes" und seiner Realisierung als „Balkansprachbund" durch die verschiedenen Balkansprachen und deren Dialekte, ebenso aber auch mit seiner Anwendung auf andere

Sprachgruppen, wie der des Donauraumes oder des Polnischen und des Litauischen. So stellte Klaus STEINKE bereits 1976 die berechtigte Frage, ob es denn
überhaupt Balkanismen gebe. Die amerikanischen Sprachwissenschaftler Ernest
SCATTON und J. AUGEROT (1976/1977: 77) fragten im selben Jahr nach Balkan-
phänomen, lokal oder universell vertreten, wobei es den beiden Autoren vor allem
um die Frage nach der geographischen Verbreitung dieser sprachlichen Erscheinungen ging: „We would like to submit that everything which emerges as common
in the phonology of Bulgarian and Rumanian – or at least in the fragment of them
we have considered here – represents linguistic universals, either in the absolute
sense or in the sense of being the most natural, the most likely, the usual case". Bereits 1974 hatte Norbert REITER (1975) in einem aufsehenerregenden Vortrag während des III. Internationalen Südosteuropakongresses in Bukarest unter einem später anderweitig veröffentlichten Titel seine grundsätzliche Ablehnung des Balkansprachbundes und damit auch der Vorstellung von Balkanismen international bekannt gemacht.[1]

Erstmalig taucht wohl in der wissenschaftlichen Literatur der Terminus „Bal-
kanismus" in einem 1925 in Paris veröffentlichten Beitrag von Aleksandr
SELIŠČEV (1925) auf, während der bulgarische Sprachwissenschaftler Ljubomir
MILETIČ (1937) in einer Abhandlung zur Frage der Verdoppelung des Objektes den
Terminus „Balkanismus" zwar gebraucht, im konkreten Fall des verdoppelten
Objektes im Bulgarischen aber abgelehnt hat. Eine eindeutige Beschreibung der
Balkanismen hat Henrik BIRNBAUM (1965: 43) gegeben, wenn es bei ihm heißt:
„Als Merkmale des balkanischen Sprachbundes, kurzerhand auch Balkanismen ge-
nannt, gelten in erster Reihe die nichtlexikalischen Übereinstimmungen, d.h. die
von Sandfeld in seiner dritten Gruppe zusammengefassten Erscheinungen. Dabei
handelt es sich vornehmlich um im engen Sinne grammatische, also morpholo-
gisch-syntaktische Übereinstimmungen, wozu noch einige gemeinsame phra-
seologische – also nur im weitesten Sinne grammatische, syntaktische Züge treten.
Dabei spielen die etwaigen Ähnlichkeiten im Lautsystem einzelner oder mehrerer
Balkansprachen für die Konstituierung eines balkanischen Sprachbundes nur eine

---

1 In dem während des III. Internationalen Kongresses für Südosteuropaforschung, Bukarest, 4.–10. September 1974 gehaltenen Vortrag führte Norbert Reiter u.a. aus: „Die
   Einrichtung der Nationalstaaten war zugleich die Abschaffung der die balkanische
   Soziallandschaft bis dahin dominierenden Gesellschaftsspitze. Statt einer gab es nun
   deren mehrere. Die mit der Emanzipation gekoppelte Etablierung der Idiome der
   jeweiligen ethnischen Mehrheit als Staatssprache bedeutete die Unterbrechung des
   sprachlichen Assimilierungsprozesses."
   An dieser Stelle führte N. Reiter in einer Anmerkung weiter aus: „An dieser Stelle, so
   sagte ich, sei es mit dem balkanischen Sprachbund aus. Zwar existiere er noch, aber als
   Leiche, oder anders, aber fast gleichwertig ausgedrückt, er gehe in höheren Einheiten
   auf.

untergeordnete Rolle". Strikt vermieden wurden die Termini „Balkansprachbund"
und „Balkanismus" von Günther Reichenkron in seinem 1962 erschienenen Beitrag
zum Typus der Balkansprachen, dafür spricht er von „gemeinsamen sprachlichen
Zügen" bzw. auch „Übereinstimmungen" unter den Balkansprachen[2]. Dass die sogenannten „Balkanismen" nicht auf den Bereich der Balkanhalbinsel beschränkt
bleiben, sondern teilsweise auch im südlichen Italien zu finden sind, hatte der Münchener Romanist Gerhard Rohlfs 1967 in einer in Albanien erschienenen Abhandlung gezeigt, gefolgt von einer im folgenden Jahr von J. B. Pellegrini veröffentlichten Abhandlung, wo u.a. ausgeführt wird:

„Was das Keltische für Oberitalien bedeutete, war das Griechische für Unteritali-
en. Mit dem Unterschied, dass das Griechische im Süden viel länger Widerstand geleistet hat. Wie wir bereits gesehen haben, lässt sich vermuten, dass um
das Jahr 1000 noch auf drei Gebieten des Südens in ziemlicher Ausdehnung
Griechisch die vorherrschende Sprache war: in Südkalabrien, im Nordostzipfel
von Sizilien und im südlichsten Apulien ... Dass auf diesen drei Gebieten Griechisch sehr lange die dominierende Sprache war, lässt sich nicht nur aus einer
sehr großen Zahl von griechischen Reliktwörtern erkennen, die auf diesen drei
Gebieten sich forterhalten haben, sondern auch aus charakteristischen syntaktischen Erscheinungen. So wird in Südkalabrien und in Südapulien statt der sonst
üblichen Infinitivkonstruktion ein abhängiger Satz verwendet. Zum Beispiel
wird der Gedanke ‚ich wollte wissen' in Südkalabrien wiedergegeben durch
‚vulia mu sacciu', in Südapulien ‚vulia cu saccu', ‚Ich wollte, dass ich weiß'"
(PELLEGRINI 1968: 2).

Auch für das Ungarische (SCHUBERT 1983) und für das Armenische (SCHLÖSSER
1981) wurde die Frage aufgeworfen, inwieweit es dort den Balkanismen vergleichbare typologische Sprachmerkmale gebe. Sprachbundbildende Merkmale wurden
auch für den Bereich des Baltikums von Th. STOLZ (1991) in Erwägung gezogen.
   Um Theorie und Wirklichkeit der Balkanismen in Vergangenheit und Gegenwart näher zu treten, sind vor allem drei Fragenbereiche aufzuwerfen:

1. Ist der Begriff „Balkanismus" auch ohne den „Balkansprachbund" denkbar?
2. Sind „Balkanismen" spezifisch balkansprachliche Gemeinsamkeiten oder auch
   Übereinstimmungen von Balkansprachen mit anderen Sprachen, die außerhalb
   der Balkanhalbinsel beheimatet sind und nicht an die Balkansprachen grenzen?
3. Inwieweit stimmen die „Balkanismen" tatsächlich oder auch nur scheinbar
   untereinander überein?

---

2 „Mit diesen Sprachen: Rumänisch-Albanisch-Bulgarisch ist bekanntlich der Kern der
   Balkansprachen gekennzeichnet. Alle übrigen südosteuropäischen Sprachen nehmen
   dann nur noch an einzelnen Zügen der Balkansprachen teil" (REICHENKRON 1962: 118).

Seit Begründung der Sprachbundtheorie durch den Wiener Slawisten und Begrün-
der der Phonologie N. S. Trubetzkoy im Jahre 1928[3] gab es mehrere Anwendungen
des Sprachbundmodells auf unterschiedliche Sprachgruppen, nicht Sprachfamilien,
und zwar sowohl auf indoeuropäische als auch außerindoeuropäische Sprachen.
Innerhalb des Indoeuropäischen ist als klassisches Beispiel eben der Balkansprachbund bekannt geworden, der weite Bereiche der südslawischen Sprachen, das
Albanische und Rumänische mit seinen verschiedenen Vertretungen, mit Ein-
schränkung auch das Neugriechische mit den Dialekten dieser Sprachen umfasst.
Im Gegensatz zum Balkansprachbund hat sich die Auffassung von einem „Litauisch-polnischen Sprachbund" (FALKENHAHN 1963) sowie von einem „Donau-
sprachbund" (SKALIČKA 1968) kaum durchsetzen können, dies gilt auch für den
gelegentlich erwähnten „Banater Sprachbund". Voraussetzung für die Anwendung
des Sprachbundmodells auf mehrere Sprachen ist, dass diese Sprachen zu verschiedenen Familien gehören, um möglichst genetisch bedingte Übereinstimmungen von vornherein auszuschließen. Die Sprachen eines Sprachbundes weisen trotz
verschiedener Herkunft aber gemeinsame Merkmale auf, die durch gegenseitige
Beeinflussung, gemeinsame Substrat- oder Adstrateinwirkung, vor allem aber
durch geographische Nachbarschaft zu erklären sind. Dass das Sprachbundmodell
auch heute noch aktuell ist, zeigt z.B. ein Vortrag des amerikanischen Balkanologen George Thomas, den dieser im Mai 2008 in Banff/ Kanada zu dem Thema
"Serbo-Croatian as a Bridge between the Balkan and Central European *Sprachbünde*" gehalten hat und wo er von einer durch das Osmanische Reich bestimmten
Balkankulturzone ausging, der sich ein „mediterraner Sprachbund" und ein durch
das Habsburgerreich bestimmter deutschsprachiger Sprachbund anschließen (THO-
MAS 2010). Der Balkansprachbund und die Balkanismen werden auch in der 2006
erschienenen Abhandlung "Balkan Sprachbund and Morpho-Syntactic Features"
von Olga MIŠESKA TOMIĆ weiter verwendet, ebenso auch in dem 2010 erschienenen Buch von Susanne HASENSTAB „Das Rumänische im Kontext der Balkansprachbund-Theorie", wo ebenfalls an der traditionellen Terminologie weiterhin
festgehalten wird.
    Die Frage der Bestimmung und auch der Anwendbarkeit des Begriffes „Bal-
kanismus" beschäftigte die Sprachwissenschaft bereits seit dem V. Internationalen
Slawistenkongress in Sofia im Jahre 1963, als die Prinzipien für einen Balkansprachatlas in einem Fragebogen durch S. B. Bernštejn, A. Vraciu, M. Pavlović
und I. Pătruţ aufgeworfen wurden und bereits damals die Frage nach einer Definition des Terminus „Balkanismus" gestellt wurde, fortgesetzt 1977 mit dem in

---

3 Vgl. hierzu SCHALLER (1975: 49ff.), wo die Definition des Begriffes „Sprachbund" von
   Trubetzkoy in den schwer zugänglichen „Actes du premier congrès internationale de
   linguistes à la Haye, du 10–15 avril 1928", Leiden 1928, S. 17–18, unter „Proposition
   16" wiedergegeben wird.

Varna aufgestellten Programm eines Balkansprachatlas durch die bulgarischen Sprachwissenschaftler Chr. Choliolčev, K. Kostov und M. Sl. Mladenov[4]. Im Jahre 2002 veröffentlichte der polnische Balkanologe und Slawist Jerzy Rusek sogar einen Plan für ein Wörterbuch der Balkanismen in den südslawischen Sprachen (RUSEK 2002). Völlig zu Recht hat Petja Asenova in ihrem 1999 erschienenen Beitrag „Balkanski lingvističen atlas (predloženija za izrabotvane na koncepcija)" auf die dringende Notwendigkeit einer wissenschaftlichen Festlegung des Terminus „Balkanismus" gedrungen, wobei sie eine praktische und elastische Formulierung forderte, die „Arbeitscharakter" haben sollte und auch aus theoretischer Sicht annehmbar sein sollte, z.B. „schodstvo meždu dva balkanski ezika (dialekta) na koeto u da e ezikovo ravnište" (ASENOVA 1999).

Wie weit reichen nun aber in Europa die weitgehend untersuchten und immer wieder behandelten „Balkanismen"?

Angefangen bei der Zahlwortbildung von 11 bis 19, die nicht nur das die Balkansprachen direkt benachbarte Ungarische mit dem Bildungstyp „eins auf zehn" bis „neun auf zehn" erfasst, nämlich von „tizenegy" (11) bis „tizenkilenc" (19), sondern weit darüber hinausgehend nicht nur alle slawischen Sprachen, sondern das geographisch weitab von der Balkanhalbinsel gesprochene Lettische erfasst, wo ganz entsprechend den slawischen Sprachen sich zu „desmit" (10), die Zahlwörter „vienpadsmit" (11) bis „devinpadsmit" (19) finden, während im benachbarten und als baltische Sprache nächstverwandten Litauischen keine solchen Zahlwortbildungen zu finden sind, ebensowenig im Neugriechischen, wobei das Altgriechische aber Ansätze zu einer solchen Zahlwortbildung zeigte, die in der weiteren Entwicklung des Griechischen aber wieder verschwunden sind.

Ein ähnlicher Fall liegt mit der analytischen Steigerung der Adjektive in den Balkansprachen vor. Bekanntlich finden sich auch im Russischen vergleichbare Bildungstypen, sogenannte „unechte" Komparativtypen, z.B. „ljudi postarše", etwa wiederzugeben mit „ältere Leute", auch litauisch „didis" und „po-didis" mit der Bedeutung „groß" und „ziemlich groß", im Lettischen „pasauss" mit der Bedeutung „ziemlich trocken". Gegenüber den echten Komparativen im Russischen, Litauischen und Lettischen, synthetisch gebildet, muss hier eben eine Bedeutungsdifferenzierung vorliegen, da solche Formen mit „po" bzw. „pa" sonst überhaupt keine Funktion mehr hätten und daher auch schon verschwunden wären. Es wird damit deutlich, dass „Balkanismen" nicht nur sprachliche Erscheinungen einer bestimmten geographischen Region umfassen, sondern für eine bestimmte Sprachtypologie charakteristisch sind, und es überrascht daher nicht, wenn der amerikanische Sprachwissenschaftler Howard I. Aronson in seinem 2007 erschienenen Vortrag „The Balkan Linguistic League, ‚Orientalism' and Linguistic Typology" (ARONSON 2007) sogar das Englische aus typologischer Sicht als eine Balkanspra-

---

4 In: *Balkansko ezikoznanie* XX, 1–2, 1977, S. 65–71.

che klassifiziert, denn dort finden sich u.a. Futurformen mit „wollen", gclcgentliche Objektsverdopplungen, analytische Steigerungen, die Vermischung von Ziel- und Ortsangabe. „English as a Balkan language" ist in seinen Ausführungen ein ganzer Abschnitt mit entsprechenden sprachlichen Belegen gewidmet, wo er u.a. ausführt:

> "Typologically, English is about as distant from the Balkan languages as it is possible to get. And yet, when we look for 'Balkanisms' in English, we find enough similarities to make a case for English as a Balkan language. But since, as just mentioned, English in no way typologically resembles the Balkan languages, we must conclude that with two major exceptions (identical marking of possession and the indirect objects. Significantly lacking in English, and the lack of an infinitive), the traditional Balkanisms (which are found elsewhere in Western and Central Europe) serve rather imperfectly to delimit a geographical area, rather than a typological area. Thus, there is a circularity in the definition of the Balkan languages: they are Balkan because they are spoken in the Balkans. And I would hazard, this circularity is due, in no small part, to their 'otherness' of the Balkans described above" (ARONSON 2007: 11–12).

Auch im deutschen Sprachraum finden sich gelegentlich „Balkanismen", z.B. Parallelen zur Verdopplung des Objektes in den Balkansprachen. „Seht ihn, den Mann mit der komischen Kleidung", wobei eine affektbetonte Sprecherhaltung angenommen werden kann. Was den Zusammenfall von Genitiv und Dativ als weiteren „Balkanismus" betrifft, sei hier die Wendung „Dem Freund sein Haus" anstelle von schriftsprachlichem „Das Haus des Freunds" angeführt.

Der Vergleich der Balkansprachen und ihrer Balkanismen mit anderen europäischen, insbesondere germanischen und baltischen Sprachen, zeigt uns, dass sich aus dieser Sicht wohl drei Kategorien von „Balkanismen" anführen lassen:

1. Balkanismen, die keine Parallelen in nichtbalkanischen Sprachen aufweisen, z.B. der Ersatz des Infinitivs durch entsprechende Nebensätze, die sich für die Balkansprachen nur durch die Beeinflussung seitens des Griechischen erklären lässt. Hier dürfte es sich um einen Balkanismus handeln, der sich innerhalb der Balkansprachen erst entwickelt hat, der aber bis nach Süditalien gewirkt hat, weil sich dort die griechische Sprache über einen längeren Zeitraum gehalten hat.

2. Balkanismen, deren Parallelen in anderen europäischen Sprachen auf genetische Übereinstimmungen hinweisen, nämlich der bulgarische Komparativ, der sich mit seinen analytischen Entsprechungen sowohl in den anderen Balkansprachen als auch im Russischen, Litauischen und Lettischen findet, ferner die Bildung der Zahlwörter von 11 bis 19 in den Balkansprachen, in allen slawischen Sprachen sowie im Lettischen zu finden ist.

3. Balkanismen, deren Parallelen zu anderen europäischen Sprachen wohl zufällig sein dürften, aber typologisch als gleichwertig zu betrachten sind, so die Verwendung von nachgestelltem und kopulativem Artikel in einem Teil der in Frage stehenden Balkansprachen und in skandinavischen Sprachen.

Es bleibt schließlich noch die Frage anzudeuten, ob man den traditionellen Begriff „Balkanismus", auf die Balkansprachen beschränkt, weiterhin so anwenden kann (HINRICHS 1999). Dies ist wohl in Frage zu stellen, bei weiter verbreiteten sprachlichen Übereinstimmungen sollte man besser von „Europäismen" sprechen, bei Übereinstimmungen, die offensichtlich auf den Bereich der Balkansprachen beschränkt bleiben, sollte man aber auch weiterhin von „Balkanismen" sprechen, bei „Balkanismen", die sich auch in anderen europäischen Sprachen nachweisen lassen, könnte man zukünftig vielleicht von „Eurobalkanismen" sprechen.

Literatur

ARONSON, H. I. (2007): The Balkan Linguistic League, "Orientalism" and Linguistic Typology. In: *Kenneth Naylor Memorial Lecture Series* 4. Ann Arbor, New York. 1–77.

ASENOVA, P. (1999) Balkanski lingvističen atlas (predloženija za izrabotvane na koncepcija). *Săpostavitelno ezikoznanie* XXIV, 2/3.117–120.

BIRNBAUM, H. (1965): Balkanslavisch und Südslavisch. Zur Reichweite der Balkanismen im südslavischen Sprachraum. *Zeitschrift für Balkanologie* 3. 12–63.

BIRNBAUM, H. (1966): On typology, affinity, and Balkan languages. *Zbornik za filologiju i lingvistiku* 9. 18–19.

FALKENHAHN, V. (1963): Die Bedeutung der Verbalrektion für das Problem eines litauisch-polnischen Sprachbundes. *Zeitschrift für Slawistik* 8. 893–907.

HASENSTAB, S. (2010): *Das Rumänische im Kontext der Balkansprachbund-Theorie. Vergleichende sprachwissenschaftliche Untersuchung des Rumänischen, Französischen, Spanischen und Italienischen im Hinblick auf gemeinhin als Balkanismen bezeichnete morphologische und syntaktische Eigenheiten des Rumänischen.* München.

HINRICHS, U. (1999): Die sogenannten ‚Balkanismen' als Problem der Südosteuropa-Linguistik und der allgemeinen Sprachwissenschaft. In: U. Hinrichs (Hrsg.): *Handbuch der Südosteuropa-Linguistik.* Wiesbaden. 429–462.

MILETIČ, Lj. (1937): Udvojavane na obekta v bălgarskija ezik ne e „balkanizăm". In: *Spisanie na Bălgarskata Akademija na Naukite* LVI, 28. 1–20.

MIŠESKA TOMIĆ, O. (2006): *Balkan Sprachbund and Morpho-Syntactic Features.* Dordrecht (= Studies in Natural Language and Linguistic Theory, Vol. 67).

MLADENOV, S. (1928): *Geschichte der bulgarischen Sprache.* Berlin, Leipzig.

PELLEGRINI, B. (1968): Convergence italo-balcaniche negli elementi di origine orientale. In: *Annali delle Facoltà di Magistero dell' Univ. di Palermo.* 1–35.

REICHENKRON, G. (1962): Der Typus der Balkansprachen. *Zeitschrift für Balkanologie* I. 91–122.

REITER, N. (1975): Die Balkansprachen in sozialer Sicht. *Zeitschrift für Balkanologie* XI, 2. 65–70.

RUSEK, J. (2002): Słownik balkanizmów w językach południosłowiańskich. In: *Z polskich studiów slawistycznych X. Językoznawstwo*. Warszawa. 213–212.

SCATTON, E.; AUGEROT, J. (1976/1977): Balkan phenomena, local or universal. *Balkansko Ezikoznanie* XIX. 43–47.

SCHALLER, H. W. (1975): *Die Balkansprachen. Eine Einführung in die Balkanphilologie*. Heidelberg.

SCHLÖSSER, R. (1981): Balkanismen im Armenischen? *Balkan-Archiv* N.F. 6. 83–93.

SCHUBERT, G. (1983): Ein weiterer „Balkanismus" im Ungarischen? *Zeitschrift für Balkanologie* 19, H. 1. 106–117.

SELISCEV, A. (1925): Des traits linguistiques communs aux langues balkaniques: un balkanisme ancien en bulgare. *Révue des études slaves* 5. 38–57.

SKALIČKA, V. (1968): Zum Problem des Donausprachbundes. In: *Ural-Altaische Jahrbücher* 40. 3–9.

STEINKE, K. (1976): Gibt es überhaupt Balkanismen? *Balkansko ezikoznanie* XIX, 1. 21–35.

STOLZ, Th. (1991): *Sprachbund im Baltikum? Estnisch und Lettisch im Zentrum einer sprachlichen Konvergenzlandschaft*. Bochum.

THOMAS, G. (2010): Serbo-Croatian as a Bridge between the Balkan and Central European *Sprachbünde. Balkanistika* 23 (= The Banff Papers). 371–388.

Языковые союзы и балканизмы сегодня: вспоминая Н. С. Трубецкого

Татьяна В. Цивьян (Москва)

„Wien – das Tor zur Balkanhalbinsel – die Wiege der Balkanlinguistik mit Bartholomäus Kopitar und Franz Miklosich, ihren wegweisenden ersten Fachvertretern im 19. Jahrhundert, der Universität Wien und der Österreichischen Akademie der Wissenschaften – ein idealer Tagungsort für die Internationale Kommission für Balkanlinguistik beim Internationalen Slawistenkomitee!" – эмоциональное утверждение организаторов, и я к нему не только присоединяюсь, но и позволяю себе продолжить: «Где, как не в Вене и не в Венском университете вспоминать Николая Сергеевича Трубецкого, основателя теории языковых союзов, давшей основу новому подходу к ареальной типологии и к балканистике как теории!»[1]

Небольшое отступление, прямого отношения к теме как бы и не имеющее. По воспоминаниям В. Н. Топорова (устная беседа), Петр Григорьевич Богатырев, наш замечательный фольклорист, сотоварищ Трубецкого и Якобсона по Пражскому лингвистическому кружку, на вопрос, каким был Трубецкой в жизни, ответил: «Настоящий аристократ!», а на вопрос, что значит «настоящий аристократ», подумав, сказал: «Настоящий демократ!». *Аристократический демократизм* (или *демократический аристократизм*) – оксюморон, но одновременно это и первый шаг преодоления бинаризма оппозиций, преодоления, которое на втором шаге оборачивается сходством, вплоть до слияния.

Этот эпизод я привожу, в частности, по тому поводу, что сам Н. С. ТРУБЕЦКОЙ (1923), который ввел понятие и термин „языковой союз" в противопоставление «языковой семье») (*Sprachbund – Sprachfamilie*)[2], был склонен

---

1 О роли Н. С. Трубецкого в науке см. обширную работу В. Н. Топорова (ТОПОРОВ 1989, 1990).

2 «Предположение, что индоевропейское семейство получилось благодаря конвергентному развитию первоначально неродственных друг другу языков (предков позднейших «ветвей» индоевропейского семейства), отнюдь не менее правдоподобно, чем обратное предположение, будто все индоевропейские языки развились из единого индоевропейского праязыка путем чисто дивергентной эволюции» (ТРУБЕЦКОЙ 1958: 68). О взглядах Трубецкого на «индоевропейскую проблему» см. подробно МАКАЕВ 2004, гл. 2 «О соотношении генетических и типологических критериев при установлении языкового родства».

позднее рассматривать в качестве «типологической общности» индо-европейскую языковую семью (1939, см. русскую версию Трубецкой 1958). Развитие ностратического языкознания и есть, в сущности, развитие идей Трубецкого, как бы в опровержение сформулированной им самим оппозиции родства/сродства (в терминах Р. Якобсона), или помещение ее в гораздо более широкую и плодотворную перспективу.

Итак, идеи Трубецкого о языковых союзах были прорывом в теории ареальной типологии, и я в который раз подчеркиваю известное, но, как мне кажется, до сих пор недостаточно воспринятое: балканский языковой союз Трубецкой привел в качестве *Musterbeispiel*, образец яркий, но не единственный (яркость его была подкреплена книгой Сандфельда, обобщающей собранные ранее балканские данные, SANDFELD 1930).

Напомню, что понятие, или, точнее, инструмент языкового союза применялся и применяется к самым разным сочетаниям языков. Кроме Балкан, в этот круг входят балтийские языки (в контакте со славянскими, я имею в виду балто-славянский языковой союз), языки Волго-Камского региона, Кавказа, Центральной и Средней Азии, Индостана, древней Европы, Евразии в целом (вначале без учета языков Юго-Востока Азии) – и список открыт. В 2005 году в рамках проекта Института языкознания РАН «Языковые союзы Евразии и этнокультурное взаимодействие (История и современность)» вышла статья «Языковые союзы и ареалы языковой и этнокультурной конвергенции на территории Евразии» (ЭДЕЛЬМАН, ЦИВЬЯН 2005), в которой была сформулирована «итоговая» точка зрения на современное состояние заявленной проблемы. Имелась в виду теория языковых союзов и «союзоподобных» образований и возможно более полный учет такого рода контактных (конвергентных) гнезд в пространственной и временно́й (синхронической и диахронической) перспективе Евразии. Приведу окончание статьи, содержащее важные и, как мне кажется, остающиеся более чем актуальными выводы.

Поскольку сложение союза, как и его возможный распад, как уже говорилось, не однократный и целенаправленный акт, мы теперь можем видеть (и/или реконструировать) некоторые механизмы сложения и распада союзов и/или вхождения новых языков в уже сложившийся союз. Таково, например, появление признаков вхождения в союз у языков, пришедших в ареал позднее других (примеры таджикских диалектов на Памире, осетинского и армянского языков на Кавказе; ср. также «балканизацию» тюркских языков, сефардского, цыганских диалектов на Балканах). С другой стороны, обнаруживаются следы существовавшего когда-то языкового союза, который затем распался (примеры дардско-индоарийского „единства“, тесного скифско-южнорусского союза или скифско-западнославянского взаимовлияния, которое приближалось к ситуации языкового и этнического союза, впоследствии растворившегося). Наблюдается и такое явление, как намечавшийся союз, который еще не состоялся или не имеет перспектив состояться в дальнейшем, поскольку новые социолингвистические условия нарушают конвергентную тенденцию, вызывая иные процессы в ареале. Имеются и другие новые существенные наблюдения над языковыми союзами и вообще над разными конвергентными образованиями на территории Евразии, над их историей и над социальными и этнокультурными причинами их появления и/или распада.

Все это дает новый фактический материал для теоретического осмысления данного явления и для выработки более строгих определений языкового союза, конвергентной группы, зоны конвергенции, степени конвергенции и т. д., то есть явлений, находящихся на стыке типологии, ареальной лингвистики, этно- и социолингвистики, культурной антропологии. Последнее обстоятельство указывает на перспективность разработки данной темы с охватом других языковых союзов и ареалов языковой конвергенции, и не только на территории Евразии (21–22).

Балканистика стала своего рода полигоном для испытания методов типологического анализа. Это впоследствии создало определенный перекос в восприятии и концепта языкового союза, и статуса балканских языков и породило сомнения в целесообразности существования балканистики как самостоятельной теоретической дисциплины. Периодически возникает вопрос (и он возникал и на этой конференции), сто́ит ли расширять парадигму лингвистических понятий, вводя термин *языковой союз*, если он, как будто, может быть приложен к одному единственному примеру. Мне этот вопрос представляется анахронизмом, и такой „приговор“ теории языковых союзов (и соответственно концепту балканского языкового союза) заставляет с большим сожалением признать, что идеи Н. С. Трубецкого об ограниченном ареально языковом сообществе – *Sprachbund*, в противопоставлении *Sprachfamilie*, развитые Р. Якобсоном и другими членами Пражского лингвистического кружка, оказались воспринятыми лишь поверхностно. В частности, не было в достаточной степени обращено внимание на принцип сугубой к о н в е н ц и о н а л ь н о с т и концепта языкового союза, открывающего новые измерения и новые интерпретации языкового пространства, включая выход за его собственные пределы, не претендуя при этом на нахождение истины в последней инстанции: «что и как происходит *на самом деле*».

Что бы ни говорить о направленности науки на поиски истины, мне кажется, всегда следует помнить, что наука начинается с классификации, т.е. систематизации материала. Если классификация удачна, она открывает пути к новым знаниям и новым возможностям.

К сказанному о важности классификации – своего рода *мотто* (из переписки Трубецкого с Якобсоном): «Когда какое-нибудь общепринятое мнение разрушают путём приведения нового фактического материала, – то с этим ещё можно примириться. Но когда нового фактического материала не приведёшь, а просто покажешь, что старый, всем известный материал гораздо лучше и проще объяснять как раз наоборот тому, чем это принято, – то вот это-то и вызывает раздражение».

Обычно в связи с понятием языкового союза цитируется выступление Трубецкого на первом съезде лингвистов в Гааге в 1928 г. Мне кажется более существенным процитировать пространный фрагмент из работы Трубецкого о Вавилонской башне (ТРУБЕЦКОЙ 1923: 116–119), в которой он и предложил понятие языкового союза.

«Случается, что несколько языков одной и той же географической и культурно-исторической области обнаруживают черты специального сходства, несмотря на то, что сходство это не обусловлено общим происхождением, а только продолжительным соседством и параллельным развитием. Для таких групп, основанных не на генетическом принципе, мы предлагаем название языковых союзов

Такие союзы генетически друг с другом неродственных лингвистических семейств имеются по всему земному шару. При этом часто бывает, что одно и то же семейство или одиноко стоящий язык принадлежит сразу к двум союзам или колеблется между двумя соседними союзами, играя, таким образом, ту же роль, что переходные говоры в генетической классификации. Таким образом, принимая во внимание обе возможные группировки языков, генетическую (по семействам) и негенетическую (по союзам), можно сказать, что все языки земного шара представляют некоторую непрерывную сеть взаимно переходящих друг в друга звеньев, как бы радужную. И именно в силу непрерывности этой языковой радужной сети и в силу постепенности переходов от одного ее сегмента к другому общая система языков земного шара при всем своем пестром многообразии представляет все же некоторое, правда, только умопостигаемое, единое целое. Таким образом, в области языка действие закона дробления приводит не к анархическому распылению, а к стройной гармоничной системе, в которой всякая часть, вплоть до мельчайших, сохраняет свою яркую, неповторяемую индивидуальность, и единство целого достигается не обезличением частей, а непрерывностью самой радужной языковой сети.

И все же распределение и взаимные соотношения культур основаны, в общем, на тех же принципах, что и соотношения языков, с тою лишь разницей, что то, что в культуре соответствует семействам, имеет гораздо меньше значения, чем то, что соответствует союзам. Культуры отдельных соседних друг с другом народов представляют всегда целый ряд черт, сходных между собой. Благодаря этому среди данных культур обозначаются известные культурно-исторические зоны, – например в Азии зона мусульманской, индостанской, китайской, тихоокеанской, степной, арктической и т. д. культур. Границы всех этих зон взаимно перекрещиваются, так что образуются культуры смешанного или переходного типа. Отдельные народы и части народов специализируют данный культурный тип, внося в него свои специфические индивидуальные особенности. В результате получается та же радужная сеть, единая и гармоничная в силу своей непрерывности и в то же время бесконечно многообразная в силу своей дифференцированности.

Таковы результаты действия закона дробления. При кажущейся анархической пестроте отдельные национальные культуры, сохраняя каждая свое неповторяемое индивидуальное своеобразие, представляют в своей совокупности некоторое непрерывное гармоническое единство целого. Их нельзя синтезировать, отвлекаясь от их индивидуального своеобразия, ибо именно в сосуществовании этих ярко индивидуальных культурно-исторических единиц и заключается основание единства целого. Как все естественное, природное, вытекающее из Богом установленных законов жизни и развития, эта картина величественна в своей непостижимой и необъятной сложности и вместе с тем сложной гармоничности. И попытка человеческими руками разрушить ее заменить естественное органическое единство живых ярко индивидуальных культур механическим единством безличной общечеловеческой культуры, не оставляющей места проявлениям индивидуальности и убогой в своей абстрактной отвлеченности, явно противоестественна, богопротивна и кощунственна.»

Мы видим, что Трубецкой оказался Bahnbrecher'ом и в том, без чего сейчас культурную антропологию и этнолингвистику представить уже нельзя – он, по сути, говорит о модели мира и о картине мира, универсальным кодом которой является язык. Для современной балканистики это более чем актуально. Не менее актуален и взгляд Трубецкого на человека/личность и ее индивидуацию. Здесь видится то главное, что и закладывает основы концепта балканской модели мира.

Трубецкой был одним из основателей евразийства, общественного и философского течения, возникшего в русской эмиграции в 20-е годы XX века, и имел в виду евразийскую, а не балканскую ситуацию, когда говорил о понятии л и ч н о с т и: его он считал «одним из самых важных в евразийской теории» (Трубецкой 1927):

«Одним из самых важных понятий евразийского учения (...) является понятие *личности* (...) *личностью* (...) является не только отдельный человек, но и народ ... сравнительное изучение внешнего проявления нескольких соседних друг с другом этнологических личностей позволяет делать заключения о характере духовного родства между этими личностями (...)

исследование [этого духовного родства] ведется сразу несколькими науками – географией, антропологией, археологией, этнографией, статистикой, историей, историей искусства и т.д. (...) общим предметом этого исследования является именно данная конкретная многочеловеческая (многонародная) личность в ее физическом окружении.»

Конечно, эти его „евразийские“ мысли были ориентированы прежде всего на Россию. При этом в русской ипостаси многонародной личности для Трубецкого был важен прежде всего *анализ*, выделение составляющих (в самом общем плане — выделение „востока“ и „запада“, иранского, туранского, финноугорского элемента и т.д.). Балканское же воплощение многонародной личности (с которым Трубецкому пришлось соприкоснуться биографически) поставило перед ним иную проблему: проблему *синтеза*. Здесь, в балканском культурном пространстве ситуация оказалась иной: неповторимые и неразложимые личности как бы сливали свои индивидуации в особого рода единство. И, вполне органично, изучение этого единства было начато с уровня языка – строительного элемента личности, инструмента особого рода, являющегося одновременно и субъектом, и объектом творчества (*agens* и *patiens*); ср. человек как *agens* и *patiens* собственной модели мира.

Собственно говоря, эти пространные цитаты, эти мысли Трубецкого содержат для меня ответ на вопросы, которым посвящена наша конференция и которые объявлены ее организаторами:

«Since Trubetzkoy (1923), if not earlier, linguistics speak of a "Language Union" ("Sprachbund") or a "Balkanic Language Union" when speaking about south-eastern European languages. Ever since Sandfeld presented these so-called Balkanisms, many researchers (Reichenkron 1962, Schaller 1975, Solta 1980, Asenova 1989, Reiter 1994, Hinrichs 1999, Mišeska-Tomić 2006) have further contributed to this line of research. Thus, most focus on the entirety of Balkan languages and seek to explain them as the expression of mental and pragmatic structures. In contrast, our conference will now focus on the question of how actual and appropriate this approach may seem today».

Мне кажется, что этот подход остается более чем актуальным, что выработанная веками и в самых разных исторических условиях конструкция «единство с сохранением разнообразия или разнообразие с сохранением единства» остается столь же прочной, и сила ее в том, что она не только изменяется и приспосабливается к ситуации, но сохраняет свою, если можно так сказать, главную идею – индивидуацию многонародной личности в разных ипостасях, в том числе и языковых (см. выше, у Трубецкого – «радужная сеть, единая и гармоничная в силу своей непрерывности и в то же время бесконечно многообразная в силу своей дифференцированности»).

Эту прекрасную идею изначально сформулировал Николай Сергеевич Трубецкой.

Литература

Макаев, Э. А. (2004): Общая теория сравнительного языкознания. М.

Топоров, В. Н. (1990, 1991): «Николай Сергеевич Трубецкой – ученый, мыслитель, человек (к столетию со дня рождения)» *Советское славяноведение*, 1990. №6, 51–84; 1991. № 1, 78–95.

Трубецкой, Н. С. (1923): «Вавилонская башня и смешение языков» *Евразийский временник*, кн. 3. Берлин. 107–124.

Трубецкой, Н. С. (1927): *К проблеме русского самопознания*. Париж.

Трубецкой, Н. С. (1958): «Мысли об индоевропейской проблеме». *Вопросы языкознания*, № 1. 65–77.

Эдельман Д. И.; Цивьян, Т. В. (2005): «Языковые союзы и ареалы языковой и этнокультурной конвергенции на территории Евразии» *Языковые союзы Евразии и этнокультурное взаимодействие (История и современность)*. М. 10–22.

Civjan, T. (1999): „Weltmodell und Weltsicht in Südosteuropa". In: U. Hinrichs (Hrsg.): *Handbuch der Südosteuropalinguistik*. Wiesbaden (= Slavistische Studienbücher. Neue Folge. Bd.10). 1019–1048.

Sandfeld, K. (1930): *Linguistique balkanique. Problèmes et résultats*. Paris.

Balkanisms in the Context of the Markedness Theory of Linguistic Change

Olga M. MLADENOVA (Calgary)

Balkanisms are at the core of Balkan linguistics. The term, since Kristian Sand-feld's groundbreaking work (1930), refers to similarities among the Balkan standard languages, their regional varieties and the languages spoken by minorities in the area; to those similarities that are the outcome of convergent development due to centuries of language contact. Even though various, partially coinciding, lists of mostly morphosyntactic but also semantic, lexical and phonological balkanisms have been presented in a number of surveys and comprehensive studies, there is no agreement among researchers as to the status of individual phenomena as "balkanisms" because it depends on their assessment as internal evolutions vs. borrowings and there can be different, sometimes contradictory and usually indirect criteria that are brought to bear on this assessment. I would like to show how this situation can improve if balkanisms are approached from the vantage point of the Markedness Theory of Linguistic Change.

My paper consists of three parts. First, I briefly outline Henning Andersen's Markedness Theory of Linguistic Change as presented in his three contributions to the 2001 edited volume *Actualization* (ANDERSEN 2001a, b, c). In the second part, I give examples of changes relevant to Balkan linguistics whose status as marked or unmarked have been determined previously. Finally, I propose a program for the study of balkanisms within the framework of the Markedness Theory of Linguistic Change.

Markedness Theory of Linguistic Change

When we attend to the actual chronological attestation of historical linguistic changes, we notice that *actualization* – or the orderly progression of change – is not only the sole observable aspect of change but is also grammatically conditioned. More specifically, there is a correlation between the types of environments in which phonological, morphosyntactic, lexical-semantic or other innovations occur along a chronological continuum and the *markedness values* of the parameters involved.

Markedness is a cognitive principle that underlies the organization of diverse semiotic systems, including all areas of grammar. The special relation that obtains between the marked member of an opposition and its unmarked counterpart is due to the fact that the exclusive and symmetrical oppositions of logical *contradiction*, *contrariness* or *converseness*, as the case may be, are simultaneously combined with the asymmetry that is characteristic of the inclusive relation of *hyponymy*. *Male*, for example, is at the same time the contradictory opposite of *female* and the hypernym of hyponyms *male* and *female* (see Table 1).

Table 1: Types of oppositions

	A (unmarked)	B (marked)
Contradictory opposites (binary): One can only be either A or B; there is no third option.[1]	'male'	'female'
Contrary opposites (scalar): There is neutral ground between A and B.	'wide'	'narrow'
Converse opposites: If A is the converse opposite of B, then B is the converse opposite of A.	'parent of *y*'	'child of *x*'

Of the two relations that characterize any opposition, the primary one is that of inclusion. An inclusive relation automatically obtains between any concept that is formed (marked member) and the conceptual space that surrounds it (unmarked member). So, for instance, when two co-variant allomorphs are assigned to two complementary sets of environments, they are initially construed as an inclusive opposition; therefore, one of the allomorphs (the unmarked one) would be allowed to substitute for the other and might in time completely replace it.

Unmarked terms of an opposition are simultaneously superordinate and subsumed, inclusive and included, whereas marked terms are always subsumed and included. Markedness values define synchronic systems but are also closely involved in the actualization of change.

Combinations based on markedness equivalence embody a Principle of Markedness Agreement, which can be formulated as follows: Marked elements naturally occur in marked environments whereas unmarked elements cluster in unmarked environments. This orderly distribution of default category values facilitates speech processing, allowing attention to be focused on the meaningful variables. It should be kept in mind that markedness values are not universal but system-specific: thus, the fact that a given linguistic element is marked in one language does not necessarily mean that it is marked in another. Furthermore, markedness values must be a component of the network of association, which is part of every speaker's competence.

---

1   True contradictions are perceived as a type of contraries in which the intermediate area between the two opposites is not supported by experience and hence is not conceptually formed but remains virtual.

Change imposed on the system from without (as in situations of language contact) typically progresses from marked to unmarked environments; change growing within the system (as in internally motivated changes) moves in the opposite direction. In other words, in different kinds of change, innovative variants are assessed by speakers differently – as marked or unmarked in relation to established variants – and hence, in tune with the Principle of Markedness Agreement, they are compatible with different environments. When a marked innovative variant is widely accepted in a speech community, it may, at some point, be judged to be unmarked – through a reanalysis by new cohorts of learners, for instance. If the innovative variant was at first limited to specific marked environments, its reinterpretation as unmarked allows it to spread to unmarked environments and thus eventually to supersede the old variant. Such a change in a variant's markedness value is referred to as a *markedness shift*. It shows that markedness values are not necessarily stable throughout the history of a given language system.

Table 2: Types of linguistic change

	Within a single linguistic system	In the context of language contact
Pragmatically motivated change (aims to achieve a communicative goal)	Coinage	Borrowing
	Remedial change (avoidance of a dysfunctional expression)	
Unintentional change	Extension	Transference – influence of L2 on L1 (superstratum effects)
		Interference – influence of L1 on L2 (substratum effects)
	Evolutive change (through base-grammar reanalysis)[2]	

One can make sense of differences in actualization in terms of the two layers inherent in individual speakers' grammars: the base grammar (an internally coherent structure of productive rules) and an additive system of usage rules. In the internally motivated evolutive change, the usage rules are gradually adjusted to incorporate an innovation that is unmarked in relation to the productive rules of the core

---

2   The presumed locus of reanalysis is language acquisition.

grammar and that is therefore first admitted exclusively to unmarked environments; only as the innovation loses its novelty does it spread from unmarked contexts to marked contexts. In the externally motivated change, by contrast, usage rules are directly modified to conform to the external model; the innovation is pragmatically motivated and occurs first in the most salient, most monitored marked environments, from which it may spread, as it loses its novelty, to less salient unmarked environments. Similar interactions between base grammar and additive usage rules can be reconstructed for any of the types of linguistic change presented in Table 2. Clarification changes typically spread from marked to unmarked environments, whereas obscuration changes are typically actualized earlier in unmarked than in marked environments.

Marked and unmarked linguistic changes have different starting points and follow their different characteristic paths schematically described in the following flow charts.

Stages of a marked linguistic change
(Invisible stage) initial innovation in usage rules > (invisible stage) multiple adoptions over time within varied populations of speakers > (visible stage) actualization in each population's output > (invisible stage) markedness shift > (invisible stage) establishment of the innovation in base grammar > (invisible stage) adoptions > (visible stage) actualizations.

Stages of an unmarked linguistic change
(Invisible stage) initial innovation in base grammar > (invisible stage) multiple adoptions over time within varied populations of speakers > (visible stage) actualization in each population's output;

Given these alternations of invisible and visible stages of evolution, it becomes exceedingly clear that the study of the only tangible element (actualization) is the key to understanding the process of change.

Morphosyntactic change in Bulgarian

I will now briefly present the outcomes of three studies of morphosyntactic change in Bulgarian and situate them within the framework of Andersen's Markedness Theory of Linguistic Change. These changes have been discussed in more detail in other publications.

Loss of case

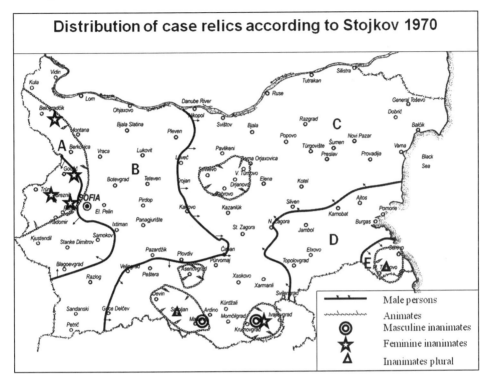

Map 1

Map 1 shows Stojko Stojkov's findings regarding the distribution of case relics in Bulgaria (STOJKOV 1970). By interpreting areal data as diachrony unfolding in space, in tune with a basic tenet of linguistic geography, Stojkov reconstructs the path from Stage I attested in Old Bulgarian with its full-fledged case system to Stage III (lack of case inflection) characteristic of Standard Bulgarian and the innovative West and Southeast Bulgarian dialects (areas B and D on the map). The more conservative Bulgarian dialects in areas A, C and E represent the intermediate Stage II and show the partial loss of case inflection. Based on the conservative dialects, Stojkov concludes that plurals must have lost their case endings before singulars, neuters before masculines and feminines, and inanimates before animates, and that masculine personal names and kinship terms preserved remnants of their case inflection longer than any other categories.

Rise of the definite article

I reached similar results to those of Stojkov regarding the sequence of implementation of identifiability-based overt definiteness on the basis of a statistical analysis of three homilies of the Tixonravov damaskin: *St. Symeon the Stylite, Apostle Thomas* and *St. Demetrius* (MLADENOVA 2007: 132). Masculine singulars with 12.5% coverage of the expected positions lagged significantly behind feminines (69.94%), neuters (69.91%) and plurals of all genders (68%), as did animates (13.38%) in comparison with inanimates (60.8%).

In both processes, therefore, animacy, gender and number governed the actualization of change: the groups that were the first to acquire a definite article were also the first to lose case inflection, and the groups that stuck with case inflection to the last lagged behind in the rise of the definite article.

Grammatical categories such as animacy, gender and number enable humans to categorize and classify the entities of the real world surrounding them and thus deal with information overload. The opposition between the more information-rich, moveable and variable cognitive entities (the figure-like ones) and their static, presupposed counterparts (the ground) can be described linguistically in terms of animacy, gender and number. Figure-like and ground-like noun classes form a continuum, with terms for typical figures, such as animates and especially male persons, at one end and typical grounds – rendered by collectives, plurals, mass nouns and singular count inanimates – at the other. It was the more figure-like noun classes, then, that were the last to lose their case inflections and the last to acquire the definite article.

Viewing figure and ground in terms of markedness, we can see that figure is the marked member of the opposition and ground the unmarked one: until a figure has been perceived by the observer, everything in a given scene is ground. Latent figures emerge from the ground, which as any unmarked term may encompass the whole or be reduced to a part of it (MLADENOVA 2009).

As unmarked innovations, actualized in unmarked environments first, these two Bulgarian morphosyntactic changes are assigned the status of internal changes in Andersen's model.

Evolution of the Bulgarian passive voice

Speakers of Bulgarian have the choice of expressing the passive voice with a participial construction or with a reflexive verb. However, participial passives were more broadly used in the Old Bulgarian period than in the Modern Bulgarian one, and the use of reflexive passives has steadily decreased over the Modern period. The criteria that determine the possibility of passivization and the choice of passive are the following: (1) the specificity/genericity of the real-world event designated by the sentence, (2) the availability of an agency that exerts control over the action, and (3) the correlation between the hierarchies of referents, semantic roles and syntactic positions (МЛАДЕНОВА 2010).

At its pre-literacy stage, Bulgarian had reflexive verbs that could, to some extent, express a passive meaning as well as present and past passive participles that, in constructions with the verb 'to be', expressed state. As with any other spoken language, speakers of Bulgarian did not often reach for the passive voice.

The adequate translation of the liturgical texts in the ninth century required a more versatile passive voice than was possible in Old Bulgarian. Under the influence of Greek, which had used participial passive since its classical period, Bulgarian participial constructions acquired the ability to designate processes and were used in analytic tenses. Reflexive passives may also have been employed more broadly than previously. At this stage, the two forms of the passive had complementary distribution. Eventually, a reanalysis of the passive voice in terms of genericity/specificity took place. A shift in the perception of the two passives came to the fore: the participial and the reflexive passives were now seen as equally capable of expressing specific, non-specific and generic states of affair. Later, at a time preceding the seventeenth century, the two passives were specialized: participial passives were excluded from generic use. So, inside the broad non-specific category, the participial passive was the marked member of the opposition and the reflexive passive its unmarked counterpart. After the seventeenth century, change affected only reflexive passives designating specific situations. This evolution is presented in Table 3.

Table 3: Distribution of the reflexive and participial passives in generic and specific contexts

	Generic context	Non-generic context	
		Non-specific context	Specific context
11th century	reflexive passive participial passive	reflexive passive participial passive	reflexive passive participial passive
17th century	reflexive passive	reflexive passive participial passive	reflexive passive participial passive
20th and 21st centuries	reflexive passive	reflexive passive participial passive	participial passive

In the seventeenth century, speakers of Bulgarian could use reflexive passives to designate specific states of affairs no matter whether referents subjected to the action were in control of it or not. Currently, reflexive passives are only possible if these referents are in control of the action. Furthermore, the retreat of reflexive passives from use was correlated with the quantificational characteristics of both agent and patient as presented in Table 4. Referents at the leftmost end of the scale were affected first and those at its rightmost end were affected last.

Table 4: Relevant quantificational characteristics of agents and patients in passive constructions

Singulars					Plurals
Count nouns	Aggregates	Abstracts	Collectives	Mass nouns	
I rank	II rank	III rank	IV rank	V rank	VI rank

These two criteria (the availability of an agency that exerts control over the action and the correlation between the hierarchies of referents, semantic roles and syntactic positions) must have played a role in actualization at the early stages of this evolution as well, although further research is necessary to confirm this.

In the contemporary language, only predicates designating controlled specific states of affairs whose referents have a ranking coinciding with the ranking of the semantic roles performed by them can still be expressed by reflexive passives. The ranking of referents and their semantic roles, however, does not affect the distribution of participial passives. Therefore, within this segment, the reflexive passive is marked and the participial passive is unmarked. Between these two stages of the evolution, a markedness shift has occurred.

The reflexive passive is currently also retreating from the designation of specific states of affairs. It is a viable option now only when there is a noticeable contrast in the ranks of the referents performing the two semantic roles.

The evolution of the passive voice in Bulgarian is therefore an instance of a marked change that affects marked environments first. Given the cultural background of the change, we can assume that it occurred in the context of Greek-Bulgarian literary contact.

Program proposal for the study of balkanisms

As shown by the previous examples, Balkan linguistics can benefit tremendously from this understanding of change as a projection of synchronic variation onto the diachronic axis, taken in conjunction with the Principle of Markedness Agreement. The study of the actualization in individual Balkan languages of the inventory of phenomena classified as balkanisms in the linguistic literature can help us determine their status with a hitherto unparalleled precision. Observations in the attested progression of Balkan linguistic changes can be conducted in a systematic way and accurately assessed within the framework of Andersen's Markedness Theory.

Before interpreting the overall state of affairs, the actualization of morphosyntactic balkanisms must be subjected to individual analysis in each of the Balkan languages. The results that Stojkov and I have reached regarding the three changes in Bulgarian described above may – but need not – coincide with the situation in other Balkan languages. Ideally, the results of the study of balkanisms in each of the Balkan languages would be published in a collection of monographs, with each volume devoted to a particular morphosyntactic phenomenon. The individual chapters would be written by specialists in the respective languages, and each volume would open with an introduction summarizing the outcomes of the individual analyses and presenting conclusions about the status of the phenomenon under discussion.

Moreover, as Darina Mladenova's ongoing study of tomato terms implies (MLADENOVA 2010), this framework could also advance the analysis of lexical and semantic change in multilingual areas like the Balkans. Although shared lexical and semantic features have contributed as much as morphosyntactic balkanisms have to the Balkan *Sprachbund* (АСЕНОВА 2003), they are the underdog in Balkan linguistics precisely because within traditional lexicological parameters, researchers have found it difficult to conclusively prove their status as "balkanisms". By allowing a uniform treatment of lexical, semantic, morphosyntactic and phonological commonalities, Henning Andersen's Markedness Theory of Linguistic Change could elevate Balkan linguistics to an unprecedented level of sophistication.

References

ANDERSEN, H. (2001a): Actualization and the (Uni)directionality of Change. In: *Actualization: Linguistic Change in Progress*, ed. H. Andersen. Amsterdam & Philadelphia, John Benjamins. 225–248.

ANDERSEN, H. (2001b): Introduction. In: *Actualization: Linguistic Change in Progress*, ed. H. Andersen. Amsterdam & Philadelphia, John Benjamins. 1–19.

ANDERSEN, H. (2001c): Markedness and the Theory of Linguistic Change. In: *Actualization: Linguistic Change in Progress*, ed. H. Andersen. Amsterdam & Philadelphia, John Benjamins. 21–57.

MLADENOVA, D. (2010): From Linguistic Geography toward Areal Linguistics: A Case Study of Tomatoes in the Eastern Balkans. *Balkanistica* 23. 181–236.

MLADENOVA, O. M. (2007): *Definiteness in Bulgarian: Modelling the Processes of Language Change*. New York & Berlin, Mouton de Gruyter.

MLADENOVA, O. M. (2009): On Morphosyntactic Change in Bulgarian: Case and Definiteness. *Diachronica* 26/3. 408–436.

SANDFELD, K. (1930): *Linguistique balkanique – problèmes et résultats*. Paris, Mouton.

STOJKOV, S. (1970): Formele cazuale nominale în limba bulgară. *Romanoslavica* 17. 129–152.

АСЕНОВА, П. (Ред.) (2003): *Актуални проблеми на балканското езикознание: аспекти на изследването на общобалканската лексика. Доклади от международната конференция, София 30.09.-01.10.2001 г.* Велико Търново, Faber.

МЛАДЕНОВА, О. М. (2010): Болгарский язык на полпути от залога неактивного к залогу пассивному. В: *Глаголната система на балкнските езици – наследство и неология*. П. Асенова, А. Петрова и Ц. Иванова, ред. Велико Търново, Faber. 177–218.

Conjunction Calquing – A Heartland Balkanism

Victor A. FRIEDMAN (Chicago)

It has been well established that conjunctions, like discourse particles, with which they overlap, are subject to borrowing among languages, and, moreover, there is a hierarchy in the likelihood of borrowing according to which disjunctives such as 'but' are more likely candidates than alternative conjunctions such as 'or' which are in turn more likely to be borrowed than combinatory conjunctions such as 'and'. MATRAS (1998) explains this hierarchy in functional-pragmatic terms, the basic idea being that the more of a cognitive break or disconnect in the discourse, the more likely the intrusion of a form from another language that is in some way dominant.[1] Disjunctive alternative conjunctions like either/or, neither/nor, etc. have not been examined in this light but seem to follow the same patterns as simple conjunctions. The borrowing of conjunctions among the Balkan languages has received only limited attention, but the calquing of conjunctions has received none at all. In this paper, I shall demonstrate not only that conjunction calquing is possible and occurs, but that it does so under current conditions that continue the Balkan linguistic league despite a century or more of nation-state boundaries. This in turn helps us to nuance concepts such as *dominance* and *prestige*.

WEIGAND (1923/24, 1925) was the first to notice certain similarities between the Albanian admirative (*mënyra habitore*) and what he called Bulgarian (in modern terms, Balkan Slavic) admirative usage and suggested that the Balkan Slavic usage was the result of Albanian influence. He described the Albanian admirative as an inverted perfect and cited example (1), transcribed here as in the original, in both articles:

(1) To bilo xubavo v grada! (Bulgarian)
    Kjen-ka bukër ndë kasaba! (Albanian)
    'How fine town life is!'

The 1925 article generated denials of Albanian influence on Bulgarian by ROMANSKI (1926) and BEŠEVLIEV (1928), but it was cited approvingly by SANDFELD (1930: 119–120). Earlier assertions that the Albanian admirative derived from an unattested inverted future have been definitively rejected by DEMIRAJ (1971), who

---

1 *Dominant* in this sense is broadly conceived as situational, social, or cognitive. MATRAS (1998) gives a variety of excellent examples illustrating the various ways in which the term *dominant* can be understood, a point to which we shall return.

also demonstrates the fact that the admirative is attested in its current form (albeit with variable semantics) in the earliest Albanian writers (see also FRIEDMAN 2010). FRIEDMAN (1980, 1981, 2005) gives an exhaustive summary of previous discussions for Albanian, Bulgarian, Macedonian, and Turkish and also demonstrates the fundamental differences between the Balkan Slavic and Turkish phenomenon, on the one hand, and the Albanian, on the other. The Albanian admirative is marked for non-confirmativity, i.e. surprise (which requires a contrary expectation, i.e. a previous state of nonbelief), doubt or disbelief, or implication that the information is inferred, reported, etc. It constitutes a distinct set of paradigms in which the present, although derived historically from an inverted perfect, is now a true present. The past nature of the Balkan Slavic phenomenon can be seen in the fact that any of the Albanian past admiratives (imperfect, perfect, and pluperfect) can substitute for the present admirative precisely in contexts where Balkan Slavic has an admirative use of the perfect.[2] This can be seen from (2a–e), where (2a) is the original Bulgarian, (2b) is the Macedonian translation – both with admirative usage of the past *bil* – while (2c–d) are Albanian translations of the same Bulgarian sentence using a perfect and pluperfect admirative, respectively, and (2e) is a translation of a similarly admirative usage of the plural *bili* with an imperfect admirative:

(2) a. *Brej, hepten magare bil tozi čovek.* (KONSTANTINOV 1895 [1973]: 88, 89)
     b. *Brej, epten magare bil toj čovek!* (KONSTANTINOV 1967: 91, 93)
     c. *Bre! gomar i madh paska qënë ky njeri!* (KONSTANTINOV 1975: 96)
     d. *Ore, fare gomar paskësh qënë ky njeri!* (KONSTANTINOV 1975: 98)
        'What an ass that guy is!'
     e. *Ama njerëz fare pa mend qënkëshin këta ...* (KONSTANTINOV 1975: 24)
        'What fools are these ...'

By contrast, as I have demonstrated elsewhere (e.g., FRIEDMAN 1981, 1986, 2005) the Balkan Slavic admiratives are actually non-confirmative uses of the unmarked past or perfect whose non-confirmativity is derived from the contrast with a marked confirmative past. In the Albanian of Macedonia, however, we find a new development of the admirative, viz. the replacement of the 3 sg. present optative of 'be' *qoftë* X, *qoftë* Y with the 3 sg. pres. admirative of 'be' *qenka* X, *qenka* Y in the meaning 'be it X or be it Y' or 'whether X or Y'. I will argue here that this is a Balkanism connected with Macedonian influence that derives from an Albanian reinterpretation of a Macedonian optative usage of the Macedonian verbal *l*-form.

---

2 Another argument for the pastness of the Balkan Slavic usage is the fact that a question with no past reference can use the present admirative in Albanian but not the Balkan Slavic admirative usage of the unmarked past, e.g. Albanian *Ku qenka mjeshtri?* but not Macedonian **Kade bil majstorot* for 'Where is the boss?'

As such, it is a relatively rare example of a calqued rather than copied (borrowed) conjunction.[3]

The Macedonian verbal *l*-form is descended from the Common Slavic resultative participle, which in Old Church Slavonic (*ceteris paribus,* the equivalent of Common Slavic for our purposes here) was used to form the perfect, pluperfect, conditional, and future perfect. In Macedonian, unlike Bulgarian, the *l*-form lost its ability to function attributively, but it remained in use for the perfect, pluperfect, and conditional. At some late stage in Common Slavic, i.e. before the rise of the opposition confirmative/non-confirmative, what was the *l*-participle developed an optative usage in the third person singular to replace the third singular imperative which, being homonymous with the second singular imperative, was lost. According to VAILLANT (1966: 97), such usage is found in Czech as well as throughout South Slavic and thus must have arisen prior to their separation. The popular Bosnian/Croatian/Serbian/Montenegrin toast *živ(j)eli* as well as the use of the use of invariant *bilo* in the meaning of 'any', e.g. *bilo ko(j)* = *koj i da e* 'anybody' are examples of such optative usage. It is worth noting that in its meaning of 'any', East Slavic *(-)bud'/budz'* and Polish *bądź* seem to preserve the an old optative usage of the third singular imperative.

For Polish, however, TOPOLIŃSKA (2008) points out uses of *bylo* that also look optative, as in example (3):

---

3   CAMAJ (1984: 163) makes the important point that in both older and modern Albanian writers, the subjunctive present admirative can be used in the protasis of irreal conditionals, as in his example *të fryke era, s'kishim me ndejë jashtë* 'If the wind were blowing, we would not sit outside'. NEWMARK, HUBBARD and PRIFTI (1982: 86) also cite the irreal conditional use of the imperfect and pluperfect subjunctive admirative, e.g. ... *fluturojnë e sillen ca re të vogla, të zeza pis, sikur të qenkëshin tym prej dinamiti* '... there fly around and roam about a few small clouds, pitch black, as if they actually were dynamite smoke' and *Sikur e gjyshja të mos paskëshin nxjerrë kokën nga qerrja ... kushedi sa gjatë do të kishte mbetur ashtu ...* 'If his grandmother had not actually stuck her head out of the cart ..., who knows how long he would have remained like that ...' These modal uses are connected with usages in some of the earliest attested admiratives (see DEMIRAJ 1971) and are, I would argue, a development that is entirely distinct from the non-confirmative meaning (see also LIOSIS 2010 on the modal fate of the admirative in Arvanitika). As CAMAJ (1984: 187) points out, the Albanian optative itself is an internal Albanian development with close morphological ties to the aorist (which, we can add, is the one paradigm absent from the admirative). It would appear that expressions of desire and *irrealis* were in a state of relative flux in Albanian for some time before the attestation of our earliest documents. Nonetheless, the phenomenon we are examining in this article is based on a later Albanian system, where both optative and admirative have achieved their current states, but at the same time a new development is possible.

(3) było nie było, zrobimy to (Polish)
     'kako da e, kje go napravime toa' (Macedonian gloss)
     'No mater what, we will do it.' (lit. let it be or not be/
     how it is, we will do it.)

She compares this to usages of *buło* in Ukrainian and *bio*, etc. in the former Serbo-Croatian, such as (4):

(4) Bilo doć! = 'ko ti je kriv što nisi došao' (BCS)
     'You should have come' = whose fault is it you didn't come

VAILLANT (1966: 97) attributes such uses of the *l*-participle to an elliptical optative composed of *da* plus the conditional (3 sg. *bi* plus *l*-participle), e.g., Macedonian *Dal ti Bog dobro!* literally 'May God grant you [that which is] good!'. He also notes that Russian uses of the type *pošël* 'Let's go' have nothing to do with the South and West Slavic phenomenon under consideration here but are rather expressive uses of the past (cf. colloquial English *We're outa here'*). It thus seems to be the case that we are dealing with an old isogloss that spread from South to North to include West Slavic and even Ukrainian, but not Russian.

In Macedonian, the *l*-form was reinterpreted as a perfect rather than an elliptical conditional and can thus occur in other persons with the auxiliary of the old perfect rather than the conditional marker, e.g. *Da ne sum te videl!* literally 'May I not have seen you!', i.e. I'd better not see you [around here]. In the course of subsequent centuries, the perfect meaning of the old present resultative perfect using the *l*-form in Macedonian came into competition with that paradigm's non-confirmative meaning, which arose as a result of the development of marked confirmativity in the synthetic pasts (see FRIEDMAN 1986 for detailed discussion). In southwestern Macedonian, with the rise of a new resultative perfect using the auxiliary *ima* 'have' and the neuter verbal adjective, the old perfect using the present of 'be' plus the verbal *l*-form became restricted to non-confirmative usage and, in the extreme southwest, disappeared almost entirely. To the north and east of the Ohrid-Struga region up to the river Vardar (and beyond, since World War Two), the old and new perfects are in competition, and the old perfect using the verbal *l*-form is an unmarked past, but with a chief contextual variant meaning of non-confirmativity (see FRIEDMAN 1977 for detailed explanation).

At the same time, with all these developments, a remnant of the old Late Common Slavic use of the *l*-participle as an optative (without, n.b., an auxiliary in all the languages where it occurs) developed in Macedonian and Bulgarian into a disjunctive alternative conjunction using the third person singular neuter of 'be' *bilo ..., bilo ...* in the meaning 'whether ..., or ...'[4] In its meaning, this construction

---

4 Some speakers of BCS accept the *bilo ... bilo ...* construction, and it is attested in
   literature, but other modern speakers today reject such usage.

corresponds to the Albanian use of the 3 sg. present optative *qoftë ..., qoftë* .... In modern Albanian, the optative is more or less limited to expressions such as *rrofsh!* 'thank you' (literally, 'may you live'), *me nder qofsh* 'you're welcome' (literally 'may you be with honor') and a variety of other formulae, blessings, and curses that can use any verb in any person, such that the paradigm is very much alive albeit quite restricted in function. These functions, however, are very tightly connected to the desiderative function of the optative. As such, it rarely occurs outside this function, and when it does, e.g. in the expression *në qoftë se* 'if', it can always be replaced by some other locution (*në, po, po të*, etc.).

In the Albanian of Macedonia (but not that of Kosovo, Montenegro, Albania, or Greece)[5], it appears that the combination of restriction of the Albanian optative to wishes combined with the surface similarity of the Macedonian optative use of the *l*-form to its non-confirmative use, especially with the verb 'be' as in the example from Weigand cited for Bulgarian above (the Macedonian would be the same, *mutatis mutandis*, see FRIEDMAN 1981, 1986 for further discussion), has resulted in a calqued replacement of *qoftë* by *qenka* in the meaning of 'whether ..., or ...'. Thus, for example, an Albanian politician from Tetovo talking with a colleague in Skopje about the importance of investment made the point that nationality was irrelevant: *qenka shqiptar, qenka amerikan, qenka maqedonas* ... '[it doesn't matter] whether it's (= let it be) an Albanian, an American, or a Macedonian ...'. The Macedonian for *qenka* here would be *bilo*, while standard Albanian would use *qoftë* in this position.

As indicated above, based on evidence from a variety of languages (MATRAS 1998), we have here an interesting and relatively rare example of calquing as opposed to ordinary borrowing in a conjunction. Thus, for example, in the hierarchy of borrowed conjunctions in Romani (and elsewhere), 'but' is most likely to come from the most recent contact language, 'or' from an older contact language, and 'and' is least likely to be borrowed (ELŠÍK and MATRAS 2006: 185). Consistent with this hierarchy, colloquial Macedonian and Albanian share Turkish *ama* for 'but' (literary Albanian *por* and literary Macedonian *no*), but have native expressions for 'or' and 'and'. Moreover, in the context of nineteenth and twentieth century nation-state politics, neither Macedonian and Albanian in what is today the Republic of Macedonia occupied positions of prestige prior to World War Two. In terms of the concept of *dominance*, therefore, this calque argues for a source in situations where Macedonian had some sort of contextual dominance not associated with prestige or politics. As MATRAS (1998: 322) makes clear, dominance can be pragmatically conditioned by a variety of factors such as topic, addressee, and conversational expectations that do not necessarily involve prestige. If the first

---

5   I wish to thank Rexhep Ismajli of the Academy of Arts and Sciences of Kosova and the University of Prishtina for confirming that this usage is limited to Macedonia.

occurrence of the calque was the result of the cognitive dominance of Macedonian in a bilingual speaker, the subsequent spread of the construction to the Albanian dialects of Macedonia in general could have been promoted by other factors. Given that that Albanian optative is used most often for expression of the speaker's desire, its use in a conjunction that expresses indifference or alternatives rather than actual wish may have been contributed to its vulnerability to the calqued alternative. The fact that this Albanian usage is a calque and not a borrowing – and at the middle level in the hierarchy of likelihood – points to a long-standing local bilingualism between the Albanian and Macedonian language communities of the type that give rise to the Balkan sprachbund. Such a calque also demonstrates both the accessibility and the vulnerability of verbal forms when used in the function of other parts of speech. Finally, it is the Albanian calque that illuminates the grammatical complexity of the Macedonian structure.

References

BEŠEVLIEV, Veselin (1928): Kăm văprosa za taka narečena 'admirativ' v bălgarski ezik. *Makedonski pregled* 4, 1. 174–177.

CAMAJ, Martin (1984): *Albanian Grammar*. Harrassowitz: Wiesbaden.

DEMIRAJ, Shaban (1971): Habitorja dhe mosha e saj. *Studime filologjike* 8 (=25), 3. 31–49.

ELŠÍK, Viktor; MATRAS, Yaron (2006): *Markedness and Language Change: The Romani Sample*. Berlin: Mouton de Gruyter.

FRIEDMAN, Victor. A. (1977): *The Grammatical Categories of the Macedonian Indicative*. Columbus: Slavica.

FRIEDMAN, Victor. A. (1980): The Study of Balkan Admirativity: Its History and Development. *Balkanistica* 6. 7–30.

FRIEDMAN, Victor. A. (1981): Admirativity and Confirmativity. *Zeitschrift für Balkanologie*, 17, 1. 12–28.

FRIEDMAN, Victor. A. (1986): Evidentiality in the Balkans: Macedonian, Bulgarian, and Albanian. *Evidentiality: The Linguistic Coding of Epistemology* (Advances in Discourse Processes, Vol. 20), ed. by Johanna Nichols and Wallace Chafe. Norwood, NJ: Ablex. 168–187.

FRIEDMAN, Victor. A. (2005): Admirativity: Between Modality and Evidentiality. *Sprachtypologie und Universalienforschung*, 58, 1. 26–37.

FRIEDMAN, Victor A. (2010): The Age of the Albanian Admirative: A Problem in Historical Semantics. *Ex Anatolia Lux: Anatolian and Indo-European Studies in Honor of H. Craig Melchert*, ed. by R. Kim, N. Oettinger, E. Rieken, M. Weiss. Ann arbor: Beech Stave Press. 31–39

HAMP, Eric P. (1994): Albanian. In: R. E. Asher (ed.): *The Encyclopedia of Language and Linguistics*. Oxford: Pergamon Press. 65–67.

KONSTANTINOV, Aleko (1895): Baj Ganjo. Sofija: Penčo V. Spasov.

KONSTANTINOV, Aleko (1967): Bay Ganjo, transl. Gjorgji Caca. Skopje: Kultura.

KONSTANTINOV, Aleko (1975): Baj Gano, transl. Dhurata Xoxa. Prishtina: Rilindja.

LIOSIS, Nikos (2010): If only Arvanitika had an admirative mood! Between evidentiality and counterfactuality. *Zeitschrift für Balkanologie* 46, 2. 184–202.

MATRAS, Yaron (1998): Utterance Modifiers and Universals of Grammatical Borrowing. *Linguistics* 36. 281–331.

NEWMARK, Leonard; HUBBARD, P.; PRIFTI, P. (1982): *Standard Albanian*. Stanford: Stanford University.

ROMANSKI, Stojan (1926): Review of Weigand 1925 q.v. *Makedonski pregled* 2, 3. 143–145.

SANDFELD, Kristian (1930): *Linguistique balkanique*. Paris: Klincksieck.

TOPOLIŃSKA. Zuzanna (2008): Było pomyśleć wcześniej. *Z Polski do Macedonii*, I. Kraków: Lexis. 166–172.

VAILLANT, A. (1966): *Grammaire comparée des langues slaves*, III, 1. Paris: Klincksieck.

WEIGAND, Gustav (1923/24): The Admirative in Bulgarian. *The Slavonic Review* 2. 567–568.

WEIGAND, Gustav (1925): Der Admirative im Bulgarischen. *Balkan-Archiv* 1. 150–152.

YLLI, Xhelal (1997): *Slavisches Lehngut im Albanischen*. Munich: Otto Sagner.

Convergence and Causation in Balkan Slavic

Ronelle ALEXANDER (Berkeley)

1. Statement of the problem

What has caused the striking similarities among Balkan languages? Two words in this sentence ("caused" and "languages") identify issues that continue to plague the discipline.

The first issue is that of causation. It is now generally agreed that one cannot unambiguously identify the single source language – whether it be an ancient substrate, a peripheral but prestigious language, or one of the current member languages – which gave rise to any one of the "Balkanisms". Rather, these similarities evolved as a result of intense communicative contact among speakers of the several languages over a period of centuries. It stands to reason that if there are a number of people living in close proximity who know each other's languages imperfectly if at all, but who need to communicate, these people will develop ways to do it. The various adaptive shifts that come about in these complex communicative situations accumulate over time to produce changes in everyone's speech patterns. This overall process is usually referred to by the very general term "convergence", and it is the accretion of these processes which leads to the results we refer to today as "Balkanisms".

But when people talk of the "cause" of a change, they tend to think in terms of the Western logical "cause and effect" model, according to which the cause of something is its source. This is certainly part of the reason why many Balkanists still (perhaps unconsciously) continue to look for a single source for any one Balkanism. Thus, despite the clear awareness that most Balkanisms cannot be traced back to a single source, and that the best we can do is to think in terms of multiple causation and the reinforcement of parallel developments, many Balkanists still look for "something" (usually in one specific language) that exerted the influence which gave rise to the change. And in fact, there do exist several instances where one of the shared features indeed does seem to be traceable to a single source. If, for instance, (a) geographical and historical evidence allows us to presume intense contact between Language A and Language B; (b) we know that Language A had greater social prestige during the majority of the presumed contact period; (c) the feature in question is documented in Language A from very early times; and (d) the feature in question is documented in Language B only more recently – then ought we not be able to assume that Language A is the source of the phenomenon in Language B? Below I will examine two concrete instances where it has been generally assumed that this is the case.

In doing so, I will have occasion to address the second issue, which is that of language. For fairly obvious reasons, the "Balkanisms" which linguists study are the crystallized results of convergence changes which took place gradually over many centuries. That is, the data which Balkan linguists analyze are drawn from the modern Balkan languages, and furthermore from the standard forms of these languages, again for the obvious reason that grammars and dictionaries of standard languages allow one easy access to material that is reliable and verifiable. At the same time, the (standard) form of any one of these language is a system which was formulated purposefully, and quite recently, during the period of Romantic nationalism. It represents only one form of the language in question (and often an idealized one at that).

One cannot do Balkan linguistics properly on the basis of standard language data alone. It is imperative that dialectal material be included in the analysis, no matter how difficult access to such data may be. Not only does this immediately allow a much broader scope of analysis, but the data themselves have been gleaned from the speech of conservative traditional speakers whose communicative interactions, while not reproducing the original contact situation, nevertheless resemble it more closely than do those of literate educated speakers. Furthermore, data of the standard languages allow only a superficial understanding of each phenomenon. With respect to Balkan Slavic alone, none of the major "Balkanisms" can be even properly defined without reference to the broad span of dialectal variation. When historical development is at issue, such data are even more vital. One cannot address the issue of "causation", therefore, without taking a view of "language" that necessarily embraces the broad scope of dialectal variation.

Of course, data from modern dialects do not allow us to completely recapture the sequence of changes which led to the modern state of any one Balkanism, nor are they the only relevant factor. The question of causation continues to be complex. The best we can do is to find a middle ground between the easy (but incorrect) solution that any one Language A is "obviously" the source for the existence of a Balkanism, and the despairing (and unnecessary) "solution" that no real answer can ever be found. The road to this middle ground consists in taking a judicious view of the number of factors involved in any one instance. My remarks on the case studies which follow – both of which have generally been interpreted as instances where one other concrete language is "obviously" the source for the corresponding phenomenon in Balkan Slavic – should be seen in this light.

2. Case study: evidentiality in Balkan Slavic

The topic of the first case study is very well known, and has been extensively analyzed. It has been called many names, the most common of which is the "evidential mood". It is a striking feature of both Macedonian and Bulgarian, present in the standard languages as well as in most dialects, and it is frequently assumed to have been borrowed into Balkan Slavic from Turkish. The circumstances surrounding its rise in Balkan Slavic satisfy the four criteria noted above, namely (a) Turkish and Balkan Slavic were in contact throughout the duration of the Ottoman presence in the Balkans, (b) as the language of the overlords, Turkish clearly had higher prestige, (c) the *-miş* forms of Turkish (the equivalent to the evidential mood) are attested in Turkic from a very early date, and (d) the development of this category in Balkan Slavic clearly post-dates the Ottoman arrival.

But when one looks more closely, one sees that the situation is much more complex. Both Victor Friedman and Grace Fielder have contributed immensely to our understanding of the rise of this category in Balkan Slavic. In an early, groundbreaking paper, Friedman showed that the similarities between the two systems were deceptive, pointing out not only how the category functions differently in each of the two systems (Slavic and Turkish), but also how the salient features in each system were following a very different path, such that what was archaic in the one was innovative in the other, and vice versa (FRIEDMAN 1978). This paper was based on material from the standard languages. In an earlier paper, however (FRIEDMAN 1976), he had traced the development of the Macedonian *imam*-perfect, tracking the several stages through dialectal gradation. He expanded this discussion in a later paper (FRIEDMAN 1988), showing how the expansion of the *imam*-perfect in Macedonian was closely bound up with the development of the evidential. Dialectal data were critical to the argument in both papers.

It was Grace Fielder, however, who brought all the elements together in a convincing hypothesis about the diachronic relationship between the rise of the *imam* perfect, the loss of the auxiliary in the *sum* perfect (the inherited perfect tense), and the development of the evidential. Focusing on the full range of Balkan Slavic, from far eastern Bulgarian dialects to far western Macedonian dialects, she showed how the complex interaction between these three systemic elements formed a coherent whole (FIELDER 1996). What made her diachronic explanation so convincing was the consistent way in which she was able to track each of the three changes through the dialectal gradation from east to west. Furthermore, all of the changes were fully motivated within Balkan Slavic itself; the explanation did not make reference to any factor outside of Slavic.

Yet it is clear that Turkish had to have played some sort of role, and both of these authors returned to this question. Fielder addressed this issue directly in a paper comparing Turkish and Bulgarian, but intending the argument, *mutatis mutandis,* to be applicable to Macedonian as well (FIELDER 1999). Analyzing in some detail the function of the forms in question in narrative strategy and finding significant differences between the two systems, she proposed that "what was borrowed from Turkish … was not a new morphosyntactic category … but rather a discourse function" (ibid: 82). This, in her view, is an instance of "conceptual convergence" rather than linguistic convergence. Several years earlier, Friedman had outlined a similar scenario for the development of Balkanisms, proposing that "discourse functions are not merely subject to borrowing but serve as entry points for the development of structural change" (FRIEDMAN 1994: 110). Although no explicit mention was made of the source of borrowing, Friedman's argumentation was, as in earlier works, based upon a careful study of the gradation in dialectal variation. A decade later, however, in a major study on evidentiality in the Balkans that included attention to dialectal variation (FRIEDMAN 2004), he hypothesized that "regions with heavy concentration of Turkish speakers in urban centers served as sources of innovation" for the grammatical encoding of evidentiality (ibid: 125), and concluded that an analysis of its rise and spread "requires an account that considers sociolinguistic factors and dialectal distribution at various levels of the grammar" (ibid: 126).

As the above brief survey demonstrates, the significant scholarly attention paid to this particular issue has yielded very fruitful results. A simple model of "cause and effect" must be ruled out: because the function and development of evidentiality in the two systems is so different, it cannot have been borrowed directly into Balkan Slavic from Turkish. Once one moves beyond pure structural comparisons into the domain of pragmatics and sociolinguistics, however, one cannot deny the role of Turkish influence. But this is something quite different from causation pure and simple. It is highly significant that Friedman identified the source of innovation not as a language (Turkish), but rather as the multilingual region itself. In other words, it was the fact of inevitable and sustained contact, and its sociolinguistic result – the various sorts of ongoing convergent processes – that was the "cause".

3. Case study: "double accent" in Balkan Slavic

The topic of the second case study is in the realm of phonology, and is much less well known, given that it is not present in either of the Balkan Slavic standard languages. This is the "double accent" of southern Balkan Slavic, which is found in numerous dialects. It is most widely and consistently attested in a compact area of southern Balkan Slavic adjacent to (and overlapping with) Greek territory, and is generally assumed to have arisen under influence from Greek. Here, too, that which we know of its rise in Slavic satisfies the four criteria given earlier. Namely, (a) the region in which it occurs (southwestern Bulgaria, southeastern Macedonia, and adjacent Slavic-speaking areas within Greece) is one where Greek and Slavic were in constant contact, presumably since the arrival of the Slavs in the Balkans; (b) Greek has long been a prestige language in the region, first as the official language of the Byzantine state which held sway in the area, and then as that of the Ottoman-anointed administrators of all Orthodox peoples during Ottoman times; (c) such accentuation is attested in Greek since Classical times, and (d) the migration of Slavs to the Balkans post-dates the Classical period, and there is no suggestion of any such pattern in the Common Slavic that Slavs brought with them (actual records of such accentuation in Balkan Slavic are necessarily quite recent, since accented popular speech is recorded with any faithfulness only in relatively recent times).

Indeed, the similarity is quite striking, at least on the surface level. In both Greek and Balkan Slavic, words of four syllables or more receive a second stress, according to a very noticeable rhythmic (trochaic) pattern. But closer analysis shows the situation to be much more complex. The second accent appears in Greek almost always in instances of true augmentation, when the boundary of a word group is extended by the addition of a clitic or clitic-like element to the right. In Balkan Slavic, however, the second accent can appear in numerous contexts – without boundary extension (that is, in single words, sometimes even trisyllables), with boundary extension to the right, and with boundary extension to the left. Furthermore, double accent is found over a much broader area than the region in which it is best known (the compact area closest to the Greek border), and in a number of different rhythmic patterns. I have verified the above claims both through a thorough study of Balkan Slavic dialectal material, and through my own Balkan Slavic field recordings made primarily in Bulgaria (ALEXANDER 2004) but also in certain regions of Macedonia. I have also paid particular attention to one type of double accent – that found in negated verb phrases – which is attested not only throughout Bulgaria but also beyond its borders, both in Macedonia (ALEXANDER 1991–1993) and among Slavic speakers in Greek and Turkish Thrace (ALEXANDER 1999).

Thus, just as in the first case study, here too the patterns of dialectal variation and gradation suggest a complex of internal developments that are not consistent with simple borrowing from a source language. Furthermore, the various instantiations of double accent in Balkan Slavic appear to have affected the overall historical development of Balkan Slavic prosodic structures in purely internal ways (ALEXANDER 1993: 192–197, ALEXANDER 1994: 34–38); at the same time one must note that the dialects most affected are those located nearest to the area of most intense bilingual contact. In areas further away from this contact zone, this type of accentuation developed in different ways, but all still at the dialectal level. Only one of these patterns was "grammaticalized" and made part of the Bulgarian literary standard: the requirement of a second accent on a preverbal clitic following negation (as in *kázvat mu* 'they tell him' vs. *ne mú li kázvat* 'don't they tell him?'). The fact that this pattern is internalized at some deeper level is seen in its extension to a broader range of constructions at the dialectal level; furthermore, as a recent experiment showed, this pattern is an innovation that appears to be spreading (ZHOBOV, ALEXANDER & KOLEV 2004).

At the same time, the basic similarities between Greek and Slavic, within what must be assumed to have been the core contact region, make it impossible to deny some sort of influence from Greek. But is it a simple case of cause and effect? Can this and other prosodic patterns that have been called a "general Balkan *Redetakt-rhythmus*" (REICHENKRON 1962: 99–102) be traced directly and unambiguously to a Greek source? Common sense tells us that here too the "cause" would be the fact of contact itself.

4. Concluding remarks

What caused the similarities among Balkan languages? Embedded within this question are several more basic ones, such as: Must the term "cause" in this context always imply a donor and a recipient? Do the similarities between two or more languages, at whatever level, always imply some sort of causal relationship? Can one conceive of "language" in this instance as an abstract entity, or must one necessarily look at multiple levels? In each case, the answer is the one which eschews simplicity. With respect to causation, we can only agree with Lindstedt, who observes that the "cause" of the Balkan convergence area is "the multilingual contact situation itself, to the extent that the traditional notions of 'source language' and 'target language' may not always be applicable" (LINDSTEDT 2000: 231). And with respect to languages, it is abundantly clear that the greater amount of dialectal variation one is able to study, the more insight one gains into each one of these separate instances of convergent change.

References

ALEXANDER, Ronelle (1991–1993): The Balkan Nature of Macedonian Stress Phenomena. *Makedonski jazik* 42–44. 105–114.

ALEXANDER, Ronelle (1993): Remarks on the Evolution of South Slavic Prosodic Systems. *American Contributions to the Eleventh International Congress of Slavists*, ed. R. Maguire and A. Timberlake. Columbus: Slavica. 181–201.

ALEXANDER, Ronelle (1994): The Prosodic Systems of Balkan Slavic: A Partial Typology. *Zbornik za filologiju i lingvistiku* 27. 23–40.

ALEXANDER, Ronelle (1999): Word Order and Prosody in Balkan Slavic Dialects: The Case of Thrace. *Dialektologija i lingvistična geografija*, ed. V. Radeva et al. Sofia: Univerzitetsko izdatelstvo. 61–73.

ALEXANDER, Ronelle (2004): The Scope of Double Accent in Bulgarian Dialects. *Revitalizing Bulgarian Dialectology*, ed. R Alexander and V. Zhobov. Berkeley: Global, Area, and International Archive. 192–208. Retrieved from: http://escholarship.org/uc/item/9hc6x8hp.

FIELDER, Grace (1996): The Relationship between the *ima* ('have') Perfect, the *sum* ('be') Perfect, and Auxiliary Loss in Macedonian and Bulgarian. *Studii za makedonskiot jazik, literatura i kultura / Studies in Macedonian Language, Literature and Culture*, ed. V. Stojčevska-Antik et al. Skopje: Univerzitet "Sv. Kiril i Metodij". 177–185.

FIELDER, Grace (1999): The Origin of Evidentiality in the Balkans: Linguistic Convergence or Conceptual Convergence? *Mediterranean Language Review* 11. 59–89.

FRIEDMAN, Victor (1976): Dialectal Synchrony and Diachronic Syntax: The Macedonian Perfect. *Papers from the Parasession on Diachronic Syntax*, ed. S. Steever at al. Chicago: Chicago Linguistic Society. 96–104.

FRIEDMAN, Victor (1978): On the Semantic and Morphological Influence of Turkish on Balkan Slavic. *Chicago Linguistic Society: Papers from the Fourteenth Regional Meeting*, ed. D. Farkas et al. Chicago: Chicago Linguistic Society. 108–118.

FRIEDMAN, Victor (1988): Morphological Innovation and Semantic Shift in Macedonian. *Zeitschrift für Balkanologie* 24,1. 34–41.

FRIEDMAN, Victor (1994): Variation and Grammaticalization in the Development of Balkanisms. *CLS 30, Papers from the 30th Regional Meeting of the Chicago Linguistics Society*, vol 2: *The Parasession on Variation in Linguistic Theory*, ed. K. Beals et al. Chicago: Chicago Linguistic Society. 101–115.

FRIEDMAN, Victor (2004): The Typology of Balkan Evidentiality and Areal Linguistics. *Balkan Syntax and Semantics*, ed. O. Mišeska-Tomić. Amsterdam: Benjamin. 101–134.

LINDSTEDT, Jouko (2000): Linguistic Balkanization: Contact-Induced Change by Mutual Reinforcement. *Studies in Slavic and General Linguistics* 28. 231–246.

REICHENKRON, Günther (1962): Der Typus der Balkansprachen. *Zeitschrift für Balkanologie* I. 91–122.

ZHOBOV, Vladimir, Ronelle ALEXANDER, and Georgi KOLEV (2004): Hierarchies of Stress Assignment in Bulgarian Dialects. *Revitalizing Bulgarian Dialectology*, ed. R. Alexander and V. Zhobov. Berkeley: Global, Area, and International Archive. 226–240. Retrieved from: http://escholarship.org/uc/item/9hc6x8hp.

Die Balkanismen in geolinguistischer Sicht
Ein erster Schritt

0. Einleitung

Die wissenschaftliche Lage um die Balkanismen (BK) im Jahre 2010 ist durch folgende Merkmale charakterisiert:

1. BK sind grammatisch und typologisch, in ihrer Varianz und in ihrer Extension vollkommen durchdekliniert (ACEHOBA 2002; MIŠESKA TOMIĆ 2006).
2. BK sind im Rahmen der gängigen linguistischen Paradigmen dargestellt worden (Überblick in HINRICHS 1993). Ein Schwerpunkt besteht im historischen Paradigma; ein Defizit in der Generativen Linguistik und der Linguistischen Pragmatik.
3. Es gibt eine Vielzahl von Einführungen in die Disziplin, die im Prinzip keine Wünsche mehr offenlassen (z.B. von H.-W. Schaller, G. R. Solta, J. Feuillet, K. Steinke, E. Banfi, P. Asenova, O. Mišeska Tomić, W. Fiedler).
4. So gut wie alle Erklärungen für die Genese der BK sind genannt, von der Substrattheorie (SOLTA 1980) bis hin zur Hypothese der frühen Kreolisierung und Simplifizierung von Sprachstrukturen (HINRICHS 2002, 2004a). Anerkannter Favorit ist heute eine multifaktorielle Erklärung mit dem Schwerpunkt auf der Kontaktlinguistik.
5. Die Geschichte der Balkanlinguistik ist lang und bis in alle Details ausgeleuchtet (SCHALLER 1999). Es gibt inzwischen unübersehbar viele Listen von Balkanismen; Trend ist, dass die Listen länger werden und auch auf Standard Average European (SAE)-Strukturen ausgreifen (s. das Modell in HETZER [2010] im Anhang).

Neue Erkenntnisse über Balkanismen kann man heute angesichts der Forschungslage nur noch erlangen,

a. wenn ihre *grammatische Interaktion* untereinander (BK 1 ↔ BK 2 ↔ ...) diachron und synchron untersucht wird; im Zentrum sollten hier Grammatikalisierungsprozesse und die kognitiv-semantischen Funktionen stehen;
b. wenn ihr *Status innerhalb der Gesamtgrammatik* einer Einzelsprache gewichtet und dann vergleichend genauer bestimmt wird;
c. wenn sie *eurolinguistisch* abgeglichen werden, und zwar als linguistischer Faktor innerhalb der Sprachbundmodelle, als Varianten in den Nonstandard- und

Standardsprachen Europas und eventuell als Modellfall für zukünftige Konvergenzprozesse in Europa;

d. **wenn sie *geolinguistisch* abgeglichen werden.** Das stärkste Argument für dieses umfangreiche Projekt besteht in dem Faktum, dass BK strukturell im Prinzip ‚*uneuropäisch*' sind – wenn man den SAE-Standard und die Sprachtypen Osteuropas zugrunde legt. Sporadisch mögen sie in vielen Weltgegenden auftauchen, ob nun zufällig oder nicht. Von einer globalen Perspektive wäre deshalb der größte Erkenntniszuwachs zu erwarten. Denn Balkansprachen sind offenbar jeweils unterschiedliche Mischungen aus dem SAE-/EUROTYP-Faktor und dem BALKANFAKTOR – was gerade ihre typische Eigenart ausmacht und sie zu einem eigenen ‚EUROTYP BALKAN' zusammenschließt.

a) und b) sind eine Zukunftsaufgabe der systemlinguistisch und standardologisch arbeitenden Balkanlinguistik; c) und d) sind Aufgaben der Arealtypologie und einer globalen Typologie.

Zu c):

Wenn man die europäischen Standardsprachen ansieht, sind BK

– *in ihrem für den Balkan charakteristischen Verbund* im Europa *außerhalb* des Balkans absolut nicht vorhanden: es gibt im übrigen Europa keine ‚Balkansprache' im typologischen Sinn;

– jedoch, außerhalb eines Verbundes, vereinzelt auch wieder „regelmäßig": Kasusverlust, Deflexion und Kongruenzabbau sind schon seit langem allgemein-westeuropäische Phänomene, desgleichen z.B. der analytische Komparativ mit Partikeln (hier überschneiden sich sozusagen die westeuropäische und die balkanische Tendenz zum Analytismus). Ein Futur mit dem Inhalt WOLLEN, der sich auf dem Wege zur Partikel befindet, gibt es im Englischen, ebenso Phänomene einer UBI/QUO-Fusion. Andererseits sind typische BK wie z.B. der sogenannte Infinitiversatz durch konjunktionalen Nebensatz mit Verbum finitum schon fast wieder singulär balkanisch (s. aber unten Farsi!).

– BK haben ansonsten meist Zufallscharakter und stehen typologisch isoliert innerhalb einer einzelnen Sprache da. So ist es mit den oft zitierten Vorzeigebeispielen: dem nachgestellten Artikel im Schwedischen und Baskischen; desgleichen im Armenischen (SCHLÖSSER 1981), dem doppelten Objekt im Spanischen, dem Infinitiversatz im Ungarischen (SCHUBERT 1983), dann mit Infinitiversatz, Artikel und *evidentiality* im Romani (MATRAS 1994). Im näheren Umkreis des Balkans sind diese BK meist historisch sekundär und beruhen auf lokaler Interferenz;

– Weiter ist zu klären, inwieweit der alte Sprachbund-Begriff, der ja vom Balkan herkommt, auf das Areal Europa überhaupt anwendbar ist, vice versa (Diskussion in STOLZ 2010), ob es hier Überschneidungen gibt und wo sich beide Typen von Sprachbünden grundsätzlich voneinander unterscheiden. (Dies läuft letztlich auf die Frage hinaus, ob der Sprachbund-Begriff sich überhaupt in die Zukunft retten lässt). Der Kreuzpunkt wird hier das traditionelle Standard Average European-Modell und seine Revision sein. (In entwickelten SAE-Modellen [HASPELMATH 2001] spielen die BK als spezielle Sprachzüge so gut wie keine Rolle.)

Die europäischen *Nonstandards* – obwohl noch kaum auf balkanoide Züge untersucht – scheinen schon ein bunteres Bild anzudeuten. Soweit zu sehen, sind bis jetzt identifiziert (einige Details in HINRICHS 1990):

1. der nachgestellte Artikel im historischen Kroatisch;
2. der nachgestellte Artikel in russischen Dialekten;
3. Balkanismen als nichtkodifizierte Varianten oder Durchkreuzungen mit dem Standard im Altbulgarischen (HINRICHS 1984);
4. so gut wie alle Balkanismen in den modernen südserbischen Dialekten;
5. das doppelte Objekt in Soziolekten (Umgangssprache) des Russischen, Polnischen, Čechischen (АНГЕЛОВА 1990, ЛАПТЕВА 1976, passim);
6. verstreute balkanoide Züge in oralen Nonstandards des Englischen (dazu KORTMANN 2009, passim);
7. UBI/QUO-Vertauschung und etliche analytische Deflexionsphänomene in der neueren gesprochenen deutschen Umgangssprache, die oft ‚balkanoide' Züge tragen (HINRICHS 2009).

Die Gründe für das sporadische Auftauchen von BK in einzelnen Subvarietäten (oder: für Durchkreuzungen mit dem Standard) können verschieden sein. Außer dem Faktor *Zufall* ist wohl Interferenz zwischen Nachbarsprachen das naheliegende, vertikal ein Ausstrahlen von Substrukturen nach unten nach oben. Ich vermute bei 2 frühe Interferenz mit finnougrischen Sprachen, bei 3 Durchkreuzungen von Kopisten mit dem tatsächlich gesprochenen Altbulgarisch des 11. Jh. (Diglossie), bei 4 Interferenz mit benachbarten Balkansprachen, bei 5 und 6 Einfluss der spontan-kolloquialen mündlichen Syntax, bei 7 eine Mischung aus Interferenz mit Migrantensprachen, Bilingualismus, Rückeinfluss des Migrantendeutsch, Ökonomie (Reduktion von semantischer Komplexität), Trend zur Syntagmatisierung, Kopie aus der Kolloquialsyntax und „Spielen" mit un/markierten Varianten als Signal für akut-beschleunigten Sprachwandel.

Die Erfassung von Nonstandards in der europäischen Arealtypologie ist, wie angedeutet, noch weitgehend Desiderat (KORTMANN 2009). Da Nonstandards aber durch die Bank analytischer sind als die kodifizierten Standards, ist hier immer ein höherer ‚Balkanfaktor' zu erwarten. Vermutlich ‚verstecken' sich noch viele weitere balkanähnliche Phänomene in den gesprochenen Nonstandards der europäischen Standardsprachen.

In diesem Beitrag liegt der Schwerpunkt auf d), also auf dem geolinguistischen Blick. Es ist ein erster Schritt.

Belegt sind BK oder balkanoide Phänomene bis jetzt z.B. in vielen Kreolsprachen (HINRICHS 2004a), im Armenischen (SCHLÖSSER 1981) und im Persischen (s. Anhang); es ist damit zu rechnen, dass sie weltweit auftauchen, wenn auch nicht in einem intensiven Verbund wie in den Balkansprachen. Als Musterfall hierfür kann man den nachgestellten Artikel in afrikanischen Sprachen nennen (z.B. Ewe, Wolof, Mende u.a.). Von der Erhellung der Genese einschlägiger Züge *außerhalb Europas* kann in jedem Fall ein erheblicher Erkenntniszuwachs für die Balkanlinguistik erwartet werden. Denn man wird erst dann endgültige Klarheit über die weltweit offenbar einmalige Spezifik des Balkansprachbundes in Europa gewinnen, wenn genug einschlägige Daten aus vielen Sprachen in der Welt gesammelt und ausgewertet sein werden.

Im folgenden soll anhand von fünf ausgewählten BK (bestimmter Artikel, Kasusabbau, Komparativ, Futur I, Renarrativ/*evidentiality*; s. die neueste Liste im Anhang nach HETZER 2010) gezeigt werden, wie man eine weltweite Synopse von sprachlichen Strukturen balkanlinguistisch ausnützen kann. Dies ist ein erster Schritt in Richtung auf das anspruchsvolle Zukunftsprojekt der weltweiten Abklärung der sogenannten BK und typologisch verwandter Strukturen. Die Grundlage hierfür bildet der ‚World Atlas of Language Structures‘ (‚WALS‘) (HASPELMATH 2005), der sich insgesamt auf einen Fundus von 2600 Sprachen stützt und 142 Sprachzüge weltweit untersucht. Einige tangieren die BK direkt (s.u.). Für den Balkan (und sekundär auch für Europa) ergibt sich allerdings beim Arbeiten mit WALS prinzipiell das Problem, das für balkanlinguistische Erfordernisse oft nicht genau genug aufgelöst wird/werden kann. (Hiermit war durchaus zu rechnen, weil Balkan wie Europa letztlich nur kleine Sprachenecken auf der Weltkarte sind.)

Für die ausgewählten Balkanismen 1.–5. und ihre folgende Kommentierung vergleiche man die WALS-Karten im Anhang. (Die Autoren in Klammern haben den betreffenden Sprachzug für das WALS-Projekt bearbeitet.)

1. Der bestimmte Artikel (DRYER 2005)

‚Bestimmter Artikel‘ meint *grosso modo* (was hier genügen mag) ‚Determiniertheit‘ plus ‚anaphorische Funktion‘ in Kontext, Kotext oder Weltwissen hinein. Nach dem für den bestimmten Artikel von DRYER verwendeten *sample* ist das Verhältnis von Artikelsprachen zu artikellosen Sprachen 336 : 230. Eine genauere Auflösung auf die Artikel-Varianten zeigt die in die Karte eingeblendete Tabelle (‚legend‘). Die Sprachen selbst werden im WALS unter einem Spezial-link einzeln aufgezählt. Auffällige Ballungszentren von Artikelsprachen sind Westeuropa (Englisch, Französisch, Deutsch), Mittelafrika in einem breiten Gürtel, der pazifische Raum und der Westrand von USA und Kanada. Typische „exotische“ Artikelsprachen wären hier z.B. Ewe, Lakota-Sioux, Hawaiianisch und viele Kreolsprachen.

Weiße Flecken liegen vermehrt in Nordasien, Südamerika und Indien; in Europa haben auch die meisten slavischen Sprachen keinen bestimmten Artikel.

Dryer differenziert nicht nach der *Position* des Artikels relativ zum Nomen. Hier kann man sich aber an typologische Indizien halten: Sprachen mit Artikel*affix* (84 im *sample*) hängen dieses wohl (ausschließlich?) an das Nomen an, was genau balkantypisch ist. Solche Sprachen finden sich massiv im arabischen Raum, in Mittelafrika, im Kaukasus; Beispiele sind Kurdisch, Armenisch, Persisch, Arabisch, dann Schwedisch und finnougrische Sprachen in Russland. Postposition von freien, d.h. nicht-agglutinierenden Artikeln gibt es in vielen Kreolsprachen (*nom la* ‚der Name‘, St. Lucian-Kreol) und Indianersprachen (*wičaša ki* ‚der Mann‘, Lakota-Sioux).

Balkanlinguistisch interessant ist Position drei (roter Kreis auf der Karte): *definitive affix*, weil auch die relevanten Balkansprachen hauptsächlich ein solches verwenden und weil das *Affix* in aller Regel *post*poniert steht (mit künstlichem Bindestrich): bulg. *жена-ma* ‚die Frau‘, rum. *oraş-ul* ‚die Stadt‘, alb. *djal-i* ‚der Junge‘ etc. Das Bulgarische hat einen morphologisch transparenten Artikel, Makedonisch sogar dreifach; Rumänisch (*fata* ‚das Mädchen‘) und Albanisch sind im Femininum auch fusionierend (*vajza* ‚dass.‘), was auf höheres Alter hinweist. Albanisch hat offenbar potentiell alle drei Artikelpositionen: vorangestellt (eher selten) in *të shkruarit* ‚das Schreiben [*Tätigkeit*]‘; nachgestellt in *djali* ‚der Junge‘; und zwischengestellt (‚Gelenkartikel‘) *djali i mirë* ‚der gute Junge‘, wobei Affix und Autolexem gemischt auftreten, ähnlich in rum. *omul cel bun* ‚der gute Mensch‘. Systemisch gesehen ist das nachgestellte Affix die unmarkierte und produktive Artikelvariante. Typologisches Merkmal für Balkan wäre neben ‚nachgestelltem Affix‘ schließlich auch noch ‚Varianz‘ der Artikelausdrücke und ‚Kombination von Artikelsorten‘.

Der Balkan lässt sich in globaler Sicht und typologisch (Postposition/Affix) lose assoziieren mit dem benachbarten Raum weiter im Osten: Kaukasus, arabischer Raum, Kurdistan. Der nachgestellte Artikel wäre also vor dem Hintergrund *Europa* neben ‚Balkanismus‘ auch so etwas wie ein *Orientalismus* (ohne hier direkte areale Implikationen anzusetzen).

2. Kasus (IGGESEN 2005)

Ein ziemlich großer Teil der von IGGESEN für das *feature* ‚Kasus‘ ausgewerteten Sprachen hat keine morphologischen Kasus, sondern markiert syntaktische Beziehungen anders, z.B. durch die Wortfolge oder gar nicht. Untersucht wurden 261 Sprachen, davon haben 100 keine Kasus, also um die 40%. Kasuslose Sprachen überwiegen im afrikanischen Zentralgürtel, im indonesischen Raum, China, ganz Amerika; alle Kreolsprachen sind kasuslos. Aber auch Westeuropa ist im Laufe der Zeit eine Zone ohne morphologische Kasus (geworden). Kasussprachen sind, mehr oder weniger stark, konzentriert in Osteuropa (Ungarisch, Russisch), in

Nordasien, hier vor allem als finnougrische und Turksprachen, aber auch im dravidischen Indien und in Australiens Aborigini-Sprachen mit 9, 10 und mehr Kasus.

Europa ist grob geteilt in eine konservative kasusreiche Zone im Osten und eine progressive kasuslose Zone im Westen (Details s. die Beiträge in HINRICHS 2004). Das Deutsche steht mit seinen vier Kasus zwar numerisch in der Mitte, weist aber heute deutliche Symptome des Kasusabbaus und damit eine Annäherung an die westlichen Nachbarsprachen auf.

Der Balkan präsentiert eine bunte Melange und ist am wenigsten einheitlich, bezogen auf die BK. Und hier ist ein einschlägiger Balkanismus strenggenommen nur historisch zu formulieren, nämlich als Tendenz zum Abbau der alten Kasusparadigmen des Lateinischen, Altgriechischen und Altslavischen unter einer sich beschleunigenden Drift in Richtung Analytismus. Der Balkan ist, so gesehen, eine Übergangzone oder eine Exklave mit einem eigenen Kasusprofil, das sich im Einzelnen weiter ausdifferenziert:

1. Bulgarisch und Makedonisch haben keine Kasus, sind typologisch progressiv und verhalten sich hier im Prinzip wie Englisch und Französisch, indem sie eine analytische Kasusmarkierung anwenden.
2. Rumänisch hat zwei morphologische Kasus und stellt sich hier zu einem offenbar stabilen Typus in der Welt, der im Prinzip aus einem Obliquus als Casus generalis besteht und einem sogenannten Nominativ, der oft nicht markiert ist.
3. Neugriechisch hat drei Kasus mit einem erhaltenen Genitiv als Zugeständnis an die attische Tradition.
4. Albanisch hat je nach Auslegung 4–5 Kasus und hält sich viel auf seinen Ablativ zugute. Eingerechnet werden muss hier Kasussynkretismus im Paradigma besonders der determinierten Formen.

Das Areal Balkan stellt mit seinem Kasusprofil einen Sonderfall im Areal Europa dar, wird aber sicher der allgemein-europäischen Tendenz der Kasusreduktion und des Übergangs zu syntagmatischen Techniken der Markierung weiter folgen.

3. Futur I (DAHL / VELUPILLAI 2005)

Futur kann man auf vier verschiedene Weisen ausdrücken:

1. morphologisch-synthetisch-flexivisch wie in latein. *cantabo*
2. syntaktisch-analytisch mit Hilfsverb wie in engl. *I will take*, oft mit Subjektzwang
3. partikelanalytisch wie in bulg. *ще направя*
4. periphrastisch und metonymisch, z.B. durch Präsens plus indizierende Adverbien.

DAHL/VELUPILLAI untersuchen nur nach plus oder minus, also ob vorhanden oder nicht. Weltweit halten sich die Sprachen die Waage und es gibt keine großräumigen kompakten isomorphen Areale. Man sehe aber auf das Großareal Indien-Türkei-Kaukasus *mit* flexivischem Futur, das Gebiet China bis hinunter nach Java *ohne*. Europa hat historisch das ererbte indogermanische synthetisch-flektierende Futur abgebaut („Aversion"), was wohl einer langen typologischen Drift hin zum Analytismus geschuldet ist. Ausnahmen liegen, wie so oft, an der Peripherie: Baltisch und Keltisch.

Auch der Balkan ist heute flexionsfuturfrei, deshalb stellen Dahl/Velupillai hier auch zu Westeuropa keinen signifikanten Unterschied fest. Löst man feiner auf, kommt der Unterschied ans Licht. Das balkanische „typologische Ziel" besteht zweifelsfrei in einer ganz uneuropäischen Konstruktion, nämlich dem Cluster aus starrer <u>Partikel</u> und Verbum finitum im Präsens: bulg. *ще пее*, griech. *θα τραγουδάει (er wird singen)*. Die Parallelen zu Kreolsprachen sind hier unübersehbar (s. Anhang). Eine gewichtige Variante ist der albanisch-rumänische Typus, der offenbar alt ist und aus den Dialekten stammt. Er imitiert den Infinitivsatz mit Konjunktion und ist dreigliedrig: alb. *<u>do të</u> mendoj*; rum. *o să merg*. Der oft angeführte Balkanismus „Inhalt WOLLEN" hinter der Partikel ist etymologisch und für die Stufen der balkanischen Grammatikalisierungsprozesse zwar interessant, typologisch aber unerheblich. In den Kreolsprachen ist der *modale* Inhalt für Partikeln, also die Inhalte WOLLEN, KÖNNEN, MÜSSEN der Hilfsverben, hochreduziert und partikularisiert vertreten in den sogenannten Tempus-Modus-Aspekt-Systemen (‚TMA') der Verben. Auf diesem Feld mag die Erkenntnisausbeute aus einem weltweiten Abgleich besonders groß sein.

4. Komparative (STASSEN 2005)

Das Kapitel ‚Komparativ' zeigt noch einmal exemplarisch die Schwierigkeiten auf, die sich ergeben, wenn man WALS wirklich konsequent für Europa und den Balkan nutzen will. Wir haben klar eine sehr weitmaschige Auflösung der Sprachzüge und ihrer geographischen Verbreitung, was die Nutzung für die Areale Europa und Balkan einfach einschränkt. Weltweit ist wohl der Typus *Locational Comparative* am weitesten verbreitet, Typ türk. *o ben-<u>den</u> daha büyük* ‚er ist größer als ich', semantisch *VON MIR MEHR GROSS*; der *Exceed*-Typus (semantisch HAUS 1 GROSS *ÜBERSCHREITEN* HAUS 2) konzentriert sich hauptsächlich in Afrika, der *Conjoined*-Typus (semantisch DIESES HAUS GROSS ↔ JENES KLEIN) vor allem in Südamerika.

Europa ist ein Hort des von WALS sogenannten *Particle Comparative*, worunter jedoch sowohl der Typ engl. *bigger* als auch der Typ griech. *πιο καλός* subsummiert werden, was typologisch problematisch und terminologisch irreführend ist. Wenn man feiner auflöst, hat man hier klar den alten synthetischen Typus und den neuen analytischen Typus in Europa, die *innerhalb Europas* durchaus so etwas wie eine charakteristische Opposition bilden. Sicher kann man sagen, dass der von STASSEN in WALS verwendete europäische Komparativ-Typus morphologisch am dichtesten komprimiert ist. Weltweit bildet dieser Typus jedoch die schwächste Gruppe und kommt außerhalb Europas nur verstreut vor. Europa und der Balkan haben also keinerlei Anteile an anderen Komparativ-Typen und bilden somit zusammen ein kompaktes Areal für sich. Will man das Sub-Areal Balkan weiter auflösen, ergibt sich, wie oben angedeutet, eine typische Binnendifferenzierung:

1. der sogenannte synthetische Komparativ nach engl. *smaller* und serb. *kraći* ohne und mit Fusion. Schwerpunkt für ersteren sind Deutsch und Englisch, für letzteren Osteuropa bzw. Zentraleuropa/Ostmitteleuropa.
2. der analytische Komparativ 1, nach engl. *more intensive*, frz. *plus grande*. Schwerpunkt ist Westeuropa.
3. der analytische Komparativ 2, d.h. der echt balkanische Typus mit starrer Partikel plus Positivum wie rum. *mai bun*, alb. *më mirë* ‚besser‘.

Die einzelnen Typen reflektieren historisch verschiedene Stadien der Analytisierung des alten synthetischen idg. Komparativs. 1. ist das europäische Auslaufmodell. In den slavischen Sprachen z.B. ist heute der Typ 2 überall auf dem Vormarsch: russ. *более интересно*; serb. *više interesantan* etc. Im Deutschen bahnt sich langsam eine Konkurrenz aus 1. und 2. an, im Sinne des neuen Typus /*mehr eigenständig*/ aufkosten des alten Typus /*eigenständiger*/, was wahrscheinlich durch wachsende Sprachkontakte und den dadurch ausgelösten Neoanalytismus erklärt werden kann. Typ 3 zeigt das Endstadium der Reduzierung und Grammatikalisierung und vielleicht den europäischen Typus der Zukunft.

5. Evidentials (DE HAAN 2005)

Im Sample von DE HAAN (418 Sprachen) gibt es etwas mehr Sprachen, die *evidentiality* grammatisch kodieren, als solche, die dies nicht tun (237 : 181). Grammatische *evidentiality* ist weltweit eine fakultative Option, was im Areal Europa ganz besonders deutlich wird. Auffällig (und angesichts der Fülle an oralfundierten Sprachen verwunderlich) ist, dass Afrika fast als weißer Fleck dargestellt ist; *particle evidentials* sind offenbar in beiden Amerikas zuhause, z.B. in vielen ‚Indianersprachen‘.

Wenn man Europa maximal ansetzt, sind jedoch im Areal – bis auf *particle evidentials* – alle Typen der grammatischen Kodierung von *evidentiality* aufzufinden:

1. Sprachen ohne (grammatische Kodierung von) *evidentiality*, z.B. Ungarisch
2. Sprachen mit verbalem Affix für *evidentiality*, z.B. Lettisch
3. Sprachen, in denen *evidentiality* Teil des Tempussystems ist, z.B. Bulgarisch

4. Sprachen, in denen *evidentiality* lexikalisch durch Modalwörter wiedergegeben werden kann, z.B. Deutsch

5. Sprachen mit gemischten Typen grammatischer *evidentiality*, z.B. Schwedisch, Albanisch

Der Balkan ist eine Zone, die diese Merkmale aufweist:

1. *Evidentiality* ist, wenn vorhanden, Teil des Tempussystems oder mit ihm assoziiert, was weltweit eher selten ist (Details in FRIEDMAN 1999).

2. *Evidentiality* hat ihren referentiellen Schwerpunkt in der Vergangenheit, was auch formal zum Ausdruck kommt (Ausnutzung von Perfektformen etc.). Dies ist weltweit *nicht* unbedingt die Regel.

3. *Evidentiality* weist in der Sprache X im Prinzip keine Mischtypen auf. Hinweisen muss man aber auf den albanischen Admirativ, der offenbar verschiedene formale <u>Bildungsweisen</u> zulässt, vgl. synthetisches *punua̱ka* ‚er arbeitet ja‘ mit verbalem <u>Affix</u> und analytisches *paska punuar* ‚er soll gearbeitet haben‘ mit <u>Modallexem</u> und Partizip Präteritum Passiv.

6. Fazit

Alle Balkanismen sollten in einer größeren Monographie weltweit abgeklärt werden, soweit es jetzt möglich ist. Der WALS sollte dabei den äußeren Rahmen bieten, die Feinauflösung kann auf die balkanlinguistische Fachliteratur sowie auf die WALS-Spezialliteratur der Einzelzüge (und jede einzelsprachliche Grammatik) zurückgreifen. Möglich und wünschenswert wäre, auch den eurosprachlichen Abgleich, besonders auf der Ebene der oralen Umgangssprachen und Nonstandards, mit voranzutreiben. Dieses Vorgehen würde zu einer weiteren Entmystifizierung des Balkansprachbundes beitragen, neue Einsichten zur Ätiologie bringen und Paradigmen auf den Plan rufen, die bis jetzt noch eher unberücksichtigt sind, für den Balkan aber hohes Erkenntnispotential haben, z.B. Theorien der Simplifizierung von Sprachstrukturen im Interesse der Optimierung mündlicher oder mehrsprachiger Kommunikation durch den Ausgleich von Defiziten in L2 oder L3. Vor diesem Hintergrund darf man gespannt sein auf den in Arbeit befindlichen ‚Atlas of Pidgin- und Creol Language Structures‘ *APICS* und die dort untersuchten Sprachzüge, dessen Erscheinen für 2011 angekündigt ist (HASPELMATH et al. 2011). Forschungsziel wäre, den Balkansprachbund „zu entzaubern" und zu belegen, dass die vielgerühmten Balkanismen der Output sind von sprachreduktiven Prozessen unter dem langwährenden Dach einer einmaligen, historisch begrenzten kulturell-kommunikativen Symbiose.

Anhang 1: Karten

Karte 1: Der Artikel (DRYER 2005)

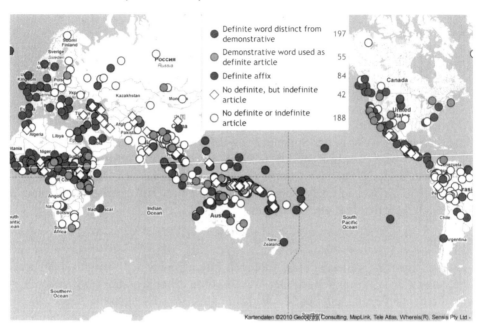

Karte 2: Morphologische Kasus (IGGESEN 2005)

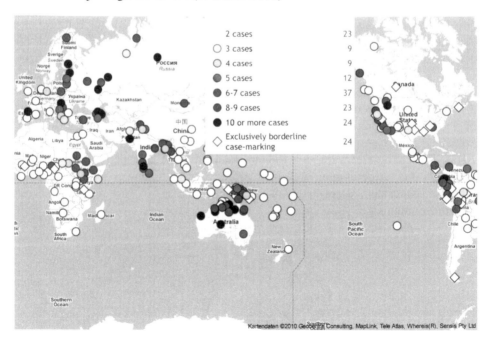

Karte 3: Futur I (DAHL / VELUPILLAI 2005)

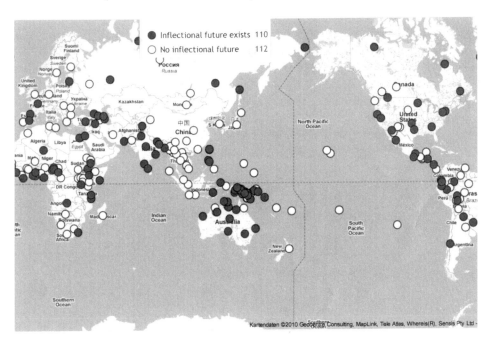

Karte 4: Komparativ (STASSEN 2005)

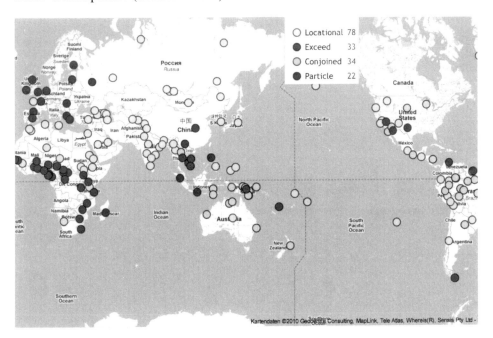

Karte 5: Grammatische Kodierung von *evidentiality* (DE HAAN 2005)

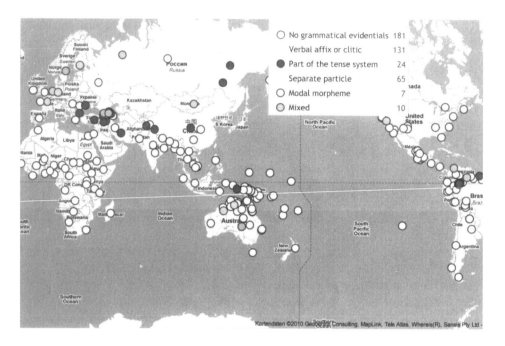

Anhang 2

I. Neueste Liste der Balkanismen nach HETZER (2010), mit kommentierenden Ergänzungen (U.H.). *Fett*: In diesem Beitrag behandelt

1. Phonem /ə/, orthographisch: ë, ъ, ă, э (alb., bulg., rum., moldauisch): alb. *shtëpi* ‚Haus'
2. **Nachgestellter bestimmter Artikel (determinierte Form): bulg.** град*ът*
3. **Gelenkartikel (nach einem subst. Beziehungswort) (vor einem Adjektiv): alb.** *djali i mirë* ‚der gute Junge'
4. **Verminderung der Anzahl der Kasus bis hin zur Aufgabe jeglicher synthetischer Kasusmarkierung: bulg.** *на жена*
5. Bewahrung der Kategorie des Neutrums oder Entwicklung der Kategorie der Heterogenität (‚Ambigenie', Sing. mask., Plural fem.): rum. *lucru : lucrurile*
6. Possossivpronomen durch Personalpronomen im (Genitiv oder) Dativ ersetzt: griech. *ο φίλος μου* ‚mein Freund'
7. Indeklinable Partikel (bzw. Adverb) statt Relativpronomen: mak. *Функци-jama што ja има контекстот*
8. Bildung der Zahlen 11–19 nach dem Muster ‚eins auf zehn': bulg. *двана̲десет*
9. Pronominale Verdopplung des (Dativ- oder) Akkusativ-Objekts: alb. *e merr autobusin* ‚ich nehme den Bus'
10. **Aufgabe synthetischer Komparationsformen und des Suppletivismus: bulg.** *по-добре* ‚besser'
11. Gerundium (Verbaladverb) statt Partizip der Gleichzeitigkeit
12. Ersetzung des Infinitivanschlusses in zusammengesetzten verbalen Prädikaten durch finite Formen im Konjunktiv: griech. *πρέπει να πάω*
13. **Bildung des Futurs mit einer erstarrten Form des Verbs ‚wollen': bulg.** *ще вървя* < abulg. *хощетъ*
14. Bewahrung synthetischer Temporalformen der Vergangenheit (Imperfekt und Aorist neben Perfekt und Plusquamperfekt): bulg. *написаше; написа*
15. **Umdeutung von Perfektformen als Modus (der Fremdbezeugtheit bzw. Evidenz): bulg.** *написал*
16. Gemeinsamer Wortschatz: (a) Substratwörter, (b) Turzismen bzw. Gräzismen

II. Balkanoide Phänomene in einigen Kreolsprachen im Vergleich mit Balkansprachen

Fett: Im Beitrag behandelt; KS = Kreolsprachen; BS = Balkansprachen; E = Englisch-basiert, F = Französisch-basiert, P = Portugiesisch-basiert, H = Niederländisch-basiert.

1. Analytismus mit Partikeln

KS: TMA-Systeme/Verb, z.B. Hawaii (E): *he **bin** walk* ‚er ging‘; *he **go** walk* ‚er wird gehen‘, *he **stay** walk* ‚er geht gerade‘; *he **bin** **stay** walk* ‚er ist eine Zeitlang gegangen‘; *he **bin** **go** **stay** walk* ‚er wäre gegangen‘;

BS: Nomen und Verb: *b. **на** жена; **по**-добре; къщата **му**; **ще** вървя; **да** чакам* etc. / → Polysemie und strenge Wortfolge bei Kumulation! /

2. Nachgestellter Artikel

KS: Schwerpunkt F-Kreols, vgl.: Lesser Antill. (F): *wat **la*** ‚Ratte die‘; St. Lucian (F): *nom **la*** ‚Name der‘, *lekòl **la*** ‚Schule die‘, *ŝapo **a*** ‚Hut der‘, *fi **ja*** ‚Tochter die‘ *tab **la*** ‚Tisch der‘; Principé (P): *meza **sɛ*** ‚Tisch der‘; Tok Pisin (E): *man **ia*** ‚Mann der‘

BS: bulg. *града**т**/града* ‚Stadt die‘; *жена**та*** ‚Frau die‘; *дете**то*** ‚Kind das‘; *мъже**те*** ‚Männer die‘; rum. *oraşul* ‚Stadt die‘; *femeia* ‚Frau die‘; *stelele* ‚Sterne die‘; alb. *qytet**i*** ‚Stadt die‘; *shok**u*** ‚Genosse der‘; *gruaja* ‚Frau die‘; *shqiptar**ët*** ‚Albaner die‘

3. Komparativ mit Partikel

KS: Guadeloupe (F) ***pli** vit*; Sri Lanka (P): ***mais** роисо*; Hawaii (E): ***more** better*; Negerhollands (H): ***mehr** grot*

BS: alb. ***më** mirë*; rum. ***mai** bun*; griech. ***пιο** καλός,* bulg. ***по**-добър*

4. Ausdruck von Possessivität durch nachgestellte Kurzformen von Personalpronomen

KS: Principé (P) *kaso **mɛ*** ‚Hund mich‘ = ‚mein Hund‘, Papia Kristang (P): *chapeu **yo*** ‚Hut mich‘; Neomelanesisch (F): *māmā **li*** ‚Mutter ihn‘; Saramaccan (E): *di oto **ɛn*** ‚das Auto ihn‘

BS: bulg.: *стаята **ми*** ‚Wohnung mir‘; *усмивка **му*** ‚Lächeln ihm‘; griech. *о φίλος **µου*** ‚der Freund mir‘; *η ψυχή **της*** ‚die Seele ihr‘; serb. *kuća **mu*** ‚Haus ihm‘, im Sinne von ‚meine Wohnung‘, ‚sein Lächeln‘ etc.

5. Lexifizierung der Reduplikation

KS: Sranan (E): ***taytay*** ‚Seil‘ zu *tay* ‚binden‘; ***freyfrey*** ‚Insekt‘ zu *frey* ‚fliegen‘; Sierra Leone Krio (P): ***bronbron*** ‚verbrannte Kruste‘ zu *bron* ‚brennen‘; ***dorodoro*** ‚Sieb‘ zu *doro* ‚sieben‘; Saramakka (E): ***libi-libi*** ‚lebend‘ zu *libi* ‚leben‘; Haiti (F): ***bɛl bɛl*** ‚sehr schön‘ zu *bɛl* ‚schön‘, ***sale sale*** ‚sehr salzig‘ etc.

BS: alb. ***lloj lloj*** ‚allerlei‘ zu *lloj* ‚Gattung‘, rum. ***rău-rău*** ‚ernsthaft böse‘ zu *rău* ‚schlecht‘; bulg. ***рано-рано*** ‚ganz früh‘; griech. ***σιγά-σιγά,*** türk. ***yavaş-yavaş*** ‚allmählich‘, zu *σιγά* ‚langsam‘ etc.

6. Evidentialität (EVID)

KS: Hawaii (E): **+EVID**: *John bin go Honolulu **for** see Mary.* ‚John ist nach Honolulu gefahren, um Mary zu treffen‘, *ist zu hören.* **–EVID**: *John bin go Honolulu **go** see Mary.* ... *und wird Mary treffen‘. Dies ist sicher.*

Mauritius (F): **+EVID**: Li ti desid *pu* **mâz** lavian. ‚Er beschloss *wohl*, Fleisch essen zu gehen'. **–EVID**: Li ti desid *al* **mâz** lavian. ‚Er beschloss, Fleisch essen zu gehen'

Jamaica (H): **+EVID**: I gaan *fi* **bied**. ‚Er ging, *scheint's*, um zu waschen'. **–EVID**: I gaan *go* **bied**. ‚Er ging waschen'

BS: Bulg.: **+EVID**: Той *обичал Ø* да пие бира. ‚Er *soll* gern Bier *getrunken haben*'. **–EVID**: Той *обича* да пие бира. ‚Er trank gern Bier'

Alb.: **+EVID**: Artani e *paska rregulluar* biçikletën. ‚Artan hat *offenbar* das Fahrrad bereits repariert'. **–EVID**: Artani e *ka rregulluar* biçikletën. ‚Artan hat das Fahrrad repariert'. → HINRICHS (2004a)

III. Einige ‚balkanoide' Phänomene aus dem Neupersischen (Farsi; in latein. Umschrift)

1. Infinitiversatz: man mituwānam berawam /*raftan/ ‚ich kann dass ich gehe' /*gehen/; vgl. alb. duhet të shkoj
2. Futur mit WOLLEN: chāham kard ‚ich will = werde machen' < chāstan ‚wollen'
3. UBI für QUO: befarmājid indzhā! ‚Kommen Sie hier (=HIERHER)!' kodzhā mirawid? ‚wo (=WOHIN) gehen Sie?' (Umgangssprache)
4. Postponierter Artikel: betontes é: chāneé ‚das Haus'; babaé ‚der Vater'; dāneshdzhué ‚der Student' (Umgangssprache); pesar-i ‚der Junge', ‚ein Junge'
5. Possessive mit enklitischen Kurzpronomen: dast-am ‚meine Hand'; ketāb-at ‚dein Buch'; pesar-etan ‚Ihr [2. Pl.] Sohn' (hier mit künstlichem Bindestrich) etc.; vgl. bulg. ръката ми ‚meine Hand', книгата ти ‚dein Buch', къщата им ‚ihr [3. Pl.] Haus' (enklitisch)
6. Doppeltes Objekt: pesar-i ke u-ra didam ‚Der Junge, den ich IHN sah'
7. Lexik: chosh āmadid! ‚gut angekommen!' = ‚willkommen!' bulg. добре дошли!
   → HINZ (1971, passim); BEHZAD/DIVSHALI (2007: 346f.)

Literatur

АНГЕЛОВА, Искра (1990): Наблюдение върху двойното допълнение в българския език (върху материал от разговорната реч и от други славянски езици). В: *Съпоставително Езикознание* 4-5. 93–96. /Das doppelte Objekt in nordslav. Sprachen/

АСЕНОВА, Петя (2002): *Балканско Езикознание. Балканизми.* Велико Търново. /Ausfüllung des Balkansprachbundes/

BEHZAD, Faramarz; DIVSHALI, Soraya (2007): *Sprachkurs Persisch.* 6. Aufl., Bamberg.

DAHL, Östen; VELUPILLAI, Viveka (2005): The Future Tense. In: HASPELMATH / DRYER / GIL / COMRIE (eds.) (2005), chapter 67. http://wals.info/feature/67.

DRYER, Matthew S. (2005): Definite Articles. In: HASPELMATH / DRYER / GIL / COMRIE (eds.) (2005), chapter 37. http://wals.info/feature/37.

FRIEDMAN, Victor A. (1999): Evidentiality in the Balkans. In: Uwe Hinrichs (Hrsg.): *Handbuch der Südosteuropa-Linguistik.* Wiesbaden. 519–543.

HAAN, Ferdinand de (2005): Coding of Evidentiality. In: HASPELMATH / DRYER / GIL / COMRIE (eds.) (2005), chapter 78. http://wals.info/feature/78.

HASPELMATH, Martin (2001): The European linguistic area: Standard Average European. In: Martin Haspelmath et al. (eds.): *Language Typology and Language Universals. An international handbook.* Vol. 2, Berlin, New York. 1492–1510. /Das entwickelte Modell des SAE/

HASPELMATH, Martin; TROCKNER, Matthew S.; GIL, David; COMRIE, Bernard (Hrsg.) (2005): *The World Atlas of Language Structures.* Max Planck Digital Library. München. http://wals.info/features

HASPELMATH, Martin et al. (Hrsg.): *The Atlas of Pidgin and Creole Languages Structures.* Angekündigt für 2011.
http://lingweb.eva.mpg.de/apics/index.php/The_Atlas_of_Pidgin_and_Creole_Language_Structures_(APICS)

HETZER, Armin (2010): Das südosteuropäische Areal. In: HINRICHS (Hrsg.) (2010): 457–474. /Neueste Liste der Balkanismen/

HINRICHS, Uwe (1984): Ist das Altkirchenslavische eine Balkansprache? In: *Zeitschrift für Balkanologie* 20, 2. 142–160. /Balkanismen im Altkirchenslavischen/

HINRICHS, Uwe (1990): Das Slavische und die sogenannten Balkanismen. In: *Zeitschrift für Balkanologie* 26, 1. 43–62. /Balkanismen in den (nord)slavischen Sprachen/

HINRICHS, Uwe (1993): Ziele und Wege der Balkanlinguistik. In: Uwe Hinrichs et al. (Hrsg.): *Sprache in der Slavia und auf dem Balkan. Festschrift für Norbert Reiter zum 65. Geburtstag.* Göttingen. 101–115. /Balkanismen in den verschiedenen Paradigmen/

HINRICHS, Uwe (1994): Balkanische Konvergenz und das Standard-/Nonstandard-Problem. In: Uwe Hinrichs, Norbert Reiter, Jiřina van Leeuwen-Turnovcová (Hrsg.): *Standard und Substandard in Osteuropa und Südosteuropa.* Berlin. 96–113. /Balkanismen im Nonstandard vieler Sprachen/

HINRICHS, Uwe (1999): Balkanismen – Europäismen. In: Norbert Reiter (Hrsg.): *Eurolinguistik. Ein Schritt in die Zukunft.* Wiesbaden. 85–109. /Balkanismen als Europäismen/

HINRICHS, Uwe (2002): Können Balkanlinguistik und Kreolistik voneinander profitieren? In: *Balkansko ezikoznanie* XLII/2. 147–157. /Begründung der kreoloiden Hypothese für Balkanismen/

HINRICHS, Uwe (Hrsg.) (2004): *Die europäischen Sprachen auf dem Wege zum analytischen Sprachtyp*. Wiesbaden. /Substantiierung der historischen Drift Synthetismus > Analytismus/

HINRICHS, Uwe (2004a): Orale Kultur, Mehrsprachigkeit, radikaler Analytismus. Zur Erklärung von Sprachstrukturen auf dem Balkan und im kreolischen Raum. Ein Beitrag zur Entmystifizierung der Balkanologie. In: *Zeitschrift für Balkanologie* 40, 2. 141–174. /Begründung der kreoloiden Hypothese für Balkanismen ff./

HINRICHS, Uwe (2009): Sprachwandel oder Sprachverfall? Zur aktuellen Forschungssituation im Deutschen. In: *Muttersprache* 1. 47–57. /‚Balkanoide' Phänomene in der modernen deutschen gesprochenen Umgangssprache/

HINRICHS, Uwe (Hrsg.) (2010): *Handbuch der Eurolinguistik*. Wiesbaden.

HINZ, Walther (1971): *Persisch. Praktischer Sprachführer*. 5. Aufl., Berlin, New York.

IGGESEN, Oliver A. (2005): Number of Cases. In: HASPELMATH / DRYER / GIL / COMRIE (eds.) (2005), chapter 49. http://wals.info/feature/49.

KORTMANN, Bernd (2009): Die Rolle von (Nicht-Standard-)Varietäten in der europäischen (Areal-)Typologie. In: Uwe Hinrichs et al. (Hrsg.): *Eurolinguistik. Entwicklungen und Perspektiven. Wiesbaden*. 165–187. /Plädoyer für die Einbeziehung von Dialekten und Soziolekten in die Eurolinguistik/.

ЛАПТЕВА, Ольга А. (1976): *Русский разговорный синтаксис*. Москва. /Balkanoide Züge in der Syntax der gesprochenen russischen Umgangssprache/

MATRAS, Yaron (1994): Structural Balkanisms in Romani. In: Uwe Hinrichs, Norbert Reiter, Jiřina van Leeuwen-Turnovcová (Hrsg.): *Standard und Substandard in Osteuropa und Südosteuropa*. Berlin. 195–210. /Infinitiversatz, Artikel, *evidentiality* im Romani/

MIŠESKA TOMIĆ, Olga (2006): *Balkansprachbund. Morphosyntactic features*. Dordrecht. /Ausfüllung des Balkansprachbundes/

SCHALLER, Helmut-Wilhelm (1999): Geschichte der Südosteuropa-Linguistik. In: Uwe Hinrichs (Hrsg.): *Handbuch der Südosteuropa-Linguistik*. Wiesbaden. 91–116.

SCHLÖSSER, Rainer (1981): Balkanismen im Armenischen? In: *Balkan-Archiv* N.F. 6. 83–93.

SCHUBERT, Gabriella (1983): Ein weiterer „Balkanismus" im Ungarischen? In: *Zeitschrift für Balkanologie* 19, 1. 106–117.

SOLTA, Georg R. (1980): *Einführung in die Balkanlinguistik mit besonderer Berücksichtigung des Substrats und des Balkanlateinischen*. Darmstadt.

STASSEN, Leon (2005): Comparative Constructions. In: HASPELMATH / DRYER / GIL / COMRIE (eds.) (2005), chapter 121. http://wals.info/feature/121.

STERN, Dieter (2006): Balkansprachen und Kreolsprachen: Versuch einer kontakttypologischen Grenzziehung. In: *Zeitschrift für Balkanologie* 42, 1–2. 206–225. /Kritik der kreoloiden Hypothese für Balkanismen/

STOLZ, Thomas (2010): Sprachbund Europa – Probleme und Möglichkeiten. In: HINRICHS (Hrsg.) (2010): 397–424. /Kritik des alten Sprachbundbegriffes; Geschichte der Arealtypologie in Europa; Neuanwendung auf Areal Europa/

Können linguistische Ordnungsversuche, beispielsweise Balkansprachen, auf ewig gültig bleiben?

Jürgen KRISTOPHSON (Hamburg)

Die Linguistik untersucht etwas und benennt dieses dann. Dieses "Etwas" nennt man zunächst Sprache bzw. einen Teilaspekt davon. Diese unklaren Ausdrücke haben ihren Grund darin, dass es keine völlig überzeugende Definition vom Untersuchungsgegenstand der Linguistik gibt. Eine solche Definition ist auch nicht zwingend erforderlich. Nimmt man Sprache als Evidenz, so weiß jeder, ob Linguist oder nicht, was gemeint ist. Sprache ist kein Spezialfall von Zeichensystem, sie ist primär. Dass man Sprache gerne als ein solches gesehen hat, liegt wohl an der Verwechslung von Sprache und Schrift. Schrift ist natürlich ein Zeichensystem, das gleichzeitig eine erste Analysemöglichkeit von Sprache bietet. Es gibt durchaus Grenzwerte bei der Deutung optischer Zeichen. Als die Hieroglyphen noch nicht entschlüsselt waren, war es unsicher, ob sie Ornamente oder Bilder zur Wiedergabe von Informationen oder eben doch Ansätze oder sogar ein System zur Wiedergabe von Lauten, also von Sprache, darstellen sollten. Ähnlich verhielt es sich mit den Runen, die als Buchstaben zur Lautdarstellung dienen konnten oder, wenn durch Zufallsgenerator erzeugt, zur Weissagung. Die „feu" Rune diente als Lautzeichen für „f" oder eben als Orakel, dann hatte sie Bedeutung „feu" (= Vieh), gemeint war eine Voraussage über den Erwerb von Reichtum. Dieses Beispiel möge für den Begriff Zeichensystem stehen, das entweder, wenn es Schriftcharakter hat, relativ exakt lautlich zu realisieren ist, oder, wenn es Piktogrammcharakter hat, variabel, aber nicht willkürlich zu versprachlichen ist.

Damit sei dem Begriff Sprache genüge getan. Sie ist als akustischer Eindruck, als Gespräch, wahrnehmbar oder als optischer, als Text. Nun gibt es sehr viele Gespräche und auch genug Texte, die die Menschen klassifizieren müssen, zunächst in verständlich und in unverständlich. Das wäre die erste und banalste Benennung „eigene Sprache" : „Fremdsprache". Aber selbst diese Opposition ist nicht so eindeutig. Für einen Serben ist Bulgarisch zwar nicht eigen, aber auch nicht ganz fremd, ja sogar etwas verständlich. Man kann anfangen zu suchen, warum Serbisch und Bulgarisch nicht ganz fremd aber auch nicht ganz gleich seien. Dies hat man natürlich längst gemacht. Die Begründung dieser Unterscheidung braucht hier nicht ausgeführt zu werden, aber ein Ergebnis besteht darin, dass man die Art einer Menge von Sprechern und Schreibern zu sprechen und zu schreiben, mit „serbisch" benennt bzw. die Art einer anderen Menge von Menschen, die von der ersten abweicht, „bulgarisch". Merkwürdig ist es schon, dass man einer unbekannten Anzahl von Gesprächen, deren Form und Inhalt eigentlich niemand kennt, einen Eigennamen zuteilen kann, der von den Sprechern in der Regel akzeptiert wird. Die Linguistik begründet die Berechtigung dieses Namens und gibt ihm eine Art Signalement. Damit wird eine Sprache geradezu eine Institution, die handeln kann, sie kann besitzen (z.B. Vokale), sie kann entlehnen (= ausleihen) oder verleihen, sie kann sich ausbreiten, verändern, sogar aussterben. Tatsächlich ist es aber so, dass die Sprache nichts tut, es sind die Sprecher, die alles tun. Dies ist im Grunde bekannt, aber der allgemeine, auch linguistische Sprachgebrauch legt den Institutionscharakter der Sprache nahe. Es wäre adäquater zu sagen, Serben benutzen sieben Kasus statt das Serbische habe sieben Kasus.

Die Benennung einer Sprache postuliert, dass es Einzelsprachen gibt. Dabei entsteht sofort das Problem, wo hört die Einzelsprache auf und wo fängt die nächste Einzelsprache an. Ist „šopski" noch Serbisch oder schon Bulgarisch, wenn man nach Osten geht? Geht man nach Westen lautet die Frage, ob es noch Bulgarisch oder schon Serbisch ist. Unabhängig davon wie sicher man Einzelsprachen voneinander abgrenzen kann, erhalten Sprachen außer dem Eigennamen noch zusätzliche Namen, die über Geschichte, Struktur und Typ etwas aussagen sollen, also z.B. indogermanisch, slavisch, flektierend, agglutinierend, analytisch, synthetisch usw. Es ist bekannt, dass etwa die Strukturen von Sprachen sich ändern können oder aber, wenn nur deskriptiv gearbeitet wird, durchaus gemischte Strukturprinzipien beobachtbar bzw. manche Phänomene unterschiedlich interpretierbar sind. Ist z.B. das serbokroatische Futur „biću", „bićeš" synthetisch, „-ć-" als Futurkennzeichen, wie die serbische Orthographie das nahelegt, oder agglutinierend, wie es die kroatische Orthographie meint mit „bit ću", oder sogar analytisch, denn es gibt auch Formen wie „ja ću biti". In der bulgarischen Schriftsprache ist die Futurkennzeichnung zu einer Partikel „šte" geschrumpft. Ist das nun eine analytische Form oder etwas anderes? Es gibt durchaus Varianten für die Futurbildung, wie „šte ... da, „šteš ... da", sicherlich eher analytisch, aber „ima ... da" verhält sich schon wie „šte", denn „ima" bleibt für alle Personen gleich. Zusätzlich gibt es Formen, die wie die serbokroatischen aussehen „napravi šta, napravi šteš" usw. Sind diese Formen etwa agglutinierend? Könnte man diese Phänomene als Tendenz zum Analytismus nennen? Die Futurbildung im Bulgarischen kann also variieren, aber die Benennung der Bildungsart bereitet Schwierigkeiten, ist sie synthetisch, analytisch oder agglutinierend. Diese Schwierigkeiten zeigen nur, dass eine Sprache nicht zwingend idealtypisch agglutinierend, flektierend oder einem anderen Strukturprinzip konsequent folgend beschaffen sein muss. Gerade das Auftreten einzelner vom vorherrschenden strukturellen Typ abweichender Züge kann ein Indiz für eintretenden Sprachwandel sein. Auch wenn man primär deskriptiv arbeitet, bemerkt man zumindest Veränderungsansätze, die man mit

Ausdrücken wie Regel : Ausnahme, produktiv : unproduktiv, benennt. Man wird sich damit abfinden müssen, nicht für alles eine geeignete Nomenklatur zu finden.

Nun hat die Linguistik nicht nur deskriptiv unter synchronem Aspekt gearbeitet, sondern auch dezidiert unter diachronem. Auch unter diesem Aspekt hat sie Sprachen untersucht, verglichen und ist zu Benennungen gekommen. Auch hier redet man von ähnlichen Sprachen, und wenn man Gründe für die Ähnlichkeit aufzeigen kann, spricht man in biologischen Metaphern von Sprachfamilien, Tochtersprachen, Stammbäumen u.a. Der Idealfall besteht dann, wenn sich von einer Ausgangssprache, belegt oder erschlossen, durch zunehmende, aber relativ regelmäßige Divergenz neue Sprachen oder Sprachgruppen entwickeln. Solche Idealsprachfamilien wären Latein als Ausgangssprache und die romanischen Sprachen als Nachfolger oder Urslavisch als rekonstruierte Ausgangssprache mit den Nachfolgern, den frühen slavischen Einzelsprachen (gut belegt nur Altbulgarisch) und den neuen slavischen Einzelsprachen. Lateinisch und Urslavisch lassen sich noch zu einer früheren Familie Indogermanisch vereinen. Die Frage, die man sich nun stellen muss, lautet: Sind die Benennungen slavisch, romanisch, indogermanisch noch gültig für heutige Sprachformen? Oder anders formuliert, einmal slavisch, immer slavisch. Da Begriffe wie „Sprachfamilie" biologische Metaphern darstellen, kann man die menschliche Familie in ihrer Generationenabfolge als Vergleich heranziehen. So sind Cousins und Cousinen über ein gemeinsames Großelternpaar definiert und gelten als verwandt. Gilt die Verwandtschaft aber noch bei Cousins und Cousinen zweiten und dritten Grades, etwa als Ehehindernis oder im Erbrecht? So ist zu fragen, wie indogermanisch, slavisch bzw. romanisch noch die uns interessierenden Sprachen seien. Das ältere Slavisch, also Altbulgarisch im Besondern, bewahrt noch recht gut seinen indogermanischen Charakter, ja es war sogar eine wichtige Quellensprache zur Rekonstruktion des Indogermanischen. Als gut indogermanisch kann man noch die Deklinationsklassen, die Verbalmorphologie und große Teile des Wortschatzes ansehen. Dies hat sich aber bis heute schon sehr verändert, ein gutes Beispiel ist etwa das Element „-ov-". Es war ursprünglich mit dem Themavokalwechsel der u-Deklination verbunden, heute aber dient es als Kennzeichnung des Genitiv Plural einiger russischer Deklinationsklassen, als Verstärkung der Belebtheitskategorie im slavischen Westen oder als Kennzeichnung des Plural einsilbiger Substantiva im Süden. Dies bedeutet, dass die ererbte und im alten Slavischen erhaltene Funktion des -ov-Elementes in den slavischen Neusprachen nicht mehr existiert. Der Gebrauch des Elements ist also weder indogermanisch noch slavisch sondern eine russische, polnische, tschechische oder bulgarische Eigenart. War dieses Beispiel eher ein Einzelfall, so steht es doch für Veränderung in zahlreichen Bereichen der slavischen Morphologie.

Insgesamt haben die slavischen Sprachen noch viel vom indogermanischen Charakter bewahrt; auch das gemeinsame slavische Erbe, besonders im Wortschatz, aber auch in der Morphologie ist erhalten geblieben. Starke Unterschiede haben sich in der Phonetik ergeben, zu nennen sei der Grad der Palatalisierung, Vokalquantität oder ihr Fehlen, Akzenttypen. Die innerslavischen Verschiedenheiten lassen sich aber als unterschiedliche lokale Entwicklungen, sogar mit einer sprachgeographischen Ratio, nachzeichnen und erlauben immer noch von einer slavischen Sprachfamilie mit einer Slavität zu reden. Dies gilt natürlich nur sprachlich, nicht etwa kulturell und sozial.

Für das Rumänische gilt Ähnliches wie für das Bulgarische. Das Rumänische bewahrt sehr gut das lateinische Verbalsystem, das allerdings das indogermanische verändert hatte. Das Nominalsystem, das gerade im Lateinischen noch einen gut erkennbaren indogermanischen Charakter besaß, ist ähnlich wie in den anderen romanischen Sprachen verändert worden, aber auf eigenartige rumänische Art. Griechisch baut ebenso im Nominalsystem ab, aber nicht so weitgehend wie das Romanische. Das Verbalsystem verändert sich durch Entwicklung eines Aspektsystems, bewahrt aber noch ein synthetisches Mediopassiv. Insgesamt sind die synthetischen Züge in der Morphologie noch stärker ausgeprägt als im Bulgarischen und im Rumänischen. Albanisch muss so genommen werden, wie es ist. Entwicklungslinien können nicht gezeichnet werden. Hiermit sind also durch Nennung einiger Sprachen schon Ausblicke auf die balkanischen Sprachen gemacht worden. Es ist zunächst zu fragen: Verdienen die sogenannten Balkansprachen überhaupt ein besonderes Interesse? Sie tun dies durchaus, allein schon aus wissenschaftshistorischen Gründen. Die Idee von Sprachbund, Arealtypologie usw. wären ohne die Entdeckung gemeinsamer Züge in den sogenannten Balkansprachen nicht schon so früh gewonnen worden. Besonders auffällig waren die gemeinsamen Züge der Balkansprachen an sich nicht, sie waren aber durch gemeinsame Entwicklung erklärbar. Altgriechisch, Altbulgarisch und Lateinisch hatten diese Züge nicht, die erst, teilweise sogar belegbar, in den letzten tausend Jahren entstanden sind.

Ist also Balkanität, vorausgesetzt es gibt so etwas, eine Erkenntnis, die unter diachronem Aspekt oder unter synchronem Aspekt gewonnen wurde?

Betrachtet man rein deskriptiv balkanische Sätze mit gleichem Inhalt, so hat man schon lange festgestellt, dass sie sehr ähnlich, um nicht zu sagen gleichartig strukturiert sind, vgl. das folgende Beispiel (Lexikon tetraglosson v. Daniil Moschopolitis, KRISTOPHSON 1974: 70):

neugriechisch: I jineka opu echi dhaktilidhia dhen prepi na zimoni
aromunisch: mul' earea ți are neale nu pripseaşte se frimită
bulgarisch: ženata što imat părsteni ne prilegat da mesit
albanisch: gruaja qi ka unazë nukë gjan të gatuanj
Satztyp (Art.) Substantiv (Art.) rel. Part. V.S. Neg. V. Part. V.

Dies hätte nicht gestört, wenn man nicht gewusst hätte, dass altgriechische, altbulgarische und lateinische Sätze anders gebildet gewesen wären. Es ist also anzunehmen, dass Balkanität eher über eine postulierte gleichartige Veränderung älterer stärker verschiedener Satztypen sich zu neuen weit ähnlicheren Satztypen entwickelt hat. Auch die morphologischen Möglichkeiten werden ähnlicher. Die Grunderkenntnis der historischen Sprachwissenschaft war die Annahme von zunehmender Divergenz, was auch zu den Veränderungen der neuen Balkansprachen passte. Vergleicht man aber die Balkansprachen untereinander, so stellt man Konvergenzerscheinungen fest, die sogar Sprachfamiliengrenzen überspringen konnten. Sofort wurde natürlich nach den Gründen für diese Veränderungen gesucht. Man vermutete sie im Vulgärgriechischen, Vulgärlatein oder besonders gern im Substrat, von dem man allerdings nicht wusste, welche Sprache es gewesen sein noch wie diese Sprache ausgesehen haben könnte. Literarischer Einfluss scheidet wohl aus, da die beiden wichtigsten Literatursprachen, Griechisch und Kirchenslavisch, in einer archaisierenden Form verwendet wurden, die gerade die modernen Entwicklungen unterdrückte. Es ist schon eher anzunehmen, dass die Mischung von Sprechern verschiedener Sprachen zu verschiedenen Zeiten an unterschiedlichen Orten zu den angenäherten Strukturen aller beteiligten Sprachen geführt hat. Dieser Prozess dauert fast ein Jahrtausend, er wurde durch die Nationalbewegungen beendet. Seit dem 19. Jahrhundert beginnt eine systematische Entmischung. Entscheidend waren für die sprachliche Entwicklung die Grenzziehungen von 1912/13 und 1918/19.

Von diesem Zeitpunkt an gibt es für alle Staaten der Region eine Art Binaritätsprinzip, Staatssprache : Minoritätensprache, wobei der Rechtsstatus der Minoritätensprache unterschiedlich geregelt sein kann. Man wird davon ausgehen dürfen, dass Einsprachigkeit eher die Regel ist, ein Schulwesen ist normal, das Analphabetentum spielt keine allzu große Rolle mehr, die Kenntnis einer Nachbarsprache beginnt gegen null zu tendieren, mit gewissen Ausnahmen im jugoslawischen Gebiet, wo etwa im Kosovo und in Makedonien noch Serbischkenntnisse vorhanden sind. Fremdsprachenkenntnisse gibt es natürlich, sei es als Bildungserlebnis, sei es als Gastarbeiterdasein, aber sie betreffen in erster Linie die europäischen Großsprachen Englisch, Französisch, Deutsch, in Albanien auch Italienisch. Vielleicht gibt es noch bei albanischen Gastarbeitern in Griechenland Neuanfänge des alten balkanischen Multilingualismus. Insofern ist die zwar nur angenommene, aber doch wahrscheinliche Ursache für die Entstehung und Entwicklung von Balkanität, nämlich bi- und multilinguale Sprechergruppen in Südosteuropa, nicht mehr vorhanden. Balkanität kann nur noch als Erbteil in den betreffenden Sprachen angesehen werden.

Worin soll aber jetzt die Balkanität der Balkansprachen bestehen? Diese Frage hat bei grundsätzlicher Annahme gemeinsamer Strukturprinzipien die Suche nach den Balkanismen ausgelöst. Die gemeinsamen Strukturprinzipien waren evident und unbestritten, aber einem ursächlichen Zusammenhang für die Entwicklung solcher Prinzipien wurde durchaus widersprochen. Eigentlich wollte kein Einheimischer eine Balkansprache sprechen. Vor allem suchte man ähnliche Phänomene anderswo und machte damit im Grunde die Sprachbundidee überhaupt erst fruchtbar, wie das als klassisch zu wertende Zitat von PUŞCARIU (1943: 201) „trotzdem spricht niemand von einer ‚Alpenlinguistik', um Romanen und Germanen zum gleichen ‚Sprachbund' zusammenzufassen", ungewollt das Richtige sagt. Natürlich sollte und könnte man das, vgl. KRISTOPHSON 1993, da wo genau dieser Bund, eigentlich ungeplant, zustande gekommen ist. Nun ist es tatsächlich so, dass die Kritiker am Balkanbund insofern recht haben, dass das Besondere an den Balkansprachen so ungewöhnlich nicht ist, sondern tatsächlich nur, wie schon erwähnt, wenn man aus klassischphilologischer Perspektive das Neugriechische, aus romanistischer das Rumänische, aus slavistischer das Bulgarische betrachtet. So fällt der postponierte Artikel auf, der aber im Neugriechischen fehlt, im Rumänischen und im Albanischen gibt es zusätzlich den Adjektiv- und Genitivartikel, den das Bulgarische wieder nicht kennt. Postponierte Artikel gibt es zudem auch außerhalb des Balkans. Den generell fehlenden Infinitiv gibt es in erstarrten Formen fast überall, im Rumänischen partiell auch den echten Infinitiv. Das Futur wird eben nicht nur mit „wollen" gebildet bzw. mit davon abgeleiteten Kurzformen oder Partikeln, sondern auch mit „haben". Die Verteilung der Varianten ist teils lokal eingeschränkt, teil modal abgetönt. Exklusive Balkanismen sind seltene Randerscheinungen, die keinen spezifischen Sprachtypus ergeben (s. SOBOLEV 2003). Balkanismen sollten also nicht definiert werden, sondern als Beziehungsgeflecht verschiedenster Erscheinungen, Abstufungen, Überschichtungen, Variationsmöglichkeiten, Ausfransungen, Frequenzverkettungen verstanden werden. Das eben Geäußerte lässt sich sehr einfach am Vokalinventar feststellen, fünf Grundvokale ohne Quantitätsopposition „a", „e", „i", „o", „u", mit möglicher Reduktion in unbetonten Silben, dazu rumänisch „ă", und „î", letzteres aber nicht in allen Dialekten, bulgarisch ebenso ein „ă", albanisch „ë" und ein zusätzliches „y", aber nicht in allen Dialekten. Negativ lassen sich die balkanischen Inventare gegen das Türkische mit "ü", „ö", gegen das Ungarische mit "ü", „ö" aber auch mit Vokalquantitäten und das Serbokroatische mit den fünf Vokalen „a", „e", „i", „o" „u" aber mit Vokalquantitäten und mit musikalischem Akzent abgrenzen. Für den Wortschatz gilt dagegen eine stärkere Bewahrung des eigenen Erbwortschatzes, innerbalkanische Entlehnungen sind fast nur Slavismen, am stärksten im Rumänischen, schwächer im Albanischen, am schwächsten im Neugriechischen. Neograzismen gibt es überall, aber schwächer, autochthone Wörter verbinden Albanisch und Rumänisch, in den anderen Sprachen sind sie als exotische Raritäten einzustufen. Außerbalkanische Entlehnungen sind die Turzismen, überall vorhanden, Hungarismen, nach Süden abnehmend. Westeuropäismen gehören natürlich der neueren Zeit an, sie gelten als eben wenig interessant, passen aber doch auf den Balkan, denn sie verhalten sich kaum anders als die alten Lehnwortschichten.

Die Westeuropäismen bilden ein Netz von Entlehnungen, Lehnübersetzungen und von westeuropäischen motivierten Eigenbildungen. Genau genommen ließen sich die Balkansprachen auf dieser Basis zusammenbinden und vergleichen, nur findet der Kontakt nicht innerbalkanisch sondern einzelsprachlich über Direktkontakt mit Westeuropa in erster Linie auf literarischem Wege statt. Wir sind hier also nicht auf die Hirtenterminologie angewiesen (s. KAHL 2007).

Eine kleine Vokabelliste von einigen allgemeinen Termini aus dem Verkehrswesen soll dieses belegen.

	rumänisch	neugriechisch	bulgarisch	albanisch
Schiff	corabie	καράβι	кораб	karavë, anije
Dampfer	vapor	βαπόρι	параход	vapor
Automobil	automobil	αὐτοκίνητον	автомобил	automobil
Lastwagen	camion	καμιόνι	камион	kamion
Autobus	omnibus, tramcar	μποῦσι	автобус, рейс	omnibus
Motorrad	motocicletă	μοτοσυκλέττα	мотоциклет	motoçikletë
Fahrrad	bicicletă	ποδήλατον	велосипед	biçikletë
Flugzeug	aeroplan, avion	ἀεροπλάνον	самолет	aeroplan, avion
Eisenbahn	cale ferată, drum de fier	σιδηρόδρομος	железница	hekurudhë
Zug	tren	τραῖνο	влак	tren
Schiene	şină	σιδηροτροχιά	релса	shinë, binar
Weiche	ac, macaz	κλειδί	стрелка	shigjetë, këmbyes
Lokomotive	locomotivă	ἀτμομηχανή	локомотив	lokomotivë
Wagon	vagon	βαγόνι	вагон	vagon
Tram	tramvai	τράμ	трамвай	tramvaj
Triebwagen	automotor	ὠτομοτρίς	мотриса	autovagon
Fahrkarte	bilet	μπιλιέττο	пътен билет	biletë, udhëtimi

Die Liste zeigt eine starke Orientierung am Französischen, das fast das Gewicht des Türkischen angenommen hat. Auch die Lehnübersetzungen in die eigene Sprache sind eher nach dem französischen Vorbild geschehen. Besonders zu erwähnen ist der Ausdruck für „Weiche", französisch „aiguille" dazu als Nachbildung italienisches „ago", rumänisches „ac", russisches „strelka", auch ins Bulgarische übernommen, albanisches „shigjetë", griechisches „κλειδί". Rumänisches und albanisches „bicicletă", „biçikletë" könnte auch über italienische Vermittlung gelaufen sein, u.U. aber nur über die Schrift. Auch aus dem Englischen stammende

Begriffe sind über das Französische nach Südosteuropa gelangt. Englische Wörter sind also als Gallizismen anzusehen, ähnlich den Turzismen, die auch arabische und persische Wörter umfassten. Die Reslavisierung des Bulgarischen lief weitgehend über das Russische (strelka, relsa) oder sogar über das kroatische „željeznica", „vlak", letzteres im Kroatischen aus dem Tschechischen übernommen, wobei tschechisches „vlak" eine Lehnübersetzung des deutschen „Zug" darstellt. Einige dieser Neologismen sind Eigenbildungen mit dem fremden Material, z.B. albanisches „autovagon". Im Russischen findet ein komplizierter Prozess der morphologischen Eingliederung statt, englisches „rails" wird zu russischem „rel's", wird aber nicht als Plural erkannt und erhält darum ein russisches Pluralsuffix, wird zu „rel'sy", von dem sekundär ein neuer Singular „rel'sa" f. bzw. „rel's" m. gebildet wird. Die Form „rel'sa" wird ins Bulgarische als „relsa" übernommen. Die morphologische Eingliederung, Genus- und Deklinationsklassenzuweisung ist je nach Wort und Sprache verschieden. Die griechische Orthographie gliedert die neuen Wörter nach griechischen Vorstellungen ein also „μοτοσυκλέττα" mit Ypsilon, „ὠτομοτρίς" mit Omega.

Prinzipiell verhalten sich die Balkansprachen wie andere europäische Sprachen, neue Begriffe werden, hier meist aus dem Französischen oder über dieses entlehnt oder, eher selten, durch freie Eigenbildung geschaffen. War hier nur ein kleiner Ausschnitt des modernen Wortschatzes vorgestellt, der aber keiner spezifischen Fachsprache angehört, so signalisiert dieser Ausschnitt doch eine weitere Europäisierung der Balkansprachen. Hatte man seinerzeit für die Balkansprachen eine strukturelle Ähnlichkeit und dieser vorausgehend auch eine Annäherung zuerkannt, so sollte nicht vergessen werden, dass die Balkansprachen durchaus als neueuropäische Sprachen einzuschätzen sind (KRISTOPHSON 1993), vielmehr als ihre westlichen Nachbarn, die slavischen von Polen bis Montenegro und die ugrischen in Ungarn. Alle diese Sprachgruppen unterlagen mittelalterlichen lateinischen und sonstigen westeuropäischen sprachlichen Einflüssen. Sie nahmen am literarischen und kulturellen Leben Europas viel intensiver als die Balkanländer teil, trotzdem näherten sich die Sprachen der Zwischenzone nicht so stark an die neueuropäischen wie die Balkansprachen. Sprachliche Konvergenz muss nicht zu kultureller Konvergenz führen, wie umgekehrt sprachliche Divergenz nicht kulturelle Konvergenz verhindern muss. Eine gewisse Übereinstimmung von sprachlicher Balkanität und balkanischer Zivilisation gilt sicher noch im 19. Jahrhundert, aber seitdem wurden doch weitgehende Reformen in allen Bereichen durchgeführt, es entwickelten sich ausgebaute Literatursprachen, es folgten die Alphabetisierung der Bevölkerung, starke Veränderungen des wirtschaftlichen und sozialen Lebens. Dies alles geschah aber im Rahmen der neuen Nationalstaaten jeweils ohne Rücksicht auf die Nachbarn. Als Gemeinsamkeiten bestanden nur noch die Ausgangspunkte und die Problemlage, die in etwa die gleichen waren. Dies erschloss sich aber nur dem Beobachter von außen. Der Blick von außen hatte im 19. Jahrhundert die

Balkansprachen als Einheit erkennen lassen, als relative Einheitlichkeit ihrer Entwicklung von ihren Vorstufen und damit verbunden als Trennung von den anderen Gliedern der entsprechenden Sprachfamilien. Balkanität war also schon zur Zeit ihrer Entdeckung ein Ergebnis diachron ausgerichteter Forschungen. Erst in der Folge entwickelte sich die Kontakt- und Areallinguistik, altväterlich Sprachbundforschung genannt. Als Ergebnis sollte man akzeptieren, dass es Balkanität gab, die natürlich auch noch fortdauert. Man sollte sie aber nicht genau definieren, sondern von einem Netz von Eigenschaften reden, die sich über die dazugehörenden Sprachen verteilen, überall unterschiedlich, lokal und stilistisch häufig sein oder auch ganz fehlen können. Beispiele wären etwa die unterschiedlichen Futurbildungen, Behandlung des Infinitivs, die Objektverdoppelung usw.

Der innerbalkanische Sprachkontakt ist aber für die Gegenwart als beendet anzusehen. Eine Bedingung für den alten Sprachkontakt war, dass man die jeweils andere Sprache in Ansätzen gelernt hatte. Es war nicht wie bei den Slaven, wo eine rudimentäre primitive Verständigung noch panslavisch möglich ist. Sprachkontakt findet heute überwiegend mit den europäischen Großsprachen statt, schon mehr als ein Jahrhundert. Die nationale und sprachliche Homogenisierung in den einzelnen Staaten setzt sich fort. Die heutigen Standardsprachen und die in ihnen verfassten Texte entfernen sich immer mehr von den Sprachen der Folklore. Literarische Texte, die das archaische ländliche Milieu zum Thema haben, sind schon mit Glossaren ausgestattet. Sicherlich wird aus Gründen der Expressivität, auch in der Presse, manches Balkanische wie Turzismen, archaische Satzkonstruktionen, erhalten bleiben.

Somit lässt sich abschließend behaupten, Balkanität gibt es als Relikt, als wirkender Faktor ist sie nicht mehr anzusetzen. Es gibt sie also noch, aber mit einem „ja, aber" zu versehen, wobei das „aber" immer größer wird. Die schöne Mahnung, natürlich von Goethe: „Was du ererbst von deinen Vätern, erwirb es, um es zu besitzen" wird also nicht beachtet. Man hatte den Balkan ererbt, aber man wollte ihn nicht haben, d.h. auch pflegen und bewahren. Immerhin bleibt noch genug Erbmasse.

Literatur

KAHL, Thede (2007): *Hirten in Kontakt. Sprach- und Kulturwandel ehemalige Wanderhirten (Albanisch, Aromunisch, Griechisch)*. Wien, Berlin.

KRISTOPHSON, Jürgen (1993): Ein neuer Beitrag zur Sprachbunddiskussion. In: *Zeitschrift für Balkanologie* 29. 1–11

KRISTOPHSON, Jürgen (1996): Numerische Bestimmung der Position des Rumänischen als Glied einer Sprachfamilie und eines Sprachbundes. In: M. Iliescu, S. Sora (Hrsg.): *Rumänisch: Typologie, Klassifikation, Sprachcharakteristik. Bulkan-Archiv* NF, Beiheft Bd. 11, Südosteuropa-Schriften Bd. 14. 25–33.

KRISTOPHSON, Jürgen (2001): Das Ende der Geschichte, in: „Was ich sagen wollte …“. In: B. Igla, Th. Stolz (Hrsg.): *Festschrift Norbert Boretzky. Studia typologica* 2. Berlin. 101–114.

KRISTOPHSON, Jürgen (2001): Das Bulgarische als Glied einer Sprachfamilie und eines Sprachbundes. In: *Balkansko ezikoznanie* XLI, 2. 113–121.

KRISTOPHSON, Jürgen (2008): Ist das Bulgarische noch eine Balkansprache? In: *Balkansko ezikoznanie* XLVII 2–3. 171–176.

KRISTOPHSON, Jürgen (2009): Ist das Rumänische noch eine Balkansprache? In: Th. Kahl (Hrsg.): *Das Rumänische und seine Nachbarn*. 81–94.

СОБОЛЕВ, Андрей Н. (2003): *Малый диалектологический атлас балканских языков. Пробный выпуск*. München.

Summary

Linguists denominate features of languages in structural or historical, e.g. analytic, synthetic, agglutinative etc. or Indo-European, Slavic or even Balkanic. In reality pure structural types often do not exist, but rather mixed or indefinable.

Also to be called into question is the eternity of Indo-European, Slavic or Balkanic denomination, as the respective groups are continually changing. The Balkanic languages had developed some similar structural features caused by a mutual contact phase, however there are no exclusive Balkanic peculiarities.

The Balkanic languages should be regarded as new European languages. Furthermore, the intrabalkanic contacts have ended and each Balkanic language relates independently to West European languages, mostly French. So Balkanity can be defined today as heritage, but no longer as a linguistic factor.

Welche Zukunft hat der Balkansprachbund?

Klaus STEINKE (Erlangen/Kraków)

Der Terminus *Balkansprachbund* besitzt mittlerweile seinen festen Platz in der sprachwissenschaftlichen Terminologie, und er hat von N. S. TRUBETZKOY während des 1. Internationalen Linguistenkongresses 1928 in Den Haag diese viel zitierte, immer noch gültige und inhaltlich kaum wesentlich erweiterte Definition erhalten:

> Unter den Sprachgruppen sind zwei Typen zu unterscheiden: Gruppen, bestehend aus Sprachen, die eine große Ähnlichkeit in syntaktischer Hinsicht, eine Ähnlichkeit in den Grundsätzen des morphologischen Baus aufweisen, und eine große Anzahl gemeinsamer Kulturwörter bieten, manchmal auch äußere Ähnlichkeit im Bestande der Lautsysteme, – dabei aber keine systematische Lautentsprechungen, keine Übereinstimmung in der lautlichen Gestalt der morphologischen Elemente und keine gemeinsamen Elementarwörter besitzen, – *solche Sprachgruppen nennen wir Sprachbünde*. Gruppen, bestehend aus Sprachen, die eine beträchtliche Anzahl von gemeinsamen Elementarwörtern besitzen, Übereinstimmungen im lautlichen Ausdruck morphologischer Kategorien aufweisen und, vor allem, konstante Lautentsprechungen bieten, – *solche Sprachgruppen nennen wir Sprachfamilien*.
>
> So gehört z.B. das Bulgarische einerseits zur slawischen Sprachfamilie (zusammen mit dcm Serbokroatischen, Polnischen, Russischen, u.s.w.), andererseits zum balkanischen Sprachbund (zusammen mit dem Neugriechischen, Albanesischen, und Rumänischen).
>
> Diese Benennungen, bezw. diese Begriffe sind streng auseinanderzuhalten. Bei der Feststellung der Zugehörigkeit einer Sprache zu einer gewissen Sprachgruppe muß der Sprachforscher genau und deutlich angeben, ob er diese Sprachgruppe für einen Sprachbund oder für eine Sprachfamilie hält. Dadurch werden viele voreilige und unvorsichtige Äußerungen vermieden (TRUBETZKOY 1930: 18).

Eine wesentliche Ergänzung erfuhr sie erst durch die Unterscheidung von *Divergenz* und *Konvergenz* bei der Interpretation der Phänomene. Als exemplarisch hierfür können die Überlegungen von N. REITER 1978 in seinem grundlegenden Aufsatz „Balcanologia quo vadis?" angeführt werden. Der Balkansprachbund ist demnach ein *Konvergat*, das aus verschiedenen *Konvergenten*, den Balkansprachen, gebildet wird. (Die Sprachfamilie ist hingegen ein *Divergat*, das sich in verschiedene *Divergenten* aufspaltet.)

Wie die Beiträge auf der Tagung „Balkanisms today" erneut gezeigt haben, bleibt der Sprachbund auch weiterhin primärer Gegenstand der Balkanlinguistik, wobei sich die Forschung aber längst nicht mehr allein auf die Untersuchung der klassischen Balkanismen beschränkt, sondern sich sehr aktiv und erfolgreich an der allgemeinen Methodendiskussion der Linguistik beteiligt. Vor allem die in den vergangenen Jahrzehnten entstandenen verschiedenen „Bindestrichlinguistiken" wie Sozio-, Ethno-, Kontaktlinguistik sowie Kreolistik und Pidginforschung haben viel zur Implementierung neuer Untersuchungsansätze und grundlegend zur Erweiterung des Forschungshorizonts beigetragen.

Als historisch orientierte philologische Disziplin richtet die Balkanlinguistik naturgemäß ihren Blick vornehmlich in die Vergangenheit. Die Entstehung und Entfaltung des Balkansprachbundes werden irgendwann in der Vergangenheit angesiedelt. Die Ansichten darüber, *wie, wo, warum* und *wann* die entscheidenden Prozesse abliefen, differieren bekanntlich immer noch erheblich. Und die Interpretation der sprachlichen Fakten erhält durch neue theoretische Ansätze ständig frische Impulse.

Doch wie ist es um den Balkansprachbund heute bestellt? Es wird hier nicht nach seiner Bedeutung als Forschungsgegenstand, sondern als weiterhin existentes sprachliches Phänomen gefragt. Oder anders formuliert: *Funktioniert der Sprachbund noch immer?* Natürlich ist das eine Fragestellung, die den Sprachhistoriker kaum interessiert, da er nur nach den Gründen für die Entstehung der Balkanismen oder des Balkansprachbundes sucht. Über ihre Entstehung herrscht wohl soweit Übereinstimmung, dass die sprachlichen Gemeinsamkeiten auf einen engeren Kontakt zwischen den Balkanvölkern zurückzuführen sind. Als mittlerweile weitgehend überholt kann die vor allem von rumänischen Linguisten vertretene Auffassung gelten, dass für die Entwicklung der sogenannten Balkanismen kein Sprachbund notwendig war. Damit wird von uns nicht in Abrede gestellt, dass sie jeweils sprachspezifisch ausgeformt wurden. Das hat an sich schon B. KOPITAR 1829 mit seiner oft zitierten Formel „nur eine Sprach f o r m herrscht, aber mit dreyerley Sprach m a t e r i e " gemeint.

Die Existenz eines Sprachkontakts allein reicht jedoch nicht aus. Er muss zudem intensiv und sehr lang andauernd gewesen sein, um einen Sprachbund zu initiieren. Die notwendige Voraussetzung für einen derartigen, zu einem Sprachbund führenden Kontakt mit einem defizitären Multilingualismus hat auf der Balkanhalbinsel nach allgemeiner Auffassung bestanden. Ob es nun aber die altbalkanischen Völker, das Römische Imperium, das Byzantinische oder das Osmanische Reich waren, welche den günstigen äußeren Rahmen für diesen Sprachkontakt konditionierten oder alle zusammen und noch einige weitere Faktoren, darüber gehen die Meinungen immer noch auseinander. Mit dem Niedergang des Osmanischen Reichs verändert sich dann die sprachliche Situation auf der Balkanhalbinsel fundamental.

Den folgenschweren Umbruch in seiner Existenz erlebte der Sprachbund gegen Ende des 18. Jahrhunderts. Um diese Zeit beginnen sich die verschiedenen nationalen Wiedergeburtsbewegungen in Südosteuropa zu formieren. Sie erhalten entscheidende Anregungen von der sich nach der Französischen Revolution in Westeuropa verbreitenden nationalen Idee. Die Sprache wird in diesem Kontext zum grundlegenden Kennzeichen der Nation. Deshalb wird sie auch zum zentralen Thema aller nationalen Bewegungen auf der Balkanhalbinsel. Die Aktivisten der Wiedergeburt von Adamantios KORAIS bis Vuk KARADŽIĆ, von Pajsi HILENDARSKI bis Samuel KLEIN/MICU und Gheorghe ŞINCAI kämpfen zudem nicht nur für eine neue, gemeinsame Schriftsprache, sondern immer gleichzeitig auch für die Dignität ihrer Muttersprache (und damit implizit ihres Volkes). Diese basierte zumindest auf der Ebenbürtigkeit oder sogar auf der Überlegenheit über die anderen Sprachen in der Nachbarschaft. Der Gebrauch der neuen vereinheitlichten Nationalsprache sollte allgemein verpflichtend werden und alle daneben existierenden Varietäten sowie die anderen Sprachen verdrängen.

Die immer lauter werdende politische Forderung der nationalen Wiedergeburtsbewegungen ebenfalls nach einem eigenen Staat für ihr Volk oder ihre Nation findet dann schnell in der bekannten Trias *ein Volk – ein Staat – eine Sprache* ihre prägnante Losung. Man kann dieses Motto gleichzeitig als Grabinschrift für den Balkansprachbund verwenden. Denn die oben erwähnten Reiche waren alle im Unterschied zu den bald entstehenden neuen Nationalstaaten noch *multiethnisch, multikonfessionell* und *multilingual*. Überall ist nun aber die Tendenz zu erkennen *multi* durch *mono* zu ersetzen, was bekanntlich wegen der komplexen Bevölkerungsstruktur auf der Balkanhalbinsel besonders schwierig war bzw. ist. Während man die sprachliche Entwicklung bis zum 18. Jahrhundert als Verfestigung des Sprachbundes betrachten kann, setzt nun die Entwicklung vom *Multilingualismus* zu *Monolingualismus* in den neu entstandenen Balkanstaaten ein. In der Terminologie von N. Reiter 1978 heißt das, dass nun der Übergang von mehreren Konvergenten (Balkansprachen) zu einem Konvergat (Balkansprachbund) oder zu einer gemeinsamen Balkansprache abgebrochen wurde.

Die Veränderungen im sprachlichen Umfeld, d.h. zunächst die sich ändernden makrohistorischen Gegebenheiten ab dem 18. Jahrhundert, können hier nur kursorisch ohne Anspruch auf Vollständigkeit und eine abschließende Gewichtung hinsichtlich ihrer Relevanz für den Balkansprachbund skizziert werden. Bereits die Gründung der neuen Balkanstaaten führt zu ersten Abwanderungen von minoritär gewordenen Volksgruppen und zeichnet deutlich den Weg zu ihrer fortschreitenden Monoethnisierung vor. Die anderssprachigen Gruppen werden zunehmend als „Schädlinge" im eigenen Volkskörper betrachtet, die man loswerden muss. Im Gefolge der Balkankriege kommt es daher aus ethnischen und konfessionellen Gründen zu umfangreichen Vertreibungen anderer Volksgruppen. Der griechisch-türkische Konflikt der 1920er Jahre ist ein weiterer Höhepunkt und führte schließlich zum massenhaften Exodus der Griechen bzw. Christen aus Kleinasien und der Türken bzw. Muslime aus Thrakien. Das vorläufig letzte Kapitel dieser langen Kette stellen die zahlreichen ethnischen und konfessionellen Säuberungen während der jüngsten jugoslawischen Bürgerkriege dar.

Die Folgen sind offensichtlich. Tendenziell treten überall monoethnische und monolinguale Nationalstaaten an die Stelle multiethnischer und multilingualer Imperien. Da die Monoethnisierung selten durch einfache Grenzziehungen zu verwirklichen ist, werden ethnische Säuberungen als legitimes Mittel angesehen, um das Ziel, eine homogene Volksgemeinschaft zu schaffen, zu erreichen. Das führt immer wieder zu Spannungen und Kriegen zwischen den Balkanstaaten, wobei die in den Nachbarstaaten verbliebenen Minderheiten zu Geiseln der Politik werden.

Flankiert werden die ethnischen Säuberungen immer von einer rigorosen Schulpolitik, die de facto die jeweilige Staatssprache zur alleinigen Unterrichtssprache macht oder zumindest massiv favorisiert. Auch die abweichende Konfession kann sich schnell als Störfaktor erweisen und zu gewaltsamen Missionierungen führen. Dazu kam es z.B. verstärkt im Gefolge der Maßnahmen des Živkov-Regimes in Bulgarien gegen die türkische Minderheit. Die Skala der ethnischen Konflikte reicht von der Unterdrückung über die Vertreibung bis zur physischen Vernichtung der störenden Minderheiten.

Was hat sich nach diesen Vorgängen hinsichtlich des Sprachbundes geändert? Der enge Sprachkontakt zwischen den Balkanvölkern hat merklich abgenommen. Es gibt heute nur wenige Bewohner der Balkanhalbinsel, die neben der jeweiligen Muttersprache noch andere Balkansprachen lernen. Die Kenntnis der Nachbarsprachen scheint von Generation zu Generation geringer zu werden. Doch es gibt auf der Balkanhalbinsel immer noch keine vollkommen monolingualen Staaten. Überall findet man weiterhin Reste von Minderheiten. Ist sie zu groß, kommt es zur Kantonisierung wie in Bosnien und de facto wohl ebenfalls in Makedonien.

Generell ist also der Zerfall des gemeinsamen Sprachraums auf der Balkanhalbinsel zu konstatieren. Mittlerweile gibt es dort keine dominante Herrschaftssprache und keine überregionalen Verkehrssprachen mehr. Türkisch hat seine Stellung als dominante Herrschaftssprache verloren, und Griechisch die einer Verkehrssprache. Ihre Stellen haben die modernen Nationalsprachen eingenommen, welche die verbliebenen Minderheiten in der Schule lernen müssen und neben ihrer Muttersprache im Alltag verwenden.

Symptomatisch für die Veränderungen scheint mir folgende persönliche Beobachtung zu sein. Anfang der 1970er Jahre habe ich auf einem griechischen Campingplatz beobachtet, wie ein Grieche und ein Serbe sich nur auf Deutsch miteinander verständigen konnten, das sie wohl als Gastarbeiter in Deutschland

rudimentär gelernt hatten. Die Muttersprache ihres Nachbarn verstanden sie hingegen nicht. Inzwischen wird in solchen Situationen wohl meist schon Englisch benutzt. Auf jeden Fall ist vom alten Sprachbund nicht mehr viel geblieben. Die
Entwicklung läuft eher auf einen neuen Sprachbund, auf einen *Eurosprachbund* zu,
den Reiter zuletzt im Auge hatte. Die zunehmende europäische Integration hinterlässt natürlich ebenfalls in den Balkansprachen ihre Spuren. Allerdings wird alles
von den Auswirkungen der Globalisierung überlagert, die vielleicht auf einen
globalen Sprachbund zusteuert, wie Pessimisten meinen.

An dieser Stelle soll zur Veranschaulichung der sprachlichen Verhältnisse ein
kurzer Überblick über die aktuelle Situation in den Balkanstaaten eingefügt werden. In *Albanien* gibt es eine kleine makedonische und eine größere griechische
Minderheit. Die Größe der letzten Gruppe ist ein Politikum und daher nicht exakt
zu fassen. Für diese beiden anerkannten Minderheiten existieren Minderheiten-
schulen. Alle Minderheiten sowie auch die kleinen nicht offiziell anerkannten
ethnischen Gruppen lernen natürlich ebenfalls Albanisch in der Schule. Als
Gastarbeiter erwerben viele Albaner in Griechenland und Makedonien ferner
Grundkenntnisse in den Sprachen der Nachbarn. In *Bulgarien* gibt es immer noch
eine größere türkischsprachige Minderheit, die übrigens erheblichen politischen
Einfluss hat und in der Schule neben Türkisch auch Bulgarisch lernt. Andere ethni-
sche Gruppen haben keine eigenen Schulen und sprechen überwiegend Bulgarisch
(z.B. die zahlreichen Zigeuner). Die Bulgaren verfügen indessen kaum noch über
Türkisch- oder gar Griechischkenntnisse, da sie selten als Gastarbeiter in die
Nachbarländer gehen. Nur in Griechenland scheint es eine größere Zahl von
bulgarischen Saisonarbeitern zu geben. In *Makedonien* stehen sich slavische
Makedonier und Albaner gegenüber. Die Albaner haben inzwischen ihre eigenen
Schulen, verstehen aber überwiegend noch Makedonisch, während die slavischen
Makedonier selten Kenntnisse des Albanischen besitzen. Die gegenwärtige Situa-
tion kann auf eine Kantonisierung hinauslaufen. In *Griechenland* gibt es nur Griechen oder, genauer, orthodoxe Griechen, wie es offiziell heißt. Dem widerspricht
freilich die Tatsache, dass Türken bzw. Muslime nach dem Vertrag von Lausanne
von 1923 sogar offiziell als Minderheit anerkannt sind. Immer noch geleugnet wird
hingegen, dass es auch Albaner und Slaven gibt. Unter diesen nicht existenten
Minderheiten, die natürlich alle Griechisch lernen müssen, regt sich inzwischen
Widerstand. Die Griechen selber lernen natürlich nicht die Sprachen der nicht
existenten Minderheiten, sondern höchstens Englisch und eventuell noch Deutsch.
Ähnlich ist wohl auch die Situation in *Serbien*, wo nach dem Bürgerkrieg die
Monoethnisierung weiter fortgeschritten ist. Zum Schluss nach ein Blick auf
Rumänien, wo nur noch die Ungarn und Szekler eine relevante Minderheit darstel-
len. Die Gruppe der Deutschen ist nach massiven Auswanderungen während des
Ceauşescu-Regimes und nach der Wende fast zur Bedeutungslosigkeit ge-
schrumpft. Die Verhältnisse sind kompliziert. Schon in kommunistischer Zeit gab

es für die Minderheiten einen weitreichenden Schutz, der zumindest auf dem Papier weiter existiert. Allerdings macht das raue innenpolitische Klima heute seine Aufrechterhaltung zusehends schwieriger, wie die virulenten Spannungen mit Ungarn zeigen. Nur selten sprechen die Rumänen noch die Sprachen der mitwohnenden Nationalitäten.

Im Rückblick lässt sich folgendes feststellen:

1. Der Balkansprachbund muss als dynamisches Phänomen verstanden werden, da der untersuchte Gegenstand – primär die *Sprache* – einem ständigen Wandel unterworfen ist und nach dem Wegfall wichtiger Voraussetzungen die Konvergenz an Kraft verliert. Oder auf eine kurze Formel gebracht: *Der Balkansprachbund ist tot, es lebe die Balkanlinguistik!* Der Balkanlinguist sollte in seinen Untersuchungen – und das sehe ich als ein Ergebnis der bisherigen Ausführungen für die Theorie – den Sprachbund stärker als dynamische Erscheinung sehen. Denn er ist von äußeren Umständen abhängig, die sich mehr oder weniger schnell ändern können.

2. Mit der Bildung der Nationalstaaten hat eine sprachliche Parzellierung der Balkanhalbinsel eingesetzt. In den neuen Staaten gibt es jeweils eine dominante Herrschaftssprache. Zwar sind sie noch nicht vollkommen monoethnisch und monolingual geworden, aber der Übergang vom Multilingualismus zum Monolingualismus ist überall erkennbar. Die Minderheiten werden von den jeweiligen Herrschaftssprachen dominiert und ihre Angehörigen sind zwangsläufig mehr oder weniger bilingual.

3. In der Zukunft könnte der Eurosprachbund oder auch ein globaler Sprachbund die Nachfolge des Balkansprachbundes in Südosteuropa – und nicht nur hier – antreten.

Literatur

KOPITAR, Bartolomej (1829): Albanische, walachische und bulgarische Sprache. In: *Jahrbücher der Literatur* 46. 59–106.

REITER, Norbert (1978): Balcanologia quo vadis? In: *Zeitschrift für Balkanologie* 14. 177–224.

REITER, Norbert (1994): *Grundzüge der Balkanologie. Ein Schritt in die Eurolinguistik.* Berlin.

STEINKE, Klaus (1998): Balkanlinguistik als linguistisches Propädeutikum. In: *Die Welt der Slaven* XLII. 161–172.

STEINKE, Klaus; VRACIU, Ariton (1999): *Introducere în lingvistica balcanică.* Iaşi.

TRUBETZKOY, Nikolaj Sergeevič (1930): Über den Sprachbund. In: *Actes du premier congrès international de linguistes à la Haye, du 10.–15. avril 1928.* Leiden. 17–18.

Die Herausbildung der Wortklassenterminologie in den Balkansprachen[1]

Thede KAHL (Jena/Wien), Michael METZELTIN (Wien)

Einleitung

Geht man von dem ältesten abendländischen Grammatikbeschreibungsversuch aus, demjenigen des Grammatikers Dionysios THRAX (2. Jahrhundert v. Chr.), bestehen die „Sätze" (λόγος) eines Diskurses aus der Zusammenstellung (σύνθεσις) von „Wörtern" (λέξις), die einen „in sich vollendeten Gedanken ausdrücken" (διάνοιαν αὐτοτελῆ δηλοῦσα). Aufgrund verschiedener morphologischer, syntaktischer und semantischer Kriterien teilt Dionysios Thrax die satzbildenden Wörter in verschiedene Kategorien ein. Seitdem ist es üblich, die Wörter einer Sprache in Wortklassen oder Wortarten einzuteilen. Im Prinzip kann man die Lexeme einer Sprache klassifizieren nach ihrer

- phonetischen Form
- morphologischen Variabilität
- Affigierbarkeit
- Semantik
- syntaktischen Kombinierbarkeit
- Mobilität im Satz
- Austauschbarkeit in derselben Satzposition
- Funktion in einem Satzschema.

Die in der europäisch geprägten Sprachwissenschaft traditionell verwendeten Wortklassen sind das Ergebnis des Versuches, die Lexeme aufgrund ihrer möglichen morphologischen, syntaktischen und semantischen Aspekte in Gruppen aufzuteilen, deren Erkennung die Satzrezeption und -produktion erleichtern, denn die Satzglieder haben als Kern bestimmte Wortarten. Daher werden diese Wortklassen auch Redeteile (alb. *pjesët e ligjëratës*, gr. μέρη του λόγου, rum. *păr-*

---

1 Der vorliegende Beitrag ist ein Teil eines größeren Projektes über eine neue vergleichende Grammatik der Balkansprachen, das unter der Leitung von Thede Kahl und Michael Metzeltin und der Beteiligung von Gerhard Neweklowsky und Claudia Romer an der Balkan-Kommission der Österreichischen Akademie der Wissenschaften initiiert worden ist. Für eine nähere Beschreibung des Projektes verweisen wir auf KAHL/LINDENBAUER/METZELTIN (2010).

țile de vorbire, bulg. *части на речта*, serb. *sastav reči*, türk. *konuşma parçaları*)
genannt. Die von der griechischen und lateinischen Grammatik übernommenen
Wortklassen sind nicht unbedingt universal, wie zum Beispiel Bantusprachen zei-
gen, in denen die Wortklassen überwiegend nach Präfixen kategorisiert werden.
Die Anzahl der Wortklassen kann schwanken (z.B. durch die Existenz oder das
Fehlen eines Artikels), und ihre genaue Abgrenzung muss wegen möglicher
Polyfunktionalität bestimmter Wörter in den verschiedenen Grammatikographien
nicht einheitlich sein. So kann das albanische *në* als Konjunktion (ob, wenn) oder
Präposition (in, nach), das griechische *καλά* als Adverb (gut) oder Substantiv (Gü-
ter), das rumänische *drept* als Substantiv (Recht), Adjektiv (gerade), Adverb (geradezu) oder Präposition (als), das bulgarische *слаб* als Substantiv (schwache Note),
Adjektiv (schwach), Adverb (schlecht) betrachtet werden. In den indogermanischen Sprachen ist es üblich, die Wortklassen in veränderliche (flektierte Wortklassen: Substantive, Adjektive, Pronomina, Artikel und Verben) mit Deklination oder
Konjugation und unveränderliche (unflektierte Wortklassen: Adverbien, Präpositionen, Konjunktionen, Interjektionen) zu unterscheiden. In einzelnen Grammatiken wird neben den traditionellen Kategorien auch eine Klasse ‚Partikeln' behandelt.

Die Terminologie in den einzelnen Sprachen

Im Folgenden soll versucht werden, das Entstehen der Wortklassenterminologie in
den Balkansprachen (im weiteren Sinne) Albanisch, Griechisch, Rumänisch,
Aromunisch, Bulgarisch, Makedonisch, Serbisch und Türkisch aufgrund der frühen
und der standardisierenden Grammatikographien aufzuzeigen.

Albanisch

Die ersten grammatischen Beschreibungen des Albanischen stammen von italie-
nisch- und deutschsprachigen Autoren. Francesco Maria de LECCE (1716: 3) sieht
in seinen *Osservazioni grammaticali nella lingua albanese* (Roma, 1716) für das
Albanische acht Wortkategorien vor, und zwar: „Nome, Pronome, Verbo, Partici-
pio, Preposizione, Adverbio, Interiezione, e Congiunzione". In seinem Werk *Die
Sprache der Albanesen oder Schkipetaren* unterscheidet J. v. XYLANDER (Frankfurt am Main, 1835) folgende Wortkategorien:

1. *Hauptwort und Artikel*
2. *Eigenschaftswort*
3. *Fürwort*
4. *Zeitwort*
5. *Zahlwert*
6. *Umstandswort*

Wenig später unterteilt Johann von HAHN in seinen *Albanesischen Studien* (zweites Heft, Jena, 1854) die Wörter in folgende Klassen, die sich auch bei späteren Autoren (z.B. Gustav MEYER 1888) finden:

1. *Artikel*
2. *Substantiv*
3. *Adjectiv*
4. *Numeralia*
5. *Pronomina*
6. *Verbum*
7. *Präposition*
8. *Adverbien und Conjunctionen*
9. *Ausrufungen (im Anhang)*

Sami FRASHËRI (1886) scheint in der *Shkronjëtore e gjuhësë shqip* die Grundlage für die entsprechende Terminologie im Albanischen gegeben zu haben. Angelo LEOTTI (1915: 8) unterscheidet in seiner auf dem toskischen Dialekt basierenden *Grammatica elementare della lingua albanese* folgende Kategorien (*parti del discorso*):

1. *articolo / nyj*[2]
2. *sostantivo o nome / emërë*
3. *aggettivo / miémërë*
4. *pronome / përémërë*
5. *verbo / folje*
6. *avverbio / mifolje*
7. *preposizione / parje*
8. *congiunzione / lidhje*
9. *interiezione / thirje*

Die Grammatik der albanischen Sprache (*Gramatika e gjuhës shqipe*, 2002: 37–38) des Instituts für Sprach- und Literaturwissenschaft (Instituti i gjuhësisë dhe i letërsisë) der Albanischen Akademie der Wissenschaften unterscheidet folgende Wortklassen:

1. *emri* (das Substantiv)
2. *mbiemri* (das Adjektiv)
3. *numërori* (das Numerale)
4. *përemri* (das Pronomen)
5. *folja* (das Verb)

2　Die kursiv geschriebenen Bezeichnungen vor und nach einem Querstrich (/) stammen von den zitierten Autoren, die nicht kursiven Übersetzungen in Klammern von den Autoren dieses Beitrages.

6. *ndajfolja* (das Adverb)
7. *parafjala* (die Präposition)
8. *lidhëza* (die Konjunktion)
9. *pjesëza* (die Partikel)
10. *pasthirrma* (die Interjektion)

Griechisch

Die erste Grammatik des Neugriechischen (im Sinne der gesprochenen Volkssprache) wurde vor 1550 von Nicolas SOPHIANOS als *Γραμματικὴ Εἰσαγωγή* verfasst, aber erst 1874 von Émil Legrand veröffentlicht. Sophianos unterscheidet folgende neun Wortklassen:

1. *Ὄνομα* (Nomen)
2. *Ἄρθρον* (Artikel)
3. *Ὀνόματα ἀριθμητικά* (Zahlwörter)
4. *Ῥῆμα* (Verb)
5. *Μετοχῆ* (Partizip)
6. *Ἀντωνυμία* (Pronomen)
7. *Προθέσεις* (Präpositionen)
8. *Ἐπίῤῥημα* (Adverb)
9. *Σύνδεσμος* (Konjunktion)

Eine entsprechende lateinische Terminologie liefert Simon PORTIUS in seiner 1638 verfassten *Gramatica linguae graecae vulgaris*: „Cum octo sint Orationis partes, Articulus scilicet, Nomen, Pronomen, Verbum, Participium, Praepositio, et Conjunctio, de iis singillatim habendus erit sermo [...]" (Kap. III). Auch Alexandros MAVROKORDATOS behandelt in seiner *Γραμματικὴ περὶ συντάξεως* (Grammatik über die Syntax, 1745) acht Wortklassen (*Ἄρθρον, Ἀντωνυμία, Ὄνομα, Ῥῆμα, Μετοχῆ, Ἐπίῤῥημα, Σύνδεσμος, Προθέσεις*).

Spätestens seit den 40er Jahren des 20. Jahrhunderts gibt es in Griechenland Institutionen, die für die Herausgabe von Schulbüchern zuständig sind und auch normative Grammatiken („Staatsgrammatiken") herausgeben, so wie der Οργανισμός Εκδόσεως Διδακτικών Βιβλίων (Verband für die Herausgabe von Lehrbüchern). Die Athener Akademie scheint keine normative Grammatik herausgegeben zu haben. Normierende Grammatiken sind von Manolis A. TRIANTAFYLLIDIS am Ινστιτούτο Νεοελληνικών Σπουδών (Institut für Neugriechische Studien) herausgegeben worden. In seiner *Μικρή νεοελληνική γραμματική* (Kleine[n] neugriechische[n] Grammatik, 1965, dem Nachfolgewerk der *Νεοελληνική γραμματική*, 1941) unterscheidet der Autor z.B.:

1. *το άρθρο* (der Artikel)
2. *τα ουσιαστικά* (die Substantive)
3. *τα επίθετα* (die Adjektive)

4. *οι αντωνυμίες* (die Pronomina)
5. *τα ρήματα* (die Verben)
6. *επιρρήματα* (Adverbien)
7. *οι προθέσεις* (die Präpositionen)
8. *σύνδεσμοι* (die Konjunktionen)
9. *επιφωνήματα* (die Interjektionen)

Rumänisch

Die erste, zwar nicht gedruckte Grammatik des Rumänischen (*Gramatica rumânească*) wurde 1757 von Dimitrie EUSTATIEVICI verfasst. Er unterscheidet zwischen folgenden Redeteilen (*părţile voroavei*):

1. *numele* (das Nomen)
2. *în loc de numele* (Pronomen)
3. *graiul* (das Verb)
4. *împărtăşirea* (das Partizip)
5. *înainte-punerea* (die Präposition, einschließlich der Präfixe)
6. *spreghrăirea* (das Adverb)
7. *în mijloc-aruncarea* (die Interjektion)
8. *împreunarea* (die Konjunktion)

Nach der ersten gedruckten Grammatik, *Observaţii sau băgări-dă-seamă* von Ianache VĂCĂRESCU (1787), sind die Wörter in neun Redeteile zu gliedern, und zwar in „*articol* adică *încheerea, nome* adică *nume, pronome* adică *pronume, verbu* adică *graiu, partiţipie* adică *părtăşire, propoziţione* adică *propunere, adverbiu* adică *spre graiu, congiunţione* adică *legare*, şi *interieţione*".

Die Academia Română (Rumänische Akademie) gibt seit 1954 normierende Grammatiken des Rumänischen heraus (*Gramatica limbii române*). In der zweiten Ausgabe von 1966 (§ 9) werden folgende Redeteile unterschieden: „Cuvintele din limba română se grupează în zece clase, lexicale şi gramaticale în acelaşi timp, numite părţi de vorbire: substantivul, articolul, adjectivul, pronumele, numeralul, verbul, adverbul, prepoziţia, conjuncţia şi interjecţia". Diese Reihenfolge der Wortklassen (*clase de cuvinte*) wird auch in der stärker fachtechnisch ausgerichteten Ausgabe von 2005 beibehalten, in der allerdings kein eigener Teil für den Artikel vorgesehen ist:

1. *Substantivul* (das Substantiv)
2. *Adjectivul* (das Adjektiv)
3. *Pronumele* (das Pronomen)
4. *Numeralul* (das Numerale)
5. *Verbul* (das Verb)
6. *Adverbul* (das Adverb)
7. *Prepoziţia* (die Präposition)

8. *Conjuncţia* (die Konjunktion)
9. *Interjecţia* (die Interjektion)

Aromunisch

Das Aromunische hat bis heute keine normierende Instanz. Die erste publizierte Grammatik wurde 1813 von Michael BOJADSCHI (*Γραμματική ρωμανική, ήτοι μα-κεδονοβλαχική / Romanische, oder Macedonowlachische Sprachlehre*) verfasst und weist rumänisierende Tendenzen auf. Bojadschi unterscheidet folgende Wortklassen (S. 16). Seine Bezeichnungen sind nur griechisch und deutsch, weshalb ein aromunisches Fachvokabular diesbezüglich nicht eingeführt wird.

1. *τὸ Ἄρθρον / Das Geschlechtswort*
2. *τὸ Ὄνομα / Das Nennwort*
3. *ἡ Ἀντωνυμία / Das Fürwort*
4. *τὸ Ῥῆμα / Das Zeitwort*
5. *ἡ Μετοχῆ / Das Mittelwort*
6. *ἡ Πρόθεσις / Das Vorwort*
7. *τὸ Ἐπίρρημα / Das Nebenwort*
8. *ὁ Σύνδεσμος / Das Bindewort*
9. *ἡ Παρένθεσις / Das Empfindungswort*

Eine rezente deskriptive aromunische Grammatik, verfasst von Iancu IANACHIEV-SCHI-VLAHU (*Gramatica simplă shi practică*, 1993), verwendet eine neue aromunische Terminologie internationaler Prägung und spricht von:

1. *numa / substantivu* (Substantiv)
2. *adjectivu* (Adjektiv)
3. *articulu / nodu* (Artikel)
4. *pronuma* (Pronomen)
5. *verbu* (Verb)
6. *adverbu* (Adverb)
7. *prepozitionu* (Präposition)
8. *conjuctionu / ligatura* (Konjunktion)
9. *interjectsionu* (Interjektion)
10. *numeralu* (Numeral)
11. *particul* (Partikel)

Bulgarisch

Ein früher Versuch, das Bulgarische zu beschreiben, wurde vom bulgarischen Mönch Neofyt, genannt Neofit RILSKI, unternommen (*Волгарска граммати*ка, 1835). Die Wortklassen heißen bei ihm *части те на-слобо то*, er nennt derer acht:

1. *Имѧ то / Nomen*
2. *Прилагателни те имена / Adjektiv*
3. *Мѣстоименїе та / Pronomen*
4. *Глаголатъ / Verbum* (einschließlich *Причастїе / Partizipium*)
5. *Нарѧчїето / Adverbium*
6. *Предлогатъ / Prepositio*
7. *Союзатъ / Coniunctio*
8. *Мѣждометїе то / Interactio*

Die Aufzählung entspricht den Kapiteln des Bandes. Das Partizip wird als Unterkapitel des Verbs und im Gegensatz zur kirchenslawischen Grammatik von Meletij SMOTRYC'KYJ von 1619 (*Граммаꙗки славенския правилное Сѵнтагма*), die er als Quelle verwendet, nicht als selbstständige Wortklasse behandelt.

Für das heutige Bulgarisch scheint es keine verbindliche Akademie-Grammatik zu geben. Es gibt Standardwerke der neuen bulgarischen Sprache, die die Schriftsprache beschreiben, ohne jedoch deutlich normativen Charakter zu haben. Das Lehrbuch von Demetrius W. GAWRIYSKY unterscheidet (1910: 17) in seiner *Bulgarischen Konversations-Grammatik für den Schul- und Selbstunterricht* folgende Wortklassen (*частитѣ на рѣчьта*):

1. *членъ / der Artikel*
2. *съществително име / das Hauptwort*
3. *прилагателно име / das Eigenschaftswort*
4. *мѣстоиме / das Fürwort*
5. *числително име / das Zahlwort*
6. *глаголъ / das Zeitwort*
7. *нарѣчие / das Umstandswort*
8. *прѣдлогъ / das Vorwort*
9. *съюзъ / das Bindewort*
10. *междуметие / das Empfindungswort*

Die Grammatik der bulgarischen Schriftsprache von Stojan STOJANOV (1964) gibt folgende Klassen an, die auch von anderen Autoren angegeben werden:

1. *съществително име* (Substantiv, einschließlich bestimmtem Artikel = *членуване на съществителните имена*)
2. *прилагателно име* (Adjektiv)
3. *числително име* (Numerale)
4. *местоимение* (Pronomen)
5. *глагол* (Verb)
6. *наречие* (Adverb)
7. *предлог* (Präposition)
8. *съюз* (Konjunktion)

9. *междуметие* (Interjektion)
10. *частица* (Partikel)

Makedonisch

Die im Auftrag des Volksrates der jungen Teilrepublik Makedonien bereits im Januar 1946 in Skopje herausgegebene und zur Schulbildung bestimmte *Македонска граматика* von Krume KEPESKI geht auf die folgenden Klassen ein:

1. *именки* (Substantive)
2. придавки (Adjektive)
3. броеви (Zahlen)
4. заменки (Pronomina)
5. *глаголи* (Verben)
6. прилози (Adverbien)
7. предлози (Präpositionen)
8. сврзници (Konjunktionen)
9. *извици* (Interjektionen)

Die Grammatik der makedonischen Literatursprache von Blaže KONESKI (*Граматика на македонскиот литературен јазик*, 1967), die die Grammatikographie des Makedonischen bis heute maßgeblich prägt, unterscheidet die folgenden Kategorien:

1. *именка* (Substantiv, einschließlich bestimmtem Artikel (*член, членски форм*) in einem Kapitel zur Unbestimmtheit und Bestimmtheit der Substantive (*определеноста и неопределеноста на именките*))
2. *придавка* (Adjektiv)
3. *броеви* (Zahlen)
4. *заменки* (Pronomina)
5. *прилог* (Adverb)
6. *глагол* (Verb)
7. *предлози* (Präpositionen)
8. *сврзници* (Konjunktionen)
9. *частици* (Partikel)
10. *модални зборови* (Modalwörter)
11. *извици* (Interjektionen)

Im seinem *Lehrbuch der makedonischen Sprache in 50 Lektionen* unterscheidet Wolf OSCHLIES (2007: 29) die folgenden Kategorien:

1. *именки* (Substantive)
2. *член* (Artikel)
3. *заменки* (Pronomina)
4. *придавки* (Adjektive)

5. *глагол* (Verb)
6. *броеви* (Zahlen)
7. *предлози* (Präpositionen)
8. *прилози* (Adverbien)
9. *сврзници* (Konjunktionen)
10. *частици* (Partikel)
11. *модални, начински зборови* (Modalwörter)
12. *извици* (Interjektionen)

Serbisch

Ein früher Versuch, das Serbische zu beschreiben, wurde vom serbischen Sprachreformer Vuk Stefanović KARADŽIĆ (*Писменица сербскога іезика*, 1814) unternommen:

1. *име* (Substantiv)
2. *мѣстоименіе* (Pronomen)
3. *глагол* (Verb)
4. *причастіе* (Adjektiv)
5. *нарѣчіе* (Adverb)
6. *предлог* (Präposition)
7. *соіуз* (Konjunktion)
8. *междометіе* (Interjektion)

Ðuro DANIČIĆ (1850) publizierte 1850 in Wien die *Мала српска граматика*, in der die folgenden Wortkategorien mit verschiedenen Bezeichnungen behandelt werden:

1. *Самоставне ријечи (имена суштествителна, substantiva)*
2. *Придјеви (имена прилагателна, adjectiva)*
3. *Бројеви (имена числителна, numeralia)*
4. *Замјенице (местоименија, pronomina)*
5. *Глаголи (verba)*
6. *Предлози (praepositiones)*

Die 1908 von Emil M. MUŽA verfasste *Praktische Grammatik* unterscheidet neun Redeteile (*деоба речи*):

1. *именица / Hauptwort / Substantiv*
2. *придев / Eigenschaftswort / Adjectiv*
3. *заменица / Fürwort / Pronomen*
4. *број / Zahlwort / Numerale*
5. *глагол / Zeitwort / Verbum*
6. *предлог / Verhältniswort / Präposition*
7. *прилог / Umstandswort / Adverb*

8. *свеза / Bindewort / Conjunction*
9. *усклик / Empfindungswort / Interjection*

Die normative Zeitgenössische serbokroatische Grammatik von Mihailo STEVANO-
VIĆ (*Савремени српскохрватски језик,* 1991) unterteilt in:

1. *именице* (Substantive)
2. *придеви* (Adjektive)
3. *заменице* (Pronomina)
4. *бројеви* (Zahlen)
5. *глаголи* (Verben)
6. *прилози* (Adverbien)
7. *предлози* (Präpositionen)
8. *везници* (Konjunktionen)
9. *речце* (Partikeln)
10. *узвици* (Interjektionen)

Türkisch

Die Grammatikographie des Türkischen dürfte in ihren Anfängen durch die Domi-
nanz französischer Terminologie und in geringerem Maße anderer westeuropäi-
scher Terminologien geprägt worden sein. Im Späteren erfährt sie eine Erweiterung
durch arabische und persische Traditionen. In seiner *Grammatik der türkisch-
osmanischen Umgangssprache* unterscheidet P. J. PIQUERÉ (1870) z.B. folgende
Wortklassen:

1. *Hauptwort*
2. *Beiwort* (unterschieden in Eigenschaftswort und Bestimmungswort, letzteres
   bestehend aus Zahlwörtern, anzeigenden, zueignenden, unbestimmten und
   fragenden Beiwörtern)
3. *Fürwörter*
4. *Zeitwort*
5. *Adverbium* oder *Nebenwort*
6. *Postpositionen*
7. *Bindewörter* oder *Conjunctionen*
8. *Ausrufungswort* oder *Interjection*

Adolf WAHRMUND gibt im Inhaltsverzeichnis seines Werkes *Praktisches Handbuch der osmanisch-türkischen Sprache* (1884, 1. Ausgabe 1869) die folgenden
Kategorien an:

1. *Hauptwort*
2. *Eigenschaftswort*
3. *Zahlwort*
4. *Fürwort*

5. *Zeitwort*
6. *Partikel* (*Postpositionen, Conjunktionen, Adverbien, Interjektionen, persische und arabische Partikeln*)

Eine Aufstellung der Wortklassen mit genauerer Einteilung bietet Jean DENY in der Cinquième partie (*Parties du discours*) des Inhaltsverzeichnisses seiner *Grammaire de la langue turque (dialecte Osmanli)* (1921: 1206–1216), und zwar:

Livre I. *Nom*
   1) *Nom variable (substantif, pronom)*
   2) *Nom invariable (adjectif, adverbe)*
   3) *Noms de nombre*
   4) *Noms dérivés d'un autre nom* (d.h. *diminutifs, dérivés proprement dits*)
Livre II. *Verbe*
   1) *Verbe substantif*
   2) *Du verbe turc en général. Racines verbales*
   3) *Suffixes verbaux de dérivation expriment la voix (ou modificateurs)*
   4) *Suffixe verbaux désinentiels. Conjugaison*
   5) *Verbes complexes et verbes composés*
Livre III. *Verbe dérivés d'un nom et nom s dérivés d'un verbe*
Livre IV. *Particules*
   1) *Postpositions*
   2) *Conjonctions*
   3) *Interjections*

Faruk TIMURTAŞ verwendet im Inhaltsverzeichnis seiner *Osmanlı Türkçesi Grameri* (Grammatik des Osmanisch-Türkischen, 1979) für die Oberbegriffe arabische Terminologie, für die Unterkategorien auch türkische (im Folgenden kursiv und fett hervorgehoben) und zur Verdeutlichung französische Übersetzungen:

1. *isim* (Nomen bzw. Substantiv)
2. *fiil* (Verb)
3. *sıfat* (Adjektiv; es folgen die verschiedenen Arten von Adjektiven, zuerst in arabischer bzw. türkisch-arabischer Terminologie mit türkischer Syntax, dann in Klammern die älteren Formen in arabischer Terminologie mit persischer Syntax, dann die französische Übersetzung)
   işaret sıfatları / = sıfât-ı işâriyye / adjectifs démonstratifs
   sayı *sıfatları / = sıfât-ı adediyye / adjectifs numéraux*; früher, nicht näher spezifiziert, als Substantiva betrachtet, daher *ism-i aded*, Pl. *esma-ı a'dâd / noms des nombres*
   soru *sıfatları / sıfât-ı istifhâmiyye / adjectifs interrogatifs*
   belirsizlik *sıfatları / sıfât-ı mübheme / adjectifs indéfinis*
4. *zamir* (Pronomen)

5. *zarf* (Adverb)
6. *edat* (Partikel)
    son çekim *edatları* / *postpositions*
    bağlama *edatları* / *conjonctions*
        tekit (**berkitme**) *edatları* (nicht übersetzt; enthält Bekräftigungspartikeln
        ‚auch', ‚sogar', ‚eben', ‚eben dieser')
        soru edatları (nicht übersetzt; enthält Fragepronomina)
        nida (**ünlem** / *interjection*)

Die Grammatik des modernen Türkisch schließlich von Haydar EDISKUN (*Türk Dilbilgisi*, 1985) verbindet arabische und türkische Terminologie miteinander:

1. *isim* (Substantiv)
2. *sıfat* (Adjektiv, enthält auch Pronomina in attributiver Position)
3. *zamir* (Pronomen, nur in substantivischer Position)
4. *fiil* (Verb)
5. *zarf* = *belirteç* (Adverb, enthält auch Frageadverbia)
6. *edat* (Partikel, einschließlich Postpositionen und Adverbia und Verbalformen)
7. *bağlaç* (Konjunktion, wörtl. Verbindungswort, Neologismus)
8. *ünlem* (Interjektion, wörtl. Ausruf, Neologismus)

Kommentar

Die europäische Grammatikographie geht auf die philologischen Bemühungen der alexandrinischen Schule zurück. Obwohl Bezeichnungen verschiedener Wortarten schon bei PLATON (z.B. im *Kratylos*, 425a, 431c) und bei ARISTOTELES (z.B. in der *Poetik*, Kap. 20) vorkommen, dürften die zwei wichtigsten Werke, auf denen die traditionelle Grammatik beruht, die Τέχνη γραμματική (Grammatische Kunst) von Dionysius THRAX (2. Jahrhundert v. Chr.) und Περὶ συντάξεως (Über die Syntax) von Apollonios DYSKOLOS (2. Jahrhundert n. Chr.) sein. Dionysius Thrax unterscheidet im § 11 acht Redeteile: „δὲ λόγου μέρη ἐστὶν ὀκτώ· ὄνομα, ῥῆμα, μετοχή, ἄρθρον, ἀντωνυμία, πρόθεσις, ἐπίρρημα, σύνδεσμος" (Der Redeteile sind acht; Name/Substantiv, Rede/Verbum, Teilnahme/Partizip, Gelenk/Artikel, ‚Fürname'/Pronomen, Aufstellung/Präposition, ‚Aufverb'/Adverb, Verbindung/Konjunktion). Bei Apollonios Dyskolos kommen die Redeteile in den Paragraphen 12 bis 35 mit den gleichen Bezeichnungen und in der gleichen Reihenfolge wie bei Dionysius Thrax vor. Bei den meisten Bezeichnungen dürfte es sich um ältere Wörter mit fachspezifischer Bedeutung handeln, im Fall von ἀντωνυμία und ἐπίρρημα scheint es sich um Neuschöpfungen zu handeln. Bei Dionysius Thrax sind die Wortkategorien auch inhaltlich näher erläutert:

a. ein Name/Substantiv ist ein deklinierter Redeteil, das einen Körper oder eine Handlung/Sache bezeichnet (§12).

b. die Rede/ das Verbum ist ein dekliniertes Wort, das Zeiten, Personen und Zahlen aufzeigt und Handlung oder Leidenschaft ausdrückt (§13).

c. Die Teilnahme/ das Partizip ist ein Wort, das Eigenschaften sowohl von Verben als auch von Substantiven hat (§15).

d. Das Gelenk/ der Artikel ist ein deklinierter Redeteil, der der Beugung der Namen voran- oder nachgestellt wird (§16).

e. Der ‚Fürname'/ das Pronomen ist ein Wort, das anstelle des Namens steht und auf bestimmte Personen hinweist (§17).

f. Die Aufstellung/Präposition ist ein Wort, das allen Wortteilen in Zusammensetzung und Zusammenstellung (=Satz) vorangestellt wird (§18).

g. Das ‚Aufverb'/Adverb ist ein ungebeugter Redeteil, der entlang der Rede/ dem Verb gesagt oder zur Rede/ zum Verb hinzugefügt wird (§19).

h. Die Verbindung/Konjunktion ist ein Wort, das Gedanken ordnend verbindet und die Lücken des Ausdruckes vervollständigt/ die Verständnislücken schließt (§20).

Dionysios scheint der erste zu sein, der sich über die Redeteile und ihre Erfassung genauere Gedanken macht, wobei er morphologische Kriterien (z.B. Deklinierbarkeit), semantische Kriterien (wie beim Nomen und Verb) und syntaktische Kriterien (wie beim Artikel) heranzieht. Er gibt auch bereits Unterklassen vor wie z.B. die Unterscheidung in acht Typen von Konjunktionen. Schon bei ihm zeigt sich die Schwierigkeit, die Unterscheidungskriterien für jede Klasse konsequent anzuwenden. Als besonders schwer zu erfassen und zu definieren stellen sich Kategorien wie Adverb und Konjunktion heraus. Das Adjektiv wird bei Dionysios unter den Namen/Substantiven und die Interjektion unter den Adverbien geführt.

Die lateinische Grammatikographie führt die griechische Tradition weitgehend fort. Aelius DONATUS (4. Jahrhundert n. Chr.) zählt in seiner *Ars Minor* (Kleine Kunst (der Grammatik)) die folgenden *partes orationis* auf: *nomen, pronomen, verbum, adverbium, participium, coniunctio, praepositio, interiectio*. Priscianus Caesariensis oder Priscian (6. Jahrhundert n. Chr.) unterteilt in seinen *Institutiones grammaticae* die *partes orationis* in leicht geänderter Reihenfolge in *nomen, verbum, participium, pronomen, praepositio, adverbium, interiectio, coniunctio*. Beide Autoren führen das Adjektiv (bei PRISCIAN II, 13 mit der Bezeichnung *adiectivum*) unter den Nomina auf. Bei PRISCIAN (II, 15–17) finden wir außerdem eine ausführliche Besprechung der möglichen Anzahl von Wortkategorien, die zwischen zwei und elf schwanken kann, wobei Nomen und Verbum eine zentrale Stellung einnehmen: „Partes igitur orationis sunt secundum dialecticos duae, nomen et verbum, quia hae solae etiam per se coniunctae plenam faciunt orationem, alias autem partes ‚syncategoremata', hoc est consignificantia, appellabant". Priscians Werk war über Jahrhunderte das Referenzwerk für den Grammatikunterricht. Die Adjektive als eigene Kategorie werden erst von der Grammaire générale des 18. Jahrhunderts ausgearbeitet. Das Referenzwerk hierfür ist die *Grammaire géné-*

rale von Nicolas BEAUZÉE (1767), der diese Wortart in Livre II, chapitre III, 290–291 folgendermaßen beschreibt:

> «C'est sur ce méchanisme métaphysique qu'est fondée la nécessité des *Adjectifs*, espèce de mots ainsi nommés d'*adjectum*, supin d'*adjicere* (ajoûter); en sorte qu'*adjectivus* (adjectif) signifie proprement *qui sert à ajoûter*. C'est caractériser très-bien la distinction de cette espèce de mots, puisqu'ils servent en effet à modifier les noms appellatifs, en ajoûtant à l'idée de la nature commune qu'ils énoncent quelqu'autre idée accidentelle. (…) Or il n'y a que deux choses qui puissent être modifiées dans la signification des noms appellatifs, savoir la compréhension & l'étendue: de là deux espèces générales d'Adjectifs, que j'appelerai *Adjectifs physiques & Articles*.»

Systematische Terminologien der Wortarten für die südosteuropäischen Sprachen entstehen für das Neugriechische im 16. Jahrhundert (Sophianos), für andere Sprachen erst im 18. oder 19. Jahrhundert. Diese Terminologien basieren vor allem auf Lehnübersetzungen, wobei es schwierig ist festzustellen, ob die griechische oder lateinische Tradition oder beide als Vorlage gedient haben. Sprachen mit geringerer schriftlicher Tradition weisen eine weniger gefestigte Terminologie auf. Teilweise verwenden die Verfasser der hier berücksichtigten Grammatiken sowohl eine unterschiedliche Terminologie als auch eine unterschiedliche Reihenfolge der Merkmale. Das Adjektiv tritt im Allgemeinen als eigene Kategorie auf. In einzelnen Terminologien kommt auch die Kategorie Partikel vor. Meistens lässt sich eine grobe Zweiteilung in nominale und verbale Kategorien erkennen, wobei die Tendenz zu beobachten ist, mit dem Nomen zu beginnen. Dies könnte auf die Intuition zurückzuführen sein, dass Sätze grundsätzlich aus Haupt- und Zeitwörtern bestünden (PLATON, *Kratylos*, passim).

Albanisch

Im Fall des Albanischen spricht Julius PISKO in seinem Werk *Kurzgefasstes Handbuch der nordalbanesischen Sprache* (1896: III) noch von einem „vollständigen Mangel einer Schriftsprache" und verwendet in seiner nordalbanischen Grammatik wie auch schon Johann von HAHN (1854) und Gustav MEYER (1888) keine albanische, sondern eine lateinisch-deutsche Terminologie (Substantiv, Adjectivum etc.). Bei den heutigen albanischen Bezeichnungen der Wortkategorien dürfte es sich um Lehnübersetzungen handeln (z.B. *mbi* ‚auf/über' + *emri* ‚Name' > *mbiemri* ‚Adjektiv'; *ndaj* ‚bei/gegen' + *folja* ‚Verb' > *ndajfolja* ‚Adverb'). Die Grammatik der Albanischen Akademie der Wissenschaften gruppiert die Wortklassen in die zwei großen Gruppen *fjalë të mëvetësishme* (selbstständige Wörter: *emri*, *folja*, *mbiemri*, *numërori*, *përemri*, *ndajfolja*, *pasthirrma*) und die *fjalë të pavetësishme* (unselbstständige Wörter: *parafjala*, *lidhëza*, *pjesëza*). Die Kategorie Partikel ist in der heutigen Grammatikographie eher unüblich. Darunter versteht die Grammatik der Akademie Adverbien, die heute aus pragmatischer Sicht unter der Bezeichnung ‚Modalpartikeln‘ untersucht werden. Das Albanische kennt einen postponierten bestimmten Artikel, der zwar von LEOTTI (1915) als eigene Kategorie vorgesehen ist, der aber von der Grammatik der Akademie nicht eigens als Wortklasse aufgestellt wird (S. 37), vermutlich weil die Agglutinierung so stark ist, dass der Artikel eher als Teil des Nomens betrachtet wird. Auch SOLANO beschreibt in seinem *Manuale di lingua albanese* (1972: 15) den albanischen Artikel als „determinazione del nome" mit „suffissi", die an die „desinenze flessive" angehängt werden. Andere Grammatiken (z.B. das *Lehrbuch der vereinheitlichten albanischen Schriftsprache* von HETZER/FINGER 2006: 35–36) unterscheiden außerdem einen sogenannten Gelenkartikel, der Attribute auf ein vorangehendes Wort bezieht (z.B. *gruaja e mirë* ‚Frau-die die schöne‘). Hingegen enthält bereits von HAHNs Werk (1854) einen einschlägigen Paragraphen mit dem Titel „Von dem besitzanzeigenden Artikel".

Griechisch
Die älteste neugriechische Grammatik (SOPHIANOS) unterscheidet neun Wortklassen. Die Adjektive werden als solche im Gegensatz zu den Zahlwörtern nicht explizit behandelt. Unter den Konjunktionen werden koordinierende und subordinierende aufgezählt. Portius, der nur noch acht Klassen vorsieht, definiert die Adjektive zwar als eigene Klasse („Adiectiva sunt quae propriis ac substantivis nominibus praefiguntur"), behandelt sie aber in einer Appendix zum Kapitel über das Nomen (Kap. IV). Die Zahlwörter scheinen bei ihm nicht mehr als eigene Kategorie auf. Auch MAVROKORDATOS spricht von acht Redeteilen, wobei er bei dem Problem der nominalen und pronominalen Übereinstimmung die Unterscheidung in οὐσιαστικόν (Substantiv) und ἐπίθετον (Adjektiv) vornimmt. Bei dieser Gelegenheit erwähnt er auch die Kategorie des Pronomens; die Kategorie der Zahlwörter findet bei ihm ebenfalls keine eigene Erwähnung. Vergleichen wir die älteste neugriechische Grammatik mit der heutigen normierenden Form (z.B. TRIANTAFYLLIDIS) können wir insofern eine Modernisierung feststellen, dass nicht nur die Zahlwörter, sondern auch das Partizip nicht mehr als eigene Kategorien vorhanden sind, dagegen die Kategorien der Adjektive und Interjektionen hinzukommen. Auffällig ist auch, dass sich inzwischen die neuere Bezeichnung des Substantivs als ουσιαστικόν durchgesetzt hat, anstelle des älteren ὄνομα, was an einem Einfluss (*substantia* > *substantivum*; cf. *ουσία* > *ουσιαστικόν*) der latinisierenden Terminologie liegen kann. Die Bezeichnung επιφώνημα für Interjektion könnte eine moderne Terminologisierung des altgriechischen Wortes ἐπιφώνημα für Zuruf/ Ausruf sein. Triantafyllidis (§ 321) teilt außerdem die Wortklassen in κλιτά (beugbare) und άκλιτα (unbeugbare) μέρη του λόγου (Wortklassen) ein. Bereits seit dem 17. Jahrhundert wird in der griechischen Grammatikographie der Artikel vor dem Substantiv behandelt.

Rumänisch

Eine Grammatikographie des Rumänischen entsteht erst im Laufe des 18. Jahrhunderts. Sowohl für die Terminologie als auch für die Beschreibungen lehnen sich die ersten Grammatiker an bestehende Grammatiken des Griechischen, des Kirchenslawischen und des Lateins an. Für die Terminologie arbeiten sie mit Lehnübersetzungen und Wortentlehnungen. Die Grammatik von Dimitrie EUSTATIEVICI (1757), der an der Theologischen Akademie in Kiew studiert hatte, enthält den Versuch, rumänische Übersetzungen für die Bezeichnungen der Wortklassen zu finden, wobei slawische (*în loc de numele* aus *мѣстоименїе?*), lateinische/ griechische (*înainte-punerea* aus *praepositio / πρόθεσις*) oder lateinische / slawische (*în mijloc-aruncarea* aus vom Autor zitierten *interjectio / междометїе*) Bezeichnungen als Vorbilder gedient haben mögen. Es fällt auf, dass das Adjektiv keine eigene Kategorie erhält, allerdings werden die Nomina in *înfiinţitori* (= Substantive) und *adăogători* (= Adjektive) unterteilt. Bezüglich des Artikels stellt er fest, dass es den *ἄρθρο / încheietură* im Griechischen und Deutschen gäbe, er aber nicht so viel Kraft (*putere*) habe wie in diesen Sprachen, weshalb er ihn im Kapitel Pronomina behandelt. Ianache VĂCĂRESCU dagegen verwendet schon, vermutlich unter italienischem Einfluss, die moderne latinisierende Terminologie, auch wenn er sie zusätzlich etymologisch erklärt. Als eigene Kategorie erscheint das Adjektiv unter den Wortarten in der einflussreichen *Граматикъ ромѫнеаскъ* von D. I. ELIAD' von 1828 (Nachdruck als RĂDULESCU 1980): „Aşa dar vedem' că ca să facem' o vorbire sau un' cuvînt intreg' avem' de trebuinţă zece feluri de ziceri, care se-zic' părţi ale cuvîntului, şi care sînt: Substantivul', Pronumele, Adjectivul', Articolul', Verbul', Partiţipi'a, Prepoziţi'a, Adverbul', Conjugativul' şi Interjecţi'a" (S. 6). Die Anzahl der unterschiedenen Wortklassen schwankt bis heute, die Gründe dafür hatte schon Theoktist BLAŻEWICZ in seinem Lehrbuch *Theoretisch-praktische Grammatik der dacoromanischen Sprache* (Lemberg/Czernowitz, Winiarz, 1844) erkannt: „Es gibt 8 Theile der Rede (пърцї а кувѫнтѫлѫї) und zwar:

1. Das Geschlechtswort oder Artikel (Артіколѫл).
2. Das Nennwort (Нѫмеле).
3. Das Fürwort (пронѫмеле).
4. Das Zeitwort (вербѫл).
5. Das Nebenwort (адвéрбѫл).
6. Das Vorwort (препозíціа).
7. Das Bindewort (кон'ѫнкціа).
8. Das Empfindungswort (інтерéкціа).

Andere Sprachlehrer haben bald zehn bald neun Redetheile angenommen, und zwar: das Nennwort in Haupt-, Bei- und Zahlwörter eintheilend, oder aber die Nennwörter belassend, nehmen das Mittelwort (партіцíпіѫл) der Zeitwörter als abgesonderten Theil der Rede" (S. 12–13).

Besondere Kategorisierungsprobleme gibt der bestimmte Artikel auf, für den es präpositive und postpositive Formen gibt. Die affixale postpositive Form führt immer wieder dazu, dass der bestimmte Artikel unter anderen Kategorien beschrieben wird. In der *Gramatică română* von Gavrile MUNTEANU (1860, § 34) wird er bei den Substantiven behandelt. In der Akademie-Grammatik von 2005 ist die Einordnung des bestimmten Artikels als Wortklasse widersprüchlich. Unter dem allgemeinen Kapitel „Clase de cuvinte" wird ihm ein Unterartikel gewidmet (3.4.), wie übrigens auch dem Numerale (3.1.). In der darauffolgenden ausführlichen Beschreibung kommt das Numerale noch einmal als eigenes Kapitel vor, aber nicht mehr der bestimmte Artikel. Der unbestimmte Artikel wird unter den *pronumele de cuantificare* beschrieben. Der sogenannte Genitivartikel oder possessive Artikel *al/a/ai/ale* wird als solcher in der Grammatikographie erst spät wahrgenommen: Theodor GARTNER spricht in seiner *Darstellung der rumänischen Sprache* (1904: § 97) vom „voranstehende[n] oder alleinstehende[n] artikel", Karl TAGLIAVINI in der *Rumänische[n] Konversations-Grammatik* (1938: Lektion 7) vom „präpositiven Artikel", die Akademie-Grammatik von 1966 (§ 107) von „Articolul posesiv sau genitival".

Aromunisch

Die Grammatikographie des Aromunischen beginnt mit der *Romanische[n] oder Macedonowlachische[n] Sprachlehre* von Michael BOJADSCHI (1813), in der konsequent griechische und deutsche Terminologie verwendet wird. In den Werken der aromunischen Diaspora in Österreich-Ungarn zeigen sich früh latinisierende Tendenzen. Tache PAPAHAGI verwendet in den grammatischen Ausführungen in der Einleitung seines *Dicționar dialectului aromân general şi etimologic* ([2]1974) rumänische und französische Terminologie (z.B. *substantiv/ substantif, verbul/ le verbe, articol/ article*), LAZAROU (1986), der sein Werk auf Französisch schreibt, verwendet dementsprechend französische Terminologie (z.B. *l'article. noms* (*subtasntifs* [sic], *adjectifs*), *adverbes*, etc.), während die wenigen, kurz darauf im griechisch geprägten Raum entstandenen Werke (KOLTSIDAS 1978; KATSANIS/DINAS 1990) griechische Terminologie verwenden (z.B. *Το άρθρο, Το ουσιαστικό, Το επίθετο, Οι αντωνυμίες*). In den aromunischen Kreisen außerhalb Griechenlands setzt sich eine auf lateinische bzw. rumänische Termini zurückgehende aromunische Terminologie durch (z.B. IANACHIEVSCHI-VLAHU 1993, [2]1997; CARAGIU/ SARAMANDU 2005).

Bulgarisch

Eine bedeutende slawische Grammatik der frühen Neuzeit verfasste der ruthenische Gelehrte Meletij SMOTRYC'KYJ 1619 unter dem Titel *Граммаτіки славенския правилноε Сνнтагма*. Sie erfuhr mehrere Neuauflagen und vermochte daher auch die modernen südslawischen Grammatikographien zu beeinflussen. Smotryc'-

kyj unterscheidet acht Wortklassen (*части слова*): *Имѧ, Мѣсто именїе, Глаголъ, Причастїе, Нарѣчїе, Предлогъ, Союѯъ, Междометїе*. Ferner weist er darauf hin, dass andere Sprachen, nicht aber die slawischen, auch einen *ἄρθρον* kennen würden. Außerdem verweist er auf die lateinische Bezeichnung *interiectio* für *Междометїе*.

In der Einleitung seiner *Волгарска граммати ка*, die im Vorwort als *Славенно-бо́лгарска та Грамма́тіка* bezeichnet wird, erwähnt Neofit RILSKI, dass er die Regeln „aus unterschiedlichen neuen und alten slawischen Grammatiken zusammengestellt" hätte („собрав от различни нови и вехти славянски грамматики"). Eine dieser älteren Grammatiken dürfte die von SMOTRYC'KYJ (1619) gewesen sein, da sie bezüglich ihrer Terminologie und der Anordnung der Behandlung auffällig übereinstimmen. Während Smotryc'kyj (S. 20) in seiner Beschreibung der Nomina von drei Klassen – *сꙋществителное, собирателное* und *прилагателное* – spricht, führt Rilski die *Прилагателни те имена* (Adjektive) als neue Kategorie ein. Wie Smotryc'kyj unterscheidet auch Rilski die Wortklassen in *склаnѧемы* (flektierbar) und *несклаnѧемы* (unflektierbar). Eine eigene Klasse der Artikel wird jedoch von Rilski nicht erwähnt. Die bulgarische Grammatik von GAWRIYSKY (1910: 19) führt den Artikel (*членъ*) unter den Wortarten auf, gibt aber den Hinweis, dass der bestimmte Artikel nur für die bestimmten Endungen „der Wörter verwertet wird und alleinstehend keine Bedeutung hat". GININA/NIKOLOWA/SAKASOWA (1965: 38) verwenden zwar keine eigene Bezeichnung für den Artikel, sprechen aber von *членуване на съществителните имена*: „Der bestimmte Artikel ist kein selbständiges Wort, sondern eine Partikel, die nach der Grundform des Substantivs steht und daran angehängt wird" (1965: 39). Die modernen Grammatiken des Bulgarischen behandeln das Zahlwort als eigene Kategorie. In der normierenden Grammatik von STOJANOV (1964) taucht außerdem eine eigene Klasse ‚Partikel' (*частица*) auf, wobei die Unterscheidung zwischen Interjektionen und Partikeln unklar bleibt.

Makedonisch

Einen frühen Versuch makedonischer Grammatikographie unternahm Ǵorǵija PULJEVSKI (1880) mit seiner in Sofia gedruckten *Славянско-насельениски-македонска слогница речовска*. Kurz nach der Einrichtung der Föderativen Volksrepublik Makedonien innerhalb der Föderativen Volksrepublik Jugoslawiens im Jahre 1944 erscheint in Skopje die *Македонска граматика* von Krume KEPESKI (1946). Die von ihm verwendete Terminologie lehnt sich offenbar eher an den serbischen als an den bulgarischen Sprachgebrauch an, vor allem bei derjenigen des Adjektivs und des Pronomens wird dies deutlich. Blaže KONESKI (1967) bleibt weitgehend bei dieser Terminologie und fügt zwei weitere Kategorien für die Partikeln (*частици*) und Modalwörter (*модални зборови*) ein, auch Wolf OSCHLIES (2007) bleibt in seinem Lehrbuch dieser Terminologie verhaftet, beschreibt den

Artikel aber in einem eigenen Kapitel. Der Artikel wird bei Kepeski unter der Deklination der Nomina behandelt, bei Koneski hingegen in einem Kapitel zur Bestimmtheit und Unbestimmtheit von Nomina. Für die sonst eher seltene Klasse der Partikeln gibt OSCHLIES (2007: 162) folgende Beschreibung: „Partikel geben einem Wort oder einem Satz einen besonderen Ausdruck – hinweisend, betonend, negierend, fragend usw. Rein äußerlich sind Partikel oft mit Präpositionen oder Konjunktionen identisch, doch ist ihre Bedeutung eine andere".

Serbisch

Grammatikographische Werke des Kroatischen und Serbischen entstehen seit dem 17. Jahrhundert, vor allem aber im Laufe des 18. Jahrhunderts. Die erste vollständige Grammatik scheinen die *Institutionum linguae illyricae libri duo* von Bartol KAŠIĆ (Roma 1604) zu sein. Die frühen Werke sind zumeist auf Italienisch verfasst worden (darunter Ardelio DELLA BELLA: *Instruzioni grammaticali della lingua illirica*, 1728; Josip VOLTIGGI: *Grammatica illirica*, 1803; Francesco M. APPENDINI: *Grammatica della lingua illirica*, 1808). Seit Anfang des 19. Jahrhunderts mehren sich Werke, die explizit die serbische Grammatik darstellen. Vuk S. KARADŽIĆ scheint sich in seiner *Писменица* (1814) an Meletij SMOTRYC'KYJ (1619) anzulehnen, denn beide Autoren verwenden auffälligerweise die gleiche Terminologie. Ein Terminologiewechsel scheint sich um die Jahrhundertmitte durchzusetzen, wie man bei den Adjektiven und Pronomina in der *Мала српска граматика* von Ђуро DANIČIĆ (1850) erkennen kann, in der dem Leser neben den bis dahin üblichen Bezeichnungen eine neue (serbischere?) Terminologie sowie die entsprechenden lateinischen Übersetzungen nebeneinander geboten werden. Im Laufe des 20. Jahrhunderts setzt sich, darauf aufbauend, ein neues terminologisches Modell durch, das von Karadžićs Vokabular abweicht und bis heute Gültigkeit besitzt.

Türkisch

Erste Versuche einer osmanisch-türkischen Grammatikographie entstehen im Laufe des frühen 18. Jahrhunderts (HOLDERMANN, *Grammaire turque ou méthode courte et facile pour apprendre la langue turque*, Constantinople 1730). Mit Ende des 19. Jahrhunderts liegen bereits zahlreiche Grammatiken des Osmanisch-Türkischen vor, die auf Italienisch, Englisch, Deutsch, Griechisch, vor allem aber auf Französisch verfasst wurden (s. DENY 1921: xxix–xxx). Die grammatikalische Terminologie des Türkischen scheint aber bis heute noch im Fluss und durch Neologismen weiterhin gewissen Veränderungen unterworfen zu sein. Dies zeigt sich in Wörtern wie ‚Grammatik‘, wofür im Türkischen heute allgemein neben *gramer* der Terminus *dilbilgisi* verwendet wird (Nominalkompositum ohne Possessivsuffix mit *dil* als Attribut, im Gegensatz zu *dilbilim* = ‚Sprachwissenschaft‘, aus *dil* ‚Sprache‘ + *bil-* ‚wissen‘; hinzu kommen die deverbalen Nominalsuffixe -*gI* bzw. -*Im*).

Im Türkischen können die Wortklassen weniger eindeutig voneinander getrennt werden als in den indogermanischen Sprachen. PIQUERÉ (1870: 30) hat zum Beispiel darauf hingewiesen, dass das sogenannte Eigenschaftswort verschiedene Wortklassenfunktionen übernehmen kann:

„Als Eigenschaftswort dient es [das Beiwort] zur näheren Bezeichnung der Hauptwörter, der Zeitwörter und anderer Eigenschaftswörter. Auf diese Weise vertritt es in diesen zwei letzten Fällen das Nebenwort der Art und Weise. Z.B. [...] *eji adam*, der gute Mensch; [...] *eji japmak*, gut handeln; [...] *tschok kitab*, viele Bücher; [...] *tschok fena* sehr schlecht. Das Eigenschaftswort wird bisweilen als Hauptwort gebraucht, und ist in diesem Falle denselben Regeln unterworfen".

Auch DENY (1921: § 193) bestätigt dies: «En turc, les différentes catégories grammaticales n'ont pas été différenciées aussi strictement qu'en français [...]. La ligne de démarcation qui sépare les différentes parties du discours n'est pas toujours très nettement tracée.» Dies dürfte mit der größeren Bedeutung der Affigierungen im Türkischen zusammenhängen. Es sind eher die Affixe, insbesondere die Suffixe, als die Bedeutung des Wortstammes, die die Wortklasse festsetzen. Deshalb sehen die Grammatiken ein eigenes Kapitel zu den Postpositionen vor. Die Suffixe können aus der Perspektive der anderen berücksichtigten Sprachen als eher denominal oder als eher deverbal betrachtet werden.

Allgemeine Beobachtungen

Ein Vergleich der Entwicklungen der Wortklassenterminologien in den Balkansprachen lässt eine Reihe von Problemen erkennen:

- Die Einteilungen in Wortklassen sind weder im Laufe der Geschichte der Grammatikographie noch innerhalb der Sprachen selbstverständlich oder einheitlich.
- Auch die Reihenfolge, in der die Wortklassen aufgeführt werden, schwankt (z.B. bei der Einordnung des Adverbs).
- Die Adjektive werden nicht von Anfang an als eigene Kategorie geführt.
- Die Numeralia bilden bei manchen Autoren eine eigene Kategorie, bei anderen werden sie innerhalb anderer Kategorien oder gar nicht behandelt.
- Besondere Probleme wirft die Kategorisierung des bestimmten Artikels auf.
- Gegenüber der griechischen und lateinischen Tradition fällt auf, dass die μετοχή / das *participium* als eigene Kategorie im Laufe der Zeit aufgegeben und in die Kategorie der Verben aufgenommen wird.
- Bei den südslawischen Sprachen ist die Einführung einer Kategorie ‚Partikel‘ verbreitet.

- Während in den griechischen, romanischen und albanischen Terminologien die Bezeichnungen für Adverb und Verb formal in einem Ableitungsverhältnis stehen, liegen in den südslawischen Sprachen für Adverb und Verb verschiedene Lexeme zugrunde.
- Die Definition von Wortarten im Türkischen bereitet aus der Perspektive einer indoeuropäisch geprägten Grammatikterminologie Schwierigkeiten.

Die trotz aller Unterschiede vergleichbaren Terminologien müssten in Zukunft daraufhin untersucht werden, wieweit die einzelnen Termini in den Sprachen deckungsgleich verwendet werden können und welche Rolle dabei eine globalisierende Terminologienormierung spielt.

Bibliographie

Academia Română (1966): *Gramatica limbii române*. Bucureşti (Ausgabe 2005, Band 'Cuvântul').

BEAUZEE, Nicolas (1767): *Grammaire générale ou exposition raisonnée des éléments nécessaires du langage, pour servir de fondement à l'étude de toutes les langues*. Paris.

BLAŻEWICZ, Theoktist (1844): *Theoretisch-practische Grammatik der dacoromanischen, das ist der moldauischen oder walachischen Sprache*. Lemberg / Czernowitz: Winiarz.

BOJADSCHI, Michael (1813): *Romanische, oder Macedonowlachische Sprachlehre*. Wien.

CARAGIU MARIOŢEANU, Matilda; SARAMANDU, Nicolae 2005: *Manual de aromână. Carti trâ înviţari armâneaşti*. Bucureşti: Editura Academiei Române.

DANIČIĆ, Đuro (1850): *Мала српска граматика*. У Виенни.

DANIČIĆ, Đuro (1983): *Мала српска граматика*. Nachdruck München: Sagner.

DENY, Jean (1921): *Grammaire de la langue turque (dialecte Osmanli)*. Paris: Ernest Leroux.

EDISKUN, Haydar (1985): *Türk Dilbilgisi*. İstanbul: Remzi Kitabevi.

ELIAD', D. I. [Елиад', Д. I.] (1828): *Грамматикъ ромънеаскъ*. Sibiu.

EUSTATIEVICI, Dimitrie (Braşoveanul) (1969): *Gramatica rumânească*. Bucureşti: Editura Ştiinţifică. Ausgabe des Manuskriptes von 1757 (izvodit în Bolgaria Braşovului).

FRASHËRI, Sami (1886): *Shkronjëtore e gjuhës shqipe*. Bucarest.

GARTNER, Theodor (1904): *Darstellung der rumänischen Sprache*. Halle: Niemeyer.

GAWRIYSKY, Demetrius W. (1910): *Bulgarische Konversations-Grammatik für den Schul- und Selbstunterricht*. Heidelberg: Julius Groos.

GININA, Stefana C.; NIKOLOWA, Cvetana N.; SAKĂZOVA, Ljuba A. (1965): *Bulgarisches Lehrbuch für Ausländer*. Sofia: Nauka i Izkustvo.

HAHN, Johann Georg von (1854): *Albanesische Studien: nebst einer Karte und anderen artistischen Beilagen*, Heft 2. Jena-Wien: Kaiserlich-königliche Hof- und Staatsdruckerei.

HELIADE-RĂDULESCU, Ion (1980): *Gramatică românească*. Bucureşti: Editura Eminescu.

HETZER, Armin; FINGER, Zuzana ([6]2006): *Lehrbuch der vereinheitlichten albanischen Schriftsprache*. Hamburg: Buske.

HOLDERMANN, Jean Baptiste D. (1730): *Grammaire turque ou méthode courte et facile pour apprendre la langue turque*. Constantinople.

IANACHIEVSCHI-VLAHU, Iancu (1993, [2]1997): *Gramatica simplă shi practică*. Crushuva.

Instituti i gjuhësisë dhe i letërsisë (2002): *Gramatika e gjuhës shqipe*.Tiranë.

KAHL, Thede; LINDENBAUER, Petrea; METZELTIN, Michael (2010): Vorschläge zu einer neuen typologischen Erfassung der Balkansprachen. In: Комисия по балканско езико-знание, Международен комитет на славистите (Hg.): *Глаголната система на бал-канските езици – наследство и неология. The Verbal System of the Balkan Languages – Heritage and Neology*. Велико Търново.

KARADŽIĆ, Vuk Stefanović (1814): *Писменица сербскога iезика*. У Виенни (Wien).

KAŠIĆ, Bartol (1604): *Institutionum linguae illyricae libri duo*. Roma.

KATSANIS, Nikolaos [Κατσάνης, Νικόλαος]; DINAS, Kostas [Ντίνας, Κώστας] (1990): *Γραμματική της Κοινής Κουτσοβλαχικής*. Θεσσαλονίκη.

KEPESKI, Krume [Кепески, Круме] (1946): *Македонска граматика*. Скопје.

KOLTSIDAS, Antónis M. [Κολτσίδας, Αντώνης] (1978): *Γραμματική και λεξικό της κουτσο-βλαχικής γλώσσας*. Θεσσαλονίκη.

KONESKI, Blaže [Консеки, Блаже] (1967): *Граматика на македонскиот литературен jазик*. Скопје: Култура.

LAZAROU, Achille G. (1986): *L'aroumain et ses rapports avec le grec*. Thessaloniki.

LECCE, Francesco Maria de (1716): *Osservazioni Grammaticali nella Lingua Albanese*. Roma.

LEOTTI, Angelo (1915): *Grammatica elementare della lingua albanese*. Heidelberg: Groos.

MAVROKORDATOS, Alexandros [Μαυροκορδάτος, Αλέξανδρος] (1745): *Γραμματική περί συντάξεως*. Ενετία.

MEYER, Gustav (1888): *Kurzgefasste albanesische Grammatik mit Lesestücken und Glossar*. Leipzig: Breitkopf, Gustav & Härtel.

MUNTEANU, Gavrile (1860): *Gramatică română*. Braşovŭ: Römer şi Kamner.

MUŽA, Emil M. (1908): *Praktische Grammatik der serbisch-kroatischen Sprache: Theore-tisch-praktische Anleitung für den Selbstunterricht*. 4. Aufl. Wien-Leipzig: Hartleben, VIII (Die Kunst der Polyglottie 12) (Bibliothek der Sprachenkunde).

OSCHLIES, Wolf (2007): *Lehrbuch der makedonischen Sprache: in 50 Lektionen* (= Sla-vistische Beiträge 454). München: Sagner.

PAPAHAGI, Tache (1974): *Dicţionar etimologic dialectului aromân. General şi etimologic*. Bucureşti.

PIQUERÉ, P. J. (1870): *Grammatik der türkisch-osmanischen Umgangssprache. Nebst ei-nem Anhange von einer Auswahl verschiedener Gespräche, Sprichwörter und einer Wörtersammlung in alphabetischer Ordnung. Mit genauer Bezeichnung der Aussprache*. Wien: Wenedikt.

PISKO, Julius (1896): *Kurzgefasstes Handbuch der nordalbanesischen Sprache*. Wien: Alfred Hödler.

PORZIO, Simone [Portius, Simon] (1638): *Gramatica linguae graecae vulgaris. Gramma-tikē tēs Rhōmaïkēs glōssēs. grammatica lingvæ græcæ vvlgaris*. Parisiis.

Prisciani Grammatici Caesariensis Institutionum Grammaticarum Libri XVIII, Lipsiae. In: Aedibus B. G. Teubneri, 1855.

PULJEVSKI, Ǵorǵija [Пуљевски, Ѓорѓија] (1880): *Славянско-населбениски-македонска слогница речовска*. Sofia.

RĂDULESCU, Ioan Heliade (1980): *Gramatică românească*. Bucureşti: Eminescu.

RILSKI, Neofit (1835): *Волгарска граммаmика*. Kragujevac.

SMOTRYC'KYJ, Meletij (1619): *Граммаmики славенския правилное Синтаґма*. Jevje (Vievis), zu finden unter http://litopys.org.ua/smotrgram/sm.htm (letzter Zugriff: 19.10.2011)

SOLANO, Francesco (1972): *Manuale di lingua Albanese*, hrsg. von Corigliano. Calabro: Arti Grafiche Joniche.

SOPHIANOS, Nicolas: *Γραμματικὴ Εἰσαγωγή* (Ausgabe von Émile Legrand unter dem Titel *Grammaire du grec vulgaire*. Paris: Maisonneuve, 1874).

STEVANOVIĆ, Mihailo [Стевановић Михаило] (1991): *Савремени српскохрватски језик (Граматички системи и књижевнојезичка норма*, I.). Београд: Naučna knjiga.

STOJANOV, Stojan [Стоянов, Стоян] (1964): *Граматика на българския книжовен език. Фонетика и морфология*. София: Държавно издателство Наука и искуство.

TAGLIAVINI, Karl (1938): *Rumänische Konversations-Grammatik*. Heidelberg: Groos.

TIMURTAŞ, Faruk (1979): *Osmanlı Türkçesi Grameri*. İstanbul: Umur Reklâmcılık.

TRIANTAFYLLIDIS, Manolis A. [Τριανταφυλλίδης, Μανόλης Α.] (1965): *Μικρή νεοελληνική γραμματική*. Θεσσαλονίκη: Ινστιτούτο Νεοελληνικών Σπουδών.

VACARESCU, Ianache (1787): *Observaţii sau băgări dă seamă asupra regulelor şi orindelilor gramaticii rumâneşti*. Rîmnic.

WAHRMUND, Adolf ([2]1884): *Praktisches Handbuch der osmanisch-türkischen Sprache*. Gießen: Ricker.

XYLANDER, Josef von (1835): *Die Sprache der Albanesen oder Schkipetaren*. Frankfurt a.M.: Andreä.

The Phonetics of the Balkans

Irena SAWICKA (Warsaw)

The geographical range of the Balkan phonetics does not overlap with the range of the morphosyntactic Balkanic Sprachbund. This, of course, is expected, given the general opinion that a holistic typology is not possible. Nevertheless, when in the mid-20th century balkanological studies started to develop intensively, the linguists tried to elaborate hypotheses about the phonetic Balkan type, for example, MINISSI (1982), СИМЕОНОВ (1977) and, especially, IVIĆ (1968), who considered the eastern Balkanic area, i.e. the Bulgarian-Rumanian area, as the center of the Balkanic phonetic Sprachbund. The reason was certainly the fact that the Bulgarian and Rumanian phonetics differ in some features from European phonetics; consequently, these two seem specific against the European background. However, if we look at the Balkan Sprachbund in this way, we shall see that it is quite the opposite. Balkanization in grammar means, in fact, europeization and the Southern Slavic languages differ from the Northern Slavic exactly in this very fact. When Slavs settled in the Balkans, their language gradually lost certain grammatical elements in the multilinguistic environment, preserving some other elements which were lost in the northern part of the Slavic linguistic world. The key was the approximation of the Southern Slavic grammar to the general European characteristics. This means that the properly formulated question is: *why have the Northern Slavic languages developed their own grammatical type*, and not *why has the Balkan grammar emerged*? The question of why is, naturally, very different from the question of how – and this is what the balkanologists usually deal with: *how the balkanisms emerged and how they function.*

The early history of Slavs seems to be very important in finding answers to some of these questions. Unfortunately, we do not know much about it, especially about the northern branch. However, there exist certain hypotheses which, contrary to the earlier classical ideas, are based on reliable data and constitute the starting points for further investigation of the problem. Today we already know that the Slavs came to northern Europe probably at the same time as to the South and that they were in a kind of war union with Altaic tribes (Huns or Avars are usually mentioned in the literature). Slavs served them in their incursions. This union was probably something more than just a pillage alliance, because the vocalic harmony has left a structural trace in the form of the Slavic syllabic synharmonism (see GALTON 1989, 1997, GODŁOWSKI 1999, PRITSAK 1864). Today, there even exist Altaic etymologies of the names of the most important Slavic tribes, including the very ethnonym "Slav" (see PARZYMIES 2006). This means that the development of the Slavic languages, at least in the last thousand years, on the grammatical level as well as in phonetics, proceeds from the eastern type to the western one.

The above suggests a very important role of the Slavic languages in balkanological studies. If there were no Slavic element in the Balkans, scholars would probably not notice that there is a Balkan grammar because it would be restricted mainly to Rumanian and Albanian, which are structurally linked to Latin. It is not accidental that the first to notice the Balkanic specificity was Jernej KOPITAR – a Slav and a Slovenian. As a Slovenian, he was able to discern grammatical differences because the Slovenian language is spoken in the Balkans (if we define the Balkans by non-linguistic criteria), but it is not a Balkanic language.

Thus, the Slavic linguistic material is very important in monitoring processes of balkanization, as we compare, first of all, the Balkan Slavic languages with the non-Balkan Slavic languages. The Rumanian language differs from other Romance language grammars to a lesser degree. Apart from this, the development of Slavic at the Balkans has rich documentation. Another language with quite good historical documentation is Greek, however, the Balkanic aspect is neglected in most Greek linguistic studies.

Within phonetics, as I mentioned above, the general geographical-typological divisions do not overlap with grammatical isoglosses. This is because the phonetics changes faster: purely physical assimilation is easier than the assimilation of units with semantic functions. Phonetic processes are usually restricted to sounding, whereas functional assimilation at this level (i.e. phonological) is often not so. Consequently, the phonetics undergoes changes faster, which means that the convergence is faster, but the divergence is faster too, as phonetic features may not be as stable as functional features. As a consequence we have a broad periphery where dialects are classified differently with respect to grammar and to phonetics.

As already mentioned, with regard to phonetics, the eastern part of the Balkans differs considerably from the western part. Of course, between the two typologically contrasted areas there exists a broad transitional area and, in fact, we are not able to draw a definite borderline. The western area preserves certain prosodic features (long vowels, tonal word stress), whereas the eastern part preserves a rich repertoire of palatalization phenomena (in various degrees and on various levels – allophonic and/or phonemic). Generally, the pronunciation in the east is more fluent, which manifests itself in a number of assimilations and neutralizations, mainly in the context of palatalization and the so-called vocalic reductions. Generally, we can say that the eastern part is more archaic, whereas the western one is more innovative (polytony is also gradually disappearing here). I shall not go into details now – I have written about it on many occasions (see, for example, 1997, 2007).

If we agree that the balkanization means, in fact, europeization, then it automatically means that the western group of the Balkanic languages is more Balkanic than the eastern one. Moreover, in the western group one additional region can be distinguished – I term it the Central Balkanic area – where convergence processes are extremely deep and noticeable at first glance. Geographically, this is the place where Macedonian, Greek and Albanian language elements meet. These dialects have most of the phonetic characteristics of the Western Balkanic area and, apart from that, they have a certain specificity which – against the European background – is quite extraordinary. First of all, we find there a concentration of a number of features which are opposite to the eastern phonetic type, such as: the lack of the palatalization assimilative processes, the loss of phonemic palatalization (e.g. merger of palatal and alveolar affricates), the lack of the velar fricative, a specifically Balkanic type of sandhi, a high frequency of vocalic clusters, and others. In some parts of the region traces of an old, medieval Balkanism can be found (a kind of nasal schwa). Above all, there are a number of various phenomena connected with the functioning of the famous clusters *nd*, *ŋg*, *mb*.

For Bulgarian, Rumanian, Macedonian and Albanian a phase can be reconstructed when vocalic nasalization was linked to centralization. In fact, we can even postulate the occurrence of a common Balkanic vowel similar to the nasal schwa. The time of the emergence of this [ə̃] can be determined only for Slavic, because the merger of the back nasal vowel and the back jer appeared in Slavic (mainly Bulgarian) sources from the 11th century. Albanian scholars insist that all important phonetic shifts (including rhotacism which is related to the problem in question) took place before the 7th century. Even if we agree on such a temporal localization, it must be stressed that the rhotacism which brought about the end of the existence of nasal vowels never occurred in northern Albanian. Consequently, the nasal schwa could be preserved longer in this area; moreover, one can say that in a way it exists even today in the form of the stressed [ɑ̃] which corresponds to *ë* [ə] of standard Albanian. In Rumanian, a kind of nasal, higher, centralized vowel emerged from the cluster [an] or [amC]. In its later development nasalization was lost. Today in Rumanian there is a kind of lower schwa that emerged from the unstressed [a], and a higher schwa developed from the nasal [a] before a nasal sonant, regardless of whether it was stressed or not, cf. *bîne* from Latin *bene*, *cîmp* from *campum*, etc. Rumanian *î* corresponds to southern Albanian *ë* [ə] and northern Albanian *â* [ɑ̃], cf. Alb. *mëz/mânz*, Rum. *mînz,* etc. In Bulgarian, the Old Slavic back (hard) jer fused with the back nasal vowel, cf. сън from Old Sl. *sъnъ, ръка from Old Sl. *rōka. As can be seen, only the Slavic material gives us some orientation in time. In Macedonian the back nasal vowel fused with the secondary vowel which emerged in certain contexts after the loss of weak jers. The data from Macedonian shows us that the fusion occurred after the vocalization/loss of the original jers. In Macedonian, the merger did not comprise the reflex of the strong back jer, certainly because at the time of fusion this jer already sounded like a "full" vowel (cf. Standard Macedonian сон from Old Sl. *sъnъ). Only in the so-called „*u*-dialects" (at the very north of the Macedonian language area) nasal vowels did not fuse with secondary vowels, which means that these dialects did not have such a nasal centralized vowel in their history; here, the back nasal vowel yielded [u], whereas the secondary vocalism produced [a], cf. *рука* from Old Sl. **rōka*, *ветар* from **[vetr] < Old Sl. **větrъ*, *магла* from **[mgła] < Old Sl. **mъgla*, whereas in the remaining Macedonian dialects: *рака*, *ветар*, *магла*. At the preceding stage of the development this secondary non-etymological vowel must have been centralized and extra-short at the beginning, because it developed from a syllabic variety of sonants in certain positions (in the so-called "two-peak" syllables), cf. **mъgla* > [mgla] (the loss of the weak jer and the subsequent emergence of the "two-peak" syllable, with [m] becoming in time syllabic in order to suppress the "two-peak" syllable) > [məgla] (syllabic sonant gives the cluster SV) > *магла* in Standard Macedonian and a number of dialects (further development of this new schwa). It could be a coincidence that the Old Slavic nasal vowel gave the same reflex as the secondary schwa, however, this fact shows that it should be nasal before the "vocalization". Helpful data are related to another "classical" balkanism – the ND (N – nasal sonant, D – voiced stop) clusters.

As a result of vocalic reductions (dating back as far as to Latin) these clusters occur very often in Albanian and in the southern Italian dialects. They also appear word-initially in these languages, cf. Alb. *mbret* from Latin *imperator*, *ngushtë* from *angustus*, dialectal southern Italian *nducere < inducere*, *mbrellu < ombrello*, etc. PAPAHAGI (1963) provides similar Aromanian examples: *ndreptu < in directo*, *mpartu < impartire*, but DALAMETRA's and GOŁĄB's notations suggest syllabicity of nasal sonants in initial position, cf. *'ngîrcat*, *'ndreg* (DALAMETRA 1906), *ᵊmpartu*, *ᵊŋkl'idu* (GOŁĄB 1984). These forms suggest a development such as in Dako-Rumanian, and not as in Albanian (Rum. *întreg*, *împart*, etc.). Initial ND clusters occur under Albanian influence in a number of Macedonian villages in southern Albania (cf. [mbleko]). These clusters appear word-initially also in the colloquial, emotionally marked utterances in Greek, but here the reason is not the same. In Greek, these clusters have the same systemic value as voiced stops. They are in fact combinatory variations of the voiced stop phonemes. To an untrained ear of a native speaker, the difference between [b] and [mb], [d] and [nd], etc., is not perceptible at all. Clusters ND occur in the intervocalic positions, whereas in the word-initial position varieties without prenasalization occur. However, in emotional speech ND clusters appear in this position as well, cf. [mbes epitelus] instead of [bes epitelus]. In the colloquial and dialectal Greek these clusters are perceptively and functionally equivalent to the corresponding voiced stops. One would rather expect that voiced stops and voiced fricatives form combinatory variations, because in the early history of Greek intervocalic voiced stops underwent lenition and the restriction on the occurrence of voiced stops in this context is still valid. However, today in loans and foreign words, intervocalic voiced stops are not replaced by fricatives but by ND clusters, e.g. recently I heard [paŋganini] for *Paganini*. In the colloquial Greek there are no such clusters with voiceless stops (in the domestic lexicon they have undergone voicing). Consequently, loans with intervocalic voiced stops or NT clusters are usually pronounced with ND, cf. [menta]//colloquial [menda] (of course, in the speech of educated Greeks there should exist the opposition /nd/ vs. /nt/ vs. /d/). Such a situation influenced Aegean Macedonian dialects, although in northern Greek dialects the ND clusters were later simplified to single stops (here we have [meda] instead of [menta] or [menda]). Here again the Slavic material appeared to be useful, because the Macedonian data suggest that after the loss/vocalization of Slavic jers, northern Greek dialects still had the ND clusters non-simplified.[1] Today northern Greek has new ND and NT clusters. They emerged as a result of the loss of unstressed high vowels. In several Macedonian villages in Greece and in south-western Macedonia, the Old Slavic nasal vowels are preserved in the form of ND (or NT) clusters, but nasalization (that is N) is preserved only before stops, cf. *dambi, grandi* or *dəmbi, grəndi*, etc. The link with Greek is obvious. The Slavic condition of the merger in question was centralization. First of all the Bulgarian material proves this. Besides, the secondary centralized vowel receives the same nasal reflex in the same villages and only before voiced stops – in these villages *магла* sounds [maŋgła] or [mə̃ŋgła]. Here we do not find any etymological link between nasalization and centralization. Nasalization is automatically associated with centralization.

In some villages in Aegean Macedonia nasalization may appear in other contexts too. If the Old Slavic back jer preserved its original schwa-like phonetic character, as in Bulgarian, it can also have a nasal reflex today before stops. However, such examples are very rare in Aegean Macedonia. The scope of nasalization may be enlarged also by a typical north Greek phenomenon: an infixed stop, breaking clusters of a sibilant and a sonant or a cluster of two sonants, as in Greek [xamomilo] which produces in northern Greek [xamomlu] and then [xamomblu], Slavic dialectal [ӡdrebe] instead of [ӡrebe], etc. Under the influence of this phenomenon, clusters of a nasal sonant plus fricative which emerged in Southern Macedonian after the decomposition of nasal vowels in several villages of eastern Aegean Macedonia got such an infixed stop. As a result, nasal sonants appeared before stops and, consequently, nasalization has been preserved in this context, cf. Old Slavic **gǫsь* > [gõns] > [gõnts] > [gənts]. Sometimes, in Eastern Aegean Macedonian, the same sounds developed from the original jer, cf. **bъzъ* > [bəs] > [bə̃s] > [bəns] > [bənts] > [bənts]. The infixed [b] is common in Albanian dialects in the *mr* and *ml* clusters (cf. [zəmbra] instead of *zëmra*) – the same occurs in

---

1   Although in the north-eastern dialects the shift ND > N started centuries earlier (see the evidence from Panfilic dialect).

Macedonian dialects in southern Albania, cf. [mbleko], [umbrjał], (for details see
САВИЦКАЯ 2000, 2002).

The facts described briefly above caused that the frequency of the ND clusters
in the Central Balkanic area and in the Southern Italian dialects is extremely high.
Moreover, we find here a number of options where a form may be pronounced with
D or ND or even N – this is connected with the mentioned Greek functional equivalence of these clusters with voiced stops and also with the systemic shifts of ND
into N or NN (Northern Albanian, Southern Italian) or into D (Northern Greek and
very Southern Albanian) – such forms are associated by speakers with the
unsimplified forms from the other variety of the same language. Additionally, the
sonorization of T after N is very frequent (Greek, Southern Italian, Northern Albanian).

To sum up, if we look at the Balkan phonetic type from the European perspective,
we shall see that its Eastern part has features similar to the Northern Slavic, that the
Eastern part preserves to a greater degree Old Slavic phonetic characteristics. This
means that it constitutes rather a southern extension of Euro-Asiatic phonotactic
Sprachbund. Such a Sprachbund has been described by Roman JAKOBSON (1962)
as dialects with a rich correlation of palatalization and lacking polytony. West of
the Bulgaro-Rumanian area, especially of eastern Bulgaria, the phonetic type
gradually changes and finally achieves contrastive character, whereas, additionally,
a part of the western area is distinguished by some specific features which radiate
from the center in various directions (not to the East, however).

In the southern part of the Balkanic Peninsula one more phonotactic type may
be distinguished. This area may be characterized by the open (or relatively open)
syllable pattern and the restriction on the occurrence of intervocalic voiced stops.
These features, depending on a language, appear in various degrees (obliga-
tory/facultative, more or less regular) and at various levels (standard/colloquial/
dialectal). They are present in the Southern Greek dialects and in Standard Greek.
The Greek language shares these features with other "Mediterranean" dialects,
mainly Romance (for details see PERLIN, SAWICKA 1991).

It is interesting that the Greek language participates in all the three areas distinguished. In Northern Greek, vocalic reductions and palatalizations appear, as in the
East. Southern Greek has the typical characteristics of the Mediterranean dialects
and, additionally, the most important feature of the Central Balkanic area regarding
the *nd*, *ŋg*, *mb* clusters. As the Slavic material shows these clusters still existed in
the North when the Greek and Slavic dialects came to contact.

All three areas are quite compact, but it must be stressed that the extensions of
particular features do not fully overlap. Consequently, we cannot draw definite
borderlines between the areas. As the material of the Aegean Macedonian shows,
given that phonetic features may not be stable, the most interesting are small rural

multidialectal microregions where the convergence may be deeper and where certain older features may be preserved.

References

DALAMETRA, Ioannis (1906): *Dicţionar Macedo-Român*. Bucureşti.

GALTON, Herbert (1989): Phonological causation through the system? The case of Slavic and Altaic. *Folia Linguistica Historica* X. 281–287.

GALTON, Herbert (1997): Neither universals, nor preferences – the genesis of Slavic. *Folia Linguistica Historica* XVII. 171–177.

GODŁOWSKI, Kazimierz (1999): Spór o Słowian. In: *Narodziny średniowiecznej Europy*. Warszawa. 52–83.

GOŁĄB, Zbigniew (1984): *The Arumanian dialect of Kruševo in SR Macedonia SFR Yugoslavia*. Skopje.

IVIC, Pavle (1968): Liens phonologiques entre les langues balkaniques. In: *Actes du premier congrès international des études balkaniques et sud-est européennes*. Sofia. 133–143.

MINISSI, Nullo; KITANOSKI, Naum; CINQUE, Umberto (1982): *The phonetics of Macedonian*. Napoli.

PAPAHAGI, Pericle (1963): *Dicţionarul dialectului Aromîn general şi etimologic*. Bucureşti.

PARZYMIES, Anna (2006): Ethnonymes slaves. Proposition d'étymologies altaïques. In: *Studies in oriental art and culture in honour of professor Tadeusz Majda*. Warszawa. 79–103.

PERLIN, Jacek; SAWICKA, Irena (1991): Is there a Mediterranean phonotactic community? In: *Studies in the phonetic typology of the Slavic languages*. Slawistyczny Ośrodek Wydawniczy, Warszawa. 51–63.

PRITSAK, Omeljan (1984): The Slavs and the Avars. In: *Gli Slavi occidental e meridionali nell'alto medioevo*. Centro Italiano di studi sull'alto medioevo. Spoleto. 353–432.

SAWICKA, Irena (1997): *The Balkan Sprachbund in the light of phonetic features*. Energeia, Warszawa.

SAWICKA, Irena (2007): *Arealinės fonetikos (fonètines geografijos) įvadas*. Bibliotheca Salensis, Vilnius.

САВИЦКАЯ, Ирина (2000): Об одном средневековном балканизме. In: *Материалы XXVIII Межвузовской научно-методической конференции преподавателей и аспирантов, вып. 21, Балканские исследования, част 3, март 1999*. Санкт Петербург. 25–28.

САВИЦКАЯ, Ирина (2002): Функционирование групп согласных типа НД в балканских языках. In: *Материалы конференции посвещенной 90-летию со дня рождения Агнии Васильевны Десницкой*. Санкт-Петербург. 195–198.

СИМЕОНОВ, Борис (1977): Общие черты фонологических систем балканских языков. *Балканско езикознание* 20. 53–99.

ЯКОБСОН, Роман (1962): К характеристике евроазийского языкового союза. In: *Selected writings* I. Mouton, 's-Gravenhage. 144–202.

On the Syntax of Possession in the Balkan Languages: the Elusive Nature of the External Possessive Construction

Iliana KRAPOVA (Venice)

0. Introduction

As observed by ASSENOVA (2001), Balkan languages feature four types of possessive expressions, exploiting the intricate connection between the grammatical category of definiteness and the semantic category of possession, in particular the notion of inalienable possession. In this paper, I will be concerned with what Assenova labels "Preverbal Dative + Definite article" (Strategy B. below), a construction which is also referred to as "external possession" (EP). It is often pointed out in the literature that EP has a special status in the typology of possessive constructions since the possessor argument (a true dative argument or a dative clitic, as is the case with some of the Balkan languages) forms a syntactic complex with the sentential predicate, as opposed to the more "logical" strategy A., where the possessive pronoun or clitic stands next to the noun expressing the possessum.

A. [Noun Phrase + D(efinite) A(rticle)] + possessive pronoun (tonic or clitic): all Balkan languages

a. possessive adjectives: *cartea mea, moja(ta) kniga* 'my book';
b. possessive pronouns: *prietenul lui* 'his friend', *libri i tij* 'his book'
c. personal clitic pronouns in Genitive/Dative Case: *cartea-mi, knigata mi* 'my book', *to skilí mu* 'my dog'.

(1a) [Chipu-i luminos] domina mulţimea (AVRAM/COENE 2000: 12)
(1b) [Svetloto í litse] izpăkvaše sred tălpata. 'Her bright face dominated the crowd'
(1c) Patisa kata laθos [to poδi tu]. 'I stepped on his foot by mistake' (MG, Kupula 2008: 145)

B. Preverbal Dative + [Noun Phrase + Definite Article] = Possessive Clitic Construction: all Balkan languages

(2a) I-am zărit chipul în mulţime. (Romanian, AVRAM 2000: 11)
(2b) Az í zabeljazax litseto sred tălpata. (Bulgarian) 'I spotted her face in the crowd'
(2c) Tu patisa kata laθos to poδi. (MG) 'I stepped on his foot by mistake'
(2d) I pashë fytyrën në pasgyrë. (Albanian, G. Turano, p.c.) 'I spotted her face in the mirror'

C. Noun Phrase + Definite Article (inalienable possession): all Balkan languages

(3) *a coborî ochii* ('to lower one's eyes'), *a mişca mâna* ('to move one's hand') *ngre dorën* 'I raise the hand'; *slagam pod glavata, vë poshtë kokës* 'I put (something) under the/[my] head'

D. Noun Phrase + $\emptyset_{article}$ (Bulgarian only)

(4) *zatvarjam oči* 'close (my) eyes'; *vdigam răka* 'raise (my) hand'

The Balkan EP has not been studied extensively from a typological perspective, although several studies have dealt with language-specific issues of its distribution, special semantics and syntactic properties (STATEVA 2002 for Bulgarian, SVEŠNI-KOVA 1986: 202, DINDELEGAN 1994: 129–131, AVRAM/COENE 2000: 2008 for Romanian). A major concern in the syntactic literature has been to account for the presence of the Dative clitic, which is apparently unselected by the predicate (and hence, extra-thematic), yet occupies the same position as that of the indirect object clitic in (non-possessive) clauses encoding the thematic roles of recipient, target or goal typically associated with the Dative. As illustrated by the Romanian examples in (5), the possessive and the indirect object clitic obey the same ordering constraints with respect to negation, auxiliaries, and the main verb. Moreover, both share the same morphosyntactic and phonological dependency, i.e., as enclitic or proclitic to the verb, according to language specific structural requirements:

(5a) Eu nu-i (nu îi) dădusem cheile. 'I did not give him/her the keys'
(5b) Eu nu-i (nu îi) găsisem pălăria. 'I did not found his/her hat'

Given that at least the Balkan languages to be considered here (Bulgarian, Romanian and Modern Greek) also dispose of noun phrase internal dative/genitive clitics (strategy A(c))[1], some syntacticians (notably STATEVA 2002, AVRAM/COENE 2000) have proposed to view EP as a derivative pattern. More precisely, the possessive clitic has its source within the noun phrase, to which it is semantically linked, but can sometimes "raise" to the clausal Dative position reserved otherwise for the indirect object clitic, as in (6):

XP CL$_{possessor}$ (Aux) V [noun phrase+Definite article CL$_{possessor}$]

---

1 I abstract away from issues of frequency and style. In Romanian, internal possession is very rarely used, "being felt as outdated, formal and poetic" (AVRAM/COENE 2000: 158), and has been almost entirely (with the exception of the singular paradigm, in particular 3rd person) replaced by the EP construction regardless of register and stylistic marking (*Gramatica Academiei* 1966, CORNILESCU 1995, PANCHEVA 2004: 187). Bulgarian grammars have hardly discussed external possession (cf. for a brief mention NITSOLOVA 1986; 2008: 165), although it is the norm in both educated and colloquial speech. A first look at Greek grammars uncovers few examples, cf. HOLTON et al. (1997: 194) who refer to these clitics as benefactive and malefactive genitives.

(6a) Az vidjax litseto í 'I saw her face'
(6b) Az í vidjax litseto í

Apparent evidence for such an approach comes from the ungrammaticality of examples like (7), where the external and the internal possessor position are simultaneously filled by the same clitic.[2]

(7) *Az í zărnax litseto í v tălpata.
     *I-am zărit chipu-i în mulțime. 'I her-DAT spotted her face in the crowd'

Although the "possessive raising" approach became quite popular in accounting for a subset of the EP constructions in typologically diverse languages (e.g. Hebrew, LANDAU 1999, Choktaw, DAVIES 1984, BAKER 1988), its predictive power has turned out to be limited. First, many languages instantiate the EP construction but appear to asymmetrically miss its structural correlate – the Internal Possession (IP) construction in (6a). Slavic, Romance, and Germanic have Dative possessive clitics or pronouns but they can appear only externally:

(8a) On poceloval **ej** ruku. 'He kissed her hand' (Russian, PODLESSKAYA, RA-KHILINA 1999: 512); Teklo **nam** do kuchyně. 'We had a leak in our kitchen' (Czech, FRIED 1999: 479); Slomila **mi** se čaša. 'The glass went and broke on me/My glass broke' (TOMIĆ 2009: 455)
(8b) On **lui** a coupé les cheveux. 'They cut his/her hair' (French, KAYNE 1977: 159); El gato **le** arañó la cara. 'The cat scratched his/her face' (Spanish, SÁNCHEZ LÓPEZ 2007: 153); Gli hanno rotto la macchina. 'They broke his car' (Italian).

Additionally, even if a certain language has possessive clitics in the nominal domain, it is hardly the case that the two constructions (EP and IP) are syntactically reversible or semantically synonymous so as to justify a free choice Dative placement for this language. The peculiar property of EP resides in the fact that the rela-

---

2 This possibility is available in the languages under study but under precise conditions. Doubly-filled constructions with an external clitic and an internal possessive modifier are considered pleonastic and much less acceptable or completely ungrammatical, as in Bulgarian *Az í vidjax nejnoto litse 'I saw her face'. According to AVRAM/COENE (2000) also in Romanian the construction *I-am zărit chipul său în mulțime 'I have seen his/her face in the crowd' is ungrammatical, but SVEŠNIKOVA (1986: 207) gives acceptable examples like ne regăsim, ne întîlnim în viața noastră 'we find each other, we encounter our life'. Nevertheless, she notes that such doubly-filled constructions are special, and require emphasis or focus on the possessor, so they are excluded with body parts or with some other inalienably possessed property of the human being like e.g. soul, potential, character, life where possession is taken for granted. For more examples and an analysis cf. CORNILESCU (1991: 64).

tion possessor-possessed seems only implied or in any case subordinate to the more salient "affectedness" interpretation which focuses on the effect or impact (positive or negative) that the circumstances described in the predicate have on the possessor. This pragmatic reading illustrated in (9a) from Bulgarian lacks parallels in the realm of adnominal possession (9b). This is also true of languages which lack internal possession, as in the examples in (8) above:

(9a)   Toj í skăsa pismoto. lit. 'He tore off to her the letter'
(9b)   Toj skăsa pismoto í 'He tore off her letter'

In this paper, I want to argue that the apparent complexity of the Balkan EP as it emerges from the three Balkan languages I will consider – Bulgarian, Romanian and Modern Greek (see section 2) – can be dealt with theoretically if what is thought to be a single EP construction is decomposed into two discrete instances, corresponding to a purely possessive (genitive) vs. "affected" (dative of interest) interpretation, the latter only inferentially associated with possession in ways that are familiar from other European languages, e.g. Slavic and Romance. In the last section, it will be suggested that this functional split within EP is a follow-up of the well-known dative-genitive syncretism which has conflated the two morphological forms but has nevertheless retained their distinct underlying case functions.

1. EP from a typological perspective

The "affectedness" condition, which HASPELMATH 1999 identifies as one of the two (alongside dative case marking) constraints on the realization of EP in a broader perspective, reduces to two more basic requirements: 1) that the predicate of the construction bear a benefactive or a malefactive meaning, and 2) that there be a strict semantic relationship between possessor and possessed. The combined effect of these two requirements explains the strong cross-linguistic tendency, especially among the European languages, for marking humans as possessors and inalienably possessed items as possesses, in particular body parts as they represent the prototypical member of what BALLY 1926/1996 has identified as the human "personal sphere" (cf. also WIERZBICKA 1988). The implicational nature of this tendency arises from a purely pragmatic consideration: affecting some inalienably possessed item implies affecting its possessor as well. According to BYBEE (1988), cited in an article by Kate BURRIDGE[3], this implicit sense of possession (inferred meaning) may become actual meaning by way of a semantic transfer and can thus be seen as the crucial factor for the grammaticalization of possessivity.

    Deviations from the prototypical schema may result in a different strength of the affectedness condition. Apart from variation in terms of inalienability, purely structural parameters may also affect the syntax of the construction, with reference

---

3   See www.latrobe.edu.au/linguistics/latrobepapersinlinguistics/.../03burridge.pdf.

to the type of predicates selected as affecting in each particular language. To capture cross-linguistic variation, and the relative accessibility of the various grammatical elements for EP encoding, several implicational hierarchies have been proposed:

(10a) The Animacy Hierarchy (KÖNIG/HASPELMATH 1997: 7.1)
       $1^{st}/2^{nd}$ p. pronoun $\subset$ 3rd p. pronoun $\subset$ proper name $\subset$ other animate $\subset$ inanimate
(10b) The Possessive Hierarchy (FRIED 1999: 477)
       Body part > kinship relations > close alienable entities > distant alienable entities
(10c) The Situation Hierarchy (KÖNIG/HASPELMATH 1997: 6)
       Patient-affecting $\subset$ dynamic non-affecting $\subset$ stative (KÖNIG/HASPELMATH 1997)
(10d) The Syntactic Relation Hierarchy (KÖNIG/HASPELMATH 1997: 2.6)
       PP $\subset$ direct object $\subset$ unaccusative subjects $\subset$ unergative subjects $\subset$ transitive subjects

Languages may choose to grammaticalize different cut-off points of these four universal hierarchies but the conclusion of HASPELMATH (1999) strongly suggests that EP constructions are favored cross-linguistically if they are relatively high on all of the hierarchies. In particular, European languages restrict EP to a) animate possessors (as well as the positions above "other animate" on the Animacy hierarchy, especially 1st person); b) affecting verbs denoting an event, i.e. dynamic (typically transitive) but not stative predicates (on the Situation Hierarchy); c) syntactic functions that can express the affected semantic roles of patient, theme or goal, i.e. prepositional phrases, direct objects, and (to a much less extent) unaccusative subjects (on the Syntactic Relations Hierarchy). As confirmed by a number of studies (FRIED 1999 for Czech, PODLESSKAYA/RAKHILINA 1999 for Russian, ŠARIĆ 2002 for Slavic, LAMIROY 2003, SÁNCHEZ LÓPEZ for Romance, GUERÓN 1985 for French), the common tendencies have led typologists to think that there is just one homogeneous construction, which HASPELMATH 1999 calls "the European prototype" given that "variation in Europe is not particularly great" (p. 113).[4]

---

4   The only more significant locus of variation seems to be the Inalienability Hierarchy but it is known since BALLY 1926/1996 that this very notion is flexible and membership in the personal sphere often depends on cultural, pragmatic and contextual factors that may be predominant in one language or another. Apart from body parts, also kinship terms, clothes, picture nouns and even familiar objects such as *home, car* etc. are also be available for EP construal (these are the extended inalienables of VERGNAUD and ZUBIZARRETA 1992, cf. also CHAPPELL and McGREGOR 1996: 8). Some European languages tend to be stricter than others. For example, French admits only body parts while the

2. The Balkan EP construction

In this section, I want to show that at first glance, Balkan EP strongly deviates from the European prototype in that as has already emerged from previous studies (CRISTEA 1974, ŠVEŠNIKOVA 1986, CORNILESCU 1991, MANOLIU-MANEA 1996, NICULESCU 2008 for Romanian, STATEVA 2002 for Bulgarian), there are practically no restrictions relevant to

a) the reference of the possessor (human or non-human);
b) the type of possessive relation (inalienable or alienable);
c) the type of syntactic function that the possessum can fulfill;
d) the type of verb that can enter the configuration (affecting or not).

The three Balkan languages under study will be shown to pattern alike with respect to the first three points, and to diverge with respect to d) in that only Modern Greek obeys the "affectedness" constraint regarding choice of predicate type, a feature which will be attributed to the fact that this language instantiates just one of the two constructions which I am going to posit for the other two languages.

Starting with animacy effects, the most significant property of Balkan EP is that the external possessive clitic need not refer to a human possessor; in fact, it can pick up any of the reference points on the Animacy hierarchy in (10a). In particular, as illustrated by the examples in (11), objects typically belonging to the human "personal sphere", but not exclusively so[5], can be viewed as inanimate possessors with respect to their constituent parts, basic functions or properties:[6]

---

rest of Romance seems to extend the construction also to kinship terms and to extended inalienables. See the following examples from French (i) vs. Italian (ii):

(i) a. Il me prend le bras. 'He grabs my arm' (LAMIROY 2003: 259)
        On **lui** a coupé les cheveux. 'They cut his/her hair' (KAYNE 1977: 159)
(ii) a. Mi ha preso la mano. 'He grabbed my hand'
        b. Gli hanno rotto la macchina. 'They broke his car'

Slavic languages too, judging from data presented in ŠARIĆ 2002, as well as in FRIED 1999 for Czech, occasionally extend EP to kinship terms, garments, familiar objects of possession.

5   This seems to be particularly true for Romanian where the reflexive dative construction can express the same possessive relations as the personal dative clitic, cf. e.g. (i):

(i) Soarele îşi trimitea razele. (Murd 159) 'The sun was pouring its rays'
        Cîntecul şi-a repetat vraja. 'The song repeated its charm' (SVEŠNIKOVA 1986: 202)

6   Often, as in (11) in the text, the inanimate possessor is represented by a full dative noun phrase (a prepositional phrase in Bulgarian) in addition to the dative clitic. The result is a clitic doubling structure whose function however is not to mark topicality, as in the standard case, but to resolve potential ambiguity (cf. (i)), given the lesser accessibility of inanimates for possessor encoding.

(11) Ioana **i**-a rupt (mesei) piciorul 'Ioana broke its leg (= the leg of the table). (NICULESCU 2008, 488); Njakoj í e otrjazal krakata (na masata). 'Someone has sawn off the legs of the table'; Na radioto sa mu svăršili bateriite; Radioului i s-au terminat bateriile; Tis teliosan i bataries tou radiofonou 'The batteries of the radio are consumed'.

Another remarkable feature of the possessive clitic construction is that the possessive relation encoded by the possessive dative structure need not be inalienable. (See the extensive lists presented in SVEŠNIKOVA 1986, and NICULESCU 2008 for Romanian.) Apart from the prototypical body parts, cf. (12), and kinship terms, (13), the following kinds of referents can appear as possessums in the EP construction:

a. extended inalienables such as clothes, cf. (14) and familiar objects from the possessor's environment, cf. (15);
b. permanent abstract properties or qualities, cf. (16);
c. temporary mental or psychological states (17a); functional relations (17b); objects in the near vicinity to the possessor (17c); close alienable entities (17d); actions and results (expressed by deverbal nouns) in relation to their Agents qua possessors (17e), distant alienable entities (17f), etc. (Romanian examples are from NICULESCU 2008, see also CRISTEA 1974, CORNILESCU 1991, MANOLIU-MANEA 1996).[7]

(12) Afti **tou** espasse to mikro dahtilo; Tja **mu** sčupi malkija prăst. 'She broke his little finger'
(13) Afti **tou** katestrepsan tin kori/ ti ghineka. 'They ruined his daughter/wife'
(14) Objlakox í rokljata. 'I put one her dress'
(15) Apa **i**-a distrus casa. 'The water destroyed his house'; **Tou** ehassa tin ombrella. 'I lost his umbrella'; **Sou** hrisimopiisa to stilo. 'I used your pen'; Razbixa **mi** kolata. 'They destroyed my car'; **Sou** sinkentrosa ta vivlia. 'I collected your books'
(16) Mrazja ti taja čerta na xaraktera. 'I hate this feature of your character'; Îi urăsc lipsa de respect. 'I hate her lack of respect'
(17a) Ne **mi** vgorčavaj radostta. 'Don't spoil my happiness'; Nu-**i** apreciez comportamentul. 'I don't appreciate her behavior'; Esi **mou** ekmetaleftikes tin kali diathesi. 'You spoiled my good mood'

(i) Ioana mu sčupi glavata 'Ioana broke his/its head'.

In the default case, the possessor gets interpreted as animate regardless of the grammatical function of the possessum

7 Here and elsewhere in the text the Modern Greek examples present native judgements of my informants. I thank in particular Eugenia Liosatou, and also Marika Lekkakou, for invaluable help with the data.

(17b) Ţi-am condus şeful la aeroport; Izpratix **ti** šefa na letišteto. 'I saw your boss off at the airport'

(17c) A-**şi** termina cafeaua/izpivam si kafeto 'finish one's coffee' (SVEŠNIKOVA 1986: 204)

(17d) Te sa **ni** zaeli mestata. 'They have occupied our places'

(17e) Ne **ti** priemam izvinenieto. 'I don't accept your excuse', Lupul nu-şi încetă prădăciunile 'The wolf did not stop the robbery' (SVEŠNIKOVA 1986); **Tou** diekopsa ti roi' tis skepsis. 'I interrupted the flow of his thought'

(17f) Dăždovete **ni** uništožixa rekoltata. 'The rains ruined our crops'.

It is obvious that the referents in (12)–(17) cover the entire range of elements on the possessive hierarchy in (10b), including its lowest cut-off point, distant alienable entities, as in (17f). This semantic expansion of the possessive construction reveals a consistent grammaticalization pattern reflected not only in the increased number of elements that can enter the construction but also in its greater contextual freedom. As shown by (18) from Bulgarian, even nominals that fall outside of the realm of possession (such as abstract temporal and spatial relations) can be coded as possessums:

(18)   Izgubix mu dirite/koordinatite/doverieto/vremeto/celija den.
       'I lost his traces/whereabouts/faith/time/the whole day'

It would seem therefore that the Balkan languages have gone one step further in the grammaticalizaton of possessivity, in that their EP signals not only the first and foremost relation of possession (ownership) or some pragmatic extension thereof, as in the other European languages, but practically all relations belonging to possession in a very broad sense.[8] However, the generalization of lexical meaning is just one of the ingredients of the process of grammaticalization. The other involves a reanalysis of the syntactic functions of the dative clitic in its relation to the type of predicate involved in the construction.

Judging from the above examples, it appears very plausible that the dative clitic be considered a particular case of dativus commodi/incommodi (dative of interest) expressing the beneficiary of an action, i.e., the person in whose favor or to whose detriment the action is being performed. As pointed out by a number of scholars, beneficiary datives share with the other usages of the dative a typically goal-oriented semantics. However, differently from the more prototypical dative functions (that of recipient with verbs of giving and of experiencer with experiencer predi-

---

8   As has been noted in the literature, it often appears difficult to arrive at some coherent notion of "possession". Within the cognitive framework, LANGACKER (1991) has pointed ted out that the only thing all possessives have in common is that one entity (the possessor) is invoked as a reference point for purposes of establishing mental contact with another (the possessum).

cates), the beneficiary dative is not required by the verb's valence, hence it is often viewed as an additional or extra-thematic argument which traditional grammars term 'free' dative (but see NICULESCU 2008 for an attempt to relate all usages of the dative under a single common denominator as 'entity on which the action has an indirect effect'). FRIED (1999) proposes that affectedness may evolve into ownership by way of a semantic shift which extends possessive construal into constructions where the dative is simply an additional argument that can be interpreted as affected by the circumstances described in the predicate. In (19a) for example, which constitutes an intermediate step of this process, a possessor-possessum relation can be established given that "work" is a possessible entity and the goal argument can be felicitously construed as the possessor of this entity. This possessive relation can then be further extended to contexts like (19b) where the verb is incompatible with a goal argument but the possessive relation is nevertheless available:

(19a) Preča ti (na rabotata) 'I disturb you on the work'
(19b) Vali mi na glavata/v kăštata. 'It rains on my head/in my house'

In other words, the grammaticalization of possessivity has arisen in clauses where a potentially possessible item is present which could be associated with a dative of interest reading. According to Fried, it is precisely this linking between affectedness and possession that gets conventionalized and starts off as an independent grammatical pattern. One can imagine that initially the process has affected only elements which are high on the possessive hierarchy (e.g. a body part) and on the animacy hierarchy (e.g. a human possessor; for converging data on the evolution of the possessive dative in Bulgarian, see MINČEVA 1964), and has eventually extended also to the lower cut-off points on the hierarchies, bringing the possessive construction further away from its originally dative functions but without making it lose completely the initial semantic link with possession.

An immediate proof for treating EP as a special case of dative of interest comes from the fact that, as mentioned above, in many contexts the possessive dative is still ambiguous between an affected and a possessive interpretation (see also TOMIĆ 2009 for Balkan Slavic):

(20a) Šte **ti** nareža dărvata. 'I will cut your wood/I will cut the wood for you'
(20b) Opravjam **ti** radioto; **Îți** repar radioul (NICULESCU 2008: 39); **Sou** episkevazo to radiofono. 'I am repairing the radio for you/I am repairing your radio'

An explanation in terms of ambiguity however is too narrow to account for the numerous cases where a purely possessive interpretation is available to the exclusion of the dative of interest reading. To see this, let's see how the Balkan languages perform on the situation hierarchy in (10c) in comparison to other European languages.

(10c) **The Situation Hierarchy** (KÖNIG/HASPELMATH 1997, section 6)
Patient-affecting ⊂ dynamic non-affecting ⊂ stative (KÖNIG/HASPELMATH 1997)

The situation hierarchy reflects the strength of the affectedness constraint as a function of the type of predicate selected for the EP construction. As mentioned above, Haspelmath's generalization is that cross-linguistically and in Europe in particular, the higher points of the hierarchy are favored, especially the classical patient affecting verbs, such as *open, repair, lose, lift, break, scratch, destroy, ruin,* all of which transitives.

Balkan EP however is not limited to these predicate. It is also available – and this is true to a maximum extent for Bulgarian and Romanian – with:[9]

i.   intransitives such as *walk, run, enter, flow,* unaccusatives such as *get old, lose weight, die, become red,* unergatives, such as *work, cry, laugh,* among many others;
ii. stative predicates like *see, hear, love, hate, know, remember,* among many others.

For reasons of space I cannot go into much detail, so I just illustrate these possibilities (see (21)–(22) and for more examples BACIU (1985), SVEŠNIKOVA (1986), AVRAM/COENE (2000, 2008), NICULESCU (2008)):

(21a) Teče **mu** nosăt; **Îi** curge nasul. 'His nose is running.' – Unaccusative predicates
Mi-a căzut un dinte; Padna **mi** edin zăb. 'One of my teeth fell out';
Treperjat **mi** rătsete. 'My hands are trembling';
Začervixa **mi** se buzite. 'My cheeks grew red';
I-a murit pisica. 'His cat died'.

---

9   For Romanian, NICULESCU (2008) has shown that there are few restrictions which seem to be of *lexical* nature, as some verbs do not accept the occurrence of this clitic, be it possessive or of a different type: *a constitui* ('to constitute, to be'), *a exista* ('to exist'), *a însemna* ('to mean'), *a reprezenta* ('to represent, to be'), *a spera* ('to hope'):

(i) ****Îmi** sper fericirea. '*I hope for **my** happiness' (NICULESCU 2008: 64).

Also excluded, but for an independent reason, are obligatorily reflexive verbs which cannot accommodate a second dative:

(ii) **Nu-i amintesc fata vs. Nu-mi amintesc de fata lui. 'I don't remember her face'

I thank Corina Bădeliţa for judgements and precious help with the Romanian data.

(21b) Ne **mi** raboti kompjutărăt. 'My computer doesn't work' – Unergative predicates

Zasmja **mi** se sărceto. 'My heart was happy'.

(22) Az **mu** vidjax novata prijatelka. 'I saw his new girlfriend' – Stative predicates

Az **mu** zabravix imeto. **I**-am uitat numele 'I forgot his name'

Poznavam **ti** prijatelite. 'I know your friends'

Nu-ţi sţiu adresa (LAMIROY 2003: 268, citing DUMITRESCU 1990).

As mentioned above with respect to (19b), intransitives represent the next stage of the grammaticalization of possessivity, given the absence of any benefactive/ malefactive component in their lexical semantics, of the semantic role of "patient", as well as of a goal argument. Therefore, it is only via the salient possessive relation that affectedness gets signaled, or better, inferred, in this case, which is why some authors prefer to speak of "mental affectedness"[10] in order to distinguish this more abstract way of affecting a possessor, or even to discard the connection with the beneficiary dative in favor of a possessive dative analysis. Without elaborating on this type of dative in relation to affectedness, I will treat it together with the beneficiary datives, noting that the possessive value is supplementary here and thus closer to the so-called dativus sympatheticus[11] as it is used traditionally. EP with such type of predicates is occasionally found in the European EP construction e.g.

---

10 See e.g. HASPELMATH (1999). The possessor is affected in a more abstract way by the whole situation by virtue of holding a possessor relationship with the main argument of the sentence, typically a subject or (in impersonal sentences) a prepositional phrase or both, as in (i):

(i) Edin kosăm **mi** padna v supata 'A hair fell into my soup'

Semantic information, e.g. the double possessive relation in (i), is entirely manipulated by syntactic function. According to FRIED (1999), to account for the common ground between "mental affectedness", which for her is a form of interest, and possession, a more abstract semantic relation should be used instead of "affectedness", namely 'endpoint of the event'. In any case, this kind of implicational affectedness can be considered an intermediate step between beneficiary Datives and pure possessive Datives. Note that the term "non-affecting" in (10c) is rather misleading.

11 The classical (and historically very early) usage of dativus sympatheticus, labeled by some authors dativus possessivus, is represented by (i). In such cases, the dative clitic appears with the verb *essere* and in Romanian also with *habere*, and expresses a relation between a possessor and a kinship term or some other close possession:

(i) Îmi este naş. 'He is **my** godfather'; Toj **mi** e čičo. 'He is my uncle'

Îşi are mama în spital. 'He has **his** mother in the hospital.'

I will not discuss predicative possession here. It is not clear how this type of dative is to be differentiated from dativus commodi/incommodi.

in Czech, Spanish and Italian. The pattern however is very productive in Romanian and Bulgarian, and is also available in Modern Greek (23), mainly with unaccusative verbs (parallel to those in (21a) where the possessum is coded as the subject and represents the theme argument), but also with unergatives (where the possessum is an agentive subject, as in (21b), and also (23b)).[12]

(23a) **Mou** ponì to kefali. 'I have a headache'; **Tou** kopikan ta ghonata lit. 'He felt his feet torn off'/'His feet were trembling' (Sint. 1990: 88)

(23b) De **mou** doulevi to kompiouter. 'My computer doesn't work'

From a broader typological perspective, the dividing line that sets apart Bulgarian and Romanian regards stative predicates. Crucially, one of the defining properties of statives is the absence of any inherent benefactive or malefactive semantics: the patient of e.g. a perception/experience verb like *see, hear, love* or a verb of knowledge like *know* cannot possibly be conceptualized as affected by the very act of seeing/hearing/knowing, and in consequence, the possessor cannot be cast as affected either. See (24)–(25) from Romance and Slavic. As reported by FRIED (1999), such data are consistent with the same restriction noted for other languages.

(24) Slavic
*Už iste **jim** viděli zahradu. 'Have you seen their yard yet?' Czech (FRIED 1999: 484)
*Widziałem **mu** zęby. 'I saw his teeth' Polish (WIERZBICKA 1986, cited in HASPELMATH 1999: 114)

(25) Romance
*Non **le** ho visto la faccia. 'I didn't see her face'
*Je **lui** ai oublié le nom. 'I forgot his name' French (KAYNE 1977: 159)
*Je ne **te** connais pas l'adresse; *Non **ti** so/conosco l'indirizzo; *No **te** sé/conozco la direction. 'I dont'know your address' (SÁNCHEZ LÓPEZ 2007: 168).

Romanian thus stands in contrast to the rest of Romance, as does Bulgarian to the rest of Slavic (Czech included in spite of the greater predicate range allowed in this language, to judge from FRIED 1999). In the absence of an affecting reading at least

---

12 According to HASPELMATH (1999), unergatives are inexistent in Europe but Albanian is an exception (HAPSELMATH refers to examples from O. BUCHHOLZ and W. FIEDLER: *Albanische Grammatik*, 1987). Such facts, which need further research, will turn out to be highly relevant for the overall analysis of Balkan EP. Several examples (from Giuseppina TURANO, p.c.) are given below:

Djali nuk më noton 'My child does not swim'
Nuk më punon komputeri 'My computer does not work'
?Libri nuk më ka ftuar asnjë çmim 'My book did not win a prize'
Sytë nuk më qeshin 'My eyes are not laughing'

a subset of Balkan EPs should be analyzed as possessive only and not as a special case of the dative of interest construction. I will come back to the situation in Modern Greek later.

What I want to show now, following previous work (CINQUE/KRAPOVA 2009), is that the maximal permissiveness of Bulgarian and Romanian with respect to predicate choice is an effect of conflating in a single construction what some Romance languages (French, Italian) express in two different ways: by a dative clitic (in a dative of interest construction) and by a genitive clitic (*ne/en*) in a purely possessive construction. In fact, this type of clitic is the only possible way of rendering (25) grammatical in the presence of a stative predicate, implying that one of the functions of *ne/en* in Romance is to express possession outside the realm of affectedness:

(26a) Non **ne**   conosco   l'indirizzo
      not it$_{gen}$ know-1sg   the-address 'I don't know his/its address'
(26b) J'**en** ai   oublié   le nom
      it$_{gen}$ have-1sg   forgotten   the name 'I have forgotten his/its name'

The evidence in the next section will help tease apart the dative from the genitive usage of the "possessive" clitic, applying diagnostics internal to Bulgarian, which can be extended, I believe, also to Romanian. The historical relevance of this biconstructional approach, if it is on the right track, will amount to denying the possibility of semantic bleaching of the affectedness feature in the emergence of a true possessive construction, and to claiming that in spite of the genitive-dative syncretism which has rendered the two case functions morphologically indistinguishable, they are nevertheless still well differentiated syntactically.

3. On distinguishing two EP constructions

Starting from constructions involving a dynamic (patient-affecting or intransitive) predicate, there is particularly clear evidence that the dative clitic corresponding to the beneficiary/possessor is an extra argument of the predicate and not an argument of the noun phrase expressing the possessum. In generative grammar terms, this means that the dative argument is base generated externally rather than derived by "possessor raising" from within the noun phrase. To take one example, consider idiomatic expressions such as (27a/a') from Bulgarian. If we try to substitute the external with an internal clitic, either the idiomatic reading is lost (27b/b'), or the sentence becomes ungrammatical (28b):[13]

---

13 In Romanian too the idiomatic reading is lost if we substitute the external clitic with a possessive adjective:
  (i) a. A nu-şi crede ochilor 'to not believe one's own eyes' (NICULESCU 2008)
      b. *A nu crede ochilor săi/Ioanei ('*to not believe his/Ioana's eyes')

(27a)   Ti **mi** skri topkite/šajbata. 'You really shocked/confused me'
(27b)   Ti skri topkite/šajbata **mi** (no idiomatic interpretation). 'You hid my balls/
         disk' (e.g. tennis balls, hockey disk)
(27a') Padna **mi** šapkata. 'I was extremely surprised'
(27b') Šapkata **mi** padna (v kalta). 'My hat fell (in the mud)' (no idiomatic inter-
         pretation)
(28a)   Ti **mi** xodiš po nervite. lit. 'You are walking on my nerves' ('You are get-
         ting on my nerves')
(28b)   *Ti xodiš po nervite **mi**.

The lack of symmetrical reading between the a. and the b. examples suggests that
the external clitic is not related to the noun phrase internal position; if this were indeed the case, the pairs should have been mutually reversible, contrary to fact. The
test in (27)/(28) can be replicated for all of the idiomatic expressions given in the
(unordered) lists below:

(29) Bulgarian
čupja mu xatăra ('displease someone'); *gledam si rabotata* ('mind my own business'), *gledam si kefa* ('indulge in pleasure'); *vlači mi se opaškata* ('people are
gossiping about me'); *vleze mi muxa v glavata* ('it got into my head'); *vljazăl mi e
v krăvta* ('be particularly fond of something or somebody'); *vljazla mi e glavata v
torbata* ('be in a mortal danger'); *vljazăl mi e pod kožata* ('be under someone's
influence'); *da si izbălvaš červata* ('feel bad because of something or somebody
disgusting'); *da si kăsaš glavata* ('feel bad because of something or somebody
nasty'); *ne mi miga okoto* ('not to be afraid'); *ne mi pee petelăt* 'not to be respected'; *ne mi se čuva dumata* ('have no influence, not to be respected'); *izvaždam
mu očite, vmesto da mu izpiša veždite* 'do a bad favor'; *razkaza mi se igrata* 'have
a real hard time'; *da ti padne šapkata* 'be shocked'; *sveti mi červenoto* 'have no
chance'; *plamna mi glavata* 'have a lot of trouble'; *seče mi akălăt* 'be real clever',
etc.

(30) Romanian (from NICULESCU 2008: 506)
a-şi da viaţa ('to die'), *a-i merge numele* ('to become famous'); *a-şi pierde urma*
('to get lost'); *a-şi pierde minţile/capul/viaţa/vremea* ('to lose one's mind/~mind/to
die/to lose one's time'); *a-şi pune capăt zilelor* ('to end one's life'); *a-şi pune în
gând* ('to set one's mind to something'); *a-i trece prin cap* ('to cross one's mind');
a-i ţine cuiva calea ('to follow someone'); *a-şi ţine firea* ('to keep calm'); *a-şi ţine
gura* ('to keep silent'); *a-şi vedea de treabă* ('to mind one's business'); *a nu-şi vedea lungul nasului* ('to be vane'); *a-i veni pe limbă* ('to find the words'); *a-i veni
inima la loc* ('to calm down'); *a-i veni ceasul* ('to die'); *a-i veni dracii* ('to get furi-
ous').

Note that all of the above idiomatic expressions contain a) a benefactive or malefactive verb meaning, b) a beneficiary or "sympathetic" dative, c) a human possessor, and d) a body part (or some other inalienable possession in the strict or extended sense). These are precisely the properties which form the quintessential affectedness EP pattern, or the "European prototype" in Haspelmath's terms. Parallel idiomatic constructions in Romance also require an external dative clitic that cannot be substituted by an internal possessive adjective nor by a genitive *ne/en clitic*. Cf. (31)–(32).

(31a) Luc **lui** casse les pieds. 'Luc bothers him/her' (LAMIROY 2003: 260f.)
(31b) Luc casse **ses** pieds. 'Luc breaks his/her feet' (no idiom interpretation available)
(31c) Luc **en** casse les pieds. 'Luc him$_{gen}$ breaks the feet' (no idiom interpretation available)
(32a) **Gli** hanno rotto le scatole. 'They annoyed him'
(32b) Hanno rotto le **sue** scatole. 'They have broken his boxes' (no idiom interpretation available)
(32c) **Ne** hanno rotto le scatole. 'Him$_{gen}$ they have broken the boxes' (no idiom interpretation available).

In non-idiomatic constructions the same possessive dative clitic is apparently free to occur either noun phrase-internally or externally:

(33a) Tja **mu** sčupi [$_{NP}$ malkija prăst]. 'She broke his little finger'
(33b) Tja sčupi [$_{NP}$ malkija **mu** prăst]. 'She broke his little finger'

However, the internal variant of (33) must meet a crucial requirement not holding of the external variant; namely that the noun phrase containing the possessive clitic must be definite: the possessive dative clitic cannot appear inside an indefinite phrase, a restriction known from the syntactic literature as the "definiteness restriction"[14] (PENČEV 1998: 30, FRANKS/KING 2000: 282; ASSENOVA 2001). See the contrast between (33b) and (34) below:

(34)   *Tja sčupi [edin **mu** prăst]. 'She broke a finger of his'

No definiteness requirement holds of the external variant, (34), as can be seen from (35) which is the only possible way to render (34):

(35)   Tja **mu** sčupi [edin prăst]. 'She broke a finger of his'

The availability of indefinite (partitive) possessive elements in a subset of the EP constructions, namely those involving an affecting predicate, as opposed to the

---

14 The clitic appears immediately attached to a demonstrative or to whichever element is inflected with the definite article (PENČEV 1993, FRANKS 2000: 59ff., STATEVA 2002: 660, a.o.).

obligatory definiteness feature of the same elements in the Internal Possessive construction suggests that (33a) and (33b) are not related transformationally and consequently, the external dative clitic in (35) does not have its source inside the noun phrase but is generated within the verb phrase as an additional argument of the verb rather than being moved to this position by way of raising or cliticization (cf. (6) above).

Other cases however call for an analysis in terms of possessor raising. The ungrammaticality of (36a), for example, follows from the impossibility of the clitic to appear inside an indefinite noun phrase (36b).

(36a) *Ne **mu** poznavam **edin prijatel.** 'I know a friend of his'
(36b) *Ne poznavam [edin mu prijatel].

This case contrasts with the one before since here, the external dative clitic remains affected by the definiteness restriction inside the noun phrase. If in (36a) the external clitic position is derived by possessor raising from within the noun phrase, then the "wrong" result in (36a) can be attributed to a movement out of an improper syntactic configuration (36b). This implies that whenever the definiteness restriction is respected on the noun phrase internal level, the corresponding external clitic formation is expected to be grammatical, as e.g. in (37):

(37)   Ne mu poznavam [NP-def prijatelja ~~mu~~]. 'I don't know his friend'

Similar reasoning can be made for the other EP constructions which contain a stative (non-dynamic and non-affected) predicate. The claim therefore is that precisely with these predicates will external and internal possession correspond to each other semantically and syntactically because of the mirror-like positioning of the possessive clitic. An even stronger claim is that precisely in these cases, the possessive clitic, although dative in morphology, has an underlying genitive case value which makes it compatible with Romance *ne/en*-clitic amenable to a "possessor raising" analysis as well.

Before we turn to Modern Greek, I just point out one consequence of the split approach to Bulgarian, extendable also to Romanian, EP constructions. Since the clitic in the affecting EP type is not related to a noun phrase internal position, we can expect that this latter position could be simultaneously filled. This would give rise to a double occurrence of the clitic, as in (37) and in other similar contexts involving some type of mental affectedness – once in the external position where the clitic bears a beneficiary (dative of interest) value, and a second time in the internal position where it is specialized for possession and has a genitive value.[15]

---

15 The co-occurrence of two dative clitics corresponding respectively to a dative and to a possessive argument under coreference is possible also when the clitic realizes one of the prototypical dative functions (word order and optionality apart). In (i), for example,

(38)   Umrja **mu** (...) konjat **mu** (...). 'His horse died on him' (SCHICK 2000: 191)

With pure possessive structures, on the other hand, no similar double occurrences are predicted to be possible under the possessor raising analysis suggested above, or else the sentence would end up having two coreferential clitics with the same syntactic function. We can follow the standard assumptions in the generative grammar tradition and suggest that in this case, the possessive clitic leaves an unpronounced copy in the noun phrase from which it has been raised. The relation with the overt clitic takes care of the possessive interpretation (cf. (7) above repeated here as (39a) and the structure in (39b)). For additional evidence bearing on the syntactic properties of the two EP types the reader is referred to CINQUE/KRAPOVA (2009).

(39a) *Az **í** zărnax litseto **í** v tălpata. 'I her-DAT spotted her face in the crowd'
(39b) Az [$_{VP}$**í** zărnax] [$_{NP}$ litseto **í**] [v tălpata]. 'I saw her face in the crowd'

Modern Greek also allows for the double occurrence pattern analogous to (37) with predicates of the mental affecting type such as e.g. *die* in (40):

(40)   **Tou** pethane to alogo **tou**. 'His horse dies on him'.

However, in spite of sharing this, as well as many of the other semantic or syntactic peculiarities of the Romanian and Bulgarian EP (possessed objects, nonhuman possessors, unaccusative and unergatives predicates, cf. the examples in (11)–(16), (23) above), the so-called "personal pronoun genitive" in Modern Greek does not allow, as the following ungrammatical examples show, a stative predicate (*like, see, remember, understand, know*) to appear in this construction. All of the examples in (41) have been judged ungrammatical by my informants:

(41)   *Tis** sou aressoun ta podhia. 'You like her legs'; *Tus** idha to kenourghio avtokinito. 'I saw his new car' (PANCHEVA 2004); ?? *Tou** xehasa to onoma. 'I forgot your name'; *Den **tou** thimame to prossopo. 'I don't remember his face'; *Sou** katalava tin idea. 'I got your idea'; *Den **tou** xero ton filo. 'I don't know his friend'.

The only way to render the possessive meaning in (41) is by a noun phrase internal possessive clitic:

---

the first appearance of *mu* corresponds to the recipient of *nosja* 'bring', and the second occurrence is the obligatory internal possessive argument of a kinship term, *majka mu* 'his mother':

(i) Zakuskata [**mu** donese] [majka **mu**]. / [Majka **mu**] [**mu** donese] zakuskata.
    'His mother brought him the breakfast'

This possibility gives support to the claim made in the text that the beneficiary dative belongs to the same family of dative functions.

(42)   Sou aressoun [ta podhia **tis**]; Idha [to kenourghio **tou** autokinito]; Xehasa [to
         onoma **tou**].
         Den thimame [to prosopo **tou**]; Katalava [tin idea **sou**]; Den xero [ton filo
         tou].

Given that stative predicates diagnose the presence of a true possessive structure,
Modern Greek obviously does not dispose of this pattern, so its EP is basically a
dative of interest context. As in other European languages, the beneficiary dative
can cumulate an additional possessive value due to the inferential relation between
possessor and possessed. HOLTON et al. (1997: 194) refer to this usage of the Greek
genitive as "malefactive" and "benefactive", although the distinction with the other
dative functions (e.g. the ethic dative) needs to be made more precise:

(43)   Afti **mou** skotose ton enthousiasmo 'She killed my enthusiasm'; Esi **mou**
         katestrepses ti zoi. 'You ruined my life'; **Mou** ekapses to spiti. 'You burned
         my house'; **Tou** dankosa to dahtilo. 'I bit his finger'; **Mou** ponì to kefali 'I
         have a headache'; **Sou** haidevi to kefali 'He/She caresses your head' (Sint.
         1990: 62); Ghiati mas halases tin parea? 'Why did you spoil the party for
         us?' (HOLTON et al. 1997: 194)

Restricting EP to just "affectedness" leaves the additional possessive interpretation
open to context. Also somewhat "vague" in this sense is the extent to which a certain predicate can count as affecting for the purposes of the construction. For example, the verb *like* and experiencer predicates in general do not seem good candidates for an EP construal, and sometimes even the inalienable relation does not
succeed in rendering the construction possible. *Hate* on the other hand, is acceptable to some extent, (44a), especially under emphasis, as in the second examples of
(44a). In spite of the lexical and pragmatic support, my informants would still prefer the internal possessive construal (44b):

(44a)   ?(?) **Tou** misso to haraktira /?Den **tou** misso to haraktira.
         b. Miso to haraktira **tou**. 'I hate his character'

However, in other cases a stricter inalienability (ownership) relation can provide an
interpretive clue and increase the verb's chances for entering an EP construction
and provoking the same ambiguity as in the other two Balkan languages. In (45b),
as reported by my informants, only the benefactive/malefactive reading survives,
given that no possessive relation is likely to be implied, while such reading is more
readily available in (45b) because of the ownership relation:

(45a)   **Sou** anteghrapsa to arthro. 'I copied the article for you/*I copied your arti-
         cle'.
         Cf. Prepisax **ti** statijata. 'I copied your paper/I copied the paper for you'
(45b)   Na **mou** taìsis to skilaki. 'Feed the dog for me/Feed my dog'

Although a historical scenario of the grammaticalization process in the Balkan languages is beyond the scope of this paper, I just point out that the affectedness criterion internal to Modern Greek is yet another proof that we are dealing with two separate constructions well differentiated in the other two languages: dative of interest and possessive dative. The ambiguity of the Bulgarian example in (45a) is thus only apparent. What is visible on the superficial level as "two-in one" in fact conceals two distinct underlying constructions whose syntactic properties can be successfully extrapolated in the non-ambiguous contexts we have discussed above. In other words, the emergence of a truly possessive dative cannot be said to result from a process of semantic bleaching of the affectedness feature on the possessor in the EP construction on its way to expressing pure possession; this would leave unexplained the distinct behavior of the EP constructions in Bulgarian and Romanian, as well as the special choice of Modern Greek not to follow the exact same path in the grammaticalization of possession, as opposed to the other two languages.

4. The case for dative case

For HASPELMATH (1999), the morphological dative-genitive case in the Balkan EP behaves as unambiguously dative from a structural and synchronic point of view. However, if this were so, the restrictions presented by Modern Greek would remain mysterious in the face of what would seem to be an overgenerated pattern in Romanian and Bulgarian. What I would like to suggest, as mentioned before, is that the dative clitic in the possessive construction is a genitive clitic "in disguise", while in the affectedness construction it is a true dative clitic. Following TOPOLIŃSKA (2004), I understand case "not as a morphological form, but as a syntactic relation of dependence of a noun phrase either on the verbal construction ... or on another noun phrase". The dative is an adverbal case related to predicative expressions, while the genitive is an adnominal case related to argumental expressions and although there is the additional possibility (in Bulgarian and Romanian) of expressing a possessive (genitive) relation outside of the noun phrase and on the sentence level, it is not the case that that genitive case functions switch to dative case functions. The genitive-dative case syncretism, as pointed out again by Topolińska, has unified the morphological devices of grammatical accommodation, but the syntactic functions of the adverbal dative vs. the adnominal genitive are still as visibly distinct as they have been before the merger; wherever the two cases appear "fused" from a syntactic point of view, in the contemporary languages, independent evidence can establish their different syntactic behavior.

A very brief look at the history of the construction in Bulgarian and Greek shows that in fact the two languages may have gone in opposite directions in grammaticalizing external possession. As pointed out by HORROCKS (2007), 'displaced' genitives had a crucial role in the diachronic process related to the dative –

genitive functional transfer: genitive clitics which properly belonged to the possessed noun could cliticize to the verb and end up in the position typically reserved for indirect objects and other types of datives. This allowed for their interpretation as dativus commodi/incommodi (or dativus ethicus) which quickly led to the assumption of all dative functions by the genitive clitic pronouns. By the 8th or 9th century the dative almost entirely disappeared. A process in the opposite direction must have taken place in Old Bulgarian (Old Church Slavonic), to be further extended in the period of Middle Bulgarian as a result of Balkan influence on analytic development. MINČEVA (1964) has shown that the first contexts to yield a possessive interpretation of the dative were those involving a dativus commodi/incommodi context where a dative (lexical or pronominal) argument translating the Greek genitive clitic and appearing in preposition to the noun and closer to the verb, could get interpreted as "doubly dependent" – once as signaling possession with respect to the noun, and a second time as an argument of the verb. Internal possession on the other hand heavily relied on the genitive, at least in Old Bulgarian, in the rendering of the Greek postnominal genitives, and only after the spread of the doubly dependent dative did the internal genitives get substituted by a dative. Of course, a number of questions remain unanswered pertaining to the more precise picture of these historical processes, but it seems that while in Greek (which has generalized the genitive) a reanalysis of the dative relation has taken place, in Bulgarian (which has generalized the dative) it was the genitive relation that underwent a reanalysis. Both the intrusion of the dative into the sphere of possession (in Bulgarian) as well as the assumption of dative functions by the genitive in Greek are due to some sort of syntactic displacement of the pronominal or clitic argument which has allowed the respective reinterpretation of the original case functions. This, and other issues (especially the possibility of clitic doubling of the possessive element) are essential for a better understanding of the syntax of Balkan possession but of course require much further research.

Bibliography

ASSENOVA, Petya (2001): «Observations sur la structure du texte balkanique». *Zeitschrift für Balkanologie* 37, 2. 119–135.

AVRAM, Larisa; COENE, Martine (2000): "Dative/Genitive Clitics as Last Resort". In: M. Dimitrova-Vulchanova, I. Krapova, L. Hellan (eds.): *Papers from the Third Conference on Formal Approaches to South Slavic and Balkan Languages.* (University of Trondheim Working Papers in Linguistics 34). Trondheim: NTNU Linguistics Department. 157–169.

AVRAM, Larisa; COENE, Martine (2008): "Romanian possessive clitics revisited". In: D. Kallulli, L.Tasmowski (eds.): *Clitic Doubling in the Balkan Languages.* Amsterdam: Benjamins. 361–387.

BACIU, Ion (1985): «Observations sur le datif possessif en roumain». *Linguistique comparée et typologie des langues romanes*, II. Université de Provence. 349–359.

BAKER, Mark (1988): *Incorporation: A theory of Grammatical function changing*. Chicago: Chicago University Press.

BALLY, Charles (1926): «L'expression des idées de sphère personnelle et de solidarité dans les langues indo-européennes». In: F. Frankhauser, J. Jud (eds.): *Festschrift Louis Gauchat*. Aarau: Sauerländer (English Translation in CHAPPELL/MCGREGOR 1996). 68–78.

BYBEE, Joan (1988): "Semantic substance vs. contrast in the development of grammatical meaning". *Berkeley Linguistics Society* 14. 247–264.

CINQUE, Guglielmo; KRAPOVA, Iliana (2009): "The two possessor raising constructions of Bulgarian". In: S. Franks, V. Chidambaram, B. Joseph (eds.): *A Linguist's Linguist. Studies in South Slavic Linguistics in honor of E. Wayles Browne,* Slavic Publishers: Bloomington, Indiana. 149–166.

CHAPPELL, Hilary; McGregor, William (eds.) (1996): *The Grammar of Inalienability: A typological perspective on body-part terms and the part-whole relation*. Berlin: Mouton de Gruyter.

CORNILESCU, Alexandra (1995): "Romanian Genitive Constructions". In: G. Cinque, G. Giusti (eds.): *Advances in Rumanian Linguistics*. Amsterdam, Philadelphia: John Benjamins. 1–54.

DAVIES, William (1984): "Inalienable possession and Choktaw Referential Coding". *International Journal of American Linguistics* 50. 384–402.

DUMITRESCU, Domnita (1990): "El dativo posesivo en español y en rumano". *Revista Española de Lingüística* 20, 2. 403–430.

FRANKS, Steven (2000): "The Internal Structure of Slavic NPs, with Special Reference to Bulgarian". In: *Generative Linguistics in Poland 2 (syntax and morphology)* (Proceedings of the GLiP-2 Conference). Warsaw: Institute of Computer Science, Polish Academy of Sciences. 53–70.

FRIED, Mirjam (1999): "From Interest to Ownership: A constructional View of External Possessors". In: D. Payne, I. Barshi (eds.): *External Possession*. Amsterdam: John Benjamins. 473–504.

HASPELMATH, Martin (1999): "External Possession in a European Areal Perspective". In: D. Payne, I. Barshi (eds.): *External Possession*. Amsterdam: John Benjamins. 109–135.

HOLTON, David; MACKRIDGE, Peter; PHILIPPAKI-WARBURTON, Irene. (1997): *Greek: A Comprehensive Grammar of the Modern Language* (Comprehensive Grammars). London: Routledge.

HORROCKS, Geoffrey (2007): "Syntax: From Classical Greek to the Koine". In: A. P. Christidis (ed.): *A History of Ancient Greek. From the Beginnings to Late Antiquity*. Cambridge: Cambridge University Press. 618–631.

KAYNE, Richard S. (1977): *Syntaxe du français. Le cycle transformationnel*. Paris: Éditions du Seuil (French translation of *French Syntax*. Cambridge, Mass.: MIT Press, 1975).

KÖNIG, Ekkerhard; HASPELMATH, Martin (1997): «Les constructions à possesseur externe dans les langues d'Europe». In: J. Feuillet (ed.): *Actance et valence dans les langues de l'Europe* (Empirical Approaches to Language Typology/EUROTYP, 20-2). Berlin: Mouton de Gruyter. 525–600.

KUPULA, Mikko (2008): *Adnominal Possession and Ditransitives*. Studia graeca stockholmiensia. Series neohellenica. Stockholm University.

LAMIROY, Béatrice (2003): "Grammaticalization and external possessor structures in Romance and Germanic languages". In: M.Coene, Y. D'Hulst (eds.): *From NP to DP. Volume II: the expression of possession in noun phrases*. Amsterdam: Benjamins. 257–280.

LANGACKER, Ronald (1991): *Foundations of Cognitive Grammar*. Volume II. Descriptive application. Stanford: Stanford University Press.

LANDAU, Idan (1999): Possessor raising and the structure of VP. *Lingua* 107. 1–37.

MINČEVA, Anghelina (1964) = А. Минчева: Развой на дателния притежателен падеж в българския език. София 1964.

MANOLIU-MANEA, Maria (1996): "Inalienability and topicality in Romanian: Pragmasemantics of syntax". In: H. Chappel, W. McGregor (eds.): *The Grammar of Inalienability: a Typological Perspective on Body Part Terms and the Part-Whole Relation*. Berlin: Mouton de Gruyter. 711–743.

NICULESCU, Dana (2008): "Romanian possessive dative – The limits of the structure". *Revue Romaine Linguistique* LIII, 4. Bucureşti. 485–515.

NITSOLOVA, Ruselina (1986): *Българските местоимения*. София: Наука и изкуство.

NITSOLOVA, Ruselina (2008): *Българска граматика. Морфология*. Софияр Университетско издателство „Св. Климент Охридски".

PANĂ DINDELEGAN, Gabriella (1994): *Teorie şi analiză gramaticală*. Bucureşti: Coresi.

PANCHEVA, Roumyana (2004): "Balkan Possessive Clitics: The Problem of Case and Category". In O. Mišeska Tomić (ed.): *Balkan Syntax and Semantics*. Amsterdam: Benjamins. 175–219.

PENČEV, Iordan (1998): *Sintaksis na săvremennija bălgarski knižoven ezik*. Plovdiv.

SÁNCHEZ LÓPEZ, Cristina (2007): "The possessive dative and the syntax of affected arguments". *Cuadernos de Lingüística del I. U. I. Ortega y Gasset XIV*. 153–173. http://www.ortegaygasset.edu/iuoyg/dpto/linguistica/publicaciones/cl14/sanchez.pdf.

ŠARIC, Liljiana (2002): "On the semantics of the 'dative of possession' in the Slavic languages: An analysis on the basis of Russian, Polish, Croatian/Serbian and Slovenian examples". *Glossos* 3, http://seelrc.org/glossos/issues/3/saric.pdf.

SCHICK, Ivanka (2000): "The phenomenon of possessive clitics in the Balkan Slavic languages". In: M. Dimitrova-Vulchanova, I. Krapova, L. Hellan (eds.): *Papers from the Third Conference on Formal Approaches to South Slavic and Balkan Languages*. (University of Trondheim Working Papers in Linguistics 34). Trondheim: NTNU Linguistics Department. 183–195.

Synt. (1990) = Συντακτικό της Νέας Ελληνικής, Α',Β' και Γ' Γυμνασίου, Οργανισμός εκδόσεως διδακτικών βιβλίων. Αθήνα 1990.

STATEVA, Penka (2002): "Possessive Clitics and the Structure of Nominal Expressions". *Lingua* 112. 647–690.

SVEŠNIKOVA (1986) = Т. Н. Свешникова: Об одном способе выражения посессивности в румынском языке [Вып. 10]. Славянское и балканское языкознание. Проблемы диалектологии. Категория посессивности. М. 201–208.

TOMIĆ, Olga (2009): "South Slavic clitics expressing possession". In: S. Franks, V. Chidambaram, B. Joseph (eds.): *A Linguist's Linguist. Studies in South Slavic Linguistics in honor of E. Wayles Browne*. Slavic Publishers: Bloomington, Indiana. 445–464.

TOPOLIŃSKA, Zuzana (2004): Paper presented at the 9th International Congress of the Association Internationale d'Études du Sud-Est Européen, Tirana, 30.8–3.9.2004.

VERGNAUD, Jean-Roger; ZUBIZARRETA, Maria Luisa (1992): "The definite determiner and the inalienable constructions in French and in English". *Linguistic Inquiry* 23. 595–652.

WIERZBICKA, Anna (1988): *The semantics of Grammar*. Amsterdam: John Benjamins.

Aspects of Inter-Linguistic Isosemy in the Pastoral Terminology of the Pindos Mountain Region[*]

Doris K. KYRIAZIS (Thessaloniki)

Out of the numerous possibilities at its disposal in order to name the various reference objects, language makes its own choices, which may in part coincide or differ at the inter-linguistic level. The degree of similarity is expected to be greater in languages that are genetically related or have been in direct contact with each other for a long period of time.

According to СЕМЧИНСКИЙ (1976: 36), isosemy is found in words that present isomorphism of the signifier for the expression of the same meaning or that present partial or full identity in the semantic structure of the polysemes. Isosemy may result from: 1. the genetic relation of the languages involved – генетическая изосемия; 2. their parallel evolution – независимая ассоциативная изосемия; 3. mutual borrowing – интерференционная изосемия.[1] TZITZILIS (2001) has established a series of criteria, on the basis of which we can distinguish the cases of parallel evolution from those of semantic borrowing, through loan translations (calques). This view includes cases of: 1. Calques, formed on the basis of erroneous etymological analysis; 2. Semicalques, which preserve elements of the source-language; and 3. Taking into account the manner of formation of words that present isosemy. Furthermore, depending on the case, we can apply chronological, geographic, semantic and cultural criteria. Семчинский also stresses that isosemy is related to the so called inherent form of the words, which can be structural (Gr. χέρι, Alb. dorë 'hand' – Gr. χερ-ούλι, Alb. dor-ezë 'handle') or metaphorical (χερ-ούλι / dorezë 'doorhandle'). Therefore, we should add that in the case of "primary" single-form words that do not allow comparison of their inherent form (due to the arbitrariness of the linguistic sign, compare e.g. the words dorë and χέρι 'hand', (n)drit and φέγγω 'to shine'), cases of isosemy must be sought out in the metaphorical usage of these words and on the other their derivatives (cf. Alb. drit-

[*] The field research for the study has been supported by the Austrian Science Found, project "Terminologie der Wanderhirten", projekt-no. P19406-G03, conducted by Thede Kahl.

1 Межьязыковои изосемисй нами было названо такое явление, при котором отдельные слова различных языков обнаруживают нзоморфность своей ексформы (= фономорфологической внешностн) при одиноковом значении или идентичность (полную нлн частичную) семантической структуры многозначных слов.

are 'window' and Gr. *φεγγ-ίτης* 'skylight, attic window', Alb. i *presh-të* 'green' and Gr. πράσ-ινος 'green' (*presh* / πράσο 'leek'), Gr. δεξιός – Alb. i *djathtë* 'right' and 'proper', Gr. δεμένος – Alb. i *lidhur* 'tied up' and 'impotent' (ASSENOVA 1993), as well as in the fixed word sets they form: e.g. Alb. *qime* and Gr. τρίχα 'hair' → *shpëtuam për një qime* = γλιτώσαμε **παρά τρίχα** 'we escaped by a hair's breadth', as well as *e bën qimen tërkuzë* = κάνει την τρίχα τριχιά 'turning a hair-thin string into a rope', which can be translated as 'exaggerating', but compare Alb. *është kock' e lëkurë* and Gr. είναι πετσί και κόκαλο 'is only skin and bone', where the word-order is inverted; Alb. *lesh me qime* and Gr. τρίχες κατσαρές, lit. 'hair curly', where the same meaning of 'nonsense' is given in a slightly different way. The last two as well as numerous similar examples can be considered as cases of partial isosemy.

Moreover, it is equally interesting to note cases of inherent asymmetry, not only within the limits of a single language (interdialectally), but also interlingually. For instance, in Albanian idioms spoken in the north part of Shkumbin river, the words *bukël*, *bukëlz* are used for the meaning 'weasel'; however, the same words appear in the south end of the Albanian continuum (ADGjSh II 80). We should add that several different names are used across the Albanian region to describe the animal we referred to previously, such as *nusez, nusja bukër, nusbukër, nusja e mive, bishtafurka*, etc. In Albanian, beside the words *nusezë* (< *nuse* 'bride') and *bukël* (< *e bukur* 'pretty') 'weasel', which have their counterparts in other languages (Gr. νυφίτσα, Bulg. *невестулка*, Rum. *nevestuică*, Turk. *gelincik*, Romani *bororu*, TZITZILIS 2001: 46); there are also *nusël, nuselalë, nuse e lalës*, which, in our view, may originate from the Latin *mustela (nivalis/arealis)*. We believe that in this way the existence of the *lalë/e lalës* (*lalë* 'uncle, brother') part of these words[2], which does not appear in neighbouring languages, is appropriately explained. This, of course, is a hypothesis, as we do not know the precise form of this word in Balkan Latin. If this hypothesis is accurate, then Albanian may have been the starting point for the corresponding names of the 'weasel' in other Balkan languages. This possibility is reinforced by the fact that Albanian (to be more correct, its *lingua mater*) came into contact with Latin quite early. Nevertheless, it is possible that this is a case of multiple isosemy, based on the combination of folk etymology and eu-phemictically created names used for weasel.

Although the need for a broader examination of isosemy in an interlingual level has been repeatedly expressed (SCHRÖPFER 1956: 148[3]), in this case, we will focus

---

2 Note that the word *nuse* is part of the Indo-European heritage of the Albanian language (HULD 1984: 100).

3 An Papahagis Sammlungen … kann man feststellen, dass die Verbreitung einer Redens-art, Wortprägung oder Metapher bzw. Sinnwandlung auch außerhalb des Balkans,

mainly on a specific geographic region and a basic human activity as animal breeding. This is an effort to present that there is a higher degree of isosemy in this case, compared to other semantic fields of the languages under examination. Besides the fact that the languages (and dialects) spoken in the broader Pindos Mountain region – Greek, Albanian, Aromanian and South Slavic – belong to the Indo-European language family, they are not closely related to each other. However, they have been "neighbours" for millennia, a fact that has led to development of common characteristics, among which of great interest is the contact-induced isosemy. The isosemy observed in pastoral vocabulary (PV henceforth) is part of a broader framework. As we know, stockbreeding is one of the oldest productive activities of the region's residents and pastoral terminology has been created by rural people. The broader region of Pindos Mountain range served as an area of contact for specific languages or, to be more precise, of direct contact of specific ones of their dialects. The speakers of southern Albanian idioms (labërisht, çamërisht) met here with speakers of northern, semi-northern and southern Greek idioms. They also met with speakers of Aromanian and to a lower degree with Slavic speaking populations of the area.

Attempting to rank PV by type in terms of the origin of the words it comprises, the following picture emerges:

– names that exclusively appear in one language, with generalized (Alb. *dash* 'ram', *dhi* 'goat', Gr. γάλα 'milk', βούτυρο 'butter') or restricted geographical use (Alb. *qumësht* 'milk', *gjalpë* 'butter' in southern and *tamël* 'milk', *tlyn* 'butter' in northern dialect, Gr. μαλλόρρυπον 'wool's dirt', έγγαλα 'milky goats/ sheep', Crete), etc.

– names that are loanwords from other languages of the region: Alb. dial. *mëndër* < Gr. μάντρα, Alb. dial. *nome* < Gr. νομή, Alb. *stan* < Slav. станъ, Gr. στάνη < Slav. станъ, Gr. dial. κουρίζα 'ραχοκοκκαλιά/backbone' < Alb. *kurriz*, Alb. *çoban* < Turk. *çoban*, Gr. τσομπάνος < Turk. *çoban*, etc.

– names that are common and originate from the so-called lexical Balkanisms[4], most of which form part of PV: Alb. *kaleshe*, Gr. καλέšο, Alb. *shutë*, Gr. šούτα, Alb. *shtrungë*, Gr. στρούγκα, etc.

– names that are the result of parallel or contact-induced isosemy: Alb.dial. *çalë* 'a kind of disease' (< *çaloj* 'limp') Gr.dial. κουτσαμάρα (< κουτσαίνω 'limp'), Alb.dial. *marrël* 'a kind of disease' (< *marr* 'take'), Gr.dial. παρμάρα (< παίρνω 'take'), Alb.dial. *mëlçi e zezë*, Arom. *hicat negru, h'ikat laiu* (ДОМОСИЛЕЦКАЯ 2002: 332), etc.

besonders in den nächsten genealogischen Verwandten der betreffenden Sprachen nicht berücksichtigt wird.

4   ΤΖΙΤΖΙΛΗΣ (43–56) in ΔΟΥΓΑ-ΠΑΠΑΔΟΠΟΥΛΟΥ & ΤΖΙΤΖΙΛΗΣ 2006.

The main characteristic of the broader region and the languages being examined is the fact that for the same RO (reference object), we find a combination of ways of naming that object at the intra-lingual and inter-lingual level. For example, in Albanian, apart from the words *qumësht* or *klumësht* 'milk', the word *tamël* (< Alb. *të ambël* 'sweet') appears in northern idioms, while for the word 'bile' the names *vner/vrer* (< Lat. *venenum*) and *tëmth* (< Alb. *të ëmbëlth* 'sweet') are used, of which the latter is a euphemism. A 'milk-churn' in Albanian is named *tundës, dru qumështi, filiç, trobolicë, fti, pti, mëti*, etc. (ДОМОСИЛЕЦКАЯ 2002: 384); names for 'afterbirth': ακόλουθο < Anc.Gr. ἀκόλουθος (ANDRIOTIS 1974: 81), κυττάρι < Anc.Gr. κυττάριον (ANDRIOTIS 1974: 341); names for a rich grazing area: αμαλαγιά (< αμάλαγος 'pure'), απάτητο (< απάτητος 'untrodden'), καθαρό (< καθαρός 'clean'), παστρικό (< παστρικός 'clean') in Greek; names for 'hermaphrodite': Alb. *deledash, mashkullfemërë, capodhi, mashkullore* (ДОМОСИЛЕЦКАЯ 2002: 362); names for 'herdsman': Alb. *bari, çoban, blegtor, delmer, delmetor, kullotës, ruajtës, mashnor, shelegar, shterpar, tubanik, skuter, cangadhjar, gunëdhirë, qumështor* (FjSin. 2007: 73). In interlingual level we find isosemic nouns such as Gr. κυττάρι – Alb. *shtrat*, Gr. αρσενοθήλυκο, σαρκοθήλυκο – Alb. *mashkullfemërë*, Gr. βοσκός – Alb. *kullotës* (< *kullot* 'βόσκω'), Gr. γαλάρης – Alb. *qumështor*, etc., whereas, in the broader Balkan area we can also find the following names: 'afterbirth' *pometina* (Otok, Завала, Каменица), *posl'ežina* (Пештани), *ľože* (Гега), *p'osl'ɛdәk* (Гела), *ľožę* (Равна), *mul'ojs* (Muhurr), *c'ipë* (Leshnjë), *str'oma* (Ерάτυρα), *cit'ari* (Καστέλλι), *f'uskā* (Κρανιά) (МДАБЯ III 414); 'labour's liquids' *vodeńak* (Otok, Завала, Каменица), *v'oda* (Пештани), *v'odʌ* (Гега), *p'uškʌ* (Гела), *ud'ә* (Равна), *la˞hd* (Muhurr), *l'ëngjet* (Leshnjë), *n'ir'a* (Ерάτυρα), *ner'a* (Καστέλλι), *'api* (Κρανιά) (МДАБЯ III 415), etc.

With this wealth of names at our disposal, we can locate a lot of cases of isosemy. Accordingly, tha Alb. word for 'liver' is *mëlçi*, which can also be found as *mëlçi e zezë, mushkni e zez*. The same word is found in Rum. as *ficat* (cf. Gr. συκώτι and Lat. *ficus*, Gr. σύκον 'fig'), *drobu negru, ficat laiu, ficat negru*, Arom. *h'ikat, hicat negru, h'ikat laiu* (ДОМОСИЛЕЦКАЯ 2002: 332) and as **μαύρο** πλεμόνι 'black lung' in Epirus. More than that, for 'lung' we have Alb. *mushkëri, mushkni e bardh*, **mushia e bardh**, Rum. *plămîn*, **albu h'icat**, *albul drob, drobu alb*, **h'icatu aroşu**, Arom. **hicat alb**, **h'icatu arosu** (ДОМОСИЛЕЦКАЯ 2002: 333), **mëlshi e kuqe**, *mëlshi e zezë* (Çamëri, HAXHIHASANI 1974: 74), etc. We should also refer to some examples of (partial or full) isosemy in the broader Balkan region such as: 'liver' *crna ʒigarica* (Otok), *crni drob* (Каменица), *c'ərn-ʒiger* (Пештани), *crn drop* (Гега), *č'ɔr'ʌn drop* (Гела), *č'er'ęn drop* (Равна), *mulsh'i e zez* (Muhurr), *mëlç'ija e z'ezë* (Leshnjë), *škot' m'avru* (Εράτυρα), *ihk'ati l'āI* (Κρανιά) (МДАБЯ III 630); 'fatty membrane covering the entrails' *km'aish e q'ônzit* (Muhurr), *cip dhj'ami* (Leshnjë), *čk'ep'* (Εράτυρα), *maⁿd'iʌi* (Καστέλλι), *sk''epi, kāme'asā* (Κρανιά) (МДАБЯ III 636); 'tongue-clapper' *ezìčak* (Otok), *iezìk'* (Гега), *iez'ìčę* (Равна), *gjúzë* (Leshnjë), *γlósa* (Ерáτυρα), *límbā*, *límbi* (Κρανιά), as well as *žalo* 'sting' (Каменица), *thum* 'sting' (Muhurr) (МДАБЯ III 288) (внутренияя форма "язык, язычок", "žalo").

Noteworthy is the isosemy in the way employed by shepherds in order to calculate the age of animals. Accordingly, for the animals that are born prematurely or first, the Gr. πρώιμο and Alb. *i lashtë* are used. These words appear as cases of isosemy in the Balkan area: *rańče* (Otok), *ozimče* (Завала), *p'ŗvče* (Kamenitsa), *p'o-staro jágńe* (Пештани), *izimélče* (Гега), *pərvák* (Гела), *kînxh i lasht* (Muhurr), *i láshtë* (Leshnjë), *prójmu* (Ерáτυρα), *protójeno*, *próimo* (Καστέλλι), *protu sugáru, protu n'elu* (МДАБЯ III 82–83, мотивация и внутренияя форма "ранний", "первый, перворожденный", "пережиивший зиму, перезимовавший", "покрытый шерстью"[5]).

Based on this system, an animal that has given birth for the third, fourth, fifth etc. time is named as follows: Gr. απó τρία / τéσσερα / πéντε ... αρνιά / κατσίκια or Alb. *me tre / katër / pesë ... qingja / keca* (of three / four / five ... lambs/kids). In addition to that, the Alb. word *gërshërë* / Gr. ψαλίδια 'shears' is also used, instead of the words *lambs* or *kids*, referring to the shearing of the animals. See also Gr. τριάρ'/τισσάρ' 'three or four-year-old lamb or kid' in Upland Pieria (ΔΟΥΓΑ-ΠΑΠΑΔΟΠΟΥΛΟΥ & TZITZIΛΗΣ 2006: 558, 553), and κατσίκ' απoú τρία χρόνια (ibid. 180). In Crete, according to the number of its litters, the name for the goat or the sheep is πρωτóγεννη, δίγεννη, τρίγεννη etc.; whereas, the ram and the billy-goat are called after their age δίχρονος or δυó χρονώ, τριώ χρονώ or τριώτης or τριώχτης, or δυó λασώ, τριώ λασώ. In Anogeia and Toplou Monastiri, the words δίγεννος, τρíγεννος and the words πρωτóλατος, δíλατος, τρíλατος respectively, are used to describe this matter (ΞΑΝΘΟΥΔΙΔΟΥ 1918: 270). In the broader Balkan area we find a big variety of names: *ovc'a na dr'ugo i̯'agńe, ovc'a na tr'eće i̯'agńe* (Каменица), *o̦fc'ə nʌ ft'oŗo i̯'agn'ẹ, o̦fc'ə nʌ tr''etọ i̯'agn'ẹ* (Равна), *d'ele në di shq'era, d'ele në tre shq'era* (Muhurr), *përbinj'ore* (Leshnjë), *str'ifa, triarnị'a* (Ерáτυρα), *ðefter'ojẹni, trit'ojẹni* (Καστέλλι), *mblo'arā, štr'ifā* (Κρανιά) (МДАБЯ III 417).

Isosemy emerges in the field of various animal diseases. For example, Gr. παρμáρα / Alb. *marrël* 'a disease leading from paralysis to agalactia' (πaíρω / marr 'take'), Gr. κουτσαμáρα / Alb. *çalë* 'lameness', *çalez-a* (Çamëri, HAXHIHASANI 1974: 38), (κουτσαíνω / *çaloj* 'to limp'). Isosemy appears also in names of herbs considering their use or other characteristics: Gr. φιδοβóτανο 'snake-root' (Upland

---

5 The last characteristic, "covered with wool", is quite different from the rest and it is probably the result of wrong interpretation of the adjective *i lasht*, which is not connected to the Alb. word *lesh* 'wool, fleece' but to the adjective *l lushtë* 'πρώιμος/early'. As a result *kinxh i lasht* means 'πρώιμο αρνί/early lamb'. (For the adjective and its meanings see ÇABEJ SE I 308–309).

Pieria, ΔΟΥΓΆ-ΠΑΠΑΔΟΠΟΥΛΟΥ & ΤΖΙΤΖΙΛΉΣ 2006: 581) and Alb. *bar gjarpri* 'id.', Gr. μελισσοβότανο 'melissa'– *bar blete* 'id.' (as well as *melisavato*).

In many cases, based on folklore, the names of various animal diseases or of other factors related to the well-being of the cattle are given euphemistically. Euphemisms are quite common in the languages of the region and we could say that they are one of the main sources of inter-linguistic isosemy. On this basis, we find similar formations in the languages spoken in the region: Alb. *qoftëlargu, largneshi* and Gr. ο οξαποδώ 'he-from-afar, Devil', *qoftëlargu, mospastëpjesi, bukuri i lumit* 'Devil' Myzeqe (NUSHI 1991: 24), *aj me briena* (Mal i Zi, ZYMBERI 1996: 20), το καλόν ζον 'fox' (Rhodes, ΠΑΠΑΧΡΙΣΤΟΔΟΥΛΟΥ 1969: 174), *aj i gardhit, aj i lleut, aj i nargurit, aj i paemni* 'snake' (Mal i Zi, ZYMBERI 1996: 20), *i helmuemi* 'snake' (Mal i Zi, ZYMBERI 1996: 64), *aj i malit, aj i shkâmit, aj ju gu:rt goja* 'wolf' (Mal i Zi, ZYMBERI 1996: 20), *Dora e Zotit* 'God's hand, lightning' (ZYMBERI 1996: 46).

In our opinion, words of the type λυκοσκισμένα [likoskiz'mena], λυκοφαγω-μένα [likofaɣo'mena], usually used as curses of the shepherds to their animals, are related by isosemy. The corresponding words in Albanian are given by the phrases: *ju hëngërt/çaftë ujku!* 'may the wolf eat you up / tear you apart', which are used in similar situations. These words and phrases are widely used in South Albania and Epirus and further research needs to be conducted.[6] The words and phrases we just mentioned shouldn't be treated as the same as the words of Balcanic dissemination that present isosemy: *v'ɔl'k'ǫtǫ m''ɔsu* (Гела), *ʎikofaɣoma* (Καστέλλι), *māngāt'urā di lup* (Κρανιά), that are referred to a specific RO ('what was left of the animal eaten by the wolf') (МДАБЯ III 382–3) (внутренияя форма "волчье мясо", "волчья еда").

A special interesting case of euphemism constitute the names γέννα (Μονο-δέντρι, Σούλι, Πράμαντα, Κανάλι – Epirus) and γέννος (Λιβαδιά, Δρόπολη – South Albania[7]), which derives from the Gr. verb γεννώ 'give birth to', and *ilerm-i, të lerm-it* (< Alb. *lerë*, past participle of *lej* 'give birth to') 'the vagina of the sheep or goat', that appears differently in other regions (θηλυκόν, lit. 'female', in Rhodes, ΠΑΠΑΧΡΙΣΤΟΔΟΥΛΟΥ 1969: 132, *ëmë*, lit. 'mother', in the Arvanitika dialect of Andros, ΓΙΟΧΆΛΑΣ 2000: 253), φύση (< φύω 'grow, sprout') 'penis' (Rhodes,

---

6   For example, compare Alb. *pikërënë* (= të rëntë pika/dambllaja!) and Gr.dial. (Epirus) πικοβαρεμένε (= να σε βαρέσει η πίκα/ ο νταμλάς!) as well as *farëshuar* (= t'u shoftë fara!) and σβημένε (= να σβήσεις!). Find more in KOSTALLARI 1972, ΑΝΔΡΙΩΤΗΣ 1932, QIRJAZI 2004.

7   These data can be found in the material we gathered during the field research conducted in the broader Pindos Mountain region within the framework of the program "Cultural contact and terminology of mobile shepherds" (2007–2010), with the financial support of Austrian Science Fund, see homepage: http://www.oeaw.ac.at/balkan/projekte_hirten.htm .

ΠΑΠΑΧΡΙΣΤΟΔΟΥΛΟΥ 1969: 132), *currulaq* (Çamëri, HAXHIHASANI 1974: 38), *cu-laq, curlaq* 'penis' (Alb. dial. of South Italy, GIORDANO 1963: 55). Cf. also *t' lem-it* 'pudens' (Hot, SHKURTAJ 1974: 411), *véte e déles* (Muhurr, Leshnjë), *jéna* (Καστέλλι), *bìstā* (МДАБЯ III 70), *vete* (Labëri), also *limzë* and *klemëz* 'vagina', as well as *letht (të)* and *lemcë* 'matrice degli animali', in several spots in the North Albania, linked by ÇABEJ (SE I 313) with the verb *me le* 'give birth'. It should be noted that the naming mechanism is common in above mentioned languages and originates from broader social conventions and traditions (DUKOVA 1980, ASSE-NOVA 1992, CIVJAN 2000). We should note that shepherds find it hard to speak about such things! Some of the verbs referring to the mating of domesticated animals are also formed by euphemism. The verbs *kërkon* / ζητάει, γυρεύει 'is asking', *merr cjap* / παίρει τράγο 'taking a buck' and *merr dash* / παίρει κριάρι 'taking a ram' are quite frequent in the region in question (Labëri, Çamëri, Πράμαντα, Κανάλι, Λιβαδιά, Δρόπολη), but this does not mean that there are no other words similar in meaning (e.g. *këcej* / πηδάω 'to jump') or that they are not used in other Albanian-speaking or Greek-speaking areas. For example, [the sheep] *hiqet* / Gr. τραβιέται, σέρει, *ja këcen dashi* / Gr. την πηδάει το κριάρι (Çamëri, HAXHIHASANI 1974: 72); *merr* "thuhet për delen, lopën, kur mbarsen / used for the pregnant sheep or cow" (Pukë, TOPALLI 1974: 198); *m'u ma:rr mrapa* 'is made pregnant' used euphemistically for all the animals of the Albanian-speaking populations of Monte-negro, as well as the following euphemism: *me ra n'dash* / lit. 'falls on a ram' (**ndërzehet** delja 'the ewe gets pregnant'), *me ra n'sjap* / lit. 'falls on a billy goat' (**përçitet** dhia 'the goat gets pregnant') (ZYMBERI 1996: 97). Nevertheless, we do not find such use of these verbs in the Arvanitika dialect of Andros (ΓΙΟΧΆΛΑΣ 2000: 347, verb *marr*) or such frequent use in Aegean islands. For example, in Kos, οι προυάτθες / κατσίκες γυρεύγκουν or τα ζα είναι στολ λατόν τους (ΚΑΡΑΝΑΣΤΆΣΗΣ 1994: 60), in Crete, is used the verb λάμω or λάμνω 'coire' (< Anc.Gr. ἐλάύνω): οι τράγοι/κριγιοί λάμουν τσ' αίγες/τα πρόβατα. Τα θηλυκά λάμουνται or λάσουνται (ΞΑΝΘΟΥΔΊΔΟΥ 1918: 274). Cf. also the verb σέρνου (for big animals) 'be at heat' in Upland Pieria (ΔΟΥΓΆ-ΠΑΠΑΔΟΠΟΎΛΟΥ & ΤΖΙΤΖΙΛΉΣ 2006: 510) and *helq*, *vërgon* 'coire' in Myzeqe (NUSHI 1991: 266), where the verbs *helq* and σέρνου are isosemic. This case of isosemy (ζητάει/γυρεύει) is characteristic for the broader Balkan region: *tráži* (Каменица), *kërkón* (Muhurr), *zìtise* (Καστέλλι) (МДАБЯ III 74, внутренияя форма "искать, требовать").

Let's say now a few words about the isosemy and the metaphorical usage of words. In the material that we have gathered, can be found cases of isosemy related to *realia* from the everyday activities of the cattle-breeders: μάτι της στρούγκας and *siu i shtrungës* 'eye of the pen', literally 'the point of the pen through which animals pass in order to be milked', that appear in Epirus and South Albania (see also *sy i pranverës* / 'eye of the spring', ZYMBERI 1996: 117), or cases that are related to human traits: πρόβειος / *i leshtë* lit. 'sheepish' and metaph. 'mild, good', Gr.dial.

αρνάνθρουπους 'calm and quiet man' (ΔΟΥΓΆ-ΠΑΠΑΔΟΠΟΥΛΟΥ & ΤΖΙΤΖΙΛΉΣ 2006: 187) and Alb. *është qengj* 'είναι αρνί / he or she is a lamb', Gr.dial. κουπριά lit. 'dung', metaph. 'lazy' (ΔΟΥΓΆ-ΠΑΠΑΔΟΠΟΥΛΟΥ & ΤΖΙΤΖΙΛΉΣ 2006: 353) and Alb. *plehra* 'mean' (< *pleh* 'κοπριά'), etc.

The names that are formed based on procedures of metonymy are considered as cases of isosemy as well. For instance: βδέλλα, βδελλίαση are the Greek names for fluke, the disease that attacks sheep and that according to the folk perception it is caused by leeches/βδελλες in swampy grasslands. In the same manner, in Myzeqe, central Albania, the word *moçal* means both 'swampland' and 'fluke'; whereas, the verb *moçalitet* means 'suffers from fluke', cf. Gr. βδελλιάζει (NUSHI 1991: 163). In the two previous examples, the procedure of metonymy is led by the cause to the result, but there are also cases of inverse direction. For instance, in Upland Pieria the word ϱλαβάτσα means not only 'fluke' but also 'yellow wild flowers that cause it' (ΔΟΥΓΆ-ΠΑΠΑΔΟΠΟΥΛΟΥ & ΤΖΙΤΖΙΛΉΣ 2006: 256). Continuing with the presentation of more examples, we have to add that in Myzeqe are used the Alb.dial. words *strugë* 'pen' (Gr. στρούγκα) and *strunjë* 'can used during milking' (cf. Gr.dial. στρουγκιά 'id.'); whereas, in the North-West end of the Albanian-speaking area the word *shtrug* is used for both pen (στρούγκα) and milking can (ZYMBERI 1996: 151). This can is called *mjelc* (< Alb. *mjel* 'milk, draw') in Vuthaj, North Albania (ZYMBERI ibid.) and this can be compared with the Gr. word αρμεγός 'the can used during milking' (Gr. αρμέγω 'milk, draw'), which appears in Crete (ΞΑΝ-ΘΟΥΔΊΔΟΥ 1918: 279).

The relations between isosemy and etymology present another interesting issue. As we have already seen, the existence of isosemy in a certain semantic field can provide us with better verificaton of the etymon of specific words. For example, a part of lamb's or goat's stomach, with a lot of folds, is named in Gr. βηλάρια (< βηλάρι 'strip'), δίπλες (< δίπλα 'fold'), κακοπλύτης 'part of the stomach that is difficult to wash because of its multiple folds' (ΞΑΝΘΟΥΔΊΔΟΥ 1918: 307) and in Alb. *qitap* (< Turk. *kitap* 'book'), *fletës, fletosh* (< *fletë* 'sheet'), *petës, petanik* (< *petë* 'pastry sheet'), *nânpeç* (< nând-petësh 'with nine sheets') (ZYMBERI 1996: 106), *nâtnuse* (< nând-nuse 'with nine brides') (ZYMBERI 1996: 107), etc. In çamërisht they call it *fletosh, musaf, shtatë nuse,* and *frrutat e paçait* 'the folds of stomach', where the word *frrutat* is the same with the Greek φρούτα (η) 'knitted decorations on the border of a textile', which comes from Ancient Macedonian ἀβροῦτες ὀφρῦς Hesychius (ΤΖΙΤΖΙΛΉΣ 2008: 228–230). Note that this word appears in several South Albanian idioms that are characterized by the diachronic contact with the Greek language of Epirus and West Macedonia (*frytë* 'pala në fund të një rrobe/id.' (Devoll, ΧΗΑÇΚΑ 1958: 203), *frutë* 'id.' South. Alb. (TASE 2006: 85). Another interesting case is that of the Gr.dial. words κουκουφρίκους and κουφρίκους, which mean '1. πρωτόγαλα / colostrum' and 2. 'The crust formed on the surface of boiled milk' respectively. These words are found in Upland Pieria

(ΔΟΥΓΑ-ΠΑΠΑΔΟΠΟΥΛΟΥ & ΤΖΙΤΖΙΛΗΣ 2006: 346, 361) as well as in Epirus, cf. κουκουφρίγκ' 'a type of scratch / κουλιάστρα', which is a kind of dessert made of colostrum (ΜΠΟΓΚΑΣ 1964: Α 180, see also the word κουκουφρίγκος in Ναύπακτος, Μπόγκας ibid.), κουρφίγκους/'ewe's colostrum' (Χώσεψη, Άρτα, ΜΠΟΓΚΑΣ 1964: Α 188), κόρφιγκας 'κολιάστρα' (Δέλβινο, ΣΠΥΡΟΥ 2008: 380, found as well as γκουλιάστρα, 347, and νωπούρα 'colostrum', 418), κορφίγγ(ι) 'dense pie made of colostrum' (Τζουμέρκα, ΠΑΠΑΚΙΤΣΟΣ 2006: 116, as well as ήγκαιρο 'πρωτόγαλο'/'early colostrum', 88). According to ARAVANTINOS, there are the words κολλάστρα and γλοιάστρα for 'ewe's colostrum' (1909: 50) and the word γλοιάστρα for the dessert made of ewe's colostrum (1909: 33); however, in Çamëri is used the word *groviqe* 'një lloj tëmbële që bëhet me **qumështin e parë**' [cf. Gr. πρωτόγαλα] (kulloshtrën): **klloshtrën** *e hedh në një tepsi edhe e pjek në furrë e bënet* **groviqe**' (HAXHIHASANI 1974: 49). As a result, we realize that the words κουλιάστρα/γλοιάστρα are used in Epirus for both πρωτόγαλα/colostrum and for a kind of dessert made of it; whereas in çamërisht, the first is given as *qumësht i parë* and *klloshtër* and the second is given as *groviqe* [gro'viçe], which probably derives from the Bulg. dial. word коврнг 'малко кравайче, което раздават на коледари', which is found also as кофръг, коврнк (БЕР II 512). If the interpretation given above is correct[8], then we can assume that, in the case of the words κουφρίκους/κόρφιγκας (< Bulg. кофръг), the use of the name of the product is extended to the raw material, following the exactly opposite procedure compared to the case of γλοιάστρα 'πρωτόγαλα' → γλοιάστρα 'είδος γλυκίσματος από πρωτόγαλα'.[9] As far as the word κουκουφρίγκος is concerned, there is a possibility that it is a result of intermingling of the words κουρφίγκος and κουρ'φή (κορυφή) 'ανθόγαλα'/' cream', which appear in the broader region of Epirus (ΜΠΟΓΚΑΣ 1964: Α 188) and present cases of isosemy with other Balkan languages, such as the Albanian (see **kre** [krye 'κεφαλή, κορυφή'] *tamli*, Pukë, TOPALLI 1974: 329). Accordingly, we can make the hypothesis of a possible evolution of the words *κουρφου-κουρφίγκους > *κουρκουφρίγκους > κουκουφρίγκους, based on the similar example of the words κουρφουκέφαλου (κορυφοκέφαλο) > κουρκουκέφαλου 'η κορυφή του κεφαλιού, όπου συστρέφονται οι τρίχες'/ 'top of the head where the hairs make a twist' (ΜΠΟΓΚΑΣ 1964: Α 189).

Referring to the relation between etymology and isosemy we need to examine the cases of folk etymology that are worth being examined due to the fact that they may become useful regarding the scientific etymology. For example, a folk etymology from the pastoral terminology (μαρκαλώ 'coire' < *marr kal(ë)* lit. 'take horse'), is adopted by Ανδριώτης and Μπαμπινιώτης in their etymological dic-

---

8 Note that the Romanian word *covrig* 'produs alimentar în formă de inel, de opt etc.' also derives from the Bulgarian *kovrig* (DEXLR 1998: 234).

9 For the procedure of its production see ΜΠΟΓΚΑΣ 1964: Α 180.

tionaries (1983: 200, 2010: 821 respectively), besides the fact that it has many flaws.[10] In Greek (Epirus, Macedonia, Thessaly, Peloponnesus), we find the verbs μαρκαλώ/-ίζω / μαρκαλιέμαι, προυτσαλώ/-ίζω / προυτσαλιέμαι, which derive from the Slavic (Old Slavic мръкати 'meckern, brünstig sein', bulg. пръчамъ ce 'sie paaren sich', serb. прчами 'sich begatten', MEYER 1894: II 39, 53). Furthermore, we mention the word *mëndër* 'kasolle ku mbahen dhentë me qengjat që mënden / 'cottage for the sheep and lambs that are being breast-fed', which appears in Myzeqe (NUSHI 1991: 159) and derives from the Greek word μάντρα; nonetheless, here it is connected to the Albanian word *mënd* 'breast-feed'. It is known that in Greek the word Γενάρης (< lat. januarius) / 'January' was shaped by "the influence of the verb γεννώ/'give birth', because during that period of the year the sheep give birth" (ΑΝΔΡΙΩΤΗΣ 1983: 63). In Rhodes, this month is called Γεννολοητής which has the meaning that was just mentioned (ΠΑΠΑΧΡΙΣΤΟΔΟΥΛΟΥ 1969: 159).

The sampling comparison of the PV of Pindos region and the PV of the Aegean islands region and Northern Albania, shows us that there are similarities, but there are many differences too. For instance, in Rhodes they say λάμνει 'looks for intercourse' (< Anc.Gr. ἐλαύνω), έλασε 'got pregnant', λατός (ο) 'τα πράττα είναι στολ λατόν τους' = είναι εποχή που λάμνουν/'they are going through their reproductive period', λατάρι(ν) 'stallion' (ΠΑΠΑΧΡΙΣΤΟΔΟΥΛΟΥ 1969: 132), πιάννει το ζον 'gets pregnant', γριά or γρία 'το ανθόγαλα' / 'cream' (Anc.Gr. γραῦς), πρωτόγαλη and πρωτούαλη / 'colostrum' ... 'kind of dessert' (ΠΑΠΑΧΡΙΣΤΟΔΟΥΛΟΥ 1969: 133, 179), etc. As observed by Ξανθουδίδης, a century ago, in Crete: «Ούτε αλβανικαί, ούτε σλαβικαί, ούτε βλαχικαί λέξεις ευρίσκονται εν τη ποιμενική ... ονοματολογία ...»/"The pastoral terminology does not contain Albanian, Slavic or Aromanian words ..." (ΞΑΝΘΟΥΔΙΔΟΥ 1918: 268). Moreover, in the North-West end of the Albanian speaking region appear the words *ângërr* 'membrane that covers the entrails' (GAZULLI 1941: 164), *bun* 'the part of the cottage where the sheep rest' (ZYMBERI 1996: 32), *dban* 'cottage of shepherds in mountain grasslands' (ZYMBERI 1996: 42), which are not found in the dialect of South Albania. Unlike other places, here the word *kokërr* 'grain' is used as a unit of measurement: 'Sa kokrra dele, llên-dhên-berre i ke?'/'How many sheep do you have?', instead of the word krye-krenë-krerë 'heads' (ZYMBERI 1996: 43).

The general examination of the material we have gathered leads to the conclusion that, in the level of the isosemy of the pastoral terminology, there are more

---

10 Why from *marr kalë* and not from *marr dash* or *marr cjap*; What is the etymon, for example, of the verb προυτσαλώ, which belongs to the same semantic field? To what extent has the influence of neighbouring languages in Greek, in this particular field, been examined? Note that along with the Albanian *marr dash/cjap* there are the Greek παίρω κριάρι/τράγο, that are located in a broader frame of isosemy, showed by the phrases *marr burrë / marr grua* and παίρ(ν)ω άντρα / παίρ(ν)ω γυναίκα 'παντρεύομαι'/ 'get married'.

differences between the continental and the Aegean regions of Greece than between continental Greece and specific non-Greek speaking parts of the Balkan hinterland. This ascertainment agrees with the general historical and geographic conditions and special characteristics of the regions in question. The territorial continuity of the Pindos Mountains in the Balkan hinterland facilitated the mobility and contact of the native populations, creating the conditions for diffusion and convergence of the languages of the broader region.[11] On the other hand, the inhabitants of the South Aegean islands didn't move to locations far from their homeland. As a result, their pastoral terminology remained highly conservative (many elements of the Ancient Greek survived in these idioms) and wasn't influenced by the dialects of continental Greece or the other Balkan languages.[12] It is possible that inter-linguistic isosemy is more intense within the areas where different languages/ dialects come to contact; while it is limited as we move to one-language speaking areas.

It needs to be stressed that the conclusions presented here are only indicative. Thus, conducting further research, gathering new material and enriching the theoretical background are mandatory. Basic condition for the achievement of this goal remains the composition and edition of dialectological atlases for the languages that don't have as well as conducting monographies for particular dialects[13], languages or language groups.[14]

11 Cases of isosemy such as the Gr. χειμαδιό (< χειμώνας, χειμάζω), Alb. **dimn**ishtë (< dimën, dimnoj), Gr. χειμάζω, Alb. **dimër**oj/**dimn**oj, Rum. a **iern**a, Arum. **arn**ari (ДО-
МОСИЛЕЦКАЯ 2002: 184), Gr. ξεκαλοκαιριάζω, Alb. **ver**oj, **behar**oj (ДОМОСИЛЕЦКАЯ 2002: 192) derive from the habit of the populations of the region to move their animals from the plains to the mountains and vice versa and are not found or are very limited in the Aegean islands.

12 «... Ούτε *στρούγκαν* ούτε *τσέλιγκαν* ούτε *λάγιο* ούτε *γκιόσα* ούτε *άλλα* κοινά εν τη Στερεά και τη Πελοποννήσω ποιμενικά ξενόφωνα ρήματα [= λέξεις] λέγει ούτε ακούει ούτε εννοεί ο βοσκός της Κρήτης, ενώ τουναντίον καθ' εκάστην έχει ανά στόμα το *σακάζω* ['αποκόβω το αρνί/κατσίκι απ' τη μάνα του'] και το *αρνοκλήσιν* ['έκκληση για προσφορά ζώων με σκοπό την αντικατάσταση απολεσθέντος κοπαδιού'], και τα *έγγαλα* ['γαλάρια'] και τον *στειρονόμον* ['ο βόσκων τα στείρα'] και τον *έριφον* ['κατσίκι πριν χρονιάσει κι αφού απογαλακτιστεί'] και το *αρνόθηλο* [θηλυκό αρνί πριν χρονιάσει και αφού απογαλακτισθεί'] και την *απαλλαγήν* ['πρόβατο ή γίδα μετά τη γέννα'] και το *κουμιάζω* ['κλείνω αρνί ή κατσίκι σε ειδικό χώρο για να μη φάει χορτάρι και μόνο να θηλάζει'] και τον *οδηγόν* ['ζωόμορφο στοιχειό για το οποίο πιστεύουν ότι παρακολουθεί και προστατεύει το ποίμνιον'] και τον *γάλλην* ['κριός άνευ κεράτων και κρυψόρχις']... και πλείστα άλλα αρχαιοπρεπή ονόματα και ρήματα» (ΞΑΝΘΟΥΔΙΔΟΥ 1918: 268).

13 For example, there is a need for the Modern Greek dialectological atlas. On the contrary, the recent edition of the Dialectological Atlas of the Albanian (ADGjSh, 2008) provides us with important information regarding the pastoral terminology of this lan-

Comparative semantics, and the examination of isosemy (and un-isosemy) in this framework, starts in an intralingual level, develops in a narrower level (for languages/dialects that are genetically related or have been in contact for a long time) and is directed to a broader region, covering basic semantic fields and helping us to understand the way(s) our language(s) organize(s) the world.

References

ADGjSh: GJINARI, J.; BECI, B.; SHKURTAJ, Gj.; GOSTURANI, Xh.: *Atlasi Dialektologjik i Gjuhës Shqipe* I–II, 2008. Tiranë.

ANDRIOTIS, N. (1974): *Lexikon der Archaismen in neugriechischen Dialekten*. Wien.

ASSENOVA, P. (1992): La mentalité balkanique: vues de l''homo balcanicus' sur certaines qualités humaines. *Linguistique Balkanique* XXXV, 3–4. 97–113.

ASSENOVA, P. (1993): Gr. δεμένος. Paralleles balkaniques et origins mythologiques. *Studies in Greek Linguistics*. Thessaloniki. 510–524.

ASENOVA, P. (2002): *Балканско езикознание*. Veliko Tărnovo.

БЕР: *Български Етимологичен Речник*. София, 1971–.

BURKHART, D. (1989): *Kulturraum Balkan. Studien zur Volkskunde und Literatur Südosteuropas*. Berlin, Hamburg.

CIVJAN, T. (2000): L'espace ethno-linguistique des Balkans. In: Chr. Tzitzilis, Ch. Symeonidis (eds): *Balkanlinguistik. Synchronie und Diachronie*. Thessaloniki. 53–58.

ÇABEJ, E. (1976–2006): *Studime etimologjike në fushë të shqipes*, I–IV, VI, VII, Tiranë.

ÇABEJ, E. (1976/77, 1987): *Studime gjuhësore*, I–VI, Prishtinë 1976–77, VII. Prishtinë 1987.

guage and its relations with the neighbouring languages. Accordingly, a group of words belongs to the whole Albanian speaking area (*dash* 'ram', *dhi* 'goat', *cjap* 'billy-goat', *qengj* 'lamb', *shytë* 'goat without horns', *gjizë* 'cream cheese', *ftujë, ftujake* 'one year old kid/goat', *shtrungë* 'pen', *gunë* 'sleeveless long overcoat', *stan* 'stockyard', etc.), others belong to only one dialect (tosk.: *qumësht* 'milk', *gjalpë* 'butter', *ajkë/alkë* 'cream', *kec* 'kid', *derr* 'pig', *milor* 'one year old lamb', geg.: *tambël* 'milk', *tlyn* 'butter', *maze* 'cream', *edh* 'kid', *thi* 'pig') and others present a more complex distribution (e.g. *mullëz* 'rennet', south of Shkumbin river and Kosovo; while, the word *rëndë* 'id.' north, as well as *farë djathi*. The words *tundës* και *tundje* 'milk-churn' between Vjosë and Shkumbin, north the word *mëti, pëti, fti, ti*, and in the north east end the word *tunaç*. In the northern part of Vjosa river and in its southern part the words *dubek, dybek, dibek;* whereas, in the south end the words *vlladë, çube*. The word *vathë* is found mainly in Albania; while, in Kosovo as *torisht-a*, in central Albania as *thark-a*, from Tepeleni and under the word *nome* appears. To close with, there is an interesting case in which the same word is used in both dialects with different meanings (*ajkë/alkë* 'wool's dirt' in the north and 'cream' in the south of Shkumbin river).

14 It is meant that the cases of isosemy between neighbouring dialects belonging to different languages are expected to be more than those that are located when the standard forms of these languages are compared.

DEXLR: *Dicționarul explicativ al limbii române*. București 1998.

ДОМОСИЛЕЦКАЯ, М. В. (2002): *Албанско-Восточнороманский сопоставительный понятый словарь. Скотоводческая лексика*. Санкт-Петербург.

DUKOVA, U. (1980): Gemeinsame Termini in der Folklore der Balkanvölker. *Lingustique balkanique* XXIII/2. 5–12.

Fjalor 2006: *Fjalor i Gjuhës Shqipe*. Tiranë.

FjSin 2007: DHRIMO, A.; TUPJA, E.; YMERI, E.: *Fjalor Sinonimik i Gjuhës Shqipe*. Tiranë.

GAZULLI, D. N. (1941): *Fjalorth i Ri*. Tiranë.

GIORDANO, E. (1963): *Fjalor i Arbëreshëve t'Italisë*. Bari.

HAXHIHASANI, Q. (1974): Vështrim i përgjithshëm mbi të folmen e banorëve të Çamërisë. *Dialektologjia Shqiptare* II. Tiranë. 3–132.

HULD, M. E. (1984): *Basic albanian etymologies*. Los Angeles.

KAHL, Thede (2007): *Hirten in Kontakt. Sprach- und Kulturwandel ehemalige Wanderhirten (Albanisch, Aromunisch, Griechisch)*. Wien, Berlin: LIT-Verlag.

KOSTALLARI, A. (1972): Kompozitat dëshirore dhe urdhërore të shqipes. *Studime mbi leksikun dhe mbi formimin e fjalëve në gjuhën shqipe* I. Tiranë. 153–195.

МДАБЯ. *Малый Диалектологический Атлас Балканских Языков. Серия лексическая. Том. III. Животноводство*. Ред. А. Соболев. Санкт-Петербург, München 2009.

MEYER, G. (1891): *Etymologisches Wörterbuch der albanesischen Sprache*. Strassburg.

MEYER, G. (1894/95): *Neugriechische Studien*, I 1894, II 1894, III 1895, IV 1895. Wien.

MUÇA, F. (1987): E folmja e krahinës së Konispolit. *Dialektologjia Shqiptare* V. 281–362.

NUSHI, J. (1991): *Fjalë popullore nga Myzeqeja*. Tiranë.

OREL, V. (1998): *Albanian Etymological Dictionary*. Boston, Köln.

QIRJAZI, Dh. (2004): Ndikime të shoqishoqme a zhvillime paralele? Vështrim krahasues në fjalë popullore me semantikë dëshirore të greqishtes dhe të shqipes. In: *Seminari ndërkombëtar për gjuhën, letërsinë dhe kulturën shqiptare* 22/1. Prishtinë. 248–257.

SANDFELD, Kr. (1930): *Linguistique balkanique (Problèmes et Résultats)*. Paris.

SCHRÖPFER, F. (1956): Zur inneren Sprachform der Balkanvölker. *Zeitschrift für Slawistik* I. 139–151.

СЕМЧИНСКИЙ, С. (1973): *Семантическая интерференция языков (На материале славяно-восточнороманских языковых контактов)*. Автореферат диссертации, Киев.

СЕМЧИНСКИЙ, С. (1976): Межязыковая изосемия в языках и диалектах карпатсково ареала. In: *Общекарпатский диалектологический атлас*. Москва. 36–42.

СЕМЧИНСКИЙ, С. (1977): Лексико-семантические интерференции славянсково произношения в дакороманском ареале. In: *Ареальные исследования в языкознании и этнографии*. Москва. 119–127.

SHKURTAJ, Gj. (1974): E folmja e Hotit. *Dialektologjia Shqiptare* II. 344–428.

TASE, P. (1941): *Fjalorth i Ri. Fjalë të rralla të përdorura në jug të Shqipnis*. Tiranë.

TASE, P. (2006): *Fjalor dialektor me fjalë e shprehje nga Jugu i Shqipërisë*. Tiranë.

TOPALLI, Xh. (1974): Disa vërejtje për të folmen e krahinës së Pukës. *Dialektologjia Shqiptare* II. 282–343.

TZITZILIS, Chr. (2001). Methodische Bemerkungen zu den Lehnübertragungen in den Balkansprachen. *Linguistique balkanique* XLI/1. 41–53.

XHAÇKA, V. (1958): Një shikim mbi të folmen e krahinës së Devollit. *BUSHT, Seria e Shkencave Shoqërore* 2. 196–209.

ZYMBERI, A. (1996): *Leksiku bujqësor e blegtoral i të folmeve shqipe të Malit të Zi*. Prishtinë.

ΑΝΔΡΙΩΤΗΣ, Ν. (1932): Συμβολή εις την μελέτην των ρηματικών επιθέτων της νέας ελληνικής. *Αθήνα* 44. 193–222.

ΑΝΔΡΙΩΤΗΣ, Ν. (1983): *Ετυμολογικό Λεξικό της Κοινής Νεοελληνικής*. Θεσσαλονίκη.

ΑΡΑΒΑΝΤΙΝΟΣ, Π. (1909): *Ηπειρωτικόν γλωσσάριον*. Αθήνα.

ΓΙΟΧΑΛΑΣ, Τ. (2000): *Άνδρος – Αρβανίτες και Αρβανίτικα*. Αθήνα.

ΔΟΥΓΑ-ΠΑΠΑΔΟΠΟΥΛΟΥ, Ε.; ΤΖΙΤΖΙΛΗΣ, Χ. (2006): *Το γλωσσικό ιδίωμα της Ορεινής Πιερίας*. Θεσσαλονίκη.

ΚΑΡΑΝΑΣΤΑΣΗ, Α. (1956): Ποιμενικά της Κω. *Λαογραφία Στ'.* 21–104.

ΜΠΑΜΠΙΝΙΩΤΗΣ, Γ. (2010): *Ετυμολογικό Λεξικό της Νέας Ελληνικής Γλώσσας*. Αθήνα.

ΜΠΟΓΚΑΣ, Ε. (1964–66): *Τα γλωσσικά ιδιώματα της Ηπείρου, Α΄ + Β΄.* Ιωάννινα.

ΞΑΝΘΟΥΔΙΔΟΥ, Σ. (1918): Ποιμενικά Κρήτης. *Λεξικογραφικόν Αρχείον της Μέσης και Νέας Ελληνικής, Ε'.* 267–323.

ΠΑΠΑΚΙΤΣΟΣ, Χρ. Αρ. (2006): *Από τη τζουμερκιώτικη λαλιά στη λαϊκή μας παράδοση*. Αθήνα.

ΠΑΠΑΧΡΙΣΤΟΔΟΥΛΟΥ, Χρ. Ι. (1969): Λεξικογραφικά και λαογραφικά Ρόδου. *Λαογραφία*. Παράρτημα 7. Αθήνα.

ΣΠΥΡΟΥ, Α. (2008): *Το ελληνικό γλωσσικό ιδίωμα της περιοχής Δελβίνου και Αγίων Σαράντα*. Αθήνα.

ΤΖΙΤΖΙΛΗΣ, Χρ. (2008): Τα αρχαία μακεδονικά στοιχεία στο ιδίωμα της ορεινής Πιερίας. Στο Μ. Θεοδωροπούλου: *Θέρμη και Φως*. Αφιερωματικός τόμος στη μνήμη του Α.-Φ. Χριστίδη. Θεσσαλονίκη. 225–244.

Kreativität sprachlicher Mittel im Balkanraum

Corinna LESCHBER (Berlin)

I. Einführung

An Beispielen aus der Umgangssprache, die aus selbst vorgenommenen aktuellen Erhebungen mit Sprechern mehrerer Balkansprachen stammen, werden im Folgenden – vorwiegend auf der lexikalischen Ebene – Merkmale sprachlicher Kreativität aufgezeigt. Dies berührt die Bereiche des Sprachkontaktes und der Etymologie, der Semantik und der Expressivität spezifisch umgangssprachlicher Erscheinungen, sowie die Frage, inwieweit sich Parallelen zu universell nachweisbaren Verfahren sprachlicher Kreativität ziehen lassen. Der lockere und lustige Umgang mit Sprache – der ja häufig der sprachlichen Kreativität zu Grunde liegt – ist im Allgemeinen ein geeignetes Mittel, um sich in den „Geist" einer Region einzufühlen. Mit dem vorliegenden Beitrag verbindet sich die Hoffnung, dies für das Balkangebiet verdeutlichen zu können. Insbesondere wird die Synonymenhäufigkeit für bestimmte Konzepte, die Etymologisierung von Personenbezeichnungen, Personenbezeichnungen mit sexueller Komponente und solche mit türkischer Etymologie, Beispiele für Personenbezeichnungen im Rudari-Rumänischen, und anlässlich dessen die Funktion des Schimpfens generell verdeutlicht. Es stehen umgangssprachliche Bezeichnungen für 'Geld' und 'stehlen', Slangausdrücke im Trinkermilieu, und – aus universeller Perspektive – Verfahren zur Integration entlehnter lexikalischer Elemente im Fokus, sowie die Themen Neumotivierungen und Reduplikationen, regionale und semantische Differenzierungen im Gebrauch von Turzismen, Konstruktionen mit zwei Präpositionen in der Umgangssprache, gruppeninterne Verhaltensnormen. Das Mischen von Sprachen im Diskurs, Besonderheiten des Rudari-Rumänischen, speziell bei der Bildung von Lehnverben werden beschrieben und eine typologisch seltene Erscheinung bei der Integration von Lehnverben.

Was ist sprachliche Kreativität?

Besonders die Definitionen der sprachlichen Kreativität in MUNAT (2007: XIII) rufen uns die verschiedenen Faktoren, die hierbei eine Rolle spielen, ins Bewusstsein:

> 'über welche individuellen sprachlichen Möglichkeiten ein Sprecher verfüge, z.B. Zwei- oder Mehrsprachigkeit, sein Zugriff auf mehrere Stilregister, seine

Fähigkeit zum Einschätzen der Wirkung sprachlicher Mittel im sozialen Kontext. Sprachliche Kreativität zeichne sich hiernach durch Originalität, durch das Erzielen komischer oder zumindest überraschender Effekte aus. Der *lexikalischen* Kreativität komme dabei sicher die wichtigste Rolle zu. Die Wortbildung sei ein mächtiges Mittel der lexikalischen Kreativität, wobei die Benennungsfunktion die primäre und die bekannteste Funktion sei. Daneben könnten ad-hoc-Bildungen beobachtet werden. Sprachliche Kreativität wird als fortdauernder Prozess definiert, in dem die Sprecher auf eine begrenzte Anzahl vorhandener Einheiten zurückgreifen könnten, und daraus eine [beinahe] unbegrenzte Zahl neuer und phantasievoller Lösungen schafften, um ihre momentanen kommunikativen Bedürfnisse zu erfüllen' (in MUNAT 2007: XIV nach POPE 2005: XV als „Kreativität im Sinne von CHOMSKY").

Linguistische Kreativität ist „nicht nur das Produkt der Schaffenskraft eines Sprechers, sondern eine Wechselwirkung zwischen dem Sprecher, der die Bauelemente des Systems umkombiniert, und dem Hörer, der die Bedeutung rekonstruiert, und sich dabei auf sprachliches und soziokulturelles Wissen stützt" (siehe dazu die ausführliche Diskussion in CARTER 2004). LAMB (1998: 205) definiert „wirkliche [sprachliche] Kreativität als die Erfindung neuer Lexeme für neue oder alte Konzepte, indem (uns) dies erlaubt, neue Konzepte zu erstellen, wobei auf Ideen zurückgegriffen werden kann, diese dann in unser konzeptionelles System integriert werden, und zwar in einer Weise, wie diese zuvor nicht miteinander verbunden, bzw. in einem Zusammenhang gebraucht wurden". BENCZES (2006: 7) identifiziert in ähnlicher Weise Kreativität „als unsere Fähigkeit, neue Assoziationen, Verbindungen zwischen Konzepten zu schaffen, die auf Ähnlichkeit, Analogie oder Kontiguität beruhen"; BUSSMANN (2002: 376) liefert die folgende Definition der Kontiguität: „in der Semantik [eine] Relation zwischen Lexemen, die der gleichen semantischen [...] Ebene angehören (nach MUNAT 2007: XIV). Lexikalische Kreativität wird nach MUNAT (ibd.) und LIPKA (2007: 3) als „Zusammenspiel zwischen einer gegebenen Kommunikation oder sozialen Umgebung und der Manipulation des Systems durch einen Sprecher gesehen, in dem dieser neue Wörter prägt, bestehende Ausdrücke neu- bzw. rekombiniert oder neue Konzepte formt".

Die lexikalische Innovation

Nach LYONS (cf. BAUER 1983) ist Produktivität – regel*bestimmte* Innovation, während Kreativität – regel*verändernde* Innovation ist.

Die vier Kategorien der lexikalischen Innovation sind die folgenden:
1. morpho-semantische Neologismen, hauptsächlich die Wortbildung betreffend
2. semantische Neologismen oder semantischer Transfer – wie Metapher und Metonymie
3. morphologische Neologismen, d.h. Reduktionsprozesse wie:

a) Ausschneiden (engl. clipping)
b) Mischen/Verbinden (engl. blending)
c) Akronymie (ein Akronym ist ein Kurzwort, das aus den Anfangsbuchstaben mehrerer Wörter zusammengesetzt ist)
4. externe lexikalische Innovation, d.h. auf lexikalische Entlehnungen zurückgehend (cf. LIPKA 2007: 3, LIPKA 2002: 109).

II. Erhebung und Informanten

Mit der Erhebungsmethode der teilnehmenden Beobachtung wurde der Sprachgebrauch von Sprechern mehrerer Gruppen untereinander über längere Zeiträume hinweg beobachtet, die von mehreren Monaten bis zu mehreren Jahren (mit Unterbrechungen) reichen. Dabei handelt es sich um

1. **[Mak]** Sprecher aus einer **makedonischen Gruppe**: ethnische Roma aus Makedonien/Skopje, Sprachkompetenz: Makedonisch und Türkisch im Wechsel,
2. **[Rud]** einige **rumänischsprachige serbische Rudari-Gruppen**, a) aus dem Gebiet von Paraćin/Serbien, jeweils zur Hälfte in Serbien/zur Hälfte in Deutschland lebend, ältere Verwandte ständig in Serbien lebend. Private Kontakte mit der eigenen Gruppe und mit einigen Serben, b) aus dem Gebiet von Kruševac/Serbien stammend, c) bereits als Binnenmigranten aus dem angestammten Siedlungsgebiet im südlichen Zentralserbien nach Belgrad umgesiedelt,
3. **[Serb]** eine Gruppe **serbischer Sprecher**; einige der Sprecher sind in Deutschland ansässig,
4. **[Bul]** eine **bulgarische Gruppe** perfekt dreisprachiger Roma (Bulgarisch/Türkisch/Romani) aus einem Dorf im Hinterland von Dobrič, umherziehend, hohe Mobilität, Kontakte zu bulgarischen Roma und zu ethnischen Türken.

Weitere Erhebungen sind im Trinkermilieu und unter Exhäftlingen in Sofia vorgenommen worden (cf. auch LESCHBER 2005), außerdem erfolgten Sprecherbefragungen zu türkischen Entlehnungen im Bulgarischen (LESCHBER 2007).

Die Resultate sprachlicher Kreativität und speziell die Veränderungen der bulgarischen Sprache der Presse, bzw. die Beschreibung politischer Vorgänge in der Tagespresse in der erste Dekade nach der Wende sind gründlich untersucht worden (STEINKE 2000, JORDANOVA 2000), außerdem COMATI (2009) zur Sprache der Wirtschaft, Medien, Musikkultur, und zur Stellung der bg. ʹČalgaʹ siehe sehr aufschlussreich in GEHL (2010). Den Aspekten sprachlicher Kreativität im Internetzeitalter wurde viel Aufmerksamkeit geschenkt (siehe für das Bulgarische VOITSCHIZKY 2009: 201–217).

III. Ausformungen der linguistischen Kreativität in den Balkansprachen

Linguistische Kreativität äußert sich deutlich in einer Synonymenhäufigkeit für bestimmte Konzepte, wie Personenbezeichnungen, eingeschlossen sind Anreden von Personen, Schimpfwörter für Personen, und Bezeichnungen für 'Geld' und 'stehlen'.

Die Etymologisierung von Personenbezeichnungen

Manche Bezeichnungen sind schwer deutbar, wie z.B. [Bul] bg. *бръшльо* – hier ist keine lexikografische Eintragung feststellbar, nicht in ARMJANOV (2001), und nicht im BER. Denkbar wäre zunächst ein Zusammenhang zu bg. (Vb.) *бърша* „(ab)wischen", mit Metathese, dann in etwa „Putzlappen, Putzmann" (?). Hier erhellt ein Exkurs in die bulgarischen Geheimsprachen den Sachverhalt: bg. (Maurergeheimsprache, Elešnica, Gebiet Razlog, SW) (Vb.) *бръша* „lügen", mit Metathese von *бърша*, s.o. Derivate sind *бръшàвица* „Lüge" und *бръшàр* „Lügner" (IVANOV 1986: 229). Bg. *бръшльо* ist also durch einen Wechsel des Nomina agentis-Suffixes zustande gekommen: statt *-àр* wurde ein umgangssprachliches Suffix *-льо* eingesetzt. In RADEVA (2003: 181) wird ausgeführt, dass „das Suffix *-льо* dem Stamm der motivierenden Verben angefügt wird (...) Substantive auf *-льо* werden umgangssprachlich gebraucht", wobei eine negative Konnotation dieser Wörter zu beobachten ist. Die ursprüngliche semantische Entwicklung des Verbs, hin zur Bedeutung „lügen" unterlag geheimsprachlichen Gesetzmäßigkeiten. Demnach bedeutet *бръшльо* „Lügner", was perfekt zum Kontext passt, denn der Informant beschimpft damit seinen Kumpanen, der als notorischer Lügner eingeschätzt wird. Es erfolgte ein Übergang des Wortes in regionale Varietäten, und damit einher ging aus historischer Perspektive der Verlust des geheimsprachlichen Charakters des Wortes. Nach dem Schema in LESCHBER (2009: 148) kommt der Gaunersprache eine Vermittlerfunktion für Wortgut aus dem bulgarischen historischen Argot in den Jugendslang zu. Hierbei bleibt spekulativ, inwieweit *бръшльо* noch Teil der Gaunersprache oder schon Bestandteil des Jugendslangs ist. Das Fehlen des Ausdrucks in ARMJANOV spricht für eine Zuordnung zur (historisch gebundenen) Gaunersprache, cf. LESCHBER (2009: 148–149): „(die) Gaunersprache (hat) Wortgut aus den bulgarischen historischen Argots bzw. den berufsgebundenen Sondersprachen in den bulgarischen Jugendslang übermittelt. (...) Die historische bulgarische Jugendsprache – und schließlich die moderne bulgarische Jugendsprache, die sich aus ihr entwickelte – nährten sich aus dem Wortschatz der historischen berufsgebundenen Geheimsprachen. Eine zentrale Bedeutung kommt dabei der Geheimsprache der Diebe und der Gauner zu, die eine Art Vermittlerfunktion zwischen dem Jugendslang und den bulgarischen historischen Argots einnahm".

Personenbezeichnungen mit sexueller Komponente

[Bul] bg. (masc., Pl.) *карълове* „abfällig für mehrere männliche Personen" – eine Pars-pro-toto-Bezeichnung – zu Romani *kar* „männliches Geschlechtsorgan". In der bg. Gaunersprache auch *кàрчо* (Subst. neutr.) „männliches Geschlechtsorgan". Ein Informant kannte dies als einen „Spitznamen eines Mannes in Sofia". Auf das gleiche Etymon zurückzuführende Bezeichnungen existieren in russischen, neugriechischen und deutschen Geheimsprachen (LESCHBER 2002: 74). Eine parallele Übernahme und eine hohe Produktivität weist das Rumänische auf, cf. in LESCHBER (1995: 158–159) in der rumänischen Umgangssprache *car* und *cárici* „männliches Geschlechtsorgan", wie in *freacă cariciul* „er masturbiert", ebenfalls zu Romani *kar* „id.". Varianten bzw. Derivate sind *caríci* „weibliches Geschlechtsorgan", *caricioaică* „Nymphomanin", *cariciométru*, *cariciopéd* „riesiges Sexualorgan", *a caricí* (in die IV. rumän. Verbalklasse adaptiert, mit *i*-Endung für den Infinitiv) „Geschlechtsverkehr ausüben", *cariceală* „Geschlechtsverkehr, Masturbation". Die so entstandenen Wörter haben häufig eine komische oder eine abwertende Konnotation, vgl. dazu auch die Einträge in dem Argot-Wörterbuch von VOLCEANOV (2006: 54–55).

Eine vergleichbare sexuelle Komponente enthält im Rudari-Rumänischen die in der folgenden Wendung gebrauchte Pars-pro-toto-Bezeichnung: *ai mâncát ŝevá, púlu?* Dies wird fast zärtlich-scherzhaft gebraucht durch eine Frau mittleren Alters, und ist an ein männliches Familienmitglied gerichtet, zu rum. *púlă* (familiär, vulgär) „männliches Geschlechtsteil", mit einer lateinischen Etymologie. Eher als Beschimpfung dient das Beispiel aus der serbischen Kontrollgruppe [Serb] *jávi se, jebáču!* In etwa „melde dich/ruf an, (du) Bumser", ähnlich auch die Anrede *Šibanović!* zu serb. *šibati* „mit der Rute hauen", metaphorisch für „bumsen".

Beispiele für Personenbezeichnungen im Rudari-Rumänischen

murói, muroáică	„Typ", „Tussi", z.B. in: *o muroáică de fátă*
muróiu ăla de om	„negativ konnotierte Bezeichnung für einen Mann"
vs.	
ai fost la muruiéni?	„warst du auf dem Friedhof?"
mare lúpu	wörtlich: „großer Wolf", im Sinne von „Macker"
umflátu n-are chéie	„der Angeber/Weiberheld hat keinen Schlüssel"
călduroáică	„Hure" zu rum. *căldúră* „Hitze", etc.
mincinós	„Lügner, Lügenhafter", wie in: *mincinósule, ieşti mincinós, ca turŝít, iél mínce!*

Der Bereich der Personenbezeichnungen geht in den Bereich der – häufig scherzhaften – Anreden über, vgl. als Anrede eines Mannes *turcítu! turcítule!* Zum Beispiel in den Varianten *úndže iéşti, be, turĉítule!* Auch … *turŝítule!* Und: … *da ŝe fáci, bre, Turŝítović!* – in Analogie zur serbischen Familiennamenbildung

mit *-ović*. Vergleiche rum. *a se turcí* „sich an die türkische Bevölkerung assimilie-
ren", und übrigens auch bg. *турчѐе се* (Vb. 3. Sg.) „gibt sich als Türke aus (statt
als Rom)", volkstümlich wird das Letztere durch das höhere soziale Prestige der
türkischen Bevölkerung in Bulgarien erklärt. Zu den scherzhaften und ironischen
Anreden gehört auch das zwischen zwei Roma-Männern aus der Gruppe [Serb] gebrauchte *gažó!* und *gadžó!* – dies stellt eindeutig eine Bezeichnung für Nicht-Roma
dar, cf. Romani *gadžó* „Nicht-Rom, Ehemann, Bauer, Dörfler, Herr, Hausherr"
(BORETZKY/IGLA 1994: 94–95, zur Entwicklung im rum. Slang siehe LESCHBER
1995: 161–162). Eine scherzhaft-beschimpfende und typische Anrede für eine
männliche Person ist [Rud] *vrăjálă!* und *vrăjeálă!* – in etwa „Zauberer" mit negati-
ver Konnotation, zu rum. *a vrăjí* „verzaubern, verhexen" etc. In der Kontrollgruppe
[Serb] der serbischen Sprecher konnten die scherzhaften und überhöhenden Anreden *legéndo!* „Legende!", und *prezidente!* „Präsident!", *minístere!* „Minister!" festgestellt werden. In einer rum. Kontrollgruppe trat *preşedínte!* auf. Eindeutig in den
Bereich der Beschimpfungen gehört [Serb] *... stigao ovo đubro u Berlinu, kaže* „er
sagt, dieser Müll ist in Berlin angekommen" (über eine männliche Person).

Personenbezeichnungen mit türkischer Etymologie

Der vielfältige Sprachkontakt eröffnet der Kreativität im Bereich der Personenbezeichnungen reiche Möglichkeiten, zum Beispiel mittels einer intensiven Entlehnung aus der Kontaktsprache Türkisch:
   [Bul] bg. *хайвàни* (Subst. masc., Pl.), in: *не мòга да се разбѝрам с тия
хайвàни!* „ich komme mit diesen Dummköpfen nicht klar!", DTB 267 bg. *хайвàн*
„Tier, Vieh", (koll.) „Dummkopf, verflixter Kerl", zu türk. *hayvan* „Lebewesen,
Tier, Vieh", (fig.) „dummer Kerl, Dummkopf" < arab. *hayvan* „Tier", fig. „Dummkopf". Der figurative Sinn tritt bereits in der Ursprungssprache auf. Laut einem
mündlichen Hinweis von Victor Friedman liegt ein vergleichbarer, etymologisch
verwandter Ausdruck auch im Jiddischen vor, als *khaya* bzw. *ḥaya* "living thing,
animal", pejorativ für Personen gebraucht, Neuhebräisch *xa'ja* "animal, wild person".

Die Funktion des Schimpfens

Schimpfen ist ein expressiver Sprechakt: Nach LEINFELLNER (1999) (trägt)
„Schimpfen zur Festigung der sozialen Stellung eines Sprechers in einer Kom-
munikationssituation bei (...). Er versucht also, mithilfe der Sprache das ihn umge-
bende soziale Netz zu gestalten bzw. zu festigen (...)", denn „Schimpfen ist ein
bedeutendes Mittel zur negativen Beziehungsgestaltung, es kann zur Schaffung einer gespannten Atmosphäre und zur aggressiven Distanzierung absichtlich eingesetzt werden". Durchaus möglich ist also auch ein unbewusstes Bestreben, bestehende Ungleichheitsverhältnisse mit Hilfe sprachlicher Mittel zu festigen. In der

Verhaltensbiologie ist Schimpfen eine Form des Drohverhaltens, durch Lärmen soll die eigene Stärke deutlich gemacht werden. Schimpfen kann neben einer aggressiven Funktion auch einen Rückzug markieren. Dem Schimpfen kommt eine psychische Entlastungsfunktion zu. Ein Schimpfwort soll den Beschimpften abwerten. Meist handelt es sich bei diesen abwertenden Wörtern um Substantive, gelegentlich um Adjektive. Auf welche Art geschimpft wird, ist kulturabhängig. Im Balkanraum sind Schimpfwörter aus der sexuellen Sphäre häufig vertreten, so gilt zum Beispiel das Anzweifeln der männlichen Virilität als beleidigend, bzw. die (angeblich) mangelnde Keuschheit der Frau, und das Gleichsetzen mit einem „Hund" bzw. einer „Hündin", was dann einer Beschimpfung mit einem Tiernamen gleichkommt. Letzteres lässt sich in vielen weiteren Sprachen nachweisen, z.B. im Deutschen, Chinesischen und im Russischen (MARSZK 1999: 628) sowie im Rudari-Rumänischen: *minte, căinele* „er lügt, der Hund", und ähnlich: *minte ca căinele*.

Generell gesehen sind auch die Beschimpfungen in der russischen Sprache vor allem sexuell geprägt (MARSZK 1999: 626). Zum Wesen der Beschimpfung schreibt MARSZK (1999: 628–629), nach HUGHES (1991: 7): „Flüche und Zaubersprüche seien Überbleibsel eines primitiven Glaubens an Wortmagie". Laut MONTAGU (1967: 71f.) hat „das Fluchen die Funktion einer Entladung von negativen Gefühlen". LABOV (1978) beschreibt Regeln für rituelle Beschimpfungen mit Hinblick auf die kreativen Fähigkeiten der Mitglieder einer Peer-Group (gültig für das 'Black English Vernacular'): „rituelle Beschimpfungen werden (...) benutzt, um (den) Herausforderungen innerhalb einer Peer-Group zu begegnen" (LABOV 1978: 57).

Umgangssprachliche Bezeichnungen für „Geld"

ARMJANOV (2001: 402) verzeichnet 48 Synonyme für 'Geld', nur wenige davon stellen Ableitungen voneinander dar, die meisten von ihnen sind unabhängige Bildungen. Im aktuellen Sprachgebrauch [Bul]: bg. *кинт, кùнта, 30/40 кùнта*, (cf. ARMJANOV 2001: 166) bg. *кùнта* (1) „(bg. Währung) Lev" (um 1930). BER II 372 vermerkt dazu: bg. *кинт* (südwestl., Geheimsprache der Guslaspieler) „hundert", ('Gauner'sprache der Schüler, Sofia) „Lev", *кùнта* (südwestl., Geheimsprache der Bettler) „hundert", ('Gauner'sprache der Schüler, Sofia) „Lev", *кùнти* (Pl.) (Jargon) „Geld, Leva", Derivat: *кинтàж* ('Gauner'sprache der Schüler, Sofia) „Geld", mit einem Suffix nach frz. -age. Die Etymologie ist alb. *qint, qind* „hundert" < lat. *centum* „id.". Bg. *мàнгите* (Pl. art.) für: *мангùзи* „Geld" – mit einer hohen Variationsbreite (cf. LESCHBER 2002: 71–72, dort auch weitere Quellenangaben): Bg. (Slang und Gauner-Geheimsprache, Bäcker-Geheimsprache, Musikanten-Geheimsprache, südwestl.) meist im Plural: *мангùзи* „Geld", cf. (selten, Sg.) *мангùз/мангùс, мàнгис* (Subst. masc.) „Geld", gelegentlich auch „Geldstück" – auch (um 1925) *мàнги* (Pl.) „Geld". Ein moderner Informant hält bulg.

(Slang) *мàнги* (Pl.) „Geld" für eine Art Kontamination aus *мангùзи* „id." und dem komisch konnotierten *мъ̀ни* (< engl. *money*) „id."! Im bulg. Slang kann das Verb (unvollendeter Aspekt) *мангùзя* nachgewiesen werden: 1. „jemandem beim Spiel ʿKomarʾ das Geld abknöpfen", 2. „jemanden (meist jüngeres) auf der Straße anhalten, um ihm die Taschen nach Geld zu durchwühlen" und 3. (arch., um 1946) „stehlen" – dazu die westbulg. regionale Form *мангùзим* „stehlen". Modernen Informanten ist das Verb *(аз) омангùзим* „zu Geld kommen/ich komme zu Geld" bekannt; cf. im Slang weiterhin *мангизлùя* (Subst. masc.) „Mensch mit viel Geld, reicher Mann", auch (Adj.) „reich" und (Subst. fem.) *мангизлùйка* „reiche Frau", zur Verbalwurzel Romani *mang-*, cf. *mangél* (Vb. 3. Sg.) „wünschen, wollen, lieben, bitten, ersuchen, verlangen, betteln, streben nach, versuchen", *mangín* „Besitz, Vermögen, Schatz, Reichtum; Ware, Kapital", auch „Geld" etc., Boretzky/Igla (1994: 175), Malikov (1992: 50). Mit der Endung *-ис*, analog zu bg. *чòрис* „Diebstahl" zur Wurzel Romani *čor-* wie in *čorél* (Vb. 3. Sg.) „stehlen", cf. Romani *čor* „Dieb, Räuber" etc. (Boretzky/Igla 1994: 51, 52). In Malikov (1992: 89) *čóribe* „Diebstahl", mit der bulgarischen Endung *-ис* < ngr. *-ης*, mit der auf dialektaler Ebene gewöhnlich Substantive gebildet werden, cf. in formaler Hinsicht dazu ngr. geheimsprachl. *τσόρης*. Deutsch geheimsprachl. *mangen* „betteln", schwed. Geheimsprachl. *mangare* „Bettler", *manga* „sich Geld leihen", dän. dial. geheimspr. *mangave* „betteln"; das Wort wurde auch vom bulg. Slang ins Türkische übernommen: *mangiz* „Geld". Zur Übernahme und in der Folge Produktivität dieses Etymons in der rumänischen Umgangssprache cf. Leschber (1995: 166).

Ausdrücke für das Wortfeld „stehlen"

Weiterhin zeigt das Wortfeld „stehlen" eine große Bandbreite an Ausdrücken, Armjanov (2001: 394) verzeichnet 25 synonyme Ausdrücke. Nicht verzeichnet ist ein Wort aus dem Gebrauch der Gruppe [Bul]: *шùпкам, шъ̀пкам* (Vb.) – in etwa: „[ein gestohlenes Auto] verschieben".

Beispiele für Slangausdrücke im Trinkermilieu

Bg. *шòркам* (Vb.) „saufen", cf. dazu in der bg. Maurergeheimsprache und in der Gaunersprache *шòрам, шùрам, шòркам* eigentlich „pinkeln", vgl. bg. geheimsprachl. *шор* „Wein" – dazu existieren diverse Derivate, möglicherweise zu türk. *şira, şarap* „Wein".

Phantasievolle Bezeichnungen existieren für diverse alkoholische Getränke und die entsprechenden Gefäße, z.B. bg. *академùк* in *дай ми едùн академùк* „gib mir einen Schnaps" (angeblich in Erinnerung an ein ʿgewisses Akademie-Mitglied Nedelčev, das sich damit auskannteʾ), bg. *бушòнче* „kleine Flasche mit 100 ml-Inhalt für Alkohol", bg. *гипс* „Cola mit Rum", bg. *гипсùрам се* (Vb. refl.) „sich betrinken", wie in: *гипсùрах се* „ich habe mich betrunken", bg. *къ̀нките* in: *връзвам кънките*, wörtlich: „die Kufen (der Schlittschuhe) zusammenbinden", d.h. „(wegen eines Betrunkenheitszustandes) nicht mehr laufen können", bg. *Скоросмъртница* „sehr starker, schlechter Raki"; dann mit Anspielung auf die Medizin: bg. *анестезѝрам се* (Vb. refl.) „sich betrinken", auch in ARMJANOV (2001: 20); *анестезѝран* (Adj.) „betrunken", ARMJANOV ibd.; *антибиотѝк* (scherzhaft) „Alkohol; Raki", *гроздомѝцин* „Raki", eine scherzhafte Bildung mit dem Bestandteil eines Medikamentennamens, und viele andere mehr.

Verfahren zur Integration entlehnter lexikalischer Elemente

In einer breit angelegten Untersuchung, in der die Voraussetzungen und Gesetzmäßigkeiten für die lexikalische Entlehnung bzw. den lexikalischen Transfer im Sprachkontakt von einem universellen Gesichtspunkt her untersucht wurden (HASPELMATH/TADMOR 2009), konnten mehrere Verfahren zur Adaption des neuen Elementes in die aufnehmende Sprache identifiziert werden:

1) 'Insertion' (dt. Insertion, Einfügung): das Wort wird als völlig neue Einheit eingefügt,
2) 'Replacement' (dt. Ersetzung): das Wort ersetzt ein früheres mit der gleichen Bedeutung, dieses kommt außer Gebrauch oder verändert seine Bedeutung,
3) 'Coexistence' (dt. Koexistenz): das Wort kann mit einem einheimischen Wort gleicher Bedeutung koexistieren.

Die Insertion kommt für kulturell bedingte Entlehnungen infrage, als „neues Wort für ein neues Phänomen", die anderen beiden Verfahren für sogenannte 'Coreborrowings', dt. Kern-/Kernstück-Entlehnungen.

In einem weltweiten Sample aus 41 Sprachen wurde anhand einer Liste mit jeweils 1460 Wortbedeutungen herausgefunden, dass bei der lexikalischen Entlehnung die Insertion das häufigste Verfahren ist, dann folgt die Koexistenz, während die Ersetzung am seltensten ist (HASPELMATH 2009: 49). Bei der relativen Häufigkeit lexikalischer Übernahmen im weltweiten Vergleich von Sprachen zeigte sich, dass die Sprache einer marginalisierten Minderheit, die – bildlich gesehen – unter ständigem Druck dominanterer Sprachen stand bzw. steht, die höchste Entlehnungsrate aller Sprachen aus dem Sample hat, es handelt sich um den slovakischen Romani-Dialekt von Selice mit 62,7% Entlehnungen in Hinblick auf das untersuchte Wortmaterial, während für Mandarin-Chinesisch die niedrigste Entlehnungsrate (1,2%) festgestellt wurde (die zweitniedrigste hat übrigens Althochdeutsch mit 5,8%). Chinesisch war für Tausende von Jahren die dominante Sprache seiner Region, wobei wenig Anlass zu lexikalischen Entlehnungen bestand (TADMOR 2009: 56–58). Zu den soziolinguistischen Umständen, die zur Erklärung der extremen Entlehnungsraten dienen können, gehören bei dem Romani-Dialekt von Selice die Mehrsprachigkeit der Sprecher, ihre lange Abwesenheit vom ursprünglichen Herkunftsgebiet, der Mangel einer standardisierten Sprachform bzw. Dachlosigkeit ('roof-less language'), s. ELŠIK 2009. Bei der Unterscheidung zwischen der Entlehnung von Inhaltswörtern ('content words') – Substantiven, Verben, Adjektiven und Adverbien – kommt dieser Dialekt hier auf eine Quote von 65,6%, bei den entlehnten Funktionswörtern auf 30,9%. Im Gesamtkorpus aller untersuchten Sprachen wurden Substantive zu 31,2%, Adjektive und Adverbien zu 15,2%, und Verben zu 14% entlehnt. Nomen wurden also im Schnitt doppelt so häufig wie Verben entlehnt. Bei den semantischen Feldern überwiegen die Bereiche 'Religion und Glauben' – 41,2%, 'Kleidung und Schmuck' – 38,6%, 'Haus' – 37,2%; am wenigsten wurde bei 'Verwandtschaftsbeziehungen' – 15%, 'Körper' – 14,2%, 'räumlichen Relationen' – 14,0% und 'Sinneswahrnehmungen' – 11,0% entlehnt (TADMOR 2009: 64–65). Darüber hinaus gehende Erkenntnisse zum Anteil der Entlehnungen von Personenbezeichnungen gibt es nicht.

Neumotivierung

Eine weitere Spielart der sprachlichen Kreativität ist die Neumotivierung, wie im Falle von [Bul] bg. *джòнка* (Subst. fem.) „Joint", in: *да изпỳ(ш)ем (= изпỳшим) една джòнка* – eigentlich (wie in ARMJANOV 2001: 93) „eine Art Schlag mit der Hand auf den Kopf", aber cf. bg. *джòнкам се* (ipf. Vb.) (Jambol) „sich amüsieren, sich vergnügen" (ARMJANOV: ibd.) Hier wird jedoch der formale und semantische Einfluss von engl. *joint* zum Tragen gekommen sein, das zur Neumotivierung des bereits bestehenden bulgarischen Slangwortes geführt hat.

Um eine Bedeutungsspezialisierung in Abhängigkeit von 'neuartigen Lebensbedingungen' bei der Gruppe [Rud] und bei einer rumänischen Kontrollgruppe handelt es sich bei der Bedeutung der Wendung *a mérge la ziáre* „zum Verkaufen von Obdachlosenzeitungen losgehen", für viele Informanten die einzige Möglichkeit, sich in Berlin über Wasser zu halten, und zwar in diversen Varianten: … *şi pe úrmă să meárgă la ziáre*, auch: *la ziérii* (!), etc. Das Konzept des deutschen „(guten) Rufes" wird im Folgenden eingeführt [Rud]: *nu pot să (s-) stríce rúfu!* (Vb. 3. Pl.) und: *nu poáte uómu să (s-) stríce rúfu!* „der Mann kann sich den Ruf nicht verderben!", *nu pot, că îmi strig rúfu, mă răzuméśce?* „ich kann nicht, denn ich mach mir den Ruf kaputt, verstehst du mich?"

Reduplikationen

Reduplikation ist ein morphologischer Prozess, bei dem die Wurzel oder der Stamm eines Wortes ganz oder teilweise wiederholt wird. Reduplikationen kommen in der Rede eines Informanten der Gruppe [Bul] vor: Romani: *àндре-мàндре*, cf. Romani *àндре* (Adverb loc.) „hinein, innen". Als Antwort auf die Frage, wer alles in einem bestimmten einfachen Café aufhältlich sei, antwortet derselbe Informant bg. *кỳчета-мỳчета* „Hunde etc.", evt. ähnlich wie Deutsches „Mann und Maus".

Dazu existieren zahlreiche Parallelen, z.B. im südasiatischen Sprachbund (cf. in ABBI 1992, EBERT 2001: 1533) die sogenannten Echowörter, deren Bedeutung dem Deutschen „und so" entspricht. Echo-Wörter zeichnen sich durch alternierende initiale Konsonanten aus. Reduplikation ist in den meisten Sprachen der Welt üblich, auch z.B. in australischen Sprachen der Aborigines, cf. *The World Atlas of Language Structures Online*, Chapter 27: „Reduplication". Bei den genannten Beispielen handelt es sich um eine Reduplikation, vergleichbar mit einem im Türkischen sehr verbreiteten Verfahren. Allerdings ist dies nicht die einzige Art der Reduplikation im Türkischen, bei der hier der Anfangskonsonant, der nicht *m-* ist, durch ein *m-* ersetzt wird, oder einem Anlautvokal ein *m-* vorangestellt wird. Dadurch erweitert man den ursprünglichen Sinn des Wortes. Dies kann nicht nur bei Substantiven, sondern auch Adjektiven etc. Anwendung finden; ähnlich auch im Deutschen *Kuddel-Muddel* oder *schicki-micki*, im Russischen nach einem mündlichen Hinweis von T. CIV'JAN *сумки-мумки* – in etwa „Taschen und ähnlicher Krempel". Dies wird im Russischen häufig für 'eine vom Kaukasus ausgehende sprachliche Erscheinung' gehalten, aus dem 'moslemischen Kulturraum stammend'. In der Rede eines russischen Informanten konnte das vulgäre *хуйня-муйня* – in etwa „Sch..." – festgestellt werden.

Turzismen

Im erhobenen Material lassen sich regionale und semantische Differenzierungen im Gebrauch von Turzismen feststellen: [Mak] maked. *чалъци* „Krempel", vgl. dazu die Äußerung eines Rudari-Sprechers, eines älteren Verwandten aus Serbien, der vom ungebetenen Besuch von Hunden berichtet, die auf seinem Hof alles Mögliche aufgefressen haben: *am avut niște câini aișea, și m-au mâncat tóți cealắți.* Der Sprecher fährt fort: *nu am mai putút, de múncă máre* „ich konnte nicht mehr, wegen der vielen Arbeit"; vgl. dazu bg. *чалък* (indekl. Adj.) 1. (obs.) „schief, schräg", 2. (dial.) „diagonaler Schnitt am oberen Teil des Schafsohrs als Markierung" < türk. *çalık* „schief, krumm, schräg geschnitten, störrisch, eigensinnig, pockennarbig" etc., DTB 279; die phonetische Gestalt spricht für eine Herkunft aus dem Kurdischen. Bg. *чалък* ist heute obsolet/ungebräuchlich, es kommt im Familiennamen *Чалъков* und in einigen Ortsnamen vor. Im DTB 342 wird auf serb. *čaluk* verwiesen. Das Wort tritt häufig in bosnischen Familiennamen auf. Denkbar wäre als Etymon auch türk. *çalı* (endbetont) 1. „(Dorn)busch, Strauch", 2. „Gestrüpp, Gebüsch", auch (fig.) „unbeständig, wankelmütig", „quecksilbrig". Ein weiteres Beispiel ist [Mak] maked. *ерджèнин* vs. bg. *ергèн*, (selten) *ергèнин* „Junggeselle" < türk. *ergen* „id." (BER I 503–504).

Konstruktionen mit zwei Präpositionen in der Umgangssprache

Durch eine Inversion kommt es zu einer Konstruktion, die eine doppelte Präposition aufzuweisen hat. Es gibt zwei deutlich umgangssprachlich geprägte Sätze eines Informanten der Gruppe [Bul]:

1. *òния живèе с – на Màра сестрàта* [statt: *òния живèе със сестрàта на Màра*] „der lebt mit der Schwester von der Mara zusammen"
2. *чух че е билà със (!) на Исмаил му дèт(о) плèменника – òния дèто се прàвеше на нèмец* [statt: *чух че е билà с плèменника на Исмаил …*] in etwa „ich habe gehört, dass sie mit dem Neffen vom Ismail zusammen gewesen sein soll, der, der einen auf Deutschen gemacht hat", also „der versucht hat, sich wie ein Deutscher zu benehmen".

Das zweite Beispiel ist dialektal bzw. deutlich umgangssprachlich geprägt, mit dem umgangssprachlichen Relativpronomen *дето* für *който*. In der Untersuchung von BARAKOVA (2003) werden sogenannte polypräpositionale Konstruktionen beschrieben. In BARAKOVA (2003: 368, 371) und in GEORGIEVA (2010) werden sogar Konstruktionen aus drei aufeinander folgenden Präpositionen beschrieben. Die obige Konstruktion „… с на …" ist jedoch in beiden Untersuchungen nicht aufgeführt. Eine solche Doppelung sieht BARAKOVA (2003: 374–375) [in Übersetzung und sinngemäßer Zusammenfassung, d. Verf.] „als deutliche balkanische Besonderheit. In diesen Konstruktionen zeige sich auch die universelle Tendenz zur Ökonomie der Ausdrucksmittel, die besonders für die gesprochene Sprache charakteristisch sei, und die zunehmend auf das geschriebene Bulgarische Einfluss nehme. (…) Einige der polypräpositionalen Konstruktionen bewegten sich an der Grenze des grammatikalisch Korrekten, seien jedoch zunehmend auch in der Schriftsprache anzutreffen, und illustrierten damit eine Entwicklung, die zur Umgestaltung der Schriftsprache führen könne". Die Autorin eröffnet eine weitere Perspektive, indem sie auf das Vorkommen von Konstruktionen mit der Anhäufung von zwei und drei Präpositionen in der bulgarischen Kindersprache hinweist.

Gruppeninterne Verhaltensnormen

Gelegentlich gelingt es, Hinweise auf gruppeninterne Verhaltensnormen zu gewinnen. Ein Abweichen von der Verhaltensnorm wird genau registriert (vgl. dazu: [Bul] bg. *върналите, как се държàт* „die Zurückgekehrten, wie die sich verhalten/benehmen"), was in diesem Falle Angehörige der peer-group bezeichnet, die aus dem west- bzw. mitteleuropäischen Ausland in ihr nordostbulgarisches Heimatdorf zurückgekehrt sind, und nun modifizierte Verhaltensweisen an den Tag legen. Dies wird von den Gruppenmitgliedern mit Sanktionen belegt, wie Misstrauen und Spott. Das betrifft zum Beispiel auch [Bul] bg. *òния дèто се прàвеше на нèмец –* (den) „der einen auf Deutschen gemacht hat".

Das Mischen von Sprachen im Diskurs

Besonders in der Gruppe [Bul] konnte bei Dialogen unter Gruppenmitgliedern ein mehrsprachiger Diskurs beobachtet werden. Die dreisprachigen Sprecher verfügten über gleichwertige Kenntnisse des Bulgarischen, des Türkischen und des Romani. Im Gespräch setzten sie ein gezieltes Code-Switching zwischen den Sprachen ein, häufig auch Code-Mixing mit frequenten Sprachwechseln im Satz. Dies gilt besonders für die türkisch-bulgarischen Mixing-Phänomene. Eine Matrixsprache war schwer auszumachen, so dass von einem tatsächlichen Code-Mixing ausgegangen werden kann, bei dem die Matrixsprache wechselt, im vorliegenden Falle zwischen Bulgarisch und Türkisch. In den Gesprächen ließ sich ein Muster bzw. eine Tendenz erkennen: In einem Dialog zweier Männer aus derselben peer-group folgte einer stets türkischen Begrüßung oftmals eine scherzhafte Beschimpfung in bulgarischem Slang. Dann wurde – abwechselnd auf Bulgarisch und Türkisch – Organisatorisches besprochen, dazu Details erörtert und intensiv über Dritte geklatscht. Der bulgarische Diskurs zeichnete sich durch Originalität und Komik aus. In Dialogen zwischen einem Mann und einer Frau wechselte die Frau nach einem Gesprächsbeginn auf Bulgarisch häufig in das Romani, wenn sie über den Bereich der Emotionen berichtete, sich zum Beispiel beklagte oder jammerte und in sentimentalen Erinnerungen schwelgte.

Besonderheiten des Rudari-Rumänischen

Generell können in der gesamten Gruppe [Rud] zahlreiche Dialektalismen festgestellt werden:

> *eh – dá că* bzw. *eh – dá ca* „jadoch",
> *nu m-am dus pe nichéră, că nu am báni* – statt rum. *nícăieri* „... nirgends ...", in
>   Übersetzung „ich bin nirgends hingegangen, denn ich habe kein Geld",
> *hai?* „was? wie bitte?", das möglicherweise ein (hier seltenes) Überbleibsel aus
>   dem Romani ist,
> *numíca* „nichts", möglicherweise eine Kontamination aus *nu* „nein" und *nimíc*
>   „nichts",
> *şe fáş', múico!* „was machst du, Mutter/wie geht's, Mutter!", cf. *múică* „Mutter".

Bedeutende morphologische Unsicherheiten mit einem Genuswechsel vom Femininum zum Neutrum bei der Pluralbildung können in der Gruppe [Rud] festgestellt werden: *trei proţénturi* statt rum. *trei procénte* „drei Prozent", *minúturi* statt rum. *minúte* „Minuten", *nişte problémuri* statt rum. *nişte probléme* „einige Probleme". In den Bereich der morphologischen Unsicherheiten, in Kombination mit einer Ausformung von Hyperkorrektheit fällt auch das Beispiel [Rud]: *unde ieşţéţi* „wo seid ihr", analog zu *unde (i)éşti* „wo bist du", statt korrektem rum. *unde sînteţi* (bzw. *sunteţi*).

Wie zuvor bereits erwähnt wurde, entlehnt die rudari-rumänische Varietät zahlreiche Wörter, die sich auf serbische Ausgangswörter zurückführen lassen (vgl. die Beispiele in LESCHBER 2008a: 346f.). Manche Wörter scheinen auf okkasionelle Bildungen zurückzugehen, wie [Rud] Rudari *púcă* „Hitze", zu **puka*, Akk. **puku*, wobei eine solche deverbale Ableitung bisher scheinbar nicht verzeichnet worden ist, cf. serb. *pukati* „knallen", bg. *пу̀кам* „platzen/bersten lassen, knacken", aber auch „rösten" (BER V 847–849).

Weitere Beispiele für Übernahmen aus dem Serbischen:

*ai **poverenie** în mine* „du vertraust mir",

*s-a măritat pe **drughi put*** „er hat das zweite Mal geheiratet".

Intensiv werden serbische Adverbien entlehnt:

*nu plângeá, că eu viu, **obavèzno** viu!* „weine nicht, denn ich komme, ich komme bestimmt",

*n-a vrut **víše** să mai venim* „er/sie wollte nicht mehr, dass wir kommen",

*am avut buboi ... nu e aşa de **opasnu**, numai dacă se sparge* (über eine Krankheit).

Kurios ist eine Übernahme aus dem Deutschen bei in Deutschland ansässigen Sprechern:

*aia-i **bestimmt** cazna* „das ist bestimmt die Rechnung".

Mit diesen Beispielen wird Code-Mixing mit Bestandteilen aus zwei bzw. drei Sprachen illustriert, detailliert in LESCHBER (2008b), dort auch zu der Argumentation für einen 'Fusiolekt' nach AUER (1999).

Lehnverben im Rudari-Rumänischen

Das Rudari-Rumänische hat zahlreiche aus dem Serbischen stammende Verben übernommen. In Abstimmung mit der Klassifizierung verbaler Übernahmen in WOHLGEMUTH (2009) handelt es sich um direkte Einfügungen ('direct insertion') der Lehnverben. Die direkte Einfügung ist die von den romanischen Sprachen generell am häufigsten verwendete Strategie bei der Übernahme von Verben. Der Verbstamm wird wie ein ererbter Stamm behandelt, und da das Verfahren zur syntaktischen Eingliederung in den Satz jedem Verb, ungeachtet seiner Herkunft widerfährt, wird dies nicht als gesonderte morphologische Adaption betrachtet (WOHLGEMUTH 2009: 87f., 166; vgl. dazu die Weltkarte der Sprachen, die bei Integration von Lehnverben das Verfahren der direkten Einfügung gebrauchen, WOHLGEMUTH 2009: 372).

Im Bereich der verbalen Entlehnung wird bei Sprechern des Rudari-Rumänischen ein hohes Maß an Kreativität offenbart:

vói obiasníţi „ihr erklärt" bzw. *vói îi obiasníţi* „ihr erklärt es ihr" zu **a obiasní*
< serb. *objasniti* „erklären",
zabraniéśće „verbietet" (Vb. 3. Sg.) zu **a zabraní* < serb. *zabraniti* „verbieten, untersagen".

Vergleichbare Beispiele lassen sich in der Rede eines Informanten aus einer moldavischen Vergleichsgruppe feststellen, der zahlreiche Verben aus russischen/ ostslavischen Verbalstämmen bildet und in seinen rumänisch-moldavischen Diskurs integriert.

Ein auf dem Dorf lebender Informant der Gruppe [Rud] erklärt, was er gegen die zerstörerischen Effekte von Regen und Hagel unternommen hat: *toáće popravít* „alles in Ordnung gebracht, repariert", zu serb. *popraviti* (Vb.) „gutmachen, in Stand setzen, reparieren". Weitere Beispiele aus der Gruppe [Rud] sind: *a crení* und – phonetisch adaptiert – *a câlni* „los-, abfahren" < serb. *krenuti* „in Bewegung setzen", *krenuti se* „aufbrechen, sich in Bewegung setzen", z.B. in: *câlníţi sau nu câlníţi* „fahrt ihr los oder nicht?". Ein extremes Beispiel in Hinblick auf das Code-Mixing stammt aus der Rudari-Gruppe [Rud]: *krènul ich bin* „ich bin losgefahren".

Diverse Mixing-Phänomene unter Beteiligung deutscher Verben (im Infinitiv!) konnten bei in Deutschland ansässigen Sprechern aus der Gruppe [Mak] festgestellt werden:

wohlfühlen ще правя там „ich werde mich dort wohlfühlen",
много stören прави „er stört (mich) sehr",
мой телефон spinnen „mein Telefon spinnt".

Zu extensiven Mixing-Phänomenen mit deutschen Bestandteilen aus dem Bereich der Verben in der Varietät von rudari-rumänischen Sprechern finden sich weitere Beispiele in LESCHBER 2008b:

îl fac erreichen,
o fac begleiten,
fac ausräumen,
ai făcut überstehen,
el psihic face terrorisieren, cu vorbile.

Bei diesem Integrationstypus handelt es sich um die sogenannte 'Light-Verb-Strategy' (WOHLGEMUTH 2009: 102f.).

Zu einem Sondertypus gehört bestimmt *râd'e aus, narodu* „die Leute lachen ... aus", wobei der trennbare Bestandteil *aus-* des deutschen Verbs *auslachen* beibehalten wurde, *-lachen* aber durch rum. *a râde* wiedergegeben wird. Serb. *narod* „Volk, Leute" wurde mit einem postponierten rum. bestimmten Artikel für

Maskulina versehen: -*u*. Bei dieser Wendung stellt sich die Frage, ob die Matrixsprache hier noch eine rumänische Varietät ist, oder doch bereits das Deutsche die Matrixsprache ist. Eine Parallele bietet das Beispiel [Rud] **a lua ab* „abholen" in LESCHBER (2008b: 253).

Deutsche Verben werden durchaus auch morphologisch integriert:

> *ar fi vremea să **şparim** şi noi* zu dt. *sparen,*
>
> *trebe să **'klape'***, analog zu dt. *es muss klappen*, und weitere vergleichbare Beispiele.

Ein typologisches Rarum bei der Integration von Lehnverben

In verhältnismäßig dichter geografischer Nähe zum Balkanraum ist auch der höchst seltene Typus der Paradigmen-Einfügung (paradigm insertion/paradigm transfer) zu beobachten, und zwar im Sprachkontakt Romani (Dialekt von Ajia Varvara)/ Türkisch (nach dem Beispiel aus BAKKER 2005: 9, IGLA 1996: 214–216). Dagegen, dass es sich hierbei um einfaches Code-Switching handelt, spricht, dass die gegenwärtigen Sprecher dieser Varietät nicht mehr bilingual Romani/Türkisch sind, denn ihre Vorfahren kamen bereits um 1920 aus der Türkei nach Griechenland. Die Sprecher können nicht ins Türkische 'umswitchen', da sie es nicht sprechen (WOHLGEMUTH 2009: 120). Unter Hunderten von Beispielen zur Adaption von entlehnten Verben im Sprachkontakt aus über 350 Sprachen weltweit (WOHLGEMUTH 2009: 3), konnten nur drei Beispiele für eine Paradigmen-Einfügung ausgemacht werden. Damit handelt es sich um eine seltene typologische Erscheinung. Alle drei Beispiele stammen zudem aus dem ostmediterranen Raum (cf. die Karte in WOHLGEMUTH 2009: 375). Das zweite Beispiel stammt aus einem maronitisch-arabischer Dialekt auf Zypern, der stark unter dem Einfluss des zypriotischen Griechischen steht (WOHLGEMUTH 2009: 119, nach NEWTON 1964: 47), wobei die zypriotisch-griechischen Verben im arabischen Kormakitis-Dialekt exakt so konjugiert werden, als wenn sie im zypriotischen Griechischen gebraucht würden. Das dritte Beispiel stammt aus dem nahöstlichen Domari-Dialekt des Romani aus Palästina, der aus dem Arabischen nicht nur Modalverben, Verben, sondern auch deren Flexion und weitere Merkmale entlehnt hat (MATRAS 2005: 249, WOHLGEMUTH 2009: 120). Es ist sicher kein Zufall, dass sich diese Sprachkontakte zwischen Sprachen unterschiedlicher Sprachfamilien abgespielt haben:

Indoeuropäisch	←	Altaisch
Semitisch	←	Indoeuropäisch
Indoeuropäisch	←	Semitisch.

Diese typologisch seltene Erscheinung ergänzt die zuvor genannten zwei Strategien zur Integration von Lehnverben, die 'Light-Verb Strategy' (WOHLGEMUTH 2009: 102f., 374, 377), und die indirekte Einfügung (indirect insertion) (WOHLGEMUTH 2009: 94f., 376).

IV. Bibliografie

ABBI, Anvita (1992): *Reduplication in the South Asian Languages. An Areal, Typological and Historical Study*. New Delhi.

AUER, Peter (1999): From Code-Switching via Language-Mixing to Fused Lects: Toward a Dynamic Typology of Bilingual Speech. *International Journal of Bilingualism* 3. 309–332.

BAKKER, Peter (2005): *Intertwining and Michif*. Paper/Romancisation Worldwide, Conference. Bremen.

BENCZES, Réka (2006): *Creative Compounding in English*. Amsterdam.

BIERICH, Alexander (2000): Zur gegenwärtigen Situation der substandardsprachlichen Varietäten im Russischen. In: PANZER 2000: 13–29.

BORETZKY, Norbert; IGLA, Birgit (1994): *Wörterbuch Romani-Deutsch-Englisch für den südosteuropäischen Raum*. Wiesbaden.

BUSSMANN, Hadumod (2002): *Lexikon der Sprachwissenschaft*. Stuttgart.

CARTER, Ronald (2004): *Language and Creativity: The Art of Common Talk*. London.

COMATI, Sigrun (2009): Bulgarien nach der Wende bis zum EU-Beitritt: Beobachtungen zum Sprachgebrauch aus den Bereichen Wirtschaft, Medien und Musikkultur. In: VOSS 2009: 173–191.

DTB: GRANNES, Alf, Kjetil R. HAUGE & Hayriye SÜLEYMANOĞLU (2002): *A Dictionary of Turkisms in Bulgarian*. Oslo.

EBERT, Karen (2001): Südasien als Sprachbund. In: Martin Haspelmath (Hg.): *Sprachtypologie und Universalienforschung*. HSK 20. Berlin, New York. 1529–1539.

ELŠIK, Viktor (2009): Loanwords in Selice Romani, an Indo-Aryan Language of Slovakia. In: HASPELMATH/TADMOR 2009: 260–303.

GEHL, Katerina (2010): Čalga-Kultur als bulgarische Elite-Kultur? – Zur nationalen Bedeutsamkeit eines populären Phänomens im heutigen Bulgarien. *Südosteuropa Mitteilungen* 02/2010, 50. Jg. 44–57.

HASPELMATH, Martin (2009): Lexical borrowing: Concepts and issues. In: HASPELMATH/TADMOR 2009: 35–54.

HASPELMATH, Martin; TADMOR, Uri (2009): *Loanwords in the World's Languages*. A Comparative Handbook. Berlin, New York.

HUGHES, Geoffrey (1991): *Swearing. A Social History of Foul Language, Oaths and Profanity in English*. Oxford, Cambridge.

IGLA, Birgit (1996): *Das Romani von Ajia Varvara. Deskriptive und historisch-vergleichende Darstellung eines Zigeunerdialektes*. Wiesbaden.

JACHNOW, Helmut (Hg.) (1999): *Handbuch der sprachwissenschaftlichen Russistik und ihrer Grenzdisziplinen*. Wiesbaden.

JORDANOVA, Ljubima (2000): Die sprachliche Situation in Bulgarien zehn Jahre nach der Wende. In: PANZER 2000: 273–288.

LABOV, William (1978): *Sprache im sozialen Kontext*. Bd. 2, Hg. Norbert Dittmar, Bert-Olaf Rieck. Kronberg.

LAMB, Sydney M. (1998): *Pathways of the Brain: The neurocognitive basis of Language*. Amsterdam (= Current Issues in Linguistic Theory 170)

LEINFELLNER, Katrin (1999): *Schimpfen als expressiver Sprechakt und verbal-aggressiver Ausdruck der Emotion Ärger.* Diplomarbeit/elektronisches Manuskript. Graz.

LESCHBER, Corinna (1995): Romani lexical items in Colloquial Rumanian. In: Yaron Matras (ed.): *Romani in contact.* Amsterdam/Philadelphia (= Current Issues in Linguistic Theory 126). 151–176.

LESCHBER, Corinna (2002): Semantische Vorgänge bei lexikalischen Übernahmen aus dem Romani in diastratische Varietäten des Bulgarischen. *Grazer Linguistische Studien* 58, Graz. 57–101.

LESCHBER, Corinna (2007): Die Position der Turzismen im modernen bulgarischen Jugendslang. *Zeitschrift für Balkanologie* 43/1. 41–54.

LESCHBER, Corinna (2008a): Die Rudari in Serbien: Feldforschungen zu ihrem Sprachgebrauch, Spezifika, Sprachmischung, Archaismen. In: Wolfgang Dahmen et alii (Hg.): *Grenzüberschreitungen – Traditionen und Identitäten in Südosteuropa. Festschrift für Gabriella Schubert.* Wiesbaden. 338–351.

LESCHBER, Corinna (2008b): Romanian-Serbian Code-Mixing Phenomena. In: Biljana Sikimić et alii (eds.): *The Romance Balkans/Romanski Balkan.* Belgrad. 247–260.

LESCHBER, Corinna (2009): Bulgarische und makedonische Geheimsprachen. In: Christian Efing, Corinna Leschber (Hg.): *Geheimsprachen in Mittel- und Südosteuropa.* Frankfurt/M. etc. 127–152.

LIPKA, Leonhard (2002): *English Lexicology. Lexical Structure, word semantics, and word-formation.* Tübingen.

LIPKA, Leonhard (2007): Lexical creativity, textuality and problems of metalanguage. In: MUNAT 2007: 3–12.

MARSZK, Doris (1999): Substandard. In: JACHNOW 1999: 614–638.

MATRAS, Yaron (2005): The extension of "Fusion": A test case for connectivity and language contact. In: Walter Bisang et alii (Hg.): *Prozesse des Wandels in historischen Spannungsfeldern Nordostafrikas/Westasiens.* Würzburg. 241–255.

MONTAGU, Ashley (1967): *The Anatomy of Swearing.* London, New York.

MUNAT, Judith (2007): *Lexical creativity, Texts and Contexts.* Amsterdam, Philadelphia.

NEWTON, Brian (1964): An Arabic-Greek Dialect. In: *Papers in Memory of G. C. Pappageot.* Supplement to Word 20. 43–52.

PANZER, Baldur (Hg.) (2000): *Die sprachliche Situation in der Slavia zehn Jahre nach der Wende.* Frankfurt/M.

POPE, Rob (2005): *Creativity: Theory, History, Practice.* London, New York.

RADEVA, Vasilka (Hg.) (2003): *Bulgarische Grammatik.* Hamburg.

SCHIPPEL, Larisa (2008): Geschichte von Regionalsprachen und Stadtsprachen in der Romania: Südostromania. In: Gerhard Ernst et alii (Hg.): *Romanische Sprachgeschichte.* HSK 23.3. Berlin, New York. 2532–2541.

STEINKE, Klaus (2000): Die bulgarische Sprache der Wende im Spiegel der Presse. In: PANZER 2000: 261–271.

TADMOR, Uri (2009): Loanwords in the world's languages: Findings and results. In: HASPELMATH/TADMOR 2009: 55–75.

VOJTSCHIZKI, Christian (2009): Bulgarische Chatrooms und sprachliche Innovation. In: VOSS 2009: 201–217.

VOLCEANOV, George (2006): *Dicţionar de argou al limbii române.* Bucureşti.

Voss, Christian (Hg.) (2009): *EU-Bulgaristik. Perspektiven und Potenziale*. München, Berlin (= Studies on Language and Culture in Central and Eastern Europe 6).

WALS: *The World Atlas of Language Structures Online*, http://wals.info/.

Wohlgemuth, Jan (2009): *A Typology of Verbal Borrowings*. Trends in Linguistics. Berlin, New York.

Armjanov: Армянов, Георги (2001): *Речник на българкия жаргон*. София.

Barakova: Баракова, Пенка (2003): Наблюдения върху полипредложните конструкции. *Српски језик* 8/1–2.

BER: *Български етимологичен речник* (1971–). БАН. София.

Georgieva: Георгиева, Виолета (2010/под печат): Наблюдения върху функционирането на трипредложни съчетания в съвременния български език. *Лингвистичен клуб „Проф. Борис Симеонов“*, http://lingvclub.slovo.uni-plovdiv.bg/?page_id=174 [Recherche vom 7.2.2011].

Malikov: Маликов, Яшар (2002): *Циганско-български речник*. София.

Linguistic creativity in the Balkan area

This is demonstrated by examples from colloquial speech which are the means of linguistic creativity. The examples originate from current surveys with speakers of several Balkan languages. The contribution analyses some of the methods of lexical creativity. This touches on the topics of language contact and etymology, semantics and the expressiveness of several specifically colloquial phenomena. An examination is undertaken to determine the extent to which we can trace parallels to universally applied methods of linguistic creativity.

Балканская фразеология – в поисках исследовательского подхода

Анастасия ПЕТРОВА (Велико Тырново)

1. Состояние балканских исследований в области фразеологии

Со времен Т. Папахаджи и К. Сандфелда известно – во внушительном корпусе балканских фразеологизмов различия впечатляют больше, чем сходства. В настоящее время балканская фразеология остается недостаточно исследованной областью. Отсутствует общая методология собирания, обработки и лексикографической репрезентации материала. В богатых балканских собраниях материалов Т. Папахаджи, Н. Икономова, Я. Томая, Г. Брынкуша и др. нет общего взгляда на вопрос о границах и объеме фразеологии (ср. PAPA-HAGI 1908: 113–178; SANDFELD 1930; ЦОНЕВ 1934, т. 2; ИКОНОМОВ 1968; DJA-MO-DJACONIȚĂ 1968; THOMAJ, LLOSHI, HRISTOVA, QIRIAYATI, MELONASHI 1999; BRÂNCUȘ 1999 и др.). Преобладающая часть балканских исследований связана с установлением происхождения отдельных фразеологизмов, степенью влияния турецкого и греческого языка в балканском языковом союзе, а также с установлением отдельных структурно-семантических параллелей между языками, с лексикографическим представлением фразеологии и др. под. Отсутствует дискуссия об исследовательском подходе, и основная часть исследований до настоящего момента остается в рамках классического подхода, согласно которому фразеологизмы представляют собой единицы, отличающимся константностью и традиционной повторяемостью в речи.

Новые идеи в американской когнитивной лингвистике и русской лингвокультурологии меняют перспективу исследователя.[1] Они направляют внимание на тот факт, что фразеологизмы представляют собой скорее единицы, мотивированные разными структурами знаний, и их семантика следует когнитивным моделям, заданным концептуальной системой культурной общности. Эта точка зрения на фразеологию ставит по-новому вопрос о научном подходе и методологии балканского фразеологического исследования. Настоящий доклад является попыткой найти основные параметры исследования в этой области.

---

[1] Ср. симпозиумы European Society of Phraseology (EUROPHRAS, Цюрих), исследования семинара при Институте языкознания Русской академии наук, под руководством профессораТелия, исследования Московской семантической школы и т.д.

2. Основные требования к исследовательскому подходу в балканской фразеологии

2.1. Без сомнения, когнитивная сущность научного подхода требует направить внимание на ментальную природу фразеологизмов, на их метафорическую образность и эмоционально-экспрессивную окрашенность. Фразеологизмы – результат когнитивной обработки знаний о мире, фиксированных в определенной степени и определенным способом в их структуре. Упорядочение данных происходит с креативным участием метафоры, поэтому методология фразеологического анализа в общих чертах напоминает модель метафорического процесса и использует металингвистический аппарат когнитивной теории метафоры[2]:

Модель метафорического процесса

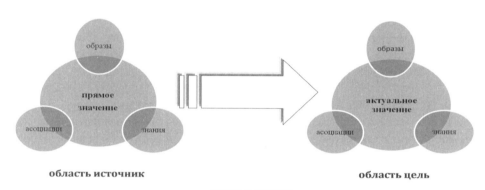

ОБРАЗ СХЕМА
(метафорическая модель)

Надо отметить, что когнитивные процедуры не переносятся автоматически на исследование устойчивых образных единиц из-за специфики их семантики и прагматики. Подобный исследовательский подход мы применили в двух исследованиях образных средств в поле 'эмоций' балканских языков (Петрова 2003, 2006):

1. систематизирование балканского фразеологического фонда, базированное на предварительно выработанной процедуре разграничения грамматических трансформаций и вариантов одного фразеологизма (сам по себе этот этап очень важен для успеха исследования, и поэтому должен быть объектом самостоятельной разработки).

---

2   В виде, в котором находим его в исследования Лейкофа, Джонсона, Търнера и др.; LAKOFF, JOHNSON 1980, 1999; LAKOFF, TURNER 1989 и др.

2. группировка в зависимости от выражаемого понятия (область цель, target domain), напр. 'глупость', 'экзистенция' и др. под., с особым вниманием к стилистической характеристике данной единицы (разг., диал., устар. и т.д.), которая может оказаться важной для установления семантического тождества или различия.

3. дополнительная группировка в зависимости от реализованного сценария, маркированного прямым значением фразеологизма. Это делает возможным установление различия или сходства областей источников (source domain) у фразеологизмов, объединенных одним и тем же сценарием.

4. анализ взаимодействия области источника и области цели, который позволяет дотигнуть до образности (образа-схемы, метафорической модели) фразеологизма. Различные точки зрения на природу образности, ее когнитивный статус и роль в понимании фразеологизма, принципиально сводимы к двум конкурирующим концепциям – „концептуально-метафорическая гипотеза" Р. Гибса, Дж. Лейкофа, М. Джонсона, З. Кьовечеша и др. и „гипотеза интерференции" К. Каччари, Р. Румиати, С. Глагсберга (цит. по Добровольским 1996: 72).

Образность – это результат взаимодействия, специфическая концептуальная структура, состоящая из привлеченной в ментальные процессы системы знаний, образов, ассоциаций и др. под., и механизмов их организации. Она является конкретным ассоциативным контекстом фразеологизма, который стал частью его плана содержания. Шаги 2, 3 и 4 позволяют установить действительное тождество между единицами обоих языков. Учете образной составляющей позволяет в ряде случаев подразделить множество идиом одного семантического поля на подмножества. Это создает предпосылки для более последовательной фиксации семантических сходств и различий между отдельными выражениями в структуре их толкования и наконец – изолировать балканизмов во фразеологии. О тождестве двух метафорических моделей можно говорить только если налицо тождество области источника, области цели и образности обоих фразеологизмов.

5. определение концептуальной области, обладающей более высокой степенью абстракции (культурная модел или концептуальная метафора) с привлечением в анализ всех вербальных и невербальных перевоплощений этой модели.

При помощи подобного когнитивно-культурологического анализа, например при концептуализации ГЛУПОСТИ в балканских языках, отчетливо выступают 4 метафорические модели, обладающие разной степенью стуктурно-семантичсского тождества между единицами:

1. Голова – это вместилище, а ум – субстанция в нем. Эта модель представлена лучше всех, она имеет три образно-схематические структуры, которые обыгрываются приблизительно в стах единицах.

1.1. В голове глупого нет ума

У глупого – пустая голова

болг. *Имам празна глава*, рум. *A avea cap sec*, гр. *Έχω το κεφάλι άδειο*, алб. *E ka kokën bosh, Kokë boshe* (пренебр.); (ср. болг. *празноглав*, рус. *пустая голова* (РБФР 200), англ. *mindless, witless, thoughtless*).

У глупого есть мало ума

болг. *Имам мозък колкото <на> врабец, Имам кокоши (патешки, пилешки) ум (мозък)* (FFB 305), рум. *A avea minte de vrabie (găină)*, гр. *Τόσο του φτάσει το μυαλό (η γνώμη)* (FFB 206), *Του έχουν βάλει τα μυαλά του γαϊδάρου* (FFB 305), алб. *I kanë hedhur trutë e gomarit* (dikujt) përb. (FFB 305); срхр. *Biti pačje pameti, Biti kratke pameti* (FFB 206).

У глупого – легкая голова

рум. *A fi uşurel de minte* (DFRB 259), срхр. *Lak je ispod kape* (FFB 42); (срв. болг. *лекомислен*, англ. *flighty, light(-minded), light-headed*).

Ум глупого не в голове

болг. *Умът ми е в краката* (ФРБЕ 2: 449), *Мисля с краката*, рум. *A gîndi cu picioarele* (DFRB 270), гр. *Δεν έχει τα μυαλά στον τόπο τους* (FFB 22), *Έχει τα μυαλά πάνω από τα μαλλιά* (FFB 305), *Έχει τη γνώμη πίσω απο το κεφάλι (λαιμό)* (FFB 255), алб. *I ka trutë në bark* (FFB 22);

Кто-то выпил ума глупого (интересная модель, только в южнославянских языках).

бълг. *Кукувица (чавка, патка, сврака) ми е изпила акъла (мозъка, пипето, ума)* (ФРБЕ: 500), срхр. *Vrana (kokoš) je komi pamet (mozak) ispila (pozobala)* (FFB 22).

Кто-то коснулся ума глупого – диалектная модель греческого и албанского языков:

Гр. и алб. диал. *Του έχει γλείψει η (α)γελάδα τα μυαλά*, алб. *Ia ka lëpirë lopa trutë (mendtë)* [dikujt] (FFB 193).

1.2. Ум-это субстанция, которая обладает определенным качеством

Ум глупого есть субстанция, которая разбрызгивается

болг. *Събирай си ума!* (ФРБЕ 262), гр. *Φτάξε τη γνώμη σου! Μάσε (μάζεψε) τη γνώμη σου!* (FFB 213), срхр. *Skupljaj pamet!* (FFB 213), алб. *Thirri mendjes!* (FFB 213), *Mbledh mëndjen!*, рум. *Adună-ţi minţile! Vino-ţi în fire!* (FFB 213), *A prinde la minte* (DFRB 503).

Голова глупого есть субстанция нехорошего качества

У глупого толстая голова: рум. *A fi gros de <la> cap* (DFRB 239), срхр. *Debela glava* (FFB 271).

У глупого квадратная голова: рум. *cap pătrat* (пренебр.) (DFRB 104), болг. – виц, с жестом, который „говорит" – 'у мальчика есть квадратная голова'.

У глупого деревянная/твердая голова: гр. *Ξερό κεφάλι* (ΛΝ 159, 259), рум. *A fi tare de cap* (FFB 271), ср. болг. *дървена глава* 'упрямость', *букова глава*; рус. *дубовая голова (башкá), елóвая (чугунная) голова* (РБФР 199–200).

У глупого вода в голове: рум. *A avea apă la cap* (DFRB 51), гр. *Του έχουν νερουλιάσει τα μυαλά του* (FFB 306).

Глупость это солома в голове

болг. диал. *Главата ми е пълна със слама* (ФРБЕ 208);

Голову нужно обработать, что-бы стала лучшей (надо варить, жарить и т.д.) болг. *Опичай си ума!, Не ми увира главата (ума)* (FFB 164).

Ум это жидкость, но у глупого ей недостает.

болг. *Наливам ум (акъл) в главата* на някого, *Наливам с фуния в главата* на някого (ФРБЕ 640), срхр. *Puniti komu glavu, Uliti komu u glavu*, гр. *(Του) το γέμισε το κεφάλι* (FFB 164), рум. *A-şi băga minţile în cap* (DFRB 636). Срв. с англ. и рус., где **ум есть твердая субстанция**: англ. *Drive/hammer/knock into s.o's head*; рус. *вбить/вбивать в голову* (РБФР 200).

Глупость – это мелкая вода, мудрость – глубокая вода.

болг. *Плитък ми е ума (акъла)* (FFB 42), срхр. *Biti plitke pameti* (FFB 303, 251), гр. *Είναι ρηχοκέφαλος* (FFB 42), алб. *Njeri me mëndje të thellë.*

Глупость – это муха в голове[3]

болг. *Главата ми е пълна с мухи (бръмбари)* (ФРБЕ 208); *Имам бръмбари (бръмбарчета, бръмбалчета) в главата си, Имам мухи в главата си* (ФРБЕ 1: 441; НГ 3: 326); Срв. *мухар* (БЕР 4: 353); срхр. *Imate bube u glavu* (FFB 255); рум. *A fi si / a avea sticleţi în cap* (DFRB 231); гр. *Είναι στο*

---

3 О. Терновская отмечает, что это выглядит фрагментом текста, относящегося к области мифологии души (срв. и У. Крайенброк-Дукова – КРАЙЕНБРОК-ДУКОВА 1988). Посколько энтомологические символы рассматриваемого типа доминируют в народных представлениях о душе, обороты речи, связанные с моделью *мухи в голове*, метафоризируют длинный ряд разнообразных внутренних состояний и настроений человека. С их помощью говорят о глупости, сумасшествии, упрямстве, легкомыслии и т.д. (ТЕРНОВСКАЯ 1988) Очень интересная модель с диахронными фрагментами.

κεφάλι του μαμούδια, букв. 'има в главата ти буболечки' (БГР 77); алб. *I ka hyrë miza në koke* (FGSS 1152).

1.3. Глупость – это физическое повреждение

Глупость – это физическое повреждение.

болг. *Ритнат в акъла* (подигр.) (ФРБЕ 256), *Ударен с лопата (мокър пещемал) по главата* (ФРБЕ 434), рум. *Bătut în cap* (DFRB 96), диал. *Bătut (lovit, pălit, trăsnit) cu leuca în cap* (DFRB 96), срхр. *Udaren mokrom čarapom*, гр. *Κουτσαίνει από τα μυαλά* (FFB 304).

Голова – это дом ума и души. У сумасшедшего/глупого – поврежденная голова.

болг. *Мърда му дъската* (FFB 268), *Хвръква (изхвръква, мръдва) ми чивията* (ФРБЕ 478), *Хлопа (мърда) ми едната чивия (дъска)* (ФРБЕ 490), *Правен-недоправен* (ФРБЕ 173), *Пробито та (че) начукано* (ФРБЕ 212) (ФРБЕ 173), *Исик' му са до̂ските, Исик' му са по̂шкине* (См., Ар., Ас., Мн., Дев. – Стойчев 1965); срхр: *Nedostaje komu treća daska* (FFB 268); рум. *A-i lipsi cuiva o doagă* (FFB 268); гр. *Του έχουν στρίψει (έχουν λασκάρει) οι βίδες* (FFB 268), *Τού στριψε η βίδα* (ΛΚΝ 272) (срв. рум. *netot, neîntreg* (Ардял) (Алексова 2005: 83).

Глупость – это физическое повреждение, которое приходит после выпивание/съедание чего-то ядливого (газа, дурмана, белены и др.)

рум. *Am băut gaz?!; Doar n-am baut gaz ca să ..., <Doar> n-am mîncat laur<i>!* (DFRB 186), *A mînca măselariţa* (DFRB 426).

Глупость приходит с ветра

гр. *Του έχει πάρει τα μυαλά ο αέρας* (FFB 306), болг. *Вятър ме носи* (ФРБЕ 1: 204), *Вятър ме вее на сляпа (бяла, сива) кобила* (ФРБЕ 204), *Вятър ме вее на гола ведрина* (ФРБЕ 204), *Вятър ме носи на бял кон* (ФРБЕ 204), *Говоря на вятъра, Вятър ме вее* (ФРБЕ 204); рум. *Vorbă (vorbe) în vînt* (FFB 308), гр. *Μιλάει στον αέρα, Μιλάει κουτουρού (στα χαμένα)*; срв. англ. *To chase the wind goose, be on fool's errand*; рус. *ветренная голова (головушка)* (РБФР 199).

2. **Ум глупого тупой, а умного – острый режущий предмет.**

болг. *Не ми сече ума (главата, акъла, тиквата, кратуната)*, рум. *A nu-l tăia capul*, гр. *Δεν κόβει το μυαλό του*, алб. *mëndje e mprehtë, mëndje thikë, Ia pret mëndja*.

3. **Ум – это живой организм**

болг. *Идва ми акъла в главата, Не ми влиза в главата (нещо)* (FFB 162), *Изскочи му ума (от главата)* (FFB 305), *Оставил го е акъла (някого)* (FFB 306), срхр. *Ne ide mu u glavu;* рум. *A nu-i intra în cap, A-i pleca mintea la plimbare, A-şi pierde minţile*; гр. *Δεν του μπαίνει στο κεφάλι (στο μυαλό), Του έφυγε το μυαλό της κεφαλής*; алб. *I ikën trutë (e kokës), I kanë rrjedhur trutë, Akoma si kanë ardhur mëntë, Si hyn në kokë [diçka].*

4. Ум – это плод, который зреет.
болг. *Зелена е главата някому*, рум. *A fi necopt la minte*, гр. *Γούρμασε η αγουρίδα (έγινε η αγουρίδα μέλι).*

Перспективность группировки по понятию и по сценарию доказана практикой. Она приводит к нетривиальным результатам при исследовании универсальных и специфических черт в сфере идиоматики (ср. DOBROVOL'SKIJ/ PIIRAINEN 2005; ПИИРАЙНЕН 1997: 92–99; ДОБРОВОЛЬСКИЙ 1996: 91; KÖVECSES 2006, 2010; OMAZIĆ 2005; БАРАНОВ/ДОБРОВОЛЬСКИЙ 1997: 11–21, БАРАНОВ/ДОБРОВОЛЬСКИЙ 2009 и др.).

2.2. Современный подход требует эллиминации оппозиции между синхронией и диахронией и рассматривание фразеологизмов и как фрагмент живого языкового процесса, и как элемент оси времени. Это предполагает исследование фразеологии не в ее идеальном статусе в словарях литературных языков, а в движении, с особым вниманием к реальным когнитивным феноменам. Идея учитывать все межкультурные и внутрикультурные (диалектные, социальные, стилевые, индивидуальные) различия и сходства присутствует и в когнитивной лингвистике, и в лингвокультурологии последнего времени (KÖVECSES 2005: 61–65; ТЕЛИЯ 1999: 17; ПИИРАЙНЕН 1997: 93; ДОБРОВОЛЬСКИЙ 1997: 45 и др.). По традиции принято связывать фразеологизм с устойчивостью, но всущности в каждом синхронном срезе „его когнитивный запас" пополняется и видоизменяется, привлекаются новые вербально-образные средства и возможности для интерпретации, смысл „достраивается" интуитивно, в соответствии с современной картиной мира. (ФЕОКТИСТОВА 1999: 175). Фрейм фразеологизма становится „объемным" (ФЕОКТИСТОВА 1999), потому что в его содержательном плане кодируется информация не только в результате взаимодействия его прямого и актуального значения, но и по причине активации его богатого образного потенциала. Хороший пример в этом отношении – модель МУХА В ГОЛОВЕ. Есть различия между активированным при возникновении единицы фреймом и фреймом в ее функционировании сегодня. В старом фрейме метафорический процесс активирует мифологические представления, которые с течением времени меняются под влиянием фразеологической агнонимии (ЖУКОВА/МАНДРИКОВА 2001; ФРЕЙДЕНБЕРГ 1987)[4]:

---

4   АОК – ассоциативно-образный комплекс, Ф – фрейм.

муха в голове

$$\Phi_1 \ (\text{муха в голове}) + AOK_1$$
$$\Phi_2 \ (\text{муха в голове}) + AOK_2$$
$$\Phi_1 \neq \Phi_2$$

С помощью компонента *муха* сохраняются ассоциативные связи со старым знанием на подсознательном уровне. Они становятся связующим звеном между актуальной информацией и мифологическими фрагментами, являясь своеобразным субстратом актуального значения, над которым надстраиваются дополнительные новые семантические элементы. Реальные когнитивные феномены связаны с культурно-языковой компетенцией коллектива, характер которой меняется во времени. Она не находит отражения в словарях, но исключительно полезна для исследователя. Чудесный пример в этом отношении – исследование БРЫНКУША 1999.

2.3. При исследовании фразеологии исключительно важно разработать процедуру достижения культурной информации в образности единицы – эта идея занимает особое место в теоретических и прикладных исследованиях русской лингвокультурологической школы (ТЕЛИЯ 1999: 17, ОПАРИНА 2007: 27–48, ТЕЛИЯ 1996: 218). В последнее время основная критика когнитивной теории связана с абсолютизацией физиологической основы метафоры и недооценкой роли культурного фактора (DOBROVOL'SKIJ/PIIRAINEN 2005; KÖVECSES 2005).

В метафорическом процессе приводятся в движение пласты знаний, принадлежащих к разным культурным слоям, которые подобно „семантическому лейтмотиву”, воспроизводятся в языковой памяти (ср. САМИГУЛЛИНА 2009). Эта культурная информация присутствует в ассоциативно-образных компонентах фразеологической семантики и проявляется в связи образов со стереотипами, эталонами, символами, мифологемами, прототипическими ситуациями и другими знаками культуры, усвоенными и воспроизводившимися во времени (ТЕЛИЯ 1996: 214, цит. по ОПАРИНОЙ 2007). Когнитивно-культурологичный анализ проникает в образность и позволяет достигнуть глубокой сущности старого концепта, следы которого живут новой „жизнью” во многих языковых средствах. Так например, в образности новогреческого выражения ἔξω φρενῶν 'обезумевший от гнева' сохраняются следы древнегреческого представления о центре мысловной и эмоциональной деятельности человека. В старых текстах αι φρένες (первоначально 'область диафрагмы, которая отделяет сердце и легкие от других внутренних органов') никогда не употребляется в качестве субъекта психической деятельности[5], поскольку осо-

---

5 В Омировите текстове думата присъства в локативни обозначения (ἐνὶ φρεσί 'въ-тре', κατὰ φρένας 'под' или περί φρένας 'около тази част от тялото').

знается как вместилище (дом) сущности человека (ИВАНОВ 1980: 89). Это ключевой концепт в мифологической и эстетической символизации греческой культуры, который не имеет эквивалента в западных языках.[6] Выражение ἔξω φρενῶν для человека, имеющего культурно-языковую компетенцию, соответствующую старому временному срезу, «рисует» картину, в которой ум или душа покидают свой «дом», и этот сценарий развертывается по когнитивной модели, очень распространенной в старой греческой культуре. В этом смысле использование культурного фактора при анализе позволяет уловить культурно «окрашенные» элементы в море универсальных фактов.

2.4. И наконец, особенно важна проблема охвата подвергнутого анализу языкового материала.

Анализ фразеологизмов должен происходить в рамках языковой системы, наряду со свободными сочетаниями, предложными выражениями, словами с метафорическим значением, грамматическими конструкциями, словообразовательными моделями и т.п., поскольку выражая определенный концепт, язык мобилизует весь свой потенциал.

С другой стороны, языковые единицы „работают” для общих культурных моделей (концептуальных метафор), обладающие кроме языковых „воплотителей” и многими еще невербальными проявлениями. Поэтому умение интерпретировать образные средства формирует особый тип компетентности, основанной на усвоении «языка» культуры посредством всех ее текстов – мифов, сказок, преданий, религиозных и художественных текстов, неязыковых систем как живопись, театр, кино и др. (ОПАРИНА 2007: 37). Например, в древнегреческом языке появляется фразеологизм ὕδωρ πίνειν 'пить воду', с переносным значением 'становиться грустным, мрачным, прозаичным'. Подобного выражения не находиться в древнеболгарских текстах, но в историко-фольклорной перспективе наткнулась на верование, рассказанное Д. Мариновым и гласящее, что «когда человек упадет в воду, сразу приходит чёрт, держит в руке маленький зеленый кувшин с водой и приглашает его выпить из него. Пока не выпьет из кувшина, человек не может утонуь» (МАРИНОВ 1994: 80). Это знакомая во многих различных культурах ассоциативная связь между идеями о *воде* и *смерти* (или *состоянии, близкого к смерти),* греки вербализовали ее.

---

6 Напоминает культурный статус концепта *hara* в японском (*hara* не просто 'живот', это положительно конотирован символ, важный центр жизни, с особым местом в светоощущении и аналогиях, базированных на старую китайскую медицину; DOBROVOL'SKIJ/PIIRAINEN 2005: 14–15).

И наконец, притягивание других индоевропейских и неиндоевропейских параллелей к балканскому материалу – это возможность выделения универсальных и этноспецифических феноменов.

В своей совокупности изложенные здесь требования оформляют облик научного подхода к балканской фразеологии как подхода комплексного когнитивно-культурологического характера. Исследование, проведенное в подобных рамках, позвóлит отчетливо очертить не только универсальность концептуальных метафор высокого уровня абстракции (generic level), но и множество невидимых на поверхности различий в ассоциативно-образных кóмплексах балканских фразеологических единиц на конкретном уровне диалектного, социального, стилевого, индивидуального картирования.

Литература

АЛЕКСОВА, В. (2005): Езикови свидетелства за значението на дома в представите на румънския народ. 10 години специалност „Балканистика". София. 79–86.

АПРЕСЯН, В.; АПРЕСЯН, Ю. (1993): Метафора в семантическо представлении эмоций. Вопросы языкознания, кн. 3. 27–35.

БАРАНОВ, А.; ДОБРОВОЛЬСКИЙ, Д. (1997): Постулаты когни-тивной семантики. ИАН СЛЯ, т. 56, 1. 11–21.

БАРАНОВ, А.; ДОБРОВОЛЬСКИЙ, Д. (2009): Принципы семантического описания фразеологии. Вопросы языкознания, 6. 21–34.

БРЫНКУША, Г. (1999): Concordanțe lingvistice româno-albaneze. Bucureşti.

ДОБРОВОЛЬСКИЙ, Д. (1996): Образная составляющая в семантике идиом. Вопросы языкознания, 1. 71–93.

ДОБРОВОЛЬСКИЙ, Д. (1997): Национально-культурная специфика во фразеологии (1). Вопросы языкознания, 6. 37–48.

КРАЙЕНБРОК-ДУКОВА, У. (1988): Представите на славяните за душата (по езикови данни). Славистичен сборник, 1988. 214.

ЖУКОВА, А. Г.; МАНДРИКОВА, Г. М. (2001): Фразеологическая агномия: к постановке проблемы. Available: http://www.philot.msu.ru/~rls2004/files/sec/99.doc. Date of access: 15.11.2008.

ИВАНОВ, Вяч. (1980): Структура гомеровских текстов, описывающих психические состояния. Структура текста, Москва. 81.

ИКОНОМОВ, Н. (1968): Балканска народна мъдрост. София.

МАРИНОВ, Д. (1994): Народна вяра и религиозни народни обичаи. София.

НИКИТИНА, С. Е. (1993): Устная народная культура и языковое сознание. Москва.

ОПАРИНА, Е. О. (1999): Лексические коллокации и их внутрифреймовые модусы. Фразеология в контексте культуры. Москва. 139–144.

ОПАРИНА, Е. (2007): Лингвокультурология: Методологические основания и основные понятия. Online. Available: http://www.auditorium.ru/books/1000/gl2.pdf; Date of access: 23.02.2007.

ПЕТРОВА, А. (2003): Езиковата метафора и балканската картина на света. Велико Търново.

ПЕТРОВА, А. (2006): Концептите в полето „радост" – сходства и различия в балканския лингвокултурен ареал. Велико Търново.

ПИИРАЙНЕН, Е. (1997): „Область метафорического отображения" – метафора – метафорическая модель (на материале фразеологии западно-мюнстерландского диалекта). Вопросы языкознания, 4. 92–99.

САМИГУЛЛИНА, А. С. (2009): „Скрытая память" слова (на примере метафорических номинаций). Вопросы языкознания, 4. 110–118.

ТЕЛИЯ, В. Н. (1996): Русская фразеология: Семантический, прагматический и лингвокультурологический аспекты. Москва.

ТЕЛИЯ, В. Н. (1999): Первоочередные задачи и методологические проблемы исследования фразеологического языка в контексте культуры. Фразеология в контексте культуры. Москва. 13–24.

ТОЛСТОЙ, И. И. (1983): О предмете этнолингвистики и ее роли в изучении языка и этноса. Ареальные исследования в языкознании и этнографии: Язык и этнос. Л. 181–190.

ФЕОКТИСТОВА, А. (1999): Культурно значимая роль внутренней формы идиом с позиций когитологии. Фразеология в контексте культуры. Studia philologica. Москва. 174–180.

ФРЕЙДЕНБЕРГ, О. М. (1978): Миф и литература древности. Москва.

ЦОНЕВ, Б. (1934): История на българския език, т. 2. София.

BRÂNCUȘ, G. (1999): Concordanțe lingvistice româno-albaneze. București.

CACCIARI, C.; RUMIATI, R.; GLUCKSBERG, S. (1992): The role of word meanings, transparency and familiarity in the mental images of idioms. Proceeding of IDIOMS. Tilburg.

DJAMO-DJACONITA, L. (1968): Contributions à la parémiologie balkanique. Actes VI. 277–292.

DOBROVOL'SKIJ, D.; PIIRAINEN, E. (2005): Cognitive Theory of Metaphor and Idiom Analysis. Jezikoslovje, 6.1. 7.

GIBBS, R. W. (1990): Psycholinguistic studies on the conceptual basis of idiomaticity. Cognitive linguistics. 1–4.

KÖVECSES, Z. (1986): Metaphors of anger, pride, and love. Amsterdam, Philadelphia.

KÖVECSES, Z. (2006a): Embodyment, Experiential Focus, and Diachronic Change in Metaphor. In: Selected Proceedings of the 2005 Symposium of New Approaches in English Historical Lexis (HEL – LEX), ed. R. W. McConchie et al., 1–7, Somerville, MA: Cascadilla Proceeding Project.

KÖVECSES, Z. (2006b): Language, mind and culture: a practical introduction, Oxford: Oxford University Press.

KÖVECSES, Z. (2010): Cultural Variation in Metaphor1. Online. Available: http://www.fulbright. hu/book2/kovecseszoltan.pdf. Date of access: 17.08.2010.

LAKOFF, G.; JONSON, M. (1980): Metaphors we live by, Chicago, London.

LAKOFF, G. (1987): Women, fire, and dangerous things. What categories reveal about the mind. Chicago.

LAKOFF, G. (1992): The Contemporary Theory of Metaphor – Online. Available: http://www.acwwu. edu/market/semiotic/lkof_met.html, Date of access: 19.08.04.

LAKOFF, G. (1993): The contemporary theory of metaphor // Metaphor and thought. Second edition. Cambridge.

LAKOFF, G.; Turner, M. (1989): More than Cool Reason: A Field Guide to Poetic Metaphor. Chicago, London: University of Chicago Press.

OMAZIĆ, M. (2005): Introduction: Why, What and How in phraseology. Jezikoslovje, 6.1. 1–5.

PAPAHAGI, T. (1908): Parallele Ausdrücke und Redensarten im Rumänischen, Albanesischen, Neugriechischen und Bulgarischen. Jahresbericht des Instituts für rumänische Sprache zu Leipzig XIV. 113–178.

PIIRAINEN, E. (2010): Common features in the phraseology of European languages: cultural and areal perspectives. Available: http://fi/100v/liitteet/1203329856-abstracts1.pdf. Date of access: 11.05.2010.

SANDFELD, K. (1930): Linguistique balkanique. Problèmes et résultats. Paris.

Източници материала

ФРБЕ: К. Ничева, С. Спасова-Михайлова, Кр. Чолакова: Фразеологичен речник на българския език., т. 1, т. 2. София 1974.

БАР: Т. Кацори, Т. Тартари, Л. Душа, С. Паско, Л. Грабоцка: Българско-албански речник. София 1959.

БГР: К. Илков, Д. Марицас, Ап. Михайлов, Д. Петкидис: Българско-гръцки речник. София 1991.

БЕР: Български етимологичен речник, т.1–5. София 1977–1996.

Стойчев 1965: Т. Стойчев: Родопски речник. Българска диалектология. Проучвания и материали, II. София.

DEX: Dicţionarul explicativ al limbii române. Bucureşti 1998.

DFRB: С. Калдиева-Захариева: Румънско-български фразеологичен речник. София 1997.

FFB: J. Thomaj, Xh. Lloshi, R. Hristova, K. Qiriayati, A. Melonashi: Fjalor frayeologjik balkanik. Dituria 1999.

FGSS: N. Rrahmani: Fjalor i gluhës së sotme shqipe. Prishtinë 1981. 1–2.

ΛKN: Λεξικό της κοινής νεοελληνικής. Θεσσαλονίκη 2002.

The Balkan Phraseology: In Search of the Research Approach

The present paper is an attempt to find an answer to the general question in the research of the Balkan phraseological corpus, namely: which is the best approach in revealing the nature of the phraseologism and hence in the development of the Balkan comparative research in this field. The idea suggested for discussion is that the traditional methods for systematization and interpreting of the phraseologisms cannot reveal their real cognitive and communicative values of units, which transfer a particular kind of cultural knowledge, accumulated during the process of their function in the language. Through them it is difficult to find the similarities and the differences between the languages of the Balkan linguistic union. The research model applicable for Balkan phraseology studies is to be found on the basis of *The Cognitive Theory of Metaphor* (LAKOFF, JOHNSON 1980, 1999; LAKOFF 1987, 1990, 1993; LAKOFF, TURNER 1989, etc.) with the suggested in it tools for analysis and its development in *The Conventional Figurative Language Theory* (DOBROVOL'SKIJ/PIIRAINEN 2005; БАРАНОВ, ДОБРОВОЛЬСКИЙ 2009, etc.).

On Some Peculiar Datives in Colloquial
Middle Ottoman Texts

Claudia RÖMER, Vienna

Some Modern Standard Turkish verbs like *başla-* "to begin" usually take the dative
with nouns, including verbal nouns like the infinitive, others like *iste-* "to want" do
not. Within Modern Turkish, case marking is sometimes liable to change, cf.

(1a) *bana   sordu*
      IDAT   askPRET3SG
      "He asked me"

(1b) *benden   sordu*
      IABL   askPRET3SG
      "id."

Both (1a) and (1b) are possible according to *Türkçe Sözlük* 1955, but according to
Türkçe Sözlük 1988 the ablative case can only be used in a context of responsibil-
ity:

(1c) *benden   sordu*
      IABL   askPRET3SG
      "He held me responsible"

NILSSON 1985: 115 draws up a list of predicates of "mental reaction" which can be
used either with the allative or the ablative according to "temporal properties of the
context"[1]:

---

1 NILSSON 1985 prefers the term allative throughout her study, which principally marks
   goal phrases (108, 110). Turkic datives in general can have various functions (local, directive, allative, and terminative; cf. JOHANSON 1998: 54). Differently, and following
   (BAZIN, BASTUJI 1976: 105) argues that she calls the dative directive throughout.
   According to her it has the functions of direction towards a place, towards a goal, towards a person, of conjunction and approaching, of the value of exchange (*beş kuruşa*
   "for five *kuruş*"), of a temporal extension (*güze doğru* "towards autumn"), stapled
   phrases (phrases enchassées, *üstüste* "one above the other"), and others. Its central value
   is «le pôle positif d'un déplacement spatial ou symbolique qui peut être représenté par
   un vecteur» (105–114, esp. 113).

(2a) *derhal*   *dediğimi*
      immediately   sayNOUN-POSS1SG-AKK

      yapacağına   *eminim*
      doFUT-NOUN-POSS3SG-DAT   sureCOP1SG
      "I'm sure that he will immediately do as I say." (ex. 249)

(2b) *derhal*   *toparlanacağımdan*
      immediately   pull oneself togetherFUT-NOUN-POSS1SG-ABL

      emindim
      surePRET1SG
      "I was sure that I would immediately pull myself together." (ex. 250)

Nilsson argues that whereas the first statement "concerns one single future event", the second one "expresses an enduring certainty".[2]

At different times, different case markers have expressed grammatical relations in phrases like

   ata bin-
   horseDAT mount
   "to mount a horse",

i.e. both the theme and goal roles can be marked by either datives or accusatives (ERDEM 2006). Therefore, principally, it can be assumed that case assignment can also have changed during the transition from Middle Ottoman via Late Ottoman to Modern Turkish.

Usually, the two phraseological verbs formed with the Arabic nominal component *'inâyet* "grace", viz. *'inâyet olun-*[3] "to be granted" and *'inâyet it-/eyle-* "to grant" are constructed with a subject or a direct object respectively. The direct object can be marked or unmarked (RÖMER 1988).

(3a) *... bâbında*   *'ahdnâme-i   hümâyûn*   *'inâyet olunub*
      ... chapterPOSS3SG-LOC   treatyIZ[4]   lofty   grantGER
      "a lofty treaty will be granted, in order to ..."[5]

But if the thing to be granted is an action verb, we find the verbal noun in –mE in the dative. The same usage is still to be observed today, cf. *Yeni Redhouse Sözlüğü*:

---

2 Cf. also NILSSON 1991: 104.
3 In the Ottoman examples we will not use any diacritics in order not to complicate reading the sentences.
4 IZ designates the Persian *izafet* construction, which is used to link two nouns, either forming a genitive compound, or linking an attribute to its head noun.
5 SCHAENDLINGER 1983: doc. 25/l. 22; doc. 32/l. 19.

"536a *inayet et-* 1. to give as a favor 2. to do as an act of grace", with -a respectively.

(3b) *bu*   *canibe*   *i'lâm itmesine*[6]
      this   sideDAT   communicateINF-POSS3SG-DAT

      'inâyet buyurıla
      grantPASS-OPT3SG
      "please do the favour of communicating [this] to our side"[7]

or with the active form of *buyur-*:

(3c) *biz bendenüze*   *bir mektûb-i*   *şerîfünüz*
      we slavePOSS2PL   one letterIZ   loftyPOSS2PL

      ile   *bildürmesine*   *'inâyet idesiz*
      with   communicateINF-POSS3SG-DAT   grace   doOPT2SG
      "please do the favour of communicating [this] to this servant of yours"[8]

If we look at examples (2a–2d), we see that there seems to be a difference in usage whether the verb is used with a substantive or a deverbal noun.

However, in the 16ᵗʰ century material used here, there can be exceptions from this apparent rule, no matter whether instead of *'inâyet* the synonymous word *himmet* is used or not. The text of the following document does not share any of the characteristics presented in this paper, and, what is more, we see that the active and passive voices are mixed up. The verbal noun in -mEK takes an accusative marker, yet the phraseological verb *himmet buyur-* 'to do the grace', 'to deign' is used in the optative of the passive voice. This is a fairly frequent phenomenon in Middle Ottoman texts near to the level of the spoken language.

(4)   *Zaranda bîrovları*   *bir baluban*   *getürdiler*
      Z.   lawyerPL   one falcon   bringPRET3PL

      bu yaz   *ki olub*   *gâyet iri olduğın*
      this summer   that   beGER very large beNOUN-POSS3SG-ACC

      dahı   *bildürmegi*   *himmet buyurıla*
      too   tellINF-ACC   grace   orderPASS-OPT3SG

      anı   *dahı*   *niçe* (!) *idelüm*
      itACC   too   how   doOPT1PL

6 In the glosses to the examples, we will use the term "infinitive" (INF) for the two deverbal nouns in -mEK and -mE exclusively. All other deverbal nouns will be called "nouns" (NOUN).
7 PROCHÁZKA-EISL/RÖMER 2007, doc. no. 50.
8 PROCHÁZKA-EISL/RÖMER 2007, doc. no. 102.

"The *birovs* (lawyers) of Zaranda brought a falcon. Could you deign to tell (your master) that this summer, as it happened, it became very large? What should we do with it?"[9]

The same seems to go for the verb *dirîğ it-* "to refuse", where we have the dative only with the infinitive, but not with substantives:

(5a)   *cümle ahvâli*   *bildürmesine*
       all circumstancesACC   announceINF-POSS3SG-DAT

       dirîğ itmeyesiz
       refuseNEG-OPT2PL
       "Do not neglect telling [us] all the circumstances"[10]

The normal construction, however, would be *dirîğ it-* "to refuse" with a direct object (with or without the accusative marker), e.g.,

(5b)   *enzâr-i*   *'âlîyenüz*   *dirîğ buyurmayasız*
       looksIZ   loftyFEM-POSS2SG   refuseNEG-OPT2PL
       "Do not refuse [us] your lofty benevolence."[11]

In 16th-century Ottoman letters of lower officials and private persons (PROCHÁZ-KA-EISL/RÖMER 2007), and to a much lesser degree in colloquial/direct speech parts of firmans of the same period (SCHAENDLINGER 1983 and 1986), unexpected datives with -mEsI/-mElErI (27 examples), -mEK (29 and 7 examples respectively), -dÜGI/-dÜKIErI (18 and 1 example[s] respectively) occur frequently when replacing the subject or direct object, e.g.

(6)   *gayrı kimesneyi*   *çıkarmağa*
       other somebodyACC   take outINF-DAT

       mümkin olmadı
       possible beNEG-PRET3SG
       "it was not possible to bring other people out"

(7)   *bu maslahat*   *te'hir*   *olunduğına*
       this matter   delay   bePASS-NOUN-POSS3SG-DAT

       eyü anlanmaz
       good understandPASS-NEGAOR3SG
       "it cannot be understood well why this matter was delayed".

---

9 PROCHÁZKA-EISL/RÖMER 2007: doc. no. 86.
10 PROCHÁZKA-EISL/RÖMER 2007: doc. no. 73.
11 PROCHÁZKA-EISL/RÖMER 2007: doc. no. 82.

In the examples above the normal *SOV* word order of Turkic languages is observed. However, we also find inverted word order, which could be interpreted as a phenomenon similar to the so-called *devrik cümle* of Colloquial Modern Turkish, or as a result of language contact[12]:

(8) *buyurmışlar   ba'zî   tâyifeye   evler   yapmağa*
orderPAST3PL   some   peopleDAT   housePL   makeINF-DAT
"They ordered some people to make houses"[13]

Under the heading of "Vermengung von Sätzen, Anakoluthe", NÉMETH (1965) gives examples of similar constructions, which according to him, are against the rules and are supposed to be of Bulgarian influence.

(9) *qızın   qarnı   buyuduğune   hiç duşekden*
girlGEN bellyPOSS3-SG growNOUN-POSS3SG-DAT   not bedABL

qalqmay
risePRES-NEG3SG
„wegen der Zunahme ihres Bauches steht das Mädchen aus dem Bett nicht auf"[14]

(10) *seçey-misin   bu çocuq   dilsiz*
seePRES-INTERR-2PSG this child   tonguePRIV

olduğuna
beNOUN-POSS3SG-DAT
„Merkst du (nicht), daß das Kind stumm ist?"[15]

(11) *ben   seç''erum   c''endumdan   karnun*
I   seeAOR-1SG   selfPOSS1SG-ABL   bellyPOSS2SG

aç(un)   olduğuna
hungry(GEN)   beNOUN-POSS3SG-DAT
„Ich sehe es an mir selbst, daß euer Magen hungrig ist"[16]

(12) *ben   zan etmemişim   buyle   geç''   olduğuna*
I   thinkNEG-PAST1SG   so   late   beNOUN-POSS3SG-DAT
„Ich dachte nicht, daß es so spät ist"[17]

---

12 On this latter possibility, see also MENZ 2000:152.
13 PROCHÁZKA-EISL/RÖMER 2007: doc. no. 106.
14 NÉMETH 1965: 115.
15 NÉMETH 1965: 94.
16 NÉMETH 1970: 53.
17 NÉMETH 1970: 36.

Without trying to give an explanation, HAZAI (1973: 458) points out a few unusual occurrences of case assignment:

(13) *arpasu   bu vilāyetlerde   yapmağa   bilmezler*
     beer   this countryPL-LOC   makeINF-DAT knowAOR-NEG3PL
     „Bier versteht man in diesen Provinzen nicht zu machen"

ADAMOVIĆ (2001: 128) quotes, among others, some sentences from Argenti's 16th century *Regola* which he interprets as showing Italian influence, as far as word order is concerned,

(14) *ſpat edeim   eſpap   verdighine*
     proveOPT1SG   things   giveNOUN-POSS2SG-DAT
     „Ich werde nachweisen, daß die (!) [ihm] die Ware übergeben hast"

Turkish infinitival double passives are investigated by KORNFILT 1988. ÖZSOY 1988 analyses the three types of Turkish infinitives within the framework of the Government and Binding Theory. Among the spatial cases (locative, ablative, directive), the directive case has the function of a "positive orientation towards a point of arrival", but not necessarily of the arrival at this point itself (BASTUJI 1976: 113). These studies, although dealing with the Turkish dative, are not helpful for elucidating our present subject.

JOHANSON 1990: 209, when discussing sentences without a first actant, e.g.,

(15) *girmek   mümkün mü?*
     enterINF possible INTERR
     "Is it possible to come in?",

also cites several expressions of necessity from other Turkic languages, e.g. Khakas

(16) *xarā   uzirɣa   kiräk*
     night   sleepAOR-NOUN-DAT   necessary
     "at night one has to sleep",

with the aorist noun/participle and the dative marker.

Similarly, an infinitive in -mā or -mAA exists in the Oghuz Turkic variety of Gagauz, spoken in Moldova, Bulgaria, and the Ukraine. This infinitive has evolved from the infinitive in -mAK plus the dative case marker -A and is believed to be contact-induced from Slavonic (DOERFER 1959: 270, MENZ 2000: 13).

(17) "ister   bolnicaya   gitmää
     want-PRS3SG   hospital-DAT   go-INF
     'She wants to go to the hospital'"[18]

---

18 MENZ 2000: 152.

Astrid Menz has shown that the use of this feature in Gagauz is especially used with same-subject sentences, whereas under the influence of Slavonic (i.e. Bulgarian and Russian) analytic modal constructions have evolved[19]. In Bulgarian Gagauz, even same-subject sentences tend to be constructed with the optative:

(18) "... istee   yašasïn   Sofyada
      want-PRS3SG   live-OPT3SG   Sofia-LOC
      '... he wants to live in Sofia'"[20]

If we look at the examples given so far, we see that many have been found in transcription texts, which basically are colloquial texts or in written texts near the colloquial level. Some examples come from the so-called Vidin Turkish dialects and some others from Gagauz.

Within Turkish dialects, the analytical construction and "the replacement of infinitival clauses by subjunctive ones" is a typical feature of West Rumelian Turkish[21]:

(19) *"Lâzımdır*   *çalışalım"* = *"Treba da rabotime"* (Macedonian)
      necessaryCOP   workOPT1PL
      "We have to work"[22]

In this example, we see the Slavonic analytic construction with the subjunctor *da*, which, in the Slavonic languages has all but completely superseded the infinitive.[23]
If the Balkan languages have lost the infinitive, and if this loss has influenced the Balkan Turkish dialects and Gagauz, how can we suppose that the constructions with the dative of nouns or infinitives in Middle Ottoman can be the result of Slavonic influence?

It appears that the infinitive, under Greek influence, "has been completely lost in ... Macedonian ... and almost completely in Bulgarian ...", but it has survived in Croatian and Serbian, though the subjunctive construction is much more frequent.[24] Croatian and Serbian infinitives, including those used with the preposition *za* in final (or purposive[25]) clauses, have been discussed by JOSEPH (1983: 136):

---

19 MENZ 2000: 153.
20 MENZ 2000: 153.
21 FRIEDMAN 2006: 38. Within Turcology, this has been discussed in various contexts, see, e.g. KAKUK 1960; KAKUK 1972: 246.
22 The example is taken from FRIEDMAN 2006: 38.
23 On the loss of the infinitive in most of the Slavonic languages and in the Balkan Sprachbund as a whole, see, e.g., TOMIĆ 2006, chapter 6 "Infinitives and Subjunctives".
24 TOMIĆ 2006: 413.
25 JOHANSON 2009: 3. I would like to thank Lars Johanson for sending me the text of this paper.

(20)   *došao sam za gledati* 'I came (in order) to see'

Contemporary Croatian and Slovenian are now under the influence of the colloquial non-standard language, cf.

(21)   *imate kaj za jesti?*[26]
       "Have you got anything to eat?"

It is this construction we have to think of as a model for the Ottoman (and Gagauz)
usage of the infinitive and other deverbal nouns together with the dative.

One of six areas where modal systems have converged under the influence of
dominant Indo-European languages is precisely the Balkans with East and West
Rumelian Turkish and Gagauz.[27] Whereas JOHANSON 2009 deals mainly with the
"Balkanisms of the South-European languages, which have replaced infinitive
constructions by finite complementation"[28], he also includes the feature of "Purposive markers, mostly dative markers added to infinitives", giving a few examples
from Gagauz.

Nearly all the Ottoman texts discussed here are related to Ottoman affairs in
Hungary or were written in Hungarian surroundings. During Ottoman rule in Hungary, administrative and military staff predominantly were of Slavic origin, be they
(new) Muslims or not. The "peculiar" datives, therefore, can be assumed to have
evolved under Slavonic influence.[29]

Bibliography

ADAMOVIĆ, M. (2001): *Das Türkische des 16. Jahrhunderts. Nach den Aufzeichnungen des
       Florentiners Filippo Argenti (1533)*. Göttingen (= Materialia Turcica. Beiheft 14).
BASTUJI, J. (1976): *Les relations spatiales en turc contemporain. Étude sémantique*. Paris.
DOERFER, G. (1959): Das Gagausische. In: Jean Deny et al. (eds): *Philologiae Turcicae
       Fundamenta*. Wiesbaden. 260–271.
ERDEM, M. (2006): Grammatical cases and thematic roles in Turkish: Historical Account.
       In: S. Yağcıoğlu, A. C. Değer (eds.): *Advances in Turkish Linguistics. Proceedings of
       the 12th International Conference on Turkish Linguistics, 11–13 August, 2004*. İzmir:
       Dokuz Eylül University İzmir. 137–150.
FRIEDMAN, V. A. (2006): West-Rumelian Turkish in Macedonia and adjacent areas. In:
       Turkic Languages in Contact. Edited by Hendrik Boeschoten and Lars Johanson. With

---

26 KUNZMANN-MÜLLER 2003: 153.
27 JOHANSON 2009: 3.
28 JOHANSON 2009: 7 argues that modal markers can easily be copied on the one hand, but
   on the other, similar patterns exist in Turkic, so that we cannot be sure if these constructions are copied structures at all: Two main clauses are juxtaposed, "(i) *Someone has a
   wish.* (ii) *May this occur*".
29 The Khakas construction in example (16) above could have been influenced by Russian.

the editorial assistance of Sevgi Ağcagül and Vildan Milani. Wiesbaden (= Turcologica 61). 27–45.

HAZAI, G. (1973): *Das Osmanisch-Türkische im XVII. Jahrhundert. Untersuchungen an den Transkriptionstexten von Jakab Nagy de Harsány*. The Hague, Paris.

JOHANSON, L. (1990): Subjektlose Sätze im Türkischen. In: B. Brendemoen (ed.): Oslo, *Altaica Osloensia. Proceedings from the 32nd Meeting of the Permanent International Altaistic Conference June 12–16, 1989*. Oslo. 193–218.

JOHANSON, L. (1998): Structure of Turkic. In: E. Csató, L. Johanson (eds.): *The Turkic Languages*. London, New York.

JOHANSON, L. (2009): Mood Meets Mood, *Morphologies in Contact Thursday, October 1st – Saturday, October 3rd, 2009, University of Bremen*, unpublished paper.

JOSEPH, B. D. (1983): *The synchrony and diachrony of the Balkan infinitive: a study in areal, general, and historical linguistics*. Cambridge (= Cambridge studies in linguistics, Supplementary Volume).

KAKUK, S. (1960): Constructions hypotactiques dans le dialecte turc de la Bulgarie occidentale, *Acta Orientalia Academiae Scientiarum Hungaricae* 11. 249–257.

KAKUK, S. (1972): Le dialecte turc d'Ohrid en Macédoine. *Acta Orientalia Academiae Scientiarum Hungaricae* 26. 227–282.

KORNFILT, J. (1988): NP-Deletion and Case Marking in Turkish. *Studies on Turkish Linguistics. Proceedings of the Fourth international conference of Turkish Linguistics, 17–19 August 1988*. Middle East Technical University, Ankara. 187–215.

KUNZMANN-MÜLLER, B. (2003): Gesellschaft im Wandel – Slovenisch im Wandel. *Slovenski knjižni jezik – aktualna Vprašanja in zgodovinske izkušnje. Ob 450-letnici izida prve slovenske knjige Mednarodni simpozij Obdobja – Metode in zvrsti. Ljubljana, 5.–7. december 2001*. Ljubljana. 147–160.

MENZ, A. (2000): Analytic modal constructions in Gagauz. *Studies on Turkish and Turkic Languages. Proceedings of the Ninth International Conference on Turkish Linguistics. Lincoln College, Oxford, August 12–14, 1998*. Edited by Aslı Göksel and Celia Kerslake.Wiesbaden. 150–158.

NÉMETH, J. (1965): *Die Türken von Vidin*. Budapest.

NÉMETH, J. (1970): *Die türkische Sprache in Ungarn im 17. Jahrhundert*. Amsterdam.

NILSSON, B. (1985): *Case Marking Semantics in Turkish* Stockholm: Department of Linguistics, University of Stockholm.

NILSSON, B. (1991): Turkish Semantics Revisited. *Turkish linguistics today*, edited by H. Boeschoten & L. Verhoeven. Leiden. 93–112.

ÖZSOY, S. (1988): On complementation in Turkish: Possessed impersonal infinitives. In: *Studies on Turkish Linguistics. Proceedings of the Fourth international conference of Turkish Linguistics, 17–19 August 1988*, Sabri Koç ed. Ankara: Middle East Technical University. 299–312.

PROCHÁZKA-EISL, G; RÖMER, C. (2007): *Osmanische Beamtenschreiben und Privatbriefe der Zeit Süleymāns des Prächtigen aus dem Haus-, Hof- und Staatsarchiv zu Wien*. Wien (= Denkschriften der Österreichischen Akademie der Wissenschaften, phil.-hist. Kl., Bd. 357).

RÖMER, C. (1998): Marked and non-marked direct objects in 16th century Ottoman documents. In: *The Mainz Meeting*, ed. L. Johanson et al. Wiesbaden. 124–134.

SCHAENDLINGER, A. C. (1983): *Die Schreiben Süleymāns des Prächtigen an Karl V., Ferdinand I. und Maximilian II. aus dem Haus-, Hof- und Staatsarchiv zu Wien.* Unter Mitarbeit von Claudia Römer. Wien (= Denkschriften der Österreichischen Akademie der Wissenschaften, phil.-hist. Kl., Bd. 163).

SCHAENDLINGER, A. C. (1986): *Die Schreiben Süleymāns des Prächtigen an Beamte, Militärbeamte, Vasallen und Richter aus dem Haus-, Hof- und Staatsarchiv zu Wien.* Unter Mitarbeit von Claudia Römer. Wien (= Denkschriften der Österreichischen Akademie der Wissenschaften, phil.-hist. Kl., Bd. 183).

TOMIĆ, O. M. (2006): *Balkan Sprachbund Morpho-Syntactic Features.* Dordrecht.

Türkçe Sözlük (1955), herausgegeben von Mehmet Ali Ağakay et al., Türk Dil Kurumu, Ankara.

Türkçe Sözlük. Yeni Baskı (1988), herausgegeben von Hasan Eren et al., Atatürk Kültür, Dil ve Tarih Yüksek Kurumu, Türk Dil Kurumu, Ankara.

Greek and Turkish Influence upon the Balkan Slavic Verb

Gerhard NEWEKLOWSKY (Wien)

The Slavic languages have inherited a verbal system which consists of a set of tenses, moods, and an opposition of verbal aspect. This system is very well attested in Old Church Slavonic. In this language we find the synthetic indicative forms of present tense, aorist, imperfect, and the composed forms of future tense, future perfect, perfect, and pluperfect. It is important to notice that the present tense of perfective verbs has the function of future tense, whereas the future tense of imperfective verbs is formed by various auxiliaries plus infinitive.

The opposition of aspect has been preserved in all Slavic languages, whereas the inherited set of tenses has changed: The East Slavic languages (Russian, Byelorussian, and Ukrainian) have lost the imperfect and the aorist tenses, also the pluperfect and future perfect, and among the Western Slavic languages a past tense (in opposition to the perfect tense) has been preserved in Sorbian (Upper and Lower), whereas the others (Czech, Slovak, and Polish) have lost the imperfect, aorist, pluperfect, and future perfect. Among the South Slavic languages the same is true for Slovenian (the pluperfect has been, however, preserved), whereas the others (Bosnian / Croatian / Serbian / Montenegrin[1], Macedonian, and Bulgarian) have preserved the Old Church Slavonic tenses (as to SCr. see below). Macedonian and Bulgarian have preserved the future perfect (futurum exactum), and additionally developed the future in the past (which in Macedonian is identical with the former), and a new mood: the mood of status (the evidential) specifying the relationship of the speaker to the narrated action. In some Croatian Čakavian dialects the imperfect tense inflection still exists, but it has changed its function from temporal into modal.

In SCr. there are two future tenses which are usually called future I and future II, but their distribution is complementary: in the independent clause future I (of pf. and ipf. verbs) is used (*pisaću* / *napisaću* "I will write"), and in the dependent clause future II (*budem pisao*) or the present tense of pf. verbs (*napišem*) is used.

According to our experience in contact linguistics, we know that language contacts may influence the development of languages. Why have two past tenses been preserved in Sorbian contrary to all the other North Slavic languages, Eastern and Western? Since the Sorbian population has been bilingual for centuries, Sorbian

---

1 Former Serbo-Croatian, henceforth SCr. Since all our examples are taken from Serbian, we will most often call the language Serbian.

and German, it may have been the German language that has been responsible for the preservation of the two past tenses, contrary to all the other North Slavic languages. Now, let us consider Balkan Slavic. Balcanologists agree that the formation of the future tense with an auxiliary derived from the verb "want" is one of the common Balkanic features. In Balkan Slavic the forms of the auxiliary stem from OCS *hъtěti*, which yielded Mac. *ќе*, Bulg. *ще*, SCr. inflectionable *ću, ćeš, će* etc.). In Greek the auxiliary is *θα*, derived from *θέλω* "want". (We will set aside the other Balkan languages.)

We will now discuss some striking morphological coincidences between Balkan Slavic and Greek, and Balkan Slavic and Turkish. It is unavoidable that some generalizations and simplifications will have to be made. As to Balkan Slavic, I will confine myself predominantly to Macedonian.

1. Coincidences between Balkan Slavic and Greek

Both language groups possess the verbal category of aspect which in both groups has very similar functions. The perfective aspect denotes the accomplishment of an action or a series of actions, whereas imperfective verbs describe the action as a process. However, there is a difference: In Slavic the formation of aspect oppositions is a matter of word formation, whereas in Greek it is rather a matter of inflection, cf. SCr. ipf. aspect *pisati* vs. pf. *napisati* "write" (the pf. aspect is prefixed), pf. *prepisati* vs. ipf. *prepisivati* "copy" (the ipf. aspect is suffixed), Greek ipf. *γράφω* vs. pf. *γράψω* "write", *υπογράφω* vs. *υπογράψω* "sign" (in Greek prefixation does not change the aspect which is usually the case in Slavic). This fact (word formation vs. inflection) may have consequences concerning the use of aspect (s. 1.2.1., 1.2.2.).

1.1. Present tense

In all Slavic languages and in Greek an action taking place in the moment of speaking can be expressed by verbs of the ipf. aspect only. In Serbian, verbs of the pf. aspect in the main clause were used to denote future actions up to the 16th century. There are remainders of this situation in the Čakavian and Kajkavian dialects, whereas in modern Russian and other Slavic languages the old situation has been preserved. In modern Serbian the present tense of perfective verbs in the main clause can be used as historical present, gnomic present or general present, but not as future tense (Белић 1999: 427). This change of function must have taken place during the 16th century or before, and it is connected with the balkanism of the new formation of the future tense. Thus, in Serbian the historical present can be expressed in both aspects. Example: *Uz rat je bio u redu oni ljudi koji su najviše narod protiv Turaka podbunjivali; a kad Nemci **učine** mir s Turcima i **vrate se** natrag, on **pristane** za njima ...* (Vuk KARADŽIĆ) "In the war he was among those men who turned the people most against the Turks; but when the Germans (i. e. Austrians, G. N.) made peace with the Turks and retreated, he joined them" (the verbs *učine* and *vrate se* in the temporal clause, *pristane* in the independent clause are perfective), **Juri** *u noći beskrajni voz od Ralje do Đevđelije* ... "In the night the endless train rushed (lit. rushes) from Ralja to Đevđelija" (past tense context, ipf. verb).

In Macedonian and Greek the present tense of perfective verbs can be used in dependent clauses only. With the historical present the ipf. aspect is used (as to Macedonian cf. КОНЕСКИ 1967: 413; FRIEDMAN 1977: 21ff., МИНОВА-ЃУРКОВА 2005: 119), e.g. Mac. *Едно време, на врвот од дрвото* **се покажува** *петокрака* "Once, on the top of the tree the five-pronged star showed up (lit. shows up)" (present tense, ipf. verb) (example from Минова-Ѓуркова); Greek *Τί έχεις αυτού να μας δείξεις, Φουτούλα; ζήτησαν να μάθουν τα παιδιά. – Ένα τσιτσικάκι,* **απαντά** *το κορίτσι* "'What have you got to show us, Foutoula?' the children wanted to know. – 'A cricket', answered (lit. answers) the girl"; *Το ψηλό κορίτσι που βγήκε από την πόρτα* **είναι** *πολύ όμορφο* "The tall girl, who came out of the door, was (lit. is) very beautiful".

The present tense functioning as the future tense (praesens pro futuro) can be used with the imperfective verb in Serbian, Macedonian, Bulgarian, and Greek, e.g. Serb. *Budući da će u našim zemljama sunce oba puta pomrčati noću, a mjesec danju, zato se ni jedno* **ne može vidjeti** (example from MARETIĆ 1931: 526) "Since in our regions the sun will eclipse twice during the night, and the moon during the day, none of them will be seen (lit. cannot be seen)", Mac. *Не* **се мажам** *дури не најдам некој со чанта да оди на работа* "I won't marry (lit. I don't marry) until I find somebody with a bag who is leaving for work" (example from МИНОВА-ЃУРКОВА 2005: 119), Greek *Η υπόθεση φτάνει, επιτέλους, στο τέλος της* "The matter will finally come (lit. is coming / comes) to an end". With the meaning of the future tense, the verb is often accompanied by a temporal adverb.

In Russian, the ipf. aspect of verbs functioning as the future tense can be used with verbs of motion only, so the previous Serbian, Macedonian, and Greek examples cannot be constructed in the same way.

1.2. Aorist and imperfect

In Macedonian and Bulgarian, as well as in Greek, the usual tenses for reporting actions and states in the past are aorist and imperfect. In SCr. the situation is somewhat different; since both tenses are marked stylistically, the neutral tense for reporting actions that took place in the past is the perfect tense. Whereas the aorist can be considered a living category in Serbian, the imperfect is alive only in the Balkan parts of Serbia and Montenegro. In Serbian, the imperfect and aorist can always be replaced by the forms of the *l*-participle.

1.2.1. Aorist

In Macedonian, the aorist can be formed with imperfective (rather rarely) and perfective verbs, e.g. *Тој* **учи, учи** *седумнаесет години* "He studied and studied for seventeen years" (ipf. verb, the process of learning is finished); *Кога* **дојде, седна веднаш и ја реши** *задачата* "When he came, he sat down and solved the task immediately" (pf. verbs). The aorist can be used in the main clause of conditional sentences: *Да не беше амнестијата,* **отиде** *Бошко во заточеништво* "If there had not been amnesty, Boško would have gone into exile"; Greek *Στη θάλασσα* **έπιασα** *και φίλους, είπε ο Αντρέας.* **Γνώρισα** *τα παιδιά των ψαράδων* "At the seaside I made (lit. caught) friends, said Andreas. I met the children of the fishermen" (pf. verbs, statements in the past).

In Serbian, Macedonian, and Greek the aorist can be used to denote actions in the very near future, e.g. Serb. **Stigosmo** "We'll arrive shortly (lit. we arrived)", **Utopih se** "I am drowning (lit. I drowned)", Mac. **Пливајте** *побргу бидејќи ве* **престигнаа** *домаќините* "Swim faster because the hosts will outrun (lit. outran) you" (from МИНОВА-ЃУРКОВА 2005: 122), Greek *Αν το κάνεις,* **χάθηκες** "If you do that, you'll be lost (lit. you were lost)" (from RUGE 1986: 157).

In Greek the aorist of an ipf. verb cannot be formed, since aspect is a morphological category. As soon as you add the aorist desinence (usually *-s-*), the verb becomes perfective.

1.2.2. Imperfect

In Macedonian as in Greek the imperfect tense denotes the course, progress or development of an action or state, e.g. Mac. *Љуба застана* (pf. verb, aorist) *кај самото езеро. Ветрот ја* **дуваше,** *ја* **пробиваше,** *ја* **прскаше** *водата. Но таа не* **обрнуваше** *внимание на ништо* "Ljuba stopped at the lake. The wind was blowing, penetrating, and splashing the water. But she was not paying attention to anything" (example from КОНЕСКИ 1967: 426), Greek **Κοίταζα, κοίταζα** *και δεν* **έβλεπα** *άκρη* "I was looking and looking, but did not see the end (of the sea)".

In Macedonian, in contrast to Greek, the imperfect can be formed from perfective verbs to denote unreal conditions or circumstances: *Да ми* **дадеше** *малку пари!* "If only you had given me some money!" Constructions like this are impossible in Greek again because of the inflectional character of the aspect opposition. In Greek (and other Balkan languages) the imperfect is used in conditional sentences: *Λίγο έλειψε να σε πατήση το άλογο. Αν δε* **βρισκόταν** *εκείνος ο καλός κύριος, θα μπορούσες να πάθης κακό* "Just an inch more and the horse would have run you over. If the good gentleman hadn't been there, you could have suffered badly" (cf. the discussion in АСЕНОВА 2002: 232f.).

1.3. Perfect

Both in Balkan Slavic and in Greek the perfect tense describes an action that took place in the past but whose consequences are evident in the present time, e.g. Greek *έχω φάει* "I have eaten (and now I am full)", cf. *έφαγα* "I ate". In the latter example the action of eating took place in the past, nothing being said about its effects in the present time. One of the meanings of the Macedonian perfect tense is resultativeness (FRIEDMAN 1977: 61). This is also true for Bulgarian:

> През целия развой на българския език старият перфект се пази добре със своето специфично значение на глаголно време, означаващо извършило се в миналото действие, последиците обаче на което се свързват с момента на говоренето (МИРЧЕВ 1963: 199).

In Macedonian there are two types of the perfect tense, the Slavic type (the *l*-form), and the Greek type with *imam* "I have" (the *l*-form has also the function of reporting unwitnessed actions, see below). The "have"-perfect increases as one moves westwards in the Macedonian-speaking territory (MIŠESKA TOMIĆ 2006: 342). In the Western dialects there is an aspectual opposition between *imam* and *sum* forms of the type *imam dojdeno* vs. *sum dojden* "I came" (МАРКОВИЌ 2007: 148). A characteristic example for the *l*-form in Standard Macedonian would be: *Многу **си пораснала*** "You have really grown" (i.e. now you are big). An example for the "have"-type perfect, expressing resultativeness: *Ах, чорбаџи, ги **немаш** харно **учено** тие деца, те устрамуват* "Oh, master, you haven't brought up (lit. taught) your children nicely, they bring shame to you", cf. the Greek "have"- type: *Εδώ στην Αθήνα **έχουμε γεμίσει** παντού φαστφουδάκια* "Here in Athens we have put in fast-food restaurants everywhere".

If one wants to express resultativeness in Serbian, the perfect tense cannot be substituted by aorist or imperfect, e.g. *(po)jeo sam* (perfect tense) "I have eaten", but *(po)jedoh* (aorist) and *jeđah* (imperfect) "I ate" (concluded action vs. process). Thus, the perfect tense includes the meanings of aorist and imperfect, but not vice versa.

1.4. Pluperfect (past perfect)

The Macedonian past perfect can be formed according to the Greek model with *imam* "have", e.g. Mac. *Даскалот Бино уште рано во средата по Велигден седна на масичето што го **имаше** сам **направено**, и го напиша следното писмо* (example from КОНЕСКИ 1967: 505) "Early in the morning on Wednesday following Easter Sunday, Teacher Bino sat to the table which he **had made** himself, and wrote the following letter", Greek *Τώρα ήρθε η σειρά του Αντρέα, για να μιλήση. Αυτός **είχε πάει** στη θάλασσα* "Now it was Andrew's turn to speak. He had gone to the seaside".

In Macedonian, the past perfect can also be formed by the *l*-form and the auxiliary *sum* "be", which in Bulgarian and Serbian is the only way to form it, e.g. Mac. *Уште пред да дојде овде, тој ја* **беше решил** *таа работа* "Before he arrived here, he had solved the problem".

1.5. Future tense and future perfect (futurum exactum)

The formation of the future tense with the auxiliary derived from "want" plus ipf. or pf. verbs is exactly the same in Serbian, Macedonian, Bulgarian, and Greek (and in other Balkan languages). It is different from Slovenian and the North Slavic languages.

In Serbian the future tense is formed by the auxiliary *ću, ćeš, će* ... (negated *neću, ...*) plus ipf. or pf. verbs depending upon the kind of action, e.g. *Sad* **ćemo se veseliti i gostiti** (ipf. verbs) "Now let's be happy and enjoy our meals"; *Pij, care, veselo, jer* **ćemo se** *sutra* **rastati** (pf. verb) "Drink merrily, o king, because tomorrow we will have to separate". There is no future perfect, if we disregard modal forms (see below).

The Macedonian future tense is formed with *ќe* (in Bulgarian *ще*) plus the forms of the present tense of pf. and ipf. verbs (negated *не ќe* or, more often, *нема да*), and the future perfect is formed with *ќe* + imperfect tense of ipf. and pf. verbs, e.g. **Ќe** *ja* **прочитам** *книгата за неколку дена* "I will read the book within a few days (and finish it)" (future tense of a pf. verb), *Можеше од него добар работник да стане; "кога* **ќe дојдеше** *времето" – си велеше сам Бино* "He could become a good worker; 'when the time comes (lit. will have come)' – said Bino to himself" (future perfect, example from КОНЕСКИ 1967: 492), Greek *Θα πηγαίνωμε μαζί περίπατο, θα σου λέω παραμύθια, θα σου* **τραγουδώ**, *θα σε* **βοηθήσω** *να γνωρίσης και μερικούς καλούς φίλους* "We'll go for walks together, I'll tell you fairy tales, I'll sing for you, and I'll help you to make a few good friends" (future tense of impf. and pf. verbs depending on the kind of action), **Θα μάθης**, *παιδάκι μου, μα όταν* **θα 'ρθη** *ο καιρός. Κάνε υπομονή* "You will learn, my child, when the time comes (lit. will have come)'. Be patient" (future and future perfect; the first verb is related to the future time, the second action is supposed to take place before the former). In Bulgarian the future perfect is of the type *ще съм / бъда написал* "I will have written".

In Macedonian and in Greek the future tense and the future perfect have also modal functions, e.g. Mac. **не ќe е** *толку добар* "he is not supposed to be that good (lit. he won't be that good)", Greek *Δε* **θα** *'ταν ο Αντώνης μας, κυρά-Κωνσταντία. Λάθος* **θα κάνετε**, *είπε ο πατέρας* "Our Antonis wouldn't have been the one, Mrs. Konstantia. I guess you are mistaken (lit. you will make a mistake), said the father" (future perfect and future tenses). In Serbian, too, there is a future perfect with modal function, e.g. *jamačno* *će i ovo prezime* **biti postalo** *od nadimka*

"Apparently also this last name may have originated from a nickname" (MARETIĆ 1931: 544).

Furthermore, the future perfect is used in the independent clause of conditional sentences, Mac. *Ако сакаше, ќе можеше* "If you wanted, you could", Greek *Πολύ θα ήθελα, να γινόμουν κι εγώ πουλάκι. – Αν γινόσουν πουλί, τότε τί εγγονούλα θα είχα*; "'I would like very much to become a little bird myself.' – 'If you became a bird, then what granddaughter would I have?'". The construction is normal in Greek and in Western Bulgarian (cf. ACEHOBA 2002: 221), i.e. the area includes Macedonian. The Slavic conditional formed with *bi* + *l*-participle does exist in Macedonian and Bulgarian, but it is considered rather bookish. The future-perfect type of the conditional is an innovation in Slavic. Gołąb in his excellent study of 1964 considers the new conditional a balkanism, since it can be found in Romanian, Aromunian, Albanian, and parts of Serbian, too. According to him, the new conditional has spread from Romanian and Aromanian over the Balkan penninsula, and not from Greek. GOŁĄB (1964: 176f.) supposes wide-spread Slavic-Romanian bilingualism, in which Dacoromanian influenced Bulgarian, and Aromunian influenced Macedonian. On the other hand, the Balkan conditional can be also found in Montenegro, i.e. in an area bordering the Albanian language, and not Romanian. In Serbian (if we disregard transitional dialects to Macedonian and Bulgarian) the Balkan conditional is not known, although there are areas of Serbian-Romanian bilingualism. Therefore, I would support the opinion that the Balkan conditional spread from Greek, which was a highly prestigeous language, and not from Romanian.

1.6. Future in the past

In Macedonian, like in Greek, the future perfect can also denote a future action from a standpoint in the past (it expresses an intention in the past), e.g. Mac. *Се збираа, ќе одеа в град* "They gathered and would go down town"; Greek *Την επόμενη μέρα θα σηκωνόταν νωρίς* "The next day he would get up early" (example from RUGE 1986: 166). In Serbian, we find similar forms in Southern (i.e. Montenegrin) dialects, e.g. *doista ga preskočiti šćaše* „he would have really jumped over it" (this and other examples from the epic folk poetry in MARETIĆ 1931: 549).

This is different from Bulgarian in which a special tense, the future in the past, is used (cf. 2.4).

Furthermore, in Mac. the future perfect is used to describe habitual actions *Тoj секоj ден ќе ја земеше книгата и ќе решаваше задачи* "Every day he would take the book and solve problems". In Greek the future perfect is at least used in habitual "when" sentences, e.g. Όταν *(θα) έρχοταν (αυτοί) θα τον συναντούσαν με χαρά "When(ever) he would come they would meet him with joy" (quoted in MIŠESKA TOMIĆ 2006: 636). This seems to be different from Bulgarian, where habitual actions can be expressed by the future tense of perfective verbs, e.g. *Ще дойде, ще седне и ще почне да разказва* "(S)he would come, sit down and begin to tell stories" (example from MIŠESKA TOMIĆ 2006: 477).

2. Correspondances with Turkish

In large parts of the Balkan peninsula Turkish was the official language between the end of the 14th century and the Balkan war of 1912. Thus, in some parts of the Balkan peninsula the Ottoman rule lasted for more than half a millenium. Turkish population was present especially in Bulgaria and Macedonia, where many inhabitants were bilingual. Therefore, it is not surprising that the Turkish language exerted an important influence upon other languages of the Ottoman Empire.

In Turkish the inventory of tenses is even more complicated than that of Macedonian and Bulgarian. There are six basic tenses: present tense, aorist, future, past tense, perfect, and continuing present tense; the derived tenses are: imperfect tense, future in the past, preterit in the past, past perfect, continuative in the past, and future perfect (e.g. ERSEN-RASCH 2004: 138–157). In Turkish there is a grammatical correlation of aspect which is restricted to the present and past tenses, and does not exist in the future tense, in the infinitive, or the imperative (cf. KOSCHMIEDER 1954: 148). What grammarians call the aorist (Turkish *geniş zaman* "broad tense") is a general present tense in contrast to the actual present tense (*şimdiki zaman* "present tense"). From both present tense stems other tenses can be derived. Thus, the difference between actual and general present tense stems does often correspond to the Slavic and Greek verbal aspects.

2.1. Present tense

The Turkish actual present is expressed by the present suffix *-iyor*, e.g. *Mektub yazıyor musun?* "Are you writing a letter?" It can also be used for the historical present, e.g. *Padişah bir gün oturmuş kahvesini **içiyor** ve bakanları ile ülke sorunları üzerine konuşuyordu* "One day the sultan sat down and drank (lit. is drinking) his coffee, and discussed the problems of his country with his ministers". The first verb *oturmuş* is the indefinite / unwitnessed perfect, *içiyor* is the actual present tense, and *konuşuyordu* is the imperfect. Furthermore, the actual present tense can be used to describe future actions, e.g. *Hüseyin yarın İstanbul'a geliyor* "Hüseyin will come (lit. comes) to Istanbul tomorrow".

The general present (or *r*-present) describes general actions, e.g. *Deniz bir kararda durmaz. Bir geri **çekilir**, bir **coşar**, bir **köpürür** ve kendini kıyıdan kıyıya **çarpar** "The sea is not steady. Once it withdraws, once it storms, once it foams, once it throws itself from shore to shore". It can also be used to describe future actions, e.g. *Duştan sonra valizleri yerleştiririz* "After the shower you'll unpack your bags".

2.2. Status

Macedonian, Bulgarian, and Turkish possess a special category of status, i. e. a category specifying the relationship of the speaker to the narrated event. The latter may be marked as nonwitnessed, or reported, or marked for the expression of disbelief (dubitative) or surprise (admirative). This category is also called evidential or category of perceptivity (in German Narrativ or Renarrativ). As to the history of the term "evidential" see FRIEDMAN (2003: 84f., and 2004: 102ff.). It is expressed in Turkish by the desinence -miş, which is also used for the formation of the perfect tense. The category of status can be found neither in Greek nor in Serbian, although it must have begun to develop in the latter. In Macedonian the marked status is expressed by means of a personal form from sum "be" or imam "have" combined with the l-form (either based on the imperfective or the perfective stem). The l-form continues the Slavic perfect; it marks number and gender. The mentioned forms are used to denote past and present actions, whereas for future actions special constructions have developed. In the Macedonian l-forms the auxiliary is omitted in the third person. A literary category, in which the narrated events are obviously not witnessed, are fairy tales. In Turkish, the miş-forms are used throughout the whole story, whereas in Macedonian and Bulgarian the narrator of the story usually uses the l-form in the introductory sentence or sentences, and then changes into the reporting tenses, aorist and imperfect. Examples: Turkish *Çok eski zamanlarda, İran'da bir şehirde Kasım ve Ali Baba adında iki kardeş **yaşarmış**. Çok fakir bir ailenin **çocuklarıymış*** "Once upon a time (lit. in very old times) in an Iranian town there lived two brothers, Kasım and Ali Baba. They were sons of a very poor family", *Bir öyküye göre Pataralılar, Büyük İskender'e Anadolu seferi esnasında kentin kapısını gönüllü **açmışlar**. Hatta, bir de karşılama töreni **düzenlemişler**. Çalgıcıların yanında onların müzik aletlerini taşıyan, köle kılığına bürünmüş savaşçılar **diziliymiş*** "According to tradition the inhabitants of Patara opened the doors of their town voluntarily for Alexander the Great during his campaign to Anatolia. Even more, they organized a reception for him. Warriors disguised as slaves carried the instruments for the musicians" (all verbs in the miş-form), an example for the admirative: *Maşallah, bağın çok **büyükmüş*** "My God, how big your vineyard is! (which I didn't expect)"; Mac. *Си **биле** двајца брака, едниот женет, а другиот неженет* "There were two brothers, one married, and the other unmarried" (beginning of a fairy tale), *Jac сум дошол да се борам сос тебе, оти ти **си бил** појунак од мене* "I have come to fight you, because you are said to be a greater hero than me", *jac **сум бил** болен* "I am / was sick (as they say)", *Toj ja **прочитал** вашата статија и многу пофално се изрази за неа* "He read your article (unwitnessed) and expressed himself very positively about it (witnessed)", an example for the admirative: *Тоа **бил** леб!* "This is bread!".

The coincidence between Turkish, Macedonian, and Bulgarian is striking. Therefore, it has been stated that the rise of the Macedonian and Bulgarian category of status has its origin in Turkish (as to Macedonian see GOŁĄB 1959: esp. 35–38, КОНЕСКИ 1981: 174). We can agree with МИРЧЕВ (1963: 208) who claims that the Bulgarian modal category of status (преизказно наклонение) was formed according to the Turkish model:

> Преизказното наклонение в българския език е възникнало по подражание на съответно наклонение в турския език. То се е развило в епоха, когато българските земи са били силно колонизирани с турско население и когато големи части от българския народ заживяват в условия на двуезичие.

According to Mirčev (МИРЧЕВ 1963: 210) the development of the two *l*-forms (imperfective vs. perfective, e.g. *ходел съм* vs. *ходил съм* "I went") originates also from the Turkish model. Macedonian examples (from FRIEDMAN 1977): *Еве зошто, во 19,55 часот* **излегол** *од дома, а околу 20,05 часот* **заврнал** *силниот дожд* "This is why, at 7:55 p.m. he went out of the house, and around 8:05 p.m. it began to rain hard" (p. 160); *Прашај ги оние, кои слушале, што* **сум зборувал**, *тие знаат што* **сум говорел** "Ask them which heard me, what I have said, they know what I said" (John 18;21) (p. 157). The use of the two verb forms corresponds to the opposition between the aorist and the imperfect tenses (*излегол, заврнал* vs. *сум зборувал, сум говорел*). Of course, the *l*-forms have additional meanings. As FRIEDMAN 2003 says for Turkish "… the *di*-past is confirmative but not necessarily witnessed, and the *miş*-past (…) has neutral and resultative as well as marked nonconfirmative (evidential) uses" (p. 100, cf. also § 4 of chapter IV in his book of 1977). The Bulgarian and Macedonian situation is very similar, although some differences can be found.

> It is obvious that the distinction between the perceptive and imperceptive columns (of quoted verb forms, G. N.) in the Balkan Slavonic languages, i. e. in Macedonian and Bulgarian, is a more recent phenomenon, and that it was unknown in the older periods, i. e. before the Turkish conquest (GOŁĄB 1959: 37).

The prerequisite for the development described above must have been the fact that the Slavic aorist and imperfect have been preserved in these languages. In Serbian, the process of a development like in Macedonian and Bulgarian must have started, but it came to an end, when the perfect took over the functions of the aorist and imperfect. In Macedonian dialects which are in close contact with Greek and Aromanian, fairy tales very often start in the imperfect or aorist, as the category of status is not alive in those dialects.

As we stated before, in Serbian the category of status has not developed. However, there is a special form of the perfect without auxiliary, which is usually used in the introductory formulae of fairy tales, and more rarely in other stories. It is opposed to the "normal" perfect with the copula. Examples from the *Српске народне приповиједетке* (Serbian folk tales) by Vuk Karadžić: **Bio** *jedan car, pa* **imao** *tri* *sina i jednu kćer* "Once there was a king, who had three sons and one daughter" (not *bio je, imao je*), **Poslao** *otac dete u vodenicu pa mu* **kazao** … "A father sent his child into a mill and said to him …". According to Grickat (ГРИЦКАТ 1954: 36) the short perfect form is used at the beginning of a story to invocate the curiosity of the hearer.

The Turkish *miş*-form has been identified with the Macedonian and the Bulgarian *l*-forms. This can be proven by other tenses which are built exactly alike in these languages.

2.3. Perfect and past perfect

The Turkish suffix *-miş* is not only marked for status but it is also used to form the perfect tense, i.e. an action in the past which continues in the present time, e.g. *Kar yağmış* "Snow has fallen", *Bir öğrencim derse vaktinde geldi, ama iyi* **hazırlanmamış** "One of my students came to the lesson in time but he has not been prepared well" (example from ERSEN-RASCH 2004: 148). The predicate of the first clause is in the past tense, the predicate of the adversative clause is in the perfect tense which refers to the present state. In the above quoted Macedonian example *Jac* **сум дошол** *да се борам сос тебе, оти ти си бил појунак од мене* the predicate of the main clause is in the perfect, meaning "I've come (and now I'm here)".

The Turkish past perfect is formed by the *miş*-suffix plus the suffix of the past tense, the Macedonian (and Bulgarian) by the *l*-form plus the past tense of the auxiliary *sum*, e.g. *Bütün kuşlar* **gelmişti**. *Toplantı başladı* "All the birds had come. The meeting began", Mac. *Sирнав низ решетката, да си го видам езерото. Сонцето го* **беше позлатило** (example from КОНЕСКИ 1967: 482) "I looked through the gratings in order to see the lake. The sun had gilded it".

Neither in the Turkish nor in the Macedonian past perfect the *miş*- and the *l*-suffixes are connected with status.

2.4. Future in the past

In Bulgarian the future in the past is formed by the imperfect of the auxiliary *съм* "be" + the conjunction *да* + the present tense of the verb, e.g. *щях да чета, щеше да четеш* … "In the past I had the intention to read", negated *не щях да чета,* or, more often, *нямаше да чета.* Example: *Вълчан тури очилата си и запреглежда книжата. И без туй* **щеше да отива** *в града – той беше решил да даде Гроздана под съд* "Vălčan put on his spectacles and looked into the book. Even without this he had the intention to go / would go down town – he had decided to accuse Grozdan at court" (Yordan Yovkov, example from СТОЯНОВ 1980: 398f.). The verbs of the first sentence are in the historical present, then comes the future in the past, and then the pluperfect. In Turkish the future in the past is formed by the future suffix *-ecek-* + the past tense suffix *-di / -ti*, e.g. *Bu ne böyle hanım? Et* *almıştım, kapama* **yapacaktın?** "What does this mean, wife? I had bought meat, shouldn't you have cooked steamed meat?" The morphological coincidence between the two languages is striking. The formation of the future in the past in Bulgarian and Turkish differs from that in Macedonian and Greek (cf. 1.5.).

In Bulgarian there is also a future perfect in the past (futurum exactum in the past): *щях да съм прочел,* a transposition of the past perfect into the future in the past, e.g. *Вчера в пет часа* **щяхме да сме привършили** *работата, ако не беше се повредила машината* "We had the intention to finish work by five o'clock yesterday, if the machine hadn't been broken" (from Стоянов 1980: 400). The Turkish equivalent is *-ecek+miş+ending,* e.g. *yapacakmışsın* "they reported you had the intention to make".

3. Conclusion

There are striking coincidences in the morphology of the verb system of the Balkan Slavic languages, Greek, and Turkish. Romanian and Albanian have not been included into our considerations. The innovations in the Balkan Slavic languages must have developed after the conquest of the Balkan peninsula by the Turks. Greek influence is evident in Macedonian. Nevertheless, there have also been convergences between Turkish and Greek.

The main results of the paper are:
– Coincidence of the use of perfective and imperfective aspect in Macedonian, Bulgarian and Greek. In Serbian the present tense of the perfective verb is used for the historical present.
– Imperfect and perfect tenses are the reporting tenses in Macedonian, Bulgarian, and Greek; in SCr. they are stylistically marked and generally substituted by the *l*-form. The imperfect of perfective verbs in dependent clauses is a special development of Macedonian and Bulgarian.
– In Balkan Slavic as in Greek the aorist can be used to describe actions in the very near future.
– The use of the perfect in Macedonian, Bulgarian, and Greek is very similar, and distinct from aorist and imperfect. It corresponds to the Turkish *miş*-form.
– In Macedonian an additional perfect tense has been developed according to the Greek model with *imam* "have". This is true for the past perfect, too.
– The future is constructed exactly alike in Greek, Macedonian, and Bulgarian; the future perfect corresponds exactly in Greek and Macedonian on the one hand, and differs from Turkish and Bulgarian, on the other.
– Future and future perfect have very similar modal functions in Greek and Balkan Slavic.

References

If not otherwise stated, Greek examples are taken from Βασιλ. Γ. Οικονομίδου, Αναγνωστικον Β' δημοτικού, and Το μοντέλο που ήξερε πολλά, Νέα Σμύρνη 2000, Turkish examples from *Türkçe Okuma Kitabı / Erste türkische Lesestücke*, ed. by C. Özcan and R. Seuß, München: dtv 1992, *Hoş Geldin / Die Türkei in kleinen Geschichten*, by C. Özcan, transl. by R. Seuß, München: dtv 1994, and *Dünya çocuklarının en çok sevdiği Masallar*, İstanbul, Macedonian examples from Stefan I. Verkoviḱ, Јужномакедонски народни приказни. Подготовил и редактирал К. Пенушлиски, Скопје 1985, and my notes from the Ohrid Summer school, Serbian examples from Vuk Karadžić's *Српске народне приповијетке*, Vienna 1853, and M. Stevanović, *Савремени српскохрватски језик,* Beograd ²1974.

Асенова, Петя (2002): *Балканско езикознание. Основни проблеми на балканския езиков съюз.* Велико Търново: Faber.

Белић, Александар (1999): *Историја српског језика: фонетика, речи са деклинацијом, речи са конјугацијом.* Београд: Завод за уџбенике (= Изабрана дела Александра Белића, 4).

Ersen-Rasch, Margarete I. (2004): *Türkische Grammatik für Anfänger und Fortgeschrittene.* 2. Auflage. Ismaning: Hueber.

Friedman, Victor A. (1977): *The grammatical categories of the Macedonian indicative.* Columbus, Ohio: Slavica Publishers.

Friedman, Victor A. (2003): *Turkish in Macedonia and Beyond. Studies in Contact, Typology and other Phenomena in the Balkans and the Caucasus.* Wiesbaden: Harrassowitz (= Turcologica, 52).

Friedman, Victor A. (2004): "The typology of Balkan evidentiality and areal linguistics". In: Olga Mišeska Tomić (ed.): *Balkan Syntax and Semantics*, Amsterdam, Philadelphia. 101–134.

Gołąb, Zbigniew (1959): "The influence of Turkish upon the Macedonian Slavonic dialects". *Folia orientalia*, 1/1. 26–45.

Gołąb, Zbigniew (1964): *Conditionalis typu bałkańskiego w językach południowo-słowiańskich, ze szczególnym uwzględnieniem macedońskiego.* Wrocław, Kraków, Warszawa (= PAN – Oddział w Krakowie, Prace Komisji językoznawstwa, 2).

Грицкат, Ирена (1954): *О перфекту без помоћног глагола у српскохрватском језику и сродним синтаксичким појавама.* Београд (= Посебна издања САНУ, 223).

Конески, Блаже (1967): *Граматика на македонскиот литературен јазик.* Скопје: Култура.

Конески, Блаже (1981): *Историја на македонскиот јазик.* Поправено и дополнето издание. Скопје: Култура.

Koschmieder, Erwin (1954): „Das türkische Verbum und der slavische Verbalaspekt". In: *Münchener Beiträge zur Slavenkunde. Festgabe für Paul Diels.* 137–149 (= Veröffentlichungen des Osteuropa-Instituts München, 4).

Maretić, Tomo (1931): *Gramatika i stilistika hrvatskoga ili srpskoga književnog jezika.* Drugo popravljeno izdanje. Zagreb: „Obnova".

Марковић, Марјан (2007): *Аromанскиот и македонскиот говор од охридско-струшкиот регион во балкански контекст.* Скопје: МАНУ.

МИНОВА-ЃУРКОВА, Лилјана (ред.) (2005): *Македонски јазик за средното образование.* VI. издание. Скопје: Просветно дело.

МИРЧЕВ, Кирил (1963): *Историческа граматика на българския език,* Второ издание. София: Наука и изкуство.

MIŠESKA TOMIĆ, Olga (2006): *Balkan Sprachbund Morpho-Syntactic Features.* Dordrecht: Springer (= Studies in Natural Language and Linguistic Theory, 67).

RUGE, Hans (1986): *Grammatik des Neugriechischen,* Köln: Romiosini.

СТОЯНОВ, Стоян (1980): *Граматика на българския книжовен език.* Трето издание. София: Наука и изкуство.

Balkanisms in Aromunian today:
A View of the Core Vocabulary

Mariana BARA (Bucharest)

1. Literary language and the core vocabulary

To understand the background of the development of a "literary standard language" – achieved in general through the texts of folk songs or other species as stories, sketches, proverbs etc. known and performed by Aromanians – it is necessary to consider the most commonly used words in this language.

There are three basic criteria for the study of the core vocabulary of a language, or the vocabulary needed for a complete every day communication on common topics, as stated for instance by SALA (1988: 13): the frequency, the number on derivates, the polysemy. This modern approach permitted further studies on Aromanian core vocabulary (ACV): the Latin items (BARA 2004) and the non-Latin ones (BARA 2007: 107–155). In my research I have adopted a fourth criterion, the dialectal spread. The results have invalidated the previous assumption ("le lexique fundamental est, en tout cas, d'origine latine" [in any case, of Latin origin] CARAGIU MARIOȚEANU 1972: 128; SARAMANDU 1984: 466) about the exclusively Latin origin of the ACV. Despite the fact that it used to be a strong bias, this assumption proved to be false being *a priori*.

Taking an inclusive approach, my studies on ACV pay significant attention to the social background of language history and transformation, as mirrored in recent Aromanian texts and recorded dialogues. My analysis shows (BARA 2007: 111–112) that the total of 2294 words is near to the mean of other Romance languages core vocabulary. From this figure, words with Latin roots are less than a half (to be exact, 878 items) i.e. 38 percent. More than half of the ACV (equal to 1416 items), or 62 percent, summed the words of Greek, Turkish origin, internal derivates, old Slavic, Bulgarian, Albanian, multiple etymology, unknown etymology, Italian, French, international neologisms. The fact that less than a half of the core vocabulary is Latin is a common feature of all Romanic languages.

According to SALA's results (1998: 517), the Latin etymological class is always in the first rank (the most populated class); even if some CVs are more Latin than others:

Catalan 50,82 %, Sardinian 50,65 %, Portuguese 45,28 %, Occitan 44,34 %, Italian 44,06 %, Spanish 39,56 %, French 36,13 %, Romanian 30,29 %.

As my analysis showed, ACV with 38 % Latin words is near to Spanish CV, and more Latin than French and Romanian core vocabularies.

While the second rank for Italian and Spanish is represented by the Medieval Latin words, in ACV this is the rank for Greek loans, 18 %. This rank in Romanian, Sardinian, French, Occitan, Catalan and Portuguese is occupied by the internal derivates. As an evidence, the second and the third ranks are split between internal derivates and cultural loans, reflecting the powerful impact of a cultural contact (Greek for Aromanian; Latin for Italian, Spanish, French, Catalan, Portuguese; Italian for Sardinian; French for Romanian). Romanian language has a special profile, with a very populated multiple etymology class (third rank).

As already mentioned, beside the differences in Latin inheritance, there are main differences in the core vocabulary amongst Romance languages stemming from adstratum and substratum vocabulary.

Despite a certain loss of vocabulary, as noticed (see KAHL 2008), we could state that ACV is still preserved in a high degree in individual vocabulary, due also to the literature (i.e. the song texts). But this issue is not the main interest of the present study.

2. Lexical Balkanisms in Romanian linguistics. Undesirable words?

Till now, the study of lexical Balkanisms in Aromanian appears to be not a preferred field of research for reasons that are detailed bellow.

CARAGIU MARIOȚEANU (1997) treated the Aromanian vocabulary in the following perspective: chronological and etymological by default, principle which places the word of Latin origin in the first position, always, regardless of its frequency and spread. Thus, in an orthographical and morphological regulatory dictionary, the etymological hierarchy induces that the first form indicated would be the recommended one. In fact, the author wished to modernize Aromanian in the same manner as Romanian linguists in the late 19th century had have modernized Romanian by replacing common words, from old Balkan origin, with words from modern French.

On this issue, ROSETTI (1986: 201) emphasized that compared to Aromanian, Dacoromanian have had acquired an European look, due to economic, politic and cultural factors. In this perspective, the author believed that the prestige of Latin language reflected on Romanian, as the prestige and brilliance of Roman Empire civilization contrasted the migratory people civilization. For ROSETTI (1986: 192, 263), aware of the bilingualism and the mobility of Balkan populations, the core vocabulary of Romanian is characterized also by the elements of Slavic and other Balkan origin, especially the Greek roots of the Byzantine culture.

While this tier of Latin (and sometimes Romanian) origin words will be thoroughly given the preference in CARAGIU MARIOȚEANU's linguistic studies, in a purist attitude that explains the fact she always rejected the "stranger" words, called "alogene/balcanice" (1997: XIV), PAPHAGI or SARAMANDU are more prudent. On this less theoretical and more ideological ground, CARAGIU MARIOȚEANU (1997: XLVIII) refuses to include those Aromanian words described as pulled out from oblivion, composite and ugly ["o aromână scoasă din uitare, compozită şi urâtă. De aceea nu le-am excerptat"].

This esthetical and strongly purist vision of a beloved, sweet, golden, dear, beautiful Aromanian language (CARAGIU MARIOȚEANU 2006: 267 – *durută, dulți, hrisusită, vrută, muşată*) is the main reason for rejecting the Balkan words and the Balkanisms as well: "tot felul de elemente slave (bulgăreşti şi macedono-slave) şi turceşti" (CARAGIU MARIOȚEANU 2006: 263), "toate gunoaiele din lexiconul armânesc" [all the trash from the Aromanian lexicon] (idem: 268).

At first glance, GOŁAB (1984) seems to be only interested in grammatical Balkanisms, but his glossary provide an important number of words from the core vocabulary, and at the same time a few number of words indicating their Balkan origin: as *groapə* "grave", or some others less sure, with an interrogative point (*kukuveáo* "owl", *mačarok* "he cat", *strungə* etc.).

I therefore will operate with the Saussurian axioms of the arbitrary and conventional nature of the linguistic sign, and of language as a social object. According to this widely accepted and widespread theory, a word should not be valued and praised in relationship with its etymology, and its social and poetic functions would not be questionable for this origin. Each word – and especially the most commonly used by a community – should be accepted in terms of historical evolution and language change.

Nonetheless, the nationalism in linguistics has stated, since the 19th century, that there is an axiological difference between words, and that words with a particular origin should be permitted to exist in one language, while other words related to other origins should be expelled. This principle was identified in the practice of purifying the vocabulary and the toponymy in all Balkan countries (with diverse degrees of intensity) with respect to the Turkish words (TODOROVA 2000: 281) after the fall of the Empire.

CARAGIU MARIOȚEANU (1997) offers a number of recommendations about the standard literary Aromanian lexicon and orthography reflecting this principle and underlying excessively their Latin shape and image: the cultivated lexicon should be Latin, the alphabet and the orthographic norms should be in detail close to Romanian ones, in compliance with the practice settled by the first Aromanian modern writers.

It is obvious that this trend constitutes a late development of the Latinist movement in Romanian linguistics, and it is a backbone of the history of Romanian language as a scientific field studied by authors with academic prestige. The ethnic

purity (whether Latin or Dacian) is also a traditional trend in Romanian culture
(BOIA 2002: 161).

For DENSUSIANU (1901: 109) the arrival of Slavs in the Balkans would trans-
form the Italian dialect or Balkan Romance in a new language. For PUŞCARIU
(1940: 174) Romanian is Latin itself, a Latin core only dressed in stranger loans,
which ca be removed. ROSETTI (1986: 75) identifies the Romanian with the Latin
continuously spoken in the Eastern part of the Roman Empire. There is an emphasis on one important element of the language, but the complexity of its vocabulary
and semantics is at the same time minimized, in order to safeguard the Latin heritage as a valuable asset whilst ensuring its development as a European, modern language.

This emancipation process from the Balkan heritage in the late 19th century is
reflected in the modernization of the Romanian vocabulary, due to the fact that a
huge amount of Slavic loans inventoried by Alexandru CIHAC's etymological
dictionary published in 1870–1879 was therefore considered inappropriate for a
Romance language. The role and place of Balkan elements in language seem to be
evaluated even today as unsuitable, depreciatory, even though the academic term
should reflect a neutral distance from the every day negative connotations (TODO-
ROVA 2000: 66–67).

3. Literary texts

For the purpose of this study, I have extracted the information relevant to the question of balkanisms in today Aromanian from recent various texts, disclosed in the
genuine language and spelling of authors from almost all the dialects: fãrsherot^u
(COLOÑIA /COLONJA, ENACHE, FUCHI, GUSHO, HRISTO, POCI), pindean^u (CEARA,
PROKOVAS, VRANA) and yrãmustean^u (CUVATA, FUDULEA, GODI, HULIANI, IOR-
GOVEANU-MANŢU, PREFTI). Despite their dialectal background, it must be said that
all the writers tend, or try and succeed in different degrees to use the vocabulary of
the so-called standard traditional language (especially by CARAGIU MARIOŢEANU
2006: 5 praising her texts, as "scrise într-o aromână curată, autentică şi bogată"
[written in a clear, authentic and rich Aromanian]). Their dialectal background mir-
rors at the same time their geographical and historical belonging to the Balkans. In
contrast to the fãrsherots ones, who are all living in Albania (except ENACHE), the
other authors are from the Diaspora (Romania, Germany, Canada and USA), with
only two exceptions: CUVATA from R. of Macedonia and HULIANI from Bulgaria.
This situation highlights some significant differences relating the vitality of
Aromanian in the Balkans and its literary achievements, compared to the same language spoken by emigrants in various areas of Diaspora.

I have selected only a short list of words – with multiple Balkan etymologies,
which could testimony about the spread of the common vocabulary and the high
level of intercomprehension among the Aromanian dialects.

4. Linguistic analysis

I will focus on the class of multiple Balkan etymology words (the entire stock is rising to 84 items, or 4 percent of the 2294 words selected in the ACV (BARA 2007: 109). From those 84 items, one could form 19 groups of languages (i.e. *angrānji, cúrmu* possibly explained from gr., alb., or it.). The languages that figure in most of these groups are: Albanian in 13 groups, Greek in 11 groups, Turkish in 9, and Bulgarian in 7. The fact that most of those words could be explained whether from Albanian, whether from Greek is a supplementary argument to the theory about the meridional ancient cradle of Aromanian language (see DENSUSIANU 1901, POGHIRC 1996).

There are some frequently used words in Aromanian that could be of Albanese or Bulgarian origin, according to PAPAHAGI: *cārtéscu, ciúciur", ciudíi, shut", umúti, vátrā.*

A group of very common words in Aromanian could be explained, according to PAPAHAGI, at the same time from Greek and from Albanese, and are related to the Epirus (BARA 2007: 113):

> *azvárna, bubúki, cāníscu, cātāndíi, cumbár", grúndi, hímā, hlámburā, lumáki, māndzā, misáli, partálā, pātúnā, pirpirúnā, trunduéscu, urnéki.*

ciudíi – ciuduséscu – ciudusít", -ă

According to PAPAHAGI, the noun could be explained cf. alb. "çudî" 'meraviglia', bg. "čudo" 'miraculum'. The noun is trissyllabic in Aromanian.

The most frequent use of the noun is the comparative adjective or adverb *(ca) ti/trā ciudii*, engl. "wonderful(lly)".

> unā artā rāmāneascā *trā ciudii* (HRISTO 1996: 20)
> chirolu va s-dishcljidā *ti ciudii* (HRISTO 1996: 95)
> *ti ciudie* tu mushuteatsā (FUDULEA 1998a: 112)
> dip *ti ciudii* (FUDULEA 2004: 122)
> ca *ti ciudii* (COLOÑIA 2004: 41)
> *ciudiili* vrurā s-facā, unā dupā altā (FUDULEA 1998a: 128)
> ca *ciudii* (COLOÑIA 2004: 9)
> anda vedz ahtări *ciudii* (VRANA 2010: 9)

The verb is derivate from the noun, and its structure is specific for this class of derivates, built with the *-iséscu* suffix (see also *buiauā > buisescu, cāpaki > cāpākisescu, lemnu > limnusescu* etc.).

> Ghiorghea Patsili arāmasi *ciudusit* (HRISTO 1996: 85)
> hoarā tutā s-*ciuduseascā* (HULIANI 2007: 106)
> ti *ciuduseshti* (HRISTO & GUSHO 2002: 119)

Ahtari njic, arap shi anustu ficior nu-am vidzutã pãnã tora! *s'ciudisea* un altu
   (FUDULEA 1998a: 46)
celniclu *s'ciudisi* di ahãtã mushuteatsã (FUDULEA 1998a: 47)
aoa s-*ciudisea* tutã soea (FUDULEA 1998b: 87)
ti-atsea mi *ciudusii* (COLONJA 2002: 150)

The verb occurs also in the first Aromanian grammar, "vrtosu me *csudisii*" (BO-
IAGI, 1813: 189) and in texts published at the end of 19th century: "s *tšudisí* multu"
(WEIGAND 1894: 232), *tšudisescu* (WEIGAND 1894: 95, 119) etc. GOŁAB (1984)
included in his glossary *mi čuduséscu* explained as "wonder".

From the contexts above, it is obvious that the noun *ciudii* is the equivalent of
engl. "wonder", "miracle" (see also VRABIE 2000). This is the main meaning of the
noun and the verb. The verses "*Ciudii, mari ciudii / Bakitsa tu Vâryârii*" are open-
ing a popular song performed at the begining of yrãmustean Aromanian wedding
celebrations in Romania.

Nevertheless, rarely it could encompass also, as in CARAGIU MARIOŢEANU
1997 the equivalent for rom. *ciudăţenie,* which is engl. "oddness". As a proof for
the meaning "wonder", "miracle", the author gave in her poems this usual exclama-
tion: "Ţi *ciudie!*" (CARAGIU MARIOŢEANU 2006: 287).

hlámbura / flámbura

The word *hlámbura* "flag" – traditional and praised item for the groom family in
Aromanian wedding celebrations – seems to become very fashionable today, as its
referent is a symbol of unity displayed in Aromanians' Balkan gatherings.

It is also a poetic word, as in the title "Meru ancrutsiljeatu pi *hlamburâ*" [apple
crucified on the stick flag] (PREFTI 1996), the image of the ceremonial wedding
flag, which cross-shaped top is adorned with three apples. For this emotional
powerful meaning, and the ideological one as well, as the flag is the distinctive sign
of a people, the word is in itself a symbolic title for poets (FUCHI 2004, GODI 2006,
HULIANI 2007). The flag is associated with the leader who carries it and the
convoy that follows it, in the journey to the bride house, or in the ceremonial wedding dances.

hlambura tsi noi avem (HULIANI 2007: 311)
hlamburã fãr'meru (IORGOVEANU-MANŢU 2009: 1) [flag without apple]
cu mirakea a nunlui tsi ascuturã *hlambura* (GODI 2006: 86) [with the passion of
   the godfather waving the flag]
iţidò popul ari *flambura* a lui (FUCHI 2004: 15) [each people has its flag]
flambura (CARAGIU MARIOŢEANU 2006: 608)
fama ţi lã u flãmbureaşti pi anumiri (FUCHI 2004: 23) [the fame waving on their
   shoulders]: This verb was created by FUCHI.

bubuki / bãbuki; bubukisescu – bãbukisitu, -ã

To the poets, it is an important word, due to its metaphorical power:

> *bubuchili* par ca cafcauri alichiti (FUCHI 2004: 14)
> ndoauâ *bubuchi* ascumti (FUCHI 2006: 30)
> cã-i mizi *bãbukisitã* (GODI 2006: 118): The noun has a derivate verb, and the past participle seems to be equally poetic.

The verb is included in the final glossary by CARAGIU MARIOȚEANU & SARA-MANDU (2005), where it is explained in Romanian: "a îmboboci, a înmuguri".

cúrmu, curmát[u], -ã – curmári

This verb is polysemantic, as explained by PAPAHAGI and by VRABIE: 1. "to (be, get) tired"; 2. "to interrupt"; 3. "to stop". It has an antonym, which will be discussed below: *discurmu*. It has also a regional fãrsherot synonym, *cãpséscu* "to stop, to put an end" (see below), and a yrãmustean synonym, *cãpãéscu* "to (be) tired": "zboarãli pi teli – *cãpãiti!*" (IORGOVEANU-MANȚU 1997: 12), "mintea mea *cãpãitã* di nisomnu" (IORGOVEANU-MANȚU 1997: 40), "minduierli-a noasti cã-pãiti" (IORGOVEANU-MANȚU 1997: 62), "*cãpãits* di ahãnta alãgari" (CUVATA 1990: 284). The verb *mi kurmu* "get tired" and the adjective from past participle *kurmat* "tired" is nonetheless registered also for the yrãmustean dialect, see the glossary in GOŁAB 1984.

> unã *curmari* a truplui (HRISTO & GUSHO 2002: 102)
> regimlu otoman avea cãpsitã (*curmatã*) cu leadzi cãnticlu eretic (pãngãn) (HRISTO & GUSHO 2002: 128)
> lu-avea *curmatã* (HRISTO 1996: 30)
> imna *curmats* cata lac (HRISTO 1996: 54)
> u vidzu fatsa *curmatã* shi traptã al Toli Patsili (HRISTO 1996: 84)
> *curmat* cãt nu si spuni (HRISTO 1996: 88)
> mânjli / canâoarâ *curmati* (IORGOVEANU-MANȚU 1997: 94)
> ma ligãturã nu li *curmarã* cu hoara (POCI 2007: 12)
> ligãturã cu hoara s-*curmã* (POCI 2007: 13)
> Nia ts-u *curmarã* (COLONJA 2002: 137) [they prohibited Nia to you, she will not become your wife]
> tuti va nâ si *curmã* (CARAGIU MARIOȚEANU 2006: 277)

Characteristically, from the infinitive derives an abstract noun:

> nisomnulu, *curmarea* (IORGOVEANU-MANȚU 1997: 50)

The vitality of this verb is underlined also by the frequency of the idiomatic expression (*mi*) *curmă njila,* engl. "be strongly touched (have compassion)", as in the following extracts:

ăl *curma* njila (FUDULEA 1998b: 36)
Niculachi, *curmat* di njilă (FUDULEA 2004: 43)
furlu […] ăl *curmă* njila (FUDULEA 1998a: 65)

All those meanings are registered in the pindean Aromanian spoken in Olympus and beautifully illustrated by PROKOVAS 2006. I have transliterated in brackets:

μι κούρμου του ανίφουρου [mi *curmu* tu anifur^u]
Χίου κουρμάτου [hiu curmatu]
Νι ισă λίμπα ναφουάρă ντι κουρμάρια [nj ishă limba nafoară di *curmarịa*]
κουρμάτου, βătăμάτου ντι λούκρου [curmat^u, vătămat^u di lucru]

WEIGAND (1894: 267–268) recorded the following text (adapted to current rules of writing):

atsel tsi alagă multu / va să s *kurmă* kurundu

The verb is identified as usual and widely spread and therefore included in the final glossary by CARAGIU MARIOŢEANU & SARAMANDU (2005), where it is explained in Romanian: "a obosi, a pune capăt".

discúrmu, discurmát^u, -ă – discurmári

This verb, meaning "to rest, to relax, to repose", is an antonym for *curmu* (1). WEIGAND (1894: 178) recorded it in a fairy tale: "Pul'lu […] pi lumăk' si *diskurma*".

tut eara mushat shi ti *discurma* (HRISTO 1996: 28)
birbiljilu sh-si *discurmă* (IORGOVEANU-MANŢU 2004: 30)
cupiili-a tali tu eali s-*discurma*! (IORGOVEANU-MANŢU 2004: 70)
μι ντισκούρμου (PROKOVAS 2006) [mi discurmu]
discurmarea di năinti di somnu (IORGOVEANU-MANŢU 2004: 21)

Identified as usual and widely spread, *discurmu* is included in the final glossary by CARAGIU MARIOŢEANU & SARAMANDU (2005), where it is explained in Romanian: "a se odihni, destinde".

nicurmát^u

This is an antonym covering the three meanings of *curmat^u*, "tireless", "relentless", and „unstoppable":

lucrători *nicurmaţ* (FUCHI 2006: 107)

cărtescu, cărtit[u],-ă – cărteari

Being semantically very nuanced, the verb has contextual meanings that make it quite difficult to explain. As a transitive verb, it is "to reprove", "to reprimand", "to rebuke", but also "to trouble", "to discomfort", "to discommode", "to derange", "to prejudice". As a reflexive verb, it is "to get upset".

> vruta [...] ku gura nu s greašte / ku mânle nu s *kărteašte* (WEIGAND 1894: 161)
> țiva nu-lu *cârteaşti* (IORGOVEANU-MANȚU 1997: 58)
> mi *cărtii* arău di zboarăli a lui (COLONJA 2002: 147)
> mea 'nă boați mi *cărteaşti* (COLOÑIA 2004: 65)
> naca ti *cărtish* (FUDULEA 1998a: 131)
> nu-l *cârtea* (FUDULEA 1998b: 32)
> μι *κăρτί* γκρά̣ιλου τσί τζίσισι̱ (PROKOVAS 2006) [mi cărti graịlu tsi dzâsish[i]]
> σι *κăρτί* ό̣μλου (PROKOVAS 2006) [si cărti omlu]
> νου *κăρτιά* λούκριλι (PROKOVAS 2006) [nu cărtea lucrili]
> s-nu țiva s-li *cârtească* vârnu (ENACHE 2004: 22)

Usual and widely spread, *cărtescu* is included in the final glossary by CARAGIU MARIOȚEANU & SARAMANDU (2005), and explained in Romanian as monosemantic: "a deranja". However, the adjective *cărtit[u],-ă* from past participle is "upset", "infuriated" or "disturbed".

> λου αφλά̣ι ακάσă μούλτου *κăρτίτου̱*" (PROKOVAS 2006) [lu aflai acasă multu cărtit[u]]

nicărtit[u], -ă

The antonym for the adjective has only the meaning: "whole", "untouched" (see PROKOVAS 2006: *νικăρτίτου̱*) and „in order, undisturbed" (about objects).

I chose only those examples due to the formal constraints of the present study. However, the Aromanian literature can offer an unlimited number of contexts in which words form the VRA appear with their current form and meaning. Nevertheless, for the purposes of this study, the above examples are sufficient to highlight the vitality and importance of the Balkanisms for the literary language.

5. Conclusions

In this study, I have highlighted some of the most commonly used Aromanian words that have a Balkan etymology. The occurrences of each of these words in today Aromanian literature and in electronic communication media in Aromanian have been discussed. In particular, it has been noted that the Balkanisms are able to maintain a good communication among the Aromanians living in different states and to contribute to the establishment of the literary standard language. All of the words studied are old, popular and also a part of the Aromanian language and cultural patrimony.

Today, the Aromanian is a regional language, and in terms of number ofspeakers a severely endangered one. Its Balkan heritage is also important for the special status of a language still spoken in various states of the region, as a background and a tool for the mutual comprehensibility. This heritage would permit the growth of the literary variant and the spread of it, with more chances to be accepted than neologisms from one or another language.

Built as it is by history, in its „natural" linguistic environment, Aromanian language offers a significant core vocabulary shared by speakers of all dialects, and its literature is open to adopt new words from every language in contact. Further analysis – especially on corpora – will illustrate other features of this language.

References

BARA, Mariana (2004): *Le lexique latin hérité en aroumain dans une perspective romane.* Lincom Europa Verlag, München.

BARA, Mariana (2007): *Limba armânească. Vocabular şi stil.* Cartea Universitară, Bucureşti.

BOIA, Lucian (^{3}2002): *Istorie şi mit în conştiinţa românească.* Humanitas, Bucureşti.

CARAGIU MARIOTEANU, Matilda (1972): «La romanité sud-danubienne: l'aroumain et le mégléno-roumain». Reprinted in: *Aromânii şi aromâna în conştiinţa contemporană*, 2006, Academia Română, Bucureşti. 113–129.

DENSUSIANU, Ovid (1901): *Histoire de la langue roumaine. I. Les origines*, in: *Opere*, edited by B. Cazacu et alii, Vol. II. Minerva, Bucureşti. 1975.

GOLAB, Zbigniew (1984): *The Arumanian Dialect of Kruševo in SR Macedonia SFR Yugoslavia.* Macedonian Academy of Sciences and Arts, Section of Linguistics and Literary Sciences, Skopje.

KAHL, Thede (2008): "Does the Aromanian have a chance of survival? Some thoughts about the loss of language and language preservation". In: Institute for Balkan Studies (ed.): *The Romance Balkan*, Serbian Academy of Sciences and Arts, Belgrade. 123–140.

PAPAHAGI, Tache (^{2}1974), *Dicţionarul dialectului aromân – general şi etimologic.* Academia RSR, Bucureşti.

POGHIRC, Cicerone (1996), "Romanizarea lingvistică şi culturală în Balcani. Supravieţuiri şi evoluţie". In: Neagu Djuvara (ed.): *Aromânii. Istorie. Limbă. Destin.* Fundaţia Culturală Română. Bucureşti. 13–49 [first published in 1989, Paris].

PUŞCARIU, Sextil (1940): *Limba română. I. Privire generală.* ed. 1976. Minerva, Bucureşti.

ROSETTI Al. (^{6}1986): *Istoria limbii române. I. De la origini pînă la începutul secolului al XVII-lea.* Bucureşti.

SALA, Marius (1988) (coord.): *Vocabularul reprezentativ al limbilor romanice.* Bucureşti.

SARAMANDU, Nicolae (1984): "Aromâna". In: *Tratat de dialectologie românească*. Craiova.

TODOROVA, Maria (2000): *Balcanii şi balcanismul* (translated by Mihaela Constantinescu & Sofia Oprescu). Humanitas, Bucureşti.

Sources

BOIAGI, Mihail G. (1813): Γραμματική ρωμανική ητοί μακεδονοβλαχική, *Romanische oder Macedonowlachische Sprachlehre*. Wien [ed. 1988: *Gramaticã aromãnã icã macedovlahã*, Freiburg i. Br.].

CARAGIU MARIOŢEANU, Matilda (2006): *Poeme aromâne*. Academia Română, Bucureşti.

CARAGIU MARIOŢEANU, Matilda; Nicolae SARAMADU (2005): *Manual de aromână. Carti trã învițari armâneaşti*. Academia Română, Bucureşti.

CEARA, Ilie A. (2001): *Singur pi calea a banãljei*. Cartea Aromână, Constanţa.

COLONJA, Ilia (2002): "Lunjinã shi aumbrã". *Rivista di Litiraturã shi studii armãni*. Vol. XXIII. No 2. 119–166.

COLOÑIA, Ilia (2004): *Bunã-vã dzua, rãmâñi*. Tirana.

CUVATA, Dina (1990): *Sãrmãnitsa*. Cartea Aromână, Syracuse, NY.

ENACHE, Toma (2004): *Picurarlu a ideilor*. Fundaţia Culturală Aromână "Sfânta Ana", Bucureşti.

FUCHI, Spiru (2004): *Cântiți barbari. Poemi*. Suțata "Aromâñl'i ditu Albania", Tirana.

FUCHI, Spiru (2006): *Alchimia dipiraril'ei. Poezii*. Calc, Tirana.

FUDULEA, Cola (1998a): *Aeshtsâ armânj – oaminj dit pirmiti. I. Pirmituseri dit Balcanj*. Cartea Aromână, Constanţa.

FUDULEA, Cola (1998b): *Aeshtsâ armânj – oaminj dit pirmiti. II. Pirmituseri dit Românie*. Cartea Aromână, Constanţa.

FUDULEA, Cola (2004): *Aeshtsâ armânj – oaminj dit pirmiti. III. Alti pirmituseri dit Balcanj*. Cartea Aromână, Constanţa.

GODI, G. (2006): *Doruri shi mirãki*. Dacris, Constanţa.

HRISTO, Andon (1996) (translator) Dimu Tarusha: *Lilicea sãndzinatã*. Cartea Aromână, Fayetteville, NY– Constanţa.

HRISTO, Andon; GUSHO, Jani (2002) (translators) Dhori Falo: *Trayedia ali Muscopoli*. Cartea Aromãnã, Syracuse NY (printed in Tirana).

HULIANI Grâmusteanlu, Ghiorghi alu (2007): *Vrearea ti armânami. Poezii*. F.C.A. Sfânta Ana, Bucureşti.

IORGOVEANU-MANŢU, Kira (1997): *Ahapsi lingvisticâ. Poemi armâneştâ / Condamnare lingvisticã. Poeme armâne*. Bucureşti.

IORGOVEANU-MANŢU, Kira (²2004): *Steaua di doru*. Freiburg i. Br.

IORGOVEANU-MANŢU, Kira (2009): *Idheea* (unpublished manuscript).

POCI, Spiro (2007): "Hoara 'Andon Poci'". *Fãrshãrotu*. No 2 (26). 12–13.

PREFTI, Mihali (1996): *Meru ancrutsiljeatu pi hlamburã*, Freiburg i. Br.

PROKOVAS 2006 = Προκόβας, Κώστας Ε (2006): *ΛΕΞΙΚΟ της Κουτσοβλαχικής του Λιβαδίου Ολύμπου. Λέξεις, ιστορία, παράδοση και λαϊκός πολιτισμός*, Θεσσαλονίκη.

VRABIE, Emil (2000): *An English-Aromanian (Macedo-Romanian) Dictionary*. Mississippi University.

VRANA, Yioryi (2010): *Isturia cu Tomislu* (unpublished manuscript).
WEIGAND, Gustav (1894): *Die Aromunen. Ethnographisch-philologisch-historische Unter-suchungen über das Volk der sogenannten Makedo-Romanen oder Zinzaren. II. Volks-literatur der Aromunen.* Leipzig. Greek version consulted: *Οι Άρωμουνοι (Βλάχοι)*, ΕΚ-ΔΟΤΙΚΟΣ ΟΙΚΟΣ Αδελφών Κυριακίδη α.ε., Θεσσαλονικη. 2004.

A New View on the Latin Origin of Romanian *(f)sat* 'village', Aromanian *fsat* 'ditch' and Albanian *fshat* 'village'

Adrian PORUCIUC (Iaşi)

In memory of Georg Renatus Solta († 2005)
and in celebration of his *Einführung* (1980)

0. The origin of the Romanian (henceforth Rm.) word *sat* 'village' (with an obsolete variant *fsat*) and the latter's relationship with the Albanian word *fshat* 'village' is an issue that has been strongly debated for more than a century (see details below). The result was that many outstanding philologists came to regard Rm. *sat* as a word of "doubtful" origin. In this article, by reinterpretation of older data and by addition of new ones, I aim to demonstrate (1) that Rm. *sat* 'village' is a direct continuator of Latin *fossatus* (rather than *fossatum* – see below), (2) that Alb. *fshat* stands for a very early borrowing of the same Latin word, and (3) that, for historical and linguistic reasons, Arom. *fsat* 'ditch, trench' (itself a continuator of Lat. *fossatus*) appears to have semantically "lagged behind" Rm. *sat* and Alb. *fshat*.

1. In his impressive *Einführung* (1980: 64), Georg Renatus SOLTA states that, second to the "substrate question", a main issue of Balkan linguistics should be the one of "Latin influence".[1] Then the Austrian scholar concisely resumes REICHENKRON's vision of the various effects of that influence (1980: 66):

> It was G. Reichenkron who very nicely [*hübsch*] explained how the [Southeast European] languages in the making were penetrated by East Romance in all possible ways. Latin is visible as *interstratum* in Greece, where Vulgar Latin words, as well as word-building elements, entered colloquial language. Romance acted as *substratum* in the case of later-coming peoples such as Hungarians, Slovenes, Croatians and Serbians. A higher degree of influence is manifest in Albanian, in which case one may apply the term of *adstratum*. The Dalmatian language reached the level of *completeness* [...], but without achieving a written standard. The highest stage, namely *written standard – literary language – national language*, materialized only in Romanian.[2]

---

1   „Nach der Frage des Substrates [...] ist nun das zweite Hauptthema zu behandeln, der lat. Einfluß in den Balkanländern" (SOLTA 1980: 64).
2   All translations from various languages into English are my own.

In the present article, by analysing the fortune of a Latin term (or, possibly, of two variants of it) on Southeast European soil, I will practically illustrate particular effects of the multi-graded Latin influence observed by Reichenkron and by Solta.

1.1. In regard to the particular etymological case I chose to discuss in this article, the first scholarly approach to it is represented by the *fšat* entry of Gustav MEYER's etymological dictionary of Albanian (1891). Whereas Meyer's assumption of a derivation of Alb. *fšat* 'Dorf' (that is, *fshat* 'village') from Lat. **massatum* (< Lat. *massa*)[3] was far from turning into a definitive etymology[4], his indication of an Albanian origin for Rm. *sat*[5] enjoyed some success (see below), though it was not generally accepted.

In more recent times, a top authority in the history of Albanian, Eqrem ÇABEJ (1982: 198), added further complication to the relationship between Rm. *(f)sat* and Alb. *fshat*, as he aimed to demonstrate that *fshat* actually reflects an internal-Albanian derivation, and that it belongs to an autochthonous lexical family:

> Une autre [famille] est formée par *gërshet, këshet* «tresse, natte», *shet* «cheveux», avec *shetkë* «criniére», *sheça-t* «chevelure» […], tous, vraisemblablement, avec *fshat* «village», représentant des nouvelles formations de *shat* «houe».

Interestingly, even in Çabej's autochthonist vision (with reference to Alb. *shat* 'hoe', rather than to Lat. *fossa* and *fossatum*), Alb. *fshat* remains somehow attached to the notions of "digging" and "ditch". But, in another passage of the same book (1982: 277) we find *fshat* as member of another Albanian lexical family, united by a "sweeping" notion (see *fshij* 'to sweep with a broom'):

> C'est sous les deux formes, *f-* et *v(ë)-*, […] que se présente un autre élément formatif, dans des cas évidents tels que *fsheh* «cacher, receler», *fshij* «balayer, netoyer, épouisseter, essuyer», […] *vdes* «mourir», *vgjollë* «grande auge où l'on donne au bétail le sel […]», et dans quelques autres moins clairs à première vue, comme […] *fshat* «village», *veshkë* «rein, roignon» […], et d'autres de cette catégorie.

The rather confusing arguments by which Çabej wanted to make *fshat* appear as an Albanian derivative (with an *f-* prefix) can hardly be regarded as acceptable. As I will demonstrate below, a multitude of arguments support the idea that both Alb.

---

3 „Die Anlaute *fš-*, und *pš-* lassen sich, wie sonst, in *mš-* vereinigen. Das Wort [fshat] stellt ein lat. **massatum* von *massa* vor […]" (MEYER 1891, s.v. *fšat*).

4 From what I can get from a concise statement of SOLTA 1980: 169, Jokl was the only notable linguist who defended Meyer's etymology of Alb. *fshat*. In his turn, CIORĂNESCU (2001, s.v. *sat*) states that the "derivation from Lat. *fixatum*" (a rather peculiar solution proposed by Giuglea) appears to be "improbable, even more than the one from Lat. **massatum*" (that is, Meyer's proposition).

5 Meyer closes his *fšat* entry by a laconic statement (with no further comment): „Daraus rum. *sat* 'Dorf'".

fshat and Rm. *(f)sat* are of Latin origin. Nevertheless, I still have to come up with lots of arguments in order to demonstrate that idea, since today's state of etymological affairs is practically the same as three decades ago, when SOLTA observed that the etymology of Alb. *fshat* "ist sehr umstritten" (1980: 133, footnote 369). It is in the same book where SOLTA (1980: 169) commented on the disputed connection between Alb. *fshat* and Rm. *sat*, as presented in Ciorănescu's etymological dictionary of Romanian.

Actually, Ciorănescu's dictionary (conceived in Spanish, in the middle of the 20th century, and published in Romanian translation as late as 2001) provides a concise review of the main etymological approaches to Rm. *sat*, regarded by many (and by Ciorănescu himself) as a word of "doubtful origin" (see below). CIORĂN-ESCU's presentation (2001, s.v. *sat*) indicates the most important directions along which various scholars tried to explain the word under discussion: (1) as a continuator of Lat. *fossatum* (< *fossare* < *fossa*); (2) as a borrowing of Alb. *fshat* (which is, actually, Meyer's vision); (3) as a continuator of a Lat. *satum* (< *serere* 'to sow').[6]

1.2. After MEYER 1891, it was MEYER-LÜBKE's REW that probably played an influential role in the imposition of the idea that Rm. *sat* should be interpreted as a borrowing from Albanian. In entry 3461, *fossātum* ("Graben", "Kastell"), Meyer-Lübke gives a series of Romance continuators of the Latin term under discussion (Fr. *fossé*, Prov. *fosat*, O.Port. *fossado*, etc.), to which he adds "ngriech. *fussaton*" and "alban. *fšat* (> rum. *sat*) 'Dorf'". In regard to other mainstream views reflected in Meyer-Lübke's presentation (3461), worth mentioning is his focus on the *military* sense of certain Romance heirs of Lat. *fossātum* (for example, "apg. *fossado* 'Heer', eigentlich wohl 'Befestigung'"); also, the final parenthesis of the same entry deserves attention, since by it Meyer-Lübke rejects, for (unexplained) phonetic reasons, the possibility that Rm. *sat* could derive directly from Lat. *fossātum*.[7] (Nevertheless, as I will point out below, an evolution such as *fossatum* > **fusatu* > *fsat* > *sat* cannot be regarded as "hardly possible," whatever Meyer-Lübke's reasons may have been to present it like that.) I must also mention that the REW entry immediately preceding *fossātum,* namely 3460 *fossa* 'Graben', also deserves atten-

---

6 In regard to the origin of Rm. *(f)sat*, I will not unnecessarily complicate things by mentioning too many other etymological views that contributed nothing but supplementary uncertainty. I will mention, however, two radical (and hardly credible) views. The former is part of the reconstructivist vision of Reichenkron, who imagined a Dacian **visato* in order to explain Rm. *sat* (see criticism in ROSETTI 1986: 548). The latter belongs to Boján, according to whom neither between Alb. *fshat* and Rm. *(f)sat*, nor between the two Romanian variants, *fsat* and *sat*, are there any demonstrable connections (see BOJÁN 1969, as quoted in ROSETTI 1986: 182, and in VĂTĂȘESCU 1997: 423).

7 Here is the most important part of the parenthesis under discussion: „Rum. *sat* unmittelbar aus dem Lat. [...] ist lautlich kaum möglich ..."

tion, not only because Meyer-Lübke opens the list of Romance continuators[8] by a rare Romanian dialectal word, "Transylvanian *foasă*" (which I have not been able to find anywhere else), but also because *fossa* ('ditch') and its heirs can be made direct use of in this discussion (see below).

1.3. IVĂNESCU, in his *Istoria limbii române* (ed. 2000: 365), chose to follow Philippide (rather than Meyer-Lübke) in considering that the form of *fsat* indicates passage through Albanian:

> Thus, Old Romanian *fsat* 'village' (> *sat*), which comes from Lat. *fossatum* 'settlement surrounded by a ditch' (for protection against enemies, that is, as a kind of fortress) shows a phonetic evolution specific to Albanian: the disappearance of an unstressed *-o-* in front of the stressed syllable (cf. Alb. *fšat*). It is true that the same phonetic phenomenon occurs, sporadically, in Romanian too; nevertheless, in the case of the word under discussion, that phenomenon must be regarded as Albanian, since it is regular in that language (see Philippide, *Originea românilor*, II, p. 642). The fact that, in Albanian, it was around the year 1000 that *s* turned into *š*, obliges us to draw the conclusion that the term came into Romanian before that time.

However, the idea of a necessary passage through Albanian should not be regarded as compulsory for an etymological clarification of Rm. *sat*. As ROSETTI demonstrates, in his own history of Romanian (1986 – see especially the subchapter "Grupuri de consoane", p. 481–482), an evolution such as *fossatum* > [**fusatu*] > *fsat* > *sat* (with my bracket added) was not unusual in earlier Romanian. Actually, as I will demonstrate by other examples below, a "weakening" (or "reduction") of unstressed *o* to *u* (such reduction eventually leading to syncope, in many cases) is common enough in the history of Romanian[9], and it may represent a feature of "Balkan Latin", or even a feature of substratal resurgence (that is, a perpetuation of a Paleobalkan speech habit).[10] However it may be, I can hardly imagine the sur-

---

8   That list (in REW 3460) includes It. *fossa*, Friul. *fuese*, Fr. *fosse*, Prov. *fossa*, Span. *huesa*, as well as derivatives such as two very significant Portuguese terms, *fossar* 'to dig' and *fossão* 'plough'. In regard to the last one, see Romulus' ritual ploughing discussed below.

9   As mentioned in STEINKE/VRACIU 1999: 100, P. Ivić and V. Georgiev, separately, observed the phenomenon of vocalic reduction, that is, the shift of "the vowels *e* and *o* to *i* and *u*, respectively, in northern Greek, Macedonian, Bulgaria and Romanian dialects". I must also add that, in Romanian, there occurs a reduction of *a* to *ă* too, by shift of stress: see *cásă* 'house' > *căsúță* 'little house', or *a náște* 'to give birth' > *născút* 'born'. In regard to Balkan *schwa* as substratal element or as independent development in Balkan languages (see discussion in SCHALLER 1975: 128–129), I will not go into detail here.

10   In that respect, "weakenings" of unstressed *o* to *u* could be deduced from certain Thraco-Dacian variants of proper names and appellatives given in DEČEV's corpus

vival, as such, of a word with the form *fsat* in today's standard Romanian, since a word introduced by the consonantal cluster *fs-* would be unique in that language.[11] Aromanian speakers, however, have preserved not only their particular *fsat* 'ditch', but also many other Latin-originated words (or variants of words) introduced by clusters of voiceless consonants such as *cs-, ct-,* or *mş-,* produced by syncope (that is, by dropping of unstressed vowels) – see, for example, Arom. *csare* (< *kisare* 'pounding' < Lat. *pisare* 'to pound'), *csut* (< *cusut* 'sewn'< *cos* 'I sew' < Vulg.Lat. **cosere* 'to sew' < Lat. *consuere* 'to sew together'), or *mşeat* (< *muşeat* 'beautiful' < **furmuşeat* < Vulg.Lat. **(in)formosiatus* < Lat. *formōsus* 'well-shaped, beautiful'). Aromanian syncopes of that kind continued to occur in more recent times too, as we can deduce from syncopated variants of certain Modern Greek and Turkish loans, such as *ftină* 'pot' (< *vutină* < Mod.Gk. *βουτίνα*), or *fşeki* 'cartridge' (< *fişeki* < Turk. *fişek*).[12]

1.4. In many dictionaries and philological studies we may find that Daco-Rm. *(f)sat* (< Lat. *fossatum*) has an Aromanian variant, *fsat*, which is usually given without any indication of the fact that the meaning of the Aromanian word is 'ditch', not 'village'.[13] Rather confusing is the situation in PAPAHAGI's dictionary

---

(1957): *Drobeta*, Δρουβητίς, *Drubeta*; *Dorostorum*, Δουρόστρον, *Durosteron*; ῥομφαία, *rumpia*, etc.

11 The form *fsat* (as obsolete variant of *sat* 'village') would quite obviously stand as singular in today's standard Romanian, since there is no other word with an initial *fs-*cluster in either CIORĂNESCU 2001 or MDA 2002 (vol. II, D–H). That the initial *fs-*cluster had become uncomfortable for Daco-Romanian speakers already in medieval times is indicated by a very interesting attestation, mentioned by ROSETTI (1986: 759): at a certain point of sixteenth-century *Psaltirea Hurmuzaki*, there is a reference to *tote ferile sfatelor*, which obviously means 'all beasts of villages', since (as Rosetty accurately indicates) *sfatelor = fsatelor*. What we have there is most probably an adjustment of the uncomfortable form *fsat*, by a conflation with the Slavic loan *sfat* ('counsel, council') which was – and still is – a word of general use in Daco-Romanian (not also in Aromanian).

12 I extracted my Aromanian examples from PAPAHAGI 1974.

13 Unlike Daco-Rm. *sat*, which had to "compete" with substratal *cătun* 'hamlet' (a quite similar competition being visible in Albanian, between *fshat* and *katund*), in Aromanian the analogous competition was between *hoară* '(stable) village' and *cătun* 'hamlet, (seasonal) village'. A whole article can be written on the possibility that Arom. *fsat* (unlike Drom-Rm. *(f)sat*) might have remained with the original meanings of 'ditch' – that is, without a shift to 'village' – simply because, in very early times, Aromanians borrowed Gk. *χώρα* (cf. PAPAHAGI 1974, s. v. *hoară*) and they generalized the use of that loan as designation for stable villages. However, without going into detail, I will just mention the rather unexpected term *hoară* 'gathering, farmstead, household' in the *Daco*-Romanian idiom spoken (still in the middle of the 20th century) by heirs of Daco-

of Aromanian (1974), which gives both *sat* 'village' and *fsat* 'trench' (the latter being simply referred to another Aromanian word, *fusate* 'trench'). We can quite easily dismiss the possibility of a genuine Aromanian word *sat* 'village', since, as Papahagi mentions (s.v. *sat²*)[14], the *only* attestation of that noun occurs in a text published in a magazine of the early 20th century (*Lumina*, 1903–1908), and we may suspect that the text under discussion was substantially influenced by standard Romanian.[15]

Actually, for this discussion, what really counts is not the phantom word given by Papahagi as *sat²*, but rather the Aromanian word *fsat* that is frequently mentioned (usually without its Aromanian meaning) in etymological discussions on the origin of Daco-Rm. *(f)sat* 'village'. In the case of the neuter noun *fsat* (pl. *fsate*), Papahagi gives the meaning of 'trench' then he simply refers the word to the Aromanian feminine noun *fusate* (pl. *fusăț*) 'trench', in which case the single meaning given by Papahagi in Romanian ("tranșee") is followed by three meanings in French: «fossé, tranchée, rempart». Papahagi comments neither on the gender difference between the two words (or variants, in his opinion), nor on the fact that *fsat* shows syncope, whereas *fusate* shows only reduction of *o* tu *u*. As for the origin of *fusate*, Papahagi makes no reference to Lat. *fossatum* (that is, to the term regarded as origin of Daco-Rm. *(f)sat*, according to the Romanian mainstream vision). The Aromanian scholar gives only "cf. Gk. φουσάτο 'castra, fossa munita' [...]; Alb. *fusatë* 'fortezza, rocca'" [actually *fushatë*][16], then he decisively indicates the origin as "< it. *fossato*". However, to consider that both Arom. *fusate* and Arom. *fsat* (as variant of the former, in Papahagi's vision) are of Italian origin is unacceptable, for several reasons.

First of all, It. *fossato* (unlike Arom. *fusate*) shows no sign of reduction in its unstressed *o*, which did not turn to *u*, but remained with the original quality visible in Lat. *fossatum*. On the opposite, Modern Greek φουσάτο – like its direct

Romanians colonized by the Russian Empire on the Bug during the 18th century (GOLO-PENȚIA 2006: 198, 199, 816). More research is needed in that respect.

14 PAPAHAGI (1974) gives that noun as *sat²*, since there also is a homophonic *sat¹* ('satiety') in his dictionary. In regard to the etymology of *sat²* 'village', Papahagi simply mentions Daco-Rm. *sat*, and he closes the entry by a bold question mark.

15 In such a case, Papahagi's observation that "today the word [*sat²*] is unknown" (among Aromanians, that is) appears to be quite superfluous.

16 In fact, the Albanian term under discussion is the same as the one given as *fushatë* 'campaign' in DURO/HYSA 1995, or the one given by Meyer as *fušatε* 'multitude', under *fušε* [that is, *fushë*] 'plain, field'; for the latter, Meyer (with justified hesitation) indicates derivation from Lat. *fūsum* 'stretched [< *fundere*]. In my opinion, if one intended to present the Albanian terms *fushatë* and *fushë* as related (and as both derived from Latin), then the most credible origins would be Lat. *fossatum* (or *fossatus*) and Lat. *fossa*, respectively. But this would be an idea for another article.

predecessor, the Byzantine military term φουσσάτον (< Lat. *fossatum*) – shows reduction of unstressed *o* to *u*, which reflects, as I have already mentioned above, a speech habit specific to Balkan idioms; the same feature most probably was already specific to "Balkan Latin" too.[17] Therefore, the idea that Aromanians could get their *fusate* only by borrowing It. *fossato* is hard to believe. We may also have doubts about Papahagi's presentation of Arom. *fsat*[18] as mere variant of *fusate*. The former (with a form affected by a type of syncope that is quite common in Aromanian) represents, in my opinion, a term of more general use, inherited directly from a Latin derivative of *fossa*, whereas *fusate* may reflect the φουσσάτον of Byzantine Greek. I will, however, not exclude the possibility that the Aromanian feminine noun *fusate* (cf. Alb. *fushatë* 'campaign') could develop directly from a Balkan Latin *fossata* 'fortifications' (as plural of the military term *fossatum*). Phonetically speaking, one may also assume that *fusate* shows only vowel reduction, not syncope, simply because it has been less frequently used, so it has not come to show as "worn out" as *fsat*. I will pay more attention to the latter, in connection with Daco-Rm. *(f)sat*.

2. In *Micul dicţionar academic* (MDA-IV, 2003), Rm. *sat* graphically appears as a word with one current meaning surrounded by obsolete ones: "1. (obs.) tent; 2. (obs.) rudimentary dwelling; 3. (by extension) human settlement composed of tents; 4. (current usage) rural human settlement whose inhabitants are mostly peasants (agriculturalists) [...]; 9. (obs.) fortress [...]; 14. (obs.) sanctuary; 15. (obs.) cultivated field".[19] (It is quite obvious that both the order and the formulation of meanings are quite different from Ciorăneascu's – see below.) In regard to form, MDA-IV mentions *fsat* as an obsolete variant of *sat*, and it also mentions *Psaltirea Hurmuzachi* (written in the 16th century) as the document that contains the earliest attestation of Rm. *(f)sat*. Nevertheless, there are onomastic proofs that indicate an even earlier date for the use of the appellative under discussion.

Speaking of onomastics, let me first give a short passage from ÇABEJ's above-mentioned book (1982: 237):

---

17 As I have suggested above, the regular reduction of certain unstressed vowels may reflect a Vulgar Latin tendency, but it may also reflect a lingering substratal speech habit. In that respect, I will add that reductions of unstressed *o* to *u* can also be found in certain Albanian words of Latin origin (see the material provided by VĂTĂŞESCU 1997), such as Lat. *colare* > alb. *kulloj* ('to filter, to strain'), Lat. *molaris* > Alb. *mular* ('millstone'), or Lat. *orare* > Alb. *uroj* 'to wish (well)' – cf. Rm. *a ura*.

18 I would rather write it *fsatu*, a form that more accurately renders the typical Aromanian – and dialectal-archaic Daco-Romanian – pronunciation with a so-called "whispered" vowel at the end.

19 I abbreviated the rather confusing mixture of meanings and phrases in the *sat* entry of MDA. The numbers I skipped (5–8, 10–13) represent phrases that contain Rm. *sat*.

Certains noms de lieux sont importants aussi pour la socio-linguistique [...]. Quelques-uns ont l'importance pour la distribution dialectale du lexique, la géographie des mots, comme *Fshat* dans le Nord ...

As I will point out below, place names certainly *can* provide interesting socio-linguistic clues as to the origin and evolution of the SE European terms that represent the subject of this article.

2.1. More concretely, a village name such as Alb. *Fshat* mentioned by Çabej can be referred not only ("internally") to the Albanian appellative *fshat* 'village', but also to ancient SE European names, such as the name of a settlement mentioned by a recent historian, POHL (2005: 119), in a discussion on barbarian *foederati* that were allowed to settle on Roman soil (my italics):

> ... in der selben Provinz [*Dacia ripensis*] fanden zwei Attilasöhne ein neues Siedlungsgebiet, deren hunnische Gefolgschaft noch zu Jordanes' Zeiten unter den lateinischen Namen Sacromontisii und *Fossatisii* bekannt war.

Seventy years before Pohl, the great linguist Ernst GAMILLSCHEG (1935: 237–238) had found an opportunity to mention a sixth-century hybrid (Gothic-Latin) name of a settlement, and to use it as an argument in favor of the derivation of Rm. *sat* from Lat. *fossatum*:

> Die zum Teil auch in der Prokopianischen Liste [des 6. Jhdts] angeführten Festungen *Mareburg, Stiliburg, Alikaniburg, Skulkoburg, Lakkoburg* in der Gegend des Eisernen Tores stammen [...] von den gleichfalls ostgermanischen Herulern [...]. *Gesilafossatum* am 'Haemus Mons' im nördlichen Thrakien [...] ist dagegen wieder gotischer Herkunft. *fossatum* ist die ostromanische Bezeichnung für 'Dorf' (rum. *sat*). Die Namensbildung entspricht dem Typus *Sunna-villa* im ältesten südfranzösischen Siedlungsgebiet der Westgoten ...

Certainly, without precise archaeological proofs in regard to those particular places, it would be hard for anyone to decide whether settlements such as the ones called *Fossatisii* and *Gesilafossatum*, respectively, were military camps *or* common settlements. But the fact remains that, as early as the 6th century, Lat. *fossatum* could be used as a component of place names, just as Rm. *sat* was used in (quite a number of) place names recorded in more recent times.

2.2. To illustrate the present-day situation of Romanian place-names transparently based on *sat*, I will first mention that in the GHINEA dictionary (2000) I could count 127 such place names, of which no less than 72 appear as *Satu(l) Nou*, plus (twice) the derivative *Satnoeni* (whose original reference was to inhabitants of newly founded settlements with transparent names of the *Villanova* or *Neuville* type). Besides the 72 above-mentioned ones, there are tens of other villages with names based on *sat*, in all parts of Romania.[20] The appellative *sat* is visible in a multitude of colorful (and historically meaningful) combinations, such as *Sat Bătrân* (*sat* + *bătrân* < Lat. *vet(e)ranus*), *Satchinez* (*sat* + *chinez* – cf. Slav. *knjaz*), *Satu de Necaz* ("Village of Trouble"), *Satulung* ("Long Village"), *Satu Mare* ("Big Village"), *Satu Mic* ("Small Village"), *Saturău* (*sat* + *rău* < Lat. *reus*), *Satu Vechi* ("Old Village"), etc. There are village names such as *Sătucu* and *Săticu*, based on diminutive derivatives (*sat* > *sătuc, sătic* 'little village'), and there also are several villages called *Săcel* and *Săcele*, those names being based on a less transparent diminutive derivative, which deserves special attention, for several reasons (see below). To return to the main line of this article, I must observe that the abundance of such Romanian village names[21] as the ones above cannot represent, by itself, a decisive argument in a discussion on the origin and evolution of Romanian appellative *sat*, mainly because most of the names given above were recorded as late as modern times. However, several of the Transylvanian *sat*-based village names included in SUCIU's remarkable toponymic dictionary (II, 1968) do benefit from early attestations that can provide solid arguments for this discussion.

The onomastic material of Suciu's dictionary is fascinating, since it is a true mirror of the Transylvanian interethnic configuration, as controlled by successive officialdoms. Quite many of the place names in that dictionary are given in diachronically arranged variants, and in several languages: Romanian, Hungarian and German, sometimes also with first versions that represent literal translations into Medieval Latin (the chancery language of Transylvania, and of the Hungarian Kingdom). In many cases it is quite difficult to say in which language the name of a village was originally conceived, since one may doubt that the language of a first attestation was actually the language of conception. Here are some examples in point: one of the many villages that Romanians call *Satul Nou* was first recorded as *Nova Villa* (1332), then, successively, as *Villa Nova* (1333), *Wyfolu* (1453), *Újfalu* (1733), and *Neudorf* (1854); today's *Satul Mic* (near Lugoj) was first recorded as *Satulmic* (1717), then it got a new spelling, *Szatulmik* (1818), and it was eventually translated into Hungarian as *Lugoskisfalu* (1913); yet another village, of the numerous ones called *Satu(l) Mare* in today's Romanian, was first recorded (1566) under a hybrid (Romanian-Hungarian) name, *Marefalwa* (Rm. *mare* 'big' + Hung. *falwa*,

20 For Romanian village names based on the appellative *sat*, see also IORDAN 1963: 195–197.
21 To the village names presented above, several Romanian family names based on *sat* can be added. CONSTANTINESCU 1963, s.v. SAT, gives the Romanian surnames *Satu, Sătoi* and *Săteanul* (which transparently means "The Villager"). However, in regard to the particular case of *Satu*, IORDAN (1983, s.v. *Satu*) has doubts about a derivation from Rm. *sat*: "I cannot see how this appellative [*sat*] can turn into a person name". Therefore, Iordan proposes Bulg. *Sato* as origin of Rm. *Satu* (but he tells us nothing about the origin and the status of the Bulgarian name under discussion).

now *falu* 'village'), which survived in local Hungarian as *Máréfalu* (1854), from which local Romanians developed a compromise version, *Marefalău*.

2.3. Undoubtedly, of the many Transylvanian village names based on the appellative *sat*, the ones that can provide really significant clues as to the age and evolution of that appellative on Daco-Romanian soil are *Săcel* (which designates five villages, in five different counties) and *Săcele* (as name of a now urbanized settlement, near Braşov). One *Săcel* (in Maramureş) was first attested as *keneziatus Kys Zachal* in 1453; another one, in the Cluj County, appeared in early documents first as *Zenchel* (1444), then as *Sechel* (1475). But, although it was attested a little later than the ones above, the name of *Săcele* (recorded as *Sătcele* in 1482) is most interesting of all, both historically and linguistically. A remarkable fact is that *Săcele*, a plural form, was meant to function, as "collective name" (according to Suciu) for a union of villages, which most probably made up a *keneziatus* in early medieval times. That special situation is also reflected in the Hungarian name of the same complex settlement, *Hétfalu* "Seven Villages".[22] By their attestations in documents (see above), *Săcel* and *Săcele* take us as far back as the 15th century. Nevertheless, their forms indicate that the appellative the two toponyms are based on was in use in Romanian at a much earlier date. I take into account that a derivation from a simplex to a firmly fixed diminutive takes a long time, and that the turning of such a common-use diminutive into a *series* of place names may take even longer. More to the point, of all the toponymic elements discussed in the paragraph above, at least one, *Săcel*, is quite significant for this discussion. The village name *Săcel* (as well as *Săcele*, first recorded as *Sătcele*) doubtlessly reflects the contracted diminutive form *sătcel*, from *săticel* 'little village', from *sat* 'village'. One implication would be that certain Transylvanian Daco-Romanians had simplified the archaic form *fsat* to *sat* before the 15th century.

2.4. In fact, by its early attestation, the Romanian diminutive appellative *săticel* appears to be almost as old as *fsat* (the archaic variant of *sat* 'village'), taking into account that MDA-IV gives, separately, *săticel* (< "*sat* + *-icel*") as recorded in 1618. Besides *săticel*, the same dictionary also gives the contracted variant *sătcel*, which shows syncope of the unstressed *i* in the original diminutive suffix.[23] From the standpoint of word-formation, the unsyncopated form *săticel* displays a diminu-

---

22 As indicated by SUCIU (1968, s.v. *Săcele*), the seven names of the original settlements united in the super-village of *Săcele* are still remembered by local Romanians: *Baciu, Turcheş, Cernat, Satulung, Tărlungeni, Zizin, Purcăreni*.

23 IORDAN (1963: 195, footnote 7) referred to another diminutive of *sat*, namely *sătucel*, which appears to have turned into *săcel* (by a type of syncope that can be referred to a tendency of Vulgar Latin, according to the same scholar). Notable is that Iordan used the example of the evolution *sătucel > săcel* among the arguments by which he aimed to reject Weigand's opinion according to which Rm. *Satu Mare* (Hung. *Szatmár*, attested as *Zathmar* in 1213) could be explained as derived from "a Germanic name **Satmar*".

tive (double) suffix of certain Latin origin (-*ic-ell-*), since it obviously is the same as the one that survives in It. *monticello*, as (uncontracted) continuator of Lat. *monticellus* (see ERNOUT/MEILLET, s.v. *mōns, montis*). It so happens that – besides Romanian diminutive derivatives such as *vânticel* < *vânt* 'wind' and *firicel* < *fir* 'thread, grain, stalk' – Romanian also has *muncel* 'hillock', which stands for a contracted continuator of the above mentioned Lat. *monticellus*. And, also, it so happens that, in contrast with its Italian cognate (*monticello*), Rm. *muncel* has a form that reflects effects of both contraction (by dropping of -*ti*-) and reduction of unstressed *o* to *u*. The latter alteration recalls the effect of an archaic speech habit, to which I have already referred above.

2.5. In the light of the arguments above, what I can assume at this point is that the term *sat* 'village' has a remarkably strong position in Romanian, and that its form, meanings and derivatives (including very significant onomastic ones) present it as very old in the Romanian language. However, for an objective-accurate study, one should not overlook the fact that there is a gap of almost one millennium between sixth-century *Gesilafossatum* and fifteenth-century *Sechel* [= *Săcel*] and *Sătcele*. Also, one cannot neglect the fact that the "doubtful" derivation of Daco-Rm. *(f)sat* from the Latin military term *fossatum* has not been clarified by specialists in the history of Romanian and of Balkan Romance.

3. In the above-mentioned *sat* entry of MDA-IV (2003), only the traditional etymological solution of a direct derivation of Rm. *(f)sat* ("cf. Alb. *fshat*") from Lat. *fossatum* is mentioned. The solution adopted by the authors of MDA actually reflects the etymological solution proposed, among others, by Gamillscheg (see above), by ROSETTI (1986: 182, 481, 759) and, more recently, by Sala.

3.1. Sala starts his comments on the origin of Rm. *sat* by echoing the opinion of the predecessors who regarded *sat* as a word of "doubtful origin", and he ends by asserting the direct derivation of Rm. *sat* from Lat. *fossatum* (SALA 2006: 214 – my translation, and my addition of brackets):

> It [Rm. *sat*] is a word of doubtful origin. [...]. Everybody knows its current meaning, 'rural settlement'. But there also are two obsolete meanings, 'field' and 'fortress' [...].The mainstream etymology indicates Lat. *fossatum* 'ditch' as its source. That etymology takes into account: [1] the old variant of the term, *fsat*; [2] the existence of the term in Aromanian too [as *fsat* 'ditch', that is]; [3] the existence of Albanian *fsat* [actually *fshat*], which means the same thing [as Daco-Romanian *sat*]. [...] In conclusion, *sat* is an old word, of Latin origin, with an etymon (*fossatum*) that has been accepted by most linguists.

Nevertheless, for all assertive statements such as Gamillscheg's, Rosetti's and Sala's, one could hardly consider that the doubts about the derivation of Rm. *(f)sat* from Lat. *fossatum* have vanished, and we can see those doubts lingering in the views of two other scholars, Cioranescu and Mihăescu.

3.2. The very order chosen by Ciorănescu (2001, s.v. *sat*) for the presentation of the main meanings of Rm. *sat* indicates his own etymological option: "1. (obs.) tilled plot of land, field; 2. (obs.) landed property, farm, landholding; 3. rural settlement [as current meaning in Daco-Romanian]; 4. (slang.) prison". After the enumeration of those meanings, Ciorănescu mentions – as variants of one and the same word – Rm. (obs.) *fsat*, Arom. *fsat*. For an etymology, Ciorănescu presents the origin of *sat* as "doubtful", since, in his opinion, the word only "seems" to derive from Lat. *fossatum* 'ditch', either directly (as assumed – according to Ciorănescu – by Bogrea, Tiktin, Daicoviciu, Candrea, Scriban, Rosetti), or by the intermediation of Alb. *fshat* (as assumed by Cihac, Meyer, Densusianu, Domaschke, Battisti, Meyer-Lübke).

Ciorănescu's intention was to present the obsolete meaning 'tilled plot of land' as capital for a conclusion in regard to the origin of Rm. *sat*. He considers, in the same *sat* entry, that "the derivation from Albanian is difficult", and "the one from Latin does not appear to be easier". Moreover, he considers that "the purely military Latin term *fossatum* (> Neo-Gk. φουσσάτον 'encampment, army' > Arom. *fusate* 'ditch') could hardly be preserved in an area characterized by total lack of medieval fortifications".[24] Finally, Ciorănescu presents the etymology he regards as most plausible: "One should rather start from Lat. *satum*, from *sero* [*serere*] 'to plant, to sow'". Nevertheless, he also (rightly) observes that the latter etymological explanation (first proposed by Cipariu, in the 19th century) "would be sufficient, if no proof existed of the obsolete form *fsat*, which is difficult to explain". True enough, no serious etymological interpretation of Rm. *sat* can possibly ignore the existence of the earliest recorded form, *fsat*.

3.3. Significant facts on Rm. *(f)sat* are to be found in Haralambie Mihăescu's comprehensive book (in French) on the fortune of Latin in SE Europe. Mihăescu (1993: 57) expressly placed himself among the ones who had doubts about the mainstream etymology of Rm. *sat*:

> Une chose reste encore douteuse, la dérivation de l'albanais *fshat* «village, région» et du roumain *sat* «village» du latin *fossatum*, tant au point de vue de la forme que sous l'aspect sémantique. [...] Les descendants romans de *fossatum* en Occident ne connaissent que les sens de «fossé, tranchée, rempart, armée», de même les emprunts en grec byzantin et en néogrec (φοσσᾶτον, φουσσᾶτον, φουσᾶτο). Les sources historiques et archéologiques montrent que le camp militaire romain et byzantin était dressé de règle dans un espace restreint. On n'a point de preuve qu'il ait existé quelque part des fossés défensifs autour des villages [...].

---

24 Ciorănescu's doubts and arguments are presented as such by Solta (1980: 169). In regard to Ciorănescu's illustrative examples, I must observe that φουσσᾶτον (which he presents as origin of Arom. *fusate*) is not exactly "Neo-Greek", but Byzantine Greek.

In support of the idea in the last two sentences, Mihăescu adds footnote 133 (on the same page), in which he mentions, with no comments, two historiographical studies signed by R. GROSSE, namely *Die römisch-byzantinischen Marschlager vom 4.–10. Jahrhundert* (BZ, 22, 1913, p. 90–121) and *Römische Militärgeschichte von Gallienus bis zum Beginn der byzantinischen Themenverfassung* (Berlin, 1920).

Although I have not been able to get to Grosse's works, I can observe that their very titles present Grosse as a specialist in Roman-Byzantine military matters. And I think it probable that Grosse (directly or indirectly) contributed much to the appearance of serious doubts about the possibility of a development of terms meaning 'village' (namely Rm. *(f)sat* and Alb. *fshat*) from a Roman term (*fossatum*) that designated a type of military fortification. Anyway, with or without Grosse's direct influence, one mainstream idea of the mid-20th century appears to have been that, for an interpretation of Rm. *(f)sat* and of Alb. *fshat* as terms of Latin origin, the *only* possible source (however doubtful) was the military term *fossatum*. Illustrative is the fact that PUȘCARIU (in his *Limba română*, first published in 1940)[25], included *sat* among Latin-originated Romanian terms with military meanings. In that respect, Pușcariu draws the following conclusion (1976: 356): "Even the name of Rm. *sat* comes from Lat. *fossatum*, whose meaning was 'a place surrounded by ditches', that is, 'a fortified place'". Nevertheless, as I will demonstrate in the final part of this article, neither was the meaning of *fossatum* exclusively military, nor was it the *only* Latin term that can account for the origin of Rm. *(f)sat* and Alb. *fshat*.

4. As I will point out in the following paragraphs (which are actually the ones meant to launch the *new* etymological interpretation announced in the title of the present article), the insistent reference to the Latin *military* term *fossatum* 'ditch (as element of fortification)' in etymological explanations of Rm. *(f)sat* and Alb. *fshat* reflects an inaccurate interpretation, or at least an incomplete one. By a stroke of luck[26], I have come upon facts that can enable us to get rid of the traditional etymological "doubts" in regard to the Latin origin of Rm. *(f)sat* 'village' and Alb. *fshat* 'village'.

4.1. First of all, it appears that *fossatum* (that is, the Latin word commonly indicated as probable origin of Rm. *(f)sat*) was not an exclusively military term, but ra-

---

25 I make use of the 1976 edition of PUȘCARIU's capital work.

26 True specialists in etymology know that, as a rule, definitively credible are not the etymologies that one painstakingly searches for, but rather those one simply comes upon by chance. The stroke of luck I have just referred to above materialized in the fact that, some time ago, I was invited to write a review of the Romanian translation of Chouquer and Favory's dictionary of Roman *gromatics* (a field I was quite unfamiliar with at that moment). It was the CHOUQUER/FAVORY dictionary (2006) that, by many of its entries, opened my way to a new etymology of Rm. *(f)sat* and Alb. *fshat*, as I will demonstrate in this part of the present article.

ther one primarily used in Roman cadastral procedures. One can draw such a conclusion even from the arrangement of the formula by which the Ernout/Meillet dictionary, s.v. *fodiō*[27], presents the usages of *fossātum* ('fossé'): «langue des arpenteurs et des militaires». In the same entry, many other examples illustrate the exceptional abundance and solidity of the Latin lexical family that centered upon *fodiō* and *fossa*. Worth observing is the secondary fourth-conjugation form *fodire* (besides classical *fodere*), which accounts for Fr. *fouir* 'to dig'. Also, quite remarkable is the rich series of derivatives from *fossa* (*fossare, fossatum, fossor, fossura, fossilis, fossarius, fossorius,* etc.), several of which are marked as "rural" and/or "popular".[28] However, in regard to *fossa*, for the argumentation line of the present article, there is something fundamental to be found (in the same dictionary) not under *fodiō* 'to dig', but under *mūrus* 'wall':

> On rattache généralement à *mūrus, pomoerium* [...] «espace consacré en dedans et en dehors de l'enceinte de Rome», puis «boulevard d'une ville»; cf. Varr., L.L. 5, 143, *oppida condebant in Latio Etrusco ritu multi, i. e. iunctis bobus, tauro et uacca, interiore aratro circumagebant sulcum ... ut fossa et muro essent muniti. Terram unde exsculpserant, fossam uocabant et introrsum iactam, murum. Post ea qui fiebat orbis, urbis principium; qui, quod erat post murum, postmoerium dictum.* [...] Mais la forme [*pomoerium*] fait difficulté. Les rites de la fondation d'une ville sont étrusques.

Although, in connection with the contents of the passage from Varro, I should focus mainly on *fossa*, I will first comment on the end of that quotation. A generally known fact is that – not only in the practices of boundary marking (Lat. *līmitātiō*), but also in the ritual implications of those practices – the Romans appear to have diligently imitated the Etruscans. No wonder that the CHOUQUER/FAVORY dictionary of gromatics (ed. 2006) includes a separate entry on *disciplina etrusca*, with the following definition:

---

27 Thr Indo-European status of Lat. *fodiō* – and, implicitly, its connection with a radical **bhedh-* 'to dig' – is revealed by the list of cognates (in other Indo-European languages) given in the ERNOUT/MEILLET dictionary, s.v. *fodiō*.

28 Lat. *fossa* has well attested heirs especially in West Romance languages, which contain both direct continuators and borrowings of the Latin word under discussion. For instance, according to COROMINAS, (1967, s.v. *fosa*), Spanish has a "hereditary" variant, *huesa* 'grave', as well as a "cultism", *fosa* 'excavation, grave'. As for French, it has *fosse* «excavation, trou, tombeau», first attested in the 11th century (cf. BAUMGARTNER/ MÉNARD 1996, s .v. *fosse*). The French term was borrowed into Romanian under the form *fosă* (as in *fosă nazală* 'nasal fossa'), that neologism being certainly better known to present-day Romanian speakers than the shadowy "Transylvanian" *foasă* 'ditch' mentioned in MEYER-LÜBKE's REW (3460).

Etruscan lore; according to some authors […], it designates the Etruscan haruspicial theory on the division of the world, a theory out of which the art of arpentage appears to have been born; it was compulsorily mentioned at the beginning of every treatise on boundary marking.[29]

4.2. VARRO's description of the Roman boundary-marking ritual (of Etruscan origin) insists on the furrow ploughed around the territory of the city to-be. One important ritual requirement appears to have been that the cow and the ox yoked to the primitive plough (*aratrum*) should be of white colour. We are also given to understand that the ritual furrow was meant to symbolically represent the fortification – a combination of ditch (*fossa*) and wall (*murus*) – that was to be subsequently raised around the city. In that respect, whereas Ovid presents Romulus as ploughing the ritual furrow around the Palatine (in a manner very similar to the one presented by Varro)[30], the historian Livy, in describing the foundation of Rome, presents Romulus not as a ritual ploughman, but as a hero who built the wall proper and who consecrated it by fratricide.[31]

However the real event may have looked like, a reputed specialist in early Roman history, Raymond BLOCH (1960: 48–49), started from both Ovid and historic-archaeological facts in his own presentation of the foundation of Rome:

> Other authors, such as Ovid in Book IV of the *Fasti*, describe in detail the rites practised during the actual foundation. Romulus marked out the line of the city walls by ploughing a furrow round the Palatine with a ploughshare. Harnessed to it were a pure white cow and a bull. Along this primordial furrow the citizens then laid the foundation of the new wall. This was the origin of the *pomoerium* of the city, the sacrosanct, taboo zone that surrounded the main body of the city with an effectual frontier protected by its divine associations. The entire history of Rome dates from this basic ceremony, which took place on April 21, 747, according to some, 753 according to others. Each year April 21 was commemo-

---

29 In regard to Etruscan antecedents, mark also also that the very name of *gromatics* derives from the name of a cadastral instrument, *grōma* (of probably Greek origin), which probably reached the Romans through "Etruscan intermediation" (cf. ERNOUT/ MEILLET 1985, *s. v. grōma*).

30 Here is Ovid's presentation of Romulus's performance: "To mark the wall by the plough, he chose a propitious day./ *Pales* was drawing near; it was then that work was started./ […] He marked the wall by a furrow, by pushing the mould board;/ White were the cow and the ox yoked together./ The king prayed: '*Jupiter*, father *Mars*, mother *Vesta,*/ Give me your help, for I want to found a city!'" (*Fasti* IV – my translation after ed. 1965: 139–140, and my italics).

31 "Another legend also spread, namely that Remus jumped over the newly built wall, as he wanted to make a mockery of it, and Romulus killed him and uttered these words: 'May all thus perish who henceforth dare jump over the walls built by me!'" (TITUS LIVIUS, *Ab urbe condita*, I, 7 – my translation after ed. 1976).

rated by a solemn and ancient ceremonial on the Palatine, the ritual of *Palilia* (or *Parilia*) dedicated to Pales the pastoral god. The aim of the shepherds' feast was to ensure the safety and fertility of the animals, and it was inevitably linked with the memory of the time when the prosperity of the new village depended on its herds.

One must observe that Varro, Ovid and Livy referred to a ritual foundation of an *urban* settlement, in which case the "primordial furrow" symbolically prefigured the fortification to-be. We can, however, assume that such a furrow was ploughed also when ancient people founded a modest rural settlement, which also needed boundary marking. It is for such aspects, and especially for a credible view on the Roman procedures of boundary marking, that the Chouquer/Favory dictionary (DTEG, 2006) provides data of inestimable value.

4.3. Most entries of DTEG represent terms that anyone with sufficient knowledge of Latin may consider as familiar. But, for such words, the dictionary under discussion gives rare technical senses, specific to the field of Roman gromatics. In DTEG one may discover, for instance, a family of related terms such as *fossa* 'ditch', *fossula* 'little ditch (as boundary marker)', *fossatus* 'ditch (as boundary marker)', *fossatus Augusteus* 'a type of ditch called Augustan, which was dug along arpentage lines'. I must observe that DTEG attaches no military sense to any term of the lexical family under discussion. I could rather say that the members of the *fossa* family reflect, however indirectly, what usually happened *after* Roman military campaigns, taking into consideration that DTEG, s.v. *fossa* 'ditch', gives the following supplementary clarification: 'a boundary-marking element in *ager occupatorius*'. And, if one looks *ager occupatorius* up in DTEG, one will find out that the formula under discussion refers to 'land whose native inhabitants were chased away, such land being subsequently declared *ager publicus* and made available for free occupation and for cultivation by the conquerors' – as simple as that.

4.4. So, both historians and etymologists preoccupied with the fortune of words such as Rm. *(f)sat* and Alb. *fshat* should start from certain terms, senses and contexts presented in DTEG. More concretely, an important part of the material included in that dictionary practically imposes the idea that the Latin term on which both *(f)sat* and *fshat* appear to be based did not actually refer to any fortifications, but rather to the usual Roman procedure of boundary marking in *ager occupatorius*, on the point of being turned into *ager publicus*. Historically speaking, one should not overlook the fact that Illyria and Dacia were among the territories whose natives offered fiercest resistance to the Romans, so the latter had all reasons to turn as much of those territories as possible into *ager publicus*, by the procedure described above. That procedure, in the light of the cadastral terminology given in DTEG, certainly implied foundation of new settlements, for Roman veterans and colonists. A settlement of that type could rightly be called *fossatus*, since its boundaries were technically-ritually marked by *fossae*. Taking all these facts into account, we should not consider it curious that it was with populations of former Illyria and Dacia that terms such as *fshat* and *(f)sat*, respectively, survived with the basic meaning of 'village' to our days. Also, we should not find it surprising that it was in a territory once known as *Dacia antiqua* where (without any parallel in the Romance world)[32] two important Latin words showed a kind of convergent evolution: *fossatus* 'ditch (as boundary marker)' grew into Rm. *(f)sat* 'village' and and *veteranus* 'experienced soldier' grew into Rm. *bătrân* 'old, old man, elder'.[33] As late as modern times, Rm. *sat* continued to designate the most specific Daco-Romanian kind of rural settlement (as a territorial unit),[34] while *bătrân* continued to designate not only mere old men, but also prestige members of village assemblies that represented supreme local authority.[35] Such facts provide a perspective from which we may develop some clearer understanding of the installation of Latinophone settlements (of a *fossatus* type) in SE Europe, and of the subsequent role those settlements played in the emergence of SE European Romance (as well as in the infusion of a huge amount of Latin vocabulary into "proto-Albanian").

32 Romance languages have not preserved Lat. *vicus* as designation of a rural settlement. In West Romance languages, as designations of rural settlements we find derivations from Lat. *villa* (cf. Fr. *village*), or from Lat. *populus* (cf. Span. *pueblo*). It is only in Romanian and in Albanian (as a non-Romance language) where Lat. *fossatus* grew into terms meaning 'village', namely *(f)sat* (as Romanian continuator) and *fshat* (as Latin loan in Albanian).

33 I have, again, reasons to point out striking lexical differences between Daco-Romanian and Aromanian. Whereas *sat* 'village' is certainly among the most widely spread and best known words in Daco-Romanian, the single (and dim) attestation of what PAPAHAGI (1974) gives as Arom. *sat²* 'village' makes it look like a phantom word (see above). Similarly, whereas *bătrân* 'old, old man, elder' (< Lat. *veteranus*) has a quite strong position in Daco-Romanian, Arom. *bitîrnu* 'old' (an obvious cognate of Daco-Rm. *bătrân*) is presented by Papahagi as "an anaemic word, in comparison with its synonym, *ausu*".

34 I insist on the territorial aspect mainly because, unlike other SE Europeans (Aromanians included), Daco-Romanians would organize their communities not so much on the basis of blood relationship (of a clan type), but rather on the basis of communal ownership of territorial units (including, as a rule, arable land, pasture, forest and water sources). For earlier Daco-Romanians – just as for the Romans and the Etruscans of ancient times – fixation of boundaries of such territorial units had ritual-magic significance, as pointed out by STAHL (2000: 176, chapter „Structura religioasă a teritoriului sătesc românesc" – see also below).

35 Quite a lot of Romanian medieval documents mention *oamenii buni şi bătrâni* ("the good and old men") as decision makers in Romanian villages.

4.5. Since the method I adopted for the making of this article is unavoidably interdisciplinary, I will eventually add some ethnological facts too. First, I will make use of the bird's eye view of STAHL 2000, a volume that provides a keen comparative survey of SE European "tribes and villages", with a special focus on "social, magic and religious structures" (as indicated by the subtitle of the volume under discussion). Among other things, Stahl points out structural differences between two main types of SE European rural ways of life: (1) the one represented by mobile kin- and interest-oriented communities[36], with a dominantly pastoralist system of subsistence, as manifest with (fewer and fewer) Aromanians and Albanians; (2) the one represented by dominantly sedentary-agricultural communities of the Daco-Romanians and the South Slavs.[37] In regard to the former, I will quote a passage from the chapter in which STAHL (2000: 176) discusses the "religious structure" of the communal landed property of Romanian[38] villages:

> Once established, the boundaries [of a Romanian village] acquire characteristics that are political and, at the same time, magic. Within, where the human community lives, there lies the space that the boundary protects against the foreigner, the stranger, the one who comes from elsewhere. [...] Whatever enables one to recognize the double character of a boundary, which, in being social and political, also becomes magic? First of all, the operation of boundary marking takes a special form; in being performed – along their common boundary – by villages neighboring on each other, that operation is attended by curses against possible intruders [...].

A much more concrete view, or, rather, a number of significant glimpses of the plough-marked boundaries of traditional Romanian villages may be extracted from the extremely valuable answers to the questionnaires of the Romanian Ethnographical Atlas (*Atlasul Etnografic Român*), as rendered by GHINOIU (2001: 327–328) in

36 For specific features of mobile-pastoralist communities of the *fara* type, see PORUCIUC 2009, as well as certain subchapters of KAHL 2006 and KAHL 2007.

37 The similarity between Daco-Romanians and Slavs, in regard to traditional-rural way of life, should not appear as surprising, if we agree with Shevelov, who concisely presents the following SE European ethnogenetic processes: "... if present day Bulgarian emerged as a Sl speaking country in the Middle Ages, it is not because the Roman speaking population inhabiting the area before the Sl invasions were expelled or annihilated physically, but because Sl overcame Roman during a prolonged period of competition. Sl was absorbed into Rm in Romania, and Rom was absorbed into Sl in Bulgaria" (SHEVELOV1964: 160). Also, what a recent Austrian historian says about the Slavic low-profile *Lebensweise*, which proved to be "amazingly successful" (*erstaunlich erfolgreich*) through the troubled period of *Völkerwanderungen* (POHL 2008: 141), can very well be applied to the Daco-Romanian population, which, in Shevelov's vision, had to enter a "coterritorial" relationship with the expanding Slavs.

38 Actually, in that subchapter Stahl refers exclusively to features specific to *Daco*-Romanian villages.

a subchapter on customs regarding the settlement of "a village's communal owner-ship" (*moşia satului*). The villagers of Oltenia (SW Romania), who formulated the statements given below, appear to be in possession of very significant details – transmitted from generation to generation, by word of mouth – in regard to the original foundation of their own villages. The first statement (by an inhabitant of Orodel, Dolj County) makes us remember what Romulus is said to have done in the mid-8th century BC:

> They [the founding settlers] marked the ground by ploughing a furrow around it, and, from a fixed point, they threw an ax in several directions. The original village lay in the valley of the Orodel brook […]. It was moved here because of the Turks. Around here there were big forests. People also moved here because of the plague. They came with two white buffaloes [*doi bivoli albi*], with two candles fixed on the horns of each. The buffaloes went around, and however much land they could round in one day became the ownership of the village [*moşia satului*]. The boundary was marked all around by a plough furrow [*brazdă de plug*].

An informant from another village of the same province (Perişani, Vâlcea County) was able to provide incredibly precise details about the way his own village had been founded, in the 19th century:

> They did the boundary settlement [*ocolniţa*] like this: the elders [*bătrânii*], the forefa-thers [*moşii*] took each a knapsack full of earth on their backs, and they went around, under the oath that no one should trespass on the boundary. The settlement is still ob-served nowadays [after about 150 years, that is], especially in regard to pasture. […] They were bound by an oath: that none of them should lay down the sack of earth [*sacul cu pământ*] that they carried on their backs, and that whoever trespassed on the bound-ary settlement might turn to earth.[39]

In a subsequent subchapter, on customs regarding the settlement of a village's pre-cincts (*vatra satului*), GHINOIU 2001 gives statements of the same kind, coming from other Oltenian villages (Bratuia, Isverna, Igoiu, Scorniceşti, etc.); worth mentioning is that, in referring to village foundations, no informant failed to men-tion the "plough furrow" as fundamental marker.

Undeniably, especially from a *Wörter und Sachen* perspective, there are incredi-ble similarities between what Romans remembered about the foundation of their

---

39 In my translations of the last two quotations from GHINOIU 2001, I introduced some brackets with the original Romanian terms and phrases. My intention, in that respect, was to point out (for the sake of Balkan linguistics) the fascinating way in which Romanian villagers, in referring to fundamental features of their communities, make use of terms that come from rather diverse sources: Latin (*sat* 'village', *bătrân* 'elder', *sac* 'sack', *pământ* 'earth'), Palaeo-Balkan (*moş* 'forefather', *vatră* 'hearth, village pre-cincts'), Slavic (*brazdă* 'furrow', *ocolniţa* 'boundary settlement'), and even Old Ger-manic (*plug* 'plough').

city and what Romanian villagers remember about what their forefathers did when they founded a new village (in earlier modern times). Nevertheless, one should not expect such rural Romanians (most of them uneducated peasants – *țărani*) to also know about the foundation of Rome, about Romulus's furrow, or about what Roman arpentors did when they marked a portion of *ager publicus* that was to become communal property of of a new community. What I selected from among the answers to the questionnaires of the Romanian Ethnographical Atlas (see quotations above) may be regarded, most generally, as a reflection of what BURKERT, in referring to Greece, presented as "the inertial force of peasant culture and peasant custom" (1985: 13). It is by that force that not only the custom of furrow-boundaries, but also terms such as Rm. *(f)sat* and Alb. *fshat* – both meaning 'village', and, in my opinion, both derived from Lat. *fossatus* 'ditch (as boundary marker)' – survived in territories inhabited by Daco-Romanians and Albanians, respectively.

5. I will stop here, although I am aware of the fact that certain details need more discussion. Among other things, more could be written on the socio-historical and linguistic circumstances that account for the fact that (unlike Daco-Rm. *sat* and Alb. *fshat*) Arom. *fsat* remained with the original meaning of 'ditch', without shifting to 'village'.[40] Supplementary interpretations can also be added in regard to the parallel (or convergent)[41] evolutions of Lat. *fossatum* ('ditch' > 'military fortification' > 'army, campaign') and Lat. *fossatus* ('a boundary-marking furrow' > 'a rural settlement founded in a newly occupied territory') in Romance and in Balkan languages. The arguments given above may become starting points for a whole series of future discussions.

References

BAUMGARTNER, Emmanuèle; MENARD, Philippe (1997): *Dictionnaire étymologique et historique de la langue française*. Paris: Le Livre de Poche.

BLOCH, Raymond (1960): *The Origins of Rome*. New York: Praeger.

BURKERT, Walter (1985): *Greek Religion*, transl. J. Raffan. Boston: Harvard University Press.

CHOUQUER, Gérard; FAVORY, François (2006): *Dicționar de termeni și expresii gromatice* (DTEG), transl. M. Alexianu. Iași: Casa Editorială Demiurg.

---

40 Some explanations for the situation under discussion are foreshadowed in PORUCIUC 2009 and 2010.

41 I take into account, at this point, that the current sense of Rm. *sat*, as well as some of the latter's obsolete senses ('sanctuary', 'cultivated field') can be referred to the ritual-magic furrow I have discussed above, whereas other obsolete senses of the same Romanian word ('tent', 'settlement made of tents', 'fortress') suggest a connection with the element of fortification designated by Lat. *fossatum*.

CIORĂNESCU, Alexandru (2001): *Dicţionarul etimologic al limbii române*, transl./ed. T. Şandru Mehedinţi, M. Popescu Marin. Bucureşti: Saeculum.

CONSTANTINESCU, N. A. (1963): *Dicţionar onomastic românesc*. Bucureşti: Editura Academiei.

COROMINAS, Joan (1967): *Breve diccionario etimológico de la lengua castellana*. Madrid: Gredos.

ÇABEJ, Eqrem (1982): *Studime etimologjike në fushë të shqipes*, I. Tiranë: Akademia e Shkencave.

DEČEV (Detschew), Dimităr (1957): *Die thrakischen Sprachreste*. Wien: Rohrer.

ERNOUT, Alfred; MEILLET, Antoine (1985): *Dictionnaire étymologique de la langue latine*. Paris: Klincksieck.

GAMILLSCHEG, Ernst (1934–1935): *Romania Germanica – Sprach- und Siedlungsgeschichte der Germanen auf dem Boden des alten Römerreiches*, I–II. Berlin: de Gruyter.

GHINEA, Eliza; GHINEA, Dan (2000): *Localităţile din România – Dicţionar*. Bucureşti: Editura Enciclopedică.

GHINOIU, Ion et al. (2001): *Sărbători şi obiceiuri*, Vol. I, Oltenia. Bucureşti: Editura Enciclopedică.

GOLOPENTIA, Anton (2006): *Românii de la est de Bug*, II, ed. S. Golopenţia. Bucureşti: Editura Enciclopedică.

IORDAN, Iorgu (1963): *Toponimia romînească*. Bucureşti: Editura Academiei.

IORDAN, Iorgu (1983): *Dicţionar al numelor de familie româneşti*. Bucureşti: Editura Ştiinţifică.

IVĂNESCU, Gheorghe (2000): *Istoria limbii române*, ed. M. Paraschiv. Iaşi: Junimea.

KAHL, Thede (2006): *Istoria aromânilor*. Bucureşti: Tritonic.

KAHL, Thede (2007): *Hirten in Kontakt. Sprach- und Kulturwandel ehemalige Wanderhirten (Albanisch, Aromunisch, Griechisch)*. Wien, Berlin: LIT-Verlag.

LIVIUS, Titus (1976): *Ab urbe condita (De la fundarea Romei)*, transl. P. Popescu Găleşanu. Bucureşti: Minerva.

MEYER, Gustav (1891): *Etymologisches Wörterbuch der albanesischen Sprache*. Strassburg: Verlag von Karl J. Trübner.

MDA – *Micul dicţionar academic*, 2003, Vol. IV, ed. M. Sala et al. Bucureşti: Univers Enciclopedic.

MIHAESCU, Haralambie (1993): *La romanité dans le Sud-Est de l'Europe*. Bucureşti: Editura Academiei.

OVID (Ovidiu) (1965): *Fastele*, transl. I. Florescu, T. Costa. Bucureşti: Editura Academiei.

PAPAHAGI, Tache (1974): *Dicţionarul dialectului aromân – Dictionnaire aroumain (macédo-roumain)*. Bucureşti: Editura Academiei.

POHL, Walter (2005): *Die Völkerwanderung – Eroberung und Integration*. Stuttgart: Kohlhammer.

POHL, Walter (2008): *Eastern Central Europe in the Early Middle Ages – Conflicts, Migrations and Ethnic Processes*, ed. C. Spinei, C. Hriban. Bucureşti: Editura Academiei/ Brăila: Editura Istros – Muzeul Brăilei.

PORUCIUC, Adrian (2007): Review: "Gérard Chouquer, François Favory: *Dicţionar de termeni şi expresii gramatice* (traducere şi cuvânt înainte de Marius Alexianu). Iaşi: Casa Editorială Demiurg, 2006. *Arheologia Moldovei*, XXX. 391–393.

PORUCIUC, Adrian (2009): „Vechiul germanism *fara* păstrat în română şi în alte limbi sud-est europene". In: *Lucrările celui de-al doilea simpozion internaţional de lingvistică, Bucureşti, 28/29 noiembrie, 2008*, ed. N. Saramandu, M. Nevaci, C. I. Radu. Bucureşti, Academia Română, Institutul de Lingvistică "Iorgu Iordan – Alexandru Rosetti", Bucureşti, Editura Universităţii. 167–180.

PORUCIUC, Adrian (2010): „Rom. *sat* ca derivat din termenul lat. *fossatus* folosit în arpentajul roman". In: *Lucrările celui de-al treilea simpozion internaţional de lingvistică, Bucureşti, 20-21 noiembrie 2009*, ed. N. Saramandu, M. Nevaci, C. I. Radu. Academia Română, Institutul de Lingvistică „Iorgu Iordan – Alexandru Rosetti". Editura Universităţii din Bucureşti. 129–136.

PUŞCARIU, Sextil (1976): *Limba română*, I, ed. Ilie Dan. Bucureşti: Minerva.

ROSETTI, Alexandru (1986): *Istoria limbii române*. Bucureşti: Editura Ştiinţifică.

SALA, Marius (2006): *Aventurile unor cuvinte româneşti*, I. Bucureşti: Univers Enciclopedic.

SCHALLER, Helmut Wilhelm (1975): *Die Balkansprachen – Eine Einführung in die Balkanphilologie*. Heidelberg: Carl Winter. Universitätsverlag.

SHEVELOV, George Y. (1964): *A Prehistory of Slavic – The Historical Phonology of Common Slavic*. Heidelberg: Carl Winter. Universitätsverlag.

SOLTA, Georg (1980): *Einführung in die Balkanlinguistik mit besonderer Berücksichtigung des Substrats und des Balkanlateinischen*. Darmstadt: Wissenschaftliche Buchgesellschaft.

STAHL, Paul H. (2000): *Triburi şi sate din sud-estul Europei – Structuri sociale, structuri magice şi religioase*. Bucureşti: Paideia.

STEINKE, Klaus; VRACIU, Ariton (1999): *Introducere în lingvistica balcanică*. Iaşi: Editura Universităţii "Alexandru Ioan Cuza".

SUCIU, Coriolan (1967–1968): *Dicţionar istoric al localităţilor din Transilvania*, I–II. Bucureşti: Editura Academiei.

VĂTĂŞESCU, Cătălina (1997): *Vocabularul de origine latină din limba albaneză în comparaţie cu româna*. Bucureşti: Institutul Român de Tracologie, Bibliotheca Thracologica XIX.

A new view on the Latin origin of Romanian *(f)sat* 'village', Aromanian *fsat* 'ditch'and Albanian *fshat* 'village'

According to several outstanding philologists, an earlier etymological interpretation of Romanian *(f)sat* 'village' as continuator of Latin *fossatum* 'ditch (as element of fortification)' (cf. Aromanian *fsat* 'ditch' and Albanian *fshat* 'village') should be regarded as "doubtful." The doubt under discussion appears to have been caused mainly by the consideration of Latin *fossatum* as a "purely military" term, which could, according to the same critical specialists, hardly develop a meaning such as 'village' in a territory without evidence of fortified rural settlements. However, as this author points out, no attention has been paid to an important family of Roman cadastral terms, including *fossa* and *fossatus* (both based on the Latin verb *fodere/fodire* 'to dig'). The arguments in the final part of the present article sustain the idea that, for both Albanian *fshat* and Romanian *sat*, a more credible etymological explanation can be formulated by reference to Latin *fossatus* 'ditch (as boundary marker)', rather than to the Latin military term *fossatum* 'ditch (as element of fortification)'. One should take into consideration that, after successful military campaigns of Roman legions, the newly established *ager occupatorius* (that is, the conquered land, whose hostile inhabitants had been chased away) was transformed, by cadastral specialists, into *ager publicus*, pieces of which were allotted to Roman veterans and colonists. It was the boundaries of such plots of land that were marked by furrows or ditches designated as *fossa, fossula*, or *fossatus*, the last one appearing to be the true origin of Albanian *fshat* 'village' and Romanian *(f)sat* 'village'. Certain obsolete meanings of the Romanian word (such as 'cultivated field', or 'sanctuary') actually recall the legendary foundation of Rome, by a *fossa* ploughed by Romulus around the Palatine. However, other meanings of Romanian *(f)sat* – such as 'tent', 'camp', or 'fortress' – do suggest that we should continue to take into consideration a "participation" of the Latin military term *fossatum* in the making of the polysemantic field of the Romanian word under discussion. In conclusion, whereas Aromanian *fsat* (for its own reasons) remained with the primeval meaning of Lat. *fossatus* 'ditch', Daco-Romanian *sat* (as direct continuator of *fossatus*) and Albanian *fshat* (as borrowing of the same Latin word) reflect a semantic shift that eventually led to the current meaning of both – 'village'.

Aromanian Elements of an Albanian *argot**

Elton PRIFTI (Potsdam)

The results of numerous Romance – Albanian contacts have partly determined the linguistic history of the Western Balkans. However, while modern Romance research on the Albanian-speaking area is still in its early stages, various important linguistic and cultural issues remain to be studied. The differentiated analysis of Romance elements in Albanian varieties is one of them. Indeed, the description of the romanity of Albanian has until now almost always been limited to standard Albanian. Yet it is the *non-standard varieties* of Albanian where the most significant traces of Romance – Albanian linguistic contacts are conserved. A very rich though neglected sector is that of the continuous and dynamic interaction between Aromanian and Albanian. In this context, a particular aspect is the Aromanian influence on some Albanian *argots*, namely *Purisht* and *Dogançe*. A systematic analysis of this influence brings forth relevant cognitions, also from a theoretical point of view. Several aspects of the Aromanian influence on *Purisht* could be considered as balkanisms.

1. Brief notes on Albanian *argots*

The intensive contacts and the interaction between all Southeastern European languages take a tangible and dynamic form in the field of the *argots*. Descriptions of the mutual influences between languages and *argots* in Southeastern Europe must first take into account the dynamics of the correlations between various *cryptolectic units*. The concept of 'unit' can be related to two main aspects:

1. The *base language*, on which the various *argots* are based, e.g. the Albanian based cryptolects,
2. The *artisan group*, independent of the language, on which the *argots* are based, e.g. the cryptolect unit of the South-Balkanic masons.[1]

---

* I am deeply grateful to the interviewees for their support, as well as to Thede Kahl for his valuable observations.

1 See e.g. JIREČEK 1876: 99–100: „(…) der Jargon [ist] an ein Handwerk gebunden, meist an die Maurerei, und was das merkwürdigste ist, die »termini technici« desselben sind keineswegs, wie man erwarten könnte, griechischen oder romanischen Ursprungs, sondern albanesisch und zwar meist dem toskischen, südlichen Dialect angehörig. Dies hängt mit dem wandernden Handwerk zusammen, dessen Heimath eben das albanesi-

A thorough study of the unit of the Albanian-based cryptolects of nomadic artisans is still missing, as even are exhaustive descriptions of the individual Albanian *argots*. All known published information about Albanian secret languages is concentrated in a handful of articles (HAXHIHASANI 1964a, 1964b and 1964c, YMERI 2002, SHKURTAJ 2004, PRIFTI 2009b). The scientific community is substantially better informed on the Albanian elements present in non-Albanian *argots* – even outside the Balkan Peninsula[2] – than those on the Albanian cryptolects themselves. There are several descriptions of non-Albanian based *argots* that contain indications on their Albanian loans.[3] These convey the impression that Albanian borrowings in the *argots* are numerous and widely diffused, similar to the Romani loans.[4] This phenomenon represents another less-known and particular aspect of Albanian interferences within the framework of the inter-Balkanic language contacts.

Contrary to the aspect of Albanian borrowings in non-Albanian cryptolects, the loans in Albanian *argots* remain almost unexplored. These loans, along with the encrypted and alienated lexemes of Albanian origin, make up the majority of their vocabulary. The repertory of languages from which the borrowings come from, as well as the detours they took and the manner in which they reached the individual *argots,* are strikingly diverse. The main source languages are Greek, Slavic-varieties, Turkish, Romani-varieties as well as Romance-varieties – particularly Aromanian.

---

sche und halbalbanesische Sprachgebiet ist, die von Albanesen umgebenen oder täglich mit ihnen verkehrenden romanischen (wlachischen) und bulgarischen Gebirgsdörfer des Pindus und der Hochländer von West-Macedonien." Furthermore, concerning, e.g. the unit of the cryptolects of the wandering boilermakers see the analysis of TRUMPER 1996a: 45–53, which also contains some theoretical considerations. An early example of such an analysis is JAGIĆ 1896.

2   See e.g. CORTELAZZO 1977 and TRUMPER (1986, 1996a, 1996b), in which the authors also identify some Balkan-Albanian loans in the cryptolects of nomadic boilermakers in Southern Italy, even in Sardinia. See also the notes in PRIFTI 2010.

3   On the Albanian elements of the South-Slavic *argots,* see the accurate bibliographic information in TAGLIAVINI 1942: 42, the brief notes on BARIĆ 1926, HRISTOVA-BEJLERI 2004, ISMAJLI 1987: 165–166, КАЦОРИ/ ДУКОВА/ АСЕНОВА 1984, PETROVICI 1934, etc. Concerning Albanian interferences in the Greek-based cants see Σάρρος 1923, but also the essays of Χρήστος Σούλης, Αθανάσιος Παπαχαρίσης and others about the Greek cryptolects μπουκουραϊκα, κουδαρίτικα, σωπικά, etc. On the Albanian elements in Italian *argots* see the general notes in PRIFTI 2010: 379–380.

4   According to TAGLIAVINI 1937: 959: "Considerevole è invece l'influsso dello zingaro se si esce dalle lingue comuni e si considerano le lingue speciali e particolarmente i gerghi (...)". On the impact of Romani on Greek varieties see e.g. TRIANDAPHYLLIDIS 1923, where some Albanian borrowings are also indicated.

2. About *Purisht*

Purisht is the secret language of the Southeastern Albanian masons, self-designated *pure* 'masters'. The first indications of the existence of *Purisht* date back to the second half of the 18th century. Its current nucleus is concentrated in thirteen villages in the region of Opar (district of Korçë, Albania). *Purisht* is also spoken among men who have migrated to urbanized centers in the vicinity, to the main Albanian cities (such as Tiranë and Durrës), as well as outside the Albanian borders, first and foremost in Greece. It is very difficult to assign even an approximate figure to the number of *Purisht* speakers. Nonetheless, the total population of 1,113 people of the municipality of Lekas, which includes almost all the localities where *Purisht* is spoken, can serve as an indicator. Any estimation must further take into account the proportionally considerable number of emigrated *Purisht* speakers.

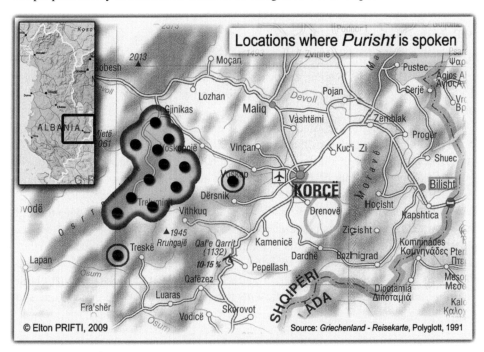

Fig. 1: *Map of the extension of the Purisht-nucleus*

An analysis of the variation-oriented data revealed that *Purisht* is normally used only by men, though it is understood perfectly by women as well. Some female speakers confirmed that they do or would occasionally use *Purisht* in specific circumstances, e.g. when they want to encrypt a conversation from Albanians that don't come from the *Purisht*-speaking area. A diagenerational differentiation is also clearly shaped. The elderly (usually born before the Second World War and

who actively and continuously used *Purisht* until the 1950s, when private business
was banned) are still able to speak a more authentic *Purisht*, though they admitted
to having forgotten a lot of it and to speaking it worse than their ancestors. It is
significant to emphasize that the *Purisht* of younger people is closely linked to an
interesting ongoing revival. This revival, accompanied by urbanization, is due to
the introduction of the free market economy, which is one of the consequences of
the radical political changes of the early 1990s in Albania. The somewhat pervasive linguistic change of this revival-phase consists mostly of numerous innovations to meet the needs of new circumstances, completing the necessary vocabulary.[5] This also happens through the adaption of new loans that are only sporadically of Romance origin. Lastly, *Purisht*, like other Albanian dialect varieties or the
languages of the minorities spoken in Albania (see e.g. PRIFTI 2009a), has been ex-
posed to the growing influence of standard Albanian.

3. Romance borrowings of *Purisht*

An analysis of *Purisht* vocabulary revealed that Romance borrowings represent the
majority of the non-Albanian elements. The Romance elements compose nearly
16 % of the registered lexical items of *Purisht* and are almost totally of Aromanian
origin.

There are only a few sporadic Romance elements that can be interpreted with
certainty as not primarily Aromanian, beginning with the substantive pur. *manxhë*
'food,' recorded only in the locality of Marjan. First of all, *manxhë* is one of the
border-crossing elements of *Dogançe* that can also be found sporadically in other
Albanian confining cryptolects. At the origin is the Italianism *mangia(re)*, which
reached Bulgarian (*манджа* / *манжа* / *манжњ*) and Aromanian (*mánǧe*) through
the intermediary of Turkish (*manca* 'food, meal, portion'), as described by TA-
GLIAVINI.[6] In all probability, this Italianism reached *Purisht* indirectly. Furthermore, pur. *xhivéllë*, 'a kind of wooden crosspiece for collecting roof joist' (recorded in Korçë from an old carpenter and *Purisht* speaker from Denas, that classified it as an archaic *Purisht* item), presents the Turkish substantive *ǧivata* 'una spe-

---

5 I registered, for example, the denomination of the cellular phone, pur. *cërre e gruthme*,
   which literally translated means 'good, fine telephone,' where the onomatopoeic substantive *cërre* more than an originally *Purisht*-term is an Albanian slang denomination
   of 'telephone.' An analogue construction is also the denomination pur. *fok(ë)tór i*
   gruthmë 'radiator', where pur. *fok(ë)tór* < pur. *fok* < ar. *fóku* 'fire' (see below).

6 According to TAGLIAVINI 1938: 119: "Potremo invece affermare con sicurezza che il
   turco *manǧa* (…) è un prestito diretto (che poi si è irradiato al bulgaro) sia perché finora
   non è stata dimostrata la sua presenza in neogreco (ciò che proverebbe poco), ma più
   che altro, perche il ⇥ turco rende direttamente il *ǧ* palatale italiano che in neo-greco
   avrebbe dato invece δζ il quale sarebbe stato reso in turco con ج."

cie di chiodo.' According to TAGLIAVINI (1938: 119), this Turkish element surely derives from the Venetian *čaveta*, and not from the Italian *chiavetta*, because of the conservation of the post-alveolar consonant. *Xhivéllë*, therefore presents an intermediated Venetianism of *Purisht*.

Another source of the Romance loans of *Purisht* has occasionally been the Judeo-Spanish of Southeastern Europe. The denomination pur. *bumbarúk* 'badly dressed man, beggar,' recorded in Gjergjevicë and Gjonbabas, is a derivation of the Judeo-Spanish *bambarúto* 'Schreckgespenst der Kinder' (WAGNER 1914: 178) < span. *barbarote*. Although evidence of this item in Aromanian or Greek is missing, it should not be excluded that the loan has been intermediated into *Purisht*. It must be emphasized that while the Judeo-Spanish varieties spoken in Greece and Turkey have occasionally been the objects of study, the Sephardic elements of Albanian varieties – especially in the area of Vlora – are still unexplored. This is a further aspect of Albanian romanity worthy of a systematic investigation.

In many cases, phonetic similarities make it very difficult to distinguish the possible Megleno-Romanian elements – or rarer still the Daco-Romanian ones – from the overwhelmingly dominant elements of Aromanian origin. The Romanian borrowing pur. *curcubé* 'rainbow,' for example, can be phonetically related to ar. *kurkubéu*, as well as to megl. *curcubéŭ*.[7]

4. Aromanian elements of *Purisht*

The significant influence of Aromanian on *Purisht* is palpable even in the following etymological interpretations about the denomination *Purisht* itself. Its origin can be found in ar. *puríe* '(a variety of) stone, porous stone' (PAPAHAGI 1996: 228), that derives from the semantically analogous Greek πωρί (Νικολαΐδης 1909: 440 and GEAGEA 1931: 196). A direct loan gr. πουρί 'limestone' could be considered as well. Another, very similar interpretation of the origin seems to be the widespread Balkan-Romani *pʰur(o)* 'old man' that has reached at least Daco-Romanian[8] and Aromanian[9] as a semantically equivalent *argot*-element. A direct borrowing of *Purisht* from Romani can be equally sustained phonetically, as well as an intermediation of Aromanian. However, to give a better-founded interpretation of this issue, more detailed and complete dialectological data are needed.

The substantial impact of Aromanian on *Purisht* becomes clearly tangible through the dynamic of the distribution of numerous elements on manifold seman-

---

7   On the correlation between the Aromanian and Megleno-Romanian forms see PAPA-
HAGI 1974: 415.

8   According to CIORĂNESCU (2002: 647) Romani *puro* / *puri* 'bătrîn' > dacorom. *puriu*
[arg.] 'tată' (> *purie* 'mamă'). Find there further bibliographical information.

9   I registered in the item ar. *purájă* 'old slut / whore, badly dressed old woman' in 2005
from an old Aromanian speaker native of Dishnicë (Albania).

tic spheres. Among them, the richest is the sphere of **fauna**, especially the sector of **domestic animals**. The substantive pur. *bolo* 'bull, ox,' for example, derives from the semantically identical ar. *boŭ / bóŭlu* (< lat. *bovus*). It is noteworthy that the *Purisht*-denomination of 'cow' is derived through the addition to the masculine form pur. *bolo* of the Albanian feminine-forming suffix *-vicë*[10], and not through any direct borrowing. Some (mainly young) speakers generally used *bolo* for both genders. A similar word-formation process characterizes the pairs *glinë - glinës*, where pur. *glinës* 'cock' < pur. *glinë* 'hen' < ar. *gl'ínă*[11] (< lat. *gallina*) or *këpre - këprác*, where pur. *këprác* 'male goat' < pur. *këpre* 'goat' < ar. *kapră* (ALiA: map 328) (< lat. *capra*). Thereby *-s* and *-ac* are diffused Albanian substantive-forming suffixes for the masculine gender. These examples further confirm that *Purisht*, in terms of morphology – as is usual for *argots* – is entirely founded on its base-language: the South-eastern Tosk-Albanian variety of Opar. It is also interesting to briefly analyse the single elements of the semantic group pur. *këltush* 'male cat', pur. *këltushe* 'cat' and pur. *këltushe njigëz* 'kitten.' Theoretically it is possible that each one of these elements derives from the respective Aromanian items *kătúṣ*[(u)] (ALiA: map 94, PAPAHAGI 1974: 356), *kătúṣe* (ALiA: map 96, NEIESCU 1997: map 15, PAPAHAGI 1974: 356) or *kătúṣ n'íku*[12], but in reality they might be derivations of one another, at least for the former two (by adding or removing the suffix *-e*: *këltush > këltushe* or *këltush < këltushe*). It is more persuasive that *këltushe njigëz* constitutes a new formation through the combining of the widely diffused and vivid adverb and adjective pur. *njikëz* 'small, little, minor, few' < ar. *n'icăz*[13] (< lat. *micus*) with the substantive pur. *këltushe*. A similar use of *njigëz* – as also illustrated in the Appendix of this paper – is widespread in *Purisht* (e.g.: pur. *këpre*

10 Suffix of Slavic origin, diffused mainly in the Southeastern Albanian varieties; concerning the suffix *-icë*, cf. ÇABEJ / XHUVANI 1962: 49–50. The analogy of the use of the suffix by forming female antroponyms like *Nestovícë* or *Vangjovícë* is interesting, which means respectively 'the wife of *Nesti* or *Vangjo*'.

11 Cf. *Atlasul Lingvistic Aromân* (ALiA) of Wolfgang DAHMEN and Johannes KRAMER, map 43. This fundamental opus for the dialectological studies of Aromanian, especially the varieties spoken in Greece, will be cited several times hereafter. Where necessary, dialectological points of interest will be mentioned only by indicating its ALiA-numerical symbol. Another linguistic atlas that will be cited sometimes in the henceforth is NEIESCU 1997.

12 Variation indicated in ALiA, map 97, only in the point 40 (Καλαρίτσι, in the Northeastern Pindus); missing in NEIESCU 1997.

13 Indicated several times in some maps of ALiA (cf. the indications in HILKER 1981: 333), as well as in the maps 32, 47, 59, 63, 73 of NEIESCU 1997. See also PAPAHAGI 1996: 188.

njigë 'kid (of the goat)', pur. *këcáf njigëz*[14] 'whelp'). On the other hand, pur. *këcaf* 'male dog,' that derives from ar. *kắțáu* (ALiA: map 91, NEIESCU 1997: map. 59) 'female dog' has been taken as the basis for pur. *këcafe* 'female dog.' While pur. *ójle* 'sheep' can be traced easily to ar. *óie* (< lat. *ovis*), the hypothesis of linking pur. *bëdë*[15] 'mule' to ar. *bắdrăn'* 'stubborn, mulish,' that I recorded in Korça and Drenova, needs further detailed examination.

The semantic sphere of **flora**, including the sector of the denomination of **foods** constitutes another important source of Aromanian loans, beginning with pur. *arbë* 'grass' < ar. *ĭárbă / eárbă* 'grass' or pur. *mere* 'apple' < ar. *méru* 'apple, apple tree' (< lat. *melum*). It is also noteworthy to mention the item pur. *merellokë* 'potato' that I registered in Lekas. This item more probably presents a borrowed ar. *mer-loc*,[16] than a *Purisht* internal combination of the two Aromanian loans *mere* and pur. *llok* 'soil' (< ar. *locu* (ALiA: map 176 (points 1, 12, 8), as a *calque* on the Albanian dialectal *mollë dheu*. This isolated variety, recorded e.g. in Qytezë (District of Devoll)[17], could probably also be an Albanian *calque* on the Aromanian form. I also registered the denomination pur. *tllokut* (*të llokut*) 'potato, verbatim: of the soil' from some other speakers. Additional lexical loans from the food-sector include pur. *grëne* 'wheat' < ar. *grînu* 'cereals, grain, ear' (ALiA: maps 37, 68, NEIESCU 1997: map 219) (< lat. *granum*), pur. *frinë / frine* 'flour' < ar. *fắrínă* (ALiA: map 353, NEIESCU 1997: map 209) (< lat. *farina*), pur. *sare* 'salt' < ar. *sare* (< lat. *sal*), pur. *llapte* 'milk' < ar. *lápte* (ALiA: map 330) (< lat. *lactem*), pur. *utru-lém* 'butter' < ar. *untulémnu* 'lard' (ALiA: map 362, PAPAHAGI 1996: 1238) (< lat. *unctum de ligno*) or pur. *kërne* < ar. *cắrne* (NEIESCU 1997: map 62, point 8) (< lat. *carnem*).

Other than Greek and Slavic loans, the majority of **technical terms** can be traced back to Aromanian, beginning with pur. *llukër / lukër* 'work' < ar. *lúcru* (ALiA: map 484, PAPAHAGI 1996: 31) (< lat. *lucrum*). From the *Purisht* substantive derives the verb pur. *llukrós* '(to) work, (to) dig,'[18] as well as the adjective pur. *llukrór* 'hardworking.' Important Aromanian loans concerning construction materials, besides the previously described pur. *llok* – include pur. *léme* 'wood' < ar. *lém/ lémnu* 'wood, tree' (ALiA: map 362) and pur. *llaspë* < ar. *láspe* 'clay' (if we sup-

---

14 The tendency to analytic forms, largely present in *Purisht*, is also an indicator of the linguistic erosion that has affected Aromanian as well, as shown by diverse examples (see e.g. *munti n'iku* 'hill', indicated in ALiA, map 30, etc.).

15 I also recorded the items pur. *bërre* 'mule, donkey' and pur. *spërr* 'donkey.'

16 In PAPAHAGI 1996: 70 indicates also the denomination *mer-dit-loc*, probably a *calque* of the construction *pomme de terre*. For more precise interpretations, further dialectological data are indispensable.

17 The variety *mollë dheu* does not appear in the map 169 ('potato') of the *Atlasi Dialektologjik i Gjuhës Shqipe* (ADGjSh), vol. II (2008).

18 Concerning this, in SHKURTAJ 2004: 136 is indicated the form *lukurás*.

pose a direct interference from Greek λάσπη). The derivation of pur. *laksho* 'water' from ar. *lák^u* (ALiA: map 24/25) 'lake, pond, ditch' (< gr. λάκκος < lat. *lacus* (PAPAHAGI 1996: 5) should be taken into consideration.

Regarding the Aromanian loans as denominations of tools, I only identified the item pur. *topore* 'a kind of hatchet' < ar. *tăpóră / tăpoáră / tupoáră* 'axe, cleaver.' Furthermore, whereas the verb 'to cut, to saw' is borrowed from Aromanian (lat. *taliare* >) ar. *tál'e / tál'i* (ALiA: map 357, NEIESCU 1997: maps 136–139) > pur. *tal*, it is important to note that the denomination of the saw pur. *prionë* derives from the Greek πριόνι, probably intermediated from Aromanian (*prión(e)*). This is effectively sustained from the fact that, according to map 367 of the ALiA, the construct ar. *tál'e ku prióni*[19] 'to saw' is indicated in fifteen villages, thirteen of them in the Pindus area. A related transformation may have also embodied pur. *domë*[20] 'house, room,' of Slavic origin, that reached *Purisht* very probably through Aromanian (*dómă*) (PAPAHAGI 1974: 497). Concerning the **domestic environment** it has to be mentioned that the item pur. *partianë* 'back house, toilet' < pur. *partís* 'to defecate' is etymologically unclear. However, it may be related to ar. *párte* or to ar. *pîrţ*. Two other important and uniformly diffused elements of this sector are pur. *fridhë* 'window' (as indicated in the Appendix of this paper) < ar. *frídă / firíδă* (PAPAHAGI 1974: 562, AA.VV. 1981: 63 to map 401 of ALiA) (< gr. θυρίδα 'small window') and pur. *ushë* 'door' < ar. *uşắ*[21] (< lat. *ustium*).

Similarly, the semantic sector of **domestic tools** contains some relevant elements, which highlight once more the relevance of Aromanian for *Purisht*. There are, for example, the items pur. *lëngúre* 'spoon' < ar. *líŋgură* (AA.VV. 1981: 66 (to map 422) (< lat. *lingula*) and ar. *căţăn / căţîn* 'dish' > pur. *këcën* 'pan, dish.' I also

---

19 The other mainly diffused form is ar. *şáră / şáRă* (or the combination ar. *tál'e ku şáră*), that has been indicated there (map 367) in seventeen localities. The fact that fourteen of them are villages located in the enclaves of the (also) Albanian speaking alloglotte minority could be more an indication of interference in their Aromanian varieties from alb. *sharrë* 'saw' (< lat. *serra*) > *sharroj / pres me sharrë* 'to saw, to cut with the saw', than of the presence of the Aromanian analogue item *şáră* 'saw'. For etymological notes about *şáră* see PAPAHAGI (1996: 392). Furthermore it is interesting to mention that two of the three remaining points are the villages Στενήμαχος and Κρύα Βρύση (Ημαθία), where major *Purisht*-Aromanian concordances are assessed, as is delineated below (Fig. 2).

20 Note the use of the term in one of the numerous *Purisht*-anecdotes, usually closely linked to the crypted character of *Purisht*: *Purelecë me bibaz/ domat pa tmaçit/ nukë drynjasin/ po lozin e këndacin!* (Louse-ridden cheap masters / their families are starving / they don't rest and sleep / but just dance and sing!).

21 Cf. NEIESCU (1997: map 69, AA.VV. 1981: 64 to map 402 of ALiA) as well as PAPAHAGI (1996: 488), that also indicates – erroneously as paroxytonis – the Albanian derivation *úshe* 'piccola capanna per cacciatori.' See alb. *ushé / ushézë*.

recorded the nearly identical pur. *këcáne* 'wall clock, watch,' that can hardly be explained in any other way than through a *Purisht* internal semantic mutation of pur.
këcën. Similar to the pair *këcën* vs. *këcáne* is the pair pur. *cëruqe* 'a kind of mocca-
sin used by peasants' vs. pur. *caruqe* 'shoelace.' The item *cëruqe* is widely diffused and solidly present in all the *Purisht* varieties; for their speakers, it is considered an important *Purisht* item, and not a dialectal Albanian term. However, the
item *caruqe* is also noted in Albanian, especially in several Albanian dialectal
varieties, including *Arbërisht* and *Arvanitika*.[22] ÇABEJ (1987: 14), partly supporting
PAPAHAGI (1996: 458), considers the origin of the Turkish *tcharyq* 'chaussure en
cuir que portent les villageois,' that reached Aromanian (*tărúhe* 'sandale des
paysans') as well as Albanian (*caruqe*) with a Greek intermediation (*τσαρούχια*),
presenting a lexical balkanism. In order to conduct a detailed etymological analysis
of pur. *cëruqe*, further and detailed dialectological data on alb. *caruqe* are necessary, taking into consideration its vitality[23] as well. Due (also) to the conservation
of [ə], it is probable that pur. *cëruqe* could have been influenced by ar. *tărúhe*. Pur.
qolë / *qole* 'leather' < ar. *k'él(i)* / *k'eáli* / *k'áli* / *k'ále* 'skin, leather' (ALiA: map
144, NEIESCU 1997: map 2) and pur. *stróle* 'clothes, pants,' reducible to ar. *stóle*
(ALiA: map 230, PAPAHAGI 1996: 370) (< gr. *στολή*) are further examples of the
Aromanian influence on this semantic sphere.

The sphere of the family contains at least two relevant Aromanian borrowings,
pur. *frat* 'brother' < ar. *fráti* / *fráte* (AA.VV.: 70 (to map 463 of ALiA) and pur.
sortë 'sister' < ar. *sóră* (AA.VV.: 70 (to map 464 of ALiA). The etymological
interpretation of some other family terms proves to be more difficult, beginning
with, for example pur. *krezhdë* 'married woman,' that can be brought in connection
to ar. *krésSte*[24] 'to ripen, ripeness' (< lat. *crescere*).

22　The form *saruqe*, indicated in JUNK 1895: 124 as *saruce* 'sorta di pantofole o pianelle',
　　and in BASHKIMI 1908: 391 as *saruk'e* 'sorta di calzari', presents according to ÇABEJ
　　1987: 14 a Northwestern Geg-variety of *caruqe*. JOKL (cf. JOKL 1927: 33–34) in a de-
　　tailed analysis traces this item back to the Magyar-lexeme *szár* 'Rohr, Schaft' that
　　reached Albanian with a Serbo-Croatian intermediation (scr. *sára* 'Stiefelschaft'); see
　　further the reviews of JOKL and TAGLIAVINI (respectively in *Indogermanisches Jahr-*
　　buch XIII (1929): 166–167 and *Studi Rumeni* 4 (1930): 156). Another variety is *carihe*,
　　that is indicated in PAPAHAGI 1996: 458, as well as in GIORDANO 1963: 51 (*caríhe* /
　　cariqe 'ciocia, specie di scarpa'). For further bibliographical indications about the pres-
　　ence of the item in *Arbërisht* and *Arvanitika* see ÇABEJ 1987: 14.
23　The limited diffusion and vitality of alb. *carúqe* has probably been conditioned from the
　　synonym alb. *opingë*.
24　Cf. ALiA: map 38. The items ar. *strínd∠ire* 'to embrace' and ar. *típur* 'bud' should be
　　respectively considered by the still unclear etymological interpretation of pur. *strinxé*
　　'bride, wife' and pur. *çipull* 'boy, son.'

The Aromanian loans of the sector of **body parts** are qualitatively significant, as demonstrated by pur. *mënë* 'hand' < ar. *mînă / mănă* (< lat. *manus*), pur. *kapllë* 'head' < ar. *cáp(lu)* (< lat. *caput*) and pur. *llënë / llëne* 'wool, hairs' < ar. *lînă* 'wool' (< lat. *lana*).

Concerning the sphere of **atmospheric phenomena** I recorded the Aromanian borrowings pur. *bumburéq* 'thunder'[25], that derives in all probability from ar. *bumbuneádză* 'es donnert,' and pur. *kurkubé* 'rainbow' < ar. *kurkubélu / kurkubéu* (ALiA: maps 37–39, PAPAHAGI 1974: 415). Furthermore, the etymological analysis of pur. *mënjë* 'morning' shows that other than being a possible derivation from ar. *măne / mîni* 'morning' (< lat. *mane*), it may also be an alienation of the base-language item alb. *mëngjez*, which is a common word-creation modality found in the Albanian cryptolects.

There are also several stable lexical items of Aromanian origin, mainly verbs, classifiable within the wider sphere of **human life**, such as pur. *pllënx* 'to cry' < ar. *plăndzi / plăndze / plîndzíre* (< lat. *plangere*) (NEIESCU 1997: map 123, PAPAHAGI 1996: 258–259), pur. *dyrnjas / drynjas* 'to sleep' < ar. *durn'ire* (< lat. *dormire*) (NEIESCU 1997: map 19, PAPAHAGI 1974: 509), pur. *murít* 'to die' < ar. *muríre* (< lat. *morire*) (NEIESCU 1997: maps 186–187, PAPAHAGI 1996: 108), pur. *zhdec* 'to shut up, to stop' (usually only in the imperative form) < ar. *skidédzŭ* 'couper, trancher' (PAPAHAGI 1996: 362), pur. *frënx* 'to break' < ar. *frîndzeáre / frîndzire* (< lat. *frangere*) (PAPAHAGI 1974: 565), pur. *sparx / sparc / spars* 'to break down' < ar. *aspártu* 'gâté, corrompu, tué' (PAPAHAGI 1974: 228) or pur. *ckul / ckulem* 'to go away, to run away' < ar. *scol* '(re)lever, réveiller, révolter' (PAPAHAGI 1996: 323). The quality of the Aromanian borrowings of *Purisht* can be illustrated in some cases also through their derivations, including the dynamics of semantic evolution, like in the case of pur. *fok* 'fire' < ar. *fóku* (< lat. *focus*). Its derivations are *fókse*[26] 'match' / *foks* 'lighter,' *fok(ë)tór* 'oven' – as well as the combination mentioned above at the footnote 8 with the adjective *i gruthmë*: *fok(ë)tór i gruthmë* 'radiator' – the verbs *fókem* 'to warm, to dry' as well as *fugós* 'to burn'[27], and from the latter the further substantive *fugosës* 'hot pepper, onion, garlic'[28], *i fugosur* 'burned'.

Another significant indicator of the influence of Aromanian on *Purisht* is the borrowing of prepositions and adverbs, which is not very frequent in *argots*. Aside from the aforementioned pur. *njikëz / njigëz*, this concerns pur. *nundro / nuntro* 'in-

---

25 In Lekas I recorded from one informant the form pur. *bumbaréq* 'God.'

26 The suffix *-e* (and the gender) are visibly influenced by the Albanian counterpart *shkrepëse*, as well as in the case of pur. *foks* 'lighter' through alb. *çakmak*.

27 According to PAPAHAGI 1974: 568 ar. *fucós* 'ardent' < dacorom. *focós*.

28 I also recorded the synonym pur. *djegës* < alb. *djeg* 'to burn,' that might have influenced it semantically, as a *calque*.

side, within' < ar. *înăuntru*, pur. *nalltë / nallto* 'above, high' < ar. *análtu / anáłtu*
'big' (ALiA: map 140) pur. *mulltë* 'a lot' < ar. *multu* (ALiA: maps 6, 7, 25, 27,
202, 228, 245, 343, 395; NEIESCU 1997: maps 14, 24, 67, 134, 187) and ar. *káldu*
'hot' > pur. *kaldë* 'warm' (ALiA: map 223) from which further derives pur.
kaldàre 'saucepan, boiler.'

5. About the origin of the Aromanian borrowings of *Purisht*

The previous analysis illustrated the qualitative and quantitative relevance of the
Aromanian elements of *Purisht*. It is essential to indicate that this phenomenon is a
result of intensive cultural contacts between Opar-Albanians and Aromanians.
Therefore it is necessary to carry out a comparative dialectological analysis by con-
fronting all forty-six aforementioned definite Aromanisms of *Purisht* – that appear
widely homogeneous in *Purisht*'s individual varieties – with their corresponding
items in the Aromanian varieties in Albania, Greece and Southwestern Macedonia.
The goal is to quantitatively delineate a spatial distribution of the concordances between them. However, care must be taken to avoid defining any individual isoglosses or conducting a microdialectological classification, primarily because of
two fundamental problems concerning the Aromanian dialectology. The first consists of the well-known difficulty of any microdiatopic classification of Aromanian[29], being the language of a mainly transhumant population.[30] The second problem is found in the narrowness of the dialectological data on Aromanian, mainly
concerning the varieties spoken in Albania.[31] The comparative analysis demonstrated in several cases substantial differences – first of all on the lexical level,
which is undoubtedly more reliable than the phonetic one – between the *Purisht*-
items and their counterparts in the geographically closest Aromanian varieties of

---

29 Cf. DAHMEN/KRAMER 1985: 8–9: „(…) von ortsgebundenen oder gar ‚bodenständigen'
    Dialekten [kann] überhaupt nicht die Rede sein (…): es findet ein ständiger Austausch
    zwischen den verschiedenen Dialekten, ja Idiolekten statt". The perception of this issue
    was delineated already in WEIGAND 1894: 341–344.

30 Traditionally most of the Aromanians moved seasonally with their livestock from the
    higher pastures in the mountains, where they spent the summer months, to the lower
    plains where they passed the winter. This phenomenon was quite common among
    Aromanians in Albania at least until the 1950s.

31 The dialectological data material on the Aromanian varieties spoken in Greece arises
    exclusively from ALiA; those spoken in Macedonia from ALiA and NEIESCU 1997. The
    dialectological data on the Aromanian varieties spoken in Albania, that arises only
    partly from NEIESCU 1997, have been completed through some of my own restricted
    investigations. Hereby I verified the concrete diffusion of the forty-six definite afore-
    mentioned Aromanisms of *Purisht* on the varieties of the (mainly) sedentary Aromani-
    ans of Dishnicë, Plasë, Voskopojë and Shipskë. The highly advanced linguistic erosion,
    which has affected their Aromanian, hampered the task.

Shipskë, Plasë, Dishnicë and in some cases also Korçë[32], e.g. ar. (Shipskë) *otún'ǎ* vs. pur. *bumburéq* < ar. *bumbuneádzǎ, t"éli* (NEIESCU 1997: map 2) vs. pur. *qole*, ar. *máțâ / pǎsǎ* (NEIESCU 1997: map 15) vs. pur. *këltushe*, ar. *lócuri* (NEIESCU 1997: map 176) vs. pur. *lloku*, etc. On the other hand, as the map below clearly indicates, the main concordances are to some Aromanian varieties spoken near Βέροια, Καστοριά and Φλώρινα, in the Σούλι-area (Prefecture of Θεσπρωτία), or in the Northwestern-Pindus-area. The item pur. *kurkubé* 'rainbow', for example, corresponds to the Aromanian *kurkubéu / kurkubélu*, recorded mainly in the aforementioned areas[33], while in the rest of the localities the form *béu* mostly dominates. The tendency becomes more apparent in the case of pur. *topóre*, which according to ALiA appears only in the Aromanian varieties near Βέροια, as well as in the Northwestern Pindus and in some Southeastern-Thessalian localities.[34] Similarly, the counterpart Aromanian forms of pur. *utrulem* < ar. *untulémnu* appear only in Στενήμαχος (Ημαθία), Παραπόταμος and Πλαταριά (Θεσπρωτία) as well as in five other localities (ALiA: map 362, points 41, 38, 48, 88 and 73) of the Pindus-area. There are also some phonetically based concordances that could give further support to this tendency, such as the *Purisht* items *frinë*[35], *grëne*[36], *ojle* (ALiA: map 322, the points 50, 51, 52, 56, 93, 36; 56, 51, 17 and 63), *fridhë* (ALiA: map 401, the points 17, 32, 33, 36, 43) etc.

It is evident that the Aromanian varieties of the coastal regions conserve the most concordances. Furthermore, it must be stressed that the areas of Πρέβεζα, of Myzeqe as well as of Ημαθία were important winter-grazing regions for the transhumant Aromanians. In the summertime they would move to the mountainous grazing areas of Τζουμέρκα (see also KAHL 2007: 292) Pindus, Gramoz or – more

---

32 It is erroneous to consider the main urban centers of Albania, where disseminated Aromanians live, as more or less homogeneous dialectological points of Aromanian, reliable by any microdiatopic differentiation. Even in the case of Korçë, where the consistent and solid Aromanian community lives partly concentrated in its district, it is possible to speak only of a linguistic heterogeneity.

33 Cf. ALiA map 348. These forms appears in the points: 1, 20, 21 (near Bitola), 64, 18, 78, 2, 65, 36, 77 and 3 (in the Greek Macedonian territory), 93 and 56 (in Θεσπρωτία) and everywhere in the Pindus, but not in the area of Gramoz.

34 Cf. ALiA, map 348, the points 65, 13, 36, 77, 3; 41, 67, 79, 66, 70, 44, 73 and 7, 53, 80. In the other points appear the forms *χǎngáre, țǎpátǎ, bálțǎ, lustó, vǎreáu, sǎțîri, kamǎ, kǎțút, kǎcúgu*, etc.

35 Cf. ALiA, map 353, the points 50, 51, 52, 56, 93 in the area of Σούλι as well as Κεφαλόβρυσον, Χωρίον Γράμος, Κρυσταλλοπηγή and Маловиште. In the other localities appears mainly the form *fǎrínǎ*.

36 Cf. ALiA, map 68, the points near Bitola, as well as the Pindus-area.

importantly for this analysis – the area of Ostrovicë (Opar)[37], which includes the
Purisht area. Although more dialectological information is needed, especially on
the Aromanian varieties spoken in Albania, current data indicates that the presence
of Aromanian elements in *Purisht* is due much more to the direct contact between
the Albanians of Ostrovicë and the transhumant Aromanians that settled there during the summer months than to the proximity of the former to the localities of
Shipskë, Plasë or Dishnicë, where sedentary Aromanians used to live.

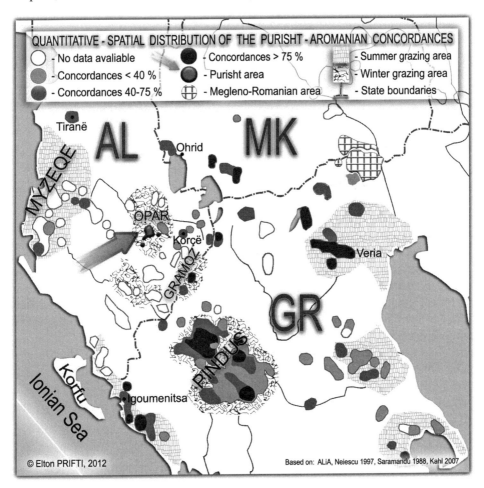

Fig. 2: *Geographical Distribution of the Purisht-Aromanian concordances*

37 An Aromanian lady that I interviewed in Korçë, born in the 1940s, on the way to the
summer-grazing, testified that her large family, like other *Krëstënjòte*-families, used to
peddle usually from Ostrovicë to Ηγουμενίτσα.

In summary, *the Aromanian borrowings of Purisht are mainly a consequence of the phenomenon of transhumance* that characterized the existence of the Aromanian population and were thus reflected in their language. Further linguistic evidence of these movements can be found in the quantity and quality of the Albanian elements in the aforementioned Aromanian varieties, as shown clearly by several maps of ALiA.[38] In the case of the area of Θεσπρωτία (Çamëria) – as well as in some other small areas – further Albanian elements must be considered due to the (pluri)linguistic contact with the Tosk-Albanian varieties in the Albanian-speaking alloglotte enclaves.[39]

As far as the diatopic differentiation of *Purisht* is concerned, its Aromanian elements appear highly uniform. However, because of their nature, the cryptolects are usually very open to lexical innovation as I noted repeatedly during fieldwork. This usually produces a strong presence of synonyms[40], as well as a marked diatopic differentiation.

6. Brief notes on variation and linguistic contact issues concerning *Purisht* and Aromanian

Concerning the variation of *Purisht*, two aspects must be considered. Firstly, in cases of advanced linguistic erosion, the speakers used to bypass the gaps in their linguistic competence (especially the reduction of the vocabulary) by paraphrasing or combining items – as illustrated above in some cases – using Albanian archaisms or even borrowing new items from other languages. Secondly, it is sometimes very difficult to specify whether an item represents a very limited diffused dialectal or archaic element of Albanian, or a *Purisht* item. It is even more difficult when it concerns *Purisht* items that are used rarely, or others that have even been irradiated from *Purisht* into the surrounding Albanian local dialects. In addition to the above notes on *carúqe*, the example of the aforementioned *xhivéllë* clarifies this point. Its extremely limited diffusion makes it difficult to classify it as a true *Purisht* element, although defined as such by the speaker himself; rather, it should be considered a local-bound Albanian dialectal form. On the other hand, in several cases frequently used *Purisht*-terms are usually considered as endemic elements of the

---

38 Particularly significant are the maps 59, 94, 95, 125, 191, etc. ALiA contains only some very sporadic indications about the relevant Albanian interferences on the Aromanian local varieties.

39 A systematic and variational in-depth analysis of the linguistic contact between Greek, Albanian and Aromanian in the Northern Greece could bring important and interesting knowledge. In KAHL 2007 some of the dynamics of this contact are described.

40 In some of the cases of synonym pairs, the synonyms of the Aromanian elements are borrowed from Greek, e.g. ar. *untulémnu* > pur. *utrulem* vs. pur. *vutur* < gr. βούτυρο, ar. *muríre* > pur. *murit* vs. pur. *pethanós* < gr. πεθαίνω.

Albanian varieties in the localities where *Purisht* is spoken, as illustrated by the re-mark of a young speaker of *Purisht*:

> "Already before I reached school-age I was aware of *Purisht*, but anyway, we did use some words of it [in the everyday-Albanian]. We were not aware that some words we used were in *Purisht*; we thought it was Albanian, dialect. For example *zhavló* [run away], or *i sparxur* [crazy], *zagobé* [jackass], *bime* [attractive young girl], or there are some words of this kind."[41]

It is important to generally highlight the linguistic contact issues between *Purisht* and local Albanian varieties. Within this framework *Purisht* has in some cases been an intermediator of Aromanian loans with very restricted diffusion on Albanian varieties of the localities where *Purisht* is spoken. Some of these interferences are irradiated even further, and have even reached the urban dialect of Korçë. This process can also be accompanied by semantic deviations. Among some speakers (mainly elderly) I recorded for example the following items: alb. (Korçë) *kapllo* 'noodle' < pur. *kapllë* 'head' < ar. *cáp(lu)*; alb. (Korçë) *bolovicanë* 'dirty place' < pur. *bolovicanë* 'cowshed' < pur. *bolo* 'bull, ox' < ar. *bóŭlu*, alb. (Korçë) *púre* 'country folks from the mountainous hinterland (pej.), somebody from Opar-area' < pur. *púre* 'carpenter, somebody from Opar-area,' etc. In terms of the intermedia-tion of Albanian lexical items in the opposite direction – through *Purisht* into Aromanian – there is currently no concrete indication.

* * *

To study appropriately the so-called balkanisms, an interdisciplinary approach is indispensable, as this paper partly illustrates. This necessity becomes more palpa-ble through the study of *argots*, which can provide important information on the multifaceted inter-Balkanic cultural and linguistic contacts. The investigations should be progressively oriented also toward the non-standard varieties. The rele-vance of an interdisciplinary approach appears evident in the case of the study of the Western-Balkan romanity, where a systematic interaction between Romance Philology and Albanology is fundamental. In this regard, the somewhat overlooked contact between Aromanian and Albanian that has been going for a long time, takes actually on significance. There is still quite a lot to be done on this multifac-eted contact thus the implementation of a variational approach is auspicious. Concluding, it is the high *dynamicity* of the inter-Balkanic language contacts, like

---

41 *"Që para se të bëesha për shkollë e dinja ç'ishte purishtja, po ndonjë llaf e përdornim edhe kshu... ndonjë llaf që theshim nuku e dinim që qe purisht; kujtonim që qe shqip, dialekt. Për shëmbull* zhavlò, *ose* i sparxur, zagobé, bíme, *ose... ka ca llafe të këtillta."* Note that the item *bime*, which is the youth-specific corresponding term of the usual *bimëz(ë)* 'unmarried woman, girl,' presents one of these elements that also testify to the existence of the aforementioned generation-oriented differentiation of *Purisht*.

in the Aromanian – Albanian case, that shows to my opinion a continuing relevant and central balkanism.

Appendix

In the following sample text written in *Purisht*, which is based on the strip *Der tapfere Schneemann* of Erich OSER's *Vater und Sohn* (extracted from *Berliner Illustrirte* 1937/4), the Aromanian elements appear underlined. Its author is the interviewee LD, born in Lekas in 1972, where he lives and works as a teacher.

Purisht	Albanian	English
Një fyk kishte një çípull njíkës.	Një baba kishte një djalë të vogël.	A father had a young son.
Ishte lodhur fqonjë múlltë dhe çípulli donte të rinte një rrast prej fqonje.	Kishte rënë shumë borë dhe djali donte të bënte një plak prej bore.	It had snowed a lot and the boy wanted to make a snowman.
Pasi e rivi grúthëm rrastin pe fqonje, në të errme, krevi kronjë dhe dyrnjási.	Pasi e bëri mirë plakun prej bore, në darkë, hëngri bukë dhe fjeti.	After he built a good snowman, in the evening, he ate and slept.
Në të mënit çípulli u lodh në fridhë të bénte rrastin prej fqonje, por ai ishte spárcur.	Në mëngjes doli në dritare të shihte plakun prej bore, por ai ishte prishur.	The following morning he looked out the window at the snowman, but it was ruined.
E rivi prapë.	E bëri prapë.	He made it once more.
Po prapë, edhe ditën tjetër rrastin prej fqonje e gjeti të spárcur.	Po prapë, edhe ditën tjetër plakun prej bore e gjeti të rrëzuar.	But again, even the next day, he found his snowman was ruined.
Zuri të pllëncte.	Zuri të qante.	He started to cry.
E bévi fyku i tij dhe ja bévi "Zhdec, se do ta béjmë kush është ai zagobéu që e sparc. Do të më rijsh mua si rrast pe fqonje, me të rríptit, me shkelje prej fqonje."	E pa i ati dhe i tha "Pusho, se do ta gjejmë kush është ai budallai që e prish. Do të më maskosh mua si plak prej bore, me sy, me këmbë prej bore."	His father saw him and said "Stop it, we will find out who the fool is that keeps ruining it. You will disguise me as a snowman, with eyes, with snow legs."
E rivi çípulli fykun si rrast pe fqonje.	Djali e maskoi të atin si plak prej bore.	The son disguised his father as a snowman.
Fyku ja bevi çípullit të tij: "Ckulu dhe bej ckúlurazi kur të lodhet ai zágoja që ta sparc!"	Babai i tha të birit: "Shko shpejt dhe shih fshehurazi kur të vijë përsëri ai budallai që ta prish."	The father said to his son: "Go quickly and hide, and watch when that fool comes back to ruin the snowman."
Pas pak te rrasti prej fqonje u lodh një çípull i mbëshëm për ta spárcur.	Pas pak plakut prej bore iu afrua një djalë i rritur për ta rrëzuar.	A moment latter a grown-up boy approached the snowman to make it fall.
Sa zuri ta spárcte, rrasti pe fqonje, që ishte fyku i rirë si rrast fqonje, ju mbet me carúge në ngërfje.	Sa filloi ta rrëzonte, plaku prej bore, që ishte babai i maskuar, i dha një shkelm me çizme në prapanicë.	When he started to push it over, the snowman-disguised father kicked him in his ass.

| *Dhe zagobéu zhavlóvi duke pllëncur.* | Dhe budallai iku duke qarë. | And the fool left in tears. |
| *Çípulli njíkës u gëzua múlltë.* | Fëmija u gëzua shumë. | The little boy was very happy. |

References

AA.VV. (1981): Verkürzter Fragebogen des Atlas Linguarum Europae (ALE). In: *Balkan Archiv* 6 (N. F.). 22–79.

BARIĆ, Henrik (1926): Miscellen. In: *Архив за арбанаску старину, језик и етнологију* III/1-2. 213–221.

BASHKIMI (1908): *Fjaluer i rî i Shcypés, perbâam préje Shocniiét t Bashkimit.* Skutari.

CIORĂNESCU, Alexandru (2002): *Dicționarul etimologic al limbii române.* București: Editura Saeculum I. O.

CORTELAZZO, Manlio (1977): Note sulle voci albanesi nel gergo dei ramai. In: *Zeitschrift für Balkanologie* XIII. 57–62.

ÇABEJ, Eqrem (1987): *Studime etimologjike në fushë të shqipes III.* Tiranë: Akademia e Shkencave e RPS të Shqipërisë (Instituti i Gjuhësisë dhe i Letërsisë).

ÇABEJ, Eqrem; XHUVANI, Aleksandër (1962): *Prapashtesat e gjuhës shqipe.* Tiranë: Universiteti Shtetëror i Tiranës / Instituti i Historisë e Gjuhësisë.

DAHMEN, Wolfgang; KRAMER, Johannes (1985/1994): *Aromunischer Sprachatlas / Atlasul lingvistic aromân* (ALiA) (II vol.). Hamburg: Helmut Buske.

GEAGEA, Chr. (1931): Elementul grec în dialectul aromîn. In: *Codrul Cosminului* VII. 207–432.

GIORDANO, Emanuele (1963): *Fjalor i Arbëreshvet t'Italisë / Dizionario degli Albanesi d'Italia.* Bari: Edizioni Paoline.

HAXHIHASANI, Qemal (1964a): Dogançja, e folmja shoqnore e zejtarëve shëtitës të rrethit të Përmctit dhe të Leskovikut. In: *Studime Filologjike* (XVIII)-I/ 2. 141–165.

HAXHIHASANI, Qemal (1964b): Elemente nga fjalori i Dogançcs, fragmente bisedash dhe tekste në këtë të folme. In: *Studime Filologjike* (XVIII)-I/ 3. 149–171.

HAXHIHASANI, Qemal (1964c): Të folmet shoqnore. In: *Studime Filologjike* (XVIII)-I/ 1. 99–125.

HILKER, Bernd (1981): Register zu den aromunischen Sprachaufnahmen (BA 2, 1997 – 6. 1981). In: *Balkan-Archiv* (N.F.) 6. 265–367.

HRISTOVA-BEJLERI, Rusana (2004): Shqipja në fjalorin etimologjik të bullgarishtes. In: AA.VV.: *Eqrem Çabej dhe kultura shqiptare.* Tiranë: Gent Grafik. 14–41.

ISMAJLI, Rexhep (1987): *Artikuj mbi gjuhën shqipe.* Prishtinë: Rilindja.

JAGIĆ, Vatroslav (1896): Die Geheimsprachen bei den Slaven. In: *Sitzungsberichte der philosophisch-historischen Classe der Kaiserlichen Akademie der Wissenschaften* CXXXIII/ V. Abhandlung. 1–80.

JIREČEK, Constantin (1876): Conventionelle Geheimsprachen auf der Balkanhalbinsel. In: *Archiv für slavische Philologie* VIII. 99–102.

JOKL, Norbert (1927): Die magyarischen Bestandteile des albanischen Wortschatzes (Wortgeschichtliche Studien aus den südosteuropäischen Sprachen). In: *Ungarisches Jahrbuch* 7. 46–84.

JUNK, P. Jak (1895): *Fialuur i voghel sccyp e ltinisct.* Sckoder.

КАЦОРИ, Тома; ДУКОВА, Уте; АСЕНОВА, Петя (1984): Към характеристиката на тайните говори в българия. In: *Съпоставително Езикознание* IX/ 1. 29–43.

KAHL, Thede (2007): *Hirten in Kontakt. Sprach- und Kulturwandel ehemaliger Wanderhirten (Albanisch, Aromunisch, Griechisch).* Wien, Berlin: Lit Verlag.

NEIESCU, Petru (1997): *Mic Atlas Dialectului Aromân din Albania şi din Fosta Republica Iugoslavă Macedonia,* Bucureşti: Editura Academiei Române.

Νικολαΐδης, Κωνσταντίνος (1909): *Ἐτυμολογικὸν λεξικὸν τῆς κουτσοβλαχικῆς γλώσσης.* Ἀθῆναι: Σακελλάριος.

PAPAHAGI, Tache (1974): *Dicţionarul dialectului aromân general şi etimologic.* Bucureşti: Editura Academiei Republicii Socialiste România.

PAPAHAGI, Tache (1996): *Dicţionarul dialectului aromân general şi etimologic* (vol. II). Craiova: Editura Europa.

PETROVICI, Emil (1934): Cuvinte argotice sud-slave de origine românească. In: *Dacoromania* VII. 175–176.

PRIFTI, Elton (2009a): Gjurmime variacionale mbi shqipen standarde një shekull pas Kongresit të Alfabetit. In: Demiraj, Bardhyl (Hrsg.): *Der Kongress von Manastir – Herausforderung zwischen Tradition und Neuerung in der albanischen Schriftkultur.* Hamburg: Dr. Kovač. 121–138.

PRIFTI, Elton (2009b): On the Romance Borrowings of an Albanian Argot. In: *Romania Orientale* 22. 277–298.

PRIFTI, Elton (2010): Alcuni cenni sugli elementi albanesi nei dialetti italiani. In: Bardhyl Demiraj (Hrsg.): *Wir sind die Deinen. Studien zur albanischen Sprache, Literatur und Kulturgeschichte, dem Gedenken an Martin Camaj (1925–1992) gewidmet.* Wiesbaden: Harrassowitz. 375–383.

Σάρρος, Δημήτριος Μ. (1923): Περὶ τῶν ἐν Ἠπείρῳ, Μακεδονία καὶ Θράκη συνθηματικῶν γλωσσῶν. In: *Λαογαφία* VII (Ζ'). 521–542.

SARAMANDU, Nicolae (1988): Harta graiurilor aromâne şi meglenoromâne din Peninsula Balcanică. In: *SCL* 39. 225–245.

SHKURTAJ, Gjovalin (2004): Për një vështrim sociolinguistik të të folmeve të fshehta të shqipes. In: *Studime filologjike* (LVIII)-XLI/ 1–2. 123–138.

TAGLIAVINI, Carlo (1937): Zingari, Lingue. In: *Enciclopedia Italiana dell'Istituto G. Treccani* XXXV. 958–959.

TAGLIAVINI, Carlo (1938): I rapporti di Venezia coll'Oriente balcanico. Cenni sulla diffusione degli elementi veneti nel lessico delle lingue balcaniche. In: *Atti della XXVI Riunione della Società Italiana per il Progresso delle Scienze (Venezia, 12–18 settembre 1937),* Vol. III, fasc. I. Roma: S.I.P.S. 115–123.

TAGLIAVINI, Carlo (1942): Le parlate albanesi di tipo ghego orientale (Dardania e Macedonia nord-occidentale). In: *Le terre albanesi redente I. Cossovo.* Roma: R. Accademia d'Italia. 1–82.

TRIANDAPHYLLIDIS, Manolis A. (1923): Eine zigeunerisch-griechische Geheimsprache. In: *Zeitschrift für vergleichende Sprachforschung auf dem Gebiete der indogermanischen Sprachen* 52. 1–42.

TRUMPER, John (1986): A proposito di alcuni albanesismi in un gergo calabrese di mestieranti. In: *Zjarri – il fuoco. Rivista di cultura albanese* XVIII/ 1–2. 35–40.

TRUMPER, John (1996a): *Una lingua nascosta. Sulle orme dei quadarari calabresi*, Cosenza: Rubbettino.

TRUMPER, John (1996b): Vindex verborum: aspetti importanti dell'elemento albanese nei gerghi italiani di mestiere. In: Pellegrini, Giovan Battista (a cura di): *Terza raccolta di saggi dialettologici in area italo-romanza.* Padova: Centro di Studio per la Dialettologia Italiana "Oronzo Parlangéli" – CNR. 109–124.

WAGNER, Max-Leopold (1914): Beiträge zur Kenntnis des Judenspanischen von Konstantinopel. In: *Schriften der Balkankommission. Linguistische Abteilung* XI. 1–186.

WEIGAND, Gustav (1894): *Die Aromunen II: Volksliteratur der Aromunen.* Leipzig: Barth.

YMERI, Mariana (2002): Zhargoni dhe dëshmitë e tij në gjuhën shqipe. In: *Gjuha Jonë* XXI/ 1–2. 22–33.

Formal and Semantic Analysis of the Compound Past Tenses in the Macedonian and Aromanian Dialects of the Ohrid Region (Republic of Macedonia)

Marjan MARKOVIKJ (Skopje)

In this paper, I shall discuss the compound past tense systems of the Macedonian and Aromanian dialects found in the Ohrid-Struga region (Republic of Macedonia). The Ohrid-Struga dialects belong to the West Macedonian dialect group. They are found in the valley region around Lake Ohrid. This linguistic area is bounded on its western periphery by the Albanian ethnographic border. A large portion of the linguistic particularities of the Ohrid-Struga dialects are the same as those to be encountered in the other Western dialects, and, as regards Balkanisms, these dialects show great similarity with the peripheral Western and South-Western Macedonian dialects.

As far as the Aromanian Ohrid dialect is concerned, we shall be concerned here mainly with the dialect of the Aromanian Farsheriots, because of the fact that they are represented in a large number in the Ohrid-Struga region, and because their dialect contains several Balkan linguistic features which are not found in any other Aromanian dialects. Their historical provenience is the area around the town of Frashëri in central Albania. A large group of Aromanian Farsheriots settled in the Ohrid-Struga region towards the middle of the nineteenth century. They settled in the villages of the Upper and Lower Belica, and a certain number settled also in the villages of Vevčani, Višni, Podgorci and Labuništa (TRPKOSKI 1986).

The Aromanian dialect in question contains certain linguistic features borrowed from Albanian, which induced interference between Macedonian and Aromanian Ohrid dialects. This interference is well manifested in the verbal system of these dialects, especially concerning the compound past tenses.

The forms of the perfect and pluperfect tenses of these dialects will be presented, and their meanings and functions will be discussed.

Table 1: Macedonian

perfect I	sum jadel
perfect IIa	imam jadeno
perfect IIb	sum jaden
pluperfect I	bev jadel
pluperfect IIa	imav jadeno
pluperfect IIb	bev jaden
pluperfect IIIa	sum imal jadeno
pluperfect IIIb	sum bil jaden

In the Macedonian Ohrid dialect the compound past tenses are formed with forms of the auxiliary verbs (*имам/сум*) – (*habere* and *esse*) and the l- or n/t-participle. The perfect tense (type 1) is constructed with the forms of the present tense of the auxiliary verb sum/esse and the l-participle, which changes according to gender and number. The perfect tense (type 2a) is formed with the forms of the present tense of the auxiliary verb *imam/habere* and the n/t-participle which does not change, that is, it is found in the neuter gender as the most unmarked form. The perfect tense (type 2b) is built with the forms of the present tense of the auxiliary verb sum/esse and the n/t-participle, which changes according to gender and number. The pluperfect tense (type 1) is constructed with the forms of the imperfect of the auxiliary verb sum/esse and the l-participle which changes according to gender and number. The pluperfect tense (type 2a and 2b) are built with the forms of the imperfect of the auxiliary verbs *imam/sum/ – habere/esse* and the n/t-participle. The pluperfect tenses (type 3a and 3b) are constructed with the forms of the perfect of the auxiliary verbs *imam/sum/ – habere/esse* and the n/t-participle.

Table 2: Aromanian

perfect a	am mă'kată
perfect b	esk mă'kat
pluperfect Ia	a'vem mă'kată
pluperfect Ib	a'rem mă'kat
pluperfect IIa	a'vuį mă'kată
pluperfect IIb	fuį mă'kat
pluperfect IIIa	am a'vută mă'kată
pluperfect IIIb	am 'fută mă'kată

In the Aromanian Ohrid dialect there also exists a large number of compound verbal constructions. The compound past tenses are built with the forms of the auxiliary verbs (*am/esk*) – (*habere* and *esse*) and the past participle. The·perfect tense (type a) is constructed with the forms of the present tense of the auxiliary verb *am/habere* and the past-participle, which does not change, that is, it is found in the feminine gender as the most unmarked form. The perfect tense (type b) is built with the forms of the present tense of the auxiliary verb *esk/esse* and the past-participle, which changes according to gender and number. The pluperfect tenses (type 1a and 1b) are constructed with the forms of the imperfect tense of the auxiliary verbs *am/esk – habere/esse* and the past participle. The pluperfect (type 2a and 2b) is built with the forms of the aorist of the auxiliary verbs am/esk – habere/esse and the past participle. The pluperfect (type 3a) is constructed with the forms of the perfect tense of the auxiliary verb am/habere and the indeclinable past-participle, while the type 3b is built with the forms of the perfect tense of the auxiliary verb *esk/esse* and the declinable past-participle.

First, let us examine the habere/esse perfect, which is common to both dialects and try to determine the functional differences between these two constructions. The perfect, formed with the auxiliary verb *imam* + n/t-participle (for Macedonian), and the perfect tense with *am* + past-participle (for Aromanian), is most frequent in both dialects. In the Macedonian Ohrid dialect this perfect may be formed from both perfective and imperfective verbs. When it is used with perfective verbs, a resultative meaning is obtained to a large degree. The *sum*-perfect is used most frequently with perfective verbs and the resultative meaning is more emphasised.

1. habere/esse perfect
   (*имам/сум* + participle; *am/esk* + participle)

Порано **имам доаѓано** тука. (imperfective verb / indefinitness)
V'lora **am vǎ'nitǎ** a'cia.

Имам дојдено и не си одам. (perfective verb / resultativity)
Am vǎ'nitǎ ši nu mi duk.

Кај тебе **сум дојден** двапати оваа недела.
Vǎ'nit esk la 'tini 'dao or a'istǎ stǎ'mǎnǎ.

Денес **сум дојден** и ќе седам до четврток.
Vǎ'nit esk as'tǎzi i u sǎ šǎd pǎn 'luni.

The construction of the type *habere* + participle is a typical Romance construction, which entered into the Macedonian language under Aromanian influence. The process of the adaptation of these constructions is explained in detail by Zbigniew Gołąb (GOŁĄB 1984). Concerning the constructions with *sum/esk* + the participle, which are represented in both Macedonian and Aromanian, I consider that they appeared because of the need for a clear expression of the opposition perfectivity-imperfectivity in the compound past tenses. This opposition in Macedonian is of morphological nature, while in Aromanian contextual. Thus, the constructions with *esk* + the participle serve as a certain approximation to the Macedonian way of comprehending the opposition perfectivity-imperfectivity in the compound past tenses.

1.1. Aspectual difference

имам/ам + participle	*сум/еск* + participle
Имам вечерано три саати.	Am cinată treị săhăc.
Благодарам, вечеран сум.	Haristo, cinat esk.
Имам седено дома два-три саати.	Am šă'ʒut a'kasă doị-treị să'hăc
Седнат сум на столот.	Šă'ʒut esk pit skamnu.
Имам доаѓано/одено од Битола	Am vă'nita/im'nată păn 'Bituli 'dao 'ʒăli.
два дена.	
Дојден сум од Битола.	Vă'nit esk păn 'Bituli.

The examples of the type *сум/еск* + *participle* cannot appear in the form **Вечеран сум три саати; *Седнат сум на столот два-три саати; *Дојден сум од Битола два дена;* where temporal determinant shows durativity, meaning that the constructions with *esse* + the participle, the indicator for (temporal) durativity of the action is blocked and perfective meaning is dominant.

Here are a few examples, where we can find aspectual differences between constructions with imperfect or aorist forms of the auxiliary *am* (have):

Imperfective meaning:
Додека работев, јадењето се **имаше варено**.
Păn luk'ram, 'gʹela s-a'**ve** '**hertă**.

Perfective meaning:
Додека работев, јадењето се **имаше сварено**.
Păn luk'ram, 'gʹela s-a'**vu** '**hertă**.

This process has extended in several directions. The basic tendency is towards those verbs which carry a certain lexical feature for perfectivity: momentary actions, inception, termination, part of some action, or a change of state. These are verbs of the type: to come, to go away, to go in, to come out, to sit down, to stand up, to lie down, etc. Even the Latin periphrastic perfect has been observed to have double meaning (perfective – imperfective) in constructions with verbs of this type (GALTON 1976).

This double meaning depends on the context. The situation in Romanian regarding the "perfect compus" is similar (MIOARA 1986). The fact that these verbs in Macedonian are intransitive, only facilitated the process of combining them in constructions with *esse*. Something similar happened with the verbs of the type *jadam* 'eat'. In the Macedonian language, the opposition perfectivity – imperfectivity with these verbs is of contextual nature, that is, these verbs are bi-aspectual. Also, depending on the context, they can be both transitive and intransitive because in themselves they can carry an object *вечерам – јадам вечера* (I dine = I eat diner). Therefore, it can be said that in both Macedonian and Aromanian exists an almost identical use of these constructions, as Macedonian was under great influence from Aromanian and accepted the Aromanian model, while Aromanian accepted several Macedonian characteristics, above all, Macedonian verbal aspect.

In the Macedonian Ohrid dialect the l-perfect (type 1) signifies a non-witnessed past action, without information concerning the moment of its development. Indeterminateness appears as a basic characteristic. A basic characteristic of the pluperfect tense is past perfect, i.e. an action which occurred prior to another past action.

Here, above all, we shall concentrate on two other meanings of the l-perfect and pluperfect. The first one is the admirative. In the Macedonian Ohrid dialect there are no formal indicators for signifying the admirative, that is, surprise. The Aromanian Ohrid dialect partially took the forms for the admirative from Albanian (where exists an entire paradigm for the admirative) and it adapted it to its own linguistic system. Such forms appear neither in the other Aromanian dialects, nor in Romanian. This phenomenon was almost unknown and was discovered by Victor Friedman from the University of Chicago during the time of our joint field research among the Aromanian Farsheriots from the Ohrid-Struga region in 1992 (FRIEDMAN 1994, 1996).

In the Aromanian Ohrid dialect, the admirative is formed by adding the particle *ka* to the participle of the main verb. *Ka*, in reality, represents the form of the third person present tense of the Albanian auxiliary verb *kam*. This particle is fossilized in Aromanian and does not decline according to person and number. The admirative constructions in the Aromanian Ohrid dialect appear in the present tense and in the compound past tenses.

Admirativity:
mac. Ти си **бил** богат човек!?
arom. Tini **'fuska** a'vut om!?
alb.   Ti **qenke** njeri i pasur!?

mac. Ти си **имал** голема куќа!?
arom. Tini **a'vuska** 'mari 'kasă!?
alb.   Ti **paske** shtepi të madhë!?

mac. Тој ја **имал вратено** колата!?
arom. Năs o **a'vuska tu'rată** 'kʹeră!?

mac. Виктор **бил вратен** од Америка!?
arom. Viktor **'fuska tu'rat** di Amerikă!?

The second meaning of the l-perfect and pluperfect tenses (type III) in the Macedonian Ohrid dialect is non-confirmativity. As it is known, non-confirmativity is a characteristic only of the Balkan Slavic languages (Macedonian and Bulgarian), Turkish, and several Caucasian languages. In the other Balkan languages (Albanian, Greek, Romanian, Meglenoromanian, Aromanian), non-confirmativity does not exist.

Because of the penetration of constructions of the type *imam/sum* + participle, the l-participle in the Macedonian Ohrid dialect more closely approximated non-confirmativity and the admirative. But the Aromanian Ohrid dialect did not have non-confirmativity and the forms of the perfect covered only renarration (indeterminateness). In this case as well, the Aromanian Ohrid dialect approximated the Macedonian understanding of non-confirmativity with the borrowing of the formal indicators from Albanian. Thus, for the signification of non-confirmativity in the perfect, it used the admirative forms taken from Albanian. For example:

mac. Кај комшиите имало куќа, што била многу сиромашна.
arom. Tu kum'šăc a've 'ună 'kasă, ci **'fuska** 'multu 'orfănă.

mac. Дедо ми порано имал илјада овци.
arom. Papu ńu a'meu v'lora **a'vuska** 'ună 'ńilʹe di oį.

mac. Тој поминал многу време во затвор.
arom. Năs **tăr'kucka** mult 'kʹiro tu hăpsă'nă.

mac. Имам слушнато дека Тома за ништо ја запалил куќата.
arom. Am av'ʒată ka Toma ti nkot o **aprin'ʒeska** 'kasa.

By this, the Aromanian Ohrid dialect is the only non-Slavic Balkan language which has non-confirmativity. Likewise, hereby it is demonstrated that there is a close relationship between the admirative and non-confirmativity. In the past, the Albanian admirative has also been used for non-confirmativity. In this framework, we can speak of an Albanian-Aromanian-Macedonian parallel.

As a result, we notice, on the one hand, tendency of the compound past tenses to arrive at a common system by using internal means or foreign influences as in the case of Aromanian which borrowed Albanian forms and models. The Macedonian Ohrid dialect, on the other hand, takes the constructions with *imam* and *sum* and fills out gaps in its own tense system. It has taken advantage of the labile position of the l-perfect and has used it for both non-confirmativity and for the admirative. The Aromanian Ohrid dialect took the Albanian forms directly for the admirative (albeit partially) and the models for the aorist pluperfect and applied them in order to approximate the Macedonian system. Thus, we now have an Aromanian-Macedonian system where the compound past tenses are almost identical.

All this demonstrates that the interference between Macedonian and the Aromanian Ohrid dialect was very strong and penetrated deeply into the structure of these dialects. By this the magnitude of the need for mutual understanding and communication is demonstrated.

Literature

Балканская филология, отв. редактор А. В. ДЕСНИЦКАЯ. Ленинград 1970.

ВИДОЕСКИ, Божидар (1988): *Југозападните македонски дијалекти со посебен осврт на битолското говорно подрачје*, посебен отпечаток, МАНУ. Скопје.

ВИДОЕСКИ, Божидар (1977): Тенденции во развојот на македонскиот дијалектен јазик во XIX и XX век. *Прилози* II 1-2. МАНУ, Скопје.

ВИДОЕСКИ, Божидар (1984): Охридско-струшките говори. *Прилози* IX 1. МАНУ, Скопје.

ВИДОЕСКИ, Божидар (1985а): Македонските дијалекти во Албанија. *Литературен збор*, год. XXXII. Скопје.

ВИДОЕСКИ, Божидар (1985b): Местото на охридскиот говор во западното наречје. *Предавања на XVII семинар за македонски јазик, литература и култура, Охрид, 3–24 VII 1984*. Скопје.

ВИДОЕСКИ, Божидар (1993): Меѓујазичниот контакт (на дијалектно рамниште) како фактор за дијалектна диференцијација на македонскиот јазик. *Реферати на македонските слависти за XI меѓународен славистички конгрес во Братислава*, посебен отпечаток. Скопје.

ГАЛТОН, Херберт (1974): Кратка теорија за македонскиот глаголски вид. *Прилози* V 1-2. МАНУ, Скопје.

ГЕОРГИЕВ, Владимир (1972): К вопросу о балканском языковом союзе. *Новое в лингвистике, выпуск* VI. Москва.

ГОЛОМБ, Збигњев (1970): За "механизмот" на словенско-романските односи на Балканскиот полуостров. *Македонски јазик*, год. XXI, Скопје.

ГОЛОМБ, Збигњев (1974): Значењето на македонскиот јазик за балканистичките студии. *Пристапни предавања на новите членови на МАНУ*. Скопје.

ДЕМИРАЈ, Шабан (1994): *Балканска лингвистика*. Скопје.

ИЛИЕВСКИ, Петар Хр. (1988): *Балканолошки лингвистички студии*. Скопје.

ЈАШАР-НАСТЕВА, Оливера (1971): Македонскиот јазик и другите балкански јазици. *Предавања на IV семинар за македонски јазик, литература и култура*. Охрид.

ЈАШАР-НАСТЕВА, Оливера (1989): Местото на македонскиот јазик во Балканската јазична заедница. *Предавања на XXII семинар за македонски јазик, литература и култура*. Охрид.

КОНЕСКИ, Блаже (1981): *Граматика на македонскиот јазик*. Култура, Скопје.

КОНЕСКИ, Блаже (1982): *Историја на македонскиот јазик*. Култура, Скопје.

КОРОНЧЕВСКИ, Анджеј (1979): Македонската конструкција имам+participium praeteriti како балканизам. *Македонски јазик*, год XXX, Скопје.

НАСТЕВ, Божидар (1988): *Аромански студии*. Огледало, Скопје.

ТОПОЛИЊСКА, Зузана (1992): За прагматичната и семантичната мотивација на морфосинтаксички балканизми. *Прилози* XVI. МАНУ, Скопје.

ТРПКОСКИ-ТРПКУ, Вангел (1986): *Власите на Балканот*. РО "Напредокв", Тетово, Скопје.

ФРИДМАН, Виктор А. (1980): Адмиративот во балканските јазици: категорија против употреба. *Македонски јазик* XXXI, Скопје.

ФРИДМАН, Виктор (2000–2001): Граматикализацијата на балканизмите во македонскиот јазик. *Македонски јазик*, бр. 51–52. 31–38.

ЧЕРНЯК, А. Б. (1990): *Арумынский язык*. Основы балканского языкознания, Ленинград.

CAPIDAN, Theodor (1932): *Aromâni, Dialectul aromân*. Academia română, Bucureşti.

CARAGIU-MARIOTEANU, Matilda (1968): *Fono-morfologie aromânâ*. Academia română, Bucureşti.

COMRIE, Bernard (1976): *Aspect*. Cambridge.

CRISTO-LOVEANU, Elie (1962): *The Romanian Language*. Columbia University.

GALTON, Herbert (1976): *The main functions of the Slavic verbal Aspect*. MANU, Skopje.

FIEDLER, Wilfried; BUCHHOLZ, Oda (1987): *Albanische Grammatik*. Leipzig.

FIEDLER, Wilfried (1968a): *Das aromunische Verbalsystem in balkanologischer Sicht*. Beiträge zur rumänischen Philologie. Berlin.

FIEDLER, Wilfried (1968b): Zu einigen Problemen des Admirativs in den Balkansprachen. *Actes du premier congrès international des études Balkaniques et sud-est européennes*, VI. Académie Bulgare des Sciences, Sofia.

GOLAB, Zbigniew (1961): Szkic dialektu Arumunów macedońskich. *Prace językoznawcze-zeszyt* 4, Kraków.

GOLAB, Zbigniew (1984): *The Arumanian dialect of Kruševo in SR Macedonia SFR Yugoslavia*. MANU, Skopje.

FRIEDMAN, Victor A. (1977): *The Grammatical Categories of the Macedonian Indicative*. Slavica Publishers, Inc., Columbus, Ohio.

FRIEDMAN, Victor A. (1981): The Pluperfect in Albanian and Macedonian. *Folia Slavica*, vol. 4, 2–3. 273–282.

FRIEDMAN, Victor A. (1983): Grammatical Categories and a Comparative Balcan Grammar. *Ziele und Wege der Balkanlinguistik*, Band 8. Berlin.

FRIEDMAN, Victor A. (1994): Surprise! Surprise! Arumanian has had an Admirative! *Indiana Slavic Studies*, vol. 7. 79–89.

FRIEDMAN, Victor A. (1996): A newly discovered grammatical form in the Arumanian dialect of Beala de Sus. *The Newsletter of the Society Farsarotul*, Vol. X, Issue 2. Trumbull CT.

IANACHIESCHI-VLAHU, Iancu (1993): *Gramatica armănească*. Crushuva.

KONESKI, Blaže; VIDOESKI, Božidar; JAŠAR-NASTEVA, Olivera (1968): *Distribution des Balkanismes en Macédonien*. Actes du premier congrès international des études Balkaniques et sud-est européennes, VI, Académie Bulgare des Sciences, Sofia.

KRAVAR, Milivoj (1980): Pitanja glagolskog vida u latinskom jeziku. *Živa antika* 6. Skopje.

MIOARA, Avram (1986): *Gramatica pentru toţi*. Bucureşti.

PAPAHAGI, Tache (1974): *Dicţionarul dialectului aroman*. Bucureşti.

TOPOLINSKA, Zuzanna (1995): *Zarys gramatyki języka macedońskiego*. Instytut Filologii Słowiańskiej, Krakow.

TRIFUNOSKI, Jovan (1971): Die Arumunen in Mazedonien. *Balcanica* II, Beograd.

WEIGAND, Gustav (1894): *Die Aromunen* I. Leipzig.

WEIGAND, Gustav (1895): *Die Aromunen* II. Leipzig.

WEINREICH, Uriel (1970): *Languages in Contact*. Mouton, The Hague.

Die Gestaltung des Direkten Objekts
im albanisch-rumänisch-spanischen Vergleich

Ina ARAPI (WIEN), Petrea LINDENBAUER (Wien)

Das Direkte Objekt aus allgemein sprachwissenschaftlicher Sicht

Die menschliche Kognition ordnet wahrgenommenen Lebewesen vor allem Handlungen und Zustände (Emotionen) / Prozesse und deren Einwirken auf andere Lebewesen oder Unbelebtes zu. Dabei führt die gedankliche Grundstruktur von Handlung zu einem Handelnden (Agens) und einem Behandelten (Patiens). Sie entspricht, je nach syntaktischem oder semantischem Fokus, folgenden Mustern:

> *semantisch*: <Handelnder + Handlung + Behandelter>
> oder
> *syntaktisch*: <Agens + Prädikat + Patiens>

In vielen Sprachen dürfte diese Vorstellungsstruktur zu einer transitiven syntaktischen Oberflächenstruktur geführt haben (mit dem Prädikat in aktiver Verbform):

> <Subjekt + Prädikat + Direktes Objekt>

Werden in einer konkreten Sprache nun das Subjekt und das Direkte Objekt mit derselben Wortklasse (Substantiven oder ihren Substituten Pronomina, Numeralia, substantivierte Satzglieder) ausgedrückt, stellt sich das Problem, wie diese beiden Satzfunktionen differenziert werden können. Die Differenzierung dürfte unproblematisch sein, wenn die Semantik des Prädikats aufgrund des enzyklopädischen Wissens des Wahrnehmenden den Handelnden und Behandelten deutlich erkennen lässt, wie in den Kombinationen:

> <Mutter – Kuchen – backen>
> <Wespe – Finger – stechen>
> <Fischer – Hai – jagen>

Vom allgemeinen Erfahrungshorizont schon weniger eindeutig sind Kombinationen wie:

> <Papagei – Kind – rufen> bzw. <Kind – Papagei – rufen>
> <Taucher – Hai – jagen> bzw. <Hai – Taucher – jagen>
> <Rabe – Fuchs – bestehlen> bzw. <Fuchs – Rabe – bestehlen>

Die lineare Bedingtheit der menschlichen Information führt zu einer Reihe von sprachlichen Gestaltungsmöglichkeiten des Direkten Objekts. Insbesonders um Personen an der Sprachoberfläche deutlich als Behandelte zu unterscheiden, stellen Sprachen folgende morphologische und/oder syntaktische Mittel zur Verfügung:

- eine bestimmte Satzgliederordnung: z.B. <Position 1: Handelnder als Subjekt + Position 2: Behandelter als Direktes Objekt>, wobei das Prädikat keine fixe Stelle in der Satzstruktur haben muss (französisch *Pierre invite Marie*)
- Die Position des Direkten Objekts innerhalb der Satzgliederordnung ist freier, wenn es eine Kasusmarkierung gibt (griechisch *Ανοίγει την πόρτα η Κρινούλα* vs. *Η Κρινούλα ανοίγει την πόρτα*, ‚Krinula öffnet die Tür‘)
- Handelnde und Behandelte werden durch Kasusmarkierungen unterschieden: z.B. Handelnder als Subjekt im Nominativ und Behandelter als Direktes Objekt im Akkusativ (lateinisch *Petrus Mariam invitat*)
- Der Behandelte oder das Behandelte wird in seiner Objektfunktion präpositional markiert (spanisch *Piedro invita a María*, *Este morfema nominal concretiza al semantema*)
- Behandelte werden als Direkte Objekte durch Klitika vorweggenommen oder wiederaufgenommen (aromunisch *preftu âl câliseashti njiclu*)

Die Markierung des Direkten Objekts (kurzer historischer Rückblick)

Die heutige Gestaltung des Direkten Objekts dürfte mit verschiedenen Phänomenen der diachronen Sprachentwicklung in Zusammenhang stehen. Wie schon das Lateinische bauten die neuentstehenden Systeme des Protoromanischen die Endungsmorphologie ab, darunter, beispielsweise in Italien und Dakien, die Subjekt-Nominativ- versus Objekt-Akkusativ-Opposition. In der Zeitphase zwischen dem Altlatein und dem Neolateinischen/ Protoromanischen dürfte sich, vielleicht unter griechischem Einfluss, der Artikel herausgebildet und allmählich die Markierung von Kasus, Genus und Numerus übernommen haben (SCHMITT 1987: 95–96, 100). In manchen Sprachen hat eine stärkere Fixierung der Satzgliederordnung die fehlende Akkusativ-Kasusmarkierung kompensiert. Sprachen wie das Rumänische und Spanische dürften hierbei aus ursprünglichen lateinischen Präpositionen (rum. *pe* < lat. PRAE, span. *a* < lat. AD) zusätzliche Ausdrucksfunktionen entwickelt haben, um den akkusativischen Kasus, insbesonders bei Bezug auf Personen und Lebewesen, zu markieren. Constantin FRÂNCU (2009: 1.4.4., 38–39) liefert uns hier Einblicke für das Rumänische, das in seiner frühesten Schriftlichkeit des 16. Jahrhunderts eine erst noch schwache Verwendung von *pre* kennt. In den frühesten religiösen Übersetzungen, v.a. wenn sie kirchenslawischen Originalen folgten, bzw. in manchen Coresi-Drucken, erschien *pre* selten als Zeichen für eine Person oder für ein personifiziertes Lebewesen als Direktes Objekt: „Acuzativul cu funcția de complement direct exprimat prin nume de persoane sau nume personificate însoţit de *pre* este slab reprezentat în textele literare, în special în cele traduse din slavonă, căci în astfel de texte construcţiile fără prepoziţia sînt determinate de originalul slavon." Dennoch dokumentieren Werke wie die moldauische *Pravila ritorului lui Lucaci* (1581) oder Übersetzungen aus dem Ungarischen oder private Dokumente des 16. Jahrhunderts bereits auch die Verwendung von Präpositionalkonstruktionen des Akkusativs, die bis Ende des 17. Jahrhunderts eine häufige Markierung des Direkten Akkusativ-Objekts geworden sein dürften (FRÂNCU 2009: 8.1., p. 140).

Die *Nueva gramática de la lengua española* (Real Academia Española, 2009) kommentiert in ähnlicher Weise die Verwendung der Konstruktion <Präposition AD + *acusativo de persona*> in noch lateinischen Dokumenten (*época preliteraria española*) und im Spanischen spätestens in Zeiten des Cid, v.a. wenn der Referent des Direkten Objekts eine Person darstellte (cf. "Veré a la mugier a todo mio solaz."). Über das Mittelalter hinaus dürfte sich diese syntaktisch und semantisch motivierte Konstruktion in der modernen Zeit stark verankert haben: "En la Edad Moderna se halla muy generalizada la tendencia a construir con la preposición *a* los complementos directos de persona, y sin preposición, como en latín, los de cosa.", auch wenn es viele Fälle von Alternanz gegeben zu haben scheint (cf. ib. 34.8a, p. 2630).

Möglichkeiten der Gestaltung des Direkten Objekts

Die Gestaltung des Direkten Objekts ist in jeder Sprache individuell ausgeformt, d.h. die Sprachbenutzer verwenden die ihnen sprachlich zur Verfügung stehenden Mittel sprachenindividuell. Nicht jede Sprache erlaubt alle Möglichkeiten. So gibt es beispielsweise im Albanischen keine präpositionale Markierung des Direkten Objekts. Andererseits ist in verschiedenen Sprachen auch die Kombination von mehreren Morphemen zugleich „erlaubt", d.h. dass die strukturellen Merkmale ein und derselben Information in Kombination auftreten können. Die strukturellen Möglichkeiten, um die Information <Direktes Objekt> auszudrücken, sind z.B. folgende:

Das Albanische verwendet die Kombination:

<Klitisierung des direkten Objekts + akkusativische Kasusmarkierung> (bei Objekten im Singular):

alb. *Pjetri **e** fton Marie**n** për një kafe* (‚Peter lädt Maria zu einem Kaffee ein‘).

alb. *Ajo [makina] ... **e** kishte lënë befas rrugë**n** ...* (‚Es [das Auto] hatte plötzlich die Straße verlassen‘, KADARE 2009: 17–18).

Das Rumänische und in geringerem Maße bzw. im informellen Stil das Spanische (cf. BUTT/BENJAMIN 1998: 11.14) kennen die Kombination:

<Klitisierung des Direkten Objekts + präpositionale Markierung + Direktes Objekt>:

rum. *Petru o invită pe Maria* (‚Peter lädt Maria ein‘).

span. *Los he invitado a los niños para comer* (‚Ich habe die Kinder zum Essen eingeladen‘ (standardsprachlich: *He invitado a los niños para comer*).

Das Albanische, Rumänische und Spanische verwenden die tendenzielle pronominale Vorwegnahme des Direkten Objekts bei Inversion der normalen Topik:

alb. *Gjyshen e donte shumë* (‚Die Großmutter liebte er/sie sehr‘).

rum. *Pe bunica o iubea foarte mult* (‚Die Großmutter liebte er/sie sehr‘).

span. *A la abuela la quería mucho* (‚Die Großmutter liebte er/sie sehr‘).

Bei invertierter Topik verwenden das Rumänische und Spanische weitere syntaktische Markierung heran:

alb. $\emptyset_{präp.}$ *Gjyshen e donte shumë* (‚Die Großmutter liebte er/sie sehr‘).

rum. *Pe bunica o iubea foarte mult* (‚Die Großmutter liebte er/sie sehr‘).

span. *A la abuela la quería mucho* (‚Die Großmutter liebte er/sie sehr‘).

Im Unterschied zum Albanischen und Spanischen kennt das Rumänische freie Varianten der Gestaltung des Direkten Objekts:

rum. *Am invitat pe copii la masă. / Am invitat copiii la masă* (‚Ich habe die Kinder zum *Essen* eingeladen‘ GLR 2005, II: 378).

Im Unterschied zum Albanischen kennt das Rumänische auch den Fall der semantisch bedingten, nicht freien Gestaltung des sich auf eine Person beziehenden Direkten Objekts:

rum. *Îl caut pe informatician* (‚Ich suche den [bestimmten] Informatiker‘) vs. *Caut un informatician* (‚Ich suche [irgend]einen Informatiker‘).

rum. *Vi-l prezint pe domnul inginer Argeşeanu* vs. alb. *Ju prezantoj zotin inxhinier* (‚Ich stelle Ihnen Herrn Ingenieur A. vor‘).

Schwierigkeiten des albanisch-rumänischen Vergleichs der Gestaltung des Direkten Objekts

Wie aus dem vorangehenden Abschnitt schon ersichtlich wird, ist die Gestaltung des Direkten Objekts, insbesonders in der Frage der präpositionalen und/oder pronominalen Objektverdoppelung, im Albanischen und Rumänischen mannigfaltig bedingt. Bezüglich der Frage der Setzung oder, respektive, Auslassung der präpositionalen Markierung des Direkten Objekts im Rumänischen sind sich die Autoren der Akademiegrammatik durchaus einer multiplen Motivation für die Auswahl einer bestimmen Konstruktion bewusst, ohne jedoch dem Nicht-Muttersprachler (alle) Lösungen oder Regularitäten systematisch anzubieten: „Regulile de construire a complementului direct cu sau fără *pe* implică ... şi dinstincţii gramaticale legate de anumite specii de pronume, de prezenţa anumitor determinanţi sau determinativi, de relaţia sintactică de dublare, de topică etc. Şi verbul este parţial ‚responsabil‘ de folosirea uneia dintre cele două construcţii." (‚Die Regeln der Konstruktion des direkten Komplements mit oder ohne *pe* impliziert ... von bestimmten Pronomen oder der Präsenz bestimmter Determinantien oder der syntaktischen Beziehung der Verdoppelung oder von der Topik abhängige grammatikalische Unterschiede etc. Auch ist teilweise das Verb „verantwortlich" für die eine der beiden Konstruktionen‘; GLR, II, 2005: 376, 382).

Zu ähnlich komplexen Schlussfolgerungen kommen in der Frage der Reduplikation[1] des Objekts im Albanischen auch Buchholz/Fiedler und Liberacka, wenn sie schreiben: „Ob sie [die Pronomen] obligatorisch oder fakultativ sind, hängt von dem Stellenplan des Verblexems ab, das aufgrund seiner Rektion auch die Art der syntaktisch-morphologischen Realisierung des Obj. bestimmt", „Die Objektsverdoppelung, die sowohl beim direkten und indirekten Objekt als auch bei Nominalgruppen im Dativ ohne Objektsfunktion auftritt, nicht aber beim Präpositionalobjekt, hängt von bestimmten Bedingungen ab, die sich in bezug auf das direkte Obj. als recht vielschichtig und kompliziert erweisen" (BUCHHOLZ/FIEDLER 1987: 436 und 440), "Në bazë të rezultateve të përfituara mund të them, që lidhja e reduplikacionit të kundrinorit me kategorinë e shquarsisë është shumë më e komplikuar sesa del nga informacionet e gramatikës shqipe" (‚Aufgrund der konkreten Ergebnisse stelle ich fest, dass die Beziehung zwischen der Reduplikation des Objekts und der grammatischen Kategorie der Bestimmtheit viel komplizierter ist als von den angegebenen Informationen in der albanischen Grammatik anzunehmen ist‘; LIEBERACKA 2009: 143; cf. auch 148).

---

1   In der im Kosovo gesprochenen Varietät des Albanischen zeigt sich aktuell die Tendenz, systematisch und fallunabhängig Klitika zu setzen. Diese Tendenz hat schon früher eingesetzt. So hat Gj. N. Kazazi aus Gjakova (Kosovo) in seinem Werk (Rom 1743) die Verdoppelung des DO einige Male vorgenommen. Demiraj kommt zum Schluss, dass sich die Regeln zur Verdoppelung des DO nicht früher als im 18. Jahrhundert festlegten. Und schon Mitte des gleichen Jahrhunderts begannen auch die ersten Versuche, andere neue Regeln durchzusetzen. Hier ein Beispiel heutigen Sprachusus: *Instituti Albanologjik i Prishtinës ... e ka një histori 57-vjeçare të mbijetesës* ‚Das Albanologie-Institut in Prishtina ... hat eine 57-jährige Überlebensgeschichte‘ (aus: *Odisejada e Institutit Albanologjik nëpër qeveritë tona*, unter: www.telegrafi.com/2id=26&a=3471 vom 22.03.2011).
Die systematische Klitisierung wird aber nicht von allen gerne getragen. Eine Systematisierung würde natürlich Ordnung im Sprachsystem schaffen. Die Objektverdoppelung ist ein Phänomen der Volkssprache, welches die Kommunikation deutlicher macht, jedoch das „ästhetische" Niveau der Sprache beeinträchtigt.

Eine Aufstellung der Gestaltungsregularitäten des Direkten Objekts im alba-
nisch-rumänischen Vergleich muss mindestens folgende Fälle berücksichtigen:

In den Fällen, in denen das Direkte Objekt durch eine Person oder ein Indefinitpronomen ausgedrückt wird, kann die Setzung oder Nicht-Setzung des kataphorischen, vorausweisenden Klitikums in Kombination mit der Präposition *pe* im Rumänischen bedeutungsunterscheidend sein. Die folgenden Beispiele sind entnom-
men aus der GLR 2005, II: 379–380:

rum. *Caut un student* (‚Ich suche einen Studierenden [ohne Bezug auf jemanden
  bestimmten]‘ vs. *Îl caut pe un student* (‚Ich suche einen [bestimmten] Studierenden‘).
rum. *Aştept nişte / câţiva elevi* (‚Ich erwarte ein paar [nicht bestimmte] Studierende‘) vs. *Îi aştept pe câţiva elevi* (‚Ich erwarte einige [ganz bestimmte] Studierende‘).
rum. *Ai mai văzut pe vreunul?* (‚Hast Du schon irgendeinen [von mehreren, nicht
  bestimmten] gesehen?‘) vs. *Ai mai văzut vreunul ca el* (‚Hast du schon jemals
  [so] einen gesehen [wie diesen]‘)?
rum. *Cautā altul* (‚Er sucht [irgend]einen Anderen‘) vs. *Cautā pe altul* (‚Er sucht
  einen [ganz bestimmten] Anderen‘).
rum. *Profesorul ascultă pe fiecare* (‚Der Professor hört jeden [x-Beliebigen] an‘)
  vs. *Profesorul îl ascultă pe fiecare* (‚Der Professor hört jeden [aus einer bestimmten Gruppe] an‘).
rum. *Am întâlnit pe unii / alţii / câţiva* (‚Ich habe einige/weitere/ein paar [unbe-
  stimmte] getroffen‘) vs. *I-am întâlnit pe unii / alţii / câţiva* (‚Ich habe einige/
  weitere/ein paar [unter Bestimmten] getroffen‘).
rum. *Am întâlnit atâţia* (‚Ich habe soviele [unbestimmte] angetroffen‘) vs. *Am
  întâlnit pe atâţia* (‚Ich habe so viele [unter ganz bestimmten] getroffen‘).
rum. *Nu vezi om pe-aici* (‚Hier siehst du keinen einzigen Menschen‘) vs. *Nu-l vezi
  pe om aici* (‚Hier/an diesem Ort kannst du dir keinen Menschen vorstellen/Du
  siehst einen [ganz bestimmten] Menschen hier nicht‘).

Während die pronominale und präpositionale Konstruktion des Direkten Objekts in
bestimmten Fällen eindeutig gewählt werden muss (rum. *I-am întâlnit pe amândoi.*
‚Ich habe beide getroffen‘), kann die Setzung oder Nicht-Setzung des kataphorischen Objektklitikums in bestimmten Fällen im Rumänischen (seltener im Albanischen) bedeutungsgleich und daher fakultativ sein:

rum. *Vulpea (l-)a păcălit pe urs* (‚Der Fuchs hat den Bären getäuscht‘).
alb. *Ai (e) mburri / ata (e) mburrën veten* (‚Er/Sie hat sich selbst gelobt‘; BUCH-
  HOLZ/FIEDLER 1987: 435).
span. *Ahora me **lo** tienes que contar **todo*** (‚Nun musst Du mir alles erzählen‘;
  obligatorisch bei *todo*, cf. BUTT/BENJAMIN 1989: 11.14.4).

Umgangssprachlich oder regionalsprachlich kann im Rumänischen – hier selbst bei Referenz auf eine Person/ein Lebewesen/etwas Personifiziertes – das vorausgehende Klitikum und/oder die Präposition *pe* wegfallen. Die GLR 2005, II: 378–379 sieht bezüglich der Gestaltung des Direkten Objekts mit Präposition (*prepoziţional*) oder ohne Präposition (*neprepoziţional*) v.a. in der familiären Sprache eine starke Fluktuation (die nicht selten auch unter Muttersprachlern Unsicherheit auslöst):

Für das Rumänische gibt uns die GLR 2005, II: 377–378 viele Beispiele, u.a.:

rum. (*O*) *Văd pe mama* („Ich sehe die Mutter') vs. alb. (*E*) *shoh nënën.*

rum. (*L-*) *Am chemat pe tata* („Ich habe den Vater gerufen') vs. alb. (*E*) *thirra babain.*

rum. *Pe toţi* [= copiii] (*i*)-*am trimis acasă* („Alle Kinder habe ich nach Hause geschickt').

rum. (*O*) *vreau pe asta / aia* („Ich will diese da').

Auch bei Inversion der normalen Topik kann bei Referenz auf ein sächliches Objekt das Klitikum ausgelassen werden:

rum. *O problemă* (*o*) *ridică scrierea cu cratimă* („Ein Problem stellt die Schreibung mit Bindestrich dar').

rum. *Un succes* (*îl*) *constituie rezultatele bune obţinute la examen* („Einen Erfolg stellen die bei der Prüfung erreichten guten Resultate dar').

Im Rumänischen erscheint die Präposition *pe* vor Direkten Objekten, die sich auf eine sächliche Kategorie beziehen, z.B. bei umgangssprachlich verwendeten Demonstrativpronomen (*asta, aia*) und Indefinitpronomen (außer *orice*) als syntaktischer Marker:

rum. *Împrumut pe oricare* („Ich verleihe jedes').

rum. *Am lăsat în urmă pe al patrulea* („Ich habe die vierte [z.B. Stadt] hinter mit gelassen').

rum. *Am citit pe Blaga* [metonymische Verwendung für das Werk] aber auch *Am citit Blaga* („Ich habe Blaga gelesen').

rum. *O iau pe asta* („Ich nehme das da'); Umgangssprachlich auch: *Iau asta. Asta vreau.*

rum. *Am cumpărat un creion. Pe al meu l-am pierdut* („Ich habe einen Bleistift gekauft. Meinen habe ich verloren').

Nur im Rumänischen alternieren frei, also bedeutungsgleich, die präpositionale Konstruktion des Direkten Objekts mit der Artikel-Konstruktion (ohne vorangehende Präposition) des Direkten Objekts:

rum. *Am invitat pe copii la masă / Am invitat copiii la masă* („Ich habe die Kinder zum Essen eingeladen', GLR 2005, II: 378).

rum. *Aşteptăm profesorul la oră / Aşteptăm pe profesor la oră* ('Wir erwarten den Professor zur Unterrichtsstunde', GLR 2005, II: 378).

Im Albanischen hat das kataphorische Klitikum die Funktion, auf ein in den Diskurs bereits eingeführtes Objekt, unabhängig von dessen kategoriellem Bezug (Person, Personifiziertes, Gegenstand) hinzuweisen. Wird ein Objekt erstmals thematisiert, verlangt das Albanische kein Klitikum, wird das Objekt nach seiner erstmaligen Einführung genannt, verlangt das Albanische die pronominale Vorwegnahme dieses Objekts:

alb. *Ditë për ditë peshkatari merrte grepin, shkonte në breg, e hidhte grepin në det, dhe priste* ('Tag für Tag nahm der Fischer die Angel, ging zum Ufer, warf die Angel ins Meer und wartete'; BUCHHOLZ/FIEDLER 1987: 441).

BUCHHOLZ und FIEDLER (1987: 443) zufolge, hat die Auslassung des Klitikums bereits eingeführter Objekte eine emphatische Funktion:

alb. *Nëna i dha Agimit një mollë e një dardhë, por djali hëngri vetëm mollën* ('Die Mutter gab Agim einen Apfel und eine Birne, aber der Junge aß nur den Apfel'; BUCHHOLZ/FIEDLER 1987: 443–444).

Das Albanische verfügt über eine deutliche Kasusmarkierung des Akkusativs (nur) im Singular Maskulin und Feminin (-*n*/-*në*). Das Rumänische und Spanische setzen hier eine pronominale und/oder präpositionale Markierung des Akkusativs ein:

alb. *Nëse ky ligj do të ishte miratuar, publiku italian ndoshta do të dinte pak ose asgjë nga skandalet që **e** kanë tronditur ven**din** gjatë vitit të fundit* ('Wenn dieses Gesetz in Kraft getreten wäre, hätten die Italiener wahrscheinlich wenig oder gar nichts von den Skandalen erfahren, die das Land in den letzten Jahren erschüttert haben'; aus der albanischen Tageszeitung *Mapo*, vom 23. Juli 2010, Seite 10).

alb. *Gratë pyesin shitësen për çmimin* ('Die Frauen fragen die Verkäuferin um den Preis'; HETZER/FINGER 2006: 82) vs. *Femeile (o) întreabă **pe** vânzătoare după piersici*.

alb. *Po presim profesorin* ('Ich warte auf den Professor') vs. *(Îl) aştept **pe** profesor*.

alb. *Pjetri thërret shokun* ('Peter ruft den Freund'; HETZER/FINGER 2006: 82) vs. *Petru îl cheamă **pe** prieten*.

Die Bedingungen, welche die eine oder andere Konstruktion auslösen oder synonyme Realisierungen erlauben, sind also syntaktische Kriterien (Akkusativ, Topik), semantische Kriterien (im Rumänischen) wie die Bestimmtheit und die Seme <belebt> / <unbelebt> des Direkten Objekts oder auch satzfunktionale und diskurspragmatische Kriterien (im Albanischen), die den Referenten als <bekannt vs. neu> oder als <+ Betonung> charakterisieren.

Das Direkte Objekt – morphosyntaktisch (satzfunktional) und semantisch erfasst

Mit dem vorliegenden Beitrag versuchen die beiden Autorinnen die Regeln und Regularitäten der Objektgestaltung v.a. des Albanischen und Rumänischen und ihre Vergleichbarkeit (oder Nicht-Vergleichbarkeit) zu erfassen, gerade weil die Grammatiken beider Sprachen die jeweiligen möglichen Objektrealisierungen für Außenstehende oder Lernende unzureichend beschreiben. Dazu werden in den folgenden Abschnitten Beispiele aus einschlägigen Grammatiken sowie aus empiri-schem Material in Form der ersten fünf Kapitel des Romans *Aksidenti* von Ismail KADARE neu zusammengestellt. Hier nicht eigens behandelt werden Fälle reiner pronominaler Nennung von Direkten Objekten und ihrer betonten (langen) Pronominalformen sowie syntagmatische Ausdrücke oder Verben der Reziprozität wie:

alb. *e pranoj* (,Ich hab es angenommen'; cf. dazu BUCHHOLZ/FIEDLER 1987: 446–447).

alb. *E vetmja gjë, që munda të bëja ka qënë pregatitja e disa tezave të shkruara. Unë i lexova **ato** shumë ngadalë dhe dy herë* (,Das einzige, was ich tun konnte, war die Vorbereitung einiger schriftlicher Thesen. Ich habe **sie** sehr langsam und zweimal durchgelesen'; BUCHHOLZ/FIEDLER 1987: 441).

alb. *e kemi kaluar shumë mirë në Shqipëri*, wörtlich: ,wir haben [es] sehr gut ge-habt/verbracht in Albanien' > ,Wir haben uns in Albanien sehr wohlgefühlt' (cf. HETZER/FINGER 2006: 33).

rum. *Te aștept **pe** tine* (,Ich erwarte dich') vs. alb. *Të pres ty.*

rum. *Se amăgește **pe** sine. **Pe** sine se amăgește* (,Er grübelt in sich hinein', cf. GLR 2005, II: 379, 380) vs. alb. *Mërzit veten.*

Das Direkte Objekt des Verbs <haben>

alb. *Unë kam tre fëmijë, një vajzë e dy djem* (,Ich habe drei Kinder, ein Mädchen und zwei Jungs', HETZER/FINGER 2006: 65).

rum. *Am (un) soț* (,Ich habe einen Ehemann').

span. *Tengo (un) marido* (,Ich habe einen Ehemann').

alb. *Ai ka (një) shtëpi në fshat* (,Er hat ein Haus auf dem Land').

rum. *El are (o) casă la țară* (,Er hat ein Haus auf dem Land').

alb. *Kam një ide* (,Ich habe eine Idee').

rum. Am o idee (,Ich habe eine Idee').

alb. *A do të keni pak kohë te lirë?* (,Werden Sie ein wenig freie Zeit haben', HET-ZER/FINGER 2006: 48).

rum. *Veți avea ceva timp liber?* (,Werden Sie ein wenig freie Zeit haben').

Da das Klitikum, wenn es gesetzt wird, und die Präposition, wenn sie im Rumänischen verwendet werden, immer in dieser Reihung (Klitikum = Position 1, Präposition = Position 2) vorkommen, und im Albanischen nur das Klitikum auf das Direkte Objekt verweisen, haben wir für die Repräsentation dieser Positionen bei Nichtsetzung der Präposition die Darstellung $\emptyset_{1=\text{Pronomen}}$ und für die Nichtsetzung des Klitikums die Darstellung $\emptyset_{2=\text{Präposition}}$ gewählt. Für das Verb <haben> ergeben sich somit folgende mögliche Gestaltungsmuster des Direkten Objekts:

$\emptyset_1$ + <haben> + $\emptyset_2$ + Person, unbestimmt

$\emptyset_1$ + <haben> + $\emptyset_2$ + Konkretum, unbestimmt

$\emptyset_1$ + <haben> + $\emptyset_2$ + Abstraktum, unbestimmt

Das Direkte Objekt als Person / Personifiziertes Lebewesen mit anderen Verben

alb. *Shoh nënën* [*në rrugë*] (‚Ich sehe meine Mutter [auf der Straße] ‘) vs. rum. *O văd pe mama.*

alb. *Thirra babain* (‚Ich lud meinen Vater ein‘) vs. rum. *L-am chemat pe tata.*

alb. *Kam parë vëllanë tënd* (‚Ich habe deinen Bruder gesehen‘).

alb. *Ju prezantoj zotin inxhinier* (‚Ich stelle Ihnen Herrn Ingenieur A. vor‘).

→ alb. $\emptyset_1$ + $\emptyset_2$ + Person im Singular bestimmt durch Akkusativdesinenz

alb. *Unë **e** shoh shpesh nëne**n*** (‚Ich sehe meine Mutter oft‘).

alb. *Unë **e** thirrisja shpesh babai**n** për darkë* (‚Ich lud meinen Vater oft zum Abendessen ein‘).

alb. *Shpresa që bombardimi të quhej i gabuar, **i** bënte të ngazëlleheshin ose të dëshpëroheshin mijëra njerëz* (‚Die Hoffnung, dass das Bombardement ein Fehler gewesen war, ließ Tausende von Menschen jubeln oder auch verzweifeln‘; KADARE 2009: 26).

→ alb. Klitikum + $\emptyset_2$ + Person im Singular bestimmt durch Akkusativdesinenz

→ alb. Klitikum + $\emptyset_2$ + Person im Plural bestimmt durch Numeral/nicht identifiziert

alb. *Profesori kritikoi disa studentë* (‚Der Professor kritisierte einige Studenten‘; BUCHHOLZ/FIEDLER 1987: 441).

→ alb. $\emptyset_1$ + $\emptyset_2$ + Person im Plural bestimmt durch ein indefinites Pronomen

rum. *Vi-l prezint pe domnul inginer Argeșeanu* vs. alb. *Ju prezantoj zotin inxhinier* (‚Ich stelle Ihnen Herrn Ingenieur A. vor‘).

rum. *L-am văzut pe fratele tău* vs. alb. *Kam parë vëllanë tënd* (‚Ich habe deinen Bruder gesehen‘).

→ rum. Klitikum + *pe* + Person im Singular bestimmt durch Eigennamen

→ rum. Klitikum + *pe* + Person im Singular bestimmt durch Possessivpronomen rum. *Mângâie câinele* (‚Er streichelt den Hund‘).

→ rum. $\emptyset_1 + \emptyset_2$ + Lebewesen im Singular, bestimmt durch bestimmten Artikel

rum. *Vulpea (l)-a păcălit **pe** urs* (‚Der Fuchs hat den Bären getäuscht‘). Vs. alb. *Dhelpra e mashtroi ariun.*

→ rum. (Klitikum) + *pe* + Lebewesen personifiziert im Singular, ohne Artikel

rum. *Caut profesor de germană* (‚Ich suche einen Deutschlehrer‘), *Căutăm informatician* (‚Wir suchen einen Informatiker‘), *Primeşte studenţi în gazdă* (‚Er nimmt Studierende auf‘; Beispiele aus GLR 2005, II: 376).

rum. *A trebuit să plimb prin ţară un cuplu de prieteni din America* („Ich musste ein [unbestimmtes] Freundespaar aus Amerika durchs Land spazieren führen"; PLEŞU 2006: 29).

→ rum. $\emptyset_1 + \emptyset_2$ + Person generisch für eine Klasse/Kategorie/Berufs-/Zivilstand von Personen

span. *Le quiere mucho a ese hijo* (‚Sie liebt diesen Sohn sehr‘; familiäre Sprache, cf. BUTT/BENJAMIN 1989: 11.14.4).

span. *... Podía concebirse que uno de ellos intentara besar **al** otro ...* ? (‚Konnte man sich vorstellen, dass einer der beiden den Anderen zu küssen versuchte ...?‘; KADARE 2009: 17).

→ span. $\emptyset_1 + a$ + Person / substantiviertes Indefinitpronomen

Das Direkte Objekt als Sache oder Abstraktum

alb. *Ditë për ditë peshkatari merrte grepin, shkonte në breg, **e** hidhte grepin në det, dhe priste* (‚Tag für Tag nahm der Fischer die Angel, ging zum Ufer, warf die Angel ins Meer und wartete‘; BUCHHOLZ/FIEDLER 1987: 441) vs. rum. **În fiecare zi pescarul lua undiţa, se ducea la mal, arunca undiţa în mare şi aştepta.*

alb. *Vizituam banesën e Habibesë. Kur **e** blenë shtëpinë, as oborri as kopshti nuk kishin një pemë* (‚Wir besuchten Habibes Heim. Als sie das Haus kauften, gab es weder im Hof noch im Garten Obstbäume‘; BUCHHOLZ/FIEDLER 1987: 441).

alb. *Gjuhëtarët **e** hartuan fjalorin e ri* (‚Die Sprachwissenschaftler haben das neue Wörterbuch erarbeitet‘; BUCHHOLZ/FIEDLER 1987: 437).

alb. ***E** kam lënë duhanin. Nuk e pi më* (‚Ich habe aufgehört zu rauchen. Ich rauche nicht mehr‘; HETZER/FINGER 2006: 56).

alb. *Atëherë po **e** dredh dhe unë një cigare* (‚Dann drehe auch ich mir eine Zigarette‘; BUCHHOLZ/FIEDLER 1987: 442).

alb. *Na thuaj ca shembuj!* (‚Sag uns ein paar Beispiele‘; BUCHHOLZ/FIEDLER 1987 443).

alb. *Maria **e** lexon shpesh këtë libër* (‚Maria liest dieses Buch oft‘).

alb. *Ajo **i** ka lexuar disa herë "Lulet e verës"* (‚Sie hat die „Sommerblumen" mehrmals gelesen‘).

→ alb. bei Informationsstrukturierung Klitikum + $\emptyset_2$ + Gegenstand, Singular, durch Akkusativ-Desinenz/bestimmten Artikel bestimmt>

rum. *Văd drumul* (‚Ich sehe den Weg').

rum. *El citeşte articolul* (‚Er liest den Artikel').

rum. *Îmbracă păpuşa* (‚Er kleidet die Puppe an').

span. [el taxi] *había abandonado de pronto la carretera* ... (‚Das Taxi hatte die Fahrbahn plötzlich verlassen'; KADARE 2009: 12).

alb. *Familjet ... blejnë vetëm tekstet shkollore* (‚Die Familien ... bezahlen nur die Schulbücher'; HETZER/FINGER 2006: 64).

alb. *Vera dhe Teuta lënë valixhet dhe dalin në balkon* (‚Vera und Teuta lassen die Koffer [stehen] und gehen auf den Balkon'; HETZER/FINGER 2006: 66).

→ alb. $\emptyset_1$ + $\emptyset_2$ + Gegenstand Plural bestimmt durch bestimmten Artikel

→ rum., span. $\emptyset_1$ + $\emptyset_2$ + Gegenstand Singular bestimmt durch bestimmten Artikel

alb. *Ai lexon një artikull* (‚Er liest einen Zeitungsartikel').

rum. *El citeşte un articol* (‚Er liest einen Zeitungsartikel').

alb. *Porosiste një uiski tjetër* (‚Er forderte einen weiteren Whisky'; KADARE 2009: 24).

rum. *Cerea alt whisky* (‚Er forderte einen weiteren Whisky').

span. *Pedía otro whisky* (‚Er forderte einen weiteren Whisky').

alb. *Një tjetër dëshmitar ... jepte ... të njëtën gjë* (‚Ein anderer Zeuge ... vermittelte ... dieselbe Version'; KADARE 2009: 18).

span. *Otro testigo ... proporcionaba ... la misma versión* (‚Ein anderer Zeuge ... vermittelte ... dieselbe Version'; KADARE 2009: 12).

rum. *Maria cumpără o carte nouă* (‚Maria kauft ein neues Buch').

alb. *Maria blen një libër të ri* (‚Maria kauft ein neues Buch').

alb. *Unë pi cigare më filtër* (‚Ich rauche Zigaretten mit Filter'; HETZER/FINGER 2006: 56).

alb. *Sillmë pe, gërshërë dhe gjilpërë ...* (‚Bring mir Faden, Schere und Nadel'; BUCHHOLZ/FIEDLER 1987: 435).

alb. „*Më ke dhënë lumturi të pakufishme ...*" (‚Du hast mir grenzenloses Glück gegeben'; KADARE 2009: 26).

alb. *... ky njeri nuk kishte gjetur qetësi* (‚Dieser Mann hatte keine Ruhe gefunden'; KADARE 2009: 26).

alb. *Ky libër përmban këngë popullore* (‚Dieses Buch enthält Volkslieder'; BUCHHOLZ/FIEDLER 1987: 435).

rum. *Colomb nu cunoscuse teamă* (‚Kolumbus kannte keine Angst').

rum. *Copiii i-au adus satisfacţii* (‚Die Kinder haben ihm Erfüllung gebracht').

span. *... este hombre no había encontrado sosiego* (‚Dieser Mann hatte keine Ruhe gefunden'; KADARE 2009: 25).

→ alb., rum., span. Ø₁ + Ø₂ + Gegenstand/Abstraktum, durch unbestimmten Artikel bestimmt oder artikellos

rum. *Critică democraţia* (‚Er kritisiert die Demokratie‘).
alb. *Kritikon demokracinë* (‚Er kritisiert die Demokratie‘).
→ alb. Ø₁ + Ø₂ + Abstraktum bestimmt durch Akkusativdesinenz
→ rum. Ø₁ + Ø₂ + Abstraktum bestimmt durch bestimmten Artikel

alb. *Merria një kënge!* (‚Stimm ein Lied an‘; BUCHHOLZ/FIEDLER 1987: 445).
alb. *Do ta kesh një hall* (‚Du wirst schon ein Problem haben‘; BUCHHOLZ/FIEDLER 1987: 442).
rum. *M-ai făcut să experimentez o bucurie nelimitată* (‚Du hast mir grenzenloses Glück gegeben‘).
span. *„Me has hecho experimentar una felicidad sin límites ..."* (‚Du hast mir grenzenloses Glück gegeben‘; KADARE 2009: 24).
→ alb. Klitikum + Ø₂ + Abstraktum bestimmt durch unbestimmten Artikel
→ rum., span. Ø₁ + Ø₂ + Abstraktum bestimmt durch unbestimmten Artikel

Das Direkte Objekt als Pronomen ausgedrückt

In Fällen pronominaler Objekt-Realisierung (einer Person oder Sache), insbesonders bei Negation, Fragepronomen und Indefinitpronomen, wird im Albanischen wie im Rumänischen ein Klitikum tendenziell nicht gesetzt, im Rumänischen tendenziell die Präposition *pe*.

alb. *Në shkollë nuk gjeti asnjeri* (‚In der Schule traf er niemanden an‘; BUCHHOLZ/FIEDLER 1987: 444).
alb. *Nuk pashë njeri* (‚Ich habe keinen gesehen‘; BUCHHOLZ/FIEDLER 1987: 444).
rum. *Nu văd pe nimeni* (‚Ich sehe niemanden‘).
span. *No he visto a nadie* (‚Ich sehe niemanden‘).
rum. *N-am întâlnit pe niciunul dintre ei* (‚Ich habe keinen von ihnen getroffen‘).
alb. *Kë po kërkon?* (‚Wen suchst du‘; BUCHHOLZ/FIEDLER 1987: 444).
rum. *Pe cine vezi?* (‚Wen siehst du?‘).
rum. *Spune-mi pe cine ai văzut* (‚Sag' mir, wen du gesehen hast‘).
alb. *Nuk gjeti (as)gjë* (‚Er hat (gar) nichts gefunden‘; BUCHHOLZ/FIEDLER 1987: 444).
alb. *Kam blerë diçka* (‚Ich habe etwas gekauft‘; BUCHHOLZ/FIEDLER 1987: 444).
alb. *Në fillim lexonte çdo libër që i binte në dorë* (‚Zu Anfang las er jedes Buch, das ihm in die Hände fiel‘; BUCHHOLZ/FIEDLER 1987: 443).
alb. *Ai përsëriste çdo fjalë* (‚Er wiederholte jedes Wort‘; BUCHHOLZ/FIEDLER 1987: 443).
alb. *Raporti i kontrollit teknik të makinës e përjashton çdo sabotim* (‚Der technische Kontrollbericht des Autos schließt jeden Sabotageakt aus‘; KADARE 2009:

19) vs. span. *El informe de la revisión técnica del vehículo excluía cualquier acto de sabotaje* (KADARE 2009: 12).

rum. *Primeşte pe oricine* (‚Er empfängt jeden‘).

rum. *Notez pe fiecare* (‚Ich notiere jede [x-beliebige] Person‘).

→ alb. <Verneinung>/<Frage>/Indefinition> + $\emptyset_1$ + $\emptyset_2$ + Pronomen/pronominales Adjektiv

→ rum. <Verneinung>/<Frage>/Indefinition> + $\emptyset_1$ + pe + Pronomen/pronominales Adjektiv

Das Direkte Objekt in markierter Satzsyntax

Sowohl im Albanischen als auch Rumänischen erfolgt bei Inversion der normalen Topik tendenziell eine obligate Klitisierung, unabhängig von der Semantik (<Person> oder <Gegenstand>) des Referenten.

alb. *Marinë e ftojnë të gjithë* (‚Maria laden alle gerne ein‘).

alb. *Gjyshen e donte shumë* (‚Die Großmutter liebte er/sie sehr‘).

alb. *Nënë e bir i gjeti fjetur* (‚Mutter und Sohn traf er schlafend an‘; BUCHHOLZ/ FIEDLER 1987: 442).

alb. *Gjithë ditën e kalonte pranë vatrës* (‚Den ganzen Tag verbrachte er an der Feuerstelle‘; BUCHHOLZ/FIEDLER 1987: 440).

alb. *Portën e oborrit mos e hap* (‚Die Hoftür mach nicht auf!‘; BUCHHOLZ/ FIEDLER 1987: 441).

alb. *Një reaksion të tillë nuk e kishte pritur kurrë* (‚Eine solche Reaktion hatte er nicht erwartet‘; BUCHHOLZ/FIEDLER 1987: 442).

rum. *Pe bunică o iubea foarte mult* (‚Die Großmutter liebte er/sie sehr‘).

rum. *Copiii i-am îmbrăcat ...* (‚Die Kinder hab ich angezogen [aber ich bin noch nicht angezogen ...]‘).

rum. *Pe Ioana am întâlnit-o la facultate* (‚Ioana habe ich an der Fakultät getroffen‘, GLR 2005, II: 381).

rum. *Pe păpuşă a îmbrăcat-o frumos* (‚Die Puppe hat er schön angezogen‘, GLR 2005, II: 381).

rum. *Pe toţi (= copii) i-am trimis acasă* (‚Alle Kinder habe ich nach hause geschickt‘, GLR 2005, II: 381).

rum. *Pe toţi i-am chemat* (‚Alle habe ich gerufen‘, GLR 2005, II: 381).

rum. *Pe câţiva îi văd zilnic* (‚Einige [unter bestimmten] sehe ich täglich‘, GLR 2005, II: 381).

rum. *Pe al patrulea l-am felicitat* (‚Den Vierten habe ich beglückwünscht‘, GLR 2005, II: 381).

rum. *Fiecare cameră am vopsit-o în altă culoare. Toţi pereţii i-am reparat* (‚Jedes Zimmer habe ich in einer anderen Farbe gestrichen. Alle Fenster habe ich repariert‘, GLR 2005, II: 381).

rum. *Acea lucrare am terminat-o* („Jene Arbeit habe ich beendet', GLR 2005, II: 381).

rum. *Dragostea ne-o țină zeii* („Unsere Liebe, mögen die Götter sie erhalten'; nach BLAGA, GLR 2005, II: 381).

rum. *Parisul l-am vizitat mai demult* („Ich habe Paris schon vor längerer Zeit besucht') vs. *Am vizitat Parisul anul trecut* („Paris hab ich schon vor längerer Zeit besucht', GLR 2005, II: 382).

rum. *Luchian-ul l-am vândut* („[Das Bild von] Luchian habe ich verkauft', GLR 2005, II: 381).

rum. *Pe păpușă o iubește mult* („Die Puppe liebt sie sehr', GLR 2005, II: 377).

rum. *Am cumpărat un creion. Pe al meu l-am pierdut* („Ich habe einen Bleistift gekauft. Meinen habe ich verloren').

span. *A alguno de vosotros os quisiera ver yo en un buen fregado* („einen von Euch würde ich gerne in einem Schlamassel sehen'; BUTT/BENJAMIN 1989: 11.14.1.)

span. *Lo que dice ... jamás lo consentiría nadie de los dirigentes ...* („Was er sagt, hätte keiner von den Direktoren je approbiert'; BUTT/BENJAMIN 1989: 11.14.1.)

→ alb. $\emptyset_1$ + DO$_{Akk.}$ + Klitikum + Verb (bei Person oder Gegenständen)

→ rum. Präp. + DO$_{Akk.}$ + Klitikum + Verb (bei Person)

→ rum. $\emptyset_1$ + DO$_{Akk.}$ + Klitikum + Verb (bei Gegenständen / Abstraktum)

→ span. Präp. + DO$_{Akk.}$ + Klitikum + Verb (bei Person)

→ span. $\emptyset_1$ + DO$_{Akk.}$ + Klitikum + Verb (bei Gegenständen / Abstraktum)

Das Direkte Objekt mit Funktion der Informationsstrukturierung

Schon BUCHHOLZ/FIEDLER (1987: 440, 441) haben auf die besondere pragmasemantische Funktion des kataphorischen Klitikums im Albanischen hingewiesen:

> „Die weiteren Bedingungen [...] für die Verdoppelungen des dir. Obj hängen in starkem Maße von den grammatischen Eigenschaften des Obj und den Gegebenheiten des Kommunikationsprozesses, insbesonders von Kontextbeziehungen, ab. Sie äußern sich vor allem in dem engen Zusammenhang zwischen der Objektsverdoppelung und der Thema-Rhema-Gliederung und den damit verbundenen Akzentregularitäten" (cf. dazu auch *Akademia e Shkencave e Shqipërisë* 2002: 259–260).

In den Diskurs neu eingeführt, wird das Direkte Objekt, unabhängig von seiner referenziellen Semantik, nicht vorweggenommen. Wird der Referent hingegen im weiteren Diskurs thematisiert, wird er klitisiert:

alb. *Kurr u err, na kthehen të shtatë xhuxhat. Kur Bardhabora i pa të shtatë xhuxhat, u tremb shumë* („Als es dunkel wurde, kehrten die sieben Zwerge zurück. Als Schneewittchen die sieben Zwerge erblickte, erschrak sie sehr'; BUCHHOLZ/FIEDLER 1987: 442).

alb. *Kaprolli hovi jashtë i gëzuar. Kur e panë mbreti me trimat e tij këtë kapruall të bukur donin ta zinin* („Der Rehbock sprang fröhlich hinaus. Als der König und sein Gefolge diesen schönen Rehbock sahen, wollten sie ihn fangen'; BUCH-HOLZ/FIEDLER 1987: 441).

alb. *Ditë për ditë peshkatari merrte grepin, shkonte në breg, e hidhte grepin në det, dhe priste* („Tag für Tag nahm der Fischer die Angel, ging zum Ufer, warf die Angel ins Meer und wartete'; BUCHHOLZ/FIEDLER 1987: 441) vs. rum. *În fie-care zi pescarul lua undiţa, se ducea la mal, Ø arunca undiţa în mare şi aştepta.*

alb. *Sot bleva një qilim të bukur* („Heute habe ich einen schönen Teppich gekauft'; BUCHHOLZ/FIEDLER 1987: 443).

alb. *Atje shesin një roman të ri të Kadaresë* („Dort verkauft man einen neuen Ro-man von Kadare'; BUCHHOLZ/FIEDLER 1987: 443).

alb. *Ai është hero aktiv, që muk pret të çlirohet nga të tjerët, por hidhet në aksione ... Kënga e partizanit të vogël i shpreh mirë këto ide* („Er ist ein aktiver Held, der nicht wartet, bis er von anderen befreit wird, sondern er geht zu Taten über ... Das Lied vom kleinen Partisanen drückt diese Gedanken recht gut aus'; BUCHHOLZ/FIEDLER 1987: 441).

alb. *Ju do t'i gjeni çdo ditë dhomat dhe krevatet të rregulluara* („Sie werden die Zimmer und Betten täglich gemacht vorfinden' (HETZER/FINGER 2006: 33).
    Cf. rum. *Veţi găsi în fiecare zi camerele şi paturile făcute.*
    Cf. span. *Van a encontrar las habitaciones y camas hechas todos los días.*
→ Bei Weiterführung des DO: alb. Klitikum + $Ø_2$ + Lebewesen / Gegenstand / Abstraktum
→ Bei Neueinführung des DO: alb. $Ø_1$ + $Ø_2$ + Lebewesen /Gegenstand / Abstrak-tum

Das Direkte Objekt wird auch dann vorweggenommen, wenn es für den/die Em-pfänger als *situativ präsent*, also bekannt, vorausgesetzt werden kann (BUCHHOLZ/FIEDLER 1987: 442–443):

alb. *Mbylle dritaren!* („Mach das Fenster (doch) zu'; BUCHHOLZ/FIEDLER 1987: 442).

alb. *Tani mund t'i hapni fletoret* („Jetzt könnt ihr die Hefte aufschlagen'; BUCH-HOLZ/FIEDLER 1987: 442).

Mit der Referenz auf <bestimmt/bekannt> bzw. <unbekannt/nicht identifiziert> er-klärt sich auch die Setzung des Klitikums im ersten Beispiel und seine Auslassung im zweiten albanischen Beispiel:

alb. *Sot ia* [= i+i] *tregova mysafirit* („Heute habe ich ihm [dem Gast] es/sie [**das** neue Museum/alle Sehenswürdigkeiten] gezeigt') vs. alb. *Desha t'i tregoj* („Ich wollte es [ein neues Museum/einige Sehenswürdigkeiten] ihm [dem Gast] zei-gen'; BUCHHOLZ/FIEDLER 1987: 445).

BUCHHOLZ/FIEDLER geben aber noch eine weitere pragmasemantische Funktion der Weglassung des Klitikums an, nämlich der Emphase und/oder des Kontrasts (1987: 443):

alb. *Nëna i dha Agimit një mollë e një dardhë, por djali hëngri vetëm mollën* (‚Die Mutter gab Agim einen Apfel und eine Birne, aber der Junge aß nur den Apfel'; BUCHHOLZ/FIEDLER 1987: 443–444).

alb. *Ne kishim pritur Agimin dhe jo Skënderin* (‚Wir hatten Agim und nicht Skënder erwartet'; BUCHHOLZ/FIEDLER 1987: 444).

Kasusdesinenz des Direkten Objekts (Singular) im Albanischen

Anders als im Rumänischen und Spanischen, beides Sprachen, die ihre nominale Flexion schon stärker abgebaut haben als das Albanische, verfügt das Albanische für die bestimmte Form des Nominativs und Akkusativs über eine noch deutliche differenzierte Kasusdesinenz (cf. die Opposition Ø vs. *-n* für Maskulin und Femi-nin in *një gjysh* ‚ein Großvater', *gjyshe* ‚eine Großmutter' und *gjyshin* ‚den Großvater' sowie *gjyshen* ‚die Großmutter'). Die morphologische Kennzeichnung des Akkusativs ist unabhängig von der Semantik des jeweiligen Direkten Objekts.

alb. *Te kjo pikë, anketuesit […] e ndërprisnin pianisten, për t'i thënë […]* (KADA-RE 2009: 28) vs. span. *los investidagores … [zero] interrumpían a la pianista para decirle …* (‚An diesem Punkt … unterbrachen die Untersucher die Pianis-tin …'; KADARE 2009: 27).

alb. *Fëmija i do shumë gjyshin dhe gjyshen* (‚Das Kind liebt seine Großeltern sehr').

alb. *Dhelpra e mashtroi ariun* (‚Der Fuchs hat den Bären getäuscht').

alb. *Lefteri nxori shaminë e fshiu fytyrën* (‚Lefter zog das Taschentuch heraus und wischte sich das Gesicht ab'; BUCHHOLZ/FIEDLER 1987: 443).

alb. *… ata e kishin lënë taksinë …* (‚sie hatten das Taxi verlassen'; KADARE 2009: 19) vs. span. *… los otros habían abandonado el taxi* (KADARE 2009: 14).

alb. *Më mirë marrim autobusin* (‚Besser wir nehmen den Autobus', HETZER/FIN-GER 2006: 76).

alb. *E bija e mbretit u gëzua shumë, kur e pa lodrën e dashur* (‚Die Königstochter freute sich sehr, als sie ihr Lieblingsspielzeug sah'; BUCHHOLZ/FIEDLER 1987: 441).

alb. *Kolombi zbuloi Amerikën!* (‚Kolumbus entdeckte Amerika'; BUCHHOLZ/FIED-LER 1987: 443).

alb. *… pasi i jepte adresën e hotelit* (‚nachdem er ihr die Adresse des Hotels hinterlassen hatte'; KADARE 2009: 25).

alb. ... *arkivisti nuk e kishte fshehur dot habinë* ('der Archivist konnte seine Überraschung nicht verbergen'; KADARE 2009: 22) vs. span. ... *el encargado de los archivos no pudo ocultar su sorpresa* (KADARE 2009: 18–19).

alb. ... *një raport mjekësor e jepte gjendjen psikike të tjetrit, krejtësisht normale* (KADARE 2009: 22) vs. span. ... *un informe médico calificaba el estado psíquico del conductor como enteramente normal* ('ein ärztlicher Bericht attestierte den psychischen Zustand des Fahrers als vollständig normal'; KADARE 2009: 18).

alb. „... *po aq herë nervozizmi yt mizor ma* [Fall von Krasis: *më + e > ma*) *ka helmuar jetën*" (KADARE 2009: 26) vs. span. „... *tantas otras veces tu sañuda irritabilidad me ha envenenado la existencia.*" ('so viele andere Male hat mir deine wutentbrannte Reizbarkeit das Leben vergiftet'; KADARE 2009: 24).

alb. ... *hetuesi i* [= dem Taxifahrer] *kishte bërë pyetjen kurth se ç'kishte ndodhur me udhëtarët pas përplasjes në tokë* ('... der Richter stellte dem Taxifahrer eine Fangfrage darüber, was denn mit den Reisenden geschehen wäre, nachdem sie in den Hang gestürzt waren'; KADARE 2009: 19) vs. span. ... *el juez le hizo una pregunta trampa sobre lo que había sucedido con los viajeros tras la caída por el barranco* (KADARE 2009: 14).

alb. ... *kjo fraza e fundit ... i kishte bërë zbuluesit shqiptarë të besonin* [zu glauben] *se kishin gjetur kyçin për shpjegimin ...* (KADARE 2009: 26) vs. span. ... *esta última frase ... empujó a los agentes albaneses a creer que habían encontrado la clave para explicar ...* ('Dieser letzte Satz ... veranlasste die albanischen Ermittler zu glauben, dass sie den Schlüssel zur Erklärung ... gefunden hätten ...'; KADARE 2009: 24).

alb. *Dalja në skenë e pianistes Liza Blumberg, mikeshë e Rovenës, kishte kthyer dyshimin e vrasjes* (KADARE 2009: 27) vs. span. *La salida a escena de la pianista Liza Blumberg, amiga de Rovena, resucitó la sospecha de asesinato* ('Das Erscheinen der Pianistin Liza Blumber, Freundin von Rovena, erweckte den Verdacht des Mordes'; KADARE 2009: 26).

→ alb. <Klitikum oder Ø₁> + Ø₂ + Person / Lebewesen / Gegenstand / Abstraktum im Singular mit Akkusativdesinenz>

Verweist das Direkte Objekt auf einen Referenten im Plural, kann dieser nur durch den Artikel ausgedrückt werden:

alb. *Ne po presim shokët* ('Wir erwarten die Freunde'; HETZER/FINGER 2006: 82).

alb. *Pjesëmarrësit kritikuan ata të kryesisë* ('Die Teilnehmer kritisierten die vom Vorstand'; BUCHHOLZ/FIEDLER 1987: 443).

alb. ... *kjo fraza e fundit ... i kishte bërë zbuluesit shqiptarë të besonin* [zu glauben] *se kishin gjetur kyçin për shpjegimin ...* (KADARE 2009: 26) vs. span. ... *esta última frase ... empujó a los agentes albaneses a creer que habían encontrado la clave para explicar ...* ('Dieser letzte Satz ... veranlasste die albanischen Ermitt-

ler zu glauben, dass sie den Schlüssel zur Erklärung ... gefunden hätten ...'; KA-
DARE 2009: 24).

→ alb. <Klitikum oder $\emptyset_1$> + $\emptyset_2$ + Person im Plural + Direktes Objekt mit
bestimmten Artikel>

Präpositionelle Markierung des Direkten Objekts (<Person/Lebewesen>, Singular und Plural) im Rumänischen

Im Rumänischen und Spanischen, welche nicht mehr über eine Nominativ von
Akkusativ unterscheidende Flexion verfügt, werden für Referenten, welche die
Semanteme [+ belebt] und [+ identifiziert/individualisiert] die Präposition *pe* (cf.
GLR 2005, II: 383) bzw. die spanische Präposition *a* gesetzt, Konstruktionen, die
es im Albanischen gar nicht gibt. Bei neutraler Wortordnung wird im Rumänischen
und Spanischen die präpositionelle Konstruktion außerdem tendenziell in Kombination mit Klitika verwendet:

rum. *Vi-l prezint pe domnul inginer Argeşeanu* (‚Ich stelle Euch/Ihnen Herrn
Ingenieur *Argeşeanu* vor') vs. alb. *Ju prezantoj zotin inxhinier.*

rum. *L-am văzut pe fratele tău* (‚Ich habe deinen Bruder gesehen') vs. alb. *Kam
parë vëllanë tënd.*

rum. *Le aştept pe fete la şcoală* (‚Ich erwarte [die] Mädchen bei der Schule').

rum. *Îl întrebăm pe un medic* (‚Wir fragen einen [bestimmten] Arzt') vs. alb. *Të
pyesim një mjek.*

rum. *Şi Emil o aduce pe Miţi, pisica lui* (‚Auch Emil bringt Miţi, seine Katze, mit')
vs. alb. *Dhe Emili sjell Micin, macen e tij.*

span. *... Podía concebirse que uno de ellos intentara besar al otro ...?* (‚Konnte
man sich vorstellen, dass einer der beiden den Anderen zu küssen versuchte
...?'; KADARE 2009: 17).

Auffälligste Tendenzen der Direkten Objektgestaltung im Albanischen, Rumänischen und Spanischen

In der rumänischen und spanischen Standardsprache „dirigiert" das DO als stärks-
ter Auslöser die referenzielle Semantik. Dabei scheinen die Seme <+ Person /
Lebewesen / personifiziert>, <+ bestimmt> und <+ identifiziert> die Oberflächenstruktur <Klitikum + Präposition + DO> zu induzieren. Sehr fest erscheint im
Rumänischen die noch standardsprachliche Kombination pronominaler mit präpo-
sitionaler Markierung. Allerdings wird mit abnehmender Semantik der Kategorien
<+ Person, + personifiziert, + identifiziert> diese Struktur aufgebrochen bzw. mit
der Setzung der Präposition (aber nicht auch des Klitikums) nur teilrealisiert. Diese
Tendenz der Weglassung des pronominalen und/oder präpositionalen Morphems
spiegelt sich übrigens auch in der rumänischen Umgangssprache wider. Auch im
pronominal ausgedrückten Direkten Objekt scheint die Semantik die Konstruktion

zu dirigieren. Die Präpositionen rum. *pe* und span. *a* werden dabei über semantische Kriterien hinaus als syntaktische Marker für den Akkusativ gesetzt.

rum. *L-am văzut pe fratele tău* vs. alb. *Kam parë vëllanë tënd* („Ich habe deinen Bruder gesehen‘).

rum. *Chem pe tata* („ich rufe den Vater‘).

rum. *Și Emil o aduce pe Miți, pisica lui* („Auch Emil bringt Miți, seine Katze, mit‘) vs. alb. *Dhe Emili sjell Micin, macen e tij.*

rum. *Vulpea (l)-a păcălit pe urs* („der Fuchs hat den Bären getäuscht‘) vs. alb. *Dhelpra e mashtroi ariun.*

rum. *Mângâie câinele* („Er streichelt den Hund‘).

rum. *A trebuit să plimb prin țară un cuplu de prieteni din America* (PLEȘU, *descripțio moldaviae*).

rum. *Caut profesor de germană* („Ich suche einen Deutschlehrer‘), *Căutăm informatician* („Wir suchen einen Informatiker‘), *Primește studenți în gazdă* („Er nimmt Studierende auf‘; Beispiele aus GLR 2005, II: 376).

alb. *Nuk pashë njeri* („Ich habe keinen/niemanden gesehen‘; BUCHHOLZ/FIEDLER 1987: 444).

alb. *Nuk gjeti asgjë* („Er hat gar nichts gefunden‘; BUCHHOLZ/FIEDLER 1987: 444).

alb. *Në shkollë nuk gjeti asnjeri* („In der Schule traf er niemanden an‘; BUCHHOLZ/FIEDLER 1987: 444).

rum. *Nu văd pe nimeni* („Ich sehe niemanden‘).

span. *No he visto a nadie* („Ich sehe niemanden‘).

In allen drei Sprachen erscheint die syntaktische Markierung durch obligate Klitisierung im Albanischen und durch obligate Klitisierung oder Präpositionssetzung mit Klitisierung im Rumänischen und Spanischen als sehr häufige Regularität, unabhängig von der referenziellen Semantik des Direkten Objekts bei Inversion der normalen Satzgliederordnung:

alb. *Marinë e ftojnë të gjithë* („Alle laden Maria gerne ein‘).

alb. *Gjithë ditën e kalonte pranë vatrës* („Den ganzen Tag verbrachte er an der Feuerstelle‘; BUCHHOLZ/FIEDLER 1987: 440).

alb. *Portën e oborrit mos e hap* („Die Hoftür mach nicht auf!‘; BUCHHOLZ/FIEDLER 1987: 441).

alb. *Një reaksion të tillë nuk e kishte pritur kurrë* („Eine solche Reaktion hatte er nicht erwartet‘; BUCHHOLZ/FIEDLER 1987: 442).

rum. *Luchian-ul l-am vândut* („[Das Bild von] Luchian habe ich verkauft‘).

rum. *Pe păpușă o iubește mult* („Die Puppe liebt sie sehr‘).

rum. *Am cumpărat un creion. Pe al meu l-am pierdut* („Ich habe einen Bleistift gekauft. Meinen habe ich verloren‘).

span. *A alguno de vosotros os quisiera ver yo en un buen fregado* („Einen von euch würde ich gerne in einem wirklichen Schlamassel sehen'; BUTT/BENJAMIN 1989: 11.14.1.).

span. *Lo que dice ... jamás lo consentiría nadie de los dirigentes ...* („Zu dem, was er sagt, hätte keiner von den Direktoren je zugestimmt'; BUTT/BENJAMIN 1989: 11.14.1.).

Während das Albanische das Direkte Objekt <Singular, bestimmt> (noch) durch eine Akkusativ-Kasus-Endung markieren kann, „kompensieren" hier das Rumänische und Spanische mit den Präpositionen rum. *pe*, span. *a*, die als syntaktische Marker für das Direkte Objekt (im Gegensatz zum Nominativ) auftreten. Über eine präpositionale Gestaltung verfügt das Albanische gar nicht:

rum. *L-am văzut pe fratele tău* („Ich habe deinen Bruder gesehen'). Vs. alb. *Kam parë vëllanë tënd.*

Während im Rumänischen und Spanischen die Klitisierung oder Präposition + Klitisierung durch Semantik und Syntax ausgelöst werden, hat das kataphorische Klitikum im Albanischen eine von jeder Semantik unabhängige transphrastische Funktion, welche ein im Diskurs eingeführtes Objekt als <neu> anzeigt – und zwar durch Nichtmarkierung –, hingegen dessen weitere Thematisierung pronominal markiert. Somit ist der Unterschied zum Rumänischen und Spanischen ein zweifacher: der Auslöser ist nicht semantisch sondern informationsordnend. Zweitens wird das Neue Element durch Nullmorphem, Bekanntes hingegen pronominal gekennzeichnet:

alb. *Thirra babain* („Ich lud meinen Vater ein' vs. rum. *L-am chemat pe tata*).

alb. *Sillmë pe, gërshërë dhe gjilpërë!* („Bring mir Faden, Schere und Nadel'; BUCHHOLZ/FIEDLER 1987: 435).

alb. *Unë e thirrisja shpesh babain për darkë* („Ich lud meinen Vater oft zum Abendessen ein').

alb. *Atëherë po e dredh dhe unë një cigare* („Dann drehe auch ich mir eine Zigarette'; BUCHHOLZ/FIEDLER 1987: 442).

alb. *Ky libër përmban këngë popullore* („Dieses Buch enthält Volkslieder'; BUCH-HOLZ/FIEDLER 1987: 435).

alb. *Do ta kesh një hall* („Du wirst schon ein Problem haben'; BUCHHOLZ/FIEDLER 1987: 442) vs. rum. *Vei avea o problemă.* / span. *Vas a tener un problema.*

Rumänisch und Spanisch zeigen sich an seiner Strukturoberfläche durch eine reichere morphologische Variation (gleicher Bedeutung) als dynamischer, Al-banisch ist stärker fixiert:

rum. *Am invitat pe copii la masă.* / *Am invitat copiii la masă* („Ich habe die Kinder zum Essen eingeladen') vs. alb. *Ftova fëmijët në tryezë.*

rum. *Aşteptăm profesorul la oră.* / *Aşteptăm pe profesor la oră* („Wir erwarten den Professor zur [Unterrichts-]Stunde') vs. alb. *Po presim profesorin.*

rum. *L-am pe prieten [aşteptându-mă] acasă.* *Am prietenul [aşteptându-mă] acasă* („Ich habe den Freund auf mich wartend zuhause').

span. *Tengo mi amigo [esperándome] en casa.* *(Lo) tengo a mi amigo [esperándome] en casa* vs. alb. *Në shtëpi kam shokun.* / *Shokun e kam në shtëpi* („Ich habe den Freund auf mich wartend zuhause').

Die unterschiedliche Objektgestaltung durch Setzung oder Nicht-Setzung des kataphorischen, vorausweisenden Klitikums kann sowohl im Rumänischen als auch Albanischen Unterschiede und Nuancen in der Bedeutung zum Ausdruck bringen. Während aber das Rumänische die Identifizierung einer Person in den Fokus rückt, markiert der Albanischsprechende nullmorphematisch die neue Information im Diskurs und betont, was er als besonders <neu>, <unbekannt>, <unerwartet> empfindet:

rum. *Ai mai văzut pe vreunul?* („Hast Du schon irgendeinen [von mehreren, nicht bestimmten] gesehen?') vs. *Ai mai văzut vreunul ca el* („Hast du schon jemals [so] einen gesehen [wie diesen]')?

alb. *Nëna i dha Agimit një mollë e një dardhë, por djali hëngri vetëm mollën* („Die Mutter gab Agim einen Apfel und eine Birne, aber der Junge aß nur den Apfel'; BUCHHOLZ/FIEDLER 1987: 443–444).

alb. *Unë pi cigare më filtër* („Ich rauche Zigaretten mit Filter'; HETZER/FINGER 2006: 56).

Bibliographie

Academia Republicii Socialiste România (1966): *Gramatica limbii române,* vol. 1. Bucureşti: Editura Academiei Republicii Socialiste România.

Akademia e Shkencave e Shqipërisë (2002): *Gramatika e gjuhës shqipe* [Grammatik der albanischen Sprache], vol. 1–2. Tiranë.

BUCHHOLZ, Oda; FIEDLER, Wilfried (1987): *Albanische Grammatik.* Leipzig: VEB Verlag Enzyklopädie.

BUTT, John; BENJAMIN, Carmen (1989): *A New Grammar of Modern Spanisch.* London: Edward Arnold.

DEMIRAJ, Shaban (1986): *Gramatikë historike e gjuhës shqipe* [Historische Grammatik der albanischen Sprache]. Tiranë: Shtëpia Botuese "8 Nëntori".

FRÂNCU, Constantin (2009): *Gramatica limbii române vechi (1521–1780).* Iaşi: Casa Editorială Demurg.

GLR 2005 = Academia Română: *Gramatică Limbii Române,* I–II. Bucureşti: Editura Academiei Române.

HETZER, Armin; FINGER, Zuzana (2006): *Lehrbuch der vereinheitlichten albanischen Schriftsprache.* Hamburg: Helmut Buske.

KADARE, Ismail (2009): *Aksidenti* in: *Vepra*, Vëllimi i shtatëmbëdhjetë [Gesamtwerk, Band 17]. Tiranë: Onufri.

KADARE, Ismail (2009): *El accidente*. Madrid: Alianza.

LIBERACKA, Kamila (2009): Reduplioni i kundrinorit në gjuhën shqipe [Die Reduplikation des Objekts in der albanischen Sprache]. In: *Gjurmime Albanologjike. Seria e shkencave filologjike* 38 (2008). Prishtinë: Shtypshkronja KGT.

PANĂ DINDELEGAN, Gabriela (2003): *Elemente de gramatică. Dificultăți, controverse, noi interpretări*. București: Humanitas.

PLEȘU, Andrei (2006): *Comèdii la porțile Orientului*. București: Humanitas.

Real Academia Española (2009): *Nueva gramática de la lengua española. Morfología. Sintaxis* I. Madrid.

SCHMITT, Christian (1987): Die Ausbildung des Artikels in der Romania. In: W. Dahmen, G. Holtus, J. Kramer, M. Metzeltin (Hrsg.): *Latein und Romanisch*. Tübingen: Gunter Narr (= Romanistisches Kolloquium I). 94–125.

Balkanisms in Modern Romanian[1]

Ingmar SÖHRMAN (Göteborg)

Are there any balkanisms in modern Romanian? It is not so easy to answer this apparently simple question. First of all, we need to define what we actually mean by the concept like *balkanism*? It is based on the idea of a Balkan *Sprachbund*, which in itself needs to be discussed. The very definition of the Balkan Sprachbund is attributed to TRUBETZKOJ (1923) and a few years later the idea was further developed by SANDFELD (1926/1930) who also created the label *Balkan linguistics* in his book on Balkan philology. WEIGAND (1925) also discussed the idea during the same period.

The idea that there were linguistic similarities between the languages spoken in South-East Europe was not new. It was a phenomenon already under discussion by linguists in the 19th century, KOPITAR (1829), SCHLEICHER (1850) and MIKLOSICH (1861). Schleicher seems to have been the first to introduce the notion of *areal linguistics*, focusing on the relationships between languages in the same geophysical environment. It is evident that the languages in question are related "genetically" as they are all Indo-European, but non-Indo-European languages like Hungarian and more specifically Turkish – and through Turkish also Arabic – also enter in the picture.

It has to be stressed that the very borrowing process often goes through several steps, and it is all too easy to just say that words like Rom., Bulg. and Serb. *mahala*, '(poor) block/neighborhood'.[2] Alb. *mahaljë* and Greek μαχαλᾶς all come from Arabic *mahalle* (cf. CIORĂNESCU 2002 [1954–66]: 484), although the most probable explanation is that it has first been borrowed into Turkish in an identical form, *mahalle*, and then from Turkish to the Balkan languages.

Let us go back to the very notion of *Sprachbund*. It indicates a common set of grammatical and lexical features due to a geophysical but not (necessarily) linguistic closeness. It constitutes a broader range of common features than ordinary linguistic influence, including categories that are normally more closed to foreign influence like phonology and morphology, while lexicon and syntax are generally

---

1   I would like to thank Dr. Antoaneta Granberg and Dr. Xhelal Ylli for fruitful and helpful discussions on this topic and I am in great debt to Dr. Larry Watts for taking the time to revise the language and suggest some pertinent improvements to this article.
2   It could also mean 'my home', 'my neighborhood' with an emotionally positive in tension.

more open and thereby easily "contaminated" by other languages. The idea of Sprachbund has later been questioned and extended to *Eurolinguistics* by linguists like Małeck and Reiter (cf. STEINKE 2005, 2008).

The Balkan characteristics of Romanian cover all four categories, but as we will see the so called closed ones (phonology and morphology) do not admit new Balkanisms. Neither do the open ones (syntax and vocabulary) or at least they rarely do so nowadays, since modern influences come from elsewhere – mainly from the Anglo-Saxon world.

Given these considerations then, how should we define *balkanism?* A preliminary definition of balkanism could be the following:

A linguistic trait or lexeme that is shared by at least three, not closely related, languages spoken in the Balkans and that is not an international borrowing or a universal phenomenon.

In order to make this definition work we first have to consider what "closely related" means, deciding, for instance, that this holds true for the relationship between Bulgarian and Macedonian or between Bosnian – Croatian – Serbian and even more so for Romanian and Moldavian where the difference is almost entirely political or ideological and not linguistic.

Secondly, we also have to view the Balkans in a linguistic, cultural and historical context (SVANBERG/SÖHRMAN 1996: 11–12) and say that, in these respects, the Balkans are Slovenia, Croatia, Serbia, Romania, Moldova and the countries southwards.

Thirdly, it is worth considering why three languages are stipulated. This seems to be a reasonable, but not always necessary, number to say that a phenomenon or lexeme is reasonably spread so that it could be considered 'general' in the Balkans but not elsewhere. Thus the existence of Turkish *kalabalık* 'crowd' in Romanian and Swedish has its historical explanation[3] but does not mean that this is a generalized lexeme, nor are all the French loanwords that were borrowed in the 19th century. They were the result of a re-romanizing process pursued by the Transylvanian School, *Şcoala ardeleană*, in order to link Romanian more clearly to the rest of the Romance languages and further re-differentiate it from its Slavic neighbors. However, it has to be born in mind that during centuries Slavic languages had contributed to the development of the Romanian vocabulary during the Middle Ages after the Roman military retreat, and words of Slavic origin constituted (and still constitutes) an important part of the Romanian lexicon.

---

3 The Swedish king Charles XII spent time in Bender after being defeated by Tsar Peter in 1709, and the Swedish troops seem to have picked up the word since it was used for a minor conflict with the Ottoman sultan.

On the other hand, we find Arabic loanwords in many Balkan languages that sometimes coincide with Spanish words, and this is, of course, a consequence of the long Muslim dominance of large parts of the Iberian Peninsula. Thus, we find words like Albanian and Bulgarian *filan* 'such, one and another' and Spanish *fulano* 'so-and-so' < Arab. *fulan* 'such' (MLADENOV 1941: 661; COROMINAS 1954: 590–591). This does not include Spanish in the Balkan Sprachbund, but the word *filan* could be seen as a Balkan lexeme although it appears only in two languages since they are only remotely related.

Having established these definitions we can take a closer look at Romanian and ask the vital question: What characterizes Romanian as a Balkan language?

Here I will just give a few examples in order to be able to discuss, later on, the question of whether there are any balkanisms in Modern Romanian. Let us take the four categories that we have discussed earlier:

Phonology:
- Close, central, unrounded vowel *â* [ɨ], earlier orthographically represented by *î*, *ô* like in *când* < Lat. *quando* 'when', *gând*, earlier written *gônd* < Hung. *gond* which has changed its meaning to 'disturbing thought, trouble' (modern *gondolat* 'thought' < *gondola* 'think') and *sfânt* 'saint, holy' < Slav. *svętŭ*.
- Schwa, i.e. the stressed, mid, unrounded vowel *ă* [ə] like *război* 'war' (< Slav. *razboi/boi*). This stressed schwa is possibly the result of Slavic influence f. ex. Bulg. *ръб* 'edge; seam', but on the other hand we find this sound in Alb. *kënga* 'the song'. There does exist an unstressed schwa in other Romance languages, like French *cela* [səl'a] 'this', but this vowel is never stressed in any other Romance language. It could well be seen as Slavic-influenced change of usage, but not necessarily as an introduction of a new sound, since it already existed in Romanian.

Morphology:
- Postponed def. art. *trenul* 'the train', *regele* 'the king' – cf. Alb. *mbretu*, Bulg. *kraljat*.
- Genitive article *un om iubitor **al** cărţilor* 'a bookloving man' (SÖHRMAN 2005).
- Possibly the disappearance of pluperfect in spoken Romanian (SÖHRMAN 2009). *Dormisem* 'I had slept' < Lat. pluperfect subjunctive *dormivissem* which in modern spoken and colloquial written language is substituted by perfect *am dormit*.
- There is no synthetic future tense but four periphrastic ones (HALVORSEN 1973).
- The adverbs coincide with the adjectives and do not use the *-ment(e)* suffix, a phenomenon that we also find in Jewish Spanish in the Balkans.

Syntax:
- Keeping the tense of the direct discourse also in indirect discourse. This is supposedly Slavic influence, but it is still the subject of debate.
- Rare use of infinitives (mainly only *putea* 'can'). The infinitives were replaced by subordinate clauses like in *Vreau să cânt* 'I want that I sing' (I want to sing).

Vocabulary:
- There are Turkish words just as in the other Balkan languages like Turk. *dolap* '(built-in) cupboard' > Alb. *dolap*, Bulg. *долап*, Greek. *ντουλάπι*, Rom. *dulap*, Serb. *dolap/долап*. There are also strange examples like Italian loanwords into Turkish that have come back as Balkanisms: It. *timone* 'rudder; helm' > Turk *dümen* > Alb. *dümen*, Bulg *дюмен*, Serb. *dumen*.

N.B. there are evidently also Greek, Slavic and Albanian influences, but we will not concern ourselves with them here. Moreover, there are also Hungarian and German loan-words and in the XIXth century an important and very conscious re-romanizing introduction of French words that changed the Romanian vocabulary considerably while, in the late XXth century, English becomes the most important loan-giver, just as it does in the rest of the world. Sometimes this linguistic cleansing did not lead to the disappearing of a lexeme but to semantic change that restricted the meaning of the Slavic loan-word, since it mainly concerned these. An example is *nevastă* 'wife' that for some time came to mean 'Slavic wife' and was ironically substituted by *soție* < possibly (but very uncertain) also Slavic *šutŭ* 'jester' (CIORĂNESCU 2002: 732).

Could we then still consider Romanian as a Balkan language? KRISTOPHSON (this volume) discusses how complex and problematic this question is and that it is actually impossible to proclaim a definitive YES or NO to it. At the same time, however, he concludes that the "suspicion" of Romanian's "balkanity" can be by no means disregarded, and his main question as to whether this linguistic notion of *Balkansprachen* as eternally valid is absolutely correct. I would thus suggest that *Balkansprachen* is a typological construct, and that this as well as any other historical feature has its temporal limits. Today, for example, it appears more appropriate to consider *Balkanism* a historical reality rather than a contemporary phenomenon. Although it still exists and it continues to be valid it is no longer productive any more – or at least it is productive only in very rare cases.

However, the Balkan Sprachbund is not a linguistic isolate. As everywhere else, there is a constant, mostly lexical, immigration into Romanian, now mainly from English as in *barwoman*. This has also led to the introduction of, although not necessarily immediate, substitution of Romanian expressions, "foreign" patterns and words, for instance, *Locuri de munca în Suedia* being substituted by *joburi în Suedia* 'jobs in Sweden' (all examples cited here are taken from *Evenimente zilei online*, Sept. 1ˢᵗ 2010). The last two examples are taken from the very same page, and it has to be said that this last is an example with synonymous expressions probably chosen to avoid a repetition of words, and possibly this gives a shorter and "cooler" final impression – or this, at least, seems to be the author's intention.

When new phenomena need new words, from where are we to get them? English is currently the main source but it is not the only one. Spanish, Arabic and Chinese have been contributing to the international vocabulary. In Romanian phenomena like *street dance* exist but often vernacular varieties may appear, just as it has in this specific case, *dans urban*. It is interesting to note that there also exists what appears to be a general tendency to create an autochthone word as in the case above, while in other instances, certain concepts are preferred since they are from English (or any foreign source) in order to lend an international or 'cooler' flavor to the text as in the case of *vacanțe **all inclusive*** which could have been written *inclusive tot* (or *toate cheltuielile* 'all costs'). This phenomenon seems to be especially frequent in advertisements.

The reason for importing loan-words can be various: semantic gaps, foreign origin and thus a fancy or 'more sophisticated' linguistic flavor, etc. Mostly, these new loan-words adapt (or perish) like in *un rugbist al naționalei de junior* 'a rugby player from the national junior team' (*Adevărul online* Sept 1ˢᵗ 2010). Given that so many complain nowadays about the English influence on modern languages, it is worth pointing out that English does not appear to be more influential than French was in the XIXᵗʰ century in Romania, despite the fact that everything is shared so quickly now with modern communication possibilities (internet, SMS etc.). We still find many French words in Romanian like *șoferul* < Fr. *chauffeur*, 'driver', *deranja* < Fr. *déranger* 'disturb' etc. There are even combinations of loan-words like in the phrase *Guvernul vrea să incurajeze angajările de tip part-time* 'the government wants to encourage the promotion of part-time jobs', where we find *angajările* and *tip* < Fr. *engager* and *type* as well as the English expression *part-time*, but old words die slowly. For example, the Slavic word *vreme* (< Slav. *vreme*) still seems to be more used than *timp* (< Fr. *temps* < Lat. *tempus*) with the exception of idioms like *tot timpul* 'all the time'.

All of this seems to indicate that there are no new balkanisms created. However, I have found what could be a possible new balkanism in the shortening of the words for the numerals 11–19. The basic numeral construction is based on the Slavic model "one-to-ten" = eleven. In Romanian 'eleven' is *unsprezece* (*un-spre-zece* 'one-to-ten'), but this is reduced to *unșpe* in spoken Romanian where the preposition *spre* is contracted to *-șpe-* and *zece* 'ten' is lost. This should be compared to Bulgarian *edinadeset* (= *edin-na-deset* 'one-to-ten') but in spoken Bulgarian this is reduced to [edin'ajse], where 'ten' *deset* vaguely remains in the contracted form *-jse*. This is also the case in Albanian. In standard language 'eleven' is *njëmbëdhjetë* (*një-mbë-dhjetë* 'one-on-ten'), but in spoken Albanian this is reduced to *njëmet*, where *-t* is what remains of *djetë* 'ten', and this is even reduced further as the closed syllable is turned into an open one, *njëme*, when somebody is counting quickly. The preposition *mbi* 'on' appears here in an alternative parallel form *mbë*. In all three languages this is a consequent development of all the numbers from 11 to 19. What we see is a semantic transfer from a postponed number to a preposition, *spre zece* > *-şpe* [< *spre*], i.e. 'to ten' > 'to', and since this phenomenon is the same in Bulgarian (*na-deset* > *-jse*) and Albanian (*mbë-dhjetë* > *met*) there is a good possibility that what we see is a modern balkanism, one of very few recent ones. In Greek the old pattern from Classical Greek has been kept 'one-ten' ἔντεκα (or ἔνδεκα) < Old Greek ἔνδεκα (ἔν-δεκα 'one-ten'). However, it remains to be seen if this trait is really a typical Balkan phenomenon or "just" a general linguistic phenomenon.

Romanian is not less Balkan, but it seems that what has been Balkan traits remain, and instead of borrowing from French (or Russian during the early Communist period, *tovarăş* 'comrade' < Russ. *товариш*) the words come from English (mainly from the US), but no more than they do in other European countries.

Conclusion

The Balkan characteristics of Romanian remain, but there seems to be little mutual lexical (or syntactic) transfer nowadays. The preliminary definition at the beginning of this article seems to hold but it is restricted by time, i.e. as for almost all linguistic developments it only works over a limited – although quite extended – period of time. What is interesting is that there are modern phenomena that still could be regarded as new balkanisms as has been discussed. Cultural and linguistic influences continue to appear from USA and EU, i.e. mainly English, but these will not make any considerable change. Romanian keeps it status as part of the Balkan Sprachbund, but this concept is "only" a diachronic typological classification that serves its purpose and reflects a reality that now belongs to the past.

Bibliography

Adevărul online Sept 1st 2010.

CIORĂNESCU, A. (2002) [1958–59]: *Dicţionarul etimologic al limbii române*. Translated and revised by T. Şandru Mehedinţi, M. Popescu Marin. Bucharest: Saeculum.

COROMINAS, J. (1954): *Diccionario critico etimológico de la lengua castellana*, vol. II. Bern: Francke.

Evenimente zilei online, Sept. 1st 2010.

HALVORSEN, A. (1973): *Essai d'une analyse des formes dites «de futur» en roumain moderne*. Bergen: Contributions norvégiennes aux études romanes.

KOPITAR, J. K. (1829): Albanische, walachische und bulgarische Sprache. *Jahrbücher der Literatur* (Wien) 46. 59–106.

KRISTOPHSON, J. (2011): Können linguistische Ordnungsversuche, beispielsweise „Balkansprachen" auf ewig gültig bleiben? This volume.

MIKLOSICH, F. (1861): Die slavischen Elemente im Rumunischen. *Denkschriften der Kaiserlichen Akademie der Wissenschaften, Philosophisch-historische Klasse* 12. 1–70.

MLADENOV, S. (1941): *Etimologičeski i pravopisen rečnik na bălgarskija knižoven ezik.* Sofia: Christo G. Danov.

SANDFELD, K. (1930): *Linguistique balkanique* (first published in Danish in 1926). Paris.

SCHLEICHER, A. (1850): *Die Sprachen Europas.* Bonn: König.

SÖHRMAN, I. (2005): Qu'est-ce que c'est que le génitif? Perspectives roumaines et romanes. In: http://www.ruc.dk/isok/skriftserier/XVI-SRK-Pub/RIL/RIL01-Soehrman 2005.

SÖHRMAN, I. (2009): Mai-mult-ca-perfectul în limba română într-o perspectivă romană şi balcanică. In: Th. Kahl (ed.): *Das Rumänische und seine Nachbarn.* Berlin: Frank & Timme (= Forum Rumänien 2). 131–139

STEINKE, K. (2005): Małecki und die Balkanlinguistik. In M. Mołecki (ed.): *Czełowiek, uczony, organizuba.* Kraków. 201–205.

STEINKE, K. (2008): Von der Balkanlinguistik zur Eurolinguistik. *Zeitschrift für Balkanologie* 44, 1. 95–100.

SVANBERG, I.; SÖHRMAN, I. (1996): Balkan I fantasi och verklighet. In: I. Svanberg, I. Söhrman (eds.): *Balkan. Folk och länder i krig och fred.* Stockholm: Arena. 11–16.

TRUBETZKOJ, N. S. (1923): Vavilonskaja bašnja i smešenie jazykov. *Evrazijskij vremennik* 3. 107–24.

WEIGAND, G. (1925): Vorwort, zugleich Programm des Balkan-Archivs. *Balkan-Archiv* 1. V–XV.

К вопросу о структурно-семантической специфике „съм/είμαι" фразеологических конструкций в болгарском и новогреческом языках

Христина МАРКУ (Комотини, Греция)

Образования с участием глагола 'съм/είμαι' представляют исключительно объемную часть языковых конструкций в обоих языках. Основанная на уже известных в лингвистике выводах (ИВАНОВА 1981, НИЦОЛОВА 1977, 1990, PETROVA 2010 и др.), данная работа является попыткой анализа в сопоставительном плане, рассматривая языковые реализации в основном на фразеологическом материале. Фразеология предоставляет богатый иллюстративный материал, обеспечивая взгляд на широкий «срез» времени, охватывая как архаические модели, так и актуальные конструкции и инновации. Многочисленность, устойчивость и диахроническая жизненность конструкций, но и языковое своеобразие, связь с глобальными понятийными категориями, структурное разнообразие, высокая частотность употребления и актуальность моделей в языке, замечательная продуктивность на разных стилевых уровнях – это основные мотивы, которые определили выбор языкового материала из сферы фразеологии.

Наряду с другим фундаментальным и „дискуссионным" глаголом – „иметь", глагол „быть" связан с рядом проблем. Невозможно рассматривать оба глагола в отдельности, не указывая на дистрибутивные или синонимические отношения при распределении функции между ними, при определении категорийно-понятийных пространств, которые они занимают. В некоторой степени данная работа связана с исследованием А. Петровой над глаголом „иметь" в болгарском и новогреческом (см. PETROVA 2010).

Неясная природа этого глагола, нестандартность его семантики и поведения неоднократно попадали в фокус внимания лингвистов (БЕНВЕНИСТ 1974, НИЦОЛОВА 1990, СТОЯНОВ 1973). Отношение между 'имам' и 'съм' в болгарском языке изменяется и для выражения экзистенции или локации с 17-го века уже наблюдается их взаимозаменимость в рамках одной и той же фразы, но с возможной специализацией одного или другого глагола в отдельных фразах. Таким же образом нарушена доминация глагола 'είμαι' в древнегреческом по сравнению с его частотностью в новогреческом (PETROVA 2010: 128–129). Типично „балканское" наличие лексемы 'имам/έχω' как в греческом, так и в болгарском языке, не отменяет и не „облегчает" многозначность и полифункциональность глагола 'съм/είμαι'. Приводя достаточное число языковых единиц, ставим перед собой цель показать состояние равновесия между глаголами 'съм/είμαι' и 'имам/έχω'. Развитие в направлении к 'имам/έχω'-синтагмам уравновешивается в обоих языках 'съм/είμαι'-конструкциями, действующими в сфере выражения экзистенции, локативности, характеризации, поссесивности. Таким образом болгарский и новогреческий языки, находясь на перекрестке культурных пространств, оказываются в одной и той же зоне пересечения языковых тенденций.

– В староболгарском языке глагол 'съм' обладал разными значениями, продолжает он быть многозначным и в новоболгарском. В РСБКЕ отражены следующие основные значения: 1. Существовать. 2. Находиться, присутствовать. 3. Находиться в каком-нибудь состоянии. 4. Как вспомогательный глагол для образования сложных глагольных форм. 5. Как копула между субъектом и его признаком. Основная функция глагола 'съм' – заявлять экзистенцию (НСБКЕ, т. III, стр. 358, цит. по Стоянов 1973: 191).

– В ΛΚΝΕ кроме выполняемой копулативной роли, значения глагола 'είμαι' представлены как несомненные функции самостоятельного экзистенциального глагола (см. ΛΚΝΕ, стр. 422). Зарегистрированы употребления глагола 'είμαι' в разнотипных конструкциях со значениями: существовать, быть живым, существовать с определенным свойством или в определенном состоянии, принадлежать, в предложных конструкциях, где проявляет отношения синонимии с глаголами носить, происходить, присутствовать, участвовать, заниматься, включаться, происходить и т.д.

На настоящем этапе исследования и в рамках конкретного изложения нас интересует возможное сопоставлении на основе структурно-семантической классификации и синтагматические и парадигматические вариации глагола 'съм/είμαι' в болгарском и новогреческом языках. Основная цель работы: сосредоточить и классифицировать конструкции с участием глагола 'съм/είμαι', опираясь на структурно-семантические критерии, принимая во внимание как грамматический и лексический статус глагола, так и семантику конструкции.

Следует выделить две основные группы конструкций с глаголом 'съм/είμαι' в качестве структурного компонента:

I. Конструкции, в которых глагол функционирует как полнозначный самостоятельный бытийный глагол для выражения „чистой" экзистенции. Основное значение этих конструкций: наличие, существование объекта.

> *Είναι κάποια πράγματα που με ενοχλούν. – **Има** някои неща, които ме дразнят.*
> *Ήταν μερικά παρόμοια περιστατικά. – **Имаше** няколко подобни случая.*

*Είναι κάποιος; – **Има** ли някой?*
*Είναι κάτι άνθρωποι μες στις συνοικίες... – **Има** (едни) хора по кварталите...*

На приведенных выше примерах уже нетрудно констатировать асимметрию по отношению к возможностям экзистенциального употребления глагола 'быть' и преобладание позиций бытийного употребления глагола 'είμαι' в новогреческом по сравнению с болгарским, где обычный эквивалент – это глагол 'има'. При выражении общей экзистенции глаголом „иметь", детерминатор локации является факультативным, но А. Петрова обращает внимание на тот факт, что в глубинной структуре высказывания всегда присутствует ситуационная детерминированность и придает ему общее значение 'когда-то/где-то/каким-то образом что-то происходит' (PETROVA 2010: 125).

Различия в дистрибуции этих глаголов в болгарском и греческом языках можно проиллюстрировать еще на следующих примерах:

*Какво **има**? – Τι είναι;*

Но сразу обратная зависимость, восстанавливая равновесие:

*Τι έχεις; – Какво ти **е**?*

Фразеологический материал подтверждает утверждение о том, что число конструкций общей экзистенции с глаголом 'съм' в болгарском языке, где генерическая экзистенция является преимущественно сферой специализации глагола 'има', довольно ограничено

*било каквото **било** – ό, τι **ήταν**, **ήταν** ...*
*тя **беше** тая, **беше** то – **ήταν** αυτό, πάει*
*все ми **е** едно, все ми **е** тая*
*и това ми **било** ...*

В греческом языке являются широко распространенными разговорные конструкции с разнообразно нюансированным прагматическим значением, но всегда с экзистенциальной семантикой:

*Μια φορά κι έναν καιρό **ήταν** ένας βασιλιάς ... – **Имало** едно време ...*
*είναι που **είναι***
*αυτός κι αν **είναι***
*εδώ **είμαστε** (και θα δεις)*
*Αυτός **είσαι**!*
Είσαι και φαίνεσαι
*Είμαι, που να μην **ήμουν***
Είμαστε για να 'μαστε!

II. Вторая группа: конструкции, в которых глагол выполняет функции копулы. Эти связочные конструкции, построенные по модели бытийных, впе-

чатляют своей численностью, своим формальным и семантическим много-
образием.

В лингвистике является преобладающим принципиальное разграничение
копулативной и самостоятельной функции глагола 'быть'. Так, Э. Бенвенист
говорит о невозможности дать удовлетворительное определение природе и
функциям глагола 'быть' из-за диалектического сосуществования двух слов,
двух функций, двух конструкций (см. БЕНВЕНИСТ 1974). Для Н. Ивановой
глагол семантически безличен по причине высокой функциональной нагру-
женности и затухания его семантики (ИВАНОВА 1981: 60). В греческой лингвистике 'εἰμαι' также считается десемантизированным, „семантически пу-
стым" глаголом (ΜΟΥΣΤΑΚΗ 1992β: 160).

В своем сравнительном исследовании болгарской и румынской фразеологических систем, Ст. Калдиева-Захариева останавливается на основной проблеме, возникающей при рассмотрении 'съм' во фразеологии „до какой степени глагол принадлежит к собственному составу фразеологической единицы
и соответственно в каком отношении находится к структуре" (КАЛДИЕВА-
ЗАХАРИЕВА 2005: 236). Автор отмечает, что в преобладающей части фразеологизмов, участвуя как компонент, глагол 'съм' является в качестве копулы,
приписывающей какой-нибудь признак „... но и в функции копулы *съм/a fi*
при-писывает обязательно и экзистенцию, имплицирует экзистенцию" (КАЛ-
ДИЕВА-ЗАХАРИЕВА 2005: 239–242). В всех употреблениях нетрудно про-
следить „интересный внутренний симбиоз экзистенциальности и копулатив-
ности", возможную диффузию доминации от одной к другой (там же, с. 240).

В действительности разграничение функции этого глагола не всегда бес-
проблемно: существует определенная, притом оправданная тенденция искать
сходство между экзистенциалными, притяжательными и копулативными
предложениями с глаголом 'съм' (ИВАНОВА 1981: 61). Грамматическая пере-
стройка конструкций, в которых бытующий предмет получает конкретную
референцию, влечет за собою изменение функции глагола 'быть': экзистен-
циальное значение преобразуется в связочное. Но характеризация бытующего
предмета – это утверждение о существовании объектов, обладающих опреде-
ленными свойствами. Категория экзистенциальности является настолько уни-
версальной и всеобъемлющей, что попытка изолировать ее и представить как
независимую была бы неуспешна, так как она является составляющей других
категорий. Понятие экзистенции определяется как безотносительная налич-
ность объекта по отношению к познающему сознанию. С другой стороны
экзистенция – это отношение атрибута к его носителю, включение класса в
класс, отнесение объекта к какому-нибудь классу, отношение тождества
(ИВАНОВА 1981: 58).

Самая внушительная группа конструкций, в которых глагол 'быть' реализируется в копулативной функции – это конструкции характеризирующие, проявляющиеся в разнообразных семантических и формальных вариациях.

1. Структурно-семантическая модель „быть чем-нибудь", „быть кем-нибудь" со значением непосредственной характеризации субъекта. В случаях непосредственной характеризации глагол 'съм' является знаком равенства, обеспечивает отношение тождества.

Данную модель можно представить внушительным числом фразеологических единиц, репрезентирующих целый ряд вариантных структурных субмоделей:

1.1. Конструкции беспредложной связи глагола с существительным. Отражающая эти конструкции схема выглядит следующим образом: S + Vbe/Vbe + S. Семантика данных конструкций обычно возникает на основе метафоры, более или менее сложной, притом роль глагола является рещающей для метафорической трансформации существительного, которое вне конкретного сочетания не является лексикализированным как постоянная метафора (КАЛДИЕВА-ЗАХАРИЕВА 2005: 247). Так как это конструкции квалифицирующие, т.е., выражающие постоянный признак или качество субъекта, нормально глагол проявляется в презентной форме, конечно не исключены и остальные темпо-ральные планы. Дополнение – всегда неопределенное.

гроб съм – είμαι τάφος
кале съм, крепост съм, бетон съм
бомба съм – είμαι μια χαρά
Бог съм! Цар съм! – Είμαι θεός! Είμαι βασιλιάς!

Вариант с негацией:

Не е цвете! – Δεν είναι λουλούδι

1.2. Группа беспредложно связанных существительных включает и структуры с двумя существительными, вариант представлен и в болгарском, и в греческом значительным числом единиц. В этих случаях наблюдаем следующие вариации схем: S + c + S + Vbe / Vbe + S + c + S.

кожа и кости съм – είμαι πετσί και κόκαλο
είναι βίος και πολιτεία
είναι τύπος και υπογραμμός
είμαι γέννημα θρέμμα
είναι μέλι-γάλα

1.3. Для обоих языков характерными являются вариации схемы с расширенным атрибутом: P + S + Vbe / Vbe + P + S.

гола вода **съм**, *стара кримка* **съм**, *стар вълк* **съм**
кръстен дявол **съм**
тиха вода **съм** – *είμαι σιγανό ποτάμι*
голяма риба **съм** – *είμαι μεγάλο ψάρι*

К этой же группе следует отнести и широко представленные в греческом языке характеризирующие генитивные конструкции: Vbe + Sgen + S.

είναι διαβόλου κάλτσα
είναι ευχής έργον
είναι της γούνας μου μανίκι
είναι ζήτημα ζωής και θανάτου

2. Конструкция со значением „быть каким-нибудь" для выражения эмоционального, умственного или физического состояния.

2.1. Характеризация путем прямого приписывания признака, свойства: при атрибуте прилагательном (*пиян съм, болен съм, нахален съм*), эти конструкции в болгарском языке выражаются чаще всего схемой: A + Vbe + pr + S.

лек съм (в главата) – *είμαι ελαφρούτσικος*
длъжки му са ръцете – *είναι μακρύ το χέρι του*

2.2. В роли атрибута могут появиться прилагательные или наречия с соответствующими структурно-синтаксическими схемами и возможными вариациями: A + Vbe / Vbe + A, Vbe + A + pr + A, Vbe + Adv, Vbe + Adv + pr + Adv.

кьор-кютюк пиян съм – *είμαι τύφλα στο μεθύσι*
тралала съм (малко)
είμαι (πολύ) κυριλέ, είμαι καθωσπρέπει
είμαι μείον – *в минус съм*
είναι απορίας άξιον
είμαι μόνος κι έρημος

2.3. Очень продуктивна в обоих языках субмодель как с пассивной, так и с активной причастной формой в роли атрибута: P + Vbe, P + Vbe + pr + S.

είμαι αποφασισμένος, είμαι δεμένος
печен съм – *είμαι ψημένος*
вързан съм (в краката)
цапнат съм в устата
врял и кипял съм

3. Структурно-семантическая модель со значением: „быть в каком-нибудь состоянии". Необходимо отметить широкую распространенность этой модели,

вспоминая и примечание Э. Бенвениста о том, что глагол *„быть"*, собственно говоря, и есть настоящий глагол состояния, ставя акцент на состояние бытующей субстанции (БЕНВЕНИСТ 1974). Достаточно иллюстративно сравнить этикетные выражения в болгарском и греческом языке:

*Как **сте**? – Πώς **είστε**;*
*Добре **съм**. – **Είμαι** καλά.*
*Какво ти **е**? – Но: Τι έχεις;*

3.1. К этой структурной модели относятся, в первую очередь, болгарские безличные конструкции для выражения психического или физического состояния. Фразеологизмы – безличные конструкции с участием наречия (Adv + Vpron + (pr) + S) – естественно не имеют параллельных έχω-образований.

леко ми е на душата
черно ми е пред очите
свито ми е сърцето
трудно е – είναι δύσκολο
безполезно е – είναι μάταιο
естествено е – είναι φυσικό

3.2. Конструкции ситуационно-детерминированной экзистенции.
Дискусионным остается вопрос о семантическо-синтаксическом статусе локально детерминированных экзистенциальных предложений и их соотношение с копулативными предложениями глагола 'быть'. Так как экзистенциальность обычно проявляется вместе с характеризацией, посессивностью, локализацией в пространстве и времени и др., то в семантической структуре высказывания возможны и другие обязательные аргументы или второстепенные предикаты (НИЦОЛОВА 1990: 236). Соотношение локативного, экзистенциального и посессивного значений считается некоторыми лингвистами а priori языковой универсалией. Локативность подразумевает указание на нахождение явлений или предметов в «сфере влияния» актанта, присутствие или отсутствие в определенном фрагменте мира некоторых объектов (ДАВЛЕТШИНА 2008: 37). Так, по отношению к новогреческому языку, на основании анализа употреблений экзистенциальных глаголов, Р. Делверуди приходит к выводу, что локативность является первичным значением глагола 'είμαι' и большая часть 'είμαι'-конструкций являются локально детерминированными (ΔΕΛΒΕΡΟΥΔΗ 1992: 429–445).

Χιόνι και πάγος είναι στους δρόμους. – Сняг и лед е/има по улиците.
Έξω είναι σκοτάδι. – Навън е тъмно.

Во фразеологии картина представляется еще более сложной. Многие фразеологические структуры являются „привидно" локативными конструкциями типа 'кто-нибудь есть где-нибудь', с обязательно эксплицированным локативным компонентом, но с семантикой характеризации. За выраженной в поверхностной синтаксической структуре локации, на глубинном уровне скрывается предикативное предложение, где глагол проявляется в функции копулы: кто-нибудь находится в определенном состоянии, которое в данный момент его характеризирует. Так например «быть на седьмом небе» – это локативно детерминированная экзистенциальная конструкция, которая по своей семантике имплицитно равняется предикативному предложению, где глагол выступает связочной функции: «быть счастливым» (КАЛДИЕВА-ЗАХАРИЕВА 2005: 240). Из возможных вариантов структурных схем самой распространенной является схема: pr + S + Vbe / Vbe + pr + S.

на прага на лудостта съм – είμαι στα πρόθυρα της τρέλας
на седмото небе съм – είμαι στον έβδομο ουρανό
с единия крак в гроба съм – είμαι με το ένα πόδι στον τάφο
на ръба на пропастта съм – είμαι στην άκρη του γκρεμού
на кеф съм – είμαι στο κέφι
във форма съм – είμαι σε φόρμα
наред съм – είμαι εντάξει
είμαι στα χάι μου; είμαι μέσα
Εκεί που είσαι ήμουνα κι εδώ που είμαι θα 'ρθεις.

3.3. Целесообразно привести некоторые субмодели, иллюстрирующие исключительное многообразие подобных метафорически или метонимически переосмысленных, квалифицирующих структур. Это конструкции с обязательным предлогом в структуре, который ограничивает экзистенцию в конкретных локальных или темпоральных рамках, выражая таким образом разнотипную „ситуационно связанную экзистенциальность" (НИЦОЛОВА 1990: 237).

είμαι για τα πανηγύρια; είμαι για γέλια – за присмех съм
είμαι για κλάματα – за съжаление съм
за шамари съм – είμαι για σφαλιάρες
είμαι επί ξύλου κρεμάμενος
δεν είμαι από χθες – не съм от вчера
είμαι ως εδώ – до тук съм
μέχρι το λαιμό – до гуша ми е
είμαι υπό έλεγχο – под контрол съм
είμαι υπό την επιρροή – под влияние съм
είμαι εκτός εαυτού – извън себе си съм

В греческом языке существует многочисленная группа интересных с синтаксической точки зрения фразеологических оборотов, представляющие собой предложные конструкции, где атрибут стоит во множественном числе: Vbe + pr + A + Pron. Семантика всех этих единиц: определенное эмоциональное или умственное состояние, нахождение, бытование в котором предопределяет характеристику субъекта.

είμαι στις μαύρες μου, είμαι στις κακές μου
είμαστε στις αγάπες μας, είναι στα μεράκια του
είμαι στα/με τα καλά μου, στα λογικά μου

4. Конструкции с доминирующей семантикой посессивности.

К частым и особенно важным употреблениям глагола 'съм/είμαι' в функции копулы относится выражение косвенной характеризации субъекта путем обозначения принадлежности, т.е. включение категории посессивности в семантический потенциал глагола. Сема посессивности явно ощутима на примерах просторечных разговорных вопросов о возрасте:

Τίνος είσαι; Ποιανού είσαι; – Чий си /Чие дете си?

4.1. Выделяются предложные конструкции (pr + (A/P) + S + Vbe, соответственно в греческом: Vbe + pr + (A/P) + S), выражающие косвенную характеристику, выявляющуюся в посессивных отношениях. О наличии эквивалентных конструкций и в румынском языке свидетельствует Ст. Калдиева, обращая внимание именно на посессивную семантику, которую они несут: „В этих случаях глагол 'съм' вместе с предлогом становятся семантическим ядром посессивности с положительным или отрицательным знаком, что позволяет синонимизировать его с глаголом 'имам' ..." (КАЛДИЕВА-ЗАХАРИЕВА 2004: 251). Мы обязаны подчеркнуть, что у преобладающей части этих структур есть эквивалентные и более фреквентные 'имам'-конструкции.

Наличие или отсутствие объекта, его притяжание или непритяжание обеспечивает субъекту определенные свойства, качества, т.е. притяжание развивается в проистекающую из него квалификацию субъекта, обладание объектом характеризует его определенным образом. Кто-нибудь есть, существует с определенным признаком, свойством, характеристикой – с голубыми глазами, с честью, с принципами. Семантические пространства глаголов 'быть' и 'иметь' пересекаются, взаимопроникаются, диффузируют в этих конструкциях.

*човек с достойнство **е** – **има** достойнство*
***είναι** άνθρωπος με αξιοπρέπεια – **έχει** αξιοπρέπεια*
с вързани очи съм – είμαι με δεμένα μάτια
с лека ръка съм – είμαι με ελαφρύ χέρι, чаще, однако: *έχω ελαφρύ χέρι*

без душа **съм** – **нямам** *душа*
εἰμαι *δίχως/χωρίς ψυχή* – **δεν ἐχω** *ψυχή*
без мозък **съм** – **нямам** *мозък*
εἰμαι *χωρίς μυαλό* – **δεν ἐχω** *μυαλό*
без пукната пара **съм** – **нямам** *пукната пара*
εἰμαι *χωρίς φράγκο* – **δεν ἐχω** *φράγκο*

4.2. В болгарском языке выделяется типичная модель (P+ pron + V +S) с участием дательно-притяжательной местоименной формы, где местоимение сигнализирует посессивность. Причастие в роли атрибута может быть активным, но чаще всего пассивные причастные формы появляется в этой позиции. Необходимо обратить внимание на редкость формальных эквивалентов в греческом языке, в отличии от румынского, например (см. КАЛДИЕВА-ЗАХА-РИЕВА 2004: 242–244).

вързани ми са очите
така ми е (било) писано
грижа ме е, еня ме е, срам ме е
кръв ми е – *είναι αίμα μου*

Дательно-притяжательная местоименная форма выражает грамматические категории лица и числа фразеологической единицы, в то же самое время „сигнализирует и наличие притяжательности" и именно эта посессивная семантика обеспечивает основания для параллелизма между данными конструкциями и фразеологизмами с участием глагола 'иметь' (КАЛДИЕВА-ЗАХА-РИЕВА 2005: 253). Ни болгарский, ни новогреческий не сохранили притяжа-тельных конструкций с участием глагола 'быть' (3л. глагола + Dat. Posses-sivus), настолько характерных для староболгарского и древнегреческого, заменяя их синтаксическими моделями с глаголом 'имам/έχω' (СТОЯНОВ 1973: 193).

Болгарский отдает предпочтение 'съм' – конструкциям (A+/pron/+Vbe+S), но по наблюдениям А. Петровой, в греческом языке, как и в албанском, определенно доминируют и радуются широкому распространению в практике образования с глаголом 'έχω' – (Vhave +Od+/pron/+Od).

тежка ми е ръката – **είναι** *βαρύ το χέρι μου* = **έχω** *βαρύ χέρι*
голяма й е устата – **είναι** *μεγάλο το στόμα μου* = **έχω** *μεγάλο στόμα*
остър ми е езикът – **είναι** *κοφτερή η γλώσσα μου* = **έχω** *κοφτερή γλώσσα*
дните ми **са** *преброени* – **είναι** *μετρημένες οι μέρες μου*
трън ми е (в очите)

4.3. Интересной в структурном и в когнитивном плане является довольно распространенная модель в греческом языке, где за глаголом 'είμαι' следует детерминированная генитивная форма существительного, обычно абстрактной, непредметной семантики. Значительная часть этих выражений имеет свои корни в катаревусе (MACKRIDGE 1990: 123). Во многих случаях возможна замена конструкциями с транзитивным глаголом 'έχω', где существительное является в роли прямого дополнения.

4.4.1. Значение „принадлежать, находиться в сфере влияния, в обхвате". Общая отражающая структурная схема: Vbe + article + Sgen. В качестве факультативного элемента может появиться в некоторых выражениях местоимение – неопределительное или показательное.

> *είναι* της δικαιοδοσίας μου – *έχω* δικαιοδοσία
> *είναι* της ηλικίας (μιας κάποιας) – *έχει* μια κάποια ηλικία
> *είμαι* κάμποσων χρονών
> *είμαι* της γνώμης – *έχω* γνώμη, срв. в болгарском: *на мнение съм –*
> *имам мнение*

Относиться к определенному классу, совокупности, категории, проявлять характерные для этого класса черты, т.е. существовать со „штампом", поставленным принадлежностью к определенной категории бытующих объектов, быть определенного качества, проявлять характерные черты. К этой модели относится выражение возраста в болгарском и новогреческом языках, где семантика принадлежности в плоскости экзистенциальной структуры ярко ощутима, особенно принимая ввиду и эквивалентные конструкции с глаголом 'иметь'. А. Петрова находит корни идеи возраста как притяжание субъекта в староболгарских и древнегреческих образцах (PETROVA 2010: 132).

> *Πόσων χρονών είσαι; – На колко години си?*

Семантику данных выражений можно представить следующим образом: субъект относится к какому-нибудь классу, категории, и это отношение обеспечивает наличие или отсутствие определенного качества (величина, возрасть, количество), способности, возможности, отношения, характеризирующие его. Эти конструкции невозможно заменить синтагмами с глаголом *έχω*.

> *(δεν) είναι* της προκοπής
> *είναι* της πλάκας
> *είναι* της ώρας, *είναι* της κακιάς ώρας
> *είναι* της μόδας – *на мода е*
> *είναι* του θανατά – είναι του πεθαμού
> *είναι* του δρόμου
> *είναι* του κουτιού, είναι της σειράς
> *είναι* της ντροπής – *за срам е*
> (примеры заняты у ΑΝΑΣΤΑΣΙΑΔΗ-ΣΥΜΕΩΝΙΔΗ/ΕΥΘΥΜΙΟΥ 2006: 24–25).

Наблюдаются и вариации схемы, расширенные конструкции: Vbe + art. + Sgen. + art. + Sgen.

είναι του σκοινιού και του παλουκιού – είναι εξώλης και προώλης
είναι του κλότσου και του μπάτσου

Возможны вариантные проявления с дополнительным компонентом притяжательным местоимением: Vbe + art + Sgen + Pron

είναι του χεριού μου – τον έχω του χεριού μου (ΛΚΝΕ, с. 1472)
είναι του γούστου μου/της αρεσκείας

Настоящее сопоставление является лишь фрагментом исследования, демонстрирующим позиции и значения глагола 'съм/είμαι' в интересующих нас языках, на ограниченном фразеологическом материале. На базе сопоставления можно привести следующие наблюдения:

1. Наличие в обоих языках образований с одинаковой структурой и общей семантикой – одни и те же семантические отношения находят одинаковое формальное выражение.
2. Преобладание общих структурно-семантических моделей, хотя и представленных различным объемом конкретных образований.
3. Одинаковый способ функционирования глагола в копулятивной функции в одних и тех же позициях (известно, что не все языки используют данный глагол для предикации тождества, не во всех языках мира сосуществуют две разные функции в одном глаголе).
4. Факт количественного перевеса конструкций с глаголом 'είμαι' с экзистенциальной функцией в греческом языке.

Даже только на фразеологическом материале глагол 'съм/είμαι' в обоих языках показывает совпадение внутриязыкового значения и сходные употребления в речи, что можно обобщить как идентичность его функционально-семантической характеристики. Хотя фразеология выявляет основные структурные и семантические модели, анализ семантики и функций данного глагола нуждается в своем логическом продолжении, на следующем этапе необходимо расширить обхват языковых данных, привлечь полный набор употреблений в речи, добиваясь максимально достоверных выводов и обобщений о месте глагола в системах обоих языков и его конкретных реализациях.

Библиография

АЛЕКСИЕВА, Б. (1992): Английските и българските екзистенциални конструкции – резултат от прилагането на различни когнитивни модели. *Съпоставително езикознание* 3. 84–91.

ΑΝΑΣΤΑΣΙΑΔΗ-ΣΥΜΕΩΝΙΔΗ, Α.; ΕΥΘΥΜΙΟΥ, Α. (2006): *Οι στερεότυπες εκφράσεις και η διδακτική της Νέας Ελληνικής ως δεύτερης γλώσσας.* Αθήνα, εκδόσεις Πατάκη.

АРУТЮНОВА, Н. Д. (1976): *Предложение и его смысл. Логико-семантические проблемы.* Москва, Наука.

АСЕНОВА, П. (2002): *Балканско езикознание.* В. Търново, Издателство «Фабер».

АСЕНОВА, П. (2005): Архаизми и балканизми в един изолиран български говор (Кукъска гòра, Албания). *10 години специалност «Балканистика».* Университетско издателство «Св. Климент Охридски». 73–79.

БЕНВЕНИСТ, Э. (1974): *Общая лингвистика,* Москва. 203–225.

ΒΛΑΧΟΠΟΥΛΟΣ, Σ. (2007): *Λεξικό των ιδιωτισμών της Νέας Ελληνικής.* Αθήνα, Κλειδάριθμος.

ДАВЛЕТШИНА, С. М. (2008): „Соотношение посессивности, экзистенциальности и лока-тивности". *Вестник Челябинского государственного у-та, вып* 37. 36–41.

ΔΕΛΒΕΡΟΥΔΗ, Ρέα (1992): Τα υπαρκτικά ρήματα στα Νέα Ελληνική: είναι/έχει/υπάρχει. *Μελέτες για την Ελληνική γλώσσα.* Θεσσαλονίκη, Α-φοι Κυριακίδη. 429–445.

ИВАНОВА, Н. (1981): Особености на екзистенциалните изречения в българския и сърбохърватския език. *Съпоставително езикознание* VI, 2. 58–62.

ИВАНОВА, Е. (2002): *Има* и *съм* в болгарских бытийных предложениях (в сопоставлении с русскими). *Съпоставително езикознание* 2. 5–24.

КАЛДИЕВА-ЗАХАРИЕВА, Ст. (2005): *Проблеми на съпоставителното изследване на българската и румънската фразеология.* София, Академично издателство „Марин Дринов".

ΛΚΝΕ: *Λεξικό της κοινής νεοελληνικής.* Θεσσαλονίκη.

MACKRIDGE, P. (1985 [1990]): *Η Νεοελληνική γλώσσα. Περιγραφική ανάλυση της νεοελληνικής κοινής.* Αθήνα, Εκδόσεις Πατάκη.

ΜΙΝΗ, Μ.; ΦΩΤΟΠΟΥΛΟΥ, Α. (2009): Τυπολογία των πολυλεκτικών ρηματικών εκφράσεων στα λεξικά της Νέας Ελληνικής: όρια και διαφοροποιήσεις. *Πρακτικά του 18ου Διεθνούς Συμποσίου Θεωρητικής & Εφαρμοσμένης Γλωσσολογίας του Τμήματος Αγγλικής Γλώσσας & Φιλολογίας του Α.Π.Θ.,* Θεσσαλονίκη (4-6/05/2007). 491–503.

ΜΟΥΣΤΑΚΗ, Α. (1993): Το λεξικο-γραμματική των ιδιωτισμικών εκφράσεων με το "βοηθητικό" ρήμα *είμαι. Μελέτες για την Ελληνική γλώσσα.* Θεσσαλονίκη, Α-φοι Κυριακίδη.

ΜΟΥΣΤΑΚΗ, Α. (1992α): Το "βοηθητικό" ρήμα είμαι και τα ρήματα που εναλάσσονται με αυτό στις ιδιωτισμικές εκφράσεις στα Ν. Ελληνικά. *Μελέτες για την Ελληνική γλώσσα.* Θεσσαλονίκη, Α-φοι Κυριακίδη. 409–428.

ΜΟΥΣΤΑΚΗ, Α. (1992β): Οι στερεώτυπες εκφράσεις με το βοηθητικό ρήμα είμαι στα νέα ελληνικά. *Μελέτες για την Ελληνική γλώσσα.* Θεσσαλονίκη, Α-φοι Κυριακίδη. 155–168.

НИЧЕВА К.; СПАСОВА-МИХАЙЛОВА, С.; ЧОЛАКОВА, Кр. (1975): *Фразеологичен речник на българския език.* София, БАН.

НИЦОЛОВА, Р. (1990): Екзистенциалните изречения с глаголите esse и habere в българския език в съпоставка с другите славянски езици. *Съпоставително езикознание* XV, 4–5. 236–242.

PETROVA, A. (2010): Linguistic-Cultural View on the Existential Functions of the Verb "to have" in Bulgarian and Greek. *The Verbal System of the Balkan languages – Heritage and Neology,* V. Tărnovo, „Faber". 121–149.

СТОЯНОВ, Ст. (1973): Синонимни изрази с глаголите *съм* и *имам* в българския език. *Славистични изследвания (сборник, посветен на 7 Международен конгрес на славистите),* III. София, изд. „Наука и изкуство". 191–199.

ΣΥΜΕΩΝΙΔΗΣ, Χ. (2000): *Εισαγωγή στην ελληνική φρασεολογία.* Θεσσαλονίκη, Κώδικας.

ФРОММ, Э. (2000): *Иметь или быть,* М.: „АСТ", 2000. http://www.psylib.ukrweb.net/ books/fromm02/index.htm. 7.08.2010.

ШВЕДОВА, Н. Ю. (2001): Еще раз о глаголе быть. *Вопросы языкознания* 2. 3–12.

Abstract:

This paper refers to the results of our research on the status and the semantic of the verb "съм/είμαι" in Bulgarian and Modern Greek languages. There is significant data of "съм/είμαι" constructions that express existentiality, characterization, location, possessiveness, in both languages. The main focus of the comparative analysis is on the structural-semantic classification, pointing out similarities and differences between the structural-semantic models.

Функционирование греческой лексемы *фа̀кел* в болгарском языке (семантический, словообразовательный и фонетический анализ)

Лиляна ДИМИТРОВА-ТОДОРОВА (София)

В болгарских диалектах широко распространена лексема *фа̀кел* с некоторыми вариантами и производными. Богатая полисемия, исторически развившаяся и установившаяся в плане содержания, является результатом разносторонних метафорических процессов, до сих пор оставшихся вне внимания исследователей болгарского языка и его диалектов.

Основное значение 'платок для головы' слова *фа̀кел* регистрировано в с. Габровица, район Пазарджик (АД), а со значением 'турецкая чалма' отмечено также в с. Радуил, район Ихтиман, и в районе города Гоце Делчев (ФИЛИПОВА-БАЙРОВА 1969: 166). В некоторых диалектах семантика лексемы *фа̀кел* значительно модифицируется и может быть обозначена как 'тонкий белый материал, который употребляется сверху сита при свадебных обрядах' (ФИЛИПОВА-БАЙРОВА 1969: 166). В этом усматривается естественная трансформация семантики: 'белый платок для головы' > 'белый платок для покрытия чего-либо' > 'тонкий белый материал, который употребляется для покрытия сита при соблюдении свадебных обрядов'. Здесь просматривается ассоциация очевидно и с вуалью невесты, о чем пойдет речь ниже (см. *факѐл* в с. Горубляне, район София).

Акцентный вариант *факѐл* чаще всего встречается со следующими значениями: 'белый платок на голову' в с. Горни Лозен, район София (АД), 'белый платок, предназначенный для молодой женщины' в Софийском районе (Сб. Софийски край 1993: 286), 'белый платок, который носят по диагонали на лбу с концами, завязанными сзади' в селах Драгалевци и Церово, район София (Сб. Софийски край 1993: 93), и в с. Гинци, район Годеч (Сб. Софийски край 1993: 109), 'вуаль для невесты, фата' в с. Горубляне, район София (АД), 'турецкая чалма или тюрбан' в диалекте Гоцеделческого района (МПр 1936: 171), 'белый платок с пестрыми кисточками, обвитый около феса' в некоторых болгарских диалектах' (ГЕРОВ 5: 471–472). Фонетический вариант *факѐль* в значении 'белая чалма' отмечен в районе города Смоляна (СТОЙЧЕВ 1965: 289). Этот вариант употребляется и в значении 'белый платок с пестрыми кисточками, обвитый около феса' в с. Плевня, район Драма (СбНУ VIII: 3.283). В Софийском районе встречается и форма *факѐле* 'женский головной платок для невесты большого размера со специфическим способом завязывания' (Сб. Софийски край 1993: 247). Эта форма вероятно от первоначального варианта *факѐла — форма ж.р. (срв. ниже вариант векѐла) и возникла на болгарской языковой почве путем ассимиляции е–а > е–е или процесса переосмысления родовой принадлежности слова.

У Найдена Герова (ГЕРОВ 5: 471) отмечены и диалектные слова факѐлец и факѐлче в форме уменьшительных образований от лексемы факѐл 'белое пятно на лбу животного; белый платок с пестрыми кисточками около феса'.

Известно и употребление слова фекѐл в значении 'вид платка' в с. Церово, район София (Сб. Софийски край 1993: 93, 109), 'белый платок, который складывают по диагонали над лбом и завязывают на затылке' в с. Драгалевци, район София (Сб. Софийски край 1993: 93, 109). Срв. и диал. фекѐл 'платок' (РРОДД 1974: 534). В Софийском районе употребляется и форма фикѐл с этим же значением (БАРБОЛОВА 2006: 114), которая соотносится с фекѐл с редуцированным е > и в позиции безударности; производным от фикѐл является и уменьшительная форма фикелчѐ в районе города Ихтимана (БАРБОЛОВА 2006: 114).

От фекѐл появилась форма векѐл (переход ф > в, как это встречается в диалектах в словах вайтòн вместо файтòн, вàлака вместо фàлака) в значении 'женский платок' в селах Долни Лозен и Суходол, район София (СбНУ XLIII: 194), в с. Волуяк, район Перник (Сб. Софийски край 1993: 93, 109), 'платок для головы' в с. Габров дол, район Брезник, в с. Беренде, район Годеч и в с. Банище, район Брезник'(АД), 'белый платок, белый платок для головы' в селах Глоговица и Костуринци, район Трън, в с. Радуй, район Перник, в с. Вердикал, район София, в селах Долно Ново село, Драготинци, Росоман и Сеславци, район София, в городе Перник, в с. Батановци, район Радомир, в с. Гърло, район Брезник, в с. Комщица, район Годеч, в городе Драгоман и в с. Драговита, Царибродский район (сегодня Димитровградский район) (АД), 'белый платок для молодой девушки' в с. Габер, район Годеч (АД), 'тонкий белый платок, с которым женщины покрывают голову во время полевых работ' в с. Богданов дол, район Перник, и в с. Филиповци, район Трън (АД), 'белый платок из тонкой ткани (перкаль, марля)' в с. Неделище, район Годеч, и в районе города Сливница (АД). Здесь можно отнести акцентные, фонетические и морфологические варианты вѐкел 'белый платок для головы', из с. Копаница, район Радомир (АД), 'летний белый платок', из города Цариброд (Димитровград) (АД), 'белый хлопчатобумажный платок для молодой девушки', из с. Брължница, район София (АД), векьѐл 'платок для головы из белой хлопчатобумажной ткани' из района города Брезник (СбНУ XLIX: 774), 'белый платок для головы' из с. Начево, район Цариброд (Димитровград) (АД), векьѐли – мн. ч. – с этим же значением из с. Гърло, район Брезник (СбНУ XLIX: 708), и векѐла 'платок' из района города Самоков (АД). Производные от *векèл* являются *векèлче* 'небольшой платок для головы' из с. Хра-бърско, район София (АД), и *векьелчè* 'белый платок' из города Самоков (АД). От *фикèл* (см. выше) путем перехода *ф* > *в* или от *векèл* путем редукции безударного *е* в *и* произошли *викèл* в значении 'женский платок', засвидетель-ствовано в творчестве писателя Крума Григорова, родом из Западной Бол-гарии (РРОДД 1974: 59), и *викьèл* 'платок' из с. Гинци, район Годеч (АД).

Слово *фàкел* и его варианты *факèл* и *фекèл* этимологизованы М. Филипо-вой-Байровой (ФИЛИПОВА-БАЙРОВА 1969: 166), авторами Словаря редких и устаревших диалектных слов (РРОДД 1974: 534) и Христом Дзидзилисом (ДЗИДЗИЛИС 1990: 34, 106). Согласно М. Филиповой-Байровой (ibidem) *фàкел* 'тонкая белая ткань, с которой покрывают сито при свадебних обрядах; ту-рецкая чалма' восходит к нгр. φάκελος 'конверт', дргр. φάκελος 'вязанка, связка', с переосмыслением значения. Хр. Дзидзилис (ДЗИДЗИЛИС 1990: 106) с основанием считает, что *фàкел* происходит не от φάκελος 'конверт', а от нгр. φακιόλι 'платок', из φακιόλιον (ΑΝΔΡΙΩΤΗΣ 1983: 395), уменьшительное от φακίολος из лат. *fasciola*, уменьшительное от *fascia* 'связка; лента'. По мне-нию Г. Психарис (цитируется по Хр. ДЗИДЗИЛИС 1990: 106) греческое слово происходит из φακιάλιον < лат. *faciale*, под влиянием βραχιόλι. По данным Хр. Дзидзилиса (ibidem) составители Словаря редких и устаревших диалектных слов (РРОДД 1974: 534) правильно выводят *фекèл* от φακιόλι, а на стр. 34 в этом же сочинении уточняется, что *фекèл* – это *фàкел* с регрессивной асси-миляцией *а–е* > *е–е*. З. Барболова (БАРБОЛОВА 2006: 97, 114) тоже выводит диалектную лексему *фàкел* и ее варианты *фекèл*, *фикèл*, *викèл* и *викьèл* из гре-ческого этимона со значением 'платок' (и в двух местах ошибочно записана греческая форма φακιδλι вместо φακιόλι).

Интересно отметить, что первоначальное значение 'платок; чалма' позд-нее развивает специализированное значение 'белый' (по мнению этнографов традиционный болгарский платок – белый, о цвете платка см. больше у Бар-боловой (БАРБОЛОВА 2006: 43–44, 69–77)), которое переносится на большее количество слов, полученных путем метафорического переноса от значения 'платок; чалма'. В отдельную группу могут быть выделены слова, созданные на основе признака 'белый', а именно: диал. *фàкел* 'белое пятно на лбу какого-нибудь животного' (ГЕРОВ 5: 471), *факèль* 'буйвол с белым пятном на лбу' в районе города Елена (ПЕТКОВ 1974: 160), и их производные *факèлист* диал. в сочетании *факèлист бùвол* 'который имеет белое пятно на лбу' (ГЕРОВ 5: 471), *факèльъс* '(о буйволе) который имеет белое пятно на лбу' – в с. Руховци, район Елена, и *факèльъста* 'которая имеет белое пятно на лбу' – тоже в с. Руховци, район Елена (ПЕТКОВ 1974: 160).

К другой семантической группе относятся варианты *фàкел* 'вид белой круглой тыквы, предназначенной для выпечки' – с. Горни Юруци, район Кру-мовград (АД), *факèл* 'белая тыква, каштанка' – город Хасково (СТОИЧЕВ

1970: 96), *факѝль* – с. Тънково, район Хасково (АД) (этот вариант происходит от первоначального *фа̀кель* с редукцией *е* > *и* в безударной позиции с перестановкой на ударении), *фекѐль* 'белая сладкая тыква' – в селах Горно и Долно Капиново, Долище, Жерка, Кирково и Шумнатица, район Кърджали (Родопски сборник 1983: 346). В с. Царино, район Крумовград, встречается и вариант *фаркѐль* 'белая тыква дла выпечки' (АД), который восходит к *факѐл* с этим же значением с эпентическим -*р*-, в связи с этим – срв. *фандра̀к* и *фандрѐк* вместо *фанда̀к* и *фандѐк*. Это значение получено из первоначального значения 'белая чалма' из-за похожести белой тыквой с формой и в некоторых случаях с цветом на турецкой чалмы.

В с. Малък Девесил, район Крумовград, встречается слово *фа̀келка* 'вид белой круглой тыквы для выпечки' (Родопски сборник 1983: 345). Она является производной от *факел* с этим же значением и в этом же говоре (см. выше). В селах Голям и Малък Девесил, Девесилово и Девесилица, район Крумовград, регистрирован и фонетический вариант лексемы *фа̀келка* с формой мн.ч. *фа̀кельки* 'крупные, овальные серые сладкие тыквы' (Родопски сборник 1983: 345).

В говоре села Девесилица, район Крумовград, употребляется слово *фа̀калька* 'белая тыква' (АД). В говоре с. Тихомир, район Крумовград, белая тыква называется *фа̀калькье* (АД), в то время как в с. Егрек, район Крумовград, она называется *фя̀калка* (АД). Звуковой облик *фа̀калька* – с ассимиляцией *а–е* > *а–а* к **фа̀келька* тоже в единственном числе засвидетельствано и в множественном числе *фа̀кельки* 'крупные, овальные серые сладкие тыквы' в селах Голям Девесил и Малък Девесил, Девесилово и Девесилица, район Крумовград (Родопски сборник 1983: 345). Облик *фа̀калькье* производный от первоначального **фа̀калькьа* (реализация *а* перед мягким *л* в неударной позиции) с переходом в *е*, что характерно для некоторых родопских говоров, к которым принадлежит и говор в районе города Крумовград (о переходе *а* > *е* см. СТОЙКОВ 1993: 134–135). Звуковой облик *фя̀калка* вероятно получен от первоначального **фа̀калькьа* (**фа̀калькя*) с метатезой *а–я* ('*а*) > ('*а*) *я–а*.

От первоначального значения 'белая чалма' из-за сходства по форме происходят и *факѐл* 'воздушная кукуруза' – села Добралък и Косово, район Асеновград (Родопски сборник 1983: 345), и *факлѝ* мн.ч. 'воздушные кукурузы' – с. Триград, район Девин, и с. Кожаре, район Смолян (АД). В селах Голям Девесил и Малък Девесил, Девесилово и Девесилица, район Крумовград, зарегистрировано и производное от *факѐл* с формой мн.ч. *фа̀кельки* 'воздушные кукурузы' (Родопски сборник 1983: 345). Это же свидетельствует, что существует или существовала форма *фа̀келка* с этим же значением.

Из-за сходства с формой турецкой чалмы в районе города Гоце Делчев называют и садовый желтый цветок *факѐл*, лепестки которого собраны в пучок, похожий на турецкую чалму (МПр 1936: 171). В селах Павелско и Хвойна, район Асеновград, и в с. Лилково, район Пловдив, зарегистрировано то же самое слово *факèл* со значением 'садовый оранжевый цветок' (СТОЙЧЕВ 1965: 289). Об этом значении срв. *тỳлипань, тулипàнь* и *тỳлпань* 'цветок тульпан' в Банате с первоначальным значением 'чалма; платок' (из-за сходства по форме) и *тулпàн* 'белый платок, платок' в районе города Еленско и в с. Килифарево, район Велико Търново. Этот цветок составляет единственное исключение в сравнении с другими словами, в которых кроме формы чалмы основной признак – белый цвет.

К этой группе можно отнести и существительное *факèль* со значением 'лохматая женщина', засвидетельствовано в говоре сел Виево, Кутела и Славеино, район Смолян (СТОЙЧЕВ 1965: 289), которое вероятно возникло по ассоциации с видом на турецкую чалму.

Многочисленные названия лексемы *фàкел* с основным значением 'платок' в плане культурологии свидетельствуют о большой роли платка в быту болгар как средство предохранения от солнца или холода и как неизменный элемент национального костюма болгарки, срв. БАРБОЛОВА (2006: 19).

По отношению к лингвистической географии могут быть сделаны следующие выводы. Слово с основным значением '(белый) платок; чалма' – широко распространено в западных говорах, в говорах западных болгарских окраин (т. называемые „переходные говоры"), в рупских говорах (более конкретно — в родопских, восточнорупских и западнорупских говорах). Следует обратить внимание и на тот факт, что только в западных говорах и в говорах западных окраин распространен звуковой облик *векèл* с вариантами и производными, а первоначальный диалектный облик, от которого произошел, *фекèл*, распространенный в этих говорах, является исключением в употреблении в некоторых родопских говорах. К семантическому кругу слова в значении 'платок, косынка' принадлежат также ритуальные значения 'свадебная вуаль' в софийском говоре и 'тонкая белая ткань, которой покрывают сито при свадебных обрядах'. Во втором значении информация поступает от М. Филиповой-Байровой (ФИЛИПОВА-БАЙРОВА 1969: 166), но, к сожалению автор, не указывает место говора. Данное слово с переносным значением 'тыква' встречается преимущественно в восточных рупских говорах и в родопских говорах, а значение 'воздушная кукуруза' развилось только в родопских говорах. Только там зарегистрировано и значение 'лохматая женщина'. В центральном балканском говоре, и более конкретно – в еленском говоре, это слово встречается только со специализированным значением 'белое пятно на лбу животного'.

Итак, в названии, связанном со значением 'женский платок', глубоко вошедшее в болгарские диалекты, отражается прошедшее греческое влияние на болгарский быт и культуру. Это греческое заимствование, однако, до такой степени воспринимается как болгарское, что служит основой при образовании производных на болгарской почве и при создании новых понятий путем метафорического перѐноса.

Библиография и сокращения

АД = Архив диалектов при Институте болгарского языка Болгарской академии наук.

Барболова, З. (2006): Имената за забрадка в българския език. Етнолингвистичен анализ. София.

БДПМ = Българска диалектология. Проучвания и материали. София 1962–.

Геров 5 = Найден Геров: Речник на българския език, т. 5. София 1978.

Дзидзилис, Хр. (1990): Фонетични проблеми при етимологизуване на гръцките заемки в българския език. София.

МJ = Македонски јазик, IX, кн. 1–2. Скопје 1958.

МПр 1936 = Македонски преглед, X, кн. 1 и 2. София.

Петков, П. Ив. (1974): Еленски речник. – БДПМ, кн. VII. София.

Родопски сборник 1983 = Т. Стойчев: Родопски речник (второ допълнение). – Родопски сборник 5. София. 287–353.

РРОДД 1974 = Речник на редки, остарели и диалектни думи в литературата ни от XIX и XX век. София.

СбНУ = Сборник за народни умотворения и народопис, т. I–LII. София 1889–1963.

Сб. Софийски край 1993 = Софийски край. Етнографски и езикови проучвания. София.

Стойков, Ст. (1993): Българска диалектология. София.

Стойчев, Т. (1965): Родопски речник. – БДПМ, кн. II. София. 119–314.

Стойчев, Т. (1970): Родопски речник. – БДПМ, кн. II. София. 152–221.

Филипова-Байрова, М. (1969): Гръцки заемки в съвременния български език. София.

Functioning of the Greek loan word *fàkel* in Bulgarian (semantic, word-formative and phonetic Analysis)

In Bulgarian dialects the word of Greek origin *фàкел* meaning 'a Turkish turban, a kind of female kerchief' is widely spread. In the presented research, multifarious variants of this word and its derivatives formed on Bulgarian soil are examined. The interesting semantic development is traced out through a metaphoric transfer of the meaning of the word *фàкел*, its variants and derivatives.

Zur Etymologie der bulgarischen Wörter
джѝджи-бѝджи, керкѝда, коркулу̀к
und der griechischen *κοκάρι, κουκάρι, κορκάρ*

Todor At. TODOROV (Sofia)

1. Lautsymbolische Herkunft von *джѝджи-бѝджи, керкѝда, коркулу̀к, κοκάρι, κουκάρι, κορκάρ*?

Die bulgarischen Wörter *джѝджи-бѝджи, керкѝда, коркулу̀к* und die griechi-schen *κοκάρι, κουκάρι, κορκάρ* sind in den Untersuchungen von Živka KOLEVA-ZLATEVA als Wörter lautsymbolischer Herkunft angegeben worden: *джѝджи-бѝджи* 'Unterhaltung' (in Сб. Заимов 2005: 268); die Variante *джиджи-биджи* mit folgenden Bedeutungen: 'verhältnismäßig neuer technologischer Gegenstand', 'den Hof machen; Liebesbeziehungen', 'verschiedene Ereignisse' (im Text: *Сед-мицата се очертаваше да започне добре. Така и започна. С ортопедично-травматологичен кабинет. Рентген-менген, снимки-мимки, а-у, джиджи-биджи. Нямам счупени пръсти.*), 'verschiedenartige, unwesentliche Informatio-nen' (im Kontext: *... публикувам информация, ала бала, джиджи-биджи ...*), 'etwas Oberflächliches' (im Kontext: *... музикално джиджи-биджи радио в претрупания от честоти ефир ...*) (in Дис. К.-Зл. 2009: 83, 87–88); in der Bedeutung 'Unterhaltung; den Hof machen' (in Дис. К.-Зл. 2009: 46); die Variante *жижѝ-бижѝ* in der Bedeutung 'eine Art Nachtisch, Pudding', 'etwas Süßes, eine Art Pudding' (in Сб. Заимов 2005: 266 und in Дис. К.-Зл. 2009: 171); *керкѝда* 'ein besonders hart gewordener Gegenstand' (nach БЕР II: 338) (in Сб. Заимов 2005: 266 und in Дис. К.-Зл. 2009: 207); *коркулу̀к* 'Vogelscheuche' (in Балк. ези-козн. XLIII, 2–3, 2003–2004: 279 und in Дис. К.-Зл. 2009: 216); *κοκάρι, κουκάρι, κορκάρ* 'Steckzwiebel' (in Сб. Заимов 2005: 264, 270 und in Дис. К.-Зл. 2009: 118, 260).

Es ist hervorzuheben, dass an den erwähnten Stellen in den zitierten Arbeiten von Živka Koleva-Zlateva die Wörter, die für uns von Interesse sind, als Wörter mit bestätigter lautsymbolischer Herkunft angegeben werden. Die Autorin hat das erste Verfahren zur „Erkennung und Untersuchung der lautsymbolischen Wörter in der Sprache" nicht durchgeführt, das Verfahren, das von ihr im zweiten Teil ihrer Dissertation („Методика на етимологизацията на звукосимволична лексика") vorgesehen wurde: „(1) Bestimmung des entlehnten bzw. ureigenen Charakters des untersuchten Wortes" (Дис. К.-Зл. 2009: 70). Es sollte überprüft werden, ob *джѝ-джи-бѝджи* (sowie seine Varianten), *керкѝда, коркулу̀к, κοκάρι, κουκάρι, κορκάρ* als Erbwörter oder als Lehnwörter aus einer Fremdsprache zu identifizieren sind. Bestandteil dieser Überprüfung ist die Ermittlung möglicher Beziehungen zu Wörtern aus anderen Balkansprachen sowie die Ermittlung vorhandener bisheriger etymologischer Erklärungen dieser Wörter. Es ist ein falsches Herangehen seitens der Autorin, Wörter bestimmten semantischen Gruppen zuzuordnen, diese Wörter unbegründet als lautsymbolisch zu bezeichnen und überheblich die bisherigen etymologischen Erklärungen zu vernachlässigen. Es muss darauf hingewiesen werden, dass in den hier erwähnten Arbeiten der Autorin über die lautsymbolischen Wörter gewöhnlich eine völlige Diskrepanz besteht, und zwar zwischen den formulierten theoretischen Postulaten und den Ansprüchen der Autorin darauf, einen Schlüssel zur Erkennung der lautsymbolischen Wörter gefunden zu haben, einerseits, und den konkreten Beispielen für lautsymbolische Lexik, andererseits. Es fehlt eine richtige Interpretation der lautsymbolischen Lexik.

2. Bisherige etymologische Erklärungen von *джѝджи-бѝджи, керкѝда, коркулу̀к, кока́ρι, коυκάρι, корка́ρ*

Über *джѝджи-бѝджи* (aus türkisch *cici-bici*), als auch über *жѝжи-бѝжи* un die Varianten *иджѝ-биджѝ, джѝджи-мѝджи, жѝжи-мѝжи* s. GRANNES/HAUGE/SÜLEYMANOĞLU (2002: 71, 100).

Über *керкѝда* 'ein besonders hart gewordener Gegenstand' wird im „Български етимологичен речник" (БЕР II: 338) lediglich vermerkt: „Unklar", allerdings wird hinzugefügt: „Vgl. *киркидя̀лка, киркидя̀лна*". Ich werfe noch ein, dass *киркидя̀лка* 'krummer Stock', *киркидя̀лна* 'schlagen, streifen' in БЕР (II: 383) mit bulg. *керкѝда* 'ein besonders hart gewordener Gegenstand' verglichen und mit gr. *κερκίδα* 'Schiffchen (in der Weberei)' verbunden werden. Nach TZITZILIS (ДЗИДЗИЛИС 1990: 85) sind *керкѝда* 'ein besonders hart gewordener Gegenstand', sowie die Wörter *κεκερѝδα* 'Erdnuss' und *κικιρѝδα* 'Erdnuss' zu verbinden mit gr. dial. *kikírda* '1. castagna mondata e arrostita, 2. frutto del carciofo selvatico, 3. cosa di poco valore, 4. donna corta e brutta'[1] und seiner phonetischen Variante, „die nach Gerhard Rohlfs von *kikí* abstammen". Tzitzilis zieht die Schlussfolgerung: „Die Beziehungen zwischen den griechischen Wörtern und dem italienischen Wort sind nicht völlig klar, unabhängig von der Herkunft der griechischen Wörter besteht jedoch kein Zweifel daran, dass sie die Ausgangsformen der bulgarischen Wörter sind". Koleva-Zlateva erwähnt die etymologische Erklärung von Tzitzilis überhaupt nicht.

Vor der etymologischen Erklärung von KOLEVA-ZLATEVA (in Балк. езикозн. XLIII, 2–3, 2003–2004: 279) liegt über *коркулу̀к* eine etymologische Erklärung im

---

1 Die Bedeutungen von *kikírda* in deutscher Übersetzung: „'1. geschälte und gebratene Kastanie, 2. Früchte der wilden Artischocke, 3. etwas von geringem Wert, 4. kleine und hässliche Frau'".

„Български етимологичен речник" (БЕР II: 641) vor, wo darauf hingewiesen wird, dass *коркулу̀к* 'Vogelscheuche' von türk. *korkuluk* mit derselben Bedeutung abstammt. Der Autor der vorliegenden Zeilen hat in einer Veröffentlichung (in Сб. Станишева 2008: 361) die Aufmerksamkeit darauf gelenkt. Dort schreibt er folgendes:

> „… unter den ‚bildnachahmenden Bezeichnungen', die ‚reduplizierte Lautkomplexe' enthalten, erwähnt Živka Koleva-Zlateva bulg. dial. *коркулу̀к* 'Vogelscheuche' (nach ГЕРОВ II: 399). Die Autorin hat nicht gemerkt, dass Геров *коркулу̀к* mit der Anmerkung *T.* (= *türkisch*) versehen hat, und dass in БЕР (II: 641) dem Wort *коркулу̀к* nicht nur mit seiner Bedeutung 'Vogelscheuche', sondern auch mit der Bedeutung 'Plankenzaun, Treppengeländer' ein Wörterbuchartikel gewidmet ist, in dem auf das türkische Etymon *korkuluk* hingewiesen wird … Sie lässt mindestens zwei wichtige Prinzipien der etymologischen Untersuchung außer Acht: das Prinzip der gewissenhaften Suche nach bisherigen etymologischen Erklärungen der behandelten Wörter, sowie das Prinzip der Wortuntersuchung im Balkankontext".

Über *коркулу̀к* schreiben auch GRANNES//HAUGE/SÜLEYMANOĞLU (2002: 152). Koleva-Zlateva entgehen aber diese Veröffentlichungen offenbar!

Die Autorin hält gr. *кокάρι*, *коυκάρι*, gr. dial. *коρκάρ* für lautsymbolische Wörter – ein Beispiel für „Formen mit totaler und partieller Reduplikation" (*коρκάρ* – mit totaler Reduplikation, *кокάρι*, *коυκάρι* – mit partieller Reduplikation), die „ein und dieselbe lexikalische Bedeutung bzw. Bedeutungen zum Ausdruck bringen, welche aus ein und derselben ursprünglichen Bedeutung abgeleitet werden" (Дис. К.-Зл. 2009: 270). Sie interessiert sich nicht für bisherige etymologische Erklärungen von gr. *кокάρι*, *коυκάρι*, *коρκάρ* 'Steckzwiebel', wie auch für mögliche Beziehungen zwischen diesen griechischen Wörtern und den bulgarischen dialektalen Wörtern *кокὰρ* 'Steckzwiebel', *ку̀карь* 'Ackerbohne', *крòкар* 'Zwiebeln zum Anpflanzen', d.h. 'Steckzwiebel' (aus Kondorbi, Kreis Kastoria, s. БДиал III: 257). In „Български етимологичен речник" (БЕР II: 532) wird bulg. dial. *кокὰр* 'Steckzwiebel' folgenderweise erklärt: „Aus türk. *kokar* 'etwas, was riecht', Part. Präs. Akt. von *kok-mak* 'riechen, duften; stinken'". TZITZILIS (ДЗИДЗИЛИС 1990: 88–89) lehnt diese Etymologie als nicht wahr ab, und leitet bulg. *кокὰр* 'Steckzwiebel' aus gr. *коκκάρι(ον)* 'Steckzwiebel' ab, Ableitung aus *кόκκος* 'Korn, Obstsamen; Kern', mit dem Suffix *-άριο(ν)*. Er weist auch auf „eine parallele Form *коρκάρι* hin, aus der arum. *curcáre* 'Steckzwiebel' stammt". Bulg. dial. *ку̀карь* 'Ackerbohne' (aus Ruždene, Kreis Drama) wird in „Български етимологичен речник" (БЕР II: 88) richtig wie folgt erklärt: „Wahrscheinlich aus ngr. *коυκκάρι*, Dimin. aus *кόκκος* 'Korn, Bohne', mit Verschiebung der Betonung auf die erste Silbe und mit -ь vom griechischen unbetonten *ι* im Auslaut. Semantisch vgl. *коυκκί*

'Ackerbohne', wörtl. 'Körnchen, Böhnchen', Dimin. aus *κόκκος*. Über die griechischen Wörter s. *Ανδριώτης* 167".

3. Ergänzungen zu den Etymologien von *джѝджи-бѝджи*, *керкѝда*, *коркулу̀к*, *кока̀рι*, *кουка̀рι*, *коркáр*

Das Wort *джѝджи-бѝджи* und seine Varianten gehen auf türk. *cici bici* '(bezogen auf einen Gegenstand) klein und zierlich' (ТурБълг 1962: 86) zurück, das durch Reduplikation des Wortes *cici* 'schön, gut; schöner Gegenstand, schönes Spielzeug' (in der Kindersprache) (ib.) gebildet wurde. Bei der Wiederholung von *cici* wird der anlautende Konsonant *c* (*дж*) durch *b* (*б*) ersetzt. Ein ähnliches Wortbildungsverfahren durch Wiederholung des ganzen Wortes, bei dem der anlautende Konsonant durch *b* ersetzt wird, gibt es auch im Bulgarischen, vgl. *кòce-бòce*, *кòсенце-бòсенце*. Türk. *cici*, wahrscheinlich von interjektionaler Herkunft, kann in der Kindersprache entstanden sein. Die breite Bedeutungspalette von *джѝджи-бѝджи* und seiner Varianten ('Unterhaltung', 'verhältnismäßig neuer technologischer Gegenstand', 'den Hof machen, Liebesbeziehungen', 'verschiedenartige, unwesentliche Informationen', 'etwas Oberflächliches' etc.) kann sich aus der Grundbedeutung von türk. *cici* 'hübsch, schön; etwas Hübsches, etwas Schönes' entwickelt haben. Es muss zugegeben werden, dass Koleva-Zlateva in ihrer Dissertation (Дис. К.-Зл. 2009: 88–89) bulg. *джѝджи* 'etwas Hübsches' (aus der Kindersprache) zitiert, jedoch nicht im Zusammenhang mit *джѝджи-бѝджи*.

Wie zu ersehen ist, ist *джѝджи-бѝджи* kein lautsymbolisches Wort, das auf bulgarischem Sprachboden gebildet wurde, wie dies den Erläuterungen von Koleva-Zlateva zu entnehmen ist, sondern ein Lehnwort aus dem Türkischen, wo das Wort aller Wahrscheinlichkeit nach entstanden ist.

Bulg. dial. *керкѝда* 'ein besonders hart gewordener Gegenstand' kann aus ngr. *κερκίδα* stammen, das außer 'Schiffchen (in der Weberei)' auch die Bedeutung 'Speiche (eine Art Knochen)' hat, mit der folgenden semantischen Entwicklung: 'Speiche' > 'Knochen' > 'hart wie ein Knochen' > 'ein besonders hart gewordener Gegenstand', vgl. die bulgarische Wortverbindung *като кокал* 'besonders hart', wörtl. 'wie ein Knochen' (zitiert in Дис. К.-Зл. 2009: 207)

Zu der oben aufgeführten etymologischen Erklärung vom Verfasser dieser Zeilen über *коркулу̀к* 'Vogelscheuche' würde ich noch hinzufügen, dass türk. *korkuluk* 'Vogelscheuche' eine Ableitung von türk. *korkmak* 'erschrecken' ist.

Ngr. *кока̀рι*, *коυка̀рι* entstehen aus *кокка̀рι*, *коυкка̀рι* mit einer Konsonantenvereinfachung *κκ > κ*. Bulg. dial. *крòкар* 'Zwiebeln zum Anpflanzen, Steckzwiebel' ist mit einer Metathese und einer Akzentverschiebung aus gr. dial. *коркáр* entstanden.

4. Abschließende Anmerkungen

In den oben zitierten Arbeiten ordnet Živka Koleva-Zlateva willkürlich die bulgarischen Wörter *джѝджи-бѝджи* (und seine Varianten), *керкѝда, коркулу̀к*, sowie die griechischen *кокári, коυкári, коркáр* der lautsymbolischen Lexik zu. Auf diese Weise erzeugt sie selbst Zweifel an der Effektivität der von ihr angewendeten Methodologie zur Erkennung und Interpretation der lautsymbolischen Lexik.

Abkürzungen und Literatur

Балк. езикозн. = Балканско езикознание. София 1959–.

БДиал = Българска диалектология. Проучвания и материали. София 1962–.

БЕР = Български етимологичен речник. София 1971–.

ГЕРОВ, Н. (1895–1904): Рѣчникъ на блъгарский языкъ. I–V. Пловдив.

Дис. К.-Зл. = Лексиката от звукосимволичен (образоподражателен) произход в етимологичния анализ (върху славянски езиков материал). – Dissertation von Živka KOLEVA-ZLATEVA zur Erlangung des wissenschaftlichen Grades „доктор на филологическите науки". Sofia, 2009. Internetlink: DisertacijaZhivkaKolevaZlateva.pdf – http://www.uni-vt.bg/1/userinfo.asp?zid=71&userid=123

Сб. Заимов = Езиковедски проучвания в памет на проф. Йордан Заимов (1921–1987). София 2005.

Сб. Станишева = В търсене на смисъла и инварианта. Сборник в чест на 80-годишнината на проф. Дина Станишева. София 2008.

ТурБълг = Турско-български речник. София 1962.

ДЗИДЗИЛИС, Хр. (1990): Фонетични проблеми при етимологизуване на гръцките заемки в българския език. София.

GRANNES, Alf; HAUGE, Kjetil Rå; SÜLEYMANOĞLU, Hayriye (2002): A Dictionary of Turkisms in Bulgarian. Oslo.

About the etymology of the Bulgarian words *джѝджи-бѝджи, керкѝда, коркулу̀к* and the Greek *кокári, коυкári, коркáр*

In the present research, the origin of the Bulgarian words *джѝджи-бѝджи* 'entertainment' (also with other meanings), *керкѝда* 'a very hard object', *коркулу̀к* 'a scarecrow' and of the Greek *кокári, коυкári, коркáр* 'seed onions' is clarified. The interpretation of the examined words as phonosymbolic by their origin is rejected. Phonetic, semantic and other peculiarities of the words are taken into consideration.

О статусе общих особенностей двух балканских языков – балканизмы они или нет?

Петя АСЕНОВА (София)

1. О понятии „балканизм"

Наряду с понятием „языковой союз", понятие „балканизм" является основным в теории балканского языкознания, оно его „теоретическое ядро" (HINRICHS 1999: 429).

Несмотря на множество предложений, выраженных за время последнего полстолетия (срв. напр. PĂTRUŢ 1963; SCHALLER 1975: 123; STEINKE 1976, 1999; ASENOVA 1980, 1991; DURIDANOV 1983; HINRICHS 1999) и попыток обобщить их в дефиниции (STEINKE 1999: 79–80), содержание этого понятия остается расплывчатым. Так, к единому решению балканское языкознание до сих пор не пришло.

По-моему единомыслие по этому вопросу совсем не обязательно, совсем не необходимо. В данном случае позитивно то, что разнообразие мнений создало разнообразие балканизмов, которое оценивает своеобразие *общих особенностей балканских языков (= балканизмы)*. Теперь балканское языкознание пользуется спонтанно сложившейся классификацией балканизмов:

1. по их распространению в языках Балканского языкового союза (БЯС) – *тотальные (общие)* или представленные во всех языках БЯС и *парциальные (частичные)* или охватывающие только три из них (DURIDANOV 1983: 62–63);
2. по степени их развития – *градуальные* (DURIDANOV 1983: 64);
3. по их принадлежности к одному или другому уровню языковой системы – *фонетические, морфологические, синтаксические* и т.д.;
4. по их значимости в системе языка. Балканизмы находятся в йерархических отношениях (ASENOVA 1992) – морфологические и морфосинтаксические оказываются релевантными для существования (или несуществования) языкового союза, как это подчеркивает Н. С. Трубецкой („eine Ähnlichkeit in den Grundsätzen des morphologischen Baus", TRUBETZKOY 1928: 18) и никем не оспаривается, поэтому более удачный термин здесь был бы *sprachbundbildende / nichtsprachbundbildende Balkanismen* (BIRNBAUM 1967: 43; SCHALLER 1975: 123).

2. О концепции представленного доклада

Она строится на утверждении двух основных положений, которые возможно представить следующим образом:

Во-первых. Принято считать балканизмами общие особенности, возникшие в процессе конвергенции балканских языков, следовательно, они являются инновациями. Пробуя составить дефиницию о балканизме на основании выраженых мнений, K. Steinke формулирует требование, что балканизмы не положено относить к индоевропейскому наследию. Сторонником этой идеи, между прочим, является и Вл. Георгиев (STEINKE 1999: 80).

Мое глубокое убеждение, что основательно считать *балканизмами* не только инновации, но и *сохранившееся и утвердившееся в процессе конвергенции индоевропейское наследие*. Эту идею и подкрепляющие ее аргументы я выразила несколько лет тому назад (напр. АСЕНОВА 1989: 230).

Чтобы подкрепить эту идею, можно сослаться и на Вл. Георгиева, который допускает, что во II-I тысячелетиях языки различных племен, населявших Балканский полуостров, начали взаимно влиять друг на друга и, быть может, это было отдаленное начало современной балканской общности. Так, в течении трех тысячелетий сложилось „языковое объединение, которое мы называем балканским языковым союзом" («communauté linguistique que nous appelons union linguistique balkanique»). Следовательно, уже в ранней античности существовало что-то вроде языкового союза (GEORGIEV 1968: 14).

Во-вторых. Общие особенности между двумя языками не являются частичными балканизмами – их появление может быть результатом влияния одного языка на другой (как например болгаро-румынские и болгаро-албанские лексикальные и словообразовательные параллели, а также греческо-арумынские параллели), но они очень показательны для отношений внутри языкового союза. Особое место занимают румыно-албанские параллели – в частности – лексика субстратного происхождения и копулятивный артикль (АСЕНОВА 1989: 231, 2002: 293). Их считают балканизмами на основании вероятно общего и древнего их происхождения.

Цель этого доклада-проанализировать албано-греческие схождения с точки зрения двух объявленных принципов и оценить до какой степени возможно (или невозможно) отнести их к балканизмам типа албано-румынских общих особенностей.

3. Греческий и албанский

На фоне языков балканского союза греческий и албанский отличаются древнейшим бытием на Балканском полуострове и уникальностью их положения в индоевропейской семье – каждый из них представляет отдельную группу.

По мнению Вл. Георгиева, в конце третьего тысячелетия до н. э. греки, обитавшие приблизительно северо-западную часть современной Греции, начали продвигаться к югу (GEORGIEV 1968: 12). По мнению Э. Чабея праалбанцы находились не далеко от греческой территории, что полностью соответствует местонахождению нынешней Албании. В XII-ом веке до н. э. греческие дорические племена были связаны с территорией Эпира. Древнейшие греческие заимствования в албанском, как известно, дорического характера. Праалбанцы вероятно были в контакте с северо-западными дорическими колонистами в поселениях *Lissos (Lezha), Epidamnos (Durrës), Amanthia, Buthroton, Byllis, Fenike* (HAMP 2007: 121; ЖУГРА, СЫТОВ 1990: 69).

Что касается места албанского языка среди индоевропейских языков, надо сказать, что не существует единого мнения, и вопрос остается открытым (срв. напр. HAMP 2007: 115–145; ДЕСНИЦКАЯ 1984: 210–220). Классификация индоевропейских языков, предложенная Вл. Георгиевым, относит греческий к центральной группе, а албанский – к восточной. Кроме того, эти две группы, генетически схожи (GEORGIEV 1981: 360–361).

Следовательно, несмотря на различия в понимании, в самое древнее время греческому и албанскому были присущи как генетические связи, так и исторические контакты. Албано-греческие языковые параллели архаического характера не были объектом особого внимания, но некоторые из них нашли место в балканистике. Приведу два примера.

Соноризация консонантных групп с назалами или переход *mp > mb*, (*nt > nd, nk > ng*) считается фонетическим балканизмом. Ей отдавалось тракийское или дако-мизийское происхождение (срв. ДЕЧЕВ 1952: 26–27; PO-GHIRC 1963: 97–100; ГЕОРГИЕВ 1977: 170–200). Но еще К. Сандфельд отметил одну существенную разницу: в греческом и в албанском эта особенность представляет «évolution qui remonte très haut», в то время как в арумынском речь идет о «influence grecque» (SANDFELD 1930: 102–103).

Интердентальные консонанты θ (*th*) и δ (*dh*) в греческом и в албанском – индоевропейское наследие (ие. *k > θ), а в диалектах других балканских языков они встречаются в заимствованиях из греческого и албанского, как напр. в деревне Бобощица в Южной Албании (JOSEPH 2008) или в арумынском.

4. Албано-греческие схождения на высших языковых уровнях, отсутствующих в остальных языках БЯС

4.1. Морфологическая парадигматика
4.1.1. Формы неактивного залога

Во всех языках БЯС, как и в остальных индоевропейских языках, морфологическая залоговая оппозиция является оппозицией бинарного типа – немаркированная активная форма противопоставляется маркированной неактивной форме. Маркер общеиндоевропейского происхождения восходит к дативным и аккузативным формам личных (указательных) и возвратных местоимений (GEORGIEV 1975: 44, ГЕОРГИЕВ 1985: 110, DEMIRAJ 1985: 727). В болгарском и в румынском маркером служит неударное аккузативное или дативное место-имение:

- в болгарском – это неизменяемое возвратное местоимение *се/си* как во всех славянских языках;
- в румынском – это изменяемое по лицу и по числу личное местоимение *mă / îmi* ; *te / (î)ţi* ; *ne / ni* ; *vă / vi* и возвратное *se / (î)şi* как в романских языках.

Греческий и албанский являются не только единственными среди балканских, но и среди индоевропейских языков, у которых местоименный маркер инкорпорирован в глагольной форме в качестве флексии. В результате получилась морфологизированная синтагма. Таким образом активное и неактивное спряжение глаголов морфологически противопоставляются:

- в греческом – во всех формах спряжения: наст. вр. *δένω / δένομαι* 'свяжу / свяжусь'; имперфект *έδενα / δενόμουν*, аорист *έδεσα / δέθηκα*, подчин. накл. (сов.в.) *να δέσω / να δεθώ* 'связать' / 'связаться', инф. (употребляемый только в составе сложных прошедших времен) *δέσει / δεθεί*, напр. перфект *έχω δέσει / έχω δεθεί*, деятельное прич. *δένοντας*, страдательное прич. *δεμέ-νος*;
- в албанском – в настоящем времени: *laj* 'мыть', *hap* 'открывать' / *la-hem, hap-em* и в имперфекте *la-ja, hap-ja / la-hesha, hap-esha*.

Кроме описанных форм, во всех языках БЯС употребляются описательные причастные формы (вспомогательный глагол „есть" + причастие прошедшего времени): алб. *ёshtë / ishte hapur*; болг. *е / беше отворен*; рум. *este / era deschis* 'есть / был открыт'; гр. *είναι / ήτανε δεμένος* 'есть / был связан'.

В данном случае важно отметить, что функционирование возвратных и причастных форм неактивного залога противопоставляют балканские языки: с одной стороной стоят греческий и албанский, у которых предпочтительны возвратно-местоименные формы, а с другой – болгарский и румынский, где преобладают описательно-причастные формы (ASENOVA 2000: 36–38). Срв. напр. выражения-клише, с одной стороны гр. *απαγορεύεται το κάπνισμα* = алб. *ndalo-het duhani*, а с другой – болг. *пушенето забранено* = рум. *fumatul este oprit*; 'Курить запрещается'; гр. *δεν αποκλείεται* = алб. *nuk përjashtohet* // болг. *не е изключено* = рум. *nu este exclus* 'не исключено'.

4.1.2. Формы третьеличного местоимения

В разных группах индоевропейских языков, включительно во всех языках балканского союза, третьеличные местоимения восходят к указательным, факт соответствующий статусу третьего лица, которое находится вне акта коммуникации.

Употребление указательных местоимений в качестве третьеличных известно в староболгарском (ДОБРЕВ 1982: 175), сохранилось частично в болгарских диалектах во Фракии (БОЯДЖИЕВ 1991: 78). Но только в греческом и в албанском процесс обособления двух групп местименний до сих пор не закончен. В албанском роль третьеличного местоимения исполняется указательным местоимением удаления *ai/ay, ajo, ata, ato*, а в греческом – в основном указательным местоимением близости *αυτός*, а также указательным местоимением удаления *εκείνος*.

В этом случае архаическое состояние, сохранившееся в греческом и в албанском, иллюстрирует отдаленное начало формирования участков индоевропейской прономинальной системы.

4.2. Синтагматика. Функционирование глагольных форм
4.2.1. Аорист – основное время рассказа в прошлом

Жизненность функционально-семантического противопоставления между аористом и перфектом и преобладание аориста над перфектом является частичным балканизмом, представленным в албанском, болгарском и греческом. Аорист является основным временем балканского рассказа в прошлом. Несмотря на то, что употребление аориста в греческом более активно, чем в албанском, между двумя языками существует общность в значениях аориста, совершенно невозможные в болгарском. Достаточно отметить следующие из них:

– результативное значение аориста, срв.
   гр. *...γιά να μην λες, πως σ'έφαγα άδικα, ας πάμε και στην κρίση.*
   гег. *...mos të thush se të **hangra** pa faj, eja të shkojm në gjygj.*
   тоск. *... që të mos thuash se të **hëngra** kot, le të vemi në gjyq.*
   болг. *... че **съм те изял** без право ...* (WEIGAND 1928: № 17);

– гномический аорист, срв.
   гр. *Εκύλησε ο τέντζερης και **βρήκε** το καπάκι.*
   алб. ***Gjeti** tenxherja kapakun.*
   болг. ***Търколила се** тенджерата, **намерила** си похлупака.*
   'Одного поля ягоды.', букв. 'Кастрюля нашла свою крышку.'

Остаюсь при ранее высказанном в другом месте убеждении, что каждому болгарскому аористу соответствует аорист в албанском и в греческом, но не наоборот (подробно ASENOVA 1997).

4.2.2. Экзистенциальные функции глагола „иметь"

Выражение экзистенции при помощи глагола „иметь" характерная особенность балканских языков (см. BUCHHOLZ 1989).

На этом общебалканском фоне очерчивается компактный греческо-албанский ареал, где вместо оценочных экзистенциальных конструкций при помощи глагола „есть", предпочитаются экзистенциальные *иметь*-конструкции, которые можно определить как реляционные (BUCHHOLZ, FIEDLER 1987: 460). Экзистенция в этом случае заявляется как притяжание объекта субъектом, напр.

> гр. *Έχω την μάννα μου άρρωστη.* 'У меня мать больна.' по сравнению с
> *Η μάννα μου είναι άρρωστη.* 'Моя мать болна.';
> алб. *E kam vajzën të bukur.* 'У меня красивая дочь.' по сравнению с
> *Vajza ime është e bukur.* 'Моя дочь красивая.'

В доказательство албано-греческой специфики можно сослаться еще на балканские мудрости как:

> алб. *Rrena i **ka** këmbët të shkurta.* = болг. *На лъжата краката **са** къси.*
> 'Вранье не споро, потухнет скоро.', букв. 'У лжи ноги короткие.'
> алб. *E **ka** gjuhën (gojën) brisk.* = гр. *Έχει τη γλώσσα ξυράφι.*= болг.
> *Езикът му **е** бръснач.* , букв. 'Язык у него как лезвие бритвы.'

В албанском и в греческом посредством конструкции того же самого типа можно выразить родственную связь, социальную или профессиональную близость, поэтому основательно их определить как *habere ethicus*. Ограничусь здесь фатической формулой:

> *Τι τον έχεις;* = *ç'e ke?*= арум. *ţi lu ai?* 'quel est ton rapport avec lui' (SAND-
> FELD 1930: 203), соответствующая болгарскому *какъв ти е той?* 'Кем он тебе
> приходится?', напр. *Τι τον έχεις τον Γιάννη;* (срв. болг. *Какъв ти е Яни?*) 'Кем
> тебе приходится Яни?' – *Τον έχω αδελφό.* (болг. *Брат ми е*) (более подробно
> АСЕНОВА 2008).

5. Синтаксические конструкции интенсификации

В синтаксисе балканских языков, особенно в народно-разговорной речи, функционируют неизменяемые релятивы местоименного происхождения (*дето, που, që, се*), которые вводят разные типы подчинненных предложений. Поэтому их основательно называют *relativum generale* (PO ХАУГЕ 1977) или *абсолютные релятивы* (*relatifs absolus*, см. ASENOVA 1983: 7). По причине идентичности их функций в балканских языках Й. Линдстедт даже предлагает смотреть на них как на "кандидатов" одиннадуатого балканизма в его десятичленном листе балканизмов (LINDSTEDT 1998: 95–96).

Но только в албанском и в греческом эти абсолютные релятивы являются инструментами построения особых конструкций интенсификации качества. Речь идет о восклицательных предложениях типа *Ωραία **πού'**ναι η ζωή!* 'Как хороша жизнь!' При помощи вопросительного местоимения качество как бы рамкируется: *Τι καλά **που** είναι!* 'Как это хорошо!' *Sa shpejt **që** ecën.* 'Как быстро они идут!', а экспрессивность выражения усиливается (ASENOVA 1984).

6. Фрагменты фразеологии

Из необъятности общей балканской фразеологии остановлюсь только на двух албано-греческих параллелях (без сомнения их гораздо больше), отсутствующих в болгарском и румынском, в которых находим застывшую примитивную концептуализацию объективого мира.

6.1. Кровь является символом жизни и родства в разных культурах и языках, в том числе и в языках балканского союза. На Балканах, кроме того кровь хипостаза примитивного представления о генетической идентичности – по просхождению или приобретенная. Ритуал приобретения братства идентичен на Балканах с времен автохтонных племен и выполняется посредством физического принятия смешенной крови.[1]

В греческом и в албанском этот балканизм вербализирован в выражениях:

kam pirë gjak (me dikë), τα αίματά μας σμίξανε 'наши крови смешились = мы побратимы'

έχω πιεί αίμα (με κάποιον) 'я пил кровь (с кем-то) = я побратим с кем-то'.

Если сошлемся на рассуждения Т. В. Цивьяна, можем заключить, что в болгарском и в румынском этот балканизм, оставаясь засвидетельствованным только в культурном пласте ритуальной практики, существует «скрыто», в то время как в греческом и в албанском он в «готовом виде» (ЦИВЬЯН 1990/2005: 153).

Кровное отомщение (вендета) интерпретируется в албанском и в греческом как возвращение чего-то потерянного, отнятого (чести), которое нам принадлежит по праву, поэтому «отомстить, убить» выражается следующим образом:

e zurri gjaku (dikë) = τον έπιασε το αίμα;

---

[1] Этот ритуал описан в балканской литературе – в романе Никоса Казандзакиса *Καπετάν Μιχάλης. Λευτερία ή θάνατος* и в повести Михаила Садовяпу *Neamul Şoimareştilor.*

e morri gjakun (vrau një njeri) = παίρνω το αίμα πίσω, '(он) отомстил, букв. получил кровь (обратно)'

kemi gjak për të marrë. 'мы должны отомстить, букв. мы должны кровь получить' (ASENOVA, DUKOVA 2005: 31)

6.2. В представлениях индоеропейских племен *связывание* и *развязывание*-магические действия, вызывающие соответственно отнятие сил, невозможность двигаться, болезнь и наоборот – освобождение от ограничений, излечение. Из многих свидетельств об этом в языках и магических практиках самое древнее это хетитская (неситская) ворожба для лечения больного ребенка, описывающее деятельность богини – колдуни Камрусепа.[2] На фоне изобилия общебалканских фразем, отражающих описанные примитивные идеи, бросается в глаза уникальность одного албано-греческого фразеологизма. В сжатом виде он содержит все рассеянное в корпусе общих фразем того же вида: αυτός λύνει και δένει = *ai lidh e zgjidh atje* '(он) связывает и развязывает = он всесилен' (ASENOVA 1992a: 104–106). Судя по его наличию еще в древнегреческом εἶναι τὸ δεσμεῖν καὶ λύειν '(он) есть связывание и развязывание', возможно утверждать старинность его происхождения.

Заключение

Предлагаемые на обсуждение схождения накопились в течение долгих лет в процессе исследования разных сторон суперсистемы БЯС-а, как видно из приложенной библиографии.

1. Некоторые из них встречаются и вне албано-греческого ареала: употребление аориста напр. в арумынском, которому приписывается греческое влияние (SANDFELD 1930: 105). Особые экзистенциальные функции глагола „иметь" не чужды арумынскому и болгарским говорам в соседстве с греческим. Все-таки статус албано-греческих общностей особый – они имманентно присущи этим двум языкам (как уже упомянулось в связи с фонетическими чертами), а в остальных являются результатом внешнего влияния.

2. Определенные албано-греческие схождения являются углублением общебалканских тенденций. Такими, напр., являются: нетипичные функции аориста и экзистенциального глагола „иметь"; интерпретация побратимства и всесильности в фразеологии.

   Их можно сравнить с проанализированными В. Фридманом балканизмами (местоименные повторы дополнения и вспомогательный глагол в составе

---

2 Текст в толковании и переводе Кронассера опубликован в 1961 году (KRONASSER 1961: 160–162).

форм пересказывания), которые начинаются с дискурсно-связанных вариаций (variable discourse markers) в одном языке, укрепляются как синтаксико-грамматикализованные (syntactically grammaticalized) в другом, а в третьем – они уже морфологизированны (syntactically or morphologically grammaticalized) (FRIEDMAN 2004: 504).

3. Между албано-греческими схождениями встречаются и такие, которые сохранили первичность индоевропейского состояния, как напр. неразличимость третьеличных от указательных местоимений.

На какие рассуждения наводит нас разнообразный характер этой двусторонней близости? Можно попробовать разграничить генетически связанные (напр. третьеличные местоимения) от контакто-приобретенных особенностей (напр. конструкции интенсификации). Каким из них присудить статус балканизмов? По моему категорического ответа на этот вопрос дать невозможно. С некоторой условностью можем считать балканизмами сохранившиеся архаизмы, как морфологическое противопоставление между активным и неактивным залогами, третьеличное местоимение, фразеологизмы, раскрывающие примитивное мировоззрение, особенно *связать/развязать*.

Значимость языковых контактов, „вызывающих стремление к упрощению и унификации конструкций" (ЦИВЬЯН 2005: 154), значимость прагматичного подхода в среде многоязычных говорителей (FRIEDMAN 2004: 518) для формирования БЯС в данном случае не сработала. Ограниченно-локальный характер албано-греческого билингвизма не является фактором появления балканизмов.

Библиография

АСЕНОВА, П. (1989): *Балканско езикознание. Проблеми на балканския езиков съюз.* София, Наука и изкуство.

АСЕНОВА, П. (2008): Бележки върху *Accusativus duplex* в балканските езици. В: Sigrun Comati (Hrsg.): *Bulgaristica – Studia et Argumenta. Festschrift für Ruselina Nitsolova zum 65. Geburtstag.* München (= Band 151. Specimina philology slavicae, Bd. 151). 348–357.

БОЯДЖИЕВ, Т. (1991): *Българските говори в Западна (Беломорска) и Източна (Одринска) Тракия.* София, Университетско издателство „Климент Охридски".

ГЕОРГИЕВ, В. (1985): Трите залога в българския език: деятелен, страдателен и засебен. В: *Проблеми на българския език.* София, БАН. 98–113.

ДЕСНИЦКАЯ, А. В. (1984): Древние германо-албанские языковые связи в свете проблем индоевропейской ареальной лингвистики. В: А. В. Десницкая: *Сравнительное языкознание и история языков.* Ленинград, Наука. 210–239.

ДОБРЕВ, Ив. (1982): *Старобългарска граматика. Теория на основите.* София, Наука и изкуство.

ЖУГРА, А. В.; СЫТОВ, А. П. (1990): Албанский язык. В: *Основы балканского языкознания. Языки балканского региона*. Часть I, отв.ред. А. В. Десницкая. Ленинград, Наука. 46–99.

РО ХАУГЕ, Х. (1977): Синтактични балканизми в българския език и езиковата редундантност. *Linguistique balkanique* XXVII, 5. 380–385.

ЦИВЬЯН, Т. В. (1990): *Лингвистические основы балканской модели мира*. Москва, Наука.

ЦИВЬЯН, Т. В. (2005): *Модель мира и ее лингвистические основы*. Москва, КомКнига.

ASENOVA, P. (1980): Sur le statut des balkanismes syntactiques. *Linguistique balkanique* XXIII, 1. 9–19.

ASENOVA, P. (1983): A propos des fonctions syntaxiques des relatifs absolus dans les langues balkaniques. B: *Die slawischen Sprachen* 5. Salzburg. 5–12.

ASENOVA, P. (1984): Une construction syntaxique d'intensification en grec et en albanais. *Linguistique balkanique* XXVII, 3. 31–34.

ASENOVA, P. (1991): Contenu linguistique des balkanismes. *Zeitschrift für Balkanologie* 27. 13–16.

ASENOVA, P. (1992): Hiérarchie des balkanismes dans le système de l'union linguistique balkanique. *Kurier der Bochumer Gesellschaft für rumänische Sprache und Literatur* 17. 130–137.

ASENOVA, P. (1992a): La mentalité balkanique: vues de l'«homo balcanicus» sur certaines qualités humaines. *Linguistique balkanique* XXXV, 3/4. 97–113.

ASENOVA, P. (1997): Observations sur l'emploi de l'aoriste en grec et en albanais. *Zeitschrift für Balkanologie* 33, 2. 137–147.

ASENOVA, P. (2000): Quelques observations sur l'emploi de la diathèse non-active dans les langues balkaniques. B: *Balkanlinguistik. Synchronie und Diachronie. Akten des internationalen Kongresses*. 30. Oktober – 1. November 1997. Thessaloniki. 27–39.

ASENOVA, P.; DUKOVA, U. (2005): «Ipse ego». Moyens linguistiques de son expression balkanique I. *Linguistique balkanique* XLIV, 1/2. 29–37.

BIRNBAUM, H. (1967): Balkanslavisch und Südslavisch. *Zeitschrift für Balkanologie* 3, 1. 12–63.

BUCHHOLZ, O.; FIEDLER, W. (1987): *Albanische Grammatik*. Leipzig, Enzyklopädie Verlag.

BUCHHOLZ, O. (1989): Zu Konstruktionen mit unpersönlich gebrauchtem ‚haben' in den Balkansprachen. *Zeitschrift für Phonetik, Sprachwissenschaft und Kommunikationsforschung* 42, 3. 329–338.

DEMIRAJ, Sh. (1985): *Gramatikë historike e gjuhës shqipe*. Tiranë, 8 Nëntori.

FRIEDMAN, V. (2004): Variation and grammaticalization in the development of balkanisms. B: V. Friedman (ed.): *Studies in Albanian and other Balkan Languages*. Pejë, Dukagjini Publishing House. 503–524.

GEORGIEV, V. (1968): Le problème de l'union linguistique balkanique. B: *Actes du Premier congrès international des études balkaniques et sud-est européennes. VI. Linguistique*. Sofia, BAN.

GEORGIEV, V. (1975): Die Entstehung der indoeuropäischen Verbalkategorien. *Linguistique balkanique* XVIII. 5–56.

GEORGIEV, V. (1981): *Introduction to the History of the Indo-European Languages.* Sofia, BAN.

HAMP, E. P. (1966/2007): Vendi i shqipes. B: Eric P. Hamp: *Studime krahasuese për shqipen.* Prishtinë, Ashak. 115–145 = The Position of the Albanian. – Henrik Birnbaum, Jaan Puhvel (eds.): *Ancient Indo-European Dialects.* Los Angeles 1966. 97–121.

HINRICHS, U. (1999): Die sogenannten ‚Balkanismen' als Problem der Südosteuropa-Linguistik und der allgemeinen Sprachwissenschaft. B: Uwe Hinrichs (Hrsg.): *Handbuch der Südosteuropa-Linguistik.* Wiesbaden, Harrassowitz. 429–462.

JOSEPH, B. (2008): Општа и локална дијалектологија на Балканот: Податоци од словенските јазици. *Македонски јазик* 2008 online: http://www.ling.ohio-state.edubjoseph/publicat.htm.

KRONASSER, H. (1961): Fünf hethitische Rituale. *Die Sprache* VII. 140–167.

LINDSTEDT, J. (1998): On the Balkan linguistic type. *Studia slavica finlandensia.* Tomus XV. 91–103

SANDFELD, Kr. (1930): *Linguistique balkanique. Problèmes et résultats.* Paris, Edouard Champion.

SCHALLER, H.-W. (1975): *Die Balkansprachen. Eine Einführung in die Balkanphilologie.* Heidelberg, Universitätsverlag Winter.

SCHALLER, H.-W. (1986): Genetische und typologische Übereinstimmungen der Balkansprachen mit anderen europäischen Sprachen. *Linguistique balkanique* XXIX, 4. 61–65.

STEINKE, K. (1976): Gibt es überhaupt Balkanismen? *Linguistique balkanique* 19, 1. 21–35.

STEINKE, K. (1999): Zur theoretischen Grundlegung der Südosteuropa-Linguistik. B: Uwe Hinrichs (Hrsg.): *Handbuch der Südosteuropa-Linguistik.* Wiesbaden, Harrassowitz. 67–90.

TRUBETZKOY, N. S. (1928): Proposition 16. B: *Actes du Premier Congrès International des Linguistes.* La Haye. 17–18.

WEIGAND, G. (1928): Texte zur vergleichenden Syntax der Balkansprachen. *Balkan Archiv* IV. 53–70.

On the status of some common features of two Balkan languages. Are they balkanisms or not?

Although I support the opinion that the common features of two languages belonging to the Balkan *Sprachbund* are not balkanisms, I analyse the following morphosyntactic peculiarities of Greek and Albanian:

– non-active diathesis;
– personal and demonstrative pronouns;
– Aorist / Perfect opposition;
– existential value of the verb "to have";
– some syntactic and phraseological constructions.

And if it could be proved that the origin of these common traits is archaic, could we attribute to them the status of Balkanisms?

Balkanisms today: The Dialect of Župa (Kosovo)

Krasimira KOLEVA (Shumen)

The Area

The dialect of Župa/Zhupa is the idiom of a small Slavonic Muslim community in the western Balkan-Slavonic area in the contact zone between three large indigenous language continua: Albanian in the north-west, Macedonian-Bulgarian in the south and Serbian in the east. On the diachronic linguistic plane the population was in an environment with Aromanian and with Turkish in the historical context with memories of an imposed confessional code due to the conversion from Christianity to a heterodox Muslim practice. The community was isolated for a long time, which promoted the centripetal forces in the linguistic and cultural processes. Today, the community lives on the territory of the Republic of Kosovo/Kosova in 16 villages belonging to the geographical areas of *Župa* (12 villages) and *Podgor* (4 villages), in the district of *Prizren*, which is the centre of the municipality. In the former Yugoslavia most of the villages were in the *Sredačka Župa. Zhupa* (meaning, in this context, 'administrative region') is the eastern part of the ethnographic region of Gora, the dialects of which have been variously described as: northern Macedonian, transitional Bulgarian, *turlaški* (Bulgarian and Serbian), Šar Planina Serbian, and the population as: Slavs, Muslims, Bosniaks, Turks, Bulgarians, Serbs, Prizren Pomaks and Torbeši.

Research Context

Significant social changes are taking place in the western Balkans. These changes are having a great effect on the multiethnic linguistic and cultural situation. Convergent and divergent processes are typical for the Balkans and can be compared with one another in different parts of the area. In Kosovo they are outstripping their description. The object for research – the Prizrenska Župa and Podgor – have so far been neglected by complex scholarly projects and, judging by the data, the area has rarely been counted as part of the Gora. It is a complex and dynamic contact zone and the resources of the research with which we are familiar are inadequate, since they do not employ an interdisciplinary approach. Our point of departure was the information in the literature. Then we conducted a comprehensive excursion in 2009. There followed specialized research projects, working with informants from the entire sociolinguistic spectrum. The dialect of Župa/Zhupa is treated here as a Balkan-Slavonic sociocultural phenomenon. The mentality of *homo balcanicus* is encoded in the language of this sociocultural phenomenon. This is confirmed by the stratum of balkanisms as the focus of the text.

Empirical Material

Balkanisms today in the many and varied multiethnic regions of the western periphery of the Balkan Peninsula are the topic of our on-going fieldwork in the different states of this area. This Balkan environment is in constant flux. Our research has been conducted systematically from 2007 onwards in Macedonia, Serbia and Kosovo. This work represents the first results of a long-term research project conducted by the University of Shumen entitled *"Ethnopolitics of language and languages of politics in the Balkans"*. Our results can be compared with my research into the commonalities between us and diaspora Bulgarians. The comprehensive research excursions in the Western Balkans have focussed on the commonalities with Bulgarian roots but the research has not been limited only to those. On the basis of the material that we have collected we plan to pursue a general line of research analysing language processes in the categories of cultural anthropology (oral tales of personal and collective memories and documents by the speakers of one ethnic (literary) language / dialect in competition with other Balkan languages (Bulgarian spoken in different parts of the former Yugoslavia – compared with Serbian and "Yugoslavian" constructed as dominant with a balance between "Serbisms", "Croatisms", "Bosnianisms", as well as similar processes in Southern Serbia, Kosovo, Albania, Turkey, Greece). From this point of view the narrowly sociolinguistic and dialectological problems is integrated with parallel processes in literature, the media, art and mass culture, which is a novelty in fieldwork practice. The research is in the spirit of the promising idea connected with the concept of *homo balcanicus*, developed by V. Civjan, P. Asenova and others. It links in with the large-scale programme of the Malyj dialektologičeskij atlas balkanskih jazykov (MDABJa) / Kleiner Balkansprachatlas directed by H. Schaller and A. N. Sobolev. In October–November 2009, within the framework of the university project and with the support of the Municipality of Shumen, we examined the present-day state of the historical Slavonic communities in the Republic of Kosovo. We did this in a direct dialogue conducted by the team with representatives of all the social and age groups. Contacts with the basic informants precede work in the field and are continuing. The research project is being conducted on the territory entire of Kosovo, where these people live in compact groups, in enclaves or dispersed among the mass of Albanian speakers. According to data published by the OSCE (Organization for Security and Co-operation in Europe) in 2005, 92% of the population of Kosovo is made up of Albanians and 4% of Serbs. The recognized minorities are: Bosnians and Gorans 4%, Gypsies (Rom) 1% and Turks also 1%. (The first official census in the new state is to be conducted in 2011.) The materials from the fieldwork have been documented and it is planned to publish them.

The district

Župa is on the territory of Southern Kosovo. It is a region with a mixed population. From an administrative point of view, the region is in the district of Prizren, municipality of Prizren. It includes 16 villages: *Gorne selo, Mušnikovo, Gorno Ljubine, Dolno Ljubine, Rečane, Nebregošta, Lokvica, Manastirica, Planjane, Skorobište, Gărnčare, Ljubižde, Pousko, Jablanica, Drajčiki* and *Novo selo*. There are emigrants from *Novo selo* in the village of *Kurilo voda* in the district of Sredska Župa. The people call themselves *župci* and *gorani*, one group being contained within the other. From a geographical point of view, Župa is part of Šar Planina, south-east of Prizren, and some of these mountain villages are in the basin of the river Prizrenska Bistrica. Reaching most of them is difficult due to the features of the terrain and the undeveloped infrastructure. Only three villages – *Rečane, Mušnikovo* and *Gorne selo* – are accessible by third-category road from Prizren in an easterly direction towards Kačanec – the border crossing Blace – Skopje. Access to the other villages is by lower-category road or dirt track, which makes them practically inaccessible under unfavourable climatic conditions and during the autumn and winter people move mainly to Prizren, where their children are accommodated. It is a sparsely populated region bordering on Macedonia and the only direct connexion to Tetovo is a dirt track through a narrow gorge under Mount Kobilica (2536 m). These physical characteristics of the terrain were the only defence for the population in the past, but from an economic point of view in the 20th century they have only served to marginalize the region even more. The economy is linked with the natural surroundings. Of an area of 163 square km scarcely 10% is cultivated. More than half the terrain is made up of mountain pasture that is used for sheep. The local Šar Planina sheep's cheese is famous. There are some orchards and vineyards. The traditional building trade for which the *župci* were famous has become since long an "export item" for the majority of the male population.

The Ethnolinguistic Concept of Gora and Previous Research

Župa is the eastern periphery of the ethnographic region of Gora, which in the past was a closed ethnocultural area belonging to different polities at different times. Until 1971, the population was registered by the authorities as *Turks*, from 1971 it was included in the *Muslim nationality*, from 1996–1999, in order to prove the multicultural character of Kosovo, it was declared to be a new, unique ethnos – *goranci* (in Serbian). In the local dialect the morphological variant is *gòrani*. Their late conversion to Islam excluded in effect their participation in the national movements in the Balkans, which were accompanied by incessant migration processes.

In Gora two great cultures (Christian and Muslim) intersect. The differences have been and still are manipulated in a strongly politicized social discourse, leading to a series of crises in the recent history of the Western Balkans. The Gorans were converted to Islam relatively recently. They are Shiites, which isolates them even further by confession. The Albanians call them Torbeši. Unlike the other Slavonic Muslim communities in the Balkans, the Gorans began long ago to migrate. Entire clans have settled around the Balkans – in Macedonia, Serbia, Croatia, Turkey and Bulgaria, as well as in a number of other countries on the continent, where they are known as confectioners, kebab grillers or master builders. Around the region they are famous as sheep breeders and shepherds. They breed the well-known Šar Planina dog, which gave rise to the popular zoonym Šaro. They produce and sell cold steel (knives, swords etc.) Their customs are well preserved. The community always gathers for St George's Day (6 May) to mark the beginning of the summer and the marriage season. The migratory workers (*gurbetčii*) come home. Engagements are arranged. The wedding lasts five days and the entire village takes part. The Gorans mark their territory by means of the architectural environment. Their villages have a centre formed by the mosque and communal buildings. Their houses are built and arranged differently from those of the Albanians and the Serbs. The men organize grease-wrestling contests (*pehlivanlăk*) and horse races *(kušii)*. The music, the dances and the songs have retained their Slavonic character. The traditional costumes are varied, brightly coloured, richly ornamented and appropriate for the harsh climate. A new segment has been formed in this ethnographic layer – the emigrants' clothing. The *gurbetčii* invariably buy cameras and, due to this, the culture has been documented throughout the 20th century (cf. KOSOVA 2007). A considerable part of the linguistic and musical folklore has been written down. Some original work has been published.

Today, however, we have no synchronic data on the culture and dialects of Gora because, as is well known, a century ago (1912), the political borders divided it between Albania and Serbia. The Serbian invasion against Bulgaria during the Balkan Wars (1912–1913) removed not only Kosovo from any institutionalized Bulgarian presence in the Western Balkans for a long time. Thus Gora was excluded from the Bulgarian Dialect Atlas (BDA) and other Bulgarian research projects. It is only since the Kosovo crisis (1999) that Bulgarians have had access to this Macedonian-Bulgarian area, as a result of which some publications relating to Gora have appeared in Bulgaria (Bălgarski ostrovi 2007, GRADINAROVA 2008, MANGALAKOVA 2008).

In Albania, the community has not been officially recognized even today. The dialect and the folklore are being collected and the results published by local ethnographers. With the large bilingual dictionary of the Goran by Nazif DOKLE *Reçnik goranski (nashinski) – albanski* (DOKLE 2007), the self-determination of the language as *našinski* has been finally established. This linguistic self-determination, which is used throughout the territory of Gora, is unique from the point of view of the classification of languages. The territory of the *našinski* substandard is known in Albania as *Kuk'ska Gora* based on the name of the municipal centre (*Kukës*). The bilingual language situation is being investigated by Macedonian and Bulgarian scholars (cf. ASENOVA 2005, 2007). Recently, some places have been the object of fieldwork for the *Malyj dialektologičeskij atlas balkanskih jazykov* (MDABJa) / *Kleiner Balkansprachatlas* lead by H. Schaller and A. N. Sobolev.

Most of the territory inhabited by the Gorans today is in the Republic of Kosovo. From an administrative point of view, it is included in the district whose centre is Prizren. In the public sphere it is known as Kosovska Gora, Župa and Podgor, and in scholarly publications is found as Prizrenska Gora and Župa. The dialects in Prizrenska Gora around *Dragaš* were investigated at the end of the last century mostly by Macedonian scholars (VIDOESKI 1995) and Serbian linguists (Balkan Research 2007), mainly Radivoe MLADENOVIĆ, who was born in Prizren. Mladenović describes them as Šar Planina dialects in numerous publications, including a monograph (MLADENOVIĆ 2001). Polish balkanologists have also shown an interest in Gora in the context of the language situation in Kosovo (cf. e.g. MINDAK-ZAWADZKA 2008).

The dialect of Župa is not a familiar concept in scholarly circles. In the literature (classic works and more recent ones) relating to the population, culture and language(s) in present-day Kosovo, Župa is sometimes mentioned (usually the same few villages), but there has never been a comprehensive investigation. At the end of the last century, R. Mladenović investigated three places for the Serbian dialectological atlas: *Gorne Selo* in Župa and *Ljubižde* and *Skorobište* in Podgor. The reasons for the lack of more data (especially on the contemporary language situation) are complex and some of them are objectively justified:

- the region is difficult to access even now
- the ethnodemographic picture is dynamic – the Slavonic population is being swallowed up and the Kosovo-Albanian element is increasing greatly
- in the past, the Gora villages had a compact population, but today the number of places with a mixed population is increasing; the Albanian presence is increasing, the Serbian is decreasing
- the Macedonian-Bulgarian ethnographic and linguistic continuum in Gora was unbroken until the Kosovo crisis but it has now been destroyed by an Albanian wedge in the district of Opole, which separates Župa and Podgor from Dragaška Gora in Kosovo; today, the decreasing Gora community lives (from west to east) in the neighbouring districts of Kuk'ska Gora (in Albania) and Dragaška Gora (in Kosovo), followed by Opole, which is populated by Kosovo Albanians (within the municipality of Dragaš) and the districts of Župa and Podgor (in the municipality of Prizren) with two types of village – the predominant type so far

with a homogeneous Goran population (10) and those with a mixed population (with Serbs – 5, but with Albanians there is now 1 village).

In statistical sources, the Goran population today is registered under various headings (mainly *Bosniaks* and *Turks*). The reason for this lies in the fact that, after Kosovo was administered by UNMIK (United Nations Interim Administration Mission in Kosovo) in 1999, the Gorans in Župa and Podgor not only did not receive the administrative autonomy that they had been promised, but the larger and more heavily populated Dragaška Gora was annexed to the Albanianized Opole (a municipality between Dragaška Gora and Prizren from 1991 to 1999). The demographic balance in the municipality of Dragaš is: 43% Gorans and 57% Albanians. The NATO base with a UN mandate KFOR (The Kosovo Force) in Dragaš is Turkish (and is called "Bayazid"). The Prizren municipality is under the control of the German contingent, there are a Turkish and a Bulgarian platoon. The community in Gora, which was compact and closed under the totalitarian regime, is now faced with a new and much changed territorial demographic and linguistic situation.

The Language Situation and Language Politics

These aspects of the language are closely connected with the problem of the contemporary state of the Balkanisms in a Macedonian-Bulgarian idiom in a social milieu that is increasingly dominated by other languages (Balkan and Slavonic).

In multiethnic Kosovo the trend in the birth rate of the dominant community determines the dynamics of the language situation and for the last half-century it has been turning into an instrument of language politics (KOLEVA 2011). In Župa, the co-existence between the different ethnic groups is based on confession. As a result of the hyperdynamic demographic picture and the absence of a balanced language policy, which is a hangover from the totalitarian period, the official bilingualism (Albanian / Serbian) is not, in reality, based on parity. The aggressive foreign media presence sets the scene for new myths in the sphere of ethnic and linguistic self-identification by the population, which reflects on the language situation. The three pillars that support a community are absent; they are: *schooling* in the native language; a *spiritual institution* in a language that the people understand; and a *cultural centre* that would preserve and develop traditions. In order to obtain an education, the Gorans have to choose between Serbian and Albanian, which change places in relation to *prestige* and are in opposition to each other in their social realization and access to higher education. In Gora and Župa there has never been schooling in the native language. It is a patriarchal home language whose use by young people in the age of globalization in more and more limited. This applied also to the external migration, which is constantly increasing. In the village, schools instruction is still in Serbian. Župans that emigrate within Kosovo learn to speak Albanian. In 2006 Skopje made an unsuccessful attempt to introduce standard Macedonian for the "Islamized Macedonian" Gorans. Turkish and "Bosnian" are also available, which is tacitly tolerated (which incidentally is the situation with the limiting of Serbian in the enclaves). On the regional airwaves in Župa the local radio stations are finding new partners, such as Bulgaria, with the help of the Deutsche Welle. Cultural and educational societies are being set up. An intelligentsia is coming into being. Political activity is increasing by means of coalitions with the Albanians and the Bosniaks. For now, the Gora community has only one MP. Under the new realities, prosperity depends on speaking Albanian and the hyper-language, English. Bilingualism (home language and Serbian) is being encouraged and is even increasing. Multilingualism has reached the stage of home language (substandard) – standard Serbian – Albanian substandard (which is likely to become soon the standard under the pressure of the environment). Circumstances favour the increase of Turkish, which is not unknown, and also for instruction in Bulgarian for some of the Gorans who desire this. This is the precondition for diglossia. There is little trace of the language contacts with the Aromanians (Vlachs, Cincars), about which the Bulgarian literary figure Petko SLAVEJKOV wrote in 1860:

> "В Прилеп цинцарщината тъй прилепнала у българщината, щото ако [в]земеш да я разлепиш, живо месо трябва да късаш" [In Prilep the Cincars are so firmly wedded to the Bulgarians that if you wanted to separate them you would have to bite into living flesh].

For the educated Gorans the onomastic traces of Aromanian (toponymy and anthroponymy) are well known (IDRIZI 2008).

The Balkan Code for the Identity of Communities on the Basis of the Native Language

The reordering of the territories of the Western Balkans in the 20th century has affected Gora as well. Today, it is in two states (Albania and Kosovo) and in the south it borders on Macedonia, where in the *Tetovski Polog* (SELIŠČEV 1929, KĂNČOV 1900) there are two villages with emigrants from Gora (*Jelovene* and *Urvič*). An identity crisis is characteristic of a society in conflict. In *Prizrenska Gora*, from 1971 onwards, the Gorans have been registered as *Muslims*, and from 1993 as *Bosniaks* or *Turks*. It is significant that minority communities are designated in Serbian studies with the ambivalent term *skrivene manjine* 'hidden / concealed minorities'. In the 2008 constitution of Kosovo the community is recognized as a minority under the name of *Gorans*, but in Župa it is not only not proclaimed openly but more and more often it is disguised: a situational ethnic self-determination can be observed, coupled with a linguistic behaviour of a bilingual or multilingual type. This wavering identity is due to the lack of social traditions, to a pervasive and influential intellectual and political elite. The dominant role of confession beside an ethnic / linguistic identification has many and serious causes. Some of them are associated with the sociolinguistic marker *prestige*. It can be interpreted as a defensive reaction to a permanent critical economic situation. According to our informants, the factor of *survival* is paramount. Apart from a Turkish army contingent, there are considerable Turkish investments in Prizren. During our stay, the largest broadcasting medium became the property of a Turkish company. A man that had found employment with a Turkish firm hesitated to admit indirectly that he was a Goran; he did not wish to reveal that he spoke the dialect. In the religious sphere there are new factors that have a powerful influence on local identity and language. In the Kosovo conflict, Wahabi Muslims took part in the Albanian military organization Ushtria Çlirimtare e Kosovës (UÇK) and the official Islamic community has not distanced itself from them. In their religious practices there are intensive processes of clericalization associated with globalization. Apart from that, the Kosovo Albanians are not only Muslims. Prizren is the seat of their Catholic denomination. In Kosovo, the Albanian identity is not demonstrated by confessional markers or language but through the birth rate, which is very high and, parallel to this, through the high level of building activity, which is a consequence of the high birth rate.

The Gorans fear that the appearance of Arab Muslim schools in their villages not only interferes with the development of the local schools, but also divides the community. A recent development in the new socio-political environment in the Balkans is the practice of an increasing number of members of the Goran cultural and educational organizations to identify themselves as Bulgarians and obtain an education in Bulgaria. The mother tongue of the Gorans/Župans is only a home language and has never been studied in an institutional context. Education is obtained in other languages. For the emigrants, the native language is also limited to their home and is subject to interference. The mother tongue, as part of the Macedonian-Bulgarian continuum, has an analytical structure but preserves its archaic features. The native speakers say that there are some small differences between the dialects in Dragaška Gora and Župa and also between those of the individual villages in Župa. This is due to the natural barriers that exist in this inaccessible terrain. Adult informants recognize the languages that are spoken in Kosovo and the neighbouring states and understand their similarities and differences. The Gorans learn languages easily. Satellite transmissions give the young people the possibility to engage in contemporary communication and to speak their native language on air in the local and regional media. *Gorans* and *Goran language* are concepts that bear an ethno-ideological content at a time when politics has been accompanied by ethnic cleansing. Therefore, independently of the nationality that has been proclaimed in the country and in the foreign passport held by an emigrant, community is determined by features that are common and value-laden for all speakers:

- *Gorans* or *Župans* respectively: a geographical regional marker associated with ethnographic characteristics
- *našinci* and *našinski*: a characteristic Balkan dual code for belonging to a community with the same language and the same religion and containing the presupposition that the ethnic, linguistic and national affiliations as a whole complex of features are not identical with any other community, while at the same time they cannot be advertised. The concept *naš čovek (nače čedo / našenec / ot našite)* is well-known in the Balkan-Slavonic area as a marker of belonging to an ethnoregional community whose members do not necessarily live there but have the same mother tongue / dialect.

In conversations with our informants we deliberately used standard Bulgarian. Even though they did not always understand us perfectly, which is not surprising, they called us *svoi* ("our people"). That is a convincing linguistic explication of the mentality of the *homo balcanicus* in the opposition *"ours – foreign"*, in which language, in a specific way, plays the leading role in the field of categories connected with family or ethnic belonging.

Balkanisms

As was to be expected in this peripheral Balkan-Slavonic idiom, which functions in a transitional Slavonic dialect area, which is in contact with Albanian and which preserves vestiges of an ancient interaction with Aromanian, the list of Balkanisms is long:

- the presence of a morphologically expressed category of *definite – indefinite* with a postposed definite article: *Со момчѐто се засакàла. / So momčèto se zasakàla. Го сàкам другàратого мл'о̀го. / Go sàkam drugàratogo ml'ògo. Има три мѐтра бàсмава. / Ima tri mètra bàsmava. Ко̀лко дàваш за кàпава? / Kòlko dàvaš za kàpava? Дебѐло мѐле воденицава. / Debèlo mèle vodenicava. Шугѝштево нѐ ни се тъ̀рна. / Šugištevo nè ni se tǎrna. Што биле хул'а̀ве драйчинкиштата. / Što bile hul'àve drajčinkištata.*
- isosyntagmatic constructions in which the prepositions *ot, do, za, s* signal the most abstract and general relations, a result of the development towards an analytical structure: *Йо̀ште йѐна офца имàме **от** сой. / Jòšte jèna ofca imàme **ot** soj. Нѐ се додàвай ништо **от** куча. / Nè se dodàvaj ništo **ot** kuča. Нѐ ми се собѐруйет но̀ге **от** болѐштине. / Nè mi se sobèrujet nòge **ot** bolèštine. Сви **до** йѐдно че пàтите. / Svi **do** jèdno če pàtite. Во срѐда че по̀йм **за** Призрен. / Vo srèda če pòjm **za** Prizren. Се врàтиха **за** до̀ма. / Se vràtiha **za** dòma. Че по̀йм **за** ракийа. / Če pòjm **za** rakija. **За** пàре све биде со договòрене. / **Za** pàre sve bide so dogovòrene. До̀йде л'аф **за** жѐнене и те спо̀мнахме. / Dòjde l'af **za** žènene i te spòmnahme. Трѐбе да до̀йдеш **за** свàдба. / Trèbe da dòjdeš **za** svàdba. Не вѐли шуч'ур, ка сом ги со̀браф **со** мука. / Ne vèli šuč'ur, ka som gi*

sòbraf **so** *muka. Ми сом га сòбраф смо* **со** *йен л'аф. / Mi som ga sòbraf smo* **so** *jen l'af.*

- duplication of the object with short dative and accusative forms of the personal pronouns: *Он ми га напрàиф* **рабòтата.** */ On mi* **ga** *napràif* **rabòtata.** *Им га дàде* **книгата.** */ Im* **ga** *dàde* **knigata.** *Го имам во глàва* **името.** */ Go imam vo glàva* **imeto.** *Ми го двòйте от хисе* **дèтево.** */ Mi go dvòjte ot hise* **dètevo.** *Стèгни ги мàлко* **кошòйти** *да нè се дрàнгайе тàке. / Stègni gi malko* **košòjti** *da nè se dràngaje tàke.* **Ги** *измахнàле све* **компирити.** */* **Gi** *izmahnàle sve* **kompiriti.** *Дебèло ги сèчииш* **плòчите.** */ Debèlo gi sèčiš* **pločite.** *Кой че ги нàрчи голèми* **ве кàмене?** */ Koj če gi pàrči golèmi* **ve kàmene?** *Го извàди* **инайèт** *на мèне. / Go izvàdi* **inajèt** *na mène. Со модрèнево мàло си* **га** *исàбиф* **рабòта.** */ So modrènevo màlo si* **ga** *isàbif* **rabòta.** *Опàсно го тупа* **дàйре.** */ Opàsno go tupa* **dàjre.** *Йèне мòлци ни ги испàсоха* **постèле.** */ Jène mòlci ni gi ispàso-ha* **postèle.** *Ка го виде нèго,* **мèне** *ме жèжна. / Ka go vide nègo,* **mène** *me žèžna. Не* **ти** *трèба* **тèбе** *длък мухабèт. / Ne* **ti** *trèba* **tèbe** *tlăk muhabèt.*

- use of the relative pronoun as a general relative particle: *Тòйа* **дрàйчинец,** **што** *не рабòтаф за сèбе. / Tòja* **dràjčinec,** **što** *ne rabòtaf za sèbe. Све,* **што** *дойдòха, донèсле по нèшто. / Sve,* **što** *dojdòha, donèsle po nèšto. Нè го има на клинец* **калèмот, што** *ми го трàжиш òдма. / Nè go ima na klinec* **kale-mot, što** *mi go tràžiš òdma. Пармàчето,* **што** *сом го стàваф лàни, бèше се изкривило. / Parmačèto,* **što** *som go stàvaf làni, bèše se izkrivilo. Све* **шугиш-та, шо** *прòшле ке нас, дур не застàнет, нèма. / Sve* **šutišta, šo** *pròšle ke nas, dur ne zastànet, nèma.*

- analytical degrees of comparison in adjectives and adverbs: *И он ка нах йе* **по дл'ъгест.** */ I on ka nah je* **po dl'ăgest.** *Мàти им била* **по дранагàлеста.** */ Màti im bila* **po dranagàlesta.** *Пипèрике* **по скупе** *ги имам. / Pipèrike* **po sku-pe** *gi imam.*

- the *da*-construction in place of the infinitive and the supine: *Трèбе* **да** *биде хубаф. / Trèbe* **da** *bide hubav. Трèбе* **да** *се урàвни двòрот. / Trèbe* **da** *se uràv-ni dvòrot. Трèбе* **да** *му се рèче за парèте. / Trèbe* **da** *mu se rèče za parète. Сà-кам* **да** *отвòрим йен дуч'ан. / Sàkam* **da** *otvòrim jen duč'an. Сàкам* **да** *се жèним. / Sàkam* **da** *se žènim. Те сакàйе* **да** *сèдииш òвде / Te sakàje* **da** *sèdiš òvde.*

- optative-imperative forms with *da*: *Да сом ка тèбе! /* **Da** *som ka tèbe! Да жи-вèеш сто године! /* **Da** *živèeš sto godine!*

- analytical future tense of both verbal aspects: **Че** *остàйм йен пèнджер от гòрна стрàна. /* **Če** *ostàjm jen pèndžer ot gòrna stràna.* **Че** *имаме свàдба во година. /* **Če** *imame svàdba vo godina. Кога* **че** *се урèди кучава, нè знъм. / Koga* **če** *se urèdi kučava, nè znăm. Полèка-лека* **че** *виш ка* **че** *се давранди-саш. / Polèka-leka* **če** *viš ka* **če** *se davrandisaš.*

– simple preterital forms of the aorist and imperfect: *Се заалдерисаф от сабàх по йѐне книге. / Se zaalderisav ot sabàh po jène knige. Само два пути ми го даф кòн'а. / Samo dva puti mi go daf kòn'a. Им измахнàха и се врàтиха за дòма. / Im izmahnàha i se vràtiha za dòma. Останàхме не идано на вечѐра. / Ostanàhme ne idano na večèra. Она вѐзден се молѐше да нѐ ти биде нѐшто. / Ona vèzden se molèše da nè ti bide nèšto. Йѐна жѐна продавàше патлиджàни. / Jèna žèna prodavàše patlidžàni. Телèто бѐше млòго дебèло. / Telèto bèše mlògo debèlo.*

– an interesting balkanism in the nominal system, found only in the colloquial / dialectal speech of all Balkan languages is the various two-component numerals to designate an approximate amount, as in *pet-šest, edno-drugo*, with which it is possible to describe the Balkan concept of measure and quantity connected with the universal category of *number*: *Ми дàде йѐдна-две пàре да купим йѐдно шкѐрче. / Mi dàde jèdna-dve pàre da kupim jèdno škèrče. Два-три кòна мож да биле тòйа ден во нива. / Dva-tri kòna moz da bile tòja den vo niva. Càмо два-три пути. / Sàmo dva-tri puti. Сме имàле две-три крàве. / Sme imàle dve-tri kràve. За два-трòйца нèма гàйле. / Za dva-tròjca nèma gàjle. Имам пет-шес пàре. / Imat pet-šes pàre. Ми дàла дèвет-дèсет йàбуке. / Mi dàla dèvet-dèset jàbuke. Сме биле два-трийсе мужа и йòпе нѐ сме мòгле да го помѐштиме. / Sme bile dva-trijse miža i jòpe nè sme mògle da go pomèštime. Пòйче от два-трийсетина нѐ сме биле. / Pòjče ot dva-trijsetina nè sme bile. Йѐно деведèсе-сто йàйца йа сом ги зеф. / Jèno devedèse-sto jàjca ja som gi zef. Сме биле две-триста càмо жѐне во касабàта. / Sme bile dve-trista sàmo žène vo kasabàta. Ми трѐбе йѐно две-триста кило мѐсо. / Mi trèbe jèno dve-trista kilo mèso.*

The archaic and the new aspects of these balkanisms illustrate the typology of the uneven progress from the synthetic to the analytical structure and the relationship of *centre ~ periphery* in the contact zone. The results of interference due to bilingualism with Albanian, most notably in syntax, word order and grammatical semantics bear witness to the intensity and the direction of the processes of language contact. The isosemia like the phraseology can serve as proof of how language contacts reflect on mental categories, so that one can speak of the ethnolinguocentric *homo balcanicus*.

Tasks for Research

Investigating the dynamic processes in the ethnolinguistic and standard-language situation in the Balkans at the end of the 20th and the beginning of the 21st century is one of the contemporary priorities for research. The political aspects of the problem and the high degree of social and media attention to this problem go beyond a purely academic interest. Objective scholarly insights into these processes at a time of increasing nationalist attitudes contribute not only to realizing objective scholarly standards but also to reaching a generalized contemporary scholarly vision of the linguistic past and present of the Balkan languages and societies, a scholarly vision without nationalist stereotypes and one that corresponds with historical facts and realities. The pronounced interest of the media of all types in the Balkans requires an urgent and objective analysis of the facts in order to combat new nationalist mythologemes, superficial and manipulative "research" on language, literature and culture of Balkan ethnic communities. There are scholarly programmes such as the balkanological research of the MDABJa / Kleiner Balkansprachatlas and the contact-linguistic project EUROJOS (Językowo-kulturowy obraz świata Słowian i ich sąsiadów na tle porównawczym), which seeks to elucidate the linguo-cultural world view of the Slavs and their neighbours by using ethnolinguistic dialectology, etymology and cognitive studies and including onomastic data. Such programmes can provide insights into the contemporary facts in this linguistic and cultural "keg" – a felicitous metaphor for Terra Balcanica.

References

ASENOVA 2005 = Асенова, П: *Архаизми и балканизми в един изолиран български говор (Кукъска Гора,* Албания*).* 10 години специалност "Балканистика", Ред. Милена Калчева. София. 73–78.

ASENOVA 2007 = Асенова, П: *Бележки върху българските острови в Албания.* Българските острови на Балканите, Ред. Татяна Джокова. София. 45–51.

Balkan Research 2007 = *Kosovo and Metohija. Living in the Enclave.* Belgrade.

Bălgarski ostrovi 2007 = *Българските острови на Балканите.* София.

DOKLE, N. (2007): Reçnik goranski (nashinski) – allbanski. Fjalor gorançe (nashke) – shqip. София.

GRADINAROVA 2008 = Градинарова, Пл: *Косово, моята 2007 година.* София.

IDRIZI, S. (2008): *Aromunsko-vlaški tragovi u Gori.* http://www.archive.org/details/Aromunsko VlaskiTragoviUGori

KOLEVA 2011 = Колева, Кр. *Об языковой политике в Косово.* Власть и кодификация. Пловдив. 166–179.

KOSOVA, P. (2007): *Gora dhe veshja tradicionale e saj gjatë shekullit XX. Gora and its traditional costumes during the XX Century.* Prishtinë.

KĂNČOV 1900 = Кънчов, В.: Македония. Етнография и статистика. София.

MANGALAKOVA 2008 = Мангалакова, Т.: *Нашенци в Косово и Албания.* София.

MINDAK-ZAWADZKA, J. (2008): *Poturczeńcy od Turków strasznejsi: Odmienne wspól-noty pamięci na wspólnej (serbkiej) ławie szkolnej.* Przemilczenia w relacjach międzykulturowych. Warszawa.

MLADENOVIĆ 2001 = Младеновић, Р.: *Говор шарпланинске жупе Гора.* Београд.

SELIŠČEV 1929 = Селищев, М.: *Полог и его болгарское население.* София.

SLAVEJKOV 1860 = Славейков, П. Р.: *Смешний календар за нова година 1861.* Цариград.

VIDOESKI, B. (1998): *Dijalektite na makedonskiot jazik.* Vol. I. Skopje.

Balkanismen in den Mundarten der Slavophonen Albaniens

Xhelal YLLI (Heidelberg/Tirana)

Die Balkanlinguistik hat seit ihren ersten Ansätzen (KOPITAR 1829, MIKLOSICH 1861, SANDFELD 1930) bis heute (SCHALLER 1975, SOLTA 1980, FEUILLET 1986, DEMIRAJ 1994, STEINKE/VRACIU 1999, FRIEDMAN 2000, ASENOVA 2002) eine rasche Entwicklung erfahren. Einerseits sind das Inventar der Balkanismen und besonders ihre mundartliche Verbreitung vervollständigt und tiefer erforscht worden, andererseits hat man die Hypothesen über die Entstehung der sogenannten Balkanismen verfeinert und ausgearbeitet. Neuerdings versucht man auch, parallele oder ähnliche Erscheinungen außerhalb des Balkans zu finden, und betrachtet damit die Balkanlinguistik als Südosteuropalinguistik und einen Teil der Eurolinguistik (REITER 1994, HINRICHS 1999). Aber trotz der Erfolge, besonders im Bereich der Hypothesenbildung zur Entstehung der Balkanismen, bleiben viele Fragen der Balkanlinguistik weiterhin offen.

Es ist weitgehend bekannt, dass das enge Nebeneinander der Balkanvölker in bestimmten Arealen als Erklärung für die Entstehung vieler typisch balkanischer Eigenschaften diente, obwohl Dauer und Intensität der Koexistenz nicht leicht festzustellen sind. Eine andere Frage steht im Zusammenhang mit den jüngeren geschichtlichen Entwicklungen, einerseits mit der Entstehung der Nationalstaaten, durch die frühere Kontakte zwischen den Balkanvölkern stark eingeschränkt wurden, andererseits durch die neu entstandene Relation Überdachungssprache-Mundart, die in der Balkanlinguistik noch nicht hinreichend erforscht ist.

Für die vorliegende Untersuchung wurden zwei Gebiete – Gora und Golloborda – in Betracht gezogen. Eine Beschränkung auf diese beiden Räume liegt nahe, weil sie ähnliche geschichtliche Entwicklungen und geographische Voraussetzungen aufweisen und damit einen Vergleich ermöglichen. Die Gebiete von Gora und Golloborda sind zum Teil von slavischsprechenden Einwohnern bewohnt. Dabei sind zu den heutigen Slavophonen nicht nur die Südslaven, sondern auch die slavisierten Albaner und Aromunen zu zählen. Die Anwesenheit der Südslaven in diesen Räumen neben Albanern und Aromunen ist erst seit dem 14./15. Jahrhundert urkundlich belegt (für Gora mit den Chrysobullen von 1348 und 1355 sowie mit den türkischen Registern von 1452–55, von 1571 und von 1591; für Golloborda erst mit dem türkischen Register von 1467). Aufgrund der spärlichen Angaben aus der Toponymie (z.B. Flussname *Bushtrica* im Luma- und im Librazhdigebiet) könnte man diese Kontakte theoretisch mit den ersten Einwanderungen der

Südslaven auf den Balkan, spätestens aber mit dem 9./10. Jahrhundert ansetzen. Was die Religion betrifft, gab es im Gora des 14./15. Jh. Orthodoxe und Katholiken, und man kann den späteren Islamisierungsprozess verfolgen, wobei dieser Prozess in Golloborda schon im 15. Jh. im Gange war. Seit dieser Zeit unterscheidet man für das Dibra-Gebiet, in dem sich auch Golloborda befindet, zwischen Albanern (muslimische Albaner) und Epiroten (orthodoxe Albaner). Heute findet man nur in Golloborda noch eine kleine Gruppe von christlich-orthodoxen Slavophonen. Die frühere Anwesenheit der Katholiken ist heute dagegen nur durch Spuren in der Toponymie und in der Anthroponymie belegt (ausführlicher darüber STEINKE/YLLI 2008: 9–30; 2010: 9–34). Das ethnische Zusammenleben in beiden Gebieten überlebte in vielseitigen Ausprägungen bis in unsere Tage und erreicht damit eine Zeitspanne zwischen fünf bzw. zehn bis zu fünfzehn Jahrhunderten. Die Angaben über das Zusammenleben und die Vermischung der Bevölkerung sind selbst für die jüngere Zeit ausgesprochen spärlich. Lediglich einige wenige Eckdaten sind aussagekräftig: In den türkischen Registern des 15. Jahrhunderts findet man viele gemischte Namen wie *G'in Lazarevik'* oder *G'on Vlasik'* (PALIKRUŠEVA/STOJANOVSKI 1969: 46), die klare Hinweise auf eine Bevölkerungsmischung geben. JASTREBOV (1904: 95) berichtet über die Diskrepanz zwischen Männern und Frauen in Goras Dörfern des 18./19. Jahrhunderts, die zugunsten der Männer die Ziffern 2 bis 2,5, aber in Brod auch bis zum Fünffachen reicht. Dazu kommen die Angaben unserer Informanten auf beiden Seiten der Grenze: Die Goranen haben immer Mädchen aus den rein albanischen Nachbardörfern geheiratet. Angaben aus den heutigen Tagen liefert DOKLES (1999: 135), nach dessen Informationen im Dorf Shishtavec heute 349 Familien leben. Aus einer mündlichen Angabe der lokalen Behörden geht hervor, dass in mehr als einem Drittel dieser Familien die Partnerin eine Albanerin ist (es gibt über 120 eingeheiratete Albanerinnen). Ähnliche Erscheinungen der ethnischen Vermischung hat man auch in Golloborda festgestellt (SADIKAJ 1999: 109–110; STEINKE/YLLI 2008: 29).

Diese starke langjährige Mischung spiegelt sich in den wechselhaften Optionen der Selbstbestimmung ihrer ethnischen Zugehörigkeit wider: Vor Ort haben sich die Slavophonen von Gora und Golloborda im Jahr 1923 selbst als „Albaner" gesehen, heute definieren sie sich selbst in Gora als „nie sme našinci" und nur selten als „Albaner" oder „Bosniaken", in Golloborda hingegen als „Makedonier"/ „Bulgaren" oder „Albaner". In den betreffenden Idiomen hat sich die Vermischung noch stärker niedergeschlagen. Leider besitzen wir heute, ausgenommen Jastrebovs Volkspoesie für Gora, die aus verschiedenen bekannten Gründen nicht den Zustand der gesprochenen Mundart in der gegebenen Zeit wiedergibt[1], keine älteren Belege

---

1 Nach MLADENOVIĆ (2001: 62) spricht GOPČEVIĆ (1890: 214) kurz vor Jastrebov über ein gemischtes serbo-albanisches Idiom. Den klaren Unterschied zwischen Volkspoesie

über diese Idiome und sind deswegen gezwungen, den heutigen Zustand als Ausgangspunkt für die Erschließung zurückliegender Sprachformen zu benutzen. Die Analyse der beiden gesprochenen Idiome zeigt einerseits ein hohes Auflösungsniveau des Systems (STEINKE/YLLI 2008: 33–39; 2010: 25–28, 37–42), andererseits ein unterschiedliches Inventar der Balkanismen, sei es qualitativ oder quantitativ. Natürlich ist die Erklärung des heutigen Zustandes und damit auch der Balkanismen beider Mundarten manchmal sehr schwierig und in der einen oder anderen Art auch mit den oben erwähnten ungeklärten Fragen der Balkanlinguistik verbunden. Besonders kompliziert wird es, wenn in der jeweiligen Mundart verschiedene Ergebnisse vorliegen, obwohl auf den ersten Blick die geschichtlichen und sprachlichen Voraussetzungen dieselben waren und sind. Natürlich spielen hier nicht nur die Gemeinsamkeiten, sondern auch die Spezifika beider Gebiete eine wichtige Rolle: Gora befindet sich näher an den Übergangsgebieten zwischen dem Serbischen und Bulgarischen bzw. Mazedonischen.

Diese Problematik werden wir anhand von einigen Erscheinungen der beiden Idiome, wie dem Kasussystem, dem nachgestellten Artikel und der Perfektbildung, illustrieren.

In der Mundart von Golloborda und Gora werden die syntaktischen Funktionen des obliquen Kasus im Allgemeinen von Präpositionen übernommen; in Gora findet man weiterhin einige synthetische Kasusformen, während in Golloborda nur vereinzelte Reste vorkommen. Besonders auffallend sind einige Unterschiede innerhalb Goras, auf beiden Seiten der Grenze (vgl. MLADENOVIĆ 2001: 269–396), und zwar nicht nur hinsichtlich der Häufigkeit der Kasusreste, sondern auch hinsichtlich der Verbreitung der neuen präpositionalen Ersatzkonstruktionen. Zum Beispiel kommen die *na-Konstruktionen* nach MLADENOVIĆ im kosovarischen Gora nicht vor, dagegen sind sie in unseren Texten spärlich vertreten und in Golloborda, wo der synthetische Dativ auch als Rest nicht mehr anzutreffen ist, sind sie schon etabliert. Ebenfalls ließen sich keine Belege für die von MLADENOVIĆ (2001: 270) verzeichneten Bildungen des Typs *starcatomu, starcitim, detetomu* finden, hingegen findet man für die von ihm erwähnte Stammerweiterung (MLADENOVIĆ 2001: 292) mit *-et-* bei Personen-namen Belege:

> *íma Záľo, Zele prísuje gi víkame míje,* **Záleto** *mu pánala na éna strána* (SH: BB); *míslim bíf po stár, bíf ója Ílmo, po* **Ílmeta**, *séga Étem jé po stár* (ZA: ET); **Shéhata** *go prečékale šištejáni vo Kína, a, rázumeš* (ZA: EMa).

Ferner findet man in Borje und Shishtavec auch die Adjektivendung *-go*, die MLADENOVIĆ (2001: 279) für Brod fixiert hat:

und dem heutigen Zustand des Idioms in Gora zeigen übrigens auch die Veröffentlichungen von DOKLE (2000).

e ne móže da se víka strášlif jén čóvek, što ga púšti véra dvéste gódine pret
lúmogo (BO: ND); *ne mi káža níšto, réče, so* **drúgar lóšogo** *ne ódi po pút* (SH:
BB).

Der Unterschied zwischen den beiden Teilen Goras wäre vielleicht mit dem Einfluss bzw. der Belebung durch die Überdachungssprachen in den letzten drei bis
vier Generationen zu erklären: Auf der kosovarischen Seite wirkte das Serbische,
welches ein vollständiges Kasussystem bewahrt hat, während im albanischen Teil
die Überdachungssprache das Albanische ist, welches ein reduziertes Kasussystem
aufweist. Andererseits wäre der Unterschied zwischen Gora und Golloborda, die
eine ähnliche geschichtliche Entwicklung und zuletzt auch dieselbe Überdachungssprache haben, erst mit einem früheren stärkeren Einfluss des Makedonischen zu
erklären.

Ein Zeichen, dass sich das Kasussystem in Gora in einem starken
Auflösungsprozess befindet, ist auch die folgende Erscheinung: Anstelle des Akkusativs bzw. Casus obliqus kommt für das direkte Objekt mehrmals der Dativ vor.
Dieser fehlerhafte Gebrauch ist aber charakteristisch für das Erlernen von Fremd-
sprachen.

da ni se dáde **škólu** (CË: SD); *za zíma ímale óvde* **éne vodénice** (OE: VS); *séga*
ímame **bútin'u** (SH: FK); *vo osómnajste se zatvórilo* **gránicu**; *Rízvana íma ot*
Bród **žénu** *óvdeka* (SH: BB); *Makedónija jé Makedónija, Bugárija jé Bugárija,*
svóju gránicu *íma; smé bíle ne, nezhvillúane lúg'i,* **škólu** *ne smé ímale, túrski*
(ZA: EMa).

Andererseits sprechen für die noch nicht etablierten präpositionellen Konstruktionen in beiden Gebieten die Beispiele, in denen die obligatorischen Präpositionen
fehlen:

néma dǎrvo da présečiš i séga kúpjeme Ø **sélo** *Ø* **páre**; *já sámo súm óstana Ø*
Góre (CË: AH); *Ø* **stáro vréme** *vélit své míje dójdene smé* (KO: DM); *súšime*
na sánce, málko dǎržiš Ø **ógǎn**, *zaš ógǎn* (OR: RG); *i páre se nášle, vo n'íva*
túje kázík Ø **stáro vréme** (OG: IB); *stájile sófra i ón táva Ø* **trošénica** (SH: IM).
što íma **ot strána Ø tátko mi** *svíte si se, íma vo Skópje, támo se tíje i stríko mi támo*
počinal, i tétka mi támo íšte žívi tája (PA: JŠ).

Eine andere, für das Makedonische charakteristische Erscheinung, und zwar den
dreifachen postponierten Artikel, findet man in der Mundart von Golloborda. Allerdings ist die für die makedonische Standardsprache übliche Differenzierung des
Artikels nach den räumlichen Verhältnissen des entsprechenden Objekts zum
jeweiligen Subjekt schwer bzw. selten klar zu erkennen, wie folgende Beispiele
zeigen.

*ímat, po lóšo **méstono**, po bréžno, po bréžno, bréžno **méstoto*** (LE: FS); *sèlovo e
bìdeno sto kùk'i nàpred go vèl'e stàrite naš, sto kùk'i e bìdeno, ne e ostànato
dvàjset i kùsur kùk'i ostànato, nìšto, izbègal'e, ostànal'e stàrite, stàrite k'e ùm-
reet i nèmat, nèma nìšto drùgo, i tàko k'e se braktìsat i **sèloto*** (PA: ZJ); *se
bègani dèšime, se òdeni tìje, za màjstor ràbote vo Tiràna i nàdvor, so òvije, se
rabòteni màjsori, màjstori što ràbotet àke k'e **nàšive stàrcite**, stàrcite nàše òde*
(VE: SM).

Der heutige Zustand des Artikels in Gora ist dagegen komplizierter. SELIŠČEV
(1929: 409), VIDOESKI (1998: 312) und MLADENOVIĆ (2001: 383) gehen von der
Existenz des dreigliedrigen Artikelsystems in der Mundart von Gora jenseits der
Grenze aus. MLADENOVIĆ (2001: 356, 385) unterscheidet zwei Gebiete, und zwar
die oberen Dörfer mit allen drei Artikelformen *-t*, *-n*, *-v* und die unteren Dörfer nur
mit *-t* und *-v*. Dem entspricht das jeweilige Inventar an Demonstrativpronomen – in
den oberen Dörfern *tija*, *ovija*, *onija* und in den unteren Dörfern nur *tija* und *ovija*.
Letzteres bewertet er, wobei er hier ohne ausführliche und überzeugende Argu-
mente einen albanischen Einfluss ausschließt, als Innovation der unteren Dörfer
(MLADENOVIĆ 2001: 356). Auch Nazif DOKLE (2007), der aus Borja stammt,
behauptet, dass beim Goranischen in Albanien noch alle drei Formen im Gebrauch
sind, und gibt daher in seinem Wörterbuch jeweils die entsprechenden Formen an.
Jedoch findet man in seinen Aufnahmen fast nur den *t*-Artikel und selbst diesen
nicht regelmäßig. Man findet in allen neun Dörfern Albaniens noch eine beachtli-
che Anzahl von Beispielen mit dem Artikelsuffix *-t*, während die beiden anderen
Suffixe nur vereinzelt vorkommen; *-n* tritt nur in den beiden Dörfern Orçikël und
Oreshka und mit *-v* in Borja, Cërraleva, Orgjost, Kosharisht, Pakisht, Shishtavec
und Zapod auf.

-t-Artikel

    stárecot *rábota vi zmằrc jakiánovo, ma stáraja múabet; go pókrif **k'ŭ̀pot** na
glábằrsta* (KO: DM); *k'e zámesim, i k'e dójdet **lébo*** (OE: HS); *i k'e kúpime
jéna, li dvé ka^ej tébe i i k'e ge stájme vo **dvóro*** ; (PA: ZH); *tíja táke ká bábeta
súm rékof **vúkot** magáreto* (ZA: ES).

    *góspot táke e dál, néka zévi **ríbata*** (KO: DM); *démek **stárkata** vék'e zíma
prójde íleze na léto* (PA: ZH); *sát ki íde déčko, ki jé éno véselo, ke ja vídi **de-
vójkata** i k'e ga, k'e se* pëlqésaj; (SH: BB); *a sé dằržele pozicíon na **dằržávata***
(ZA: EMa).

    *k'e cíbe **brášnoto**, zaméstime, k'e go ispéčime* (OG: HO *k'e osóbere i k'e go
stájt da se ósoli vo **cíkoto*** (PA: ZH); *k'e se skáči na dằrvo, péma, k'e se skáči
na **dằrvoto**; mor vék'e tí méčkata tá ti se závằrte, što ti káže na **úhoto** túje* (SH:
BB); *ke te jáḋem, mu véli vúk **magáreto*** (ZA: ES).

    *táj naj stári vék'e tíja **stárite** ni úmɪele vék'e; izḃégale **stárite*** (OE: HS); *a
májkete, kój íma arnáutke, déca do pét šest gódine óni ne, ne móž da go zémet*

*jézik náš; **kózite** své săm gi izvádila* (PA: ZH); *a **nevéstite** se razbírale, se škólo nášo bílo álbanski ot kó, ot kó póčnalo* (SH: BB).

-*v*-Artikel[2]

kónof *jé prístaf;* (BO: ND); *rabótujef* famílja *své súva, **kábilef** nédelen so brávi* (OG: IB); *stóka naj gólema **kón'ef**, mágare, ímašta* (PA: ZH).

*jé **žénava** brátova mój mu; upánala nóga popánala vo éna dúpka, i trak **nógava** tíja, e nášefén k'ŭp so zláte túje* (KO: DM); *da mo vzéme nékoj drúg, or tí, kój k'e ga vídi **tărmkava** me njí fjál, a óva ési zafáteno; pot **văvnava** séga k'e ga stáješ n'a i ídeš na valáica támo, míje ga vélime, k'e ga ístia óna* (PA: ZH); *so **vódava** óna, vărti so vóda, k'e g'i tépaj so trúpoj klášni* (SH: FK); *što ímale an-síja **vizítava** váša* (ZA: EMa).

*be da, ot óvde, ot **sélovo** be naši ovde* (CЁ: BD); ***sélovo** óvde Béla go víke* (CЁ: AH); *i dóšle za dóma, i e ko lái **k'ŭpčevo** so zláto sóm go náš, ká dóšle dóma go zéli k'ŭpčeto i ne stáva so nášle po pút* (KO: DM); ***jénovo** vo, ot Košárište ímame jén* fís, *Séit, Séit, Košárišta é pójden* (OG: IB); *a vo témeli ká ne, na **dés-novo** trăna, dvá óva bráfče k'e zákoleš, k'e ga stáješ, da réceme* (PA: ZH).

*trínajsti vék, vo póčetok ot četírnajsti vék své **sélava górske** sé, sé na nóge; óvaja dévet séla, i pósle kak se narádili rábote ne znám, i próšli **sélava** vo, vo Albánija* (BO: ND).

-*n*-Artikel

kónon *támo je prístaf;* (BO: ND); *strójnik, hă, **ustrójnikon** vélit, po, po Šíšteec, ot Šíšteec; kój kógo k'e práti óstrojnik kó k'épi, ot svúje **kábilon** k'e práti i k'e ti sákat déjka; **kolómok'on**, zámesi tíje što da ti jáj, stáj vo tépsija, túri krómit, íspeči hajt; **cérvenkon**, kóprive stál ăhă* (OE: HS).

*ója **dărvana** grédi, što sé gréde, qirísh ge víkame na arnáutski, gréde se víka nášinski* (OR: RG).

*k'e ja mălzime kráva, k'e, k'e o váriš **mlékon** (alb. **qumeshti-n**?), k'e o pód-kvasiš pósle za síren'e* (OR: RG).

Aber der Artikel wird in unseren Texten sehr häufig in Positionen ausgelassen, wo seine Verwendung aufgrund des Kontextes obligatorisch ist.

*néma ká da pláti **čóvek** ká ne spíe; ga zé **stárka** naj stára vo sélo i ga óbidi da mi káže éna prikažna; váša kúk'a mi go úplaši **déte**; ká sóm stánaf na* mësim, *svéjeno mi se trésle **nógi*** (BO: ND); ***mljéko** k'e o pódkvasiš, **mléko** kíselo k'e o mătiš* (OR: RG); *a dărva ká ne, vék, vék, **vráta** ne móže da ótvoriš* (OE: HS); ***déca** óvde vo Órešek znájet i nášinski, i nášinski i arnáutski* (OE: MC); ***mléko***

---

2   Für die *v*- und *n*-Artikel sind alle Beispiele angegeben, die in den über 50 Seiten langen Texten, die wir vor Ort in spontanen Gesprächen über verschiedene Themen des Dorf-lebens aufgezeichnet haben, vorkommen.

go rabótale i go jále (OG: IB); **mléko** *támo go mắtale, go prodávale* **mléko**
(PA: ZH); *k'e go océjeme* **brášno**, *k'e go zamésime* (SH: FK); *útre k'e ídem vo*
Tíran, k'e zémem i **déte**; **kómšija** *mu dójde* **déte** *ot ásker*; **žéna** *go éskara* **déte**
zášto ne úči; **mléko** *néma mlógo máslo* (SH: NB); *ke go ézmắtit* **mléko** *kíselo a*
ot **mik'énica** *k'e ézvadit pósle so tíja*; *jéno tóa dóade, jéno tóa dóade, ká mu*
déle vúko i **vúk** *psójsa* (ZA: ES).

Für die Verwendung der verschiedenen Suffixe lassen sich auch hier, wie in
Golloborda, keine klaren Verwendungsregeln erkennen.

Generell kann man die Verwendung des Artikels im albanischen Teil von Gora
als unregelmäßig bezeichnen, während seine Verwendung im kosovarischen Teil
mit demjenigen von Golloborda gleich ist.

Eine Interpretation dieses Zustandes bleibt schwierig. Das System des Artikels
befindet sich entweder in der Auflösung, oder man hat es mit neueren Einflüssen
zu tun, die noch nicht fest etabliert sind. Die Artikelsystemauflösung könnte nur
der Einfluss einer Sprache verursachen, die selbst keinen Artikel kennt und das
wäre das Serbische. Gegen eine solche Hypothese spricht aber die Tatsache, dass
im kosovarischen Gora der dreifache Artikel bewahrt wird. Wenn man die beachtli-
che Anzahl an Beispielen mit *-t*-Artikel berücksichtigt, wäre auch die Annahme eines Einartikelsystems, wie in Prespa und im Bulgarischen möglich, aber in diesem
Fall wäre das dreifache Artikelsystem der kosovarischen Gora schwer zu erklären.
Ferner kann man auch einen Einfluss des Albanischen für die Reduzierung des
dreifachen in ein einfaches System im albanischen Gora in Erwägung ziehen.
Hinzu käme auch die Frage, warum es nicht auch in Golloborda eine ähnliche
Reduzierung gab. In allen drei oben erwähnten Erklärungsmöglichkeiten bleiben
aber die zahlreichen Beispiele ohne obligatorischen Artikel ebenfalls ohne Erklärung. Auch die Erklärung als ein noch nicht etabliertes System ist auszuschließen,
weil es keine Zwischenformen gibt, sondern die Trennung bzw. der Wechsel innerhalb der Texte desselben Informanten zwischen den Formen mit und ohne
nachgestellten Artikel klar ist. Unter solchen Umständen scheint die Annahme
plausibler, dass es zuerst eine Schicht von Südslaven gab, die keinen Artikel verwendeten (dies könnten sowohl Serben als auch Bulgaren bzw. Makedonier gewesen sein), später, nachdem sich im Bulgarischen das einfache Artikelsystem entwickelte, ungefähr im 12.–13. Jh. (ASENOVA 2002: 123ff.; KONESKI 1965: 152), kam
eine Schicht an Neuankömmlingen hinzu, und erst wesentlich später eine dritte
Schicht, die den dreifachen Artikel kannte. Aber auch in diesem Fall bliebe der
Unterschied zwischen dem albanischen und kosovarischen Gora unerklärbar.

Die Enklitika und die Verdoppelung des Objekts sind eine etablierte Größe in beiden Mundarten. Hier haben wir nur wenige Beispiele ausgesondert, in denen die
albanische neben der slavischen Kurzform interferiert:

*e zévame **vólnata**, e bérime vo vrék'e i k'e ójime v trap, kaj ímat vóda, k'e **ja** périme vo kázani* (OR: EM); *pósľe k'e **ja** ízvlača so grébeni, pósľe koj sákat šíban'i, šíbi, koj sákat préden'ak, **e** prédio* (OV: LI).

In der Mundart von Gora wird am häufigsten das in den meisten slavischen Sprachen übliche Perfekt, gebildet mit dem Hilfsverb *săm* 'sein' und dem kongruierenden *l*-Partizip, der wegen der Auslautverhärtung[3] an die Formen für Maskulina im Singular meist als *bif* vorkommt, verwendet: *săm bif* (*bil*/*a*/*o*); *si bif* (*bil*/*a*/*o*); *bif* (*bil*/*a*/*o*); *sme bile*(*i*); *ste bile*(*i*); *bile*(*i*). Die Pluralendung des Partizips ist wie im Standardmakedonischen im Allgemeinen *-le* und seltener *-li*. Das neue, im Makedonischen verbreitete Perfekt, gebildet mit den Hilfsverben *imam*/*săm* und der Form des Partizip Präteritum Passiv hat sich in der Mundart von Gora auf beiden Seiten der Grenze nicht eingebürgert.[4] Die wenigen Beispiele in den Texten sind oft fehlerhaft und scheinen auf den Einfluss des Makedonischen zurückzuführen zu sein.

Dagegen findet man in Golloborda beide Typen des Perfekts: Das neue nur im Makedonischen verbreitete Perfekt wird mit den konjugierten Hilfsverben *imam* 'haben' und *sum* 'sein' + einer nicht kongruierenden bzw. kongruierenden Form des Partizip Präteritum Passiv gebildet. Die Form mit *imam* wird vorwiegend für transitive, die mit *sum* für intransitive Verben verwendet. Diese Regel wird aber nicht konsequent eingehalten, und es gibt sogar Dubletten:

*mòjata màjka go **ìmat pràveno** ~ ja **sam napràveno** so vàruška vèľime mìje i so muštènica kìsela mnògo; svìte, svìte, sèa se dèšim **dòjdeni se** ot, dèšim nèkolko kùk'i ot Trèbišta ~ ot ònde zaš **ìme dòjdeno** ot makedònsko ko nam da endèmiše* (VE: SM).

Ferner wird auch das gemeinslavische Perfekt, gebildet mit dem Hilfsverb *sum* 'sein' und dem kongruierenden *l*-Partizip verwendet.

Anders als beim Artikel, wo ein Teil von Gora und Golloborda die makedonischen Merkmale gleich und erkennbar aufweisen, wird bei der Perfektbildung in Gora nur das gemeinslavische Modell gebraucht. Die einzige mögliche Erklärung wäre mit einem gemeinslavischen Zustand, sei es serbisch, sei es bulgarisch/makedonisch, vor der Zeit der Bildung des neuen Perfektes des Makedonischen. Aber unerklärbar bliebe in diesem Fall, warum die Mundart von Gora bei der Bildung des Artikels mitgemacht hat und beim Perfekt nicht. Ist es möglich, dass die Bevölkerungsmischung früher in dem Gebiet viel stärker war als in den Zeiten der Bildung des neuen makedonischen Perfekts?

---

3   MLADENOVIĆ (2001: 196) erläutert den Wandel des *-l* im Silbenauslaut zu *-ỹ >-в*.
4   Diese Feststellung haben schon früher VIDOESKI (1998: 315) und MLADENOVIĆ (2001: 434) für die goranische Mundart in Kosovo gemacht.

Literatur

ASENOVA, P. (2002): *Balkansko Ezikoznanie*. Veliko Tărnovo.

DEMIRAJ, Sh. (1994): *Gjuhësi Ballkanike*. Shkup.

DOKLE, N. (2000): *Gorasnski narodni pesni*. Skopje.

DOKLE, N. (2007): *Rečnik goranski (našinski) – albanski. Fjalor gorançe (naške) – shqip.* Sofija.

FEUILLET, J. (1986): La linguistique balkanique. In: *Cahiers Balkaniques*, 10. Paris.

FRIEDMAN, V. (2000): After 170 Years of balkan Linguistics: Whither the Millennium. *Mediterranean Language Review* 12. Wiesbaden. 1–15.

HINRICHS, U. (1999): Die sogenannten ‚Balkanismen' als Problem der Südosteuropa-Linguistik und der Allgemeinen Sprachwissenschaft. In: Uwe Hinrichs (Hrsg.): *Handbuch der Südosteuropa-Linguistik*. Wiesbaden. 429–462.

MIKLOSICH, F. (1861): *Die slavischen Elemente im Rumänischen*. Wien (= Denkschriften der Kaiserlichen Akademie der Wissenschaften. Philos.-historische Classe, VII).

MIRČEV, K. (1958): *Istoričeska gramatika na bălgarskija ezik*. Sofija.

KONESKI, B. (1965): *Istorija na makedonskiot literaturen jazik*. Skopje.

KOPITAR, J. (1829): Albanische, walachische und bulgarische Sprache. In: *Jahrbücher der Literatur* 46. Wien. 59–106.

MLADENOVIĆ, R. (2001): *Govor šarplaninske župe Gora*. Beograd.

PALIKRUŠEVA, G.; STOJANOVSKI, A. (1969): Debarskata oblast vo šeesetite godini od XV vek. *Glasnik na INI* XIII, 1–2. 37–55.

REITER, N. (1994): *Grundzüge der Balkanologie. Ein Schritt in die Eurolinguistik*. Berlin.

SADIKAJ, H. (1999): *Gollobordasit e Dibrës*. Tiranë.

SANDFELD, K. (1930): *Linguistique balkanique. Problèmes et résultats*. Paris.

SCHALLER, H. (1975): *Die Balkansprachen. Eine Einführung in die Balkanphilologie*. Heidelberg.

SELIŠČEV, A. M. (1929): *Polog i ego bolgarskoe naselenie*. Sofija.

SOLTA, G. R. (1980): *Einführung in die Balkanlinguistik mit besonderer Berücksichtigung des Substrats und des Balkanlateinischen*. Darmstadt.

STEINKE, K.; VRACIU, A. (1999): *Introducere în linguistica balcanică*. Iaşi.

STEINKE, K.; YLLI, Xh. (2008): *Die slavischen Minderheiten in Albanien. 2. Teil. Golloborda-Herbel-Kërçishti i Epërm*. München (= Slavistische Beiträge, 462).

STEINKE, K.; YLLI, Xh. (2010): *Die slavischen Minderheiten in Albanien. 3. Teil. Gora*. München (= Slavistische Beiträge, 474).

VIDOESKI, B. (1998–1999): *Dijalektite na makedonskiot jazik*. 3 Bände. Skopje.

Sprache und Legitimierung nationaler Ziele: Kulturwissenschaftliche Analyse zu einem ambivalenten Verhältnis[1]

Emilija MANČIĆ (Wien)

Die Nation als moderne Form der Vergemeinschaftung betrat mit der Französischen Revolution von 1789 die geschichtliche Bühne und ist daher ein relativ junges Phänomen. Die Rolle der Kriterien Sprache, Literatur bzw. nationale Kultur für die Herausbildung nationaler Identitäten und die Legitimierung nationaler Ziele bedarf folglich näher erläutert zu werden.

Nationen und nationales Bewusstsein können nach subjektivistischen Theoretikern der Nation nur unter den Bedingungen der westlichen Moderne entstehen. In seinem Hauptwerk „Nations and Nationalism" legt Ernest GELLNER (1991) die Formel des modernen Nationalismus fest. Sie lautet: eine Nation, eine Sprache, ein Staat. Der Ursprung der Nation ist laut Gellner im Übergang von der Agrar- zur Industriegesellschaft zu suchen. In den vormodernen Gesellschaften entwickeln sich zwar bereits Kulturen, aber noch keine homogenen Kulturen. In der Industriegesellschaft verändert sich das Verhältnis zwischen Macht und Kultur, und es bildet sich eine Hochkultur heraus. Die neue kapitalistische Ordnung führt zu Rationalisierung, Ordnung und Effizienz, was die soziale Mobilisierung der Gesellschaft nach sich zieht und die bestehenden hierarchischen Ordnungen zerfallen lässt. In der modernen Gesellschaft sind Lesen, Schreiben und Rechnen allgemeine Qualifikationen, die vermittelt werden von jener Hochkultur, die die neue Ordnung schafft. So entsteht eine Verbindung von Staat und Hochkultur, die als Begleiterscheinung zu kultureller Homogenität führt. So schreibt Gellner:

> „Vielmehr entsteht erst, wenn die allgemeinen sozialen Verhältnisse nach standardisierten, homogenen und durch staatliche Zentralgewalt geschützte Hochkulturen rufen – nach Hochkulturen also, die die Gesamtbevölkerung und nicht nur die Minderheiten der Elite durchdringen, eine Situation, in der klar definierte, durch Ausbildung sanktionierte und vereinheitlichte Kulturen fast schon die einzige Art Einheit bilden, mit der sich Menschen bereitwillig und häufig glühend identifizieren. Nunmehr scheinen die Kulturen die natürlichen

---

1 Teile dieses Artikels wurden in meiner Dissertation zum Thema: Die Macht der Kultur und der Narrative. Zu (post-)jugoslawischen Identitätskonzepten und ihrem europäischen Kontext, Wien 2010, publiziert.

Lagerstätten der politischen Legitimität zu sein. Erst jetzt wird jede Verletzung kultureller Grenzen durch politische Einheiten als Skandal empfunden" (GELLNER 1991: 86).

Gellner identifiziert in der staatlich organisierten Ausbildung den Hauptmotor, mit dem die Idee „Nation" verbreitet und gesichert wurde. In der Zeit der Ungewissheit und Unsicherheit, die mit dem Zerfall der neuen Ordnung einhergeht, bietet die Nation Halt und vermittelt Identität. Gellner kommt zu der Schlussfolgerung, dass Nationen nur im Zeitalter des Nationalismus definiert werden können, „denn es ist der Nationalismus, der die Nation hervorbringt, und nicht umgekehrt" (GELLNER 1991: 86). Die Verbreitung der Idee Nation verstärkt den Nationalismus, so Gellner.

Nation und Nationalismus sind nach Benedict ANDERSON (1996) als kulturelle Systeme zu betrachten. Anderson sieht auch einen Zusammenhang zwischen dem Zerfall der religiösen Gemeinschaft und des dynastischen Reiches und der Entstehung des kulturellen Systems Nation. Eine Großgemeinschaft im Mittelalter wurde durch das Medium der heiligen Schriften und deren Sprachen (Latein und Arabisch) vorgestellt, besaß aber einen ganz anderen Charakter als die vorgestellten Gemeinschaften moderner Nationen. Die Welt war nur mittels eines privilegierten Systems der Repräsentation möglich, und nur die kleine Schicht der Schriftkundigen verfügte über die „Wahrheitssprache" und hatte somit die Macht über die Deutung der Welt. Nach dem späten Mittelalter schwand der „unbewusste Zusammenhalt" von den qua Religion vorgestellten Gemeinschaften immer mehr. Zum einen trugen die Entdeckungsreisen in die außereuropäische Welt dazu bei, dass man zu unterschiedlichen Vorstellungen über das Leben gelangen konnte. Zum anderen sieht Anderson einen zweiten Grund für den Verlust religiöser Macht in der Degradierung der „heiligen Sprache" bzw. des Lateinischen selbst. Die Dynastie, die damals das einzig vorstellbare politische System war, verlor seit dem 17. Jahrhundert allmählich auch an Bedeutung. Die Legitimität bekam der Herrscher in einem Königtum ja von Gott und nicht von den Menschen, „die nur Untertanen, aber keine Bürger [waren]" (ANDERSON 1996: 27).

Laut Anderson erwies sich aber nicht nur der Zerfall der Glaubensgemeinschaften und der dynastischen Reiche als zentral, um das vorgestellte Gemeinwesen der Nation entstehen zu lassen, vielmehr war auch eine neue Wahrnehmungsform der Zeit wichtig. Die neue Form der Zeitwahrnehmung, nämlich Vergangenheit und Zukunft gleichzeitig wahrzunehmen, ermöglichte auch die Vorstellung der Nation als moderne Form der Vergemeinschaftung. Diese Transformation ist, so Anderson, auf das literarische Genre des Romans und der Zeitung, die Anderson als literarische Gattung bezeichnet (ebd.: 39), zurückzuführen, die im 18. Jahrhundert die technischen Mittel bzw. die Repräsentationsmöglichkeiten für das Bewusstsein der Nation lieferten. Die moderne Struktur des Romans verfügt über ein Darstellungsverfahren, das durch gleichzeitig handelnde Charaktere in einem gesellschaftlichen Kontext eine unmittelbare Vorstellung einer Gemeinschaft ermöglicht.

„Ein Amerikaner wird niemals mehr als eine Handvoll seiner vielleicht 240 Millionen Landsleute kennenlernen oder nur deren Namen wissen. Er hat keine Vorstellung, was sie irgendwann gerade tun. Doch er hat volles Vertrauen in ihr stetes, anonymes, gleichzeitiges Handeln" (ANDERSON 1996: 34).

In der Zeitung stehen auf der Titelseite Artikel über Ereignisse in der ganzen Welt nebeneinander, die aber meist unabhängig voneinander geschehen. Über das Lesen der Zeitung, die „dem modernen Menschen als Ersatz für das Morgengebet dient" (ANDERSON 1996: 41), bekommen die Menschen den Eindruck, dass „die vorgestellte Welt sichtbar im Alltagsleben verwurzelt ist". Das Druckgewerbe ermöglichte schließlich den Menschen die Gemeinschaftsvorstellung im Sinne einer nationalen Gemeinschaft. Nach Anderson liegen die Ursprünge des Nationalbewusstseins in der „eher zufälligen, doch explosiven Interaktion" (ebd.: 49) der kapitalistischen Produktionsweise, der technischen Entwicklung in Form des Buchdrucks sowie der Existenz von verschiedenen Sprachen. Der Buchdruck verlieh der Sprache eine neue Fixierung. Das gedruckte Buch erhielt eine unveränderte Form und konnte so räumlich und zeitlich unbegrenzt reproduziert werden. Dank der Schriftsprache konnten sich Millionen gleichsprachiger Menschen verständigen und so, laut Anderson, das eigene Nationalbewusstsein entwickeln. Dieser theoretische Hintergrund diente Anderson als Folie für die Entwicklung eines Modells zur Entstehung des Nationalismus in vier Phasen. Anderson beginnt mit den neu entstehenden Staaten Nord- und Südamerikas, wo die häufig für die Nationsbildung in Europa angeführten Kriterien, wie eine exklusive Sprache und Kultur, nicht gelten. Im 18. Jahrhundert erschienen in Amerika mehr als 2000 Zeitungen, und sie wurden zum zentralen Medium für die Verbreitung der neu entstehenden amerikanischen Nationen. In den nord- und lateinamerikanischen Kolonien entwickelten die Angehörigen der einheimischen (kreolischen) Elite ein nationales Zusammengehörigkeitsgefühl, da ihnen eine Stellung und Entfaltungsmöglichkeiten im Mutterland verwehrt waren, obwohl sie „praktisch dieselbe Beziehung zu Waffen, Leiden, Christentum und europäischer Kultur besaßen" (ebd.: 65). In Europa begann parallel zu den antikolonialen Befreiungsbewegungen in Amerika am Anfang des 19. Jahrhunderts das Zeitalter des Nationalismus, und die Vorstellung der Nation fußte hier auf der Sprache und historischen Vorbildern. Anderson identifiziert als weitere Elemente, die die vorgestellte Gemeinschaft der Nation stützen: Volkszählung, Landkarten und Museen. Sie schafften Raster, mit deren Hilfe man immer sagen könne, „dass es dieses und nicht jenes ist, dass es hier an diese Stelle gehört, und nicht an jene" (ebd.: 185). Die Vereinnahmung der Vergangenheit konnte das europäische Bild der „erwachenden" Nation erzeugen und erlaubte, das Zuspätkommen gegenüber Amerika und Frankreich zu rechtfertigen.

Im Mittelpunkt der verspäteten Nationsbildungsprozesse in Europa Anfang des 19. Jahrhunderts standen Sprache und Geschichte. Diese Konzeption, die Nation-Sein von einer exklusiven Sprache abhängig macht, übte im Europa des 19. Jahrhunderts weitreichenden Einfluss aus, der sich bald auch auf das Denken über den Nationalismus erstreckte (vgl. ANDERSON 1996).

Sprachwissenschaftler und Literaten nahmen an diesem Prozess aktiv teil. So wurde mit der literarischen Verbreitung der Geschichte der Amerikanischen Unabhängigkeitskriege und der Französischen Revolution ab den 1820er Jahren ein Modell für die Entstehung des unabhängigen Nationalstaats angeboten. Diese, wie sie Anderson nennt, „philologisch-lexikographische Revolution" (ebd.: 88) regte die Frage der Selbstbestimmung jeder Sprachgruppe an und verursachte Legitimationsprobleme für die dynastischen Herrscher.

In den Ländern des späteren Osteuropa hat schon die Epoche der Aufklärung zur Entwicklung der Standardsprache und damit moderner Literatur vor allem als Mittel zu humanen Zwecken beigetragen, doch zur Zeit der Romantik wurden Sprache, Literatur sowie Geschichte zu national-emanzipatorischen Zwecken eingesetzt.

Im Jahre 1800 war nur ein Land des späteren Osteuropas unabhängig: Russland. Andere Bevölkerungsgruppen lebten verteilt auf drei verschiedene Kaiserreiche.[2] Die Erweckung des nationalen Selbstbewusstseins begann in dieser Region als eine kulturelle und sprachliche und nicht als politische Bewegung. So erschienen die nationalen Dichter zuerst als Kodifikatoren der normierten nationalen Standardsprachen und gleichzeitig als diejenigen, die die literarischen Werke schufen, die das geistige Wesen der Nation ausdrückten (vgl. WACHTEL 2006). So bekamen in dieser Region die Schriftsteller, aber auch Linguisten und ihr Beruf eine enorme Prestigerolle. Von den Intellektuellen wurden sie kanonisiert, dann von den jungen Nationalstaaten für ihre Zwecke eingesetzt und später von den sozialistischen Regimen wiederum neu-kanonisiert. Einige der bekanntesten Namen solcher Autoren sind Adam Mickiwicz in Polen, Taras Schewtschenko in der Ukraine, Sándor Petőfi in Ungarn, Mihai Eminescu in Rumänien, Christ Botev und Ivan Vazov in Bulgarien, Petar II Petrović Njegoš in Serbien und Montenegro, Ivan Mažuranić in Kroatien und France Prešeren in Slowenien. Im 19. Jahrhundert entwickelte sich auch die ursprüngliche Idee einer Einheit aller Südslawen, die mit dem romantischen, im Grunde genommen synthetischen Kulturmuster korreliert und auf der

---

2 Gemeint sind: Österreichisch-Ungarische Monarchie, Osmanisches Reich und Königreich Preußen, da sich große Teile Polens unter preußischer Herrschaft und andere Teile unter dem Russischen Kaiserreich befanden.

Vorstellung besonders enger sprachlicher, kultureller und verwandtschaftlicher Beziehungen zwischen südslawischen Ethnien basierte.

Die reinsten Formen der Volkssprache und der Kultur, die frei von fremden Einflüssen sind, finden sich für die Romantiker bei den Ahnen der Vorzeit. Eine Befreiung der Sprache von Fremdwörtern und von fremden Einflüssen ist daher die erste Voraussetzung für die Nationalisierung eines Volkes. Die zahlreichen Beispiele am Ende des 18. und Anfang des 19. Jahrhunderts zeugen von Sprachreformen, die eine eigene „wahre" Standardsprache aus Dialekten und älteren Sprachdokumenten auszubilden vermochten. Eine bekannte Sprachreform war zum Beispiel jene in der Türkei, wo die Jungtürken die osmanische Hofsprache von persischen und arabischen Einflüssen säuberten.

Es ist bis jetzt häufig betont worden, wie sehr Sprache und besonders die Volkssprache als Ausdruck von Identität und Authentizität einer Person oder eines Volkes wahrgenommen wird. Eine normierte Volkssprache kann gesellschaftliche und ökonomische Veränderungen fördern, die modernisierend wirken und den Wünschen neu aufstrebender Eliten entgegenkommen. Sie ist zumeist Beginn oder zumindest Impuls für neue nationale, volkssprachliche Entwicklungen im Bereich der Literatur (HOPF 1997: 87). Wenn es aber um die Frage geht, welche Sprache oder Sprachvariante am besten zu einer nationalen Normsprache gemacht werden sollte, wird die Sache häufig recht schwierig. Da es zunächst völlig unklar ist, welche Identität, Substanz und welchen Umfang eine Population und deren Sprache besitzen, sind nationale und linguistische Grenzen schwer bestimmbar.

Der Begriff Sprache benötigt eine Präzisierung, da es niemals klar ist, was mit Sprache gemeint ist. Sprache kann sich auf ein System von Dialekten, auf das Vernakular im Sinne der Volksprache im Unterschied zur Standardsprache oder auf die standardisierte Literatursprache beziehen. Die inoffizielle Theorie der Sprachnation, die nach dem Schema „ein Volk, eine Sprache, ein Staat" vertreten wurde, übte einen starken Einfluss auf den slowenischen Sprachwissenschaftler Jernej Kopitar, den serbischen Sprachreformator Vuk Karadžić und die kroatische illyrische Bewegung aus. Ähnlich wie in Deutschland war die Bildung des eigenen nationalen Bewusstseins in Mittel- und Südosteuropa, das sich auf Sprache und Kultur gründete, am Anfang nicht als bloße Volkzugehörigkeit zu der eigenen Volksgruppe gedacht. Da es auf dem späteren Gebiet der serbokroatischen Sprache drei Dialekte gab, schreibt Karadžić, der damaligen Doktrin von der Gleichsetzung von Sprache und Volk folgend, den čakawischen Dialekt den Kroaten, den štokawischen Dialekt den Serben und den kajkawischen Dialekt den Slowenen zu (vgl. BUGARSKI 1986). Für die Ausbildung der späteren serbokroatischen Sprache war der štokawische Dialekt relevant. Auch die „Illyrer" wählten den štokawischen Dialekt, obwohl die meisten von ihnen Kajkavci waren. Ausschlaggebend war für eine solche Entscheidung der Illyristen ihr unitaristischer kultureller Jugoslawismus bzw. das Konzept der nationalen Vereinigung und Vereinheitlichung der

Südslawen auf kulturellem Gebiet. Die illyrische Bewegung entstand vor allem als Reaktion auf die Magyarisierung und den Versuch, die ungarische Sprache in Kroatien als obligatorisches Schulfach, als Amtssprache und Verhandlungssprache auf dem gemeinsamen Reichstag einzuführen.

Die demonstrative Übernahme des illyrischen Namens als nationaler Selbstbezeichnung seitens der Träger der kroatischen Wiedergeburt und die noch zu erörternde programmatische Übertragung dieses Namens auf alle Südslawen war jedoch Ausdruck eines Jugoslawismus, der die ethnische Einheit der Südslawen betonte und ihre kulturelle, schließlich auch politische Vereinigung anstrebte (BEHSCHNITT 1980: 135).

Sprache und Literatur waren der Bereich, in dem der unitarische Jugoslawismus verwirklicht werden sollte. Aufgrund des nationalen Ziels einer einheitlichen Schriftsprache für alle Südslawen wurde als Grundlage der einheitlichen Schriftsprache der štokawische Dialekt gewählt.

Die Klassifizierung von Vuk Karadžić wird später von einigen kroatischen Linguisten angegriffen, da in Kroatien auch eine große Bevölkerungsgruppe den štokawischen Dialekt benutzte, der in Serbien den Rahmen für die eigene sprachliche Entwicklung gegeben hat. Die kroatische Ethnizität verfügte nämlich über drei Mundarten, von denen nur Čakawisch als eigener Dialekt galt, während Kajkawisch mit der slowenischen und Štokawisch mit der serbischen Ethnie geteilt wurde. Das nationale Bewusstsein, das mit der Nation und nicht mit der Ethnizität verbunden ist, wird aber über eine Ebene konstituiert, die das ganze Territorium mittels einer sprachlichen Homogenisierung abdeckt. Diese Ebene dient dann dem Bildungswesen sowie dem administrativen und kulturellen Leben. Deswegen waren Universitäten und Schulen die wichtigsten Vermittlungsinstanzen der nationalen Idee. Gerade deshalb wurde der Illyrismus unter Slowenen und Serben von der überwiegenden Mehrheit der kulturellen und politischen Elite abgelehnt. Bei Slowenen begann die nationale Wiedergeburt, die auf der Tradition der protestantischen Schriftsteller des 16. Jahrhunderts und den philologischen Arbeiten B. J. Kopitars aufbaute. Der štokawische Dialekt erwies sich hier als besonders hinderlich, da er eben einen zentralen Integrationsfaktor der „Illyrer" darstellte. Die Serben waren ihrerseits in ihrer eigenen literarischen und religiösen Tradition verwurzelt und mit der eigenen Staatsidee, deren Bezugspunkt das Fürstentum Serbien war, beschäftigt. Im Grunde fanden die kulturellen Ziele der Illyristen nur bei Kroaten Resonanz, da der kulturelle Illyrismus in erster Linie zur Einigung der Kroaten und zur Konstituierung der kroatischen Nation auf der Grundlage von Sprache, Literatur und Kultur beitrug. „Bis zum Vorabend der Revolution von 1848 manifestierte sich der Nationalismus der Illyrer als kultureller Illyrismus und politischer Kroatismus" (BEHSCHNITT 1980: 151).

Nichtsdestoweniger unterzeichneten die bekannten kroatischen (Ivan Mažuranić, Dimitrije Demetra, Ivan Kukuljević, Vinko Pencel, Stjepan Pejaković), serbischen (Vuk Karadžić und Djuro Daničić) und slowenischen Linguisten (Franc Miklošič) am 28. März 1850 das sogenannte Wiener Abkommen auf einer Konferenz in Wien, das die Grundlage für die gemeinsame Schriftsprache der Serben und Kroaten schaffen sollte. Diese Vereinbarung war eindeutig von den Grundsätzen Karadžićs geprägt. Mit dem Abkommen wurde auch vorgesehen, die Orthografien des Serbischen und Kroatischen in lateinischer und kyrillischer Schrift so aneinander anzupassen, dass direkt aus der einen in die andere transliteriert werden kann. Man einigte sich auf den štokawisch-ijekawischen Dialekt als gemeinsame Grundlage für die kroatische und serbische Sprache. Obwohl das „Abkommen" von Privatpersonen unterzeichnet wurde und als solches keine bindende Wirkung hatte, insbesondere weil eine Ratifizierung durch staatliche Institutionen nicht stattfand, stellte es einen bedeutenden Schritt zur sprachlichen Einigung der Südslawen dar. Der kulturelle Jugoslawismus stand auch im Mittelpunkt des nationalen Konzepts des Kroaten Josip J. Strossmayer, des Bischofs von Djakovo, und seines engsten Vertrauten, des Kanonikers und ersten Präsidenten der Jugoslawischen Akademie Franjo Rački. In seinem Artikel „Jugoslovjenstvo" vertritt Rački ebenfalls die These, dass dieses Volk eine gemeinsame Geschichte, sowohl politisch als auch geistig, teilt, dass es durch dieselbe Vergangenheit verbunden wird (BEHSCHNITT 1980: 163). Die sprachliche Verwandtschaft macht für Rački die Einigung der Südslawen zum Postulat. In diesem Sinne regte Rački die Schaffung der einheitlichen Schriftsprache, die Gründung der Jugoslawischen Akademie und von Lehrstühlen der serbokroatischen Sprache in verschiedenen Städten an. Strossmayer und Rački waren vielseitig aktiv auf kultureller Ebene: Herausgabe von Büchern, Wörterbüchern, Druck von Zeitschriften usw. Strossmayer finanzierte die Gründung der Jugoslawischen Akademie (1866) und der Universität in Zagreb (1874), die der geistig-kulturellen Einigung der Südslawen dienen sollte. Die kulturelle Vereinigung aller Jugoslawen, die vor allem auf der Basis einer gemeinsame Schriftsprache erreicht werden sollte, wurde auch in die Tivoli-Resolution von 1909 aufgenommen, die auf der Konferenz der jugoslawischen Sozialisten in Ljubljana von 21. bis 22. November 1909 verabschiedet wurde. Der serbische Literaturhistoriker Jovan Skerlić befürwortete auch die Schaffung einer einheitlichen Schriftsprache, die nicht nur im Interesse der nationalen Einheit zwischen Kroaten und Serben, sondern auch zwischen Serbo-Kroaten und Slowenen sei. Er tritt für die Annahme des lateinischen Alphabets und für die Erhebung der östlichen, ekavischen Form des štokavischen Dialektes zur alleinigen Schriftsprache ein. Der berühmte kroatische Dichter Tin Ujević (1891–1955) schrieb in seinem Artikel „Narodno jedinstvo" (Die Volkseinheit):

„Es bestehe heute keine besondere Notwendigkeit, die alltägliche Tatsache, daß Kroaten und Serben eine einzige Nation sind, zu beweisen ... Ein Blut, gemeinsame Gewohnheiten, eine Geschichte gemeinsamen Ruhms und Leidens, eine Sprache, eine nationale Kultur und jenes tiefe instinktive Gefühl der Einheit,

das trotz allem Gegensatz des Glaubens und der exklusiven Namen bei allen
unseren politischen und kulturellen Führern, nannten sie sich Kroaten oder Serben, zum Ausdruck kam – diese Erscheinungen stärken uns alle in dem festen
Glauben an die nationale Einheit, der für uns alle ein Axiom bleiben muß"
(UJEVIĆ zitiert nach BEHSCHNITT 1980: 224).

Ujević erweiterte die nationale Einheit der Serben und Kroaten auch um die Slowenen, da sich Serbentum, Kroatentum und Slowenentum als solche erst selbst
verwirklichen würden, wenn sie auf einem anderen Niveau verschmelzen würden.
„Der Prozeß der Integration von Serben, Kroaten und Slowenen im zukünftigen
Jugoslawentum war die Schaffung der einheitlichen jugoslawischen Kultur- und
Staatsnation", in der, wie es Ujevićs Vergleich mit der Funktion der Schriftsprache
verdeutlichte, „alle Unterschiede in einer weiteren Harmonie ausgeglichen werden
sollten" (BEHSCHNITT 1980: 227).

Ende des 19. Jahrhunderts gelang eine erste Kodifizierung der Sprache mit dem
Erscheinen eines Wörterbuchs und einer Grammatik zur kroatischen oder serbischen Sprache. 1941, als der unabhängige kroatische Ustaša-Staat gegründet
wurde, kam es zu einer Trennung von kroatischer und serbischer Sprache, und es
wurde Purismus praktiziert. Die Idee einer gemeinsamen Sprache wurde nach dem
Zweiten Weltkrieg wieder aufgegriffen. Eine Sprachkommission legte 1954 in
Novi Sad fest, dass es sich beim Kroatischen, Serbischen, Montenegrinischen und
Bosnischen um eine Sprache mit mehreren Zentren handle. Sowohl die ijekawische
als auch die ekawische Aussprache besäßen ihre Gültigkeit, und die lateinische sowie die kyrillische Schrift wurden gestattet. Slowenisch und Makedonisch wurden
aufgrund der größeren sprachlichen Unterschiede gesondert behandelt. Dieses Ein-
verständnis war jedoch nicht von Dauer. Die Deklaration über Name und Stellung
der kroatischen literarischen Sprache aus dem Jahr 1967 hatte gerade dieses Abkommen und die auf das Abkommen zurückzuführende Entstehung der serbokroatischen Sprache infrage gestellt und sie einer Revision im Lichte des damaligen jugoslawischen Kontexts unterzogen. Eine Gruppe kroatischer Linguisten, seit
1970 unterstützt von der sogenannten Massenbewegung, forderte, dass Kroatisch
eine selbstständige Sprache werden und auch der Einfluss serbischer Wörter auf
die kroatische Sprache unterbunden werden solle. Die Deklaration wurde am
17. März 1967 in der Wochenzeitung „Telegram" veröffentlicht. Der Text der
Deklaration wurde in der Matica Hrvatska verfasst und von einigen damals
bekannten kroatischen Linguisten und Schriftstellern unterschrieben. Im Dokument
wurde dazu aufgefordert, die kroatische von der serbokroatischen Sprache zu tren-
nen. Bald danach antwortete eine Gruppe serbischer Schriftsteller mit einem
sogenannten „Überlegungsvorschlag", in dem konstatiert wurde, dass mit der
Deklaration das Wiener und sogenannte Novi-Sad-Abkommen aus dem Jahre 1954
außer Kraft gesetzt würden und somit keine gemeinsame Literatursprache von Serben und Kroaten mehr existiere (BUGARSKI 2002). Die Matica Hrvatska, die eine

führende Rolle in dieser Bewegung spielte, trat im Jahre 1971 von der Absprache von Novi Sad zurück. Als Konsequenz wurde in der Verfassung der Bundesrepublik Kroatien von 1974 der Artikel über die Bezeichnung der Sprache geändert. Der Teilrepublik Kroatien wurde das Recht, dass „jede Nation und Nationalität die Sprache mit ihrem Namen zu benennen" (BEHSCHNITT 1980: 71) könne, garantiert.

Zwischen 1980 und 1990 wurde nicht nur das Zugehörigkeitsgefühl zum jugoslawischen Staat infrage gestellt, sondern es erfolgte auch ein Rückgriff auf die „ursprünglichen" (vorjugoslawischen) Identitäten. Jugoslawien wurde allmählich zu einem Niemandsland, in dem alle Nationen bedroht waren (vgl. MILOSAVLJEVIĆ in POPOV 2001). Besonders seit 1989 setzte ein intensiver Prozess der literarischen und institutionellen Nationalisierung ein, der die Konstruktion der „wahren" bzw. „natürlichen" Identität zum Ziel hatte. Wenn etwas natürlich ist, ist es als notwendig und unausweichlich bewiesen und gilt damit auch als zeitlos und universell. Die literarischen und sprachlichen Grenzziehungen, die einmal als Einheit generierende Mechanismen funktionierten, kennzeichneten auch den Anfang einer kulturellen Konstitution, die später in die soziale Desintegration münden sollte. Die Ambivalenz der Legitimierung nationaler Ziele, die durch das Kriterium Sprache konstituiert wurde, lag darin, dass dieses Kriterium sowohl für die Bildung des eigenen nationalen Bewusstseins als auch für die Herausbildung eines integrativen Jugoslawentums diente.

„Dabei ist es allerdings weitgehend eine Frage der Definition, ob man die ekavische und die ijekavische Štokavština als zwei Varianten einer Schriftsprache oder als zwei Schriftsprachen ansieht. Diese Entscheidung fällt aber nicht nur in die Kompetenz der Linguistik, sondern sie ist – wie die Geschichte bis in die Gegenwart zeigt – zentral von der Politik in der nationalen Frage abhängig. Lag es im Interesse der Ideologen des Nationalismus, beispielweise die Unterschiede zwischen Serben und Kroaten als zwei verschiedenen Nationen zu betonen, so verwies man auf sprachliche Differenzen – wie gravierend sie im einzelnen auch gewesen sein mögen. Ging es um die Hervorhebung der engen ethnischen Verwandtschaft beziehungsweise Einheit von Serben und Kroaten – sei es im Sinne des Jugoslawismus, sei es gemäß bestimmter die Eigenständigkeit der anderen Nationen negierenden Primärformen des Nationalismus –, so wurden die sprachlichen Gemeinsamkeiten akzentuiert" (BEHSCHNITT 1980: 237).

Die „eigene" Sprache, Literatur und Geschichtsdeutung bekamen erneut Relevanz und erzeugten eine neue Dynamik, da sie in der Region seit dem 19. Jahrhundert und gemäß dem totalisierenden romantischen Kulturkonzept (vgl. RECKWITZ 2000) als konstitutive Elemente der modernen Nation galten. Wenn die beherrschenden Erklärungsmuster ihre Funktion in der Gesellschaft nicht mehr optimal erfüllen können, dann werden, wie sich auch am jugoslawischen Beispiel gezeigt hat, sowohl die herrschende Ordnung als auch die Modelle und Normen, nach denen diese Ordnung gedacht wurde, fraglich. Somit wird ein Prozess der Grenzziehung angesetzt, der ein Ergebnis menschlichen Gemeinschaftshandelns darstellt und sich im ständigen Gemeinschaftshandeln (sowohl von Institutionen als auch von Individuen) reproduziert und stabilisiert. In dieser Phase rücken die Gegensatzpaare in den Vordergrund, da allen gegensätzlichen Kategorien unter bestimmten Bedingungen eine Nicht-Identität eigentümlich ist. So dominiert nun die einem bisherigen Identitätskonzept innewohnende gegensätzliche Seite.

Bibliographie

ANDERSON, Benedict (1996): *Die Erfindung der Nation. Zur Karriere eines folgenreichen Konzepts*. Frankfurt, New York: Campus.

BEHSCHNITT, Wolf Dietrich (1980): *Nationalismus bei Serben und Kroaten 1830–1914. Analyse und Typologie der nationalen Ideologie*. München: Oldenbourg.

BUGARSKI, Ranko (1986): *Jezik u društvu*. Beograd: Prosveta.

BUGARSKI, Ranko (2002): *Nova lica jezika*. Beograd: XX Vek.

GELLNER, Ernest (1991): *Nationalismus und Moderne*. Berlin: Rotbuch.

HOPF, Claudia (1997): *Sprachnationalismus in Serbien und Griechenland: theoretische Grundlagen sowie ein Vergleich von Vuk Stefanović Karadžić und Adamantios Korais*. Wiesbaden: Harrasowitz.

MILOSAVLJEVIĆ, Olivera (2001): Jugoslavija kao zabluda. In: Nebojša Popov (Hrsg.): *Srpska strana rata. Trauma i katarza u istorijskom pamćenju*. I deo. Beograd: Samizdat.

RECKWITZ, Andreas (2000): *Die Transformation der Kulturtheorien. Zur Entwicklung eines Theorieprogramms*. Weilerswist: Vielbrück Wissenschaft.

WACHTEL, Andrew Baruch (2006): *Remaining Relevant after Communism. The Role of the Writer in Eastern Europe*. Chicago, London: Chicago University Press.

Abstract

At the end of the eighteenth century, the importance of language, so typical for Western culture since the Renaissance, was increasing. The immense weight was given to the role of language which, together with culture were held to be crucial factors for nationality and membership. As the European nation states developed, monolingualism and cultural homogeneity within the state were seen as desirable, both from the point of view of the state and individual. The article aims to inquire into the role of the language reforms in the historical development in the Balkans, and into the significance of the role of language and literature in building the belated nations, especially in the formation of national culture on the periphery of Europe. Language reforms and the debates on them reflect the factors that made the invention of a national culture so inevitable. In the "peripheral" societies in the Balkans under the Ottoman and Austro-Hungarian Empire the national culture, replacing the ethno-religious identities, acted as a sort of legitimation for the emerging nations and states by harmonizing local varieties and linguistic varia-tions. The subject matter therefore focusses on language reforms in Serbia, Croatia and Slovenia in the nineteenth century. The imaginary perception of unity based on the formation of the national language and literature at that time served both for the building of the own national awareness and of Yugoslavism before it was achieved politically. The differences between varieties in the dialects were at the time mini-mized (first unofficially by the so called Wiener Abkommen in 1850), and making the formation of one future common standard language possible, facilitating later integration of different national societies into one state (1918 and 1945). In other times (during World War II and especially after 1989) these language differences were accentuated and linked to social disunity.

List of authors / Autorenverzeichnis / Список авторов

Prof. Dr. Ronelle Alexander, Department of Slavic Languages and Literatures, University of Berkeley, USA

Dr. Ina Arapi, Institut für Romanistik, Universität Wien, Austria

Prof. Dr. Petja Asenova, Факултет по славянски филологии, Общо, индоевропейско и балканско езикознание, Софийският университет „Св. Климент Охридски", София, Bulgaria

Conf. Dr. Mariana Bara, Facultatea de Litere şi Limbi Străine, Universitatea Hyperion, Bucureşti, Romania

Dr. Tat'jana Civ'jan, Институт славяноведения Российской академии наук, Москва, Russia

Dr. Liljana Dimitrova-Todorova, Институтът за български език „Проф. Любомир Андрейчин", Секция за българска етимология, Българска академия на науките, София, Bulgaria

Prof. Dr. Victor A. Friedman, Department of Slavic Languages and Literatures, University of Chicago, USA

Prof. Dr. Uwe Hinrichs, Institut für Slawistik, Universität Leipzig, Germany

Prof. Dr. Thede Kahl, Institut für Slawistik, Friedrich Schiller-Universität Jena, Germany

Dr. Krasimira Koleva, Шуменски университет „Епископ Константин Преславски", Шумен, Bulgaria

Assoc. Prof. Dr. Iliana Krapova, Dipartimento di Americanistica, Iberistica e Slavistica, Università Ca' Foscari, Venezia, Italia

Prof. Dr. Jürgen Kristophson, Institut für Slawistik, Universität Hamburg, Germany

Dr. Doris K. Kyriazis, Αριστοτέλειο Πανεπιστήμιο Θεσσαλονίκης, Τμήμα Φιλολογίας, Θεσσαλονίκη, Greece

Dr. Corinna Leschber, Institute for Linguistic and Cross-Cultural Studies, Berlin

Dr. Petrea Lindenbauer, Institut für Romanistik, Universität Wien, Austria

Dr. Emilija Mančić, Institut für Germanistik, Universität Wien, Austria

Dr. Marjan Markovikj, Филолошки факултет „Блаже Конески“, Универзитетот „Св. Кирил и Методиј“, Скопје, Republic of Macedonia

Dr. Christina Marku, Τμήμα Γλωσσών, Φιλολογίας και Πολιτισμού Παρευξεινίων Χωρών, Δημοκρίτειο Πανεπιστήμιο Θράκης, Κομοτηνή, Greece

Prof. Dr. Michael Metzeltin, Institut für Romanistik, Wien, Austria

Prof. Dr. Olga M. Mladenova, Department of Slavic Studies, University of Calgary, Canada

Prof. Dr. Gerhard Neweklowsky, Österreichische Akademie der Wissenschaften, Wien, Austria

Assoc. Prof. Anastasija Petrova, Катедра Обща лингвистика и старобългаристика, Великотърновски университет „Св. Св. Кирил и Методий“, Велико Търново, Bulgaria

Prof. Dr. Adrian Poruciuc, Facultatea de Litere, Universitatea „Alexandru Ioan Cuza“, Iaşi, Romania

Dr. Elton Prifti, Institut für Romanistik, Universität Potsdam, Germany

Ao. Prof. Dr. Claudia Römer, Institut für Orientalistik, Universität Wien, Austria

Prof. Dr. Irena Sawicka, Instytut Filologii Słowiańskiej, Uniwersytet Mikołaja Kopernika, Toruń; Instytut Slawistyki Polskiej Akademii Nauk, Warszawie, Poland

Prof. Dr. Helmut W. Schaller, Institut für Slawistik, Universität Marburg an der Lahn, Germany

Prof. Dr. Ingmar Söhrman, Göteborgs universitet, Humanistiska fakulteten, Institutionen för språk och litteraturer, Göteborg, Sweden

Prof. Dr. Klaus Steinke, Universität Erlangen, Germany

Prof. Dr. Todor At. Todorov, Институтът за български език „Проф. Любомир Андрейчин“, Секция за българска етимология, Българска академия на науките, София, Bulgaria

Dr. Xhelal Ylli, Institut für Slawistik, Universität Jena, Germany